KEEPERS OF
THE KEYS

▲

ALSO BY JOHN PRADOS

The Soviet Estimate: U.S. Intelligence Analysis
and Russian Military Strength

The Sky Would Fall: Operation Vulture: The U.S.
Bombing Mission in Indochina, 1954

The Presidents' Secret Wars: CIA and Pentagon
Covert Operations Since World War II

KEEPERS OF THE KEYS

A History of the National Security Council from Truman to Bush

▲

John Prados

William Morrow and Company, Inc.
New York

353.0089
P883 K

It is the policy of William Morrow and Company, Inc., and its imprints and affiliates, recognizing the importance of preserving what has been written, to print the books we publish on acid-free paper, and we exert our best efforts to that end.

Library of Congress Cataloging-in-Publication Data

Prados, John.
    Keepers of the keys : a history of the National Security Council
from Truman to Bush / John Prados.
        p. cm.
    Includes bibliographical references and index.
    ISBN 0-688-07397-2
    1. National Security Council (U.S.)—History.   2. United States—
National security—History—20th century.   I. Title.
UA23.15.P73   1991
353.0089—dc20   90-26244
                                                                   CIP

24.45

Printed in the United States of America

First Edition

1 2 3 4 5 6 7 8 9 10

BOOK DESIGN BY M 'N O PRODUCTION SERVICES, INC.

To
Jill
with
Love

FOREWORD

Presidential power lies at the heart of every aspect of American government. In foreign and defense policy, so-called national security, presidential power resides in the National Security Council, or NSC. Yet for all the many, many books and other studies on aspects of American national security since World War II, hardly any have focused on the National Security Council as an expression of presidential power, or on the role of the national security adviser, the President's first lieutenant for defense and foreign policy. Historians and political scientists have looked at Presidents and their secretaries of state, at Presidents and their secretaries of defense, at Presidents and their personal staffs. National security advisers are largely neglected.

For a moment in time it seemed that the Iran-Contra affair might change all that. Here was a case in which grave flaws in standing procedures were revealed precisely within the staff of the NSC, and in which the quality of national security advice given to a President was called into question. Three years later it is clear that the inquiries resulting from the affair have followed the angles of controversy and corruption, rather than examining fundamental issues.

This is the story of the National Security Council, of the national security adviser, of his staff. It is a whale of a story, encompassing the whole history of the cold war and United States defense policy, of war in Vietnam and arms control, of Washington bureaucracies and personal frustrations. Such flamboyant advisers as Henry Kissinger and Zbigniew Brzezinski are here, but so are some of their subordinates, the NSC staff, the people who really make the system work. Beyond individuals, this is the story of the rise of an institution, the NSC staff, which has acquired power rivaling that of Cabinet officers, diplomats, and generals.

This is not a book on national security per se, or the philosophy of the national security state. As the cold war recedes, the philosophy of national security must lose much of the vitality it once possessed. Whatever the temperature of international relations, however, this nation still faces the need to integrate its defense and foreign policies, a need ever more acute as available resources become increasingly limited. The National Security Council and staff is the mechanism for achieving that integration. A practical study of where the NSC came from and what it has done seems especially timely.

An abundance of material rather than its paucity has been a problem in writing this book. Numerous declassified documents are available for the administrations up to Nixon's, and even there the record is beginning to open.

For the most recent, Reagan years, the Iran-Contra affair has generated an avalanche of declassifications and revelations that scholars will no doubt labor for many years to interpret. This record has been supplemented by congressional documents and hearings, interviews, oral histories, memoirs, and the voluminous literature on the crises with which the NSC has had to deal.

Despite its length, my account has had to pass lightly over many incidents that merit more detailed treatment, and to avoid altogether some slices of our postwar experience. Other historians will have to offer the story of the NSC in Africa, or South Asia, or more detail on relations with Europe and the Soviet Union.

I have tried to follow certain subjects through the different administrations nonetheless. One is the Vietnam War, which has been the formative experience for the postwar generation that rose to consciousness in the twilight of the cold war. A second is the NSC in the Middle East. I have retained material on Lebanon and the 1967 and 1973 wars for comparison and contrast of NSC activity at different times. An effort has been made to follow arms control through the administrations, as well as United States relations with the Third World in the Dominican Republic, Nicaragua, Cuba, Africa, Iran, and elsewhere. Many of these subjects merit more space than I can give them. No account of the NSC staff would be complete without coverage of the Iran-Contra mess, but so much has been and will be written here that I have deliberately avoided going into great detail, and have also attempted to bring out aspects of the scandal thus far ignored.

This is a story of people, not simply events, and I have tried to sketch various characters who have figured in the NSC's history. There are, of course, many individuals important to the NSC story who have been left out.

This book would have been impossible but for the help, friendship, cooperation, and assistance of many people. First I thank those who agreed to be interviewed, both on the record and off. Thanks also to the helpful librarians and staffs of the Library of Congress, Columbia University libraries, New York Public Library, Martin Luther King Library, and Wheaton Regional Library of Montgomery County. Providing invaluable assistance were staffs and archivists at the National Archives, Diplomatic Branch; the Harry S. Truman Library; the Dwight D. Eisenhower Library; the John F. Kennedy Library; the Lyndon Baines Johnson Library; the Nixon Library Project and the National Security Archive. Audio-visual archivists at these facilities as well as at the Gerald R. Ford Library and Jimmy Carter Library, furnished prompt and courteous service. Particular thanks go to archivists Herbert Pankratz at the Eisenhower Library and David C. Humphrey at the Johnson Library. Individuals who gave generous help and assistance include Gordon Adams, Scott Armstrong, Gunter Bischof, Larry Bowers, Laurence J. Chang, David Corn, Roger V. Dingman, William Geissler, Lenny Glynn, Frank Greve, Judith Henchy, George McTurnan Kahin, William H. Kincade, Abbot and William Kominers, Stephen M. Katz, Robert K. Manoff, Mark Perry, D. Gareth Porter, Thomas Powers, Joseph Prados, Ann Sierakowski, and Dan and Ellen Wasserman. These people and institutions contributed much to what is good in what follows, but I alone am responsible for the errors and oversights.

—John Prados
Washington, D.C.

CONTENTS

▲▲▲

ACRONYMS

▲▲▲

ABM
Antiballistic Missile
ACDA
Arms Control and Disarmament Agency
AID
Agency for International Development
ARVN
Army of the Republic of Vietnam
BMD
Ballistic Missile Defense
Caricom
Caribbean Community
CENTO
Central Treaty Organization
CIA
Central Intelligence Agency
CORDS
Civilian Operations and Revolutionary Development Support
CPPG
Crisis Pre-Planning Group
CT
Counterterrorist
DAO
Defense Attaché Office
DCI
Director of Central Intelligence
DIA
Defense Intelligence Agency
DOD
Department of Defense
DRV
Democratic Republic of Vietnam
EXCOM
Executive Committee
FPRI
Foreign Policy Research Institute

FRG
Federal Republic of Germany
FSLN
Frente Sandinista de Liberación Nacional
GAO
General Accounting Office
GDR
German Democratic Republic
GVN
Government of Vietnam
HEW
Department of Health, Education and Welfare
IAHRC
Inter-American Human Rights Commission
IAPF
Inter-American Peace Force
ICBM
Intercontinental Ballistic Missile
IBC
International Business Communications, Inc.
ICJ
International Court of Justice
IFIO
Interagency Foreign Information Organization
IFIS
Interagency Foreign Information Staff
IG
Interdepartmental Group
INF
Intermediate Range Nuclear Forces
ISA
International Security Affairs (of OSD)
JCS
Joint Chiefs of Staff
   (CJCS)
   (Chairman, Joint Chiefs of Staff)
JFK
John Fitzgerald Kennedy
LBJ
Lyndon Baines Johnson
MAF
Marine Amphibious Force
MAU
Marine Amphibious Unit

MIA
Missing in Action
MiG
Soviet aircraft type designator
MIRV
Multiple Independently Targetable Reentry Vehicle
MIT
Massachusetts Institute of Technology
NASA
National Aeronautics and Space Administration
NATO
North Atlantic Treaty Organization
NCA
National Command Authority
NIE
National intelligence estimate
NLF
National Liberation Front (Vietnam)
NSAM
National Security Action Memorandum
NSC
National Security Council
NSD
National Security Directive
NSDD
National Security Decision Document
NSDM
National Security Decision Memorandum
NSPG
National Security Planning Group
NSR
National Security Review
NSRB
National Security Resources Board
NSSD
National Security Study Document
NSSM
National Security Study Memorandum
OAS
Organization of American States
OCB
Operations Coordinating Board
ODM
Office of Defense Mobilization

ODSM
Office Directors Staff Meeting
OECS
Organization of Eastern Caribbean States
OEO
Office of Economic Opportunity
OEOB
Old Executive Office Building (previously called Executive Office Build-
ing, and State-War-Navy Building)
OPA
Office of Program Analysis
OPD
Office of Public Diplomacy
OSD
Office of the Secretary of Defense
OSG
Operations Sub-Group (of TIWG)
PB
Planning Board
PC
Principals Committee
PCC
Policy Coordinating Committee
PD/NSC
Presidential Directive
PDB
President's Daily Briefing (or Bulletin)
PFIAB
President's Foreign Intelligence Advisory Board
PFLP
Popular Front for the Liberation of Palestine
PICKL
President's Intelligence Check List
PL
Public law
PLO
Palestine Liberation Organization
POL
Petroleum, oil, lubricants
PPS
Policy Planning Staff
PRC
People's Republic of China
PRC
Policy Review Committee

PRM/NSC
Policy Review Memorandum
PROFS
Professional Office System (an IBM computer program; or, a note generated on this system)
PSAC
President's Science Advisory Committee
PSB
Psychological Strategy Board
RIG
Restricted Interagency Group
RVN
Republic of Vietnam
RVNAF
Republic of Vietnam Armed Forces
SAC
Strategic Air Command
SAC-G
Special Arms Control Group
SAC-PG
Special Arms Control Policy Group
SAIS
School of Advanced International Studies (of The Johns Hopkins University)
SALT
Strategic Arms Limitation Talks
SCC
Special Coordination Committee
SDI
Strategic Defense Initiative
SEATO
Southeast Asia Treaty Organization
SIG
Senior Interdepartmental Group
S/LPD
Secretary of State's Office for Latin Public Diplomacy
START
Strategic Arms Reduction Talks
STTGI
Stanford Technology Trading Group International, Inc.
SVN
South Vietnam
TIWG
Terrorist Incident Working Group

UAR
United Arab Republic
UN
United Nations
U.S.
United States
USC
University of Southern California
USIA
United States Information Agency
U.S.S.
United States Ship
VC
Vietcong
VIG
Vietnam Information Group
VIP
Very important person
VP
Verification Panel

▲▲▲

PROLOGUE

▲

"IS *THAT* U.S. POLICY?"

Ｎone of the passengers would re-
member this trip quite the way they had expected to. As the *Achille
Lauro* nosed her way up to the quay in Alexandria, most thought of
exotic Cairo and the buses waiting to take them there. Only 70 or
80 of the 750 passengers stayed aboard for an evening cruise off the
Nile Delta. On the bridge, Captain Gerardo de Rosa ordered the
routine course changes necessary to get the *Lauro* back to Alexandria
in time to meet the tour group from Cairo.

But on the morning of October 7, 1985, four armed Palestinian
gunmen entered the dining room at 8:45 A.M., in the midst of breakfast service for the remaining passengers, seized hostages, and then
took control of the entire ship. The terrorists ordered Captain de
Rosa to sail the *Achille Lauro* to Tartūs on the Syrian coast.

News of the terrorist incident spread quickly throughout the world.
In Washington there was great concern as seventy-one of the *Achille
Lauro*'s passengers were American and somewhere between eleven
and twenty of them had stayed aboard for the overnight cruise off
the Nile. At the State Department, the Pentagon, and in the intelligence community, American officials did what they could to establish
the facts of the hijacking, but orders for action would have to come
from the White House.

Washington was especially sensitive to the terrorism problem that
fall. For five years, starting with the Iranian hostage crisis, President
Ronald Reagan's administration had been preoccupied with ques-

tions of terrorism and terrorists. Only four months before, in June 1985, Reagan had been faced with another serious incident when TWA Flight 847 was hijacked to Beirut. That time the passengers were held hostage for seventeen days and a U.S. Navy enlisted man brutally murdered. Negotiations successfully ended the TWA 847 incident, but Ronald Reagan worried about the image of the United States government as passive in the face of terrorism. Reagan did not want a rerun of that affair with the *Achille Lauro* incident.

In the United States, on questions of defense and foreign affairs the President is advised by his National Security Council (NSC). According to statute, it stands above all interagency groups in government and its members consist of the Vice President, secretary of state, and secretary of defense; the director of central intelligence and Chairman of the Joint Chiefs of Staff serve as advisers. The NSC is supported by a substructure of interagency groups that Presidents arrange and rearrange at their whim, and by an NSC staff within the White House.

News of the cruise ship hijacking led to an evening meeting in Washington of the NSC's Crisis Pre-Planning Group (CPPG) on October 7. Admiral John M. Poindexter chaired the CPPG. Poindexter was deputy to Robert C. McFarlane, national security adviser and chief of the NSC staff. Both men answered directly to Ronald Reagan. The CPPG's task was to assemble action options for consideration by McFarlane, the NSC, and the President.

Along with Poindexter at the CPPG meeting that Monday night were representatives of the State Department, the Department of Defense (DOD), Central Intelligence Agency (CIA), and a young NSC staffer and Marine officer, Lieutenant Colonel Oliver North. Robert B. Oakley, director of State's office on terrorism, argued for a wait-and-see posture. Colonel North advocated a raid.

National Security Adviser Robert McFarlane conferred twice with Reagan that night. The President ordered certain precautionary military moves. At Haifa, Israel, the guided-missile-carrying destroyer *Scott* put to sea, as did the *Coronado,* the command ship of the United States Sixth Fleet, from Gaeta, north of Naples. From Little Creek, Virginia, a Navy elite counterterrorist commando unit, the

Sea-Air-Land (SEAL) Team Six, moved secretly to Akrotiri air base on Cyprus.

Reagan and McFarlane conferred again on the morning of October 8. A few hours later the raid option evaporated altogether when United States intelligence lost track of the cruise ship.

In the earlier TWA 847 incident, McFarlane had opened a special channel for direct exchange of intelligence information with the Israelis through the political-military section of his NSC staff. Colonel North was the focal point for the exchange at the NSC. When the *Achille Lauro* disappeared, McFarlane got North to reopen the channel, through the Israeli military attaché in Washington.

As the White House planners scrambled to respond, events moved swiftly aboard the *Achille Lauro.* The Palestinians forced Captain de Rosa to make for Tartūs, a port on the narrow Syrian coast. When *Achille Lauro* arrived off that harbor, the Syrians refused to allow De Rosa to enter Tartūs, despite the fact that the hijackers claimed to be with the Palestine Liberation Front, a group that Syria supported.

The hijackers became desperate, demanding that Tartūs send negotiators. At 2:42 P.M. Tartūs time, the voice of one hijacker came over the radio from the *Achille Lauro:* "Negotiators? We will start killing at fifteen hundred [3:00 P.M.]."

At 2:58 P.M. the voice came over the radio again: "We cannot wait any longer. We will start killing."

Once again at 3:23: "What are the developments, Tartūs? We will kill the second. We are losing patience."

Tartūs radio replied at 3:39 P.M.: "The ship is heading towards you for negotiations."

These radio communications were monitored by the Israelis, who feared a terrorist attempt against one of their own Mediterranean ports. The Israelis passed the information to Washington. American intelligence regained contact with the *Achille Lauro,* only to lose it again when the hijackers, apparently fearing that the Syrians were sending a warship to overcome them, ordered Captain de Rosa to move out to sea.

During their talks with the Syrians, the hijackers had been serious about their threats. They murdered a wheelchair-bound American, sixty-nine-year-old Leon Klinghoffer of Manhattan. Meanwhile, the hijackers took the *Achille Lauro* to Port Said in Egypt. There four Palestinians gave themselves up, releasing the ship and hostages in exchange for a promise of safe conduct and a plane to take them to Tunisia.

Throughout the day on October 9, spokesmen at both the White House and State Department insisted they had no independent corroboration of murders aboard the *Achille Lauro*. Then the terrorists surrendered and the truth emerged from other hostages and the crew. Reagan vowed to bring the perpetrators to justice.

On Thursday October 10, President Reagan intended a political trip to Chicago. The NSC morning staff meeting that day was interrupted with a message to the effect that the hijackers had left Egypt. McFarlane asked North to check the report with the Israelis. By 8:45 A.M., North knew that the hijackers were still in Egypt. He dashed to the White House Situation Room. There, McFarlane, about to leave for Chicago with Reagan, was receiving a final review with Admiral Poindexter, NSC Middle East specialist Jock Covey, and press director Karna Small. North delivered the new intelligence, using a euphemism for the Israelis.

"The friends have the four in Egypt," North reported. "We have confirmation. We have to do something about it."

"What can be done?" asked Admiral Poindexter.

North countered with a question: "Do you remember Yamamoto?" He was referring to an episode from World War II, in 1943, when American aircraft were able to intercept and shoot down planes bearing the admiral commanding the Japanese fleet and his staff.

Poindexter remembered Yamamoto but he was perplexed. A "Yamamoto" in the *Achille Lauro* case might involve the deaths of innocent Egyptian pilots and air crew. He made his concern explicit: "You don't want to shoot it down?"

"No," North replied, "just force it to land at [the North Atlantic Treaty Organization air base at] Sigonella, Sicily."

McFarlane was impressed. He told North to get moving on the operation.

Moments later McFarlane left with President Reagan. During their flight to Chicago on *Air Force One,* he acquainted the President with the details of the option for an airborne interception of the Egyptian airplane carrying the Palestinian hijackers.

Upon landing at O'Hare Airport, President Reagan got into trouble in an encounter with reporters. Yasir Arafat, chairman of the main Palestinian umbrella group, the Palestine Liberation Organization (PLO), was saying the PLO itself would bring the terrorists to justice. Chris Wallace, an NBC Television correspondent, asked Reagan about this at O'Hare.

"Well," Reagan replied, "I would think that if [Arafat] believes that their organization has enough of a—sort of a kind of national court set up, like a nation that they can bring them to justice and— carry that out, all right; but just so they are brought to justice."

"But you'd let the PLO punish them, then?"

"What? Yes, I said if they were determined to do that."

Reporter Sam Donaldson of ABC could see Reagan was making a significant misstatement. Official United States policy was not to recognize the PLO as a government, which meant the PLO had no judiciary or standing to punish anyone.

Donaldson tried to help President Reagan with a follow-up question. "But sir, if you would let the PLO punish them, wouldn't that be, in effect, recognizing the PLO as a governing nation, which we don't do?"

"I don't think that would necessarily follow," Ronald Reagan answered. Donaldson thought several of the President's aides looked stricken. A few moments later the television reporter sought out Robert McFarlane.

"Is *that* U.S. policy?" asked Donaldson.

McFarlane growled, "Of course it isn't."

"Then you better get him out again to correct it," said Donaldson, "because it is until he does!" (The President himself later met the press to explain, "I shouldn't have made a statement of that kind.")

In the Aegean Sea the aircraft carrier U.S.S. *Saratoga* was moved into position for an airborne interception. President Reagan made the final decision for the mission aboard *Air Force One* flying back from Chicago. About 4:15 P.M. a Chicago ham radio operator overheard a conversation between the President and Secretary of Defense Caspar A. Weinberger, who also happened to be airborne at that time, en route to his vacation home at Bar Harbor, Maine. The radio transmissions went in clear because the two planes had incompatible scrambling equipment.

An Egyptian Boeing 727 jet left Cairo with the four Palestinians aboard at almost the exact moment Reagan and Weinberger were having their talk. Israeli intelligence supplied the identity of the aircraft, using the NSC channel, within minutes of its takeoff. Powerful F-14 jet fighters intercepted the Egyptian airliner while electronic warfare planes jammed its radio transmissions. The Egyptian plane then followed American orders to fly to Sigonella.

Reagan arrived at the White House unaware of a further problem confronting American forces: Sigonella was in Sicily and the property of the Italian government. The United States needed permission to land there, not only with the airliner and interceptors, but with two large C-141 Air Force transports, carrying Delta Force counterterrorism commandos and Navy SEALs.

Also unknown to Reagan, his NSC staff had already taken steps to solve this problem. Admiral Poindexter, in the Situation Room with the CPPG, told Ollie North to get the prime minister of Italy on the telephone and get him to give permission for the planes to land. North could not get through, however, for aides to the prime minister refused to put through the call. In desperation North turned to NSC consultant Michael A. Ledeen, a personal friend of the prime minister since the 1960s. Finally getting the Italian on the phone, Ledeen quickly secured the needed permission.

When Reagan arrived at home, the Italian headache had evolved to a new stage. Once the planes landed at Sigonella, the SEALs surrounded the Egyptian airliner as the United States informed Italy it intended to file papers for the extradition of the terrorists. But Italian authorities on the scene took a dim view of U.S. Special Forces troopers' extralegal action against the airliner. Bilateral treaty law required the existence of an arrest warrant prior to an extradition request, which entailed a forty-five-day period for legal formalities.

As the American soldiers surrounded the Egyptian plane, Italian security forces surrounded the Americans and, for good measure, parked vehicles in front of the C-141s in order to block them from taking off.

In the Situation Room an instantaneous satellite communications link enabled a breathless NSC staff and a handful of senior officials to hear the action as it occurred on the tarmac at Sigonella. There was a real problem with the extradition request since the entire United States action had been based on secret intelligence passed by the Israelis, not evidence that could be used to obtain a warrant in a court of law. Attorney General Edwin Meese, deputy press secretary Larry Speakes, and Poindexter, the top officials present in the Situation Room, had no doubt that Washington could not act quickly enough to meet the exigencies of the situation at Sigonella.

Michael Ledeen got on the telephone once more, with Prime Minister Bettino Craxi, at 4:00 A.M. on October 11. Ronald Reagan even came on the line. Craxi, however, was under increased pressure once Larry Speakes revealed the American action, as he had five hours earlier. Craxi had difficulty understanding the State Department translator, so Ledeen took over. The Italian asked Reagan for information Ledeen himself had already twice provided, information the NSC consultant thought the President had not been briefed on, so he deliberately changed Reagan's statements in translating them. Ledeen mistranslated again toward the end of the conversation when Reagan pleasantly conceded it might be acceptable if the two main perpetrators were jailed; the consultant repeated an earlier American demand that all four be imprisoned. That was the denouement, for the President had no choice except to acquiesce in Italian handling of the hijackers. An incident between Italian and American troops was avoided, but the Delta Force soldiers came home empty-handed.

Thus ended the *Achille Lauro* affair, which the public relations experts insisted was a great success. The Italians went on to arrest the hijackers themselves, prosecuting them since the incident had occurred aboard an Italian vessel. The four hijackers received long prison sentences although the mastermind behind the plot, who had not participated in the actual hijacking, was quietly allowed to disappear into Yugoslavia, thence to Libya. As for Michael Ledeen's deliberate inaccuracies, Ronald Reagan later thanked him for his "helpful translation."

The National Security Council staff had worked very hard during the *Achille Lauro* affair. It had invented the option the President in fact selected, and supervised the actions of the bureaucracy that led to the successful interception of the hijackers. On the surface, where only that success was apparent, it looked like the NSC staff in its classical role. Beneath the surface, things were a little more complex, for Ronald Reagan was a President having to be saved from himself. In the short space of one day, the national security adviser had felt he had to correct the President's misstatement of United States policy, while an NSC consultant had had to mistranslate to save the President from making what he perceived as policy errors.

McFarlane and Ledeen, along with Poindexter and North, no doubt thought they were just doing their jobs, and doing them well at that. Since it was all so secret, no one could know, then, that the NSC staff was acting in place of the usual institutions of government. They were the keepers of the keys.

▲▲▲

PART I

▲

BROKERS

Harry Truman's desire drove everything in the early years of the National Security Council. Truman made the group's purely advisory status crystal clear by his refusal to attend in the first years. When the President softened and began to appear, the council gained importance. The council became the top level of a policy machine serving up ideas and recommendations, plus a sounding board where the President could listen to informed discussion about the implications of contemplated actions.

There were two streams of activity in the day-to-day operations of the National Security Council system. The more formal of the two provided for the creation of policy papers by the NSC's various departments and agencies. Once drafted, the papers went up for discussion before the full council and were then approved or rejected by the President. The second stream involved policy advice, more or less spontaneous. The two streams flowed together in 1950, a crisis year for the Truman presidency.

▲▲▲

CREATION OF THE
NATIONAL SECURITY COUNCIL

▲▲▲

During World War II the military services had had to cooperate in unprecedented ways. The war had once again shown the delicacy of the relationship between force and diplomacy. At the end of it there began a great debate over the future shape of American military organization and the degree to which the armed services ought to be "integrated" together and with the diplomats. Through the war's end the United States had had separate War and Navy departments (the air force at that time being part of the Army). Each department prepared its own plan for the postwar reorganization. The War Department plan, which President Truman initially preferred, provided for a unified military establishment under a single civilian secretary. The Navy's plan was prepared under Ferdinand Eberstadt, a close friend and confidant of Navy Secretary James V. Forrestal. The Eberstadt report recommended several integrating mechanisms at the pinnacle of government, among them a "Council of Common Defense" composed of senior national security officials, and a "National Security Resources Board," to monitor preparations for military mobilization.

President Truman's initial message to Congress on December 19, 1945, asked it to create a unified military establishment, but made concessions also to those who favored integration at the policy-making level. They included an advisory board of chiefs of staff and service commanders and, after March 1946, a national defense council. While other elements of the unification project remained controversial, the Army and Navy reached agreement on several of the integrating mechanisms. Both services advocated the "Council of Common Defense" and the "National Security Resources Board" to Truman at a White house meeting on May 13, 1946, and they told Congress of the formula in a joint letter dated May 31.

That winter, at a November 12 meeting at Forrestal's Georgetown home, War and Navy department officials agreed upon the membership for the proposed council. Both the council and the resources board were included in the recommendations of a second joint letter sent to Congress, on January 16, 1947, and in Truman's formal request for legislation made a month later. The proposed legislation became bill S.758 in the Senate and HR.2319 in the House of Representatives. Both versions dropped the "common defense" nomenclature and substituted the appellation "National Security Council."

Supporting the broad legislation for unification of the armed forces, in his testimony James Forrestal declared that the National Security Council (NSC) was "perhaps the most important feature of the bill now under consideration." Congress agreed, so the NSC was featured in the text passed on July 25. Harry Truman signed it into law the next day, and it became the National Security Act of 1947.

Walter Millis, editor of Forrestal's diaries, notes that the NSC, beginning with its initial meeting on September 26, was launched "not without certain doubts and jealousies." In fact, ten days earlier General Lauris Norstad of the Air Force had told Forrestal at lunch that Dean Acheson at the State Department was dubious "and would undoubtedly try to castrate its effectiveness." The biggest doubter, however, was Harry Truman himself, who was suspicious of anything that might intrude into presidential prerogatives. He put a trusted friend in place as NSC executive secretary, but on important matters communicated his views through White House counsel Clark M. Clifford or talked directly with Forrestal, who could speak at NSC meetings.

Later, when officials were trying to explain the NSC system to John F. Kennedy, they said that Harry Truman had relied on a critique by the Bureau of the Budget (BOB). That BOB study noted that the establishment of the NSC did not increase a President's authority or decrease his responsibility, nor did it circumscribe his freedom of choice. But, observed the August 8, 1947, study, the "objectives would be advantaged if the President refrained from attending the majority of Council meetings. This would assure the advisory nature of the Council's actions and guard against its becoming an operating body with the President pressed to resolve spot issues."

President Truman made his concept of the NSC explicit in a letter to members on July 26, 1948. The council was to be a "channel for collective advice and information" regarding just one discrete part of the President's total range of responsibilities. "With complete freedom to accept, reject and amend the Council's advice and to consult with other members of his official family," Truman wrote, "it is the prerogative of the President to determine such policy and enforce it." The sole exception would be general direction and coordination of intelligence operations, for which the NSC was legally responsible under the National Security Act of 1947.

Executive secretary for the NSC was Rear Admiral Sidney William Souers, a Hoosier in whom Truman saw a kindred spirit. Both had been reserve officers (Truman in the Army and Souers the Navy) and both entrepreneurs as well (Truman a haberdasher, Souers owner of the Piggly Wiggly department store chain and purveyor of insurance). Souers had worked in the

Office of Naval Intelligence during the war, helped Truman draft and implement the postwar reorganization of United States intelligence agencies, and been the first director of central intelligence. He returned briefly to insurance before, at fifty-six, coming to the White House to work on NSC matters. Sid Souers became Harry Truman's trusted agent responsible for monitoring the NSC. A poker-playing crony of the President's, Admiral Souers was on easy terms with Harry Truman.

For his single secretary of defense, another creation of the National Security Act, the President selected James Forrestal. An advocate of creating an NSC, Forrestal now became the catalyst in making it work. Though rarely contributing to NSC papers, Forrestal was in contact with Sid Souers almost daily during the first year. His office became the source of many of the requests for policy papers that reached Souers's desk. Forrestal assigned his special assistant, John H. Ohly, also in touch with Souers, to follow up on the subjects raised. Robert Blum, another Forrestal aide, sat as observer with the NSC consultants group, as did Major General Alfred M. Gruenther for the Joint Chiefs of Staff (JCS), the military policy body created by the National Security Act.

From its inception through the end of 1948, the National Security Council held 30 meetings, considered 79 papers, and took 166 actions, though many of the latter amounted to noting, amending, or issuing policy papers. The NSC nevertheless recommended the policies President Truman actually pursued with respect to the Greek civil war, Italy, the Berlin blockade, and China, where a United States naval base at Tsingtao seemed threatened by civil war. Through its policy paper NSC-20/4, the NSC played a formative role in approval of the plan named for Secretary of State George C. Marshall, under which the United States provided economic aid for the postwar recovery of European countries.

Some came to believe, Jim Forrestal among them, that the NSC was an unwieldy mechanism for debating policy. There were just too many members to be heard at the council, including the President, Forrestal, sub-cabinet-level secretaries for three armed services, the chairman of the National Security Resources Board (NSRB), the secretary of state, other Cabinet officers, and numerous advisers and observers. Forrestal was also unhappy as secretary of defense because he lacked power over the service secretaries, and the military were unhappy with the unrealistically small size allowed the Joint Staff that served the JCS. These concerns led Truman to request amendments of the National Security Act, amendments Congress passed and which became law on August 10, 1949. President Truman made certain additional reforms by an executive order a little over a week later.

The reorganization streamlined the national security policy machinery. They established the basic structure of the modern Department of Defense (DOD) and administratively located the National Security Council within the Executive Office of the President. The 1949 amendments pared the NSC by four members, eliminating the three service secretaries and the NSRB chairman, but added the Vice President as a member and the Chairman of the JCS and director of central intelligence as statutory advisers. Four people—the President, the Vice President, and the secretaries of state and defense—have been the NSC principals ever since.

Harry Truman's attitude toward the NSC changed with the onset of the Korean War. He began to use the council as a group of senior collaborators searching with him for the best policies. Though Truman made his initial decision to intervene in Korea outside the NSC framework, within days of the June 25, 1950, North Korean invasion of South Korea, Truman was consulting his council almost daily. In the six months immediately preceding the outbreak of hostilities in Korea, seven NSC meetings had considered twenty-four papers and taken thirty-nine actions. Between the beginning of the war and the end of 1950 (six months), there were eighteen NSC meetings discussing fifty-three papers and taking ninety-seven actions. President Truman attended almost all of them. For Harry Truman the National Security Council had achieved legitimacy.

Here was the ultimate triumph for those who had worked so hard toward the ideal of policy integration. One, James Forrestal, was not around to see these fruits of his labor. Greatly depressed despite his accomplishments, in May 1949 Forrestal had leaped from a sixteenth-floor hospital window and taken his own life. That unfortunate act, however, saved Forrestal from having to witness what his NSC would become.

FIST ON THE TABLE

▲▲▲

I n many ways the bread-and-butter work of the National Security Council was the production of policy papers. These were not mere hortatory statements of intent; rather the NSC papers became the real expression of policy from which diplomatic and other initiatives followed. The very first policy paper, which after several revisions was known as NSC-1/3, sanctioned covert American involvement in Italian politics to forestall electoral victory by the Italian Communist Party. The papers NSC-4/A and NSC-10/2, later followed by NSC-10/5, established a broader program of covert activities worldwide. American policy for Japan was established in NSC-13 during 1948 and modified the following year by NSC-13/3. Atomic weapons policy was set in September 1948 by NSC-30, which provided that the United States "must be ready to utilize promptly and effectively all appropriate means available, including atomic weapons, in the interest of national security."

The evolving cold war confrontation between the United States and the Soviet Union, epitomized in the Berlin blockade crisis of 1948–1949, was naturally a major area of NSC work. In March 1948, President Truman approved the basic policy stated in NSC-7, which provided that the "defeat of the forces of Soviet-directed world communism is vital to the security of the United States" and that "this objective cannot be achieved by a defensive policy." The Soviet policy was buttressed six months later by NSC-58, providing guidelines for dealing with Soviet-dominated Eastern Europe.

The policy papers, and there were many more of them than can be mentioned here, represented the best effort of the United States government to clarify its objectives, inventory its resources, and establish criteria for assessing progress.

The papers themselves, in the original schema for the National Security Council, were to be the responsibility of the NSC staff, located across from the White House at the Executive Office Building,* by the end of 1948. The schema provided for five top-level staffers, an equal number of assistants, plus researchers and clerical workers not to exceed a total staff of twenty. The only professional NSC staff were the executive secretary and

---

* Later the Old Executive Office Building (OEOB) which, for continuity, will be used here throughout.

33

his assistant. As a temporary measure the top staff, called consultants, and their assistants, were detailed one each by the three armed services and the State Department, which was asked to nominate a coordinator and assigned Max Bishop to the job. This expedient for filling NSC staff posts became the Truman administration's standard procedure. The staff was to maintain close contact with all concerned departments and agencies. When a policy paper was assigned, the NSC staff would map out the project, obtain the necessary facts, views and opinions from the bureaucracy, analyze the information in an effort to devise a generally acceptable solution, attempt to reconcile any remaining divergent views, and finally prepare a report for the council presenting concisely the facts, conclusions and recommendations, or alternatively, the majority and minority proposals.

All this would have been a large task even for a dedicated professional unit, but it was impossible for the NSC staff alone to produce the policy papers. With a budget of only two hundred thousand dollars, the NSC staff had neither the time nor resources to compile policy papers. More important, the staff did not have detailed knowledge on specific subjects and could not therefore represent agency views.

As time passed, NSC principals increasingly resisted the procedure of NSC staff drafting of papers, arguing that their organizations were better equipped to handle such projects. President Truman responded by more frequently assigning papers to Cabinet officials, such as the secretaries of state and defense, who would delegate ad hoc groups to do the drafting. The executive secretary soon found he had the added task of prodding the bureaucracy to produce.

In November 1949, Sid Souers told Harry Truman he needed to take care of his business interests in St. Louis. At first the President acquiesced, asking Souers to advise him by describing the traits he should look for in a National Security Council executive secretary. The admiral's reply still stands as a fine description of the qualities necessary in a national security adviser.

"*He should be a non-political confidant of the president.*" Admiral Souers wrote, "a trusted member of the president's immediate official family," but "should not be identified with the immediate staff of personal advisers."

"*He must be objective and willing to subordinate his personal views on policy to his task of coordinating the views* of all responsible officials." Souers believed that the NSC deputy was "only a servant of the president *and the other members of the Council.*" Indeed, "his job is not to sell the president an idea with which he is in sympathy, but rather to insure [*sic*] that the views of *all* interested departments and agencies are reflected."

Equally important, Sid Souers noted, "*he must be willing to forego [sic] publicity and personal* aggrandizement."

Harry Truman was apparently unable to bear Sidney Souers's departure, however, and finally refused to let him go until the admiral agreed to continue advising him. Truman announced in January 1950 that Deputy Executive Secretary James S. Lay would succeed to the position, yet the President simultaneously designated Admiral Sidney Souers as "special consultant" to the President on national security. Souers continued to attend sessions of the National Security Council, and admitted to deputy chief of Army staff General Alfred Gruenther that he was spending most of his time in Washington.

He continued to supervise the NSC staff, although by statute that job belonged to the executive secretary.

The persistence of Admiral Souers's major national security role, given the strictures of the National Security Act of 1947, could easily have triggered a personality battle within the NSC staff. That it did not is a tribute to the character of successor James Sheldon Lay. Responsibility and discretion were second nature to Lay, who viewed himself as a technician, oiling the machinery of state. A reserve Army officer, Lay was called to active duty in May 1941 and became an intelligence specialist, rising to colonel and secretary of the Joint Intelligence Committee of the Joint Chiefs of Staff. Lay first met Souers during World War II, when the latter held a senior post in naval intelligence, and worked for him in 1946, when Souers headed the National Intelligence Authority and Lay was secretary to that body. In 1947, Souers made him assistant to the NSC executive secretary.

Just as Souers had consulted with Clifford, Lay would talk with Truman's counsel Charles S. Murphy, with whom Souers had also dealt after Clifford left the White House. Lay was a close friend of Murphy's, as well as of White House staffer David H. Stowe's. All of them owned adjoining summer homes and often rode to work together.

If Jimmy Lay managed to avoid conflicts with Admiral Souers, secretaries of state and defense, Dean Acheson and Louis A. Johnson, did not. An effort to update the basic national security policy promulgated in NSC-20/4 brought conflict into the open.

Louis Johnson was a fighter and prided himself on being completely without scruples. He had been a founder of the American Legion and its national president in the mid-1930s, and served as assistant secretary of war from 1937 to 1940. Johnson was a millionaire lawyer and major fund-raiser for Harry Truman's 1948 reelection campaign. When the President was forced to find a replacement for the ailing Jim Forrestal in March 1949, he seized upon the tough-minded Johnson, whom he thought could help mount a major effort to limit the military budget.

While committing himself to austerity at the Department of Defense, one of Johnson's first moves was to discard the relatively austere office Forrestal had used at the Pentagon in favor of a more opulent suite used by the wartime secretary. Johnson also created misgivings by appointing former colleagues from the American Legion as his senior assistants in place of experienced officials. Almost immediately he canceled a major Navy aircraft carrier program, igniting a bitter interservice dispute between the Navy and

Air Force over the role of naval power versus that of strategic air attack. Johnson embarrassed Harry Truman by telling the President that Gordon Gray, then assistant secretary of the army, wanted to be appointed secretary when Gray, in fact, was preparing to leave for the University of North Carolina. (Gray saved Truman from what could have been a public relations disaster by gracefully consenting to serve a few months as secretary before leaving as he had planned.) Johnson also meddled with the NSC staff by trying to get Souers, then Lay, to assume authority for supervising other government agencies to ensure that the council's decisions were carried out. The executive secretaries, "quite properly" in Truman's view, refused to do so on the grounds that if Congress had intended that role for the NSC staff director, it would have so provided in the National Security Act.

In the meantime, international events and technological developments began to call into question America's ability to meet its security requirements with small military budgets, especially in the face of the signing of the North Atlantic Treaty in late 1949 with its considerable demands for the permanent stationing of substantial United States military forces in Europe. In addition, American intelligence received evidence that the Russians had successfully detonated an atomic bomb. The Soviet achievement sharpened American deliberations on whether to proceed with a program to create hydrogen bombs.

On December 20, 1949, Admiral Souers sent a memorandum to NSC principals pointing out that "without an integrated assessment and appraisal" of actual and potential United States military power, there could be "no certainty" that the accumulation of separate policy statements "adequately meets the requirements of our national security." Souers recommended that the NSC staff assemble a new report "with the advice and assistance of all appropriate executive departments and agencies." The National Security Council approved this project in NSC Action No. 270 on January 5, 1950.

Jimmy Lay, acting through Souers as special consultant, asked Truman to approve it. Meanwhile, since mid-1949 there had been opposition among some State Department officials to NSC staff participation in drafting policy papers, and counsel Charles Murphy now advised the President that the paper should be assigned to an ad hoc group. On January 31, Truman ordered the study but directed that it be written by the secretaries of state and defense. That day the President also approved the hydrogen bomb program and asked for an assessment of its strategic and foreign policy implications. The two projects eventually merged into a single policy paper that received the number NSC-68.

A ten-member panel formed to labor on NSC-68. The most formidable of State's detailees was Paul H. Nitze, an investment banker just turned forty-three, who had recently replaced one of the major architects of containment, George F. Kennan, as director of State's Policy Planning Staff. James Forrestal had known Nitze when both worked at the Wall Street firm

Dillon, Read and Company, and in 1940 he brought Nitze into government as an assistant. Nitze had gone on to become an economic adviser at State, and had held several wartime economic management positions in the Roosevelt administration.

In drafting NSC-68, Nitze made use of both his interest in strategic military issues and his Harvard training in economics. He was aware of arguments advanced in late 1949 and early 1950 by Leon H. Keyserling, chairman of Truman's Council of Economic Advisers, that the administration could afford to spend more if it dispensed for a few years with its preoccupation with balancing the budget. While Keyserling preferred to put money into domestic programs, Nitze favored higher military spending. Truman's directive to the compilers of the NSC policy paper to consider actual *and potential* United States resources opened the door to larger allocations for the military. In this Nitze was but following the lead of his boss Dean Acheson, who was concerned with the need to devote sufficient resources to the military in order to meet the broad range of American commitments, and who had also favored the very expensive hydrogen bomb development program.

The Department of Defense, of course, provided the other half of the policy paper drafting group, and Louis Johnson remained wedded to restricted Pentagon budgets. Johnson also took the position that nothing in the policy review should affect current policies and programs, and in the middle of the drafting process he issued guidelines for the following year's military budget that provided a dollar ceiling no higher than the fiscal year 1951 budget that had just been sent to Congress.

Conferees from State and Defense moved rapidly on the policy paper, preparing a preliminary report between February 8 and 27. Johnson's representative, retired General James H. Burns, and Acheson decided that the time had come for a conference where Acheson and Johnson could review the preliminary draft before it was put in final form for departmental review. A meeting was scheduled for March 22 in the conference room of the State Department's Policy Planning Staff, because the secretary of state did not have adequate conference facilities of his own. According to Acheson a copy of the draft went to Johnson in mid-March. Acheson himself had also been keeping President Truman abreast of the progress of the policy paper.

On the afternoon of the twenty-second, at 3:00 P.M., the members of the drafting group filed into the conference room along with Acheson. Louis Johnson entered also, with General Omar N. Bradley, Chairman of the Joint Chiefs. Attending for the White House were both Souers and Jimmy Lay along with S. Everett Gleason, deputy executive secretary of the NSC staff.

After friendly greetings, Johnson interrupted the secretary of state as soon as he began to outline the purpose of the meeting. He asked if Acheson had read the paper, and when the secretary of state replied that he had read most of it the previous day, Johnson countered that the paper had only been given to him at ten that morning. Johnson also claimed that Bradley had not read the paper either, but when Acheson offered to postpone the meeting so all would have a chance to read it, "Johnson replied that since he and General Bradley were here they might as well continue with the meeting."

Acheson, who liked Nitze because of his clear, incisive mind, then asked the policy planning chief to outline the paper and its conclusions. Nitze began saying that General Truman Landon would summarize the military implications of the study. Acheson recalled:

> Johnson listened, chair tilted back, gazing at the ceiling, seemingly calm and attentive. Suddenly he lunged forward with a crash of chair legs on the floor and fist on the table, scaring me out of my shoes. No one, he shouted, was going to make arrangements for him to meet with another Cabinet officer and a roomful of people and be told what he was going to report to the President.

The secretary of state tried to calm Johnson down, but the secretary of defense stood up and stalked out of the room ordering General Bradley to leave with him. General Burns put his head in his hands and wept.

Secretary Johnson in fact went into Acheson's own office and there summoned the secretary of state. Johnson continued to insist that he had been insulted. Acheson had had enough. "I told him since he had started to leave, to get on with it and the State Department would complete the report alone and explain why." Acheson then returned to the disrupted meeting. Within an hour Harry Truman called Acheson to express dismay, instructing that everyone proceed with the paper as though nothing had happened.

Indeed Louis Johnson was finessed on NSC-68. The final draft circulated on March 31 when Johnson was at The Hague for a meeting of North Atlantic Treaty defense ministers. The Joint Chiefs of Staff unanimously supported the paper and virtually all the interested bureaucracy signed off on it before the secretary of defense returned. Johnson was left with little choice, and he notified Truman on April 11 that he approved the policy paper. The next day Truman referred the paper, now officially NSC-68, for the council's consideration.

The paper reaffirmed the United States' objectives stated in NSC-20/4 but warned that "in the light of present and prospective Soviet atomic capabilities, the action which can be taken under present programs and plans . . . becomes dangerously inadequate in both timing and scope." Continuing present programs, NSC-68 envisioned, "would result in a serious decline in the strength of the free world," The paper presented evidence that the United States could afford to spend more for defense, advocated increased conventional forces to lessen dependence upon nuclear weapons, and discussed economic and political aspects of regional situations, primarily that in Western Europe. The policy paper held out the possibility of negotiations with the Soviets, but only "after a decision and a start on building up the strength of the free world," and mainly for the purpose of facilitating "the process of accommodation by the Kremlin to the new situation." Thus:

> In summary, we must, by means of a rapid and sustained build-up of the political, economic, and military strength of the free world, and by means of an affirmative program designed to wrest the initiative from the Soviet Union, confront it with convincing evidence of the determination and ability of the free world to frustrate the Kremlin design of a world dominated by its will. Such evidence is the only means short of war which eventually may force the Kremlin to abandon its present course of action and to negotiate acceptable agreements.

Beyond the rhetoric of its advocacy, however, NSC-68 did not in fact detail feasible military programs, outline required force levels, or provide cost data. Moreover, Louis Johnson was not the only official committed to restricted military spending. Truman's own Bureau of the Budget, with the official responsibility for producing the annual budget, held similar views. Truman himself may have been irritated at Louis Johnson, but he did not immediately approve NSC-68, instead ordering up program and cost estimates to be assembled by another ad hoc committee. Council meetings on the subject would be held through the fall of 1950 and the NSC-68 series would be extended by three more papers projecting programs and costs. Many advocates worried that Truman would not in the end accept great military spending increases. More than anything else, the factor that ultimately turned the tide was the advent of the Korean War.

"YOU COULD DEPEND
ON HIM"

▲▲▲

T here was one recommendation of NSC-68 that received almost immediate attention from President Truman and his National Security Council: a "revised and strengthened staff organization under the National Security Council" that could develop program proposals for NSC consideration. For some time Admiral Souers and Jimmy Lay had been concerned at the way the staff was evolving. Members detailed from the federal bureaucracy, who worked as a group in the NSC staff offices at the OEOB, gradually came to be seen as interlopers by their respective agencies. At the same time, the more senior "consultants" nominated by the bureaucracy held heavy departmental responsibilities. Over time the consultants devoted less and less attention to NSC business. As a result the bureaucracy more and more often submitted its recommendations directly to the council, bypassing the NSC staff, while the council more frequently referred matters to ad hoc groups rather than using the NSC staff. Souers and Lay saw the increasing isolation of the NSC staff as a significant problem and used the NSC-68 recommendation to propose changes.

In a memorandum circulated on April 17, 1950, Lay saw the new organization as existing of a "senior staff group" of designated agency representatives who would be "individuals who are clearly in a position to reflect fully and accurately the policies and views of the officials whom they represent." The senior staff members would be the points of contact between the NSC staff organization and their respective agencies and would have no other departmental responsibilities. The senior staff would have the authority to augment the staff as necessary and the existing NSC staff would be assigned as assistants to the senior group.

One significant change provided by the new scheme was that the Joint Chiefs of Staff would have their own representative on the senior staff. The lack of such representation previously had made it difficult to anticipate JCS views on a matter prior to receipt of their formal written opinions, at which point military positions would largely be locked in. Having an NSC staff member would afford the Chiefs an avenue to learn of the council's initiatives at an early stage and bring their influence to bear. While the Joint

Chiefs might have been expected to favor the proposal for this reason, in their April 20 commentary on the idea, they argued that it would be impossible for a single member to represent the views of a corporate body like the Chiefs.

On May 18 the NSC discussed the views of the Joint Chiefs and set up a special committee to make a recommendation. The committee was discharged after Harry Truman preempted further discussion by a July 19 letter to NSC members, ordering them to nominate members for "a senior NSC staff group which will be designated by me as Chairman of the Council." The senior staff arrangement was changed, however, to the extent that members would not work exclusively on NSC matters. The staff was duly designated at the sixty-third meeting of the National Security Council on August 3, 1950. The Joint Chiefs' first senior staff member was Rear Admiral E. T. Wooldridge. Thereafter the senior staff met on the average two or three times a week.

In his July 19 letter, President Truman also took action on the bothersome question of attendance at NSC meetings. During the years when Truman avoided meetings, more and more people besides the members had been going to them, including the consultants and other departmental advisers, which tended to inhibit members from expressing their views. In his July 19 letter, the President wrote, "Attendance at recent meetings of the Council has been so large that I feel it has discouraged free discussion." Truman proceeded to order that attendance be restricted to members, his NSC staff representatives, and other officials only with his specific approval.

In the meantime cooperation between the Pentagon and State Department became hostage to the tense personal relations of their chiefs. Truman had great and growing regard for his secretary of state but could not blithely ignore his secretary of defense. Harry Truman's solution was to bring in a new man he thought could be useful, specifically in smoothing out Cabinet relations on foreign affairs. That man was William Averell Harriman, then in Paris as a coordinator of the Marshall Plan aid. Harriman was a man of intelligence and discretion, rather akin to Clark Clifford, who had served both Truman and Franklin Roosevelt in a variety of tough jobs. He had been secretary of commerce in Truman's first administration. In 1948 the President considered making Harriman secretary of state but, in view of his business and economic experience, gave him the Marshall Plan task instead.

Averell was the son of Edward H. Harriman, wealthy director of the Union Pacific Railroad. He grew up at Arden House, a forty-bedroom mansion on a twenty-thousand-acre estate between Tuxedo Park and West Point, New York. A product of Groton and Yale, Averell went to work for the Union Pacific but soon left to become a shipping magnate and to form a private bank with his brother that later became Brown Brothers, Harriman & Company. An early Republican, during his Roosevelt period Averell became a Democrat and decided life was more fun that way.

41

Harriman knew almost everyone, both in Washington and internationally. He had known Dean Acheson since 1905, when Dean joined the Yale freshman crew team, which Averell coached. Truman had some concern that the press would see Harriman's return as a bid to take over Dean Acheson's job as secretary of state, but Acheson was confident in his relationship with Averell and reassured Truman.

A popular misconception of Harriman's role as special assistant has been that he became a sort of roving ambassador for Harry Truman. In fact, Harriman, with Souers and Jimmy Lay, worked harmoniously as a triumvirate of presidential advisers facilitating the activities of the National Security Council. Souers remained the observer and coordinator, while Lay saw to the smooth running of the NSC machinery. Harriman became the advocate and troubleshooter, and in this sense was the President's first real lieutenant on the NSC staff. That was Harriman's own concept of the job, as he told journalist friend Cyrus L. Sulzberger only days after his appointment, when Averell compared his role to that of Harry Hopkins under Roosevelt, with the exception that he would confine himself to foreign affairs.

Harry Truman proved to be quite happy with the arrangement. Years later, asked why he had relied upon Harriman to undertake so many delicate missions, the former President replied simply, "Because he was completely trustworthy. He'd do what you asked him to do, and you could depend on him to tell you the complete truth about what had happened."

Harriman demonstrated his energetic approach to the job within days of the appointment. The original plan had been that Averell should stay in Paris until August taking care of loose ends on the economic aid program. But on June 25 in Korea, North Korean forces crossed the 38th Parallel, a postwar demarcation line, and invaded South Korea. When Harriman learned of Truman's order for American intervention, he telephoned Dean Acheson to ask the secretary of state to clear an immediate return with the President. Harriman was on a plane to Washington soon after.

State Department Soviet expert Charles E. Bohlen accompanied Harriman on the trip, first to London to catch the plane, then across the Atlantic. It was a bumpy ride that betokened their emotions as they tried to figure out what lay ahead in Korea. Approaching New York's Idlewild Airport the plane was buffeted by a thunderstorm, suddenly losing a thousand feet of altitude. Dishes, sugar, and utensils were thrown into the aisles. Unperturbed, Harriman stood through it all in the bathroom, hat on his head, shaving. By 5:00 P.M. on June 29, Harriman was listening to the discussion at a National Security Council meeting.

It was not long before Louis Johnson tried to draw Harriman into his conflict with Acheson. On one occasion the secretary of defense offered a ride to Harriman aide Theodore Tannenwald, Jr. As they sat in the backseat of the limousine, Johnson, who had never before met Tannenwald, began to gripe about the secretary of state. Harriman himself was sitting in Johnson's Pentagon office on July 3 when the secretary of defense took a call from Republican Robert A. Taft, Truman's nemesis and one of his toughest opponents in the Senate. Johnson proceeded to congratulate Taft for a speech in which the senator had attacked Truman for not consulting Congress before the Korean intervention, and had called for Acheson's resignation. Then Johnson turned to Harriman and said that if they could get Acheson out of office, the secretary of defense would make sure Averell became the next secretary of state.

That upset Harriman, who felt that Johnson was trying to buy him. White-faced, the special assistant went immediately to Truman and reported the conversation. Harriman already felt that Taft "believes in things I consider dangerous to national security," and the incident destroyed his confidence in Louis Johnson. Averell subsequently joined with State and Bureau of the Budget officials who opposed Johnson.

As for Truman, at a Blair House meeting on July 3 the President confirmed his decision not to seek congressional backing for Korean intervention, on the grounds that the United States had a United Nations mandate to pursue the war. This decision, ultimately of great political cost for Truman, was thus partly influenced by growing animosity for Louis Johnson.

The early dilemma over congressional approval became the first of many travails involving Korea, which would occupy a considerable portion of Harriman's time as special assistant. Another, most pernicious problem, one that occasioned Harriman's first special mission for the President, was General Douglas A. MacArthur. The general was virtually a proconsul at Tokyo, simultaneously theater commander for Korea as chief of the U.S. Far East Command; United Nations commander in chief; and representative in Japan of the victors of World War II, who had yet to agree on a peace treaty for the Japanese. MacArthur had trouble with the notion of limited war in Korea and was constantly making moves that made Washington nervous. In July 1950, MacArthur visited Taiwan to suggest support for Chinese Nationalist operations against mainland China—which was anathema to American allies in the United Nations and at that time to Washington as well.

Harry Truman needed someone to talk sense to MacArthur and he sent Harriman. Averell had known the haughty general as far back as the 1920s, when MacArthur was commandant of the military academy at West Point, Harriman used to invite him to go duck hunting on the Arden House estate.

Harriman undertook a whirlwind Far East trip with mixed results. In over eight hours of discussions, he explained to the general in great detail how the Chinese Nationalists could be a liability to the United States given the danger of a split in United Nations unity over mainland China. The Nationalists could not be permitted to become the catalyst for a war between the United States and China. As a soldier, MacArthur replied, he would follow the orders of his supreme commander, yet "he accepted the President's position . . . but without full conviction." Harriman reported, "I did not feel that we came to a full agreement."

In another aspect of their discussions, Harriman proved quite useful to MacArthur. The general had devised a bold plan to break the North Korean invaders in the south by an amphibious invasion to their rear, at a port called Inchon. For numerous technical and operational reasons, the military had misgivings about MacArthur's plan. Talks with Harriman and the military officers who accompanied him helped convince Washington that the idea was feasible. Almost the first thing Harriman did when he returned was spend a full day in conference with the Joint Chiefs of Staff and other Pentagon officials. The Chiefs finally supported the concept but still opposed MacArthur's choice of target. When the invasion actually occurred on September 15, it proved an outstanding success.

MacArthur meanwhile continued to provoke. In late August he sent a message regarding Taiwan to a convention of the Veterans of Foreign Wars, which was regarded as a breach of the understanding supposedly reached in Tokyo. Truman used a previously scheduled August 26 meeting to ask senior officials whether they had had advance knowledge of the general's message. None had. Furious, the President ordered Louis Johnson to instruct MacArthur to withdraw the message.

Truman's order led directly to another spat between Johnson and Acheson. After the meeting, Johnson called the secretary of state to say that withdrawal of the message would cause embarrassment; rather it should be clarified at the Washington level. By this time Acheson was beyond compromises with the secretary of defense. He called Harriman to ask if the President had in fact issued an order. Averell confirmed Acheson's recollection, then called Louis Johnson, whereupon the President himself came on the line and dictated the message he wanted to go to MacArthur. Once more Johnson called Acheson to question the wisdom of this procedure, and once more Acheson reported this to Harriman. Truman then instructed Harriman that the cable had better go as he had dictated it. The cable did go out, MacArthur withdrew his message officially, but because it had been given in advance to the press, it was widely published anyway.

This episode did nothing for Louis Johnson within the administration. On September 1, Truman decided the time had finally come to get rid of Johnson. Five days later he spoke to General George C. Marshall about assuming the post. Marshall cautioned the President that he might be a liability, as he was still being blamed for the "loss" of China, but would follow Truman's wishes. When Johnson went to the President, after *The New York Times* printed a story that he was about to be dismissed, Truman forced him to resign. The President later told Bess Truman that Johnson cried as he signed the letter of resignation. Marshall became secretary of defense on September 21, 1950.

MacArthur meanwhile had sent United Nations forces across the 38th

Parallel into North Korea, where they were driving toward the Yalu River, the border with China and the Soviet Union. MacArthur played fast and loose with his JCS directives, sending American troops much closer to the border than had been authorized.

In early to mid-September, Truman aide George M. Elsey conceived the idea of a personal meeting of the President and the proconsul. Elsey proceeded by first gaining the support of Harriman. Truman agreed to a conference, essentially as a political stunt in a congressional election year, offering MacArthur meeting sites at Hawaii or Wake Island. MacArthur chose the latter. The meeting was scheduled for October 15. Though it has been written that Washington did little preparatory work for the Wake conference, in fact the President's briefing book for the meeting contained a variety of short papers, almost a dozen, by Defense, State, and the CIA. Harriman supervised its compilation. Harriman tried to put the general at ease by sending him a message while en route to Wake, saying he keenly anticipated seeing MacArthur again. Harriman, General Bradley, and others came off the first plane to arrive at the island and met MacArthur's plane as it landed. Harriman immediately took the general by the arm and led him to the place where Truman's plane, the *Independence,* would taxi to a halt, explaining that the President wished to hear his views on a whole range of issues.

Truman and MacArthur had a short private conversation; then the larger conference convened for almost two hours. MacArthur fielded over thirty questions, many of them from Truman, others from members of the President's party. He discounted the possibility of Chinese intervention, as did Washington at that stage of the war, and spoke on other subjects ranging from South Korean battlefield performance to United States objectives in Asia. Having done much to bring about the Wake meeting, Harriman left most of the questioning to others.

The predictions about the Chinese went sour within weeks as the People's Liberation Army entered combat, at first supposedly as "volunteers" aiding the North Koreans. The Chinese stopped MacArthur's troops in late October, then drove them back in a series of major offensives beginning a month later. In late November, Harriman joined other Washington officials in warning that United Nations probes toward the Yalu might provoke the Chinese but it was already too late; the offensive had begun.

Harriman advised the President to take the lead in presenting an analysis of the situation Americans could understand and in preserving unity among the United Nations allies. He was at the morning staff meeting on November 28 when Truman stiffened his advisers with a tough pep talk, and also accompanied the President at a briefing of the congressional leadership on December 1. Harriman took an active part in the talks with British Prime Minister Clement Attlee, who was afraid the United States was considering the use of atomic weapons in Korea. He joined with State's Paul Nitze to support an option for conventional bombing of dams on the Yalu but opposed expanding the war beyond that. Truman reassured Atlee but refused to publicly rule out the use of any types of weapons.

In the face of Chinese intervention, MacArthur continued to press, over the succeeding months, for greater freedom of action to expand the war to the mainland, bombing Manchuria and supporting Chinese Nationalist invasion attempts. During the worst days, before United Nations forces stabilized the front in Korea, the Joint Chiefs expressed lukewarm agreement with MacArthur's strategy if the United Nations was driven out of Korea. They resumed their opposition to expansion of the war once the Korean front had stabilized, but the momentary lapse emboldened MacArthur to go public with his advocacy. One of MacArthur's sallies in early 1951 effectively scuttled efforts by Truman to get Korean armistice negotiations under way.

By late March 1951 the administration was discussing what to do about the proconsul just as the general was making yet another effort to influence policy through a letter he sent to Massachusetts Republican Congressman Joseph W. Martin, the House minority leader. Martin revealed the letter in a speech on April 5 that enraged the President. Over the next five days Truman considered whether to fire MacArthur. Harriman participated in talks with Secretaries Acheson and Marshall and the Joint Chiefs and all met with the President. Harriman did not say, as has been reported by Truman himself and others, that MacArthur ought to have been replaced two years before. He did concur in the selection of Eighth Army commander General Matthew B. Ridgway to succeed the proconsul, and he assisted Truman and other NSC principals in drafting a press release that announced the action, on April 11, when news began to leak from the Pentagon before MacArthur had been officially notified of his relief.

The relief of MacArthur led to great political controversy in the United States, including calls for Truman's impeachment and a lengthy series of congressional hearings on the situation in the Far East. MacArthur, Marshall, Bradley, and other members of the Joint Chiefs of Staff, all testified at great length, as did Dean Acheson, who came under especially fierce attack. The committee did not summon Harriman, who had expected to testify and had prepared himself assiduously. Harriman's willingness to testify before a congressional committee is interesting in view of the extraordinary lengths to which future keepers of the keys would go to avoid such appearances.

Though Harriman would continue to be involved in making policy on the Korean War, as when United Nations forces returned to the 38th Parallel, the special assistant also had his finger on the pulse of a range of issues. He advised Truman, spoke up at NSC and other meetings when he felt it necessary, and maintained White House liaison with the Departments of State and Defense.

Many were the days Harriman spent closeted with Secretary Marshall or the Joint Chiefs at the Pentagon. Acheson gave Averell free run at State, where Harriman regularly attended the secretary's 9:30 A.M. senior staff meetings and any other meetings he wished, and read all important cables. The special assistant had access to any information generated by the bureaucracy. Within the National Security Council structure it was Harriman, *not* Admiral Souers or the executive secretary, who was represented on the NSC senior staff, by Army Brigadier General Frank Roberts. Staffers Samuel Berger and Richard Johnson similarly represented Harriman on several NSC working groups. When, in February 1951, Deputy Secretary of Defense Robert A. Lovett went to Acheson to lodge complaints about the operation of the NSC senior staff, he was careful to note that "a full time man of the stature of Mr. Harriman is essential." By the time MacArthur was relieved, Truman ranked Harriman in his diary as among the top four national security officials, the others being Acheson, Marshall, and Omar Bradley of the Joint Chiefs.

Despite the pressures of Korea, Harriman found time to work on the North Atlantic alliance, which in 1950 became the North Atlantic Treaty Organization (NATO). In July 1950, only days after returning to Washington, Harriman had the first of several meetings with General Dwight D. Eisenhower, then president of Columbia University, who had a wealth of specialized knowledge pertinent to NATO planning. Later that month Harriman joined Acheson in advocating to Truman an extension of economic aid to Europe beyond 1952. In December 1950, when Attlee visited Washington and the focus was on Korea, Harriman spoke of the importance of getting NATO mobilization under way and appointing a supreme commander for alliance military forces. Similarly, a couple of weeks before, when the National Security Council held a follow-up discussion of the mobilization issues broached by NSC-68, Harriman expressed himself as "not sure that enough consideration had been given to the resources of the rest of the free world." The Chinese intervention in Korea, Averell also felt, created a situation that necessitated review of NSC-68/1, as well as "the availability of forces from other nations for use in Korea." On December 16, Harriman held another meeting with General Eisenhower, now in line for return to duty as NATO commander. After Ike got the appointment, his letters to Truman often went through Harriman.

Dissatisfaction continued with operation of the NSC staff. The subject arose again at a council meeting on January 18, 1951, when the group met to consider NSC-98, a policy paper on South Asia. In their comments the Joint Chiefs recommended deletion of a foreign aid program Truman had already sent to Congress. Acheson pointed this out, whereupon General Bradley gave the Chiefs' reasons. Bradley seemed irritated. Acheson quickly responded that "he did not advocate that the Joint Chiefs of Staff be excluded from commenting on NSC papers, or that the Joint Chiefs disassociate themselves from the problems discussed in NSC papers. On the

47

contrary, it was vital to have the views of the Joint Chiefs of Staff." But papers should be prepared by the department primarily concerned with them. "What worried him," said Acheson, "was that the 'fellow' on the Senior Staff often didn't seem to know what the department thought."

Admiral Souers then reminded the council that the senior staff were supposed to be the alter egos of the bureaucracies they represented. The problem, Jimmy Lay thought, was not that the senior staff ignored departmental views but there was an "inability of the Staff to secure the views of the departments."

South Asia, specifically Iran, was the locale for Harriman's next special mission, during the summer of 1951. The government of Prime Minister Mohammed Mossadegh was nationalizing the British-owned Anglo-Iranian Oil Company (AIOC). Great Britain was in an uproar and about ready to try military intervention. On the Fourth of July, Harriman invited the British ambassador, Acheson, Paul Nitze, and others for an afternoon of sober talk on the veranda of his Georgetown home. Acheson proposed sending Averell to Teheran to get stalled negotiations moving again. Everyone thought it a capital idea except Harriman, "who appeared a most reluctant bride."

Acheson took the idea to Harry Truman the next day. The President approved the mission and immediately dispatched a cable for Mossadegh's information that he would be sending Harriman, not as a mediator, but to assist in the mutual search for a solution. Harriman arrived in Teheran on July 15 in the midst of a demonstration against AIOC in which hundreds were injured and twenty persons killed. Neither the British ambassador to Iran nor AIOC executives were pleased, but Harriman forged ahead, becoming a mediator regardless of Truman's assertion. Although Harriman failed to resolve the dispute, he did get the parties to resume a semblance of communication and, more important, induced the British to back off from military confrontation.

President Truman changed Harriman's role just as the special assistant's diplomacy drew to a close. Responding to Harriman, Acheson, and others, the President had gone to Congress for new foreign aid to be administered by a Mutual Security Administration. Truman also asked that the National Security Act be amended to make the head of the new entity a statutory member of the National Security Council. Both pieces of legislation passed, and now the President made Harriman his man for the post. In this capacity Averell was instrumental in drafting a report between October and December 1951 that helped resolve NATO doubts about its capacity for military mobilization and led to an ambitious rearmament program adopted in 1952. Harriman continued to administer American aid programs and one of his last official acts before the Truman administration left office in January 1953 was to submit a request for economic aid to Egypt.

With Harriman sitting on the National Security Council as a principal, Truman retained the benefit of his advice on all policy matters. The last of those that should be mentioned here is Indochina. In early May 1950, just about a month before Harriman became special assistant, Truman granted military aid to French forces then fighting in Vietnam, Laos, and Cambodia, and economic assistance to those three nations, then "associated states" within the French Union.

By 1952 the Truman administration was for the first time elaborating a formal statement of objectives and courses of action in Indochina. This policy paper, NSC-124/1, provided for military courses of action the United States could take in support of the French. Concerned at the emphasis in the paper, when it came up for discussion at an NSC meeting on March 6 Harriman asked if State "would parallel such [military] studies by investigating what could be done to shore up the political structure in Indochina." There was a somewhat greater emphasis on political aspects in the final paper, NSC-124/2, which Truman approved in June 1952, but Harriman's question would arise again many times in the coming years.

"A PLAN FOR NATIONAL PSYCHOLOGICAL WARFARE"

▲▲▲

In addition to their other duties, both Harriman and Admiral Souers acted as conduits, funneling concepts and proposals to the President, shelving others that seemed less helpful. Psychological warfare was one area where there were plenty of proposals, vexing the President, his advisers, and the NSC senior staff. These ranged from ideas for propaganda programs to far-out schemes for winning the cold war. Many read like Madison Avenue advertising concepts, such as an item Harriman received in late 1950 that called for "a move which is BIG, POSITIVE, DIRECT, and MAGNANIMOUS" for an "international liberation policy."

Some months later Souers came into possession of a proposal from a parapsychologist residing in Mexico City to create teams that would use psychological methods to incapacitate Soviet bloc officials as Washington directed.

Separating the wheat from the chaff had always been difficult with psychological warfare, a technique that assumed importance in World War II. But it was only at the end of the war that propaganda policy was rationalized in the United States with the institution of a national weekly directive. Afterward the armed services proposed a special group be formed under the State-War-Navy Coordinating Committee, predecessor of the NSC, to analyze wartime experience and develop doctrines and requirements for future use. Guidelines for peacetime and wartime activity were prepared by the end of 1946, and a revitalized subcommittee began to actually plan for psychological warfare in mid-1947.

Bureaucratic infighting greatly hampered postwar efforts. The State Department considered that such plans intruded on its foreign policy prerogatives. Once it had been formed, and particularly after President Truman approved NSC-4/A, the Central Intelligence Agency and its Office of Policy Coordination insisted that no overt plans conflict with their responsibility for covert psychological warfare. Attempts by the group chairman to complain to a higher level were blocked by State representatives. Only the most innocuous proposals negotiated this minefield so that, by 1949, the group had very little to show for its work.

Harry Truman was deeply interested in psychological warfare and was favorably disposed toward attempts to improve the situation. Under some pressure from the armed services, at the fourth NSC meeting, State tabled a paper regarding coordination of foreign information measures that became NSC-4. After minor revisions, on December 17 NSC Action No. 16 sent the paper on to Truman. The President approved it the next day.

The paper called for the secretary of state, through his assistant secretary for public affairs, to take the lead in information policies. The word "propaganda" was avoided. State would chair a new Interdepartmental Coordinating Staff with representatives from the other agencies and develop programs intended to influence European opinion. But the diplomats still refused to take the effort seriously; it was three months before the secretary of state selected his chairman and five until the unit was actually organized. Their first paper, written in September 1948, was little more than a notice that the secretary of state would plan and coordinate the overseas information program.

Pentagon officials continued to press for a more aggressive effort and took up the matter with Admiral Souers early in 1949. That February the NSC asked its executive secretary to report on peacetime planning for the wartime conduct of overt psychological warfare. Souers circulated the resulting paper, NSC-43, on March 9 and it was approved a few weeks later. Once more there was to be a new mechanism under State, the Interagency Foreign Information Organization (IFIO) along the lines of the NSC staff. The secretary of state would appoint the director after consultation with the NSC; he would be served by policy consultants representing State, the secretary of defense, the JCS, and others, while the staff comprised persons designated by State and the Pentagon plus liaison officers from the CIA. The IFIO replaced the information unit in existence since 1947. As its first director Dean Acheson appointed his assistant secretary for public affairs, Edward W. Barrett, former *Newsweek* editor and wartime chief of the overseas branch of the Office of War Information.

Creation of the IFIO failed to end dissatisfaction with the existing system. The Pentagon now worried about the potential for discontinuity between peacetime and wartime programs. The CIA still worried that State's overt responsibilities would impinge on its covert programs. Acheson filed a progress report on the initiative in August 1949; a month later the Pentagon commented on the principles suggested to govern the conduct of psychological warfare. In an effort to meet everyone's concerns, Barrett's staff, with approval of the NSC consultants, proposed a modified IFIO to coordinate overt and covert psychological warfare, censorship, and domestic information, with control to be exercised by the Department of Defense in theaters of military operations and by State elsewhere. Within the IFIO itself the CIA liaison would be replaced by a consultant "for matters relating to coordination with planning under the NSC-10 series" (i.e., covert operations, including psychological warfare) and the staff would now include CIA officers as well. The proposal became NSC-59. Admiral Souers circulated it on December 20, 1949. Truman approved a modified report on March 10, 1950, after the principals sent along the paper under NSC Action No. 283.

Thinking the organizational problem finally solved, on April 20 Truman went on to give a speech announcing a new "Campaign of Truth" as an antidote to Soviet propaganda. Just two months later the onset of the Korean War added a real wartime venue for the planning envisioned by the revised policy paper, NSC-59/1. Though plans were far from complete, information personnel and authority in the Far East were transferred from State auspices to those of General MacArthur. In Washington the IFIO wrote weekly information policy directives to govern operations in the field.

But other parts of the bureaucracy continued to oppose State Department authority over information policy. Edward Barrett's harried IFIO staff now came up with yet another proposal, NSC-74, that James Lay sent to NSC principals on July 10, barely two weeks after initiation of the hostilities in Korea. This paper recommended that State run an interdepartmental board to establish and coordinate psychological warfare in the initial stages of war, or earlier at the discretion of the President, and create a "national psychological warfare organization" for subsequent stages of war. The latter was to have independent status, authority to issue its own policy directives, and official access to the President. As its title suggested, NSC-74 aimed at "a plan for national psychological warfare."

The idea for an independent psychological warfare organization reignited the simmering dissatisfactions with the existing system. State made a start at change in mid-August, when Barrett announced reconstitution of his unit as the National Psychological Strategy Board. The military saw that as an effort to preserve State Department dominance over information policy. Both the military and the CIA argued that the body envisioned by NSC-74 should be located elsewhere in government.

This question of organization seemed an NSC matter and quickly involved the new eight-member NSC senior staff. A solution nevertheless remained elusive. The senior staff agreed that Lay should prepare a paper defining the unresolved issue of the location of responsibility for policy formulation and coordination. A draft was circulated on December 22 that senior staff examined five days afterward. The final result went to the NSC principals on December 28, scheduled for the council's consideration on January 4, 1951.

Jimmy Lay's paper quickly summarized the points of agreement among the bureaucracy; all departments and agencies executing major portions of the psychological warfare effort should be represented, while execution would be decentralized, with the Joint Chiefs responsible for military theaters and State elsewhere. The big problem was "assignment to a single official designated by the president of reponsibility at the national level for psychological policy formulation." State argued that the authority should be given to the secretary of state, to ensure continuity with the existing machinery, to take advantage of the strengthened IFIO, because psychological warfare measures needed to be closely integrated with foreign policy, and because World War II experience indicated that "an independent agency in this field would result in more serious delay and diffusion of responsibility." Others argued for an independent unit because one attached to State would lack requisite freedom of action, and would impose an additional task upon an already overburdened Cabinet officer.

Harry Truman presided as the National Security Council gathered for its seventy-seventh meeting on January 4, 1951. The agenda item on psychological strategy brought a long, desultory, and inconclusive discussion that settled nothing. Truman gave council members a month to settle their differences. Souers, Lay, and budget chief Frederick J. Lawton were no more successful garnering agreement than the NSC senior staff. In February a frustrated President removed the item from the NSC agenda and told the bureaucracy he would settle the matter himself.

President Truman's solution, set forth in a secret directive on April 4, 1951, was the creation of a Psychological Strategy Board (PSB) that would be under the direct control of the National Security Council and responsible for both overt and covert psychological operations, as provided in the directives NSC-59/1 and NSC-10/2. Like the NSC special group that managed covert intelligence operations, called the 10/2 Panel, the PSB comprised the undersecretary of state, the deputy secretary of defense, and the director of central intelligence. Sitting with the PSB would be an adviser from JCS and a director who set its agenda, drafted programs and reports, promulgated decisions, and evaluated implementation, but would not engage in actual psychological operations.

Truman offered the job of PSB director to Mark Ethridge, publisher of the *Louisville Courier-Journal*. He rejected the offer. Truman next turned to Gordon Gray, former secretary of the army and now president of the University of North Carolina. Though feeling guilty about the short time he had served at the university, Gray agreed to help set up the PSB. He began to spend half of each week in Washington and the rest in Chapel Hill.

The Psychological Strategy Board held its first meeting on July 2, 1951. The board selected Walter Bedell Smith, Truman's director of central intelligence, as chairman. Without dissent from Edward Barrett, attending as the alternate for Undersecretary of State James E. Webb, Smith observed that the function of the PSB and its staff should be to assemble a master plan for psychological warfare and then act as review board to assign aspects of the programs to specified agencies, thereafter monitoring implementation. At the PSB's second meeting in mid-August, the board decided to relate to the National Security Council in the same fashion as the NSC senior staff. Jim Webb added that "PSB must be the central place for the members to meet, discuss problems, and make policy," while "Beedle" Smith insisted that once the PSB had developed a master plan, all government psychological operations would be kept in consonance with it. Uncontrolled operations would be prohibited.

Despite the apparent enthusiasm of senior board members, Gordon Gray found the PSB director's task daunting. Almost everything about the PSB was classified: personnel, organization, even its telephone directories and scrap paper. That brought headaches as the professional staff burgeoned to 72 and total staff to 130 by mid-1952. It became by far the largest component of the NSC machinery; indeed its $500,000 budget, composed of equal contributions from State, Defense, and the CIA, dwarfed the fiscal year 1953 appropriation of $193,000 for the National Security Council and its staff.

In November 1951, Gray added a senior advisory group. Under the director were three coequal units, offices for plans and policy, for coordination, and for evaluation and review, each headed by an assistant director of the PSB. Following directives from the board, the staff assembled overall, regional, country, or issue plans that the board would then review and approve. An ad hoc panel would be formed each time a plan was ordered. The panel would work under the office for plans in assembling the program, be transferred to the coordination office during implementation, and would then end up under the evaluation office once the program had been in progress for six months to a year.

Despite progress establishing the PSB organization, Gray's work was still hamstrung by agency differences. Beedle Smith wanted a master plan, but only if it was under CIA control. His alternate, Frank Wisner, would not even come to PSB meetings. Jim Webb came to the third board meeting to take back the broad grant of role—that PSB be *the* central place to discuss and make policy—he had previously made in the name of the State Department. Paul Nitze, director of State's Policy Planning Staff, told Gray, "Look, you just forget about policy, that's not your business; we'll make the policy and then you can put it on your damn radio."

In an attempt to get the PSB members to resolve their agency differences, in November 1951 Gray began holding private luncheons where members could talk out differences prior to the monthly board meeting. In December, Gray supplied Smith and Wisner with a PSB briefing in an effort to show that the psychological warfare unit would not trespass into CIA's domain. Truman supported the PSB as best he could, but could do little to end State intransigence. Webb went along with a project on Korea, never actually implemented, and agreed to an early plan for Germany, but often withheld approvals.

Controversy surrounded the board's second major project and set the tone for much of what followed. At the August meeting, Gray suggested and the board adopted a proposal to do an inventory of cold war "weapons"—government and private media, associations, organizations, groups, and so forth—that could be used in psychological warfare. A PSB panel formed for the exercise created three subordinate groups, one to examine the policy basis; one, the intelligence available; and the last, the actual inventory. First the intelligence investigation was dropped after it aroused the ire of the CIA and its cohorts. The State Department repeatedly construed PSB inventory activities as infringements on its interests as well. The draft inventory, completed in October 1951, ran to a hundred pages. It had to be cut to seventy-seven. The Pentagon and CIA made only bland comments and suggested minor revisions. State raised basic questions, but insisted it was cooperating when it agreed to review a *three-page* inventory paper. At the December meeting of the Psychological Strategy Board, Gray resorted to the ruse of bringing in the full inventory paper but telling members it was for information only.

The master plan idea originally developed by the CIA also fell upon the rocks of the bureaucracy. Predictably, the worst objections came from State, which questioned whether such a master plan was practicable and asserted that it would infringe on basic foreign policy. Gray countered that if State was going to be intransigent, he would take the issue to the President. Knowing that Gray would be returning to the University of North Carolina in a few months, State then tried the opposite tack and overloaded the director's group with mountains of policy papers, meetings with officials, briefings on its activities, and interviews with returning ambassadors and other diplomats. The group became so inundated with information "it could not think strategically, much less write a long-range concept."

Gordon Gray returned to his university in January 1952, thereafter becoming a PSB consultant. The Psychological Strategy Board, he believed in retrospect, "was somewhat abortive." His replacement was Dr. George Allen, a medical school administrator, who was supplanted in late 1952 by Admiral Allen G. Kirk who, like Beedle Smith, had served as ambassador in Moscow.

Both proved to be less adept at maneuvers within the bureaucracy. Agency approvals became a matter of PSB liaison officers pestering officials so often they would sign off just to be rid of the matter. The device of sending out papers "for information" was used more often. In its report for the third quarter of 1952, the Psychological Strategy Board noted that it finally had under review for approval its *first* comprehensive area plan, for Germany.

A comprehensive basic plan for Japan was at the draft stage. Limited plans for the reduction of Communist power in France and Italy were in implementation and the latter had reached the evaluation stage. A plan for Soviet bloc defectors had gone through development and was funded and in implementation. Four contingency plans had been completed but were on standby pending the events that might activate them. Ten plans were in various stages of development. In comparison, between February and June 1952 State's Psychological Operations Coordinating Committee, the old Barrett group, not only did work in conjunction with the PSB, but developed or approved eight projects and was implementing twelve, including several Korea-related ones, a NATO project, one on Japan, and another pertaining to Yugoslavia.

Even at this late date, many basic questions had yet to be resolved. Thus, a seminar at the University of North Carolina was told in August 1962 that "we have not insisted on clear-cut definitions of what is psychological strategy." The speaker felt those might be possible later. "Meanwhile, psychological strategy is anything the Board approves." A typical ad hoc panel was the seven-member unit working on a contingency plan in case Korean armistice negotiations failed. It included three officers from State and one each from the armed services and the CIA. Three members were assigned to the PSB for ninety days' temporary duty; the others just attended meetings. Although this plan was in the final stages of development, it had been thirteen months since State originally requested it. In the course of its history to 1953, the Psychological Strategy Board created thirty-six of these ad hoc panels to plan forty-four projects.

Indicative of the continuing stagnation of the board was the fact that after the 1952 presidential elections the PSB gave up its formal meetings, retaining the luncheons only. The last one held during the Truman administration occurred at the Pentagon on January 15, 1953. Alcohol was available at the Pentagon, unlike other venues, and the PSB members made it a festive occasion. So ended Harry Truman's biggest NSC staff experiment.

PART II

▲

IKE'S HIDDEN HAND

Entering office in January 1953, Dwight David Eisenhower came to Washington with years of administrative experience in the U.S. Army and elsewhere. He believed in the chain of command. In his political campaign Ike had alleged stagnation in Harry Truman's foreign policy and pledged to revitalize it and the National Security Council that made it. Robert C. Cutler, the man who had drafted Ike's NSC speech, was the person the new President picked to be his special assistant for national security affairs, his man to revitalize the NSC. As for Cabinet secretaries, Ike saw them as his executive agents in administering policy. "Look here, Charlie," the President once told his first secretary of defense, Charles Wilson, "I want *you* to run Defense. We can't *both* run it. And I *won't* run it. I was elected to worry about a lot of things other than the day-to-day operations of a department."

As his executive agents, the Cabinet officers' voices resonated powerfully in Eisenhower's National Security Council, the most powerful being those of the secretaries of state and defense. Eisenhower's collaboration with Secretary of State John Foster Dulles is legendary, and led early analysts to conclude that the President's role was passive and that Dulles controlled policy. Ike was not that close to Wilson but he warmed up to later secretaries of defense. Treasury Secretary George M. Humphrey, Ike's close political adviser, was a fiscal conservative who argued at NSC meetings against foreign aid. Among NSC participants, Humphrey acquired the reputation of a "Mr. No," resisting many new program proposals.

The records of Eisenhower's NSC are replete with demonstrations of the strong views of these NSC principals. Eisenhower used the council as a sort of corporate board of directors, but there was nothing in the least passive about the President's own involvement. Eisenhower was aggressive debating at council meetings; the NSC records show him questioning facts and motives, arguing points, issuing blanket warnings, and stating intentions. His remarks could be sharp and cutting, even emotional, as Ike's blood pressure shot up and his face turned beet red.

Eisenhower possessed a vast store of technical military knowledge that enabled him to interpret proposals and debate the minute details of recommended responses. At first Ike promised that in order to give his advisers complete freedom of expression, no record would be made of NSC discussions. But the staff recognized that records were necessary as a reference point for the bureaucracy. Jimmy Lay, who stayed on under Cutler, had his deputy take notes during the NSC meetings from which "summaries of discussion" were compiled. The deputy, S. Everett Gleason, an accomplished historian and coauthor of classic histories of the United States' entry into World War II, tried hard to capture the flavor of the exchanges, often paraphrasing the NSC principals, sometimes capturing their words, always their meaning. The summaries lost some of their narrative quality in the summer of 1959, when Gleason returned to academia and was succeeded by Marion W. Boggs, an NSC staffer since 1948 and another academic, a University of Chicago political scientist who had taught at MacAlester College in St. Paul and the University of Missouri before the war. In any case, the summaries remain among the most authoritative records of the United States government. With the end of the administration they were bundled up and sent to Fort Ritchie, Maryland, with Eisenhower's other papers. Gordon Gray reminded the former President of their existence as he prepared to write his memoirs. Eisenhower made some use of the NSC records in his books, and with declassification they are now becoming available to historians.

The NSC records reveal the details of Eisenhower's responses to the crises that his administration was so frequently compelled to face.

Ike set the tone even before the beginning of his tenure as President, during his campaign, with a promise to "go to Korea" and end the war, which was still dragging on after more than a year of negotiation. Once elected, Ike involved all his NSC principals in fulfilling the Korea pledge, thereby creating a system for making policy, and a method of crisis management to which he adhered in many subsequent duels at the brink.

▲▲▲

"TANTAMOUNT TO AN EXECUTIVE AGENCY"

▲▲▲

One of the few who had to be talked into taking the job of national security adviser, Robert Cutler became the first ever to serve twice in that capacity. Though a Boston Brahmin, Bobby Cutler was a man who liked to joke and quip; he was class poet of his undergraduate class at Harvard, and a published novelist by age twenty-three. A lawyer active in Republican politics, Cutler was among those pressing Eisenhower to run for the 1952 nomination, and was then drafted in his own turn to write speeches for Ike's campaign, including one that promised reform of the NSC system. After winning the election, Eisenhower decided to appoint Cutler as his special assistant for national security affairs.

The press conference at which Ike introduced Cutler as his keeper of the keys produced some humorous repartee when one reporter asked Bobby if it was true he had written novels.

"Three, in fact," Cutler had shot back, "of which Macmillan published two when I was in my early twenties."

"What were they about?" asked the reporter.

"Why, they were about love, of course. What else would a boy of twenty write about? Wouldn't you have done that?"

The audience broke up in laughter.

In one of the campaign speeches, Ike asserted that the Truman NSC system had become moribund. There were in fact many views on how to revamp it. Even the "modern" notion of a strong national security adviser was known then, prefigured in a 1953 paper on NSC staff roles by Townsend Hoopes, later to be secretary of the air force for Lyndon Johnson. Hoopes foresaw an "executive assistant" or national security adviser who could be made a formal member of the NSC. The NSC staff could be given authority to initiate policy proposals and request studies from all agencies, formulating proposals without further reference to the bureaucracy. It could not be a staff simply comprising designees from departments, as had been Truman's NSC senior staff. "The NSC would be converted," the paper enthused, "from a coordinating body to what would be tantamount to an executive, or directive, agency."

Dwight Eisenhower never went that far. He asked Cutler for a reorganization study and a group formed to conduct it. Sid Souers, one of the principals, later recalled that they met only once and never did see an actual draft report. That paper Bobby must have done on his own.

Ike made his basic decisions within months of reaching Washington, in response to Bobby Cutler's little study group, which reported on March 16, 1953. Reiterating the language of the 1947 act, Cutler's twenty-page report observed that the functions of the council were to advise the President on the integration of military, foreign, and domestic policies; to make such recommendations and other reports as the council might deem necessary or the President require; and to perform such other functions as the President might direct for the purpose of effectively coordinating policy.

Explicit or implicit in these functions, Cutler felt, were that the council would deal only with issues affecting the national security, that it would be concerned with both actual and potential military power, and that it would not be limited to areas of agency agreement. This role was wider in some respects than that Truman had accorded his council. For Eisenhower the NSC advisers would include the secretary of the treasury, director for mutual security, and director of defense mobilization. Other participant members could be called when matters affecting them were discussed. Permanent members remained the President, the Vice President, the secretary of state, and the secretary of defense. In Cutler's scheme the policy planning function would be performed by the council itself.

Cutler recommended creating the job of special assistant for national security affairs in order to determine the agenda for NSC meetings, brief the President the afternoon prior to each meeting, control preparation of material through an NSC Planning Board, preside over that board and the flow of work, and appoint such ad hoc staff or civilian groups as might be necessary.

On March 17, President Eisenhower returned Cutler's report of the previous day with a statement of approval. Executive Secretary James Lay sent both to NSC members and advisers such as the JCS Chairman and director of central intelligence.

With Ike's backing, Cutler plunged in to revise the machinery supporting the NSC, which was judged inefficient. For example, when the administration took office, three projects had been awaiting final action for over twenty months, three for over ten months, five for more than four months, and one for more than two. Only eight projects before the council had been on the agenda for a month or less.

Cutler considered the NSC senior staff part of the problem. The staff represented the views of their departments, and as the group was chaired by the representative of the State Department, there was no way for the White House to push for completion of work.

Eisenhower's Planning Board would be chaired by Cutler; the special assistant was explicitly made responsible for preparing issues for discussion at the council. Board members would be nominated by their agencies but appointed by the President to ensure that Planning Board work would be their main duty. Board members were to brief their department heads before each NSC meeting. Policy papers before the council were first examined by the board, where Cutler made every effort to iron out agency differences before remaining disagreements went to the NSC itself. There would be 17 meetings of the Council in 1953, but Cutler presided over 120 of the Planning Board.

In effect, the Planning Board structured proposals for the National Security Council principals. The council itself was the top of what Dillon Anderson termed a "pyramid"; others called it "Policy Hill." Here proposals were modified, expanded, often rewritten, distilled, with items that could not be agreed upon passed up to the council. Such disagreements, often called "splits," went to the NSC in the form of alternate language for paragraphs or sentences listed directly in the draft NSC papers. "Every policy proposal is tested in lengthy discussions," Anderson told the Dallas Council on World Affairs in 1955, "against the views of the assistant secretaries of the several participating departments."

At the top of Policy Hill stood Eisenhower, probing logic, examining motives, looking at proposals in terms of their long-term implications, cajoling better alternatives from the departments. Very active at the NSC, Ike had to be careful not to reveal his preferences at meetings before all agencies aired their views. Ike held almost three times as many National Security Council meetings as did Truman and presided at more than 90 percent of them. Generally he missed attending only when he was sick and then Vice President Richard M. Nixon presided. Ike also tried to preserve a regular time for council meetings, Thursday at midmorning, helping officials coordinate their schedules.

This President wanted to be able to seek outside advice when he wanted it. He created a panel of NSC consultants as an outside advisory board. Among the first were business, labor, and education leaders, including the presidents of Standard Oil of New Jersey, Monsanto Chemical, the United Steel Workers, Williams College, and Cornell University. Dillon Anderson, one of the first group, succeeded Cutler as national security adviser. Two other consultants, Robert C. Sprague and James P. Baxter III, served Eisenhower in a variety of advisory capacities through both his terms in office.

President Eisenhower soured to the use of outside advisers over time. The consultants had no permanent presence in Washington, and ultimately no government authority or access. In the summer of 1954, Ike considered having the consultants alternate attending council meetings, but Cutler and staff secretary General Paul Carroll joined to discourage the idea and nothing came of it. By Eisenhower's second administration the consultants' analyses most frequently were going straight into the file cabinets.

When Eisenhower came to the White House, the staff consisted of Jimmy Lay plus twenty-two others. Of those, one was an administrative officer, one handled internal security, twelve were clerical workers and one a chauffeur-messenger. Cutler recommended and Eisenhower approved a small "special staff" on a regional basis, it came to have six to eight additional professional staff. As executive secretary, Lay continued to have formal charge of the NSC staff, but there was no question that the special assistant for national security affairs would be the senior official.

Implementation was the reverse slope of Policy Hill and there too Ike made changes. Truman had had no formal mechanism to follow up on presidential decisions; in effect, the NSC principals themselves were expected to report on implementation. Truman's only functional unit under the NSC had been the Psychological Strategy Board. But as we have seen, PSB failed to establish itself among the agencies despite its status as an NSC entity.

To rid himself of the PSB, Eisenhower typically resorted to a civilian advisory group, which he created only five days after assuming office. The President's Commission on International Information Activities was established on January 26, 1953, to survey and evaluate information activities and related policies as they affected the national security. William H. Jackson, a former CIA official and wartime psychological warfare officer, headed the commission, which included Bobby Cutler and Gordon Gray.

While the Jackson commission canvassed alternatives, holding extensive interviews with officials, media experts, publishers, and commentators, Cutler and Gray dismantled the board. Cutler, at one time a PSB consultant, thought it "a veritable mare's nest" that had to go. They recommended the creation of an Operations Coordinating Board (OCB) in place of the PSB.

Ike took action on the suggestion for an OCB, ordering his Bureau of the Budget to draft an executive order creating the new board. Under the draft, the OCB would assist in coordinating execution and operations plans for every NSC paper assigned to more than one agency for implementation. However, Attorney General Herbert Brownell, Jr., believed that these terms violated the statutes establishing the departments and agencies by placing the OCB between them and the President. Brownell had the executive order revised to restrict the OCB to advice on implementation.

On September 3, 1953, President Eisenhower issued his Executive Order 10483 creating the OCB. The Psychological Strategy Board held its final meeting the previous day in Denver, where the President was staying that summer; the first OCB meeting occurred in Washington on the seventeenth. The coordinating board took over PSB's offices in three town houses on Jackson Place, across Pennsylvania Avenue from the White House.

Eisenhower was never to be fully satisfied by the OCB. The attorney general's changes that took the OCB out of the chain of command also left the board without authority to resolve disputes or order agency actions. It became once more a forum where assistant secretaries could wage rearguard actions against policies, after their chiefs had been overruled at the NSC level. Eisenhower took a number of actions to improve OCB but none proved wholly successful. Presidential appointments, for example, did not shield OCB members returning to work at their own agencies, so departmental representatives still had an incentive to hew to their particular agency line in their dealings at the OCB. In a second executive order, number 10700 on February 25, 1957, Eisenhower administratively relocated the OCB within the NSC, then appointed his national security adviser as the OCB's chairman. The board held weekly luncheon meetings and monitored implementation through a small central staff including, in parallel to the NSC's own staff, area specialists focusing on specific global regions or functional issues.

One reason Dwight Eisenhower liked to use businessmen as NSC consultants was that the President conceived of the NSC as a sort of board of directors of the United States. But like the OCB, the NSC never fulfilled Ike's expectations. As the Planning Board sent up the policy papers, with their frequent splits and alternative language, council meetings bogged down in arguments over the implications of words, sentences, paragraphs with concrete meaning to the bureaucracy but of rather less interest to the President. In 1955, Ike saw fit to instruct NSC members, in a formal letter, that they sat on the council as his personal advisers and *not* the representatives of departments and agencies. He was never able to banish bureaucratic rivalries from the council, so instead Eisenhower, master staff planner that he was, began to use the council as a stage to play out the rivalries of Pentagon and State to policy outcomes he preferred. The NSC papers and consultant studies became props used to bring out the agency differences at council. Then the President waded in with his questions and strong declarations of intent, trying to bend the bureaucracy to his will.

Eisenhower worked to set up situations where the natural pressures on players and their sense of their own best interests led them in the directions he preferred. One day Ike repeated to aide Andrew Goodpaster what General George Marshall, quoting someone else, had once told him: "You'd be amazed how much you can accomplish if somebody else can get the credit for it." Dwight Eisenhower deliberately used that method. As the secret records of his years become available to scholars, historians are increasingly convinced that Ike worked with a hidden hand from the White House. One of its fingers was the NSC and its staff.

Another finger of Eisenhower's hidden hand, perhaps even a thumb, was his Office of the Staff Secretary. The staff secretary was the aide on top of every national security issue in the White House, especially the ones that Ike was reluctant to ventilate at the NSC. The President carefully channeled this sensitive business through the staff secretary rather than the NSC or his special assistant. The device was an offshoot of a military practice with which Ike, given his background, was familiar. That was the employment of a secretary to the general staff, who usually records decisions and then keeps track of actions pursuant to them.

"I don't think I should have to be my own Sergeant Major around here," Ike thundered one day in 1953, when he encountered a setback. "I want to have this kind of thing handled properly."

A similar incident occurred a week or two later, and Eisenhower exploded, "I said just a week or so ago I was not going to be my own Sergeant Major and I'm not." Eisenhower looked around, then pointed to his military aide, Brigadier General Paul T. "Pete" Carroll. Long familiar with Ike, Carroll had been personal aide to the general at North Atlantic Treaty Organization headquarters, and previously at the Pentagon. "I'm going to have a staff secretary," Ike rasped. "Carroll—you're it!"

General Carroll built a secretariat very quickly, one wholly independent of the NSC staff, reporting directly to the President. He coordinated all defense paperwork flowing into the Oval Office. Ike did not enjoy reading and pressed for one-page summaries, making so-called cover memoranda increasingly important. Carroll made sure that such memos were there or would add them himself. If a document seemed incomplete, he would seek more facts among the fiefdoms of bureaucracy.

A vigorous, energetic worker for religious charities, Carroll was only forty-three in January 1954 when he suffered a serious heart attack. He returned and worked through the summer but succumbed anew and died that September.

It was said of Pete Carroll that he lived mostly in the future, sometimes in the present, but never in the past. His successor ranged the full continuum. Talking with Bobby Cutler and White House congressional lobbyist General Wilton B. Persons about a successor, presidential Chief of Staff Sherman Adams was startled to find them both recommend the same person, the Army's Colonel Andrew J. Goodpaster. Cutler had worked with Goodpaster at the Pentagon during World War II, while Persons had seen him work for Ike at NATO's European command. After the glowing accounts, Adams asked the President what he thought of Colonel Goodpaster.

"I would ask nothing more than for my son to grow up to be as good a man as he is," Eisenhower replied.

Ike had known Colonel Goodpaster since the aftermath of World War II, when Eisenhower served as Army Chief of Staff and wanted to form a special unit for long-range plans. General Lauris Norstad had recommended Goodpaster, who impressed Ike so much that when Harry Truman tapped him to become the first Supreme Allied Commander of NATO, Eisenhower insisted on taking Goodpaster along as his aide. The engineer-colonel had just completed three years at Princeton earning a Ph.D. in international relations, and saw a NATO job as a perfect venue for sharpening his global vision. He stayed long after Ike left.

In 1954, Goodpaster returned to Eisenhower from San Francisco, where he had just assumed the position of district engineer. Andrew Jackson Goodpaster was thirty-eight, a model of discretion, intelligence, and efficiency. A midwesterner, born in Granite City, Illinois, Andy had attended a small college before winning appointment to West Point, from which he graduated in 1939, and then rose to command a combat engineer battalion in Sicily and Italy during the war. Repeatedly wounded, Goodpaster had won the

Silver Star and a Distinguished Service Cross. Andy returned to Washington in 1944 and assumed a Pentagon policy planning job, the first of many that would occupy much of his subsequent career. In Eisenhower's White House, Goodpaster became a fixture. The President continually widened the scope of responsibilities accorded his staff secretary. Goodpaster flourished.

Andy Goodpaster arrived at the White House in the fall of 1954. Just then the Far Eastern crisis sharpened to a flash point in the Taiwan Strait. Communist Chinese forces on the mainland, having ejected the Nationalist government there, sought to take over offshore islands the Nationalists still controlled from Taiwan. Eisenhower interposed naval forces to prevent any invasion and ensure supply of the outlying islands. In March 1955, Colonel Goodpaster was suddenly dispatched on a mission by Eisenhower: to visit Pearl Harbor with a list of top-secret questions for the Commander in Chief Pacific (CINCPAC) about prospects in the Taiwan Strait. Ike might have called the CINCPAC, Admiral Felix Stump, to Washington, but felt such a visit might attract too much attention. Goodpaster went to Pearl Harbor instead. The admiral proved confident and his estimate turned out to be right.

In later years there would be claims that Goodpaster originated the phenomenon of secret missions by national security advisers with this assignment in Pearl Harbor. Such claims ignore Harriman's missions to MacArthur and to Iran.

But on a host of questions, the staff secretary actively sought out knowledge the President desired, represented Eisenhower's views to others, and brought problems back to the President based on his own observations.

While the special assistant for national security affairs had his office across West Executive Avenue at the OEOB, Goodpaster's office was next door to the President. To some degree, the President himself acted as the traffic cop for this system, keeping the staff secretary within narrow bounds. "Now wait a minute, boys," Ike would say, "that is a policy matter. I'm not going to decide that here. If that needs consideration, bring it before the Cabinet, or bring it before the NSC. Then I'll decide."

Nevertheless, Goodpaster worked on his own as well to preserve good relations with the national security adviser and NSC assistants. When a paper crossed his desk with unexplored policy implications, Goodpaster would call Cutler or Gray instead of taking it to the President. There was no contest among his keepers for Ike's time or attempts to stake out turf within the White House. Asked for his assessment of the primacy of Dwight Eisenhower's foreign policy advisers, Goodpaster modestly lists the secretary of state, especially when that was John Foster Dulles, then the national security adviser, *then* himself, followed by the President's special assistant for cold war activities. There were always a range of other advisers, including his personal staff, the scientists, and press secretary Jim Hagerty. There were regular meetings with congressional leaders and Republican party groups. Goodpaster believes Eisenhower used Nixon primarily as a sounding board for determining public attitudes. At the time, President Eisenhower, in one of his more painful gaffes, when asked to name a major idea Nixon had contributed, told reporters in the middle of the 1960 election campaign, "If you give me a week, I might think of one."

Ike made a far worse gaffe when he approved a secret CIA spy flight over Russia on a date shortly before a scheduled major-power summit conference in Paris. In 1956, Ike had put Goodpaster in charge of the U-2 high-altitude overflight effort to gather intelligence from the Soviet Union. On May 1, 1960, which happened to be a Soviet national holiday, a U-2 plane came down or was forced down at Sverdlovsk, deep inside the Soviet Union. Since Goodpaster had always handled the U-2 decisions at the White House, the crisis, which began when the Soviets successfully captured CIA pilot Francis Gary Powers, was essentially his.

The big American mistake at the outset was a sloppy cover story, released too soon by the National Aeronautics and Space Administration (NASA), that quickly unraveled. Both Goodpaster's office and the CIA, in this case represented by Richard M. Bissell, Jr., were rusty on the NASA cover story, did not know the Russians had Powers, and had not thought through the possibilities inherent in the situation. The NASA story—that a high-altitude weather plane was missing over Turkey—quickly fell apart when the Soviets produced the pilot and the wreckage of the U-2. President Eisenhower felt compelled to accept full responsibility for the U-2 and its mission. The Soviet premier, Nikita Khrushchev, used the incident as a pretext to break up the Paris summit amid recriminations over espionage. Ike lost the major chance for obtaining an arms-control agreement, toward which he'd been building at least since 1955 along with an anticipated invitation to visit the Soviet Union.

Behind the error lay a larger management failure that could be traced only to Goodpaster and Bissell. Both were aware of the rapid progress being made in developing reconnaissance satellites, which were not subject to adversary actions, as was the Powers U-2 mission. Though the U-2 program had passed previous reviews of its vulnerability to Soviet air defenses, original estimates had been that the mission would remain viable for only two to four years, given advances in Soviet weaponry. There should have been a renewed policy review in 1960, taking into account the closeness of satellite reconnaissance capability. Nor was enough consideration given to timing the U-2 overflight so close to the anticipated Paris summit. Eisenhower's Operations Coordinating Board, whose psychological warfare and public information machinery had lain mostly dormant during the previous few years, suddenly had their hands full with the fallout from the U-2 affair.

These developments could not have come at a worse time for Eisenhower, and specifically for his NSC machinery. For the first time in its history, the NSC was under investigation by Congress; a special committee had opened public hearings on national policy machinery in February 1960, which would extend into the first year of the presidency of John F. Kennedy.

MANAGING POLICY HILL

▲▲▲

hrough all the travails of deciding policy, and all the rush to respond to crises, the atmosphere in Eisenhower's White House, the summit of "Policy Hill" remained remarkably calm. Amid the public hysteria of the late 1950s, such calm seemed eerie in a way, but it was a product of superior knowledge. The public saw only the problems. The men atop Policy Hill knew what the administration's answers were and could see Ike's hidden hand in motion. The relationships among those few men, the offices they created at the behest of the President, were the cement that welded the government bureaucracy and steered it in the direction Eisenhower determined.

It seemed to outsiders that not much was happening, an impression that predominated in contemporary press accounts and early historical interpretations of Eisenhower's role. According to this construction, Ike insisted on Cabinet government so that he could go out and play golf. One observer characterized the system as "organized absenteeism." Thus early accounts of the Eisenhower years viewed John Foster Dulles as running the foreign policy, while George Humphrey ran the government through his budgets, and Sherman Adams managed the White House.

Such accounts saw Adams as the "assistant president" have claimed that *no* paper entered the Oval Office without Adams's scrawled "OK—S.A.," that nobody entered without his permission, that Adams cleared phone calls, made most personnel decisions himself, and attended all sessions of the NSC. White House records convey a different picture. Ike made a strong distinction between national security and domestic matters and in fact very few of his defense and foreign affairs papers contain notations by Adams.

Adams did attend many NSC meetings, his own statements to the contrary notwithstanding. So did political aides Bryce Harlow and General Persons. But all of them limited themselves to the role of NSC "backbenchers" and rarely, if ever, spoke up at council meetings. In addition, available records show that Adams did not accompany the President at the equally if not more crucial Oval Office sessions on sensitive national security topics. Cutler, Carroll, and their successors kept Adams informed directly, and dutifully went to the thrice-weekly meetings of the White House staff. The working relationship was harmonious; it continued when Persons became assistant to the President and Gray and Goodpaster were the national security assistants.

Early critics also questioned whether Ike really made many changes in the NSC system. That criticism owed something to Sidney Souers, whom Cutler had invited back to Washington to participate in brainstorming sessions regarding changes in the council. As Souers recounted it to a journalist friend, "Bobby Cutler told me the purpose was to make it look as if the Eisenhower administration had made good its promise to revolutionize the setup of the council but in effect not to change the way it was being run."

A small group met at the NSC executive secretary's office on the third floor of the OEOB. "Everybody present agreed," Sid Souers recalled, "that a mistake was made in making those [1952 campaign] speeches [criticizing Truman's NSC]." Then "one member present" (Cutler) confessed to having written two of them. Souers asked Allen Dulles how it was that Foster could have been inveigled into similar statements. Dulles replied that his brother had not expected to become secretary of state at the time. After Cutler expressed a wish to be titled "director" of the NSC, Souers interjected that there should be no director, to avoid the implication that such an official could give orders to Cabinet members on the council. Souers had no objection to changing the name of the senior staff to Planning Board.

Sid Souers's understanding to the contrary, there *were* differences between Truman's senior staff and the Planning Board that were more than cosmetic. Ike made board members responsible primarily to the White House and not the agencies that had nominated them. Board members had their own agency assistants to help with the work, senior people with reliable access to the highest levels of their parent agencies. It was the assistants, rather than the board members, who were analogous to Souers's NSC senior staff. Moreover, the Planning Board was far more active than had been its predecessors, meeting on the average of three times a week. Cutler personally presided over 504 sessions of the Planning Board, two and a half times as many as had occurred throughout the Truman administration, and in all, by the time Gordon Gray took over, there had been 703 meetings of this group.

In urgent situations, a few examples of which have already been noted, the Planning Board itself would draft policy papers. This too was a departure from Truman's practice. Otherwise the agency with primary responsibility would assemble a first draft that then went to the Planning Board, where members tried to iron out agency differences. Those that could not be resolved went to the NSC as "splits." For example, meeting at the end of August 1956, the council resolved eight splits over NSC-5612 pertaining to Southeast Asia, which Ike then approved. Overall, during the Eisenhower administration the Planning Board process served up 187 numbered policy papers, including directives for NSC subcommittees, nine versions of a paper on basic national security policy, papers on many functional subjects such as foreign information programs, and 126 papers covering thirty-seven areas of the world.

Critics objected that drafting policy papers and resolving splits degenerated into sterile arguments over wording and punctuation, clearly not the real stuff of policy. But such critics were unaware of the whole panoply of national security activity, most particularly the sensitive Oval Office meetings. Moreover, Eisenhower himself saw this problem as it evolved through the mid-1950s, and in 1958 told NSC members that he wanted less discussion of splits in papers and more of policies themselves.

Part of the problem was due to the council meetings. Those gradually increased in size, which was mostly the fault of the President himself, who recognized many different categories of NSC attendance. They included the principals, other Cabinet members (like George Humphrey) whom Ike invited to attend on a regular basis, members who were invited for specific meetings of interest to their agencies, subordinates who were regularly invited, and people attending only to discuss specific items on the agenda. With the increased attendance, particularly the multiplication of subordinate "backbenchers," NSC principals found it more difficult to act not as representatives of their agencies but as personal advisers to the President, which is what Eisenhower wanted. That in turn forced the President into more frequent use of Oval Office meetings, which imposed additional demands on his time. Ann Whitman, Ike's secretary, thought the NSC the most time-consuming part of the President's work. In 1956 and again in 1958, Eisenhower took steps to reduce the size of NSC meetings and to bring the principals back to their role as individual advisers.

Whitman worried that the President, who forced himself to sit through the long meetings and briefings on papers he'd already read, was actually going to harm his health. Apparently Whitman was not the only person so concerned. Gordon Gray once held a dinner in New York for former Eisenhower staffer C. D. Jackson plus NSC consultant Walt W. Rostow. "We've *got* to do something," Gray told them. "These NSC meetings are going to *kill* the president!"

Unfortunately, as Ike himself well knew, there was no alternative. The NSC had to be there to give direction to the bureaucracy. If the policy issues were not ventilated there, one segment or another would feel that it had to try to make an end run to the President. So while others worried about the President's health, Ike focused on trying to make the NSC sessions more productive.

Critics also charged that the policy papers were inadequate since, as general statements, they failed to provide guidance for crises. However, Ike's method of responding to crises did not depend on the policy papers. Moreover, he viewed the process of planning as more important than the actual content of the papers. It sensitized officials to the views of other parts of the bureaucracy so that when questions did develop, the administration did not have to expend time relearning what it already knew. Finally, the policy papers furnished a collective body of basic policy decisions that could be referred to in routine situations.

Another departure from earlier practice came in the use of the NSC staff. Sid Souers and Jimmy Lay's small staff had scheduled and delivered papers, not much more. Harriman's people sat in on the ad hoc interagency groups for the first time, an NSC staff role that Cutler formalized. Then he added what he called the Policy Coordinating Staff, to distinguish it from Lay's executive secretariat. This included its own secretariat of four under Marion Boggs, which did the paperwork for the Planning Board in the same fashion as Lay and "Ev" Gleason for the NSC. As director, Boggs was secretary to the Planning Board and chairman of the group of agency assistants to board members.

The Policy Coordinating Staff also contained an office for internal security. To oversee such matters, Eisenhower designated an NSC representative, who chaired two major interagency committees and also channeled any communications between the NSC and the FBI. The structure of those committees had been inherited from the Truman NSC, as had the NSC representative, J. Patrick Coyne, a nine-year FBI veteran who had done such a good job on a security report Truman requested in 1947 that he had been kept on ever since, rising to GS-17, almost the top grade in the civil service, by 1958. His assistant was another former FBI man, A. Russell Ash, who would remain with the NSC until 1972. Coyne's jurisdiction encompassed several areas rather more closely related with nuclear warfare. As of July 1959, they included port security, one of the national mobilization plans, continuity of government in the event of nuclear war, and the NSC relocation plan.

Curiously enough for an administration that had begun on the high tide of McCarthyism, the keepers of the keys barely tolerated some of the sallies of FBI boss J. Edgar Hoover. Hoover liked to exploit things for maximum effect. When he came across some item, such as NSC contacts with Soviet persons, he would pass it up through Ash, mostly, or Coyne, and just sort of dump it on the special assistant's desk. If the keeper chose to do nothing, Hoover would know that and could use the knowledge to his advantage later. Cutler, for one, considered most such reports picayune and the process a nuisance. Upon receiving such a report one time, his renowned scissors came out. Cutler hefted them from one hand to the other, then furiously flung them across the office, where they stuck, quivering, in the leather couch across the way.

The final element of the policy coordinating unit, one of the most significant innovations of the Eisenhower NSC, was the Special Staff. This had a substantive function, helping Ike's keeper by preparing the briefing notes he used to introduce policy papers at the NSC, doing the special assistant's staff work related to other groups of which he was a member, and performing independent analyses of each Planning Board paper at each stage of development. To give just one illustration, in January 1954 when the Indochina policy paper NSC-177 was up for discussion, the special staff prepared a four-page memorandum for Cutler that identified two fundamental questions raised by the paper, then supplied extensive analysis, comparing the proposed policy with other NSC papers on Korea and Iran. It warned that recommendations seemed to be phrased in an either-or fashion, so that one or another *must* be selected, then outlined other possible alternatives not mentioned at all. The Special Staff analysis drew no conclusions, but simply pointed up the paper's flaws.

In 1958, Bromley K. Smith managed the Special Staff as senior member, with four analysts, an administrative assistant, and two secretaries under him. One of the analysts, Robert H. Johnson, left shortly for leave to conduct studies under a Rockefeller Public Service Award. In July 1959, Johnson was back to assist other members on South Asia and the Far East. At that time, Charles A. Haskins, another analyst, worked on missile and space programs, arms control, Pentagon strategy presentations, financial estimates for NSC papers, and Antarctica. Johnson helped Haskins on the Far East, while George Weber assisted him on basic national security policy. Phillip J. Halla handled Iraq, Tunisia, Morocco, Algeria, and with Johnson's help, South Asia. George Weber also monitored agency status reports, East-West exchange programs, merchant marine policy, and Cyprus, France, and Japan; and helped Haskins on basic national security policy. Smith ran the staff as a sort of round-robin group. When a new NSC paper came up, he assigned it to whichever staffer had the lightest workload, except that science and technology subjects were reserved for Charlie Haskins. The NSC Special Staff, and everyone else in the policy coordination unit, worked under the supervision of Everett Gleason, the Council's deputy executive secretary until he returned to academia in the summer of 1959. Marion Boggs replaced him.

The other major component of Ike's NSC was the unit handling implementation, the Operations Coordinating Board (OCB). This went far beyond Truman's Psychological Strategy Board. Indeed, psychological warfare became but one aspect of its work, handled by a six-person Information and Education Projects Staff.

Typically, once an NSC paper received approval it went to the OCB for detailed planning. There actually was a board at the head of the OCB, composed of agency representatives, each of whom would make suggestions in formulating an "operations plan." For some years the board was chaired by Robert Murphy, then Christian A. Herter of the State Department. As had the PSB, it met weekly for private luncheons followed by the formal board meetings. The truly confidential business, of which no records were kept, continued to be transacted at the lunches.

Completed operations plans went to the bureaucracy for implementation, after which the OCB was supposed to monitor progress, through Ike's man on the OCB, who carried the title NSC representative for security operations coordination. Every six months the representative, who functioned as vice-chairman of the OCB, supervised compilation of a report on the status of all programs in effect. That report was reviewed by OCB and, depending upon its agenda and other factors, by the full NSC. The OCB presentation were made the President's representatives, Frederick M. Dearborn, Jr., and later Karl G. Harr. The senior permanent OCB official was its executive officer, Elmer B. Staats.

Although the OCB worked after a fashion, Eisenhower continued to be dissatisfied with the arrangements for implementation. Since OCB could not issue orders, real problems merely bounced back to the NSC. The President tried to solve this by emphasizing independent responsibilities for board members, then by insisting that the agencies appoint higher-ranking officers to the board. Then, in 1958, he further underlined the unity of policy by absorbing the OCB staff into his NSC staff. The board gave up its offices on Jackson Place, in use since PSB days, and moved into the Old Executive Office Building. Ike's final solution, in January 1960, was to make Gordon Gray chairman of the Operations Coordinating Board.

Gray was intimate with the problems of the OCB since, between 1955 and 1957, he had been the Pentagon member of the board, attending more than forty of its meetings. Gray also got tips from Ike's representatives at OCB, Fred Dearborn and Karl Harr. Harr ended up as Gray's deputy for NSC affairs, DOD's alternate for Gray at sessions of the OCB and the Planning Board. Yet even with inside information, Gray was unable to implement policy to Ike's satisfaction.

As the years passed, there developed exceptions to the OCB's purely advisory role. The board became involved in actual implementation in areas that fell between the cracks of agency responsibility. Thus the OCB managed the space program during its earliest years, before creation of NASA, and also United States scientific explorations of Antarctica. The OCB became involved in managing the administrative services provided for the NSC by the CIA. The CIA services included everything from administering oaths to maintaining master NSC employment records, preparing NSC budget documents, even performing routine typewriter maintenance.

As it evolved, the OCB staff came to consist of five separate units. They included executive director Elmer Staats's office, which handled day-to-day management; a secretariat that serviced the board; the information projects staff for psychological warfare; and an intelligence liaison staff. The most frustrating OCB jobs, though, were undoubtedly on the so-called area staff. Area staffers, including six "representatives" and two staff officers under a "senior area representative," were the NSC's eyes and ears on the interagency panels that assembled the country operations plans for the OCB. Since the board had no decision-making powers, however, these people could do little more than pass the word on about problems or obstructions while they busied themselves preparing working group agendas and minutes.

This, then, was the crest of Policy Hill. In all, the NSC staff included thirty-seven people, the OCB staff forty. Many had been detailed from elsewhere in the federal government, as had been the case since Truman's day. In July 1958 there were eleven detailees, including four from State, four from the CIA, and one each from the Navy, the Air Force, and the USIA. In addition, various officials throughout government spent the bulk of their time doing what was called "NSC-OCB work." A December 1958 survey found a total of fifty-four professional and thirty-eight secretarial staff in this category. The largest contribution by far came from DOD and the armed services: nine professional and seven secretarial staff from the Office of the Secretary of Defense; six professional and four secretarial workers from the Joint Chiefs of Staff; seven more professionals and six secretarial staff from the three armed services. The State Department contribution amounted to six professionals and five secretarial staff, while that of the CIA stood at four professionals and five secretarial staff. In addition, large numbers of officials would be called upon from time to time for service on a specific study or working group; at the time of the December 1958 survey, for example, State people chaired thirty-three of the forty-two OCB working groups. To the total of full-time workers should be added the five members of Goodpaster's Office of the Staff Secretary. Still, in comparison with a federal bureaucracy employing over a million people, the laborers on Policy Hill seemed a small band indeed.

While the White House staff—starting with the special assistant for national security, the staff secretary, and later the science adviser—were Ike's agents in the area of national security policy-making, the President also took steps to guard against the NSC becoming too much of an ingrown body of advisers. He wanted no secret Star Chamber. One of the first things Ike had Cutler do for him was to set up the panel of private consultants, men wholly outside government, to review existing and proposed policies. He employed NSC consultants fifteen times during Cutler's tenure on subjects of interest to him.

Actually Ike explored the idea of consultants further in the fall of 1953 and again in the summer of 1954, when a valued friend repeated the suggestion. Cutler consulted John Foster Dulles and George Humphrey, then the keeper along with Pete Carroll discussed the subject with the President. Ike wanted a group of whom perhaps three could sit in at each NSC session, then function as a kind of general advisory board. Cutler warned Ike of the danger of "ivory tower advice from people without operating responsibilities," and objected to the burden of keeping such a large group continually informed, as well as of the difficulty of getting qualified people. Foster Dulles also opposed the idea of a group, and Ike finally said he would put the idea "on ice for a while."

Robert Sprague consulted on air defense for the NSC during 1956, thinking himself so much a part of the staff that he exchanged Christmas cards with Jimmy Lay, Bob Johnson, and others. A year later, as Sprague labored with the Gaither Committee, which critiqued United States defense programs, Cutler had Walt Rostow down from MIT to discuss devices for initiating new ideas within the executive branch. Rostow got a ride in Bobby Cutler's Porsche plus dinner with Cutler and Fred Dearborn of the OCB. After Rostow worked up a list of ideas, based on conversation with Dearborn, Cutler and Dearborn twice met with Jimmy Lay and Elmer Staats to consider the possibilities. By the time Gordon Gray succeeded Cutler, these had been boiled down, once again, to the panel of NSC consultants, arrangements for which were gradually worked out from the fall of 1958 to the winter of 1959. The consultants began work that spring by supplying commentaries on the NSC paper covering basic national security policy. Judging from what can be gleaned of the commentaries, they must have disappointed the President. Rather than bold new ideas, the consultants mostly confined themselves to quibbles over the wording of sentences or paragraphs.

Available NSC records show Cutler playing a major role in managing the NSC machinery. He played that role in a low-key, self-effacing fashion. When Ike complained in April 1958 that NSC discussions were becoming bogged down over the language in the papers, Cutler typically responded, "It has been my lack of skill not to evoke as sharply as you wish the *issue*, rather than the text which expresses the issue." Yet Ike saw only the end result. "Killing as it may be to R.C.," Cutler said, he already had chaired ten Planning Board meetings on NSC-5810/1, that year's basic national security paper, and there would be six more before it went to the council at the beginning of May. Cutler's example made Ike's point though—all those sessions were unable to eliminate disputes over some paragraphs of the paper, which in fact had to be held out for revision when Ike approved the rest of NSC-5810/1 on May 5. It was not until two months later that the last splits could be resolved at the council. This kind of action on policy papers certainly did not seem dynamic, and in some instances, to Eisenhower's fury, became known outside the bureaucracy. Sensitive to leaks wherever they occurred, Ike brought up at council meetings disclosures of NSC information as a formal agenda topic at least four times.

In between Bobby Cutler's two White House stints, Dillon Anderson served as special assistant for national security. He was known to Eisenhower from the postwar period, when both worked in the Pentagon on legislation for unification of the armed services. In general, NSC staff and Ike as well seem not to have been overly impressed with Anderson.

He returned to Houston in September 1956. Ike considered himself lucky to get William H. Jackson to fill in for three months until Cutler, who had already promised to return, was back on board. Jackson was a former CIA official and wartime acquaintance of the President's. Ike used him as a troubleshooter in a number of instances in 1956 and 1957. He made recommendations to the President on NSC and OCB organization in December 1956, but one of the first things Cutler did upon his return was to knock down most of them.

Gordon Gray, Cutler's final successor, was something else again. For the first time Ike had someone who was expert in national security matters. He had worked alongside the NSC with the Psychological Strategy Board, and had in the past performed delicate political chores for Ike, notably in the case of J. Robert Oppenheimer, in which Gray had adjudicated the review of the physicist's security clearance. In charge of the Office of Defense Mobilization, Gray had organized the Gaither Committee study for the President and then kept his mouth shut about its contents when former members were blabbing at the height of the Sputnik national security hysteria.

A Winston-Salem, North Carolina boy, Gordon's father, Bowman Gray, had made a fortune in tobacco and became chairman of the board of the R. J. Reynolds Company. Gordon was sent to private school, Woodberry Forest in Virginia, but state college, and managed to keep the common touch despite his family wealth. He combined modesty with intelligence, wit, and a gracious manner. A publishing magnate from age twenty-eight, when he acquired two newspapers, thoughout his life Gray remained active in communications, the Grange, and the National Trust for Historic Preservation.

It must have been ironic for Eisenhower, once a four-pack-a-day cigarette smoker who had had to give it up, to find himself working with a tobacco scion who kept packs of regular and mentholated cigarettes on either side of his ashtray and alternated between them. Where Bobby Cutler had been sharp and aggressive, Gray was graceful and gracious. Cutler would denounce ideas he didn't like, call them "asinine"; Gray was more apt to say, "That's a respectable point of view." Ike responded to Gray and repeatedly expanded his mandate and role toward the end of the administration. Gray kept his focus on how national security issues might affect the President, and repeatedly came up with new ways in which he could help. In fact, Gray became a presence behind the scenes at the White House with unparalleled access to President Eisenhower.

At their meetings, which Gray meticulously recorded in memoranda, he and Ike discussed issues and the NSC's agenda schedule plus national security organization. Gray reported on the status of policy papers and studies, discussed which ones to bring up at council meetings and why, and offered solutions to many practical or functional obstacles to policy progress.

At one typical session with the President, about a month after Gray took the post, the new special assistant had ten items for Eisenhower to consider, including a planned Pentagon report on ICBM and ABM programs that was then in preparation. The report had been delayed for a month already and was still not ready. General Nathan Twining of the JCS, seeking a reason for having the council give up its policy review, was objecting that too many military hardware items were getting on to the council's agenda. "The President," Gray drily recorded, "expressed little sympathy for the point of view," and Ike insisted that the briefing had to go on "unless the military could come up with a better way to approach the problem." Gray then excused Ev Gleason from the room and took up the Gaither report with the President, pointing out that although there were some problems with the DOD studies, it was clear that "the JCS were not eager to proceed." Gray added that the council must "be active and affirmative in its functioning" and volunteered to follow up "on any item which was discussed in the Council which appeared to need action on somebody's part." He then gave Ike an example that involved primarily a State matter and lay outside his responsibility as special assistant. Eisenhower directed Gray to take the matter up with the relevant Cabinet officer "and not to feel that I was guilty of any transgression." Ike himself was more worried about the tedium of meetings, in particular Allen Dulles's laborious and philosophical briefings, along with the excessively detailed and historical ones from brother Foster.

In January 1959, Gray proposed substituting the NSC staff for the Council, in receiving routine progress reports from OCB, as a means of lightening the principals' burdens. Ike went further and asked to receive OCB reports only when new situations arose. The President then engaged in an extended colloquy with Gray on running the NSC consultants panel. Two months later, Eisenhower conferred extensive powers on his national security adviser amid the pressures of the Berlin deadline crisis. Almost simultaneously the President called on Gray to intercede with the publisher over a leak about to be printed in *Fortune* magazine.

By early 1960, Gray and Ike were talking over a possible film or photographic essay on the NSC in operation in order to allay congressional fears that the council was becoming too powerful. The President ruled out a film, but talk of a photo feature went as far as selecting settings and subjects for pictures.

Gray remained sensitive to others' views on the NSC's role and performance. One of his first projects upon becoming national security adviser was a series of consultations with the NSC players. Gray interviewed Richard Nixon, John Foster Dulles, Attorney General William P. Rogers, Budget Director Maurice Stans, and Deputy Secretary of Defense Robert Anderson, among others. No doubt for personal reasons, the one criticism they mostly had in common was the "exclusions," Ike's practice of ruling out certain subjects and handling them in the even more select Oval Office meetings. Foster Dulles supported the practice for a number of reasons, principally that crises or day-to-day subjects were not appropriate for council discussion (and might tie the hands of the secretary of state). Gray retorted that the public, press, and Congress would naturally assume that many of these subjects, for example Taiwan, had received full NSC consideration. But the President continued to resist and was known to feel it more important that the NSC was involved in the planning process.

Gray further discussed the consultant panel idea with other NSC members, and also the practice of holding "special" meetings for briefing purposes only, and other management issues. When the consultant panel actually materialized, Gray invited both Bobby Cutler and Dillon Anderson to be members.

Vice President Nixon advised Gray on relations with the press because he felt that Cutler and Anderson had erred "in maintaining a line against any contacts." Rather, Bill Jackson had had the "sound" posture—occasionally meeting "responsible members of the press for background discussion." Gray followed Nixon's advice and established some press contacts. It was the charge of a "missile gap," that the Soviets led the United States in ICBM capability, that occasioned one of the more notable of these sessions with reporters, in early 1960 when Gray tried to convince *Time* magazine bureau chief John Steele that there was nothing to fear.

In January 1960 the President made Gray chairman of the OCB, following Robert Murphy's retirement and the repeated refusal of State's C. Douglas Dillon to take on the task. With his follow-up and scheduling powers, his broad contact with the President, his initiative at the NSC, and even his occasional press contacts and speeches to students at the armed services war colleges, Gray became de facto national security adviser though he still lacked the job title.

For all his actual power, however, Gray headed what was but a tiny speck in the government bureaucracy. The NSC and OCB staffs together numbered less than eighty, including all the secretaries and administrative people, and fewer than seventy if one excluded personnel detailed from other agencies. The NSC budget was about 90 percent personnel costs and rose slowly throughout the decade as Congress granted federal pay increases, from $155,000 in 1953 to $248,000 in 1956–1957. The absorption of the OCB almost tripled the basic budget, but even Eisenhower's last NSC budget request, at $830,000 for fiscal year 1962, did not top the million dollar mark.

One big budget issue of the period was providing guards for the NSC offices in the Old Executive Office Building. As late as 1956 they were patrolled only at night or over the weekends, with the guard post inside on the third floor of the OEOB and the service provided by the CIA. Another burning issue was replacement of the NSC's only vehicle, a 1947 Buick sedan. The council had little call to shuttle passengers, but a great need for delivery of NSC papers, etc. After 1954, when the CIA began to provide the driver and maintain the car in its motor pool, Jimmy Lay almost always asked the agency for a Ford station wagon for the NSC couriers. By 1955 the to-ing and fro-ing had became annoying and the NSC requested $2,000 to buy a new station wagon, less the trade-in value of the old Buick, and $265 for gas, oil, and maintenance expenses.

Early keepers of the keys, unlike the later national security advisers, were not shy about appearing before Congress, and regularly gave testimony supporting NSC budget requests. Council personnel who appeared before congressional appropriations committees during the 1950s included Robert

Cutler, Dillon Anderson, Gordon Gray, James Lay, Bromley Smith, and George Weber, a member of the NSC special staff. Such appearances before Congress, a result of Eisenhower's strong sense of lawfulness, would be conveniently forgotten later when the White House asserted a precedent that NSC staff were not subject to review by the legislative branch of the government. In any case, Ike had a passion for order, Gray did too, and the NSC staff accepted propriety and balance as watchwords for its work throughout the Eisenhower administration.

Throughout his White House staff, Eisenhower replicated the style of organization he created for his NSC. He channeled domestic issues through a chief of staff, titled assistant to the President, a post to which he appointed New Hampshire governor Sherman Adams. A political associate of the President's, Adams was given Cabinet rank when Eisenhower made him chief of staff. Though the press played on Adams's job title, assistant to the president, by calling him "assistant president," the governor did not fancy himself a foreign affairs expert. Adams recounts that pressing duties often prevented him from attending sessions of the NSC, though he was present at NSC and Oval Office meetings during the Tachen and Lebanese crises. Despite Ike's backing, conflict of interest charges reported by the press drove Adams from the White House in late 1958. Ike picked his congressional liaison, General Wilton B. Persons, to succeed Adams. Both got on well with the keepers of the national security keys. Jerry Persons, in particular, respected Gordon Gray and was close to Goodpaster.

In addition to formal staff procedures, the President had less formal ways to moderate among his colleagues. For one, Ike was an avid player of golf and bridge. A good deal of business got transacted on the golf course, especially Burning Tree in Washington, and at the card table. Ike reached out to figures in Congress, government, the military, the press, and business with a series of "stag" dinners he hosted at the White House. In 1958, for example, while working on defense reorganization, the President invited his Joint Chiefs of Staff. Finally, Eisenhower used quiet times, usually late afternoons or in the evening, to keep in touch with his close staff. The men would gather in the President's office, have a drink, joke or ruminate on the events of the day and immediate, upcoming problems. This group included Sherman Adams, Jerry Persons, Bobby Cutler, Gordon Gray, and John Foster Dulles, among others.

"IN A COMFORTABLE
POSITION"

▲▲▲

Alongside day-to-day questions of national security policy, Eisenhower had also to deal with acute crises that occurred with a fair degree of frequency during his administration. In the first of them, which revolved around getting the United States out of the Korean War, Ike had made much use of his NSC, working in close concert with Bobby Cutler's Planning Board. The latter unit drafted and redrafted prescriptive papers Eisenhower used to bludgeon the bureaucracy into line behind a policy all could agree upon.

The second major crisis came at Dien Bien Phu, in French Indochina, where the French were on the verge of losing their colonial war to keep Vietnam. Eisenhower wanted to support the French but found that in the heat of the moment it was too late and too difficult to marshal the political and diplomatic backing necessary for an attempt to intervene in the conflict.

Eisenhower learned the lesson of Dien Bien Phu. In subsequent crises involving Taiwan and the Middle East, the President moved at an early date to garner the political backing he wanted. He also began, again from the time of Dien Bien Phu, to conduct certain key business *outside* the NSC framework. Thus NSC meetings worked on some but by no means all aspects of the U.S. response to the successive Taiwan crises, those over Berlin, and the one that occurred after Suez, in Lebanon.

In March 1957, Congress passed a Middle East resolution with a provision permitting the use of force, allowing the President to "secure and protect the territorial integrity and political independence" of nations requesting it, against "overt armed aggression" from any nation controlled by "International Communism."

Ike's mandate, which soon was called the Eisenhower Doctrine, came at a moment of great ferment throughout this region. Egypt's Gamal Abdel Nasser's Pan-Arab appeal seemed to grow by the minute; Syria showed signs of forming an alliance with Egypt. The pro-British Hashemite monarchies, Iraq and Jordan, seemed metastable in the face of rising Arab nationalism. Then there was Lebanon, cosmopolitan center of the eastern Mediterranean, its capital Beirut almost a European city. Beneath its placid surface, Beirut teemed with currents of religious, social, and political antagonisms.

Attracted by the prospect of American aid, Lebanese President Camille Chamoun asked his own parliament to approve the Eisenhower Doctrine. At that moment, Beirut was already preoccupied by another political question: Under the Lebanese constitution, Chamoun was entitled to one six-year term that ended in 1958. He could not succeed himself.

Washington felt there was a lot at stake in the Lebanese elections. Suddenly the embassy in Beirut began reporting that Egypt and Syria were bankrolling some of the opposition candidates. Ambassador Donald Heath recommended the United States send funds to the Christian side. The administration adopted Heath's suggestion and the CIA sent an election specialist to Beirut. One of the most frequent of Chamoun's American contacts, Wilbur C. Eveland, an agency contract officer, who had cover as a staff member of the NSC's Operations Coordinating Board, would carry lists of Maronite candidates to the Lebanese president. Chamoun, knowing Lebanese politics, decided which races were important and how much the candidates would get. Ambassador Heath meddled too—he set up at least one snafu, persuading a Christian to run for a seat already being contested by another Christian. The U.S. ended up funding both political campaigns at a cost of $50,000.

By early 1958 protests had erupted in the streets, and Beirut became an armed camp. The opposition increased its demands to include the resignation of Chamoun. President Eisenhower thought the Lebanese government, with an army of nine thousand and with twenty-five hundred national police, ought to be able to handle the unrest. Military commander General Fuad Chehab, however, made no move against the rioters. Ike never understood why Chamoun didn't just fire Chehab, not realizing that Lebanese factional politics precluded such a move. Most of the Lebanese Army was Muslim while its officer corps remained predominantly Maronite; General Chehab, from an old Christian family himself, feared that the army would disintegrate if ordered into action against other Lebanese. President Chamoun finally got so anxious that his wife gave CIA contact Wilbur Eveland the family jewels for safekeeping in the vault at the United States embassy.

Chamoun stubbornly insisted he would serve out his term, not resign. He also went to the United Nations with charges that Syria and Egypt, united in an Arab republic since February 1958, were instigating and arming the rebels. From Washington, Ike had no doubt of the veracity of the charges, and felt little need to discuss the subject before the NSC. At council meetings Lebanon figured only in general reviews of the Middle East until well after the beginning of the 1958 crisis.

On July 14 the President learned of a coup in Baghdad. The crown prince had been murdered, there were serious doubts about the fate of the king, brother of Jordan's King Hussein, and his pro-British prime minister. When the news arrived in Beirut, it sent Chamoun to Ambassador Robert Mc-

Clintock with a request for intervention to protect his government. Mc-Clintock backed the request as his own recommendation, forwarding it to Washington.

News of the Lebanese request and the Iraqi coup arrived at the White House when Eisenhower was about to hold a scheduled NSC meeting. The council was to review the record of NSC Planning Board activity since 1947 and to take up the issues of military research and civil defense against nuclear war. Bobby Cutler opened as usual, with a summary of the first item on the agenda. After a short discussion of that subject, Eisenhower adjourned the meeting. The President asked NSC principals and some other advisers to stay behind, and the meeting reconvened by 9:45 A.M. This group included Cutler, Goodpaster, Gordon Gray, who was preparing to assume Cutler's role at the White House, and Sherman Adams.

Participants were caught up in the intensity of the crisis Ike revealed. "But the President himself was easy and calm," Cutler recalled, "sprawled back in the chair behind his desk in a comfortable position." Ike listened as Allen and John Foster Dulles gave the latest intelligence and diplomatic pictures. Either might have raised questions about Bob McClintock, as both are believed to have harbored doubts regarding the ambassador's perceptions and activism. Apparently neither Dulles brother saw fit to question McClintock's judgment at this point.

Ike passed relatively quickly to a long exchange with General Nathan F. Twining, now risen to Chairman of the Joint Chiefs of Staff. Which forces, how could they move? How fast? Ike "was dealing with something that he thoroughly understood. His unruffled confidence was apparent to all," as Cutler put it. "The considerable exchange between these two men was in so low a key as to seem almost casual. There was no hurling of thunderbolts." Twining "replied with a soldier's brevity. He had the answers."

Foster Dulles asked Twining for his view of the probability the Soviets might respond to a United States intervention. General Twining replied in the name of all the Joint Chiefs. "I assured him," Twining recalls, "that the Soviets would do no more than wring their hands and deliver verbal protests."

The die was cast.

With one hour's discussion, President Eisenhower determined to intervene with the Sixth Fleet and a landing of troops in Lebanon.

Called Operation Bluebat, the Lebanese intervention involved considerable American forces. The Sixth Fleet alone, under Vice Admiral Charles R. Brown, comprised seventy-seven warships including three aircraft carriers, two battle cruisers, and twenty-two destroyers.

American Marines began by occupying a perimeter around the Beirut airport. Early the second morning, when another Marine battalion began to land, the first unit marched off for the city. Admiral James L. Holloway, the amphibious commander, landed at the airport and accompanied the advancing unit, which encountered a roadblock protected by several Lebanese tanks. McClintock and General Chehab, speeding to the scene in the ambassador's limousine, passed another dozen tanks in battle positions. They arrived at the roadblock to face a determined Marine battalion commander. Admiral Holloway arrived at almost the same moment.

McClintock introduced Admiral Holloway to General Chehab. As journalists watched, Holloway declared, "General, I am ordering this column of Marines forward at once. And if there is any resistance . . ."

Holloway let his voice trail off.

Chehab asked if the Americans would break up their force into segments, allowing Lebanese jeeps to be interspersed with it. That way, General Chehab felt, "it doesn't look so much like an invading army."

When Holloway and McClintock agreed, Chehab asked for fifteen minutes to advise Lebanese headquarters to order withdrawal of its troops. The ambassador and the admiral went with Chehab to the nearest telephone. When the mission was accomplished, Holloway turned to Chehab and said, in his broken French, "And now, *mon général,* we advance *toot dee suitee!*" Holloway repeated the last phrase with a wave.

The Marine battalion column became an impromptu parade, with the ambassador's Cadillac in the lead and the Lebanese tanks joined up for the ride.

There never was any trouble with the Lebanese Army, or the rebels for that matter. By July 19 there were four Marine battalions at Beirut, while a reinforced Army airborne brigade flew in late that day. By the end of July, 10,600 American troops occupied positions centered around Beirut's international airport.

Eisenhower's envoy, Robert Murphy, arrived on the scene shortly after the climactic parade into the city. "Since Berlin in 1945," wrote Murphy later, "I had not been in a more trigger-happy place than Beirut was at that time." McClintock and Holloway met Murphy at the airport. The envoy found Chamoun tired and worried and felt that Chehab ought to be fired, but appreciated the delicate political balance within the Lebanese armed forces. Gunshots, bombings, and arson continued in the city. Murphy met with Druze chieftain Kamal Jumblatt in the Shuf Mountains; using Chehab's good offices, the envoy also saw Muslim underground figure Rashid Karami. Murphy urged an immediate presidential election in the Lebanese parliament. Such an election in fact took place at the end of July. By a margin of 48 to 8 on the second ballot, the victor was General Fuad Chehab. Murphy left Beirut shortly thereafter.

Only once the immediate crisis had passed, on July 31, did Eisenhower put Beirut on the NSC agenda. It was the 374th meeting of the council. That was only the second substantive discussion of Lebanon in the NSC during 1958.

"Well Done!" commended Admiral Holloway in an order of the day to his forces on August 3. He directed this Navy compliment to all members of the Middle East special command. Holloway's force ashore peaked at fourteen thousand in mid-August but diminished thereafter until October 25, when the last American troops left Lebanon. Operation Bluebat had cost $200 million. No Soviet response eventuated. Lebanon did not explode.

About a week after the first Marine landings, the NSC Planning Board took up the subject of the United States' future course of action in Lebanon. A working group of agency representatives got orders to prepare a discussion paper, which the Planning Board and NSC considered on July 31. During the first week of August the representatives received instructions for a further paper, which the Planning Board sent to the NSC on August 21. The council ordered revisions in the statement of the United States' policy toward the Middle East. Within three weeks a draft policy paper was on the table with the Joint Chiefs getting their crack at it. On October 16 the NSC took up the splits that remained, and on the thirtieth the council adopted appropriate amendments. Within three months the trouble in Lebanon had led to an NSC review of American policy. In March 1959 the OCB reviewed progress in Lebanon, a review noted by the full NSC. There was thus an opportunity to brief the President about lessons learned from the crisis. From beginning to end, Middle East policy had figured in eight NSC meetings and eighteen of those of the Planning Board.

For all the success of Eisenhower's intervention it was apparent to Gordon Gray, who succeeded Cutler as the main American forces arrived in Beirut, that the crisis had been handled almost entirely *outside* the NSC. Moreover, policy review had followed the crisis, not averted it, which was rather like the saying about the horse and the barn door. Gray did not miss such details. Some of his successors were not so perspicacious. Officials in Zbigniew Brzezinski's day, focusing on the fact that a decision had been made, implemented, and successfully reviewed, cited Lebanon in 1958 as the epitome of NSC crisis management, an ideal rarely attained. Those officials did not mention the fact that the fateful decision had been taken in less than an hour or made outside the council.

"THE PRESIDENT
WANTED ME"

▲▲▲

The Lebanon intervention went up for debate before the United Nations in August 1958. Almost simultaneously the arena of conflict shifted anew to the China coast. There, Ike noted for posterity, "the Communists made their next provocative move." Again the arena was the Taiwan Strait and the targets Quemoy and Matsu.

As in 1954, Washington expected this crisis. Some of the credit belongs to Gordon Gray, Ike's newly annointed special assistant for national security affairs. Gray had been keeping tabs on the Far East intelligence picture; even before becoming security adviser he asked the CIA for the latest estimates on the Taiwan Strait and of likely reactions in Asia if the United States should use nuclear weapons in that region. Intelligence was aware that the Chinese were withdrawing forces from North Korea, and increasing the troops opposite Quemoy and Matsu. Reconnaissance also revealed construction work at nearby airfields on mainland China. Then Soviet Premier Nikita Khrushchev visited Peking to meet with People's Republic of China leader Mao Tse-tung. National Security Council discussion of the China situation seemed appropriate.

Bobby Cutler may have flagged the Taiwan Strait for Gray's attention —as early as that March the CIA had warned Cutler of an approaching crisis in Far East policy, though at the time the agency had been thinking more in terms of the controversy over whether to seat the PRC at the United Nations. Gray knew there was no NSC policy paper on China in the works, but he went ahead and scheduled the Taiwan Strait for the 375th NSC session, which took place on August 7, 1958. Eisenhower accepted the agenda proposal without difficulty.

The meeting took place as planned. Four days later Eisenhower discussed the strait situation again with Gray and "suggested it might be best to have just the statutory NSC members meet with him." A few moments later Ike told Goodpaster and General Twining the same thing. Taiwan was again before the council on August 14, immediately after which occurred a special meeting on the subject, with a follow-up meeting a week later. The next day, August 22, Chinese Communist forces on the mainland opened a mas-

86

sive artillery bombardment of Quemoy and Matsu, firing twenty thousand rounds in a single day. Rarely had the NSC been better prepared for a crisis.

Ike ordered precautionary military moves, and as time wore on the shelling became almost routine. Then the arena of confrontation shifted again, to Berlin, which had been constantly monitored as a crisis zone since the early 1950s. As Ike put it in retrospect, "I had lived with this problem intermittently for the past thirteen years."

On November 13 the NSC at its regular meeting noted a threatening speech by Soviet leader Nikita Khrushchev. The action moved into the Oval Office the next day when an American convoy was halted on the Berlin access route. Ike overruled the military, who wanted to send a small force to free the detained convoy, arguing that such a course required prior consultation with our allies, for which there had not been sufficient time. The President ordered temporary termination of convoys while Washington reviewed the options, resuming them some days later. By November 20, Foster Dulles expected that Khruschev would move soon to transfer Soviet responsibilities regarding access to East Germany, and told Ike during another meeting that this would create the most complicated situation in Berlin since the 1948 blockade. The following morning Ike had press secretary Jim Hagerty make a low-key statement affirming that the United States firmly intended to maintain the integrity of West Berlin.

When the Soviets set a deadline for a German peace treaty Ike was in Augusta, Georgia, for a golfing vacation. At his cottage on the grounds of the National Golf Club, he met with his son, Major John S. D. Eisenhower, who had flown down from Washington with news of Khrushchev's note and the latest from allied capitals. John was the most recent addition to General Goodpaster's Office of the Staff Secretary.

There were two aspects to the Soviet ultimatum imposing a Berlin "deadline." First, the ultimatum certainly promised a crisis, one with much sharper nuclear implications than previous experiences. Second, Khrushchev's deadline had at least one positive aspect—it postponed the day of reckoning for six months, during which there would be time for many things.

Actual Soviet and East German behavior along the Berlin access corridors was conspicuously correct after November 27. Ike and Dulles set to work with the British, French, and other NATO allies. Ike ordered quiet military moves that Soviet intelligence was sure to detect: naval forces shifted into the NATO area; a sudden influx of replacements that brought all American units in Germany up to full combat strength; supply stocks increased to war levels. American planners worked against the May 27 (six-month) deadline date.

What the President *did not* do is significant. Ike did not make Berlin a primary preoccupation for his NSC. After discussion of the Khrushchev speech, three NSC sessions passed before Berlin came up at all. The council considered the Soviet deadline note on December 11, more than two weeks after its receipt. In the year *prior* to the crisis, the council had found time to discuss Germany only three times, in December 1957 and February 1958, in connection with a policy paper that had annexes on Berlin and East Germany. During the deadline crisis only seven of the twenty-two NSC sessions held considered Berlin. It should be noted that three of the seven discussions of Berlin were NSC special sessions, an unusually large number. Those special sessions, restricted to NSC principals and the President's invitees, were Ike's device to overcome the formality of the large regular NSC meetings.

This apparently routine activity of the National Security Council cloaked the real work that was being done on the Berlin crisis. Ike felt great apprehension about Berlin, indicated by the proportion of business he transacted outside the NSC. During the 1958 Taiwan Strait crisis, in contrast, he had allowed the full formal council a rather large role.

Ike's method of handling the Berlin crisis should have meant a reduced role for his special assistant for national security affairs. Under this President's staff system, after all, the keeper of the keys was to focus on general policy. Andy Goodpaster was the crisis man. But Gordon Gray won Ike over with his commendable discretion and efficiency, superbly demonstrated in the Taiwan Strait episode, and the Berlin deadline crisis actually brought about yet another expansion of Gray's domain.

A consequential early encounter was the first of the special National Security Council sessions. Ike adjourned the scheduled meeting early on December 11, then invited Vice President Nixon and a dozen others into his office.

There he told his assembled advisers, "In this gamble, we are not going to be betting white chips, building up the pot gradually and fearfully. Khrushchev should know that when we decide to act, our whole stack will be in the pot."

In subsequent meetings, the President went on to discuss the progress of West German rearmament (good), and the, to the President, less satisfactory status of American planning for the use of force. In January 1959, General Twining told Eisenhower that if the Soviets were to close the Autobahn, the Joint Chiefs wanted to send in an entire division, 15,000 to 20,000 troops, to make a show of force. Ike countered that a demonstration of that size would be too large to be ignored, but not big enough to fight its way to Berlin if there were serious opposition.

Hearing the JCS views from Nate Twining, Ike decided to order an interagency paper after all, not a policy paper but a study of four alternative uses of force in the Berlin crisis. The secretary of defense, JCS, State, and the CIA were to collaborate in the assessment. The alternatives ranged from a gesture along the corridors by a reinforced battalion to larger increments or different mixtures of force. Ike initially had Gordon Gray schedule the study for presentation at a special NSC session on March 5. Then the

President also scheduled an Oval Office session for Tuesday, March 17. Gordon Gray sat in on the preparatory meetings between State and Pentagon representatives throughout the intervening week.

On March 19 Gray objected that the briefing to the special NSC gathering had been flawed—in his judgment there had been poor staff work. Neither State nor Pentagon representatives had been well versed on the memorandum their departments had signed. Finally, Ike's keeper of the keys brought up the matter of the interagency paper itself. To give it its due, Gray said that the paper "advanced the ball considerably"; but some of its assumptions had not been clearly stated and many contingencies that ought to have been covered were not. Gray further complained that he had allowed State and Defense to jointly write the agenda for the March 17 meeting, only to have it arrive a half hour before the session and in the form of a memorandum to the President. That sorely tried Gray's patience with the bureaucracy. He wanted papers to go to NSC members sufficiently far in advance to allow time for their digestion. Gray insisted upon this prerogative for the President, and another special meeting was anticipated that would consider the revised alternatives paper, plus State studies on Berlin by a group under Robert Murphy.

Gray then raised the following question with the President: "Would it be desirable to have Gordon Gray assume a role in such meetings similar to that in National Security Council meetings in order to make sure that all points were covered and all differences of view were expressed?"

Ike assented.

Gray then asked Eisenhower whether the President wished him to continue to follow the contingency planning to make certain that staff work was adequate. Ike himself had repeatedly expressed concern that the United States be sure it knew exactly what it was doing in the various contingencies.

"The President," Gray noted in his record of their private meeting, "felt that he wanted me to undertake such a role."

Eisenhower's answers to Gordon Gray that March day changed the history of the National Security Council.

At his private meeting with Gordon Gray, Eisenhower permitted the emergence of the modern national security adviser, an official with virtual command powers over the range of policy planning and crisis management. Hitherto, Ike had carefully restricted his keepers of the keys to policy planning, using Goodpaster for current operations. Gray's limited function was to make crisis management flow as smoothly as did policy planning, and he largely confined himself to this. His successors have not always been so judicious; or perhaps they entertained greater ambitions. It is a measure of Andrew Goodpaster's professionalism that he adapted with such ease to Gray's intrusion into his side of the White House shop. Previously Ike had scrupulously separated his personal staff from the policy machinery; now he was allowing, indeed requiring, cooperation under difficult circumstances. Ironically, Eisenhower, the staff expert, established a precedent here for the unparalleled accumulation of power by the NSC staff. Ideas sown would be reaped in a whirlwind years later.

In the short run, Gordon Gray energized the crisis decision-making on Berlin. His new authority enabled him to assign and enforce deadlines for crisis-related work. For the first time, a security adviser would be allowed not only to participate in but to chair interagency committees. Gray told the President that the alternative-force study practically presupposed another special NSC session, and described a four-phase arrangement for dealing with the issue.

State tried to procrastinate on the Berlin matter. Acting secretary Christian Herter began voicing concern, in fact "extreme reluctance," to proceed with an interagency Berlin presentation before the full council, though he was willing to discuss it before a smaller group. His reasons for this reluctance were State's preoccupation with a visit by British leaders, insufficient time, and fear of leaks that would lead to a frozen position.

Gray did not think much of Herter's reasoning, but took the objection to the President two days before the scheduled session. Eisenhower, according to Gray's notes, "responded that he thought we had gotten to a sorry state of affairs if matters of this sort could not be discussed in the National Security Council." Gray observed, "Although I did not think the various reasons assigned had much validity, it probably would be now difficult to have the visual presentation to which State was an indispensable party."

Ike agreed to the smaller meeting. The next morning Gray came back to clarify whether Allen Dulles and General Twining should be invited. The President had no objection. "What concerned him," Gray noted, "was not so much the people usually at the Council table, but those sitting around the periphery." In the end, the State presentation was made in an Oval Office meeting and there was no NSC session on March 26.

Meanwhile, the paper on alternative uses of force encountered repeated obstacles and Gray plunged in to save it. He gave the agencies a deadline of April 9 for their contributions, and got Ike's approval to stick to that date even after the President began thinking of making another trip to Augusta during April. Gray argued that Eisenhower might want to have the presentation outside Washington, then noted the response: "The President indicated that by all means he wished the target dates to be met in these matters and if there was something worthwhile he would wish the presentation, wherever he was."

Eisenhower did take the Augusta trip, and Goodpaster and Gordon Gray flew down on April 16 to see him. Gray reported on the Berlin force study, which had finally come in from the agencies, and on the big meeting of April 11. At that meeting participants discussed how the results should be delivered to Eisenhower. Nate Twining insisted that the military paper go forward without any summary to water down the discussion or distort its conclusions. The JCS wanted to get comments from American NATO commanders, so Gray scheduled a special NSC session for April 23 to hear the report.

That special council meeting, among other things, agreed to form an ad hoc group under Robert Murphy of State to report on the Berlin situation. In another of their private conversations, on April 28, Gray asked the President if he wished Murphy to make his periodic progress reports through the special assistant for national security affairs. Herter felt the reports should come from the State Department, whereas Gray believed he himself could provide a better reporting procedure and expedite the work of the group. Ike appreciated State's concern over its turf—at length he decided to make Gray a member of the Murphy group in order to get reports on its progress without making an issue of the channel.

As the United States struggled to refine its military options, other diplomatic moves helped defuse the Berlin deadline crisis. Protracted Anglo-Soviet contacts, including efforts by Prime Minister Harold Macmillan, led to Soviet interest in a summit conference that might review the question of Germany.

However, that summit conference, eventually set for May 1960, would never take place. It became a casualty of the U-2 affair, which erupted after an American reconnaissance plane came down inside the Soviet Union in May of that year. Though the immediate crisis ebbed, Berlin, like Taiwan, remained an unresolved matter of state.

SENATOR JACKSON'S COMMITTEE

▲▲▲

I n his late forties, Henry "Scoop" Jackson was the well-established senator from Washington State. A newspaper boy as a kid, grown up to become an attorney, elected prosecutor, then to the House of Representatives at the age of twenty-eight, he watched World War II from Congress, developing into something of a defense expert. The senator was patriotic, strong on defense; he objected to Eisenhower's New Look budgets, was a critic of slow ICBM progress, and an advocate of air power. Jackson's voice had become prominent in the Democratic party. He had presidential ambitions too.

Several times through the 1950s, Henry Jackson went on television or gave speeches admonishing against allowing Soviet leads in bombers or missiles. Jackson was sometimes called "the senator from Boeing," a reference to the presence of the major defense contractor Boeing Aircraft, in Seattle, Washington.

Concerned about the whole direction of the Eisenhower administration, Scoop Jackson decided to challenge the President's use of his national policy machinery. He threw down the gauntlet at the National War College, in a speech on April 16, 1959. Ostensibly about forging a strategy for survival, Jackson's speech charged that the NSC mechanism had not and could not produce a coherent and purposeful national program. Jackson further charged that Congress knew only bits and pieces of the story and demanded an investigation.

Senator Jackson's War College speech raised hackles at the Eisenhower White House. The President was furious and so were his keepers of the keys. Ike assigned General Wilton B. Persons, his chief of staff, to coordinate the administration's response on the matter. In a point-by-point refutation of Jackson's speech, Bobby Cutler told Persons he thought Senator Jackson misunderstood the method of NSC operations, was confused by the NSC mechanism created by the 1947 National Security Act "and the capability of individuals effectively to operate that mechanism," and was just plain in disagreement with Eisenhower's national security policy.

As Ike once told Gordon Gray, Jackson's references to the NSC were really directed at him personally. There can be little doubt Eisenhower wanted to avoid congressional investigation of the NSC. Senator Jackson, however, sponsored Senate Resolution 115 (S-115) calling for an investigation, and got it through the Government Operations Committee. At the Executive Office Building, Gordon Gray and Karl Harr put together a conceptual response for the President. They recommended that "all reasonable efforts be made to avoid the adoption of the Resolution."

The keepers did offer a fallback position: If all else failed, the executive branch could offer limited cooperation in exchange for setting the ground rules. They proposed there be no testimony about substantive NSC or OCB matters; that testimony as to policy or actions would be given only by the agencies concerned; and that the NSC itself would make "full disclosure" only of the composition, organization, and procedures of the NSC, the Planning Board (PB), and the OCB. Gray and Harr preferred no talk whatever of actual policies; if Congress insisted, "an approach might be to trace hypothetical cases through the NSC-PB-OCB machinery." Several additional arguments were advanced that might reassure the senators and induce them to reduce the scope of their inquiry.

Gray's contingency planning turned out to be necessary. The Senate passed S-115; in early July it formed a Subcommittee on National Policy Machinery chaired by Henry M. Jackson. In his effort to press the investigation, Jackson accepted the essence of Ike's concerns. The senator sent "proposed guidelines" to the President on July 9. Eisenhower accepted them the next day. The restrictions placed on the Jackson subcommittee greatly favored the President. This inquiry was to be "a study, not an investigation," and would not attempt to infringe on the "Constitutional privilege of the President to obtain advice." Legislation was specifically excluded. Studies of NSC machinery would focus on purpose, composition, organization, and procedure; substance would be excluded. Testimony of present and former officials who had served on the NSC would be taken first in executive session and not released except as agreed between the White House and the Jackson subcommittee.

President Eisenhower had the upper hand dealing with the Jackson subcommittee as a result of this prior agreement. Ike was able to keep some advisers, including both Andrew Goodpaster and Gordon Gray, out of the committee room. The subcommittee could call other witnesses and focused its attention on several groups of them. One was *former* national security advisers; this group included Sidney Souers, Averell Harriman, Robert Cutler, and Dillon Anderson. Government officials appearing before the Jackson subcommittee included the secretaries of state and defense, the director of the Policy Planning Staff, and others. The subcommittee listened to retired General Maxwell Taylor, who represented a dissident view on defense, and to Admiral Arthur Radford for Ike's view.

Probably the single most significant group sought out as witnesses by the Jackson subcommittee were the panelists who had served the NSC in compiling the Gaither report. A half dozen testified, among them Robert

Sprague, James Baxter, James A. Perkins, Jim Fisk, Herbert York, and John J. Corson. Paul Nitze testified in the capacity of a former director of the Policy Planning Staff. Most of those men were by then critical of the American defense posture or national security management, or both. York represented the administration as director of defense research and engineering, and seemed more optimistic in the face of the subcommittee's questioning.

The congressional unit was officially the Subcommittee on National Policy Machinery of the Senate Committee on Government Operations. In addition to Scoop Jackson, the Democrat members were Edmund S. Muskie of Maine and Hubert H. Humphrey of Minnesota. Republican senators Karl E. Mundt of South Dakota and Jacob K. Javits of New York completed the group. A small but capable staff, "astute and sure-footed," was headed by J. K. Mansfield. Academic political scientist Richard E. Neustadt worked as a special consultant to the subcommittee, while Dorothy Fosdick, one of Scoop's people, served on the professional staff. Other Jackson people included Thomas Foley and Brewster Denny. The subcommittee spent six months investigating national security and planning a series of public hearings on the subject.

Jackson's subcommittee began its open hearings with testimony by Robert A. Lovett, former secretary of defense and member of the advisory committee to the Gaither panel, on February 23, 1960. Lovett attracted some public attention with his warning that individual executives needed to regain their authority. Following Lovett, the next day air defense expert Bob Sprague and historian Jim Baxter testified. Sprague related major conclusions of the Gaither report and argued for an improved staff for the secretary of defense.

Public interest largely dissipated as the Jackson subcommittee hearings dragged on, coming in spurts over many months. Inside the administration, however, Scoop Jackson's hearings, resuming soon after the U-2 incident, continued to be a concern for six days in May 1960 and eight in June. Ike's NSC staff kept close tabs on official plans for testimony during this period and tried to keep an eye on the Jackson subcommittee staff. On January 26, 1960, Gordon Gray was able to warn the President that an unclassified document revealing the existence of the 5412 Group—the ultrasecret administration mechanism for approving covert intelligence operations—had crept into the bibliography being used by the Jackson committee. Gray and Eisenhower worried that the investigators might express some interest in the document, and the President "was clear and firm in his response" that Jackson's staff *not* be informed of the existence of this unit.

Another facet of the NSC staff's response to the Jackson committee was to prepare an organizational history. Gordon Gray's strategy was to provide exhaustive detail on NSC routines and subordinate units like the OCB and Planning Board. Gray put executive secretary Jimmy Lay in charge of the project. Lay, in turn, took special staff member Bob Johnson off all other duties in order to assist him; they also had the assistance of Bromley K.

Smith, deputy executive secretary of the NSC and Ev Gleason's successor. By July the three had completed a single-spaced sixty-three-page account of the National Security Act, the NSC, its components, and predecessors. Their document still stands as the best single source on this period, yet is completely silent on any NSC decision made by Truman or Eisenhower.

When the history was done, Jimmy Lay sent advance copies to Sid Souers and Harry Truman. Souers replied with enthusiasm, citing Truman's statement, made "on numerous occasions," that he did not see how a President could operate without an NSC. Admiral Souers, however, found the former President inconsistent, since, "in his autobiography he casts me in the role of having been his special assistant for *intelligence* throughout my whole career in the White House."

Eisenhower's NSC staff experienced great relief when, simultaneously with submission of its NSC organizational history, the Jackson subcommittee interrupted its hearings for a year. After some months of silence, in early 1961 the Jackson subcommittee issued the first of several staff reports. It spoke of the need for a sort of "super-Cabinet" official, perhaps a first secretary of the government. Eisenhower was out of office by then, but interestingly enough, in his final volume of memoirs, which appeared in 1965, the former President advocated the creation of a similar post.

Henry M. Jackson also came out ahead as a result of the committee investigation. It won him national recognition, and from 1962 to 1965 he headed the reconstituted Subcommittee on National Security Staffing and Operations, which continued under a different name into the Nixon administration. Dorothy Fosdick rose to and remained staff director. The same senators made up the committee, which expanded to nine members, though Hubert Humphrey left in 1965 after being elected Vice President. Member Robert F. Kennedy, who joined Jackson's subcommittee later, would run for the presidency. Among other members, Jacob Javits became an important architect of the War Powers Resolution, while Edmund Muskie would serve briefly as secretary of state. This was an obscure but important unit in the Senate that national security advisers under both Johnson and Nixon were careful to address when certain changes were made in policy machinery during 1966 and 1969.

PART III

▲

KEEPERS IN CAMELOT

In his 1960 political campaign John Fitzgerald Kennedy did not charge that the NSC was moribund, but he did heed the investigators of the Jackson subcommittee. During the presidential transition, sources hinted changes might be looming for the NSC. When he appointed McGeorge Bundy as his special assistant for national security affairs on January 1, 1961, Kennedy averred he had been much impressed by the "constructive criticisms" of the Jackson group. The President-elect declared that its study provided "a useful starting point for the work that Mr. Bundy will undertake in helping me to strengthen and to simplify the operations of the National Security Council."

Strengthen and simplify? The goals seemed contradictory, for the latter could only be achieved by dismantling parts of the NSC machinery, while the former appeared impossible to accomplish with a smaller NSC staff. It was characteristic of the press, in the warm glow that prevailed after JFK's election and the excitement of the promised "New Frontier," that no one questioned Kennedy's goals for NSC reform.

In any case, no one questioned the President's right to create exactly the kind of staff he wanted. At the time Eisenhower's precedent was not appealing—his administration was almost universally held in low esteem.

SERVANTS OF THE
PRESIDENT

▲▲▲

J ack Kennedy's national security adviser moved ambitiously but with a sure step. He put his deputy to work analyzing the existing NSC policy machinery, and had a few holdovers from the Eisenhower staff write long papers distilling NSC experience with budget reviews and the like, or defending its committees and procedures. Gordon Gray advised the new man he might wish to make his office in the West Wing of the White House, as had Goodpaster, rather than at the OEOB. Gray warned against hasty decisions and put in a good word for the Operations Coordinating Board, whose abolition he knew was in the wind. So did OCB man Karl Harr. McGeorge Bundy did not immediately move to the White House but he did absorb avidly the stream of ideas and advice. He would need to. Richard Neustadt, who had until recently been on the staff of Jackson's subcommittee, told transition official Clark Clifford that Bundy would be standing in for *five* of Ike's aides, not only Gray but Jimmy Lay, Karl Harr, and Bromley Smith too. Unaccountably, Neustadt left out Andy Goodpaster, whose role was another of those "Mac" Bundy was assuming.

This was but one of the ways the Bundy appointment marked a departure. Unlike his predecessors, he was not a man of affairs but an academic— Bundy had been dean of Harvard's Graduate School of Arts and Sciences. At forty-two he was young, to this day the youngest person ever to become keeper of the keys. Purposeful, sometimes abrasive or flippant, Bundy added a new dimension to the job. In the process, he presided over an era in which the NSC *staff* began to gain power at the expense of the National Security *Council*. Though he readily acknowledged the primacy of Cabinet members and NSC principals, Mac was determined to make his staff work and supported the process by which its power grew. Preoccupied by the flood of crises and day-to-day operations, Bundy probably never noticed the sea change.

It was not that Bundy wasn't bright and perceptive. In fact the man was very much in the image of Jack Kennedy himself. Named for his paternal grandfather, McGeorge was the offspring of two of Boston's first families, the Lowells and the Bundys. He graduated from Yale, where he majored in mathematics but found time to moonlight with advanced economics courses taught by Richard M. Bissell, Jr. He was elected to Phi Beta Kappa at Yale, and before the war Bundy was honored by Harvard with selection as a junior fellow, in a special postgraduate academic program established decades before with Lowell family donations. After Pearl Harbor his local draft board rejected Bundy for poor eyesight. He managed to enlist signing waivers, then went through Officer Candidate School, to emerge as a young Signal Corps second lieutenant. For a time he worked as secretary to Supreme Court Justice Oliver Wendell Holmes. Bundy also had wider intellectual interests. He read and could quote poetry, was active in community drama groups around Cambridge, and at Groton had played the title role in Shakespeare's *Henry V.*

For a few months in 1948, Bundy worked on the Marshall Plan as a consultant to Richard Bissell, then at the Council on Foreign Relations, where he labored on a study panel chaired by Dwight Eisenhower, before accepting an instructorship at Harvard. After four years Bundy became dean of the graduate school, at age thirty-four. As dean he renewed his acquaintance with Jack Kennedy, a Harvard alumnus who was appointed an overseer of the university. Running for the presidency, Senator Kennedy spoke at Harvard's June 1960 commencement. Sitting next to Bundy on the stage, JFK talked with him of the campaign. Bundy agreed to help organize a professional and scientific political committee to support Kennedy's candidacy.

It was surprising that President Kennedy selected McGeorge Bundy over Walt Rostow as special assistant for national security affairs. Rostow had worked directly for Kennedy's campaign and authored certain political slogans JFK used to good effect. Kennedy knew Mac Bundy only slightly, from a few social encounters and from periodic visits to Harvard. Dean Rusk asked Rostow to be deputy at Policy Planning, but Walt declined, saying, "I've got a lot to do up here at MIT." One Friday Kennedy had Rostow to breakfast at his hideaway apartment on Capitol Hill. The place was crawling with assorted operatives, messengers, and the Secret Service. Rostow had come to talk about the necessity for wage and price discipline to hold down inflation. Kennedy listened seriously, then offered the deputy special assistant post, which Walt promptly accepted. Rostow still considers it one of his greatest achievements in Washington that JFK also accepted his theory on wages and prices, acting to keep them under control throughout the administration.

When John Kennedy took Bundy back to Washington as national security adviser, Dick Bissell was still there, now risen to deputy director for plans of the CIA. Glad to see an old mentor, Bundy had no idea that Bissell was about to administer a stern lesson both to himself and to the President.

Bundy's basic advice on the organization of the NSC was in final form three days after the inauguration, on January 24, 1961, when he sent the President a five-page dissertation on the subject. Bundy saw the council as the place where those principally concerned could present their final arguments, while the President could "open the subject up so that you can see what its elements are and decide how you want it pursued." The council would be a "relatively formal place" for free and frank discussion that could give senior officials "confidence that they know what is cooking and what you want." Bundy advised that the size of NSC meetings be cut back, and the interval between sessions made longer—he thought fortnightly meetings were sufficient. He suggested putting organization on the agenda for the council's first meeting, which took place on February 1. Finally, the adviser reported he was scouting through the collection of Eisenhower's NSC policy papers, along with deputy Walt Rostow, to see which of them was most urgently in need of revision.

At the same time, Bundy and Rostow canvassed within the NSC staff for ideas on staff organization. Robert H. Johnson, who was used generally as a troubleshooter, since he was one of but a few held over from Ike's NSC staff, spent the first two months working closely with Rostow on staff organization. Jimmy Lay passed along a collection of suggestions he had solicited from Ike's old staff during the period of presidential transition following the 1960 election. Charles Haskins, another of the NSC staff kept over, warned the Kennedy people to reach a clear agreement about cable distribution early on. George Weber, a staffer who did not make it in the selection, maintained that allowing the Joint Chiefs of Staff to comment on proposals in written memos, in addition to their statements at table in council meetings, gave the Chiefs one or even two extra cracks at policy. Samuel E. Belk, a holdover staffer, wanted to push for closer ties between the Planning Board (PB) and the Operations Coordinating Board (OCB).

The survivors hardly knew why they had been invited to join Bundy's staff. In Haskins's case it may have been his scientific expertise and the esteem of Jerome Wiesner, whom JFK invited to be his science adviser. Bob Johnson knew Bundy slightly, having been an instructor in the government department at Harvard who helped with Bundy's popular World Affairs course; but Johnson does not believe that had anything to do with the appointment. More likely he was invaluable because he had been the assistant to Everett Gleason; for the year he stayed on with the Bundy staff, he worked as a troubleshooter and on South and Southeast Asia and the Far East.

Whatever reason Mac had for holding on to Sam Belk, who would basically keep the Africa portfolio for five years into the 1960s, it could not have been his suggestions on NSC reform. Bundy wanted to reduce the staff, both to get away from the image of the Eisenhower NSC and to minimize the time spent on administrative matters. Belk was recommending better coordination, which usually meant *more* staff.

The President was talking about managing the council meetings himself. To Bundy that meant dispensing with the NSC Planning Board, thus quickly eliminating five positions. Mac also expected to phase out the role of the NSC executive secretary. Kennedy himself made the big call—in February, after only one month in office, the President abolished the Operations Coordinating Board (OCB). That instantly cut the size of the NSC staff by at least half. Kennedy saw the OCB as a symbol of the stagnant policies he attributed to Ike. Senator Jackson's subcommittee had further singled out OCB as the target for some of their criticisms. Here JFK satisfied the committee, which closed up after a last round of hearings intended to determine what the new administration's NSC principals hoped to accomplish. Bundy closed out the proceedings in September 1961 with a hopeful letter to Jackson that spoke vaguely of future flexibility and earnest determination.

The reductions were effected right away. Bundy brought down NSC staff personnel from seventy-one to forty-eight, though he actually *expanded* that portion of the NSC staff handling substantive subjects. The Kennedy NSC first emphasized regional or functional specialization as a staff method. Bundy staff members became the holders of portfolios, major players in given subject areas within their ken. The wide range of national security matters naturally required a fairly large professional staff. Thus staff jobs in substantive areas increased from the five on Gordon Gray's senior staff to a dozen or more.

Still, a dozen men could not manage *all* the national security business of the United States. Bundy accomplished one essential change that made everything else possible: He transformed the NSC staff from servants of the *presidency* to those of *the President*. Staff became Kennedy's eyes and ears, no longer disinterested mediators working to push papers up to the NSC level. Combined with the addition of staff portfolios in place of ad hoc assignments, which meant that the *same* NSC person would handle the White House end the *next* time a subject came up, Bundy's change brought new power to the NSC staff. Jack Kennedy demanded unprecedented loyalty from his NSC staff, and insisted they help him think politically, but he gave them great power in return.

There was also a change in national security paperwork that helped magnify the staff role. The old series of NSC policy papers were abolished. That ended not only the year-numbered series papers, at which we have looked in considerable detail, but the even more esoteric "Mill" papers, which were proposals for NSC studies, and the "P"-series of Planning Board drafts superseded by subsequent papers.

One individual who objected to the entire Kennedy NSC concept was Andy Goodpaster. After the first of several Eisenhower-Kennedy transition meetings, Ike went to General Goodpaster and told him JFK wanted him to stay after the transition as a general factotum, "a wise and good man," as Bundy told the President-elect, "tending the door and handling urgent messages silently" at the council. Goodpaster was willing to stay, though he had keenly anticipated, after many years, a field command with the 3rd Infantry Division in West Germany, of which he would be assistant commander.

Goodpaster defended the NSC policy papers. Unlike Bundy, who saw the papers only as an accumulation of work that would have to be periodically updated, Goodpaster knew they contained a bedrock of standard policy for a vast array of possible events. The general also pressed a point that Eisenhower, staff expert that he was, repeatedly made—never mix the planning and operations functions. Goodpaster argued that it was too much to abolish the formal Planning Board side of the staff *plus* his own staff secretary office; that would throw planning squarely onto the NSC staff alone, mixing with the operations role Bundy envisaged. Goodpaster further warned that the daily intelligence briefings should not be presented by the special assistant for national security affairs, the same man who was chief of planning. Kennedy experimented, at first taking his intelligence from a military aide, Major General Chester V. Clifton. It was not long before Bundy had acquired that role as well.

The former staff secretary lost on the issue of the policy papers. Kennedy intended to provide brief memoranda of approval, simple affirmations of direction rather than the cumbersome NSC papers. This new series would be called National Security Action Memoranda (NSAMs), of which Kennedy would ultimately produce 272. Goodpaster warned that the papers lacked any assessment of the threat, risks, or cost, as had been in Eisenhower's NSC policy papers, but JFK never wavered. A few weeks into the new regime, Goodpaster went on to his field command; a few months later he was promoted to major general and made a division commander.

Goodpaster next saw John Kennedy in the aftermath of the Cuban missile crisis, when he returned to Washington to help pick up the pieces as a top aide to the Chairman of the JCS. Seeing the general appear at a meeting, Kennedy strode up, shook his hand and said, "I held your command for you, didn't I?"

The Bay of Pigs came as Kennedy's first crisis, one he triggered deliberately, by sending Cuban exiles to invade their homeland. The exiles were contained and defeated by Cuban government forces in just a few days of furious fighting. Cuban Communist leader Fidel Castro and his associates, including the Argentinian revolutionary Che Guevara, were confirmed in power. Guevara happened to have been in Guatemala in 1954, when an earlier CIA covert operation did topple a national government. Making this observation, at the height of the Bay of Pigs fiasco, Bundy told another of the new NSC staffers, "It looks as if Che learned more than we from intervention in Guatemala." The record was so bad one recent historian of the Bay of Pigs has called it "the perfect failure." Mac Bundy readily concedes the flawed character of the operation and even calls it a learning experience, from which John F. Kennedy profited greatly in later acute crises.

The first thing that was clear was that the President had not focused sufficiently on the CIA's Cuban proposals. He accepted too readily the ill-informed assurances of the Joint Chiefs. Suddenly feeling he could not trust the military, Kennedy decided to make General Maxwell D. Taylor his special military representative. Taylor would have a small staff parallel to the NSC staff that would concentrate on specifically military matters. Taylor, a dissenter from Eisenhower's New Look strategy, former Army Chief of Staff, president of Lincoln Center for the Performing Arts, and a member of JFK's panel to investigate the Bay of Pigs failure, seemed to Kennedy an excellent choice for personal military adviser.

As had Ike in the U-2 affair, Kennedy graciously took responsibility for the Bay of Pigs in public. Within the administration, however, there was as much blame to hand out as anyone wanted. While the CIA was the basic culprit, the failure to monitor implementation at the White House level had clearly factored in the debacle. Eisenhower's NSC had had a specific component—the Operations Coordinating Board (OCB)—designed to guide implementation. President Kennedy wondered if an OCB could have prevented the Cuban failure. He was straightforward about it, calling up Karl Harr, Ike's assistant for the OCB, and bringing him down to the White House. The President met Harr in the Fish Room, gave him a drink, then briefly explained the flaws of implementation in the Bay of Pigs case. Finally, Kennedy wanted to know if Harr thought the OCB could have caught certain oversights in the planning. Reluctantly, Karl had to say he thought not, that the OCB had been geared for long-term issues, such as foreign aid or psychological strategy, and not able to catch the flaws in an evolving paramilitary operation. The talk ended any chance that Kennedy might resuscitate the Operations Coordinating Board. President Kennedy *did* reestablish the Foreign Advisory Board, after but two months in limbo, and he and Bundy forged ahead creating the White House Situation Room. Bromley Smith, who rose to become NSC executive secretary under JFK, castigated himself later for not fighting harder for the OCB, but the truth was it could not be saved.

The biggest White House change seemed small at the time—JFK made Mac Bundy give up his office in the OEOB and move to the basement of the West Wing. Their relationship became like Goodpaster's with Eisenhower, the national security adviser as trusted *confidant*. Kennedy also arranged quiet weekly luncheons where differences among the agencies could be fixed up with the least fuss: at the level of assistant secretary of the departments. Walt Rostow, the keeper's deputy, was designated chairman of the group which, in the tradition of OCB, carried on using a State Department dining room for the proceedings.

There was great impetus to establish a White House Situation Room after the Bay of Pigs. In their early planning Bundy and Rostow wanted a message center. Everyone from Goodpaster on down warned that you had to read the daily cable traffic if you wanted to know what was going on, so the White House had to get all the relevant material. Kennedy, who had previously ordered that he be apprised of all developments, was astonished to find out after the Bay of Pigs some of the things he hadn't been told during supposedly "careful" briefings on the CIA operation. JFK and Bundy decided to remedy the information problem with a full-blown crisis center. It would routinely receive copies of all the relevant cables and have the capability to inform the President and NSC staff when trouble broke out anywhere. Part of the center was a conference room that could handle small-group discussions. Much tinier than the Cabinet Room, where the NSC usually met, the Situation Room nevertheless would serve as venue for many fateful events in the coming years, including discussions during the *Achille Lauro* incident with which this narrative began.

Located in the former Map Room that Franklin D. Roosevelt used for his command post during World War II, the White House Situation Room was set up for much the same purpose as had been its predecessor. Captain John L. McCrea of the Navy had moved into the Map Room with a single file cabinet plus a desk in January 1942 and soon had a clearinghouse for all military and naval information for the President. Add diplomatic traffic too and you have Mac Bundy's concept for the Situation Room, which teams from the CIA and the General Services Administration labored for over six months to create, completing it in early 1962, exactly two decades after the Map Room. Often said to be in the "basement" of the West Wing, in fact the Situation Room is down two steps but at ground level, adjacent to Bundy's office.

Mac had to negotiate for messages to be automatically furnished the White House and that entailed some difficulty. After a first round, Bundy found that some things were not coming through. The President issued blunt orders. The Pentagon countered by installing more than a half-dozen tele-printers, clacking out messages from all the services and other sources. Not only was it going to be hopeless to keep up with all this material, the noise made it impossible to work. The point was not lost on Bundy, who had all the machines save one taken away. Henceforth the staff would depend on being alert to identify and request needed cable traffic.

Because of JFK's methods, access to all the necessary cables would continue to be vital to the NSC staff. One staff professional who stayed on after Ike's passage found the contrast in styles stunning: For one of Ike's NSC meetings you had to have read the policy papers; for Kennedy's one needed to master the intelligence, the cable traffic, what the newspapers were saying, *and* the gossip in the bureaucracy. To top it off, in case called on by the President, the staffer had better have a fresh idea too. A lot of the rest flowed from the cables so those were primary. As late as 1963, JFK ordered installation of pneumatic tubes linking the State Department and the NSC in order to speed the arrival of cables. Poor servicing with cables would become a recurrent irritant for NSC workers. Complaints came from time to time from such staff members or consultants as Robert W. Komer, Francis Bator, Richard Neustadt, and John Kenneth Galbraith. Distribution of materials from the Situation Room was regulated by a sign-up sheet on which staff listed their interests roughly at quarterly intervals. Bundy or his deputy could disapprove any given request for material but they operated on the principle that a staffer who could make any kind of justification for needing to know the traffic should have it.

Bundy and Walt Rostow already had gotten together in Boston before Kennedy's inauguration. Mac made no effort to cover the entire national security spectrum himself. Instead he and Rostow split up the subject areas and each acted as a sort of associate director. The Situation Room was one of Mac's projects. Rostow, who had expressed interest in planning mechanisms of all kinds, took on the bulk of the work sifting suggestions for national security organization. He also worked on all aspects of foreign economic policy, policy toward underdeveloped countries, and counterinsurgency strategy, a particular Kennedy proclivity. The range of cable traffic Rostow received in October 1961 included most of these matters plus Algeria and France, Latin America, Southeast Asia, and Berlin.

John Kennedy could function at meetings, but he was best in individual encounters. It is not surprising, then, that JFK had a dim view of a forum created by statute, the National Security Council. Just as he reorganized the machinery, there was no doubt JFK would change the group of the NSC principals and the way they worked.

Kennedy adopted most of Bundy's advice, in the first year holding twenty-one NSC meetings, almost meeting Bundy's quota of one meeting every two weeks. One year later the President had noticeably cooled to the mechanism, holding only nine NSC sessions in the first half of 1962, and just one between July and October, when Washington plunged into the biggest crisis of all, the Cuban missile crisis.

On October 14 a U-2 spy plane over Cuba took pictures identifying Soviet offensive missile bases under construction on that Caribbean island. Kennedy, who had repeatedly warned the Soviet Union against any such action, considered it a direct challenge to the United States in the Western Hemisphere. He mobilized the United States government to refine his policy options and the missile crisis followed. In a nationally televised speech on October 22 the President announced the intelligence finding, insisted the Soviet missiles be withdrawn, and declared a blockade of Cuba, euphemistically termed a quarantine, until United States demands were met.

The Cuban missile crisis has been studied exhaustively. It is still being reinterpreted in the light of new evidence. But few observers have focused on the way JFK managed his advisers in the heat of that moment. In the final stages of considering his options, between October 20 and 22, but only after days of ad hoc deliberations, the President convened the NSC three times. Then Kennedy dispensed altogether with that mechanism; there would be no more council sessions through the remainder of the year. Instead, JFK formed his celebrated "Executive Committee" (EXCOM) of the NSC, which met no less than thirty-seven times between October 23, when the NSC began keeping records, and December 17. The comparison is actually even sharper since the group that came to be called EXCOM first convened at 11:45 A.M. on October 16 and since then had been meeting two or even three times a day. Everything was ultrasecret: EXCOM had no official existence until the day Kennedy went on television, October 22, when he also signed National Security Action Memorandum (NSAM) 196, which created EXCOM as an independent NSC unit with such members as designated by the President. There are no EXCOM records for the crucial first week of the Cuban crisis, when Kennedy chose his option before going public. The one authoritative source is a set of tapes made of those meetings that occurred in the Cabinet Room, and the only tapes of this period thus far transcribed and released are of two EXCOM sessions on October 16, the first day of the full-scale brainstorming sessions, and the 28th, perhaps the climactic day of the crisis.

The transcripts make clear that even in the first surge, JFK's advisers had already identified the options worth discussion. Those were: negotiating with Khrushchev, which Secretary of Defense Robert McNamara called a "political course of action"; blockading Cuba; mounting an air strike to destroy the Soviet offensive weapons; and invading the Caribbean island. All the subsequent talk among the President's advisers ranged back and forth over the same ground, canvassing the same options, making repeated efforts to explain why the Russians were attempting this action. Though the President did not attend all the EXCOM meetings, his brother Robert F. Kennedy, who frequently chaired the group in his absence, reported thoroughly on what transpired. The President refused to make a premature decision and the repeated discussions of the options forced his advisers to air many assumptions that went unstated at the beginning.

Maxwell Taylor came to his advice early and stuck to it. The special military representative enjoyed such presidential confidence that Kennedy had recently brought him to active duty to chair the Joint Chiefs of Staff. At EXCOM, Taylor spoke for the JCS, most of whose members the President had changed after the Bay of Pigs.

"If it really threatens the United States," Taylor intoned, "then take it right out with one hard crack."

General Taylor believed the United States could wait a few days and get complete intelligence, all the necessary photography on the target sites, then move rapidly against the missiles plus Soviet and Cuban aircraft, bombers *and* fighters.

McGeorge Bundy wavered, asked a few questions, then seemed to favor Taylor's option as being more limited than an invasion of Cuba. Taylor's course of action became known as the "surgical strike" option, which received support from such advisers as Paul Nitze, now an aide to McNamara; John McCone, the director of central intelligence; and former Cabinet member Dean Acheson, whom Kennedy included in his meetings beginning October 17.

McNamara became the strongest initial proponent of the blockade option, which he refined in the debate. Certain Soviet experts like Llewellyn E. Thompson and Charles Bohlen supported him. But the State Department seemed divided. Dean Rusk was mostly silent, though he quietly favored negotiations and, according to recent revelations, would have JFK's approval at the denouement for a compromise solution if necessary to avert war. Undersecretary of State George W. Ball sided with McNamara, while his deputy, U. Alexis Johnson, favored the Taylor option. Johnson and Taylor agree that many advisers, perhaps everyone, changed their positions at least once in the following days. Indeed it was Robert Kennedy, who had first favored the surgical strike, who developed the most influential argument against it. RFK began to compare a surprise air attack with what Japan had done to the United States at Pearl Harbor in 1941. When President Kennedy himself learned from the Air Force that it could not, in fact, guarantee the success of a surgical strike, the tide turned decisively against that option.

Historians' attention has traditionally focused on the EXCOM and its deliberations, which became a continual jawboning session in Ball's State Department office when it was not meeting at the White House. The lower levels of the bureaucracy were also caught up in the action. Several interagency task forces labored to identify and plan each of the necessary steps in implementing each option. Alex Johnson prepared the scenario for further diplomatic moves by the United States when declaring the quarantine. Walt Rostow reported to JFK on lower-echelon planning for the blockade, while Adam Yarmolinsky carried McNamara's orders to responsible Pentagon officials. Work done by the NSC staff has also been ignored in many existing accounts, in part because relevant documents remain classified almost three decades after the events of the crisis. Robert Komer, for example, produced a fistful of memoranda, and collaborated with Carl Kaysen on drafts of messages that the President could send Khrushchev.

One other aspect of the Cuban crisis is worth noting, especially for a post-Reagan America, one so used to leaks of information from the ship of state: *There were no leaks about the Cuban missile crisis!* It was not that Washington was any different then; in fact, Kennedy had had problems similar to Truman's at the dawn of the NSC era. Rather, the Cuban missile crisis was viewed as the real thing, with nuclear war hanging in the balance.

The advisers who counseled John Kennedy in these dark moments became a close-knit group who let nothing out. So successful were the President and his advisers at going through the motions of business as usual that the CIA was able to host an international conference of Western intelligence agencies, long scheduled for this time in October 1962, without tipping the United States' hand. Bundy's NSC staff were similarly closemouthed. Spurgeon M. Keeny, Jr., an aide to science adviser Jerry Wiesner, was one of JFK's best experts on exactly those military technologies that figured in Cuba. Keeny would quickly have noticed extraordinary demands made on his time, yet until Kennedy's speech he observed nothing unusual.

Max Taylor disputes this view of the seriousness with which JFK's advisers saw the nuclear threat in Cuba. Writing twenty years after the event, Taylor noted, "I never heard an expression of fear of nuclear escalation on the part of any of my colleagues." According to a well-regarded and near-contemporaneous account, however, in February 1963 Walt Rostow and Paul Nitze cooperated in producing a thirteen-page critique of the Cuban crisis that specifically argued that JFK and his advisers had placed too much stress on the danger of nuclear war.

The final outcome of the crisis was fortunate. Kennedy put his naval quarantine in place, then began to exchange communications with Nikita Khrushchev. At length the Soviet leader ordered his ships that carried military equipment, including, some believe, the nuclear warheads for the Soviet medium-range missiles, to turn back before encountering the blockade. Khrushchev also held the lid down on Soviet military action when Russian airspace was violated by a misguided U-2 flight, and when Russian submarines at sea were challenged and forced to surface by the U.S. Navy.

Recent claims that Kennedy secretly prepared with Rusk for a compromise settlement are actually related to the idea of the United States quietly trading IRBMs in Turkey for the Soviet ones in Cuba. Khrushchev explicitly suggested such a trade in one of his October 27 messages to Kennedy. In order to preserve the appearance of success in Cuba, the President felt he could not openly agree to such a trade, but apparently told Dean Rusk he would if there were no alternative. A few months later the American IRBMs in fact left Turkey. The truth is that Kennedy had been trying to get these obsolete missiles, rendered superfluous by the advent of the Minuteman, out of Turkey for some time. In *two* national security action memoranda, NSAM-35 of April 1961 and NSAM-181 of August 1962, the President had ordered the identification of actions necessary to remove the IRBMs. Paul Nitze, as a matter of fact, was the Pentagon official charged with the task. During the Cuban crisis there were a few worries in EXCOM and elsewhere that bringing the IRBMs back from Turkey would impact adversely on NATO or strain United States submarine-launched ballistic missile capability, used to compensate for the IRBMs, but these fears too came to naught.

In one of his Cuban crisis messages, Khrushchev dangled the possibility that an amicable resolution might help the search for progress in achieving a nuclear test ban. Better Soviet-American relations did result from the crisis, paradoxical as it may seem. President Kennedy made a conciliatory speech at American University in the spring of 1963, then set Averell Harriman to work as a test ban negotiator. Harriman hammered out terms for a Limited Test Ban Treaty in a visit to Moscow in the summer, which he initialed on July 25. Rusk signed it at the beginning of August. Kennedy then worked closely with Mike Mansfield, Senate majority leader, and others to secure backing from the Joint Chiefs of Staff and such opponents as John McCone. The Senate approved the treaty in late September and JFK signed its instrument of ratification on October 7. The United Kingdom also agreed to and ratified the test ban treaty, which finally prohibited further nuclear testing in the atmosphere. Thus the great Cuban missile crisis brought a measure of arms control.

"THE BEST AND THE BRIGHTEST"

▲▲▲

T he Executive Committee of the NSC reflected John Kennedy's preferences for advisers, not, as has often been claimed, a desire to
work with a group smaller than the full NSC. The fact is that the
list of individuals cleared to attend the EXCOM, which was issued
along with NSAM-196, numbered no fewer than *seventy-one*. A group that
size was larger than Eisenhower's council had ever been, and compared
with the largest NSC gatherings ever held, such as the presentation of the
Gaither report. The President never intended to sit with such a large group;
rather the EXCOM concept was of a sort of floating discussion group, with
members drifting in and out as their schedules permitted. The EXCOM list
demonstrated Kennedy's penchant for going to anyone who could help for
advice, gathering around himself a constellation of brilliant, or experienced,
or dedicated advisers, a group David Halberstam aptly called "the best and
the brightest."

The missile crisis epitomized Kennedy's freewheeling style, but the system
of procuring advice had been in place from the beginning. Presiding over
it all was Mac Bundy, self-styled traffic cop steering useful papers and people
into the Oval Office, keeping others away. Bundy felt that "an appalling
percentage" of the material that came to the President from State, Defense,
the CIA, and the Atomic Energy Commission was "raw and unsatisfactory
paper-work." The stuff flowed into his small West Wing office and piled
up. Once, in early 1962, Kennedy walked into Bundy's office and, taken
aback by the clutter, wounded Mac's pride. The President called his keeper's
office a pigpen. Bundy turned around and appealed for more space, to allow
him to beef up the staff work for council meetings without cutting him off
from Bromley Smith, and for a receiving room where incoming papers could
be sorted for the President and other West Wing consumers whose needs
were met by the NSC staff.

It irked Bundy that his staff was divided between the White House and
Executive Office Building, but it was not long before Mac, having moved
to the West Wing, decided his work simply could not be done from the
OEOB. For most of JFK's first year Bundy could afford to play traffic cop

because he had, in Walt Rostow, a deputy who could handle whatever administrative matters arose in the NSC arena. Walt sat in a two-room suite (372-372A and 374) on the third floor of the OEOB, allocating the NSC staff's resources, fitting the policy problems of government to the skills of his men. But late in 1961, soon after his return from a fateful trip to Vietnam, Rostow got a chance at the job he had originally wanted and quickly left the NSC. It happened as part of a larger shuffle at the State Department, which Kennedy engineered to get rid of Chester Bowles, who was too verbose for the President, and a few others. Walt moved over to Foggy Bottom, as State was quaintly nicknamed in its new building on Virginia Avenue, and became chief of the Policy Planning Staff, elevated to a "council" under his stewardship. George McGhee, Rusk's man who had stood in Walt's way, became counselor to the secretary of state.

Perhaps ignorant of Eisenhower's hidden hand, Bundy told appointments secretary Kenny O'Donnell that his problems all came from having a President who had taken charge of foreign affairs. Mac could deal with O'Donnell about West Wing office space, but a deputy he had to find himself. Bundy's solution, coincidentally, was another of those people who had supported John Fitzgerald Kennedy early on. In fact, Carl Kaysen had joined Walt Rostow on JFK's earliest academic advisory committee, which first met at the Hotel Commander in Cambridge, Massachusetts, on December 3, 1958. The following summer, when Arthur Schlesinger decided the candidate needed someone full time who could give economic advice, he and John Kenneth Galbraith tried to recruit Kaysen, a fellow Harvard man. Kaysen, however, had just won a Ford Foundation fellowship and spent the 1959–1960 academic year in Greece.

Kaysen was even closer with Bundy than had been Rostow—both were members of Harvard's Society of Fellows in the late 1940s and faculty members in the 1950s. Kaysen had a Ph.D. in economics, had taught at the London School of Economics as a Fulbright scholar, simultaneously held a Guggenheim fellowship, and had attained tenure at Harvard in 1957.

Carl Kaysen's national security experience was as an analyst for the OSS in 1942 and an air intelligence officer through the rest of World War II. No one was going to run circles around *him*. Kennedy made one of his first defense policy errors when he went against Carl's advice. The subject was the old Gaither issue, civil defense, on which Kaysen did studies in the spring of 1961. Kaysen's paper showed the existing program to be a waste; it was based on primitive concepts of nuclear effects and on inadequate cost data. Faced with the Berlin crisis, JFK nevertheless pressed for a fallout shelter program, but one that shifted the onus of providing protection onto the citizens, who were supposed to build and stock family shelters to protect themselves. The approach smacked of salvation only for the rich, of a *sauve qui peut* mentality, and of preparation for initiating nuclear war. Kaysen and Arthur Schlesinger thought it a disaster and the latter argued the point at a defense budget meeting at Kennedy's Hyannisport, Massachusetts, home in November 1961. The President finally reversed his policy and resumed government responsibility for shelter programs.

Civil defense was just one of the subjects that Kaysen concerned himself with. Others included basic national security policy, nuclear proliferation, command and control of nuclear weapons, Berlin and NATO, Japan (plus Okinawa and the Ryukyu Islands, which many Japanese wanted returned to that nation), and economic foreign policy. Kaysen added Panama to his concerns in the summer of 1962, and the Congo that fall. On the Congo he joined with Kennedy political aide Ralph Dungan in open criticism of any deeper United States involvement. In late 1962, coincident with the Cuban crisis, China and India fought a sharp but short border war. It meant a good deal of work for Ambassador Galbraith who, with everyone in Washington diverted to Cuba, found Kaysen the highest-level official he could reach. Later, when Galbraith tried to enlist the Indian government in schemes to settle the Vietnam problem, Kaysen facetiously called them plans for a "GATO"—Galbraith's All-Purpose Treaty Organization.

Most of Carl Kaysen's time went into matters related to nuclear weapons and arms control. Here he worked closely with another Cambridge friend, Jerome Wiesner, the science adviser, and his assistant Spurgeon Keeny, Jr. Kaysen and Wiesner were both among those cleared to attend EXCOM meetings, and Kaysen provided important behind-the-scenes staff work for the group. After Khrushchev mentioned nuclear testing in one of his letters to JFK, Kaysen did a careful analysis in January 1963 that showed that a ban on atmospheric nuclear testing would not pose unacceptable national security risks. He attended meetings with the President, and of the Committee of Principals, which agreed to seek such a ban, and then worked out negotiating instructions for Averell Harriman's delegation. When roadblocks occurred, Carl would use the telephone judiciously to mobilize the right combination of countervailing opinion. Schlesinger felt that Kaysen "united cogency as a debater with intrepidity as an operator," and that "Wiesner and Kaysen, flourishing the White House mandate, were tireless in needling the bureaucracy and forcing disarmament issues; and Bundy intervened valuably at critical moments." It was Kaysen, in fact, who relayed to Bundy a suggestion from Rusk that Harriman should head the delegation.

With his academic leave drawing to a close Carl Kaysen submitted a formal resignation on June 18, 1963. At Mac's request he continued to work on certain issues, notably the test ban, and with school out for the summer Kaysen was able to work almost full time until the fall. He went to Moscow as an NSC staff member of the Harriman team. Kaysen was invaluable there as a man who could give the delegation insight into the President's own views. After the treaty was signed and went to the Senate for ratification, Kaysen became part of a small group sanctioned by Robert McNamara to supervise the administration's approach to Congress.

Another part of the task, for any deputy to Mac Bundy, was supervising

112

the work of the NSC staff, a job that, by law, belonged to the executive secretary but was never again to be exercised by that official. Bundy actually wished to eliminate the post in 1961 but soon found it indispensable instead—the executive secretary or his deputy could take the notes at council meetings, route the varied traffic of cables and memoranda, both to the NSC staff and to certain White House people, and run the secretariat under Kaysen.

White House staff constituted one layer of officialdom about which Kaysen could do nothing and even Bundy very little. There was no chief of staff to get in the way, for JFK basically acted as his own, keeping an open door to the NSC staff, especially at the end of the day. Housekeeping tasks he channeled through appointments secretary Kenny O'Donnell. The closest thing to a chief of staff was JFK's special counsel, Theodore C. Sorensen, who had served JFK since 1952 and drafted many of his speeches. So close to the President that he was often described as his alter ego, Sorensen jumped into and out of discussions whenever he wanted, on subjects as diverse as the Bay of Pigs, Berlin, Cuba, and Vietnam. Ted worked well with Mac Bundy, soliciting material from the keeper, for example, in early 1963 when invited to present the annual Speranza Lectures at Columbia University. There Sorensen argued that the function of advisers was to offset the parochialism of experts and department heads, and that staff were chosen not according to political or geographical criteria, but "for their ability to serve the president's needs and to talk the president's language."

While Sorensen ranged across the board, other Kennedy political advisers were more circumspect. One was Ralph Dungan, at thirty-seven JFK's equivalent to Andy Goodpaster as staff secretary, although he did not hold that title. Officially a manager who handed out White House staff assignments much as Kaysen did NSC ones, Dungan had a say on ambassadorial appointments. Dungan helped follow events in Latin America for the President in 1961 and the Congo the following year. During 1962 he routinely received copies of the cable traffic for Africa south of the Sahara.

Probably the best known of Kennedy's political-cum-national-security advisers was Arthur M. Schlesinger, Jr., a card-carrying member of JFK's Boston brain trust, who for years had helped scheme to put Kennedy in the White House. A distinguished historian graduated from Harvard who had also studied at Cambridge in England, Schlesinger had won the Pulitzer Prize in 1946 for a work on America in the age of Andrew Jackson. He earned great respect from the President early on by opposing the Bay of Pigs operation, and by the end of 1961 was reading the cable traffic on Western Europe and Latin America, and following Berlin, UN issues, test ban matters, and planned information policies to enhance the American image abroad. In 1962 he added NATO, Yugoslavia, Poland, and Finland to his European concerns, plus India and the Congo to his global ones. In 1963, Schlesinger monitored UN troop withdrawals from the Congo and began to follow Arab refugee issues. Given this rather extensive national security involvement, Bundy paid for some of Schlesinger's foreign travel out of NSC funds although Arthur was a White House, not an NSC, staffer.

Then there was Richard N. Goodwin, thirty in 1961, one of the President's principal speechwriters. Graduated from Tufts University he too went to Harvard, for law school, then made law review there. His facility with a pen quickly brought him to the top ranks of JFK's organization. In the White House, Goodwin followed Latin America, including the Alliance for Progress and more than a half-dozen countries, plus the U.S. Pacific Trust Territories (the islands seized from Japan in World War II), which had a national security aspect as the location of the United States ICBM test range while being a UN trusteeship. Goodwin gained notoriety for his inadvertent meeting with Argentinian revolutionary Che Guevara in the summer of 1961, and actually chaired one of the President's interagency committees for a short time. Goodwin moved on to the Peace Corps in early 1963 but would be brought back to the White House by Lyndon Johnson.

The White House advisers could walk right into the President's office, but then, so could the NSC staffers. Bundy and Kaysen did not pretend to be experts on everything and often took staffers to their meetings with JFK. Kennedy himself tried to include his NSC staff when foreign dignitaries visited from their areas of responsibility. "We were few enough," recalled Kaysen, "so that the president had some idea of who we were and what we were doing." Nevertheless on the NSC staff, then as always, there were some things that worked and some that didn't.

Something that worked, at least for a while, was the Cambridge connection, Harvard or the Massachusetts Institute of Technology. The boundary case, the one that shows the limits of how far the Boston brain trust link could be pushed, is that of Henry Alfred Kissinger. He was yet another of the Harvard professors then, a rising star during the 1950s. As a graduate student Kissinger took Bundy's course the same year as undergraduate Zbigniew Brzezinski, their course papers marked by instructor Robert Johnson. Kissinger soon worked as an instructor himself, starting with a summer school international relations seminar, and stayed at Harvard with junior rank after failing to attain a tenured position upon completion of his Ph.D. in 1954.

When Kennedy ran for the presidency, Kissinger helped Arthur Schlesinger and others with political and foreign policy advice. After the election he could have had an NSC staff job for the asking. As Bundy put it in a note, the only complication from the President's point of view "is that more than one part of the government may want to get you." Bundy and Rostow wanted Kissinger to be part of a small group they were going to put together for Kennedy's direct use.

Kissinger, however, would not give up the perquisites of academia. He talked with Bundy, but agreed only to consult, resolving the problem of others wanting his services by writing the State Department that *he* would not be available to *them*. He was going to be one of a small group of consultants working directly for John F. Kennedy.

Government consulting was work Kissinger understood. He had been a consultant to the Army's private think tank, the Operations Research Office, since 1950, and to the Joint Chiefs' Weapons Systems Evaluation Group since 1956. In 1952, Kissinger had also been a consultant to the Psychological Strategy Board and in 1955 to the Operations Coordinating Board. On February 27, 1961, Henry officially became a consultant to John F. Kennedy, *not* to the National Security Council.

The small group for Kennedy's direct use, however, never materialized. Instead, Kissinger was the *only* consultant, and he followed NATO, European issues, and Berlin. This consultancy left Kissinger in an anomalous position with regard to the rest of the NSC staff.

The other problem with Kissinger was that his link to the President did nothing to inhibit his desire to appear in public as an authority on national security issues. Henry gave lectures, taped occasional television interviews, talked to journalists. Whereas he told Bundy in March that he had thus far avoided seeing newspaper people, there were suspicious leaks in the early summer and again in the fall. The NSC staff security officer, Russell Ash, at one point, frustrated with Henry's insistence on keeping classified documents in his Harvard office, sent Bundy a note that said, "I can think of no way to avoid the suggestion that you look into this 'can of worms.' " In the fall of 1961 Kissinger resigned but Schlesinger and Kaysen intervened to keep him on tap; then Bundy rehired Henry as consultant to the council. He was still the only one.

When news leaked, in November, of the end of Henry's consultancy to JFK, allegedly owing to a sharp disagreement on Berlin policy, Kissinger insisted to *Newsweek* that he continued to support "the main lines of our policy." The extent of his NSC work was only a technical matter, related to his Harvard obligations, and "the kind of responsibilities I could assume in Washington."

There was a qualitative difference in the relationship after November 1961. The White House Communications Agency terminated its special service to Kissinger's office in Cambridge, documents were retrieved, the safe sold back to the General Services Administration. Kissinger continued to supply Bundy with ideas in a stream of memos, plus accounts of his conversations with various notables during his travels. But the problems continued as well. In January 1962, during a trip that took him to India, Pakistan, and Israel, among other nations, Kissinger gave press conferences in all three countries that provoked unfavorable public reactions, not to mention an official Egyptian diplomatic protest to the United States. The Egyptians were upset at Kissinger's comment in Tel Aviv that "recent Russian arms deliveries to the UAR [Egypt] have provoked crisis in the Middle East." The Egyptians, as a matter of fact, might have been even angrier had they known of Henry's recommendation at the time of the Suez crisis, which

he made in an October 1957 talk in New York: "The Soviet arms deal
had to be stopped by all means—even by the use of force . . . any entry
of Soviet arms into the Middle East had to lead to an explosive situation whatever the protestations of peaceful intent." As for NATO, the
White House was infuriated by certain Kissinger statements in the early
1960s on France and independent European nuclear forces in articles appearing when the United States was trying to form a NATO multilateral
nuclear force. Although Bundy wanted the benefit of Henry Kissinger's
thinking, their relationship never regained the amiability that prevailed in
January 1961.

With his ties to the Republican Rockefellers, Henry Kissinger could, at best,
only be counted among conservative Democrats. But Jack Kennedy's NSC
staff did span the American political spectrum to some degree, as illustrated
by the man who shared a secretary with Kissinger. It is overreaching to say,
as has been written, that this appointment represented an opening to the
extreme Left. That was a *post hoc* interpretation. Rather, as with other
members of his political staff such as Sorensen and Schlesinger and Goodwin, Kennedy here chose a man from the mainstream liberal tradition.

It would be more accurate to say that this appointment was an opening
to Congress, a hint that the new president would value legislative opinion
in a way Eisenhower never had. Coming from the military tradition, Ike
saw the policy prerogative as his alone. Jack Kennedy, by contrast, was
every inch a politician, having risen through Congress. This NSC staff appointment suggested to Congress that here was a President who would take
their views on national security seriously.

When Madison, Wisconsin, formerly Republican country, elected Robert
W. Kastenmeier to the House in 1958, he had hired Marcus Goodman
Raskin as a legislative assistant. Raskin was a brilliant young fellow from
Milwaukee, then twenty-four with a doctorate in jurisprudence. Kastenmeier was a liberal and quickly found a like-minded group in Congress,
one in fact that was attempting to systematize liberal thinking and distill
policies that were consistent and really solved problems. This Liberal Project
Group commissioned essays and then met to discuss them. The freshman
Wisconsin congressman lent Raskin to the group, which found his thoughtful approach invaluable. Raskin had a proclivity for philosophical views of
issues, perhaps stimulated by his training at the University of Chicago. The
group assembled a set of essays called *The Liberal Papers* of which Raskin
wrote one and helped edit others.

President Kennedy did not know Raskin as he did many of the Harvard
crew. They had met once and shaken hands at some congressional function,
but Kennedy relied on the recommendations of David Riesman, a professor
of Social Science at Harvard, and the congressional liberals in hiring Raskin
for the NSC staff. Raskin got an office outside Bundy's first one, on the
third floor of the OEOB, and was to work on disarmament issues, the United

Nations, and congressional matters. He kept these portfolios and later added Albania, Yugoslavia, and the UN trusteeship in Micronesia.

In the spring of 1961, Bundy took Raskin to meet Walt Rostow, who was being called "Chester Bowles with machine guns," and the NSC deputy wanted to know what he thought about guerrilla warfare, one of Rostow's pet subjects. Raskin wasn't very positive. Mac said, "Marc is going to be our conscience." After a few days Bundy, at one of the thrice-weekly NSC staff meetings, told Raskin he was being disruptive and that they should speak privately in the keeper's office. Raskin tried to function as an in-house critic but the pressures for conformity on the NSC staff were great and his relations with various members gradually worsened. Bundy got Raskin to take his name off *The Liberal Papers,* by now moving toward publication.

Then came a big fracas in the fall of 1961, which revolved around the basic national security policy paper, an annual exercise under Eisenhower. This time the paper became mired in the disputes over civil defense and so-called counterforce targeting, the jargon for using nuclear weapons against opposing strategic forces rather than populations. There were people at the Pentagon who argued, as would McNamara in 1962, that counterforce was preferable as a mechanism for reducing population fatalities in a nuclear war. In the Soviet context, however, this could only succeed if Russian nuclear forces could be totally eliminated. That seemed highly unlikely unless the United States actually attacked first.

Others believed that, for this reason, counterforce would never be successful. Jerry Wiesner, for example, argued that no matter how many nuclear forces the United States fielded, it would never achieve more than a deterrent posture. The basic national security policy paper, mostly drafted at the Pentagon and with the help of RAND Corporation nuclear warfare theorists, waffled so that it could be read either way.

The dispute began over civil defense, but it spilled over into the counterforce issue. It looked to Marc Raskin like a formula for starting a nuclear war. Raskin went with Carl Kaysen when the latter marshaled White House people, including Schlesinger, for the fight. The President asked for a memo. Raskin wrote one for Bundy, then had a meeting with Ted Sorensen, Elmer Staats, and a few others. But JFK was evidently influenced by fears of a liberal Republican, Rockefeller, challenge in 1964, and by advice from such conservatives as nuclear physicist Edward Teller. About a month later Kaysen showed Raskin a new draft policy paper, worked up at the Pentagon but which sounded as if it had had a last rewrite by Kaysen himself. Raskin read the paper. The counterforce argument had not been softened at all; it looked to Raskin like a first-strike war plan. He walked back into Kaysen's office, then asked Carl how he thought the United States was different from the people who had loaded the boxcars to Auschwitz.

Marc Raskin and Carl Kaysen had been very close. After the counterforce fight they hardly spoke again.

Disarmament was Raskin's real hope. The question was, would John Kennedy pursue the option earnestly? This was an administration that had nuclear theorists like Henry Kissinger on the general advisory committee of the Arms Control and Disarmament Agency (Walt Rostow, indeed, had considered giving Henry the NSC staff portfolio for disarmament). In the spring of 1961, Raskin attended a meeting at the State Department of officials and military people plus industrialists and academics. The speakers included Dean Rusk, Mac Bundy, and Paul Nitze. Raskin sat next to the president of the Atlas Powder Company, which made solid-fuel rocket motors for the Minuteman ICBM. John J. McCloy joked that the difference between Republican and Democratic administrations was that the former invited college presidents and the latter the professors. Then McCloy said, "If this group cannot bring about disarmament then no one can." Thinking of the Minuteman missiles, Raskin rolled his eyes, catching the gaze of Richard Barnet, a McCloy aide.

Meanwhile, the book *The Liberal Papers* was published under the editorship of California Democratic Congressman James Roosevelt. The book infuriated conservatives, who railed against it in Congress, as if such an expression of opinion were subversive. One fact that surfaced was that Marcus Raskin of the NSC staff had had a hand in it, even though his name appeared nowhere in the book. The key thought for Mac Bundy then became damage control and he packed Raskin off to Geneva as a member of the United States delegation at the disarmament talks. A year of this soured Raskin. He left government to take up with Richard Barnet. Together they formed the Institute for Policy Studies, a liberal think tank that moved to the left in the heat of the Vietnam controversy. It was over Vietnam, in fact, that Marc Raskin and McGeorge Bundy would have their next encounter.

It was also in Vietnam, though much later, that the career of another member of the Bundy staff would reach its apogee. Robert W. Komer came to the NSC staff from the Central Intelligence Agency, the only one of Bundy's people, at least at the level of professional staff, to do so. It did not hurt, however, that Komer had graduated magna cum laude (a Phi Beta Kappa too) from Harvard in 1942 and from the Harvard Business School in 1947. In World War II he had served in combat intelligence with the U.S. Army in Italy, then joined the CIA after earning his master's in business administration.

When the CIA formed an Office of National Estimates in 1950, specifically to write high-level national intelligence estimates, Komer was among its staff. Komer later began to specialize in Middle Eastern matters, and in 1956 was assigned by the CIA to handle its end of dealings with Eisenhower's National Security Council and Planning Board.

From the beginning the ebullient Komer, a Chicago boy, staked out a wide swath of territory for his reading of cables and papers, taking advantage of Bundy's disposition to let staff choose their subjects within some limits.

"Some people thought him brash and intrusive," Bundy recalls, "I just thought him a marvelous staff man." Komer's areas of responsibility included high-level conferences, the NATO and CENTO alliances, military aid, overseas bases (especially in Morocco and Spain), guerrilla warfare and subversion, the Near East, North Africa, the Horn of Africa, the Sudan, China, and South Asian and European affairs. He added further responsibilities over time until, when Carl Kaysen left, it was Komer who decided how to divide up what he jocularly cracked had been the empire of Darius, a reference to the Persian ruler of antiquity that a fellow Harvard graduate might be expected to grasp.

Having outlined his turf Komer proceeded to defend it vigorously. Once, in the early summer of 1961, Komer attended a disarmament meeting of the Committee of Principals at the State Department. In the car on the way over, Jerry Wiesner showed him the agenda. The Chicagoan had not even known there *was* an agenda until then. When Komer received no copy of the proposal for what became the Arms Control and Disarmament Agency (ACDA) or the Pentagon's comments on that, it was too much. He asked Bundy to issue standing orders that all disarmament papers be sent on to Komer once Mac had seen them. "The purpose," Komer wrote, "is to enable me to provide the sort of support you need and I want to give . . . if I don't even get copies of memos you write on matters you've charged me with supporting you on, how can I represent your interest around town? . . . It's no fun for me either to beard you again on a peanut issue where we've had words. But passing out the word is indispensable if we're to do a job."

Bundy agreed and issued the necessary instructions.

Still, Komer was by no means just boom and bluster. He was *effective*, in the way Kennedy's reorganized NSC staff had to be effective. A good example was West Irian, an issue that built late in 1961 and peaked early the following year. West Irian was the name for the western part of New Guinea, then a Dutch colony but coveted by Indonesia.

Achmed Sukarno laid claim to Irian as a matter of nationalism and a diversion from internal Indonesian problems. The Dutch were willing to fight and the United States likely to be dragged in. Komer watched the situation carefully with some help from Robert H. Johnson, mobilized the State Department, and got a mediation mission going under Ambassador Ellsworth Bunker. The mediator dissuaded the Dutch from fighting and got Sukarno to agree to some guarantees for the native population. Komer added Indonesia to his list of NSC staff responsibilities.

Soon after the West Irian affair Bob Komer got an unforgettable introduction to Lyndon Johnson. Kennedy and Bundy had been trying to get the Vice President to make a goodwill trip to Turkey. Johnson resisted, finally saying he would go only if JFK sent Mac along to accompany him and demonstrate the importance of the visit. Both the President and Bundy insisted that the keeper of the keys knew *nothing* about Turkey, that *the* expert on the Middle East was Komer.

The first Bob Komer heard of this was one morning in August 1962 when the phone rang on his desk. It was Bundy.

"You're going to the Middle East in forty-eight hours," Mac told the Chicagoan, "and you're going over to see the Vice President this afternoon at five P.M."

Komer spent the rest of the day trying to find out everything he could about Lyndon Johnson, then left for the appointment at LBJ's Capitol Hill office. The place was huge, the biggest thing Komer had ever seen outside the movies, with a crystal chandelier and a table that seemed forty feet long. The only people in the room were Johnson and Phillips Talbot, assistant secretary for Near East and South Asian affairs at State. Talbot was embroiled in heated argument with LBJ over policy toward India and Pakistan, which had conflicting claims over the province of Kashmir. Talbot insisted the United States must take an evenhanded approach toward the conflict. LBJ favored Pakistan.

Not knowing what was going on between the two, Komer, though an old friend of Talbot's, said he had to disagree—he favored India.

Disregarding this difference with his own view, LBJ turned on Talbot and shouted, "See? I told you so. Even the high-ranking Kennedy men don't agree with the State Department on this India-Pakistan business!"

As Komer recalled of Johnson: "We hit it off from the beginning."

On the trip itself the relationship was further cemented. Johnson visited Turkey and Iran too. At Ankara it was midsummer on the hot Anatolian plains. An accompanying State official hadn't the heart to tell LBJ that *everyone* left Ankara in August, so Komer took it on himself to do the deed. Instead, Johnson found mobs of people, over a million, and it took hours to reach the hotel downtown. "My Ankara *faux pas*," recalled Komer, "made me a lifelong friend of LBJ."

Despite, or perhaps because of, the snappy style he cultivated, Bob Komer got on quite well with colleagues on the NSC staff. Mac liked him a lot; so did Walt Rostow. When Rostow moved to State to head the Policy Planning Council, Komer took over his OEOB office suite in rooms 372-372A and 374. Later, when Rostow went to India and Pakistan on a mission to see if the Kashmir deadlock could be broken, the one man he insisted on having with him was Komer. Marc Raskin thought Komer pleasant and articulate. Michael Forrestal became a good friend. And as for Maxwell Taylor and his staff of military specialists, who were absorbed into the NSC staff when Taylor went to the JCS, Komer himself described their relations as being among the best.

But Komer exempted no one from his outspoken prescriptions. A typical example was the note he sent Carl Kaysen, who was helping prepare JFK for a press conference on June 7, 1962:

> I'm through being polite, and its [sic] about time you quit being polite too. I'm telling you, and I want you to tell the President that he's got

to tell the nation—this afternoon—that we LOVE the neutrals, that *INDIA, YUGOSLAVIA, POLAND, INDONESIA, AND THE UAR* are our ONLY true allies and that we can't conduct foreign policy if we won't help those who hate us.

The President got the word but was by no means willing to go as far as Komer wished.

The Middle East spawned what became Komer's biggest role yet, which he took on in part because no one else could be made to recognize the seriousness of the problem. It began in September 1962 in Yemen when a coup attempt led by the chief of the palace guard turned into a full-scale civil war between royalist supporters of the former Imam and so-called republican followers of the military leader. Within a month or so Gamal Abdel Nasser had sent Egyptian advisers, then combat forces, to assist the republicans, while Saudi Arabia intervened on the side of the royalists.

Bob Komer carried the hot intelligence to Bundy, but Mac told him he was too busy, and to brief the President himself. When this process continued, Yemen became known as Komer's War. At Bundy's morning staff meetings Komer took a certain amount of good-natured ribbing because of his rushing around on this seemingly insignificant issue.

Komer estimated, accurately as it turned out, that Nasser would escalate. He pushed for United States action to deter that. Kennedy went along with several such moves: American destroyers visited a Saudi port, bombers stopped in Saudi Arabia on a hurriedly organized international tour, a Special Forces (Green Beret) team was sent to provide the Saudis extra training. Komer nevertheless pressed the issue until Bundy and the President agreed to an NSC meeting on the subject, duly held on February 25, 1963. The President approved a further evolution of American policy, expressed a few days later in NSAM-227, which combined discreet military moves with a mediation attempt. Subsequently, as part of Operation Hard Surface, a U.S. Air Force squadron was stationed in Saudi Arabia as a token but concrete commitment. Meanwhile, in recognition of the previous success of the Komer-Bunker team, Ellsworth Bunker was again selected as the mediator for the United States. Bunker shuttled between Cairo and Riyadh, got the Saudis to agree to halt their support for the royalists in exchange for the Hard Surface aircraft, and achieved concessions in Cairo as well. A United Nations mission helped, and a cease-fire was announced at the end of April.

While working on such high-level policy issues Komer still found time for bureaucratic details. In May 1963 he went to Mac on the matter of White House status symbols, arguing that being on the "White House staff" rather than the NSC staff would beef up their muscle, that it made a difference using White House stationery, the telephone switchboard, and even mail services. "To the extent that we are 'NSC,' " Komer wrote, "we are vestigial remnants of a quite different operation . . . if we're in fact expediters

121

for the President rather than part of an old-style paper mill, there is virtue in accenting this distinction." This time Komer did not get his wish.

After the Bay of Pigs the CIA proceeded with a series of plots to assassinate Fidel Castro. They included contacts with Mafia figures, with disaffected Cubans such as Castro's personal pilot and other intimate associates, and, in its greatest technical refinement, efforts to get at him with exotic toxins in seemingly innocuous gifts, at least one to be given unwittingly by a mediator for the Cuban exiles, James B. Donovan. All these plots failed, the last when Donovan substituted a different gift for the one the CIA had prepared.

The assassination plots were part of a larger CIA covert operation called Project Mongoose. While there is no evidence the President was aware of and had approved the assassination efforts, the larger project was under the direct control of an NSC subcommittee, the so-called Special Group (Augmented). It was an outgrowth of the post-Bay of Pigs investigation carried out by a board that included Max Taylor and Bobby Kennedy. Among subsequent recommendations had been one for a high-level cold war planning group under the NSC, replacing the Eisenhower system, under which the 5412 Committee, an older special group, had had the responsibility for approving covert operations. The President rejected the cold war unit but formed the Special Group (Augmented) instead and made Mac Bundy its chairman, with Bobby Kennedy and Taylor among its members, and Cuba initially its *only* active program.

The President's brother was a major catalyst for Project Mongoose, prodding the bureaucracy for action, insisting upon more forceful options, visiting training bases where newly recruited Cuban exiles were being put through their paces. Among the Washington-level coordinators for the covert activity was Brigadier General Edward Lansdale, temporarily diverted from his passionate engagement in Vietnam. Details of the paramilitary operations are not important here, but they involved sabotage, coastal raids, and commando attacks. Success was minimal despite a great deal of effort.

Then the Mongoose operation got in the way of the Cuban missile crisis, a covert action in the midst of an acute nuclear crisis. Some of the CIA commandos set out for Cuba in what would very likely have looked to the Russians like the first wave of an American invasion. Bobby Kennedy accidentally learned of the incipient Mongoose mission; shortly afterward the EXCOM issued orders to halt all Mongoose activities. Lansdale was sent down to Miami to shut down the large CIA station there, effectively terminating Mongoose.

The missile crisis did not end the secret war against Castro, however. Rather, the effort was again reorganized. In early 1963 the State Department appointed a new senior coordinator for Cuban affairs while Kennedy approved establishment of an NSC Standing Group, which Mac Bundy does not recall. The officer representing the Joint Chiefs of Staff on this committee, who acknowledges existence of the group, though *he* claims it had only a superficial role, was General Andrew Goodpaster. Other members included Robert Kennedy, Ted Sorensen, George Ball succeeded by Harriman, U. Alexis Johnson, Roswell L. Gilpatric, John McCone, and Bromley Smith.

This NSC Standing Group superseded the Special Group (Augmented) and had Cuba as its top item of business throughout its existence. Its decisions by and large went directly to implementation and did not rise to John Kennedy's level. In early 1963 these included revisions of information and propaganda policy, measures to inhibit United States and allied flag merchant shipping to Cuba, changes in United States sugar import quotas, reviews of exile problems, military contingency planning, and various intelligence reports. By early June the CIA had completed what it called an integrated plan for Cuba, an eyes-only paper prepared under the direction of Desmond FitzGerald, one of the agency's top paramilitary specialists, who was chief of a special task force on Cuba. FitzGerald presented the plan at the eighth meeting of the Standing Group, in the White House Situation Room on June 18, 1963, where it was approved. Goodpaster missed the meeting but Mac and Bromley Smith did not. State people present were Averell Harriman, U. Alexis Johnson, and Edward B. Martin, the assistant secretary for Latin America. Like Mongoose, this CIA plan intended to "nourish a spirit of resistance and disaffection" culminating in thirteen major paramilitary strikes to occur between November 1963 and the following January.

As the NSC Standing Group made its hush-hush decisions, the secret of that unit's existence was already unraveling. It was Bobby Kennedy, in fact, who let the cat out of the bag, in a talk he gave in late April to the administration's interdepartmental seminar on counterinsurgency. He told the audience that the Standing Group (he called it a committee) had been "reactivated" to look into areas outside the purview of the NSC Special Group (Counter-Insurgency). On a copy of the record of this talk he sent to Brom Smith, Bundy wrote in his precise hand, "How secret can a standing group stay?"

In the meantime the President marched to the beat of a different drummer. That January, Bundy had suggested the United States explore the possibility of communicating with Castro. On April 21, Mac sent Kennedy a memo pointing out that eliminating Castro would almost certainly lead to an even more pro-Soviet government under brother Raul. The broad alternatives, Bundy wrote, were to force a non-Communist solution "by all necessary means," to seek major but more limited goals, or to move in the direction of accommodation with Castro. Kennedy's choice was the third one, and the NSC Standing Group ultimately followed him despite its paramilitary decisions. By the fall of 1963 Ambassador William Attwood would be having private talks with Cuban diplomats in New York.

Though Eisenhower had been the first to violate the terms of the 1954 Geneva agreement, the whole American involvement in Vietnam in those days was quiet enough that John Kennedy could pretend to business as usual. As with Yemen, South Vietnam was so unknown to Americans that few cared what was happening there and almost no one could have identified what in fact the United States policy was. As Kennedy entered office the United States continued to support the government of Ngo Dinh Diem while the military assistance group stood at a strength of 685 officers and men. The President intended to do whatever was necessary to maintain an anti-Communist South Vietnam, which meant continuing to obstruct the Vietnamese reunification that had been mandated under the Geneva agreement, openly challenging Ho Chi Minh's Viet Minh, which was now beginning to be labeled with the pejorative name Vietcong.

Meanwhile, the Ngo family's grip on power in South Vietnam, always authoritarian, became increasingly tenuous. Diem could no longer wholly trust his own military, the Army of the Republic of Vietnam (ARVN). Believing they were not being allowed to combat the Communists effectively, elite ARVN paratroop units launched a coup against Diem just two months before John Kennedy's inauguration. The move proved abortive when Diem was able to stall for time and bring in loyal ARVN troops, but it had been a narrow escape. Thus, as JFK entered office the Vietnam pot boiled even while Laos received most of the attention.

The first decisions seemed simple enough, just a matter of agreeing to pay for an increase in ARVN troops and an expansion of militia-type forces. Kennedy found a range of recommendations in a report by Ed Lansdale that awaited him after the inaugural. The new President favored making Lansdale the next ambassador to South Vietnam but Bob McNamara, who found Lansdale ethereal, hardly a numbers man in the new systems analysis mold, threatened to resign and prevented it. Nevertheless, though Lansdale was not then sent to Saigon, and though his personnel suggestions were not adopted, his advice found some expression in JFK's first Vietnam decisions, embodied in NSAM-52. The military advisory group expanded to over one thousand with the addition of Green Beret trainers and Air Force unconventional-warfare units.

With the growing American role, Washington wanted a better feel for events in Vietnam. Through the summer of 1961 there were repeated discussions about sending a survey mission to Saigon under Walt Rostow. That spring, meeting Diem on his Southeast Asian tour for Kennedy, Lyndon Johnson had proposed a major expansion in the United States effort. Others wanted to use Vietnam as a kind of counterinsurgency laboratory. Then, in September through his minister of defense, Diem proposed a treaty of alliance with the United States to be backed up by American combat troops. President Kennedy needed better information before he could respond to this welter of proposals.

The idea of a Rostow mission sounded fine to JFK and Bundy but did not gain equal support throughout the bureaucracy. In particular, Chester

Bowles at State was uncomfortable with Rostow's propensity for the use of force, demonstrated by his recommendations early in the Laotian crisis. Bowles complained long and vociferously, but Dean Rusk viewed Vietnam as a simple military problem, amenable to a military solution. In line with Rusk's view, JFK then selected a military man to head the survey: He was Maxwell Taylor. That choice still did not satisfy Bowles, especially when he learned the mission would include no senior people from State. It indicated, Bowles suggested, either that Rusk had abdicated State's responsibility, or that JFK, lacking confidence in State, had decided to take that responsibility away and give it to the NSC staff and his special military representative. It was Bowles himself, in fact, out of step with the White House and suspected of leaking news of the Bay of Pigs operation, who was on the way out, soon to be exiled with the grandiloquent title of President's special representative and adviser on Asian, African, and Latin American affairs. The job brought a bigger salary, a White House car, and very little else.

Maxwell Davenport Taylor, then a sixty-year-old retired full general who had been born in the central Missouri town of Keytesville, was capable of fits of pique and stunts in the best MacArthur tradition. When Kennedy first tried to bring him into the White House, a major point of contention had been over whether the job title should be "special military representative" or "*the* special military representative," with Taylor holding out for the second (and losing). He asked to be brought back to active duty, a wish the President granted. There were some disruptions to the NSC staff when Taylor took over a block of offices on the third floor of the Executive Office Building for his own staff, and some difficulties between Taylor and Carl Kaysen when it came time to figure out exactly how Taylor's staff would relate to Bundy's. Taylor agreed at first to send his staff man Colonel Julian J. Ewell along to Bundy's staff meetings, but reserved his right to change the arrangement at will. Max did choose good people who would later be absorbed into the NSC staff. Along with Ewell they were Colonel Lawrence J. Legere and Major James W. Dingeman of the Army, Lieutenant Commander Worth Bagley of the Navy, Major William Y. Smith of the Air Force, and Thomas A. Parrott of the CIA. Taylor also insisted on a salary commensurate with that of the JCS Chairman or a service Chief of Staff, and Kenny O'Donnell had to ask McNamara to free Pentagon contingency funds to supplement Taylor's general's pay.

All this would be only academic except that Max Taylor's pique affected his and Walt Rostow's survey mission to Vietnam. Max had no objection to the State Department's man on the delegation—William J. Jorden, then a relatively junior diplomat working on a white paper justifying United States involvement, was the top diplomat. The rub for Taylor was the participation of Ed Lansdale on behalf of the Pentagon. Taylor, it happened, was an old Army friend of J. Lawton Collins, the general Lansdale had bested in 1955, when Collins had wanted new Vietnamese leadership and Lansdale backed Diem. In fact, Taylor's first visit to Vietnam had occurred in March 1955 at the height of the earlier crisis. Max hadn't liked Lansdale then and now tried to limit him as much as possible.

Kennedy announced the mission on October 11, giving Rostow and Taylor three days to prepare. They met with other participants and each drew up a list of questions that seemed germane. Taylor and Rostow went over the lists, as Walt recalled it, "like two professors going over the outlines for a series of student term papers." But when it came to Lansdale, who knew something about counterinsurgency and had listed some of the most significant questions, Max had no comment at all. Soon the group was in the air winging west, with a stop at Honolulu to get the latest views from CINCPAC. It was October 18 in Saigon when the Taylor-Rostow mission landed at Tan Son Nhut airport on a humid evening. The first item of business was to be a visit the next morning with Ngo Dinh Diem. Despite knowledge of Lansdale's relationship with Diem, Taylor excluded him from the list of those who were to see the Vietnamese president. The gesture backfired, however, for a Diem aide was on hand at the airport to take Lansdale aside during the welcoming ceremonies and whisk him off for dinner and a private talk at the presidential palace that lasted late into the night. Lansdale quickly learned what Diem would tell Taylor and Rostow the next day: that he wanted American troops and large increases in United States support for the Vietnamese Army. As he always had done, Lansdale advised Diem how best to get what he wanted.

Taylor and Rostow heard it all the next day, except that Diem was deliberately ambiguous about United States troops, mentioning only the need for naval support and for a joint plan for an American troop commitment if that was ever necessary. How much Diem's ambiguity owed to Lansdale's advice may never be known.

The mission members fanned out all over the country searching for answers to their questions. Rostow mostly stayed with Taylor, who spent one day flying over the Mekong Delta and another up north near the demilitarized zone that separated North and South Vietnam. Taylor reassembled the group for a day of taking stock, then returned with Rostow and the United States ambassador to see Diem on October 24. The group finally retired to Baguio in the Philippines, where Taylor and Rostow drafted a report to supplement the three cables the general had already sent to Kennedy. Lansdale, Bill Jorden, and lesser lights wrote papers that were stapled to Taylor's opus, while Rostow wrote nothing identifiable as a separate contribution.

Commitment of Americans in various advisory and technical capacities could cure South Vietnamese weaknesses, and would remove doubts regarding the United States' resolve, according to the Taylor-Rostow report, dated November 3, 1961. In one of his eyes-only cables, Taylor put the initial number of Americans needed at no more than eight thousand. He dismissed the danger of an escalating war at the same time: "The risks of backing into a major Asian war by way of [South Vietnam] are present but are not impressive." In addition, Taylor, perhaps influenced by Rostow, who was a great advocate of the efficacy of aerial bombardment, held out for the first time the notion that bombing might be a panacea in Vietnam. Taylor cabled that North Vietnam "is extremely vulnerable to conventional bombing, a weakness which should be exploited diplomatically in convincing Hanoi to lay off." American forces committed, the report advised, should include helicopter units, more Air Force unconventional-warfare forces, engineers and logistical troops, Green Berets, naval forces, and more trainers and planners. The units could be disguised as a task force to help rebuilding after monsoon floods, and could be covered by combat troops if necessary.

The Taylor-Rostow mission became a watershed in the growing United States involvement in Southeast Asia. Though Taylor protests that "personally, I had no enthusiasm for the thought of using U.S. Army forces in ground combat in this guerrilla war," at one stroke he had moved the focus of NSC decisions from what the United States could do to enable the Vietnamese to help themselves, to what we could do for them. Taylor and Rostow were both conscious of the change, explicitly calling the anticipated new situation a "limited partnership." Moreover, the mission cables and report discussed both bombing and "covert offensive operations" into Laos and North Vietnam. Those were things that were not going to be accomplished by the ARVN acting alone.

On their return to Washington, Taylor and Rostow were immediately "put on the witness seat," as the general phrases it, to defend their recommendations. The morning after their return, Saturday, November 4, one critical meeting took place in Rusk's private conference room at State. Bob McNamara and Ros Gilpatric arrived early, to find George Ball already there. Ball took the opportunity to tell them he was appalled by the Taylor-Rostow recommendations—the United States would find itself in a conflict far more serious than Korea, "the Vietnam problem was not one of repelling overt invasion but of mixing ourselves up in a revolutionary situation with strong anti-colonialist overtones." Ball got no sympathy from the Pentagon officials, while McNamara and Rusk gave Max Taylor the impression that both were "in general accord" with his report.

The secretary of defense nevertheless strode with a bureaucrat's cautious step. After meeting with the Joint Chiefs, McNamara sent a memorandum to the President warning that the Taylor report framed the basic issue of the United States devoting itself to the "clear objective" of preventing the fall of South Vietnam and that the chances were against, "probably sharply against," doing that "by any measures short of the introduction of United States forces on a substantial scale." If the United States adopted that goal, McNamara noted, Taylor's plan constituted a suitable first step.

John Kennedy believed in the first step, but not in the warning. On November 7, at the end of a meeting on another subject, George Ball mentioned his fears to the President.

"George, you're just crazier than hell," Kennedy told him. "That just isn't going to happen."

Back at his office, Ball told his chief of staff, "We're heading hell-bent into a mess, and there's not a Goddamn thing I can do about it. Either everybody else is crazy or I am."

The President too may have had his quiet misgivings. "They want a force of American troops," he told Arthur Schlesinger, "they say it's necessary in order to restore confidence and maintain morale. But it will be just like Berlin. The troops will march in; the bands will play; the crowds will cheer; and in four days everyone will have forgotten. Then we will be told we have to send in more troops. It's just like taking a drink. The effect wears off, and you have to take another."

Formal NSC consideration came on November 15. Rusk argued against making a major commitment to "a losing horse" and opposed troops. Harriman and Ken Galbraith also opposed the troops and the former keeper went so far as to suggest a negotiated settlement supplementing the 1954 agreement. Kennedy chose a middle course, rejecting combat troops for the moment, but also any search for a diplomatic solution. His strategy for the first phase in Vietnam, stated in NSAM-111 of November 22, accepted the advisory group increases Taylor and Rostow had recommended. In an offhand crack alluding to bombing the north, JFK told Rostow, "If this doesn't work perhaps we'll have to try Walt's Plan Six." By the end of 1962 there would be 11,300 American military personnel in Vietnam.

The responsible aides on the NSC staff observed these developments with some concern. Rostow himself had been at the top, of course, under the arrangement by which he divided the world with Bundy, taking everything east of Suez. But Rostow left for the Policy Planning Council, his last memo for the President, on December 6, 1961, in which he advocated that Ed Lansdale be freed from his other work, principally the covert action against Castro, and sent to Vietnam. Robert Johnson, the Eisenhower NSC holdover, was the working-level staff analyst, but when Walt moved to State he took Johnson with him.

Carl Kaysen tried to pick up the slack afterward. But Kaysen was overextended, with too much on his plate and no working agreement with Mac Bundy as Walt had had. Even worse, there was no action officer save Worth Bagley, who worked for Max Taylor. Kaysen had his hands too full to keep a close watch on Averell Harriman, then moving toward a Laos agreement at Geneva. Something had to be done. Kennedy and Mac Bundy decided to get someone for the NSC who could both liaise with Harriman and handle Southeast Asia, a "twofer" in the idiom of a later administration.

Michael Vincent Forrestal was that someone. Son of Harry Truman's first secretary of defense, Forrestal specialized in international business transactions and had spent five months in 1958 as special counsel to a committee Eisenhower created to study foreign trade. When Arthur Schlesinger heard Mac was thinking of giving Forrestal a place on the NSC staff, he told the keeper he had known Mike a dozen years and thought the lawyer would do an excellent job. Schlesinger believed that Forrestal had broader views than his father, was hardworking and conscientious, and would be "an exceedingly good bet." Mike came down to Washington for an interview and was working at the NSC before the end of the month. "Well," the President told him, "I really want you to be my ambassador to that separate sovereignty known as Averell Harriman."

In addition, Forrestal was going to be NSC staff liaison with Lyndon Johnson and his national security man, Howard Burris, and was to watch Indochina. The last item gave Forrestal pause—his national security experience was European and Soviet. Ignorant of Vietnam at first, Forrestal could do little more than collect the views of the agencies and present them fairly. Later he began to venture more opinions of his own and became, in Bob Komer's memorable phrase, an "expediter." If Forrestal sensed something wrong or saw a problem he thought needed the President's personal attention, he would leave the OEOB, march over to the West Wing, and go see Kennedy. Appointments secretary Kenny O'Donnell would either send him right in or ingeniously sandwich him between the President's other engagements; or, if the door was open, Forrestal would walk right in.

Given the extent of military involvement in Vietnam, there was some potential for turf battles between Forrestal and the Taylor staff. The possibility increased shortly after Forrestal joined the staff, since on January 18 the President approved NSAM-124, which established one of his NSC subcommittees, the Special Group (Counter-Insurgency), with Taylor as chairman. The general selected Major James Dingeman of his staff as executive secretary, however, and this officer worked to maintain a smooth relationship with the NSC people. Dingeman seemed to have an ability to break up the logjams and get things done when others could not, helping Forrestal at critical moments. When Taylor left to become Chairman of the JCS, Dingeman and the general's other people joined the NSC staff. Dingeman retained functional specializations that included cold war programs, counterinsurgency, civic action programs, and counterguerrilla efforts worldwide, which naturally covered Southeast Asia also.

The President, the general, the White House staff, all watched as the United States sent men and spent money in Vietnam. There seemed precious little to show for it.

Rather than improving, the situation in 1963 seemed an escalating stalemate. Seeking better information, the White House sometimes had to fight the bureaucracy to find out what was going on. A few times, the NSC staff actually received false reports, but those were usually uncovered, deterring further falsification. Kennedy ordered more and more survey trips to Vietnam to seek knowledge. There were several by military officers. McNamara made repeated visits. Michael Forrestal made a visit accompanied by Roger Hilsman, who had succeeded Harriman as assistant secretary of state for Far Eastern affairs. Kennedy became more and more frustrated as the reports came back telling him that things were really not too bad, that a little more equipment, a few more advisers or dollars would make it all right.

A crisis served as a catalyst. Buddhists at the old Vietnamese imperial capital Hue were prevented from flying their flag during a celebration. Buddhist demonstrations and police actions followed one upon another as the monks became increasingly militant, to the point that one immolated himself in downtown Saigon on June 11. Madame Nhu, wife of the president's brother, then scandalized everyone by referring to the suicide as a "barbecue." Meanwhile, Operation Sunrise seemed a failure as peasants abandoned the fortified villages in which they had been resettled, usually taking the tin roofing they had been forced to buy. For weeks Forrestal had been trying to get the CIA and the military to focus on who the Buddhists were, what motivated them, and how many there might be. Acting through the Special Group (CI), on which he had been the President's personal representative since November 1962, Forrestal pushed for some answers, but got none until after the incident at Hue. Then current intelligence reports and special national intelligence estimates began to flow. Disappointed with the lack of foresight, the NSC staff man blamed himself for not having tried harder.

The President decided that something had to be done. Most in Washington equated this with getting rid of Ngo Dinh Nhu. Diem made some promises about sending Madame Nhu out of the country, which he did, and being conciliatory toward the Buddhists, an effort that failed. It was enough to satisfy Ambassador Frederick Nolting. Then Nhu, using Vietnamese Special Forces and Combat Police, in a move that had to have been agreed upon by his brother, raided the Buddhist pagodas on August 21. Many Vietnamese were outraged. Talk of a coup d'état, recurrent in Saigon for months, rose to new heights as ARVN generals actually began to plot such an action.

Nhu's pagoda raids also enraged Kennedy, who ordered a halt in United States support for the Special Forces and threatened to end all aid to South Vietnam. McNamara wanted to revive the EXCOM to deal with the crisis. Kennedy used his NSC instead. Several officials could not see how to get rid of Nhu without being prepared to threaten the end of American support for Diem, and Roger Hilsman and Averell Harriman went ahead and prepared a cable to the new ambassador to South Vietnam, Henry Cabot Lodge, with those instructions. It happened that JFK, Rusk, and the other principals were out of Washington on August 24 when Hilsman drafted the cable, so he and Harriman took it to George Ball, who had left State early that Saturday to play golf with U. Alexis Johnson, one of the four times in six years at the department that he managed to get in a game. Ball had no objections, and the President also cleared it provided that Rusk and a representative of McNamara's also agreed. They did. Bundy was also absent that day, so Mike Forrestal cleared the cable on behalf of the national security adviser.

The following Monday, director John McCone of the CIA learned of the cable, already dispatched after approval from his subordinate Richard Helms. McCone hit the ceiling, then was able to persuade McNamara and Max Taylor to rescind approvals by their subordinates as well. This flap led to a meeting of NSC principals in the Cabinet Room at the White House on the afternoon of August 27. The consensus was to modify Lodge's instructions to preclude support for a coup while leaving in place the basic threat implied in the Hilsman cable.

Thus began several months of delicate maneuvers in both Washington and Saigon, including innumerable sessions of the NSC principals though, until October 2, never a formal meeting of the National Security Council. That meeting, the 519th, followed yet another survey mission to Vietnam, this time by McNamara and McCone accompanied by Mike Forrestal. At length the United States did deal with ARVN generals plotting a coup in Saigon. Working through the CIA, whose pro-Nhu station chief had to be replaced in order to carry on, the administration gave the Vietnamese generals a green light.

In Saigon, Diem and Nhu hatched plots of their own after receiving warnings, some of them from General Harkins who learned a little of what was up. Nhu's maneuvers included feelers sent to the Vietcong and North Vietnamese, which further infuriated the Americans and helped seal his fate. There were also bizarre plans for a fake coup as cover for liquidating the offending generals and, apparently, certain Americans, especially journalists, deemed enemies of the regime. The plotting and counterplotting climaxed on November 1 when the Vietnamese generals actually carried out their coup. Diem and Nhu fled the presidential palace, but were captured the next day and murdered, apparently by an aide to one of the ARVN leaders. Kennedy had never intended to be party to an assassination, and Lodge had been careful to inform Diem of ARVN offers of a safe conduct out of Vietnam, but policy had been swept away by events. The Diem regime was over.

Diem's overthrow resulted in a military government in Saigon, but it at least offered an opportunity for change. The President was frustrated with events so far; even the Vietnamese had their doubts, and JFK had heard of certain straws in the wind—approaches to Hanoi and claims Saigon was going to ask the United States to *reduce* its advisers in the south. The latter seemed not a bad idea to Kennedy, who asked McNamara to have the Pentagon plan for reductions on the assumption that most of the United States mission in Vietnam was being accomplished. McNamara actually did assemble plans for a withdrawal, and the White House announced that an initial increment of one thousand men would be brought back before the end of 1964.

What he was going to do in Vietnam had to happen after the 1964 election, the President told Michael Forrestal, but it was time to get ready.

Years later, reconstructing the history of Kennedy's administration, paging through its formerly classified records, talking to NSC staff, it is difficult to avoid the impression that the President was learning the responsibility of power. Perhaps it had been the 1960 campaign debates with Nixon, or the 1961 confrontation with Khrushchev at Vienna, but initially Kennedy had seemed determined to demonstrate toughness, to use power if only to show that he had the option. By 1963, the frustrations of using power had become more apparent. Here was a smoother, calmer Kennedy, secretly working for rapprochement with Fidel Castro and a withdrawal from Vietnam, openly seeking a nuclear test ban treaty with the Soviets, and signing one despite the political difficulties of ratification. Kennedy's promise went unfulfilled, as the President fell before an assassin's bullet on the afternoon of November 22, 1963.

PART IV

▲

LYNDON JOHNSON'S VANTAGE POINT

Lyndon Baines Johnson, at the President's side on that final, fatal trip to Texas, had no opportunity for the kind of carefully considered planning that normally keynotes the transition from one President to the next. One moment, Lyndon and Jack were in Fort Worth, joking the morning of the Dallas motorcade. Kennedy, worried by recent opinion polls, still felt the enthusiasm of the crowds. Cheerfully, looking ahead to the 1964 elections, he told the Vice President that at least they would win in Texas and Massachusetts. A few hours later the President was dead. Kenny O'Donnell broke the news to Johnson at about 1:20 P.M., soon after his arrival at the hospital. The Secret Service advised Johnson that he should proceed to the presidential aircraft, *Air Force One*, with its secure communications and facilities for the care and feeding of chief executives. Lyndon stood to take the oath of office aboard the plane. It was approximately 2:40 P.M. That was the presidential transition.

Indeed LBJ wished to reassure the nation that all would be business as usual precisely by retaining Kennedy's people. Thus McGeorge Bundy, in the space of one budget meeting, where he happened to be at the moment of Kennedy's assassination, gained the unsought distinction of being the first national security adviser to serve two Presidents. Bundy, of course, tried to speak with the new President as quickly as possible, and succeeded in doing so soon after LBJ reached *Air Force One*. Bundy urged Johnson to return to Washington as quickly as possible. LBJ waited for the arrival of Jacqueline Kennedy with the body, but he was airborne within a few minutes of taking the oath from Sarah Hughes, a judge of the U.S. district court.

Thus began, in shock and tumult, a presidency fated to proceed through controversy and trauma to a similarly stunning end—the voluntary withdrawal of a President from politics. The fulcrum of that transformation would be Vietnam but the changes would have many aspects, from an overheating economy to downtrodden minorities rioting in the cities, to foreign crises triggering fires in the in-baskets of Washington officials. No one who began down this road on November 22, 1963, least of all Lyndon B. Johnson, could have anticipated the ultimate outcome. Johnson was, after all, a consummate politician and proven leader, a man who had played the Senate like a calliope, the fox who could persuade, cajole, and bully his way to any goal.

Overweening ambition, suspicion, a towering ego, to hear some tell it a certain dishonesty, insatiable demands for the loyalty of subordinates, all were to play a part in the downfall of Lyndon Johnson; yet they assisted his rise as well. There were excellent qualities too in this big Texan; great kindness, wit, charm, acute intelligence. He was a man who surprised those around him with an unexpected range of knowledge. Johnson did not inspire love in quite the way Kennedy did, but for America and the world, Lyndon accomplished some significant things in his time, in the areas of civil rights, voting rights, social programs; and in foreign policy, he took the first steps toward a peace in the Middle East and meaningful arms control measures. Few had expected so much from this southern Democrat, who turned out to be a progressive in a moderate's clothing.

Kennedy's national security people knew LBJ as the front man with Congress and assumed him to be ignorant about foreign policy. LBJ himself, worried about his inferiority vis-à-vis the intellectuals of the Harvard-MIT crowd. But over time the administration came to be unmistakably Johnson's, as Kennedy's people left one by one.

Ted Sorensen soon resigned; Bobby Kennedy rarely went to work and eventually would become a political opponent. Though the successive departures sometimes hurt the President, he became more clearly his own man. Lyndon Johnson felt he had a job to do and he set out to do it.

▲ ▲ ▲

OPENING CHORDS

▲▲▲

President Johnson's formal exposure to the national security prerogatives of his office came on his first morning as President, at 9:15 on Saturday, November 23, 1963. LBJ recalled that the international front that day "was about as peaceful as it ever gets in these turbulent times." Nevertheless, John McCone and R. Jack Smith of the CIA showed up to give the President a *tour d'horizon* of his work, the CIA's methods, and salient issues. The CIA director explained the device of the "President's intelligence checklist" (PICKL), the daily situation report sent to the Chief Executive summarizing the intelligence community's discoveries regarding the latest developments. These PICKL reports had been sent to the Vice President as well, but it developed that LBJ had paid no attention to them in those years. McCone agreed to brief the President personally on PICKL each morning for the next few days while senior CIA staff took care of Bundy and the rest of the White House people.

McCone's bid for access to LBJ was a classic ploy of bureaucracies competing for a President's attention, but it was not to last. Johnson preferred to do his reading at night, rather than in the morning or on weekends, so the PICKL was eventually changed to become an afternoon report. In effect, the CIA reports summed up daily events rather than bringing in the hot information. McCone lost interest in presenting them himself, while LBJ found he had more important things to do. Things also became more difficult between McCone and Bundy, who got sick of hearing the CIA director boast of his accurate premonitions before the Cuban missile crisis. Much later McCone found himself forced to complain that he was getting *no* time with the President. Bundy advised LBJ (shades of Eisenhower, who had taken much criticism for his golf) that a few rounds of golf might satisfy the CIA director.

McCone's giving up pretensions of briefing Lyndon Johnson put the onus on Mac Bundy. Not that Bundy minded—it was part of the business of a keeper of the keys. But this President, capable of towering rages, did not like to hear bad news. Mac tried putting the bad stuff on paper, sending it into the Oval Office with a messenger. LBJ would counter by refusing to speak to his national security adviser. Bundy finally found he got better results when he would "grab the microphone" and do all the talking, not letting Johnson have a chance to respond, then getting out fast while Johnson exploded.

137

"I do not recall a case," Bundy later said, "where after the initial sort of annoyance had gone past, he was not willing to read and take account of opinions that were not initially welcome. The manner here was his own and was a disservice to himself, I think, but not the real attitude of the man toward evidence."

Meanwhile, the NSC staff also worried about keeping the President informed, as well as about its ability to maneuver within the bureaucracy under this new man. Bob Komer was one of the first to weigh in, on November 27, advocating a "brief one page teaser" to LBJ on five key issues likely to arise over the next few weeks. Unaware of Johnson's predilection for overnight reading, Komer suggested a "weekender." Komer wrote Mac, "Now that the broad lines of authority have been happily resolved, I hope you will clue us juniors when opportunity arises to reestablish our acquaintance with LBJ." Komer did not know that, besides himself, Bundy, and Forrestal, few on the NSC staff had ever met the new President.

Johnson was ignorant of many things. One of them was the practice of allowing NSC staff members the right to sit in on audiences with foreign visitors. Komer and others had found the practice beginning to atrophy in Kennedy's last freewheeling months, and there were instances in which the staff was unable to follow up because it was not given records of discussions at the meetings. Hoping to get the NSC staff back into these sessions, Komer wrote Bundy, "I'm not sure it's good for State to get the idea we're no longer sitting in on these sessions with furriners. LBJ also needs [the] protection of having his own staffer there." The President soon agreed.

Lyndon Johnson had a few ideas of his own about getting advice after his sudden succession to the presidency. While in Washington for Kennedy's funeral, Dwight Eisenhower got a call from LBJ. The former President then spent a couple of hours talking to the new incumbent. LBJ told Ike he was quite comfortable with domestic affairs but less certain regarding foreign policy. What could Eisenhower suggest? There was no hesitation: Ike told Johnson he should order General Andrew Goodpaster and persuade Gordon Gray to come to the White House and "reconstruct the type of organization and procedures for national security policy and its execution which had existed in his administration." Lyndon thought it a fine idea, one he would implement, Ike later reported to Gray, but neither Gray nor Goodpaster ever heard from LBJ about the matter. Johnson did, however, begin using Andy Goodpaster as a personal intermediary with Eisenhower, periodically briefing the former President and bringing his reactions directly back to LBJ; there were forty-six visits through 1966, and at least a dozen more in 1967 and 1968. Goodpaster continued in the intermediary role while he worked for the JCS, and commanded the National War College.

Lyndon Johnson preferred, over time, to bring in new blood, beginning with Peter Jessup for intelligence and William G. Bowdler on Latin America. A new liaison officer with the JCS, Lieutenant Colonel Richard C. Bowman of the Air Force, also joined the NSC staff in 1964. New specialists on

Europe joined, including academic Francis Bator and diplomat David Klein. William Brubeck, formerly a top assistant to Dean Rusk, moved over to the NSC to handle Africa. With perceived problems in Latin America and Southeast Asia, Bundy added two more men in those areas: foreign service officer Robert Sayre to help Bowdler, and James C. Thomson, Jr., a young aide to Chet Bowles, to assist Mike Forrestal. Spurge Keeny, who continued to work for the President's science adviser, also began to give half his time to the NSC staff. Mac Bundy and Brom Smith presided over the group with aplomb.

In contrast to the speed with which he had set reporting procedures, almost two weeks went by before LBJ held his initial meeting with the NSC principals. That occasion, December 5, 1963, examined the CIA's recently completed national estimate on Soviet military capabilities. A second council session, on January 7, 1964, took up policy for Indonesia, while LBJ's third meeting on February 29 made the decision to reveal existence of the SR-71 spy plane.

These three were the only sessions of the NSC during Johnson's first hundred days in office. Jack Kennedy, though not an avid user of the council mechanism, had held NSC meetings twice as frequently during his first fourteen weeks. This was not accidental. LBJ had learned from EXCOM and the Cuban crisis; he would go for smaller, private meetings that stayed truly secret. "The National Security Council meetings were like sieves," Johnson told Doris Kearns. "I couldn't control them. You knew after the National Security Council meeting that each of those guys would run home to tell his wife and neighbors what they said to the President."

The President lived in terror of waking up the morning after to read all about it in *The New York Times*. Thus, when the first crisis happened, there was no NSC meeting at all.

ONE TRIP TOO FAR

▲▲▲

Perhaps mindful of comparisons with later keepers of the keys, McGeorge Bundy firmly insists that he was not in the business of undertaking special missions, at least not for John Kennedy. Such trips as he made were for other reasons. For example, Bundy went out to the Pacific in the early summer of 1961, but that was a field trip to see United States nuclear test sites and the ballistic missile test ranges. Mac made another trip, to Europe in 1962, but again it was not a presidential assignment.

Lyndon Johnson was different. He expected to make use of Bundy on serious occasions and did so. One of these, the only time Mac Bundy's role could be construed as that of a full-fledged presidential plenipotentiary, was his visit to the Dominican Republic in the spring of 1965. The mission was Johnson's response to what the President perceived as a crisis threatening Americans, triggered by a coup d'état in that Caribbean country. Bundy worked at first from Washington, but the President insisted upon greater efforts as the situation evolved. As a result of Bundy's mission, the NSC staff would have a more significant part to play than at any time since the Taiwan Strait crisis of 1955.

Tom Mann, recently promoted to undersecretary of state for economic affairs, first reported on the trouble in the Dominican Republic, long a nation of unsettled politics. Crippled by a stagnant economy Donald Reid y Cabral's government stumbled from one setback to another. Coup talk was rife in Santo Domingo. Amid the belly talk of splinter political groups, however, the real plot was a military one and represented a break for Juan Bosch, the former president, himself overthrown in a 1963 coup. Getting some whiffs, the CIA reported on April 11 and 12, just two weeks before Johnson's crisis began. There was enough concern at State that Ambassador W. Tapley Bennett, Jr., was recalled for consultations in Washington.

President Reid y Cabral sent his army chief of staff to arrest four of the plotters. The officers instead turned the tables, seized the camp, and marched on Santo Domingo, quickly capturing several radio stations, and promptly announced the overthrow of the Reid y Cabral government. Thousands of Dominicans poured into the streets where the rebels began distributing weapons from trucks. Reid y Cabral resigned and a provisional president

140

▲

was installed on April 25 pending Bosch's return from Puerto Rico. There were, however, military leaders who opposed the return of Bosch, principally in the air force and the Armed Forces Training Center (Spanish acronym CEFA), actually an elite combat unit with tanks, artillery, and about two thousand troops, constituting roughly half the Dominican forces in the capital area who remained loyal to the government. These forces launched a countercoup beginning on the afternoon of April 25 with aircraft bombing the presidential palace.

Military countercoup action effectively closed the Punta Caucedo airport, about twenty miles east of Santo Domingo, ending the possibility that Bosch could return to reclaim the presidency. Perhaps Bosch was waiting to see what the CEFA troops would do, since they had overthrown his own government. In any case, after the second day a Bosch return could only be negotiated between the contending factions. Rebel troops under Colonel Francisco Caamaño Deno numbered about 2,500 to 3,000, including perhaps 200 men from an elite naval frogman unit; they controlled most of downtown Santo Domingo. The CEFA troops and other loyalists pressed in on the city from the outside.

Through the weekend the President spoke frequently with Secretaries Rusk and McNamara and with Bundy, who set himself up in the White House Situation Room in order to follow developments. Midway through Sunday morning the President ordered a special unit of the Atlantic Fleet, Task Force 44.9 (commanded by Captain James A. Dare) to assume position off the coast of Santo Domingo but to stay out of sight. Thick fog over the Catoctin Mountains prevented Bundy and LBJ's other advisers' flying up to Camp David on helicopters for an afternoon meeting, one that originally was to have dealt with Vietnam, so the President motored to the foot of the mountains and boarded a helicopter himself, returning to the White House in time for a session in the Cabinet Room. By this time the two sides were fighting in Santo Domingo.

So far the situation was delicate but, from the United States perspective, not entirely out of control. Ambassador "Tap" Bennett was on his way back to his post, while LBJ ordered a larger Navy-Marine amphibious group, six vessels including the helicopter carrier *Boxer* under Vice Admiral Kleber S. Masterson, to Dominican waters from Puerto Rico. Americans were asked to assemble for evacuation the next day at the Hotel Embajador. The State Department on April 26 fielded numerous requests from other countries for assistance in evacuating their nationals as well.

On Tuesday, April 27, the CEFA troops and other loyalists made concentrated attacks into the city, then stalled. At the Hotel Embajador, where the only protection consisted of a few embassy consular officers plus an unarmed Marine radio team, an anti-Communist Dominican radio personality appeared with bodyguards and demanded to be evacuated too. Though he was refused, rebel radio asked supporters to enter the hotel and capture the man. Soon a mob of armed Dominicans went to the hotel, which some entered. Americans and others awaiting evacuation were terrified. A senior rebel officer arrived and restored order.

The general atmosphere in Santo Domingo and the Embajador incident evidently alarmed Tap Bennett so much that the ambassador made a series of fateful on-the-scene decisions. He did nothing in the moments after the loyalist troops stalled, thus missing the best opportunity yet to arrange a cease-fire. Equally important, he pulled out the stops on reporting to Washington, increasingly allowing his communications people to use the very highest priority United States government precedence, code-named Critic, for cables home. On Tuesday, April 28, developments in Santo Domingo were significant but not critical: The evacuation now proceeded smoothly while the rebel forces, which had seemed exhausted the previous day, had recovered their vigor. A military junta of four loyalist colonels was put together at San Isidro air base outside the city and they frantically radioed a request to the U.S. embassy for military intervention in their favor. It was not reported in a Critic, but the embassy produced no less than four such cables. The tide of Critics plus the request for intervention seems to have stampeded Washington.

A few days later, LBJ said it was "just like the Alamo." But the President's actions betrayed his feeling of insecurity, which made him especially vulnerable to panicky embassy reporting. Normally Johnson rarely entered the White House Situation Room, yet as events unfolded in the crisis he went there several times.

At 3:50 P.M., shortly before the planned Vietnam session with Bundy, Rusk, and McNamara, Tom Mann got Mac Bundy on the phone to inform him of Bennett's latest report, which was that the Dominican chief of police (who had aligned himself with the San Isidro junta) felt he could no longer protect the evacuation. Mac replied that the military balance still favored the junta but said he would inform the President, which he did about a half hour later. Mann opposed landing any American Marines and Bundy agreed with him. At 5:14 P.M., barely an hour after Bundy related this development to LBJ, one of Bennett's Critics came, reporting the situation deteriorating rapidly, American lives in danger, and that everyone in the embassy agreed intervention was necessary.

President Johnson received the cable as he met with his NSC principals. Bill Moyers, a special assistant, and George Ball had joined the group. Johnson read the cable then told his people he would not stand by and see American lives lost. No thought was given to whether the Dominican rebels might be as willing to protect Americans as the junta, as in fact they had, the previous day at the Hotel Embajador. Johnson was moved by the rumors of looting and rioting, while his advisers unanimously agreed protection should be provided for the evacuation effort.

The President asked McNamara to alert military forces. The Pentagon had already done that, with orders to the 82nd Airborne Division at Fort Bragg the previous day, and with the 3rd Battalion, 6th Marines standing by offshore. When LBJ ordered a landing, four hundred Marines quickly set up a perimeter around the evacuation site. Johnson also asked Rusk to inform the OAS and Latin countries of the United States' action, a task that quickly preoccupied Ball and others, and told Bill Moyers to set up a meeting with congressional leaders for that evening.

In preparation to justify this use of force, LBJ began to consider his rationale. In his memoirs Johnson concedes that the San Isidro junta was self-proclaimed, but argues that "more than any other organization it represented the authority of the Dominican Republic." On the night of April 28, and in his public defenses of the decision for weeks afterward, LBJ relied more on the argument that the rebel forces were Communists and that no Communist state could be allowed to establish itself in the Western Hemisphere.

Both arguments are flawed. The San Isidro junta was only another faction, a military faction at that, with no more legitimacy than any other. In terms of democratic process the pro-Bosch forces, cleverly calling themselves "constitutionalists," were attempting to restore the mandate of the 1962 elections with a commensurately greater claim to legitimacy. The Communist argument was completely off base. That very day LBJ had received Vice Admiral William F. Raborn, a new director of central intelligence replacing McCone. Raborn walked into this crisis blind, knowing neither his own organization nor anything about the Dominican Republic. Asked to look into claims of Communists among the rebel forces, Raborn made a few calls around the CIA headquarters at Langley, then told LBJ the CIA had identified three Communists among the rebel leadership. With a little more time, a few days later, the CIA supplied a list of fifty-seven supposed rebel leaders. Basing his claims on that data, Johnson laid it on thick: Moscow- and Cuba-trained Communists were running the movement; Cuban intelligence helped with guns, plans, and money; fifteen hundred of about four thousand rebel forces came from Communist political parties. In his speeches, the President elevated his argument against allowing Communist states to the level of the "Johnson Doctrine."

The major CIA report on Communist participation in the Cuban revolt was completed on May 7. Mac Bundy sent it along to LBJ without even holding it long enough to read himself. The CIA proved able to identify only three military positions established by Communists, so-called strongpoints in houses, significantly enough, each at the home of the leader of one of the various Dominican Communist factions. The report contains no claim that Communists provided over a thousand troops, though it does state that Communists had a leading role in one key rebel attack. An appendix on Cuban involvement cites *no* activity directly related to the 1965 rebellion and indeed presents the story of one Dominican trained in Cuba whom the Cubans specifically *prohibited* from engaging in guerrilla activities.

By the time of this CIA report, which expanded the list of alleged Communist leaders in the revolt to eighty-three (or eighty-nine in another draft), the lists were already being exposed to ridicule in the press. Asked by reporters, Tap Bennett was unable to identify a single one of the persons on the CIA list active in the rebel command. Two of the Communist parties represented on the list were tiny; the other had in fact *opposed* Bosch in the 1962 elections. Several of the individuals named were not even in the country: One was a former ambassador of deposed dictator Rafael Trujillo who had never been regarded as a Communist; another was thought to have some "very special" connections with "certain Americans." This failure to supply credible justification for LBJ's action very likely contributed to Admiral Raborn's downfall at the CIA. That director was gone in only a year.

The President nevertheless used these justifications when meeting with the congressional leadership. That consultation, which did not affect LBJ's decision, was also Hubert Humphrey's first exposure to the matter. President Johnson continued to keep his Vice President in the dark. Humphrey was not in evidence the next day, April 29, when, through several incremental decisions, LBJ expanded the military intervention into a massive operation.

At the Pentagon the wheels were already turning. Secretary McNamara had taken the precaution earlier of examining the existing contingency plans with the Joint Chiefs and Deputy Secretary Cyrus R. Vance. Johnson's decisions on April 29 meant those plans would have to be implemented. The President first determined to commit the entire available Marine force, totaling about two thousand troops of the 4th Marine Expeditionary Brigade. Finally that evening, in a Cabinet Room session between 7:30 and 9:10 P.M., the President ordered in the full 82nd Airborne Division, explicitly basing that action upon the alleged Communist threat.

Far below the exalted heights of the President sat his NSC staff man for Latin America, William Bowdler, a forty-one-year-old naturalized citizen born in Argentina. He had fifteen years' experience with the State Department, and had been stationed at the Havana embassy during the crucial years of the Cuban revolution, 1957 to 1961. He had gained direct experience with the Dominican Republic when on temporary duty there in 1961. The intervention plans LBJ had cooked up smelled like a recipe for charges of Yankee imperialism. Bowdler and a few others, such as State Department desk officer Harry Shlaudeman, began to raise questions about the Dominican decisions.

Such cautionary voices did evoke some responsive chords. On April 29, as LBJ escalated his commitment, aide Bill Moyers and diplomat George Ball called up John Bartlow Martin, a protégé of Adlai Stevenson's, and Tap Bennett's predecessor as ambassador. Moyers and Ball wanted Martin to come down to Washington and consult, so they arranged with Colonel James Cross, the President's military aide, for an Air Force Jet Star executive aircraft to be sent to pick up Martin, who was in Washington by 6:30 A.M. on April 30. He met with Bowdler in the Situation Room and began reviewing the cable traffic. Martin was already too late—four and a half hours earlier the first battalion of United States paratroopers had begun landing at San Isidro air base.

As Martin began consultations in Washington, in the Dominican Republic the intervention gained momentum. Vance and Ball gathered at State's crisis center to monitor the overnight movements. Earlier Vance had vetoed a military proposal for a parachute drop of the 82nd Airborne soldiers, gambling on an unopposed landing at San Isidro. The junta controlled the base and it turned out to be a safe bet. Later the Army discovered its maps had been outdated and inaccurate—there would have been major casualties had an air drop been attempted. Both Marines and Army troops were flown in, some 13,400 during the first week, over 1,000 more later on, with no mishap worse than a blown tire on a C-130 after landing. General Bruce Palmer of the Army commanded the force, which peaked in early May at more than 28,000 troops.

Johnson watched all this closely, frequently going down to the Situation Room to see the latest reports. When Bromley Smith, thinking he could spare LBJ the trouble, told the President the NSC staff would cull Palmer's cables and send the best of them up to him, the gesture went unappreciated. Johnson sent back a note, Smith recalled, that read something like "if you gents don't want to give the President of the United States the information he wants, I'll have to find other ways of acquiring the information I need." In fact, LBJ proved tireless, especially on the telephone—by May 11 he had logged eighty-six calls to Mac Bundy, fifteen to Rusk, twenty-one to McNamara, twenty-eight to Tom Mann, ten to Admiral Raborn, and ten to the Situation Room. Nor was the press ignored: Recipients of Johnson telephone calls or appointments to see him included John Chancellor, Charles Mohr, Mary McGrory, Chalmers Roberts, Harry Reasoner, Cyrus Sulzberger, and Frank Stanton. The President found time for several speeches defending his policy, a televised statement to the nation, sixteen meetings with groups of advisers, three with congressional leaders, twenty-two with individuals. There were a half-dozen one-on-one sessions with Bundy, a late-night visit to McNamara's home, on another day a dinner at home with the secretary of defense. "What I had failed to anticipate," records George Ball, "was President Johnson's increasing absorption in the Dominican problem, to the point where he assumed the direction of day-to-day policy and became, in effect, the Dominican desk officer." Through all this there was never a meeting of the NSC.

One emissary sent to Juan Bosch in Puerto Rico was the President's close friend Abe Fortas, soon to be nominated to the Supreme Court. Fortas kept in touch with George Ball at State using the aliases "Mr. Davidson" and later "Mr. Arnold." Fortas remained in close touch with Johnson as well, to the extent of forty telephone conversations between April 25 and May 11.

John Martin also remembers LBJ running the operation like a State desk officer, and talking to Johnson on the phone at least once, sometimes several times, a day. Prior to May 11, however, according to records compiled by presidential aide Jack Valenti, *none* of LBJ's 225 logged telephone calls were with Martin. The former ambassador perhaps communicated through Mac Bundy, or Valenti's records may be incomplete.

McGeorge Bundy and associates became the American mediators. Martin's best had not been good enough. Taking a leaf from his Panamanian book, in which he had dispatched high-level observers to the Canal Zone, Lyndon Johnson tried a new tack. It was a special mission to the Caribbean island, headed by McGeorge Bundy and Cyrus Vance. Accompanying them were Tom Mann and Jack Vaughn, recently promoted to assistant secretary of state for Latin American affairs. The importance of the mission sharpened after May 13, when Colonel Caamaño's rebels, believing the United States had violated the cease-fire lines, got into a firefight with American troops. General Antonio Imberts Barreras's CEFA troops seized the moment to abrogate the cease-fire themselves and it became a thing of the past. Imbert also ordered an air attack on the rebel radio station, which in fact went instead against the United States embassy. American reporters covering the fighting saw Imbert forces being allowed past United States checkpoints in the demilitarized corridor to attack the constitutionalists.

Bundy's mission made a stop in Puerto Rico where Mac and Vance went off to meet Juan Bosch. As a first step, they were able to get Bosch's agreement to allow a Dominican political figure to stand in for him in a caretaker government that could supervise new elections. Then it was on to Santo Domingo for the tough part. Very closely held, United States officials denied there was any mediation mission at all until a reporter chanced to see Mac sitting behind the desk when he peeked through an embassy window.

Soon after revelation of the mission, the United States announced that Bundy would stay on in the Dominican Republic "indefinitely" until the situation was resolved. Mac began meeting with Silvestre Antonio Guzmán, a surrogate for Bosch, at a little pink house on Calle Benito Monción, and separately with General Imbert. The latter was furious that the Americans would seek his help, then ask him to step down in favor of a provisional government. In his phone calls to Washington, Bundy initially referred to Imbert as "Napoleon," but later switched to "Frankenstein." President Johnson's keeper of the keys also met Colonel Caamaño, who was reluctantly willing to go along with a provisional government under Guzmán.

General Imbert remained the real stumbling block to settlement of the Dominican crisis. The United States could have forced a resolution, but only by putting pressure on Imbert to get him to resign. This Lyndon Johnson was not prepared to do. In less than two weeks Mac Bundy's indefinite mission drew to a close. About the only positive result was enlightenment for Mac, fluent in Spanish, who was able to see both sides up close, shorn of the filters inherent in reading ambassadorial reporting or CIA distillations.

Bundy spoke to reporters on background a week after his arrival; he offered the basic analysis that the Dominican crisis was "an interrupted civil war."

Mac returned to Washington on May 26, his place eventually to be taken by an OAS mission that included Ellsworth Bunker. The mission, or Bunker alone, met with Caamaño some forty-eight times and with Imbert or his representatives fifty-three, finally resulting in a provisional government installed on September 3, 1965.

Lyndon Johnson would always remain sensitive about the Dominican episode, presenting several defenses of his actions and ordering aide Jack Valenti to assemble material on his leadership during the crisis. The President ordered the State Department to prepare a white paper justifying the necessity for intervention. In fact, the crisis opened fissures between Johnson and important political allies, such as Senator J. William Fulbright (D-Ark.) chairman of the Foreign Relations Committee, who charged that the administration had overreacted. The loss of the support of Fulbright and many others would haunt Lyndon Johnson, especially as he endeavored to conduct a war in Southeast Asia. The consequences were significant. The NSC staff had tried to warn its boss, but he had not been willing to listen. Mac Bundy later asked that Bill Bowdler be given a State Department commendation.

LYNDON'S APPARAT

▲▲▲

At the time, most political commentators expected that Lyndon Johnson, unlike John Kennedy, would never be a foreign policy President. Even in retrospect many historians of the era, and even some analysts of national security issues, underestimate the degree to which Johnson involved himself in these affairs. Of course LBJ had set an immense domestic agenda, and dreamed above all of what he came to call the "Great Society," in which poverty would be eradicated and equal opportunities would be open to all races. Johnson also had a lengthy list of legislative projects begun by JFK, now left to him to push through Congress. But Johnson's continuing presence at the NSC table, starting as Vice President, as the Vietnam imbroglio deepened, showed him that in national policy some things had to be done so other things could proceed. Had he any inclination to ignore international issues, it was beaten down during the Panamanian troubles of January 1964, which demonstrated that the lack of a policy could be positively dangerous in international affairs. The Dominican crisis, if nothing else, was an early illustration of just how far Johnson would go in conducting foreign policy business by himself.

Lyndon Johnson's foreign policy role has been underestimated for at least three reasons. The first derives from the accurate perception of Johnson as a political animal. Since Johnson began to prepare for the 1964 election almost immediately after his succession to the presidency, his involvement in foreign affairs was muted during his first year in office. A second reason is that the full record resides in highly classified sources that are only now, to a limited extent, becoming available to scholars. Finally, to some degree Johnson hid his own role by his manner of operation—numerous private conversations, subtle and hidden efforts made to influence the media; playing cards close to the vest, as in his use of Abe Fortas, a private citizen, in the Dominican episode—a by no means isolated instance; finally, his careful restructuring of the NSC and its staff work.

Lyndon's restructuring added to the changes Jack Kennedy had already wrought, creating something Harry Truman would never have dreamed of. Kennedy had changed the relationship of President and NSC staff, making those men expediters of the President's will, lieutenants at a lower level than the keeper of the keys. Now Johnson changed the relationship between President and NSC principals. He did it by creating a new forum for national security decisions, a forum where Johnson called the shots and decided who would attend, unfettered by the exigencies of the National Security Act. The people LBJ selected to come to these meetings, who included the NSC principals from State and the Pentagon, became the President's collaborators in setting policy, almost a cabal to run the government; while undesired voices went unheard. Dean Rusk and Robert McNamara, and their colleagues whom Johnson selected, acquired more power than their Cabinet predecessors had ever had.

There was nothing new, of course, in the device of Oval Office meetings. In fact, the NSC principals had usually met crises in this setting. But Eisenhower and Kennedy's Oval Office meetings had been ad hoc affairs, called to meet the emergency of the moment or to discuss a matter deemed too sensitive to ventilate at the council. Truman and Eisenhower insisted on pushing the daily business of government through the NSC mechanism because that seemed proper for *policy*. Kennedy did the same, not because he had any theory of national security administration, but because the council forum freed him from the routine business so he could focus on the special situations.

Both Ike and JFK had had briefing sessions of the NSC too, and both had tried to do something about the large *size* of meetings, which they no doubt thought related to leaks from the council, but neither set out to emasculate the mechanism. Johnson did, and substituted a forum where, attended by a mere handful of trusted minions, he made the real decisions. He staged the NSC meetings merely to get the bureaucracy to ratify the course he had selected or to implement the programs he had begun. It has often been said that LBJ was a consensus President, that he wanted everyone to agree on the course chosen, but in national security decisions consensus applied to his chosen few. There was plenty of dissension, often reflected at the NSC, among the wider bureaucracy.

Johnson's private forum was the Tuesday Lunch. Sometimes the group did not meet at lunchtime, and sometimes not on Tuesdays, but it did both often enough to acquire that nickname. Dean Rusk, Bob McNamara, and Mac Bundy gathered with the President for the first Tuesday Lunch at 1:00 P.M. on February 4, 1964, when the smoke had barely cleared over the Panama Canal Zone. Actually LBJ was bringing to the White House a practice he had initiated in the Senate, when the participants had been his colleagues and the business of the day the legislative calendar. Johnson would later brag that there had never been a single leak from a Tuesday Lunch.

Lest anyone in the bureaucracy miss the point, in May 1964 LBJ began to schedule his Tuesday Lunches immediately following NSC meetings. In connection with the first of those sessions, that of May 5, Mac Bundy advised his boss that should discussion of the agenda take less than the allotted hour, the principals ought to adjourn to lunch. When the situation in Vietnam began to escalate, starting with the Gulf of Tonkin incident, in August

1964, McNamara presented no more than a brief description at the NSC meeting and the real discussion followed at lunch. The President called a second meeting for the evening, but the Joint Chiefs' execute message to CINCPAC went out *before* the council session. Tuesday Lunch topics typically included Cuba, nuclear weapons production and use, Western Europe, Cyprus, the Dominican crisis, the Indian-Pakistani war over Kashmir, NATO, and nuclear proliferation negotiations with the Soviet Union. Throughout the existence of the Tuesday Lunch, the bread-and-butter item on its agenda remained the Vietnam War.

Much of the government bureaucracy hated the institution of the Tuesday Lunch, though opinions differ as to why. One argument is simply that so many were excluded. Though this view has a certain plausibility, the individuals who *needed* to be there, the NSC principals, *were* there. The true task of the bureaucrats was to inform those principals so they could represent the views of their departments and agencies. Johnson regarded NSC attendance as a reward he could bestow for loyalty, as his treatment of Hubert Humphrey vividly demonstrates, and ultimately the bureaucracy resented him for it.

Detailed study shows that the number who attended the Tuesday Lunches gradually increased over time; members added included the director of central intelligence and Chairman of the Joint Chiefs plus Johnson's personal advisers like Bill Moyers. Bromley Smith thought the lunches one of the most valuable pieces of machinery he had ever encountered. Walt Rostow, soon to become a regular attendee, and Richard Helms of CIA, who only achieved that status much later, agree. Rostow notes: "Clashing, exploratory, or even frivolous views could be expressed with little bureaucratic caution and with confidence no scars would remain."

The other standard complaint is that the lunches left the bureaucracy mystified, that their confidentiality, one of the advantages LBJ perceived, meant that no one knew what decisions were being made. In fact, there were no formal summaries of discussion or minutes. But as soon as they got back to their offices, Rusk, McNamara, and the others would be besieged by their assistants until they described the latest decisions. Since there *were* agendas, and often agency position papers as well, the officials who had prepared the NSC principals could not just be put off. In addition, Bundy and his successor, right after lunch, usually called senior associates at State and the Pentagon to inform them of needed actions. The keepers of the keys did a good deal of doodling on their agenda papers, but they frequently noted significant points or decisions, and they were perfectly capable of reciting those to officials not present. Moreover, Bill Moyers, according to at least one participant, did take notes at the lunches he attended, though they do not figure among Johnson's presidential papers. So did Bromley Smith.

Perhaps the real problem for the bureaucrats was the radical decline in the production of written guidance for the government. Kennedy had approved National Security Action Memoranda (NSAMs) at a rate of about ninety a year. In the five years of his presidency, Lyndon Johnson produced fewer than a hundred NSAMs, for an average of less than nineteen per year. Especially in the later period, many of Johnson's NSAMs were no more than one- or two-paragraph items assigning the highest national priorities to the development or production of particular technologies or weapons systems, as required by budget law. It was really Kennedy rather than Johnson who had been responsible for the change in the character of NSC policy papers. But this combined with Lyndon's downgrading of the council meetings served to befuddle at least some bureaucrats.

In the early weeks of Johnson's administration, Brom Smith began to notice that he had less business. His basic task was to funnel the paper coming to the NSC, to ensure that memos were properly "staffed." Suddenly the flow seemed to be drying up. Smith's antennae went up immediately as he began to suspect the bureaucracy of attempting end runs to the President by by-passing the NSC staff; it was not for nothing that Brom had been executive secretary to Ike's OCB for two years before the advent of Bundy. With the Kennedy staff still in place in the immediate aftermath of the assassination, Smith had good lines into the White House. He set out to see what he could do.

Brom Smith turned out to be partly right but mostly wrong. There had been some minor league pushing at the limits, the kind of testing to be expected with any new Chief Executive. The true reason for the shift, however, was LBJ's preference for the telephone. Smith clarified the lines of authority, then settled back into his work. When the President initiated the Tuesday Lunch mechanism, Smith threw himself into the task of establishing the paperwork—agendas, position papers, and the like—to back them up.

This was typical for Brom Smith, who relished process rather than substance and fancied himself an expert at administrative management. Originally from a small town in Iowa, he had gone to college at Stanford then on to graduate work at the Sorbonne in Paris and the Zimmern Institute in Geneva. In the early 1950s he became an adviser to NATO headquarters under General Eisenhower, then returned to Washington as a member of State's Policy Planning Staff. Soon afterward, with Ike in the White House, Bobby Cutler hired Brom for the NSC staff, and in 1959 the President appointed him executive secretary of the Operations Coordinating Board. As a concession to OCB fans when the board was abolished, Mac Bundy selected Smith for executive secretary of the full council once JFK entered office.

Mac had originally thought Brom's job ought to be eliminated, but it was too much for Bundy to lead NSC discussions while also attempting to follow them for the purpose of maintaining the record. Smith did that happily. A few months later, amid extensive informal discussions among the NSC staff of which portfolios to assume, Mac was a little puzzled to discover that Brom considered himself fully employed without having any substantive area of expertise. Over time though, the utility of an administrative manager became evident to Bundy, who was freed from having to follow the progress of paperwork. Mac's successor agreed, calling Smith "knowledgeable, wise, wholly discreet, and reliable."

Bromley Smith would stay on through both the Kennedy and Johnson administrations, living in Georgetown near Dean Acheson. Smith was almost certainly one of the first sounding boards for Acheson's throaty critique of the Cuban missile crisis decision making. Though himself rather conservative, such experiences failed to quench Brom's appetite for serving on the NSC staff. In 1965, as a matter of fact, Mac Bundy got it into his head that Smith might be ready for a change, and talked to Dean Rusk about finding him a suitable ambassadorship. As soon as he heard about it, Smith accosted Bundy to protest that his wife, an architect, was in the middle of several important projects and could not possibly leave. Indeed Brom was still in the Executive Office Building when Henry Kissinger returned to town three years later.

Thus Brom Smith made the transition from Kennedy to Johnson without skipping a beat. Mac Bundy did too, though perhaps he got some help from the family Democrat, older brother Bill. Since his CIA days in the early 1950s, William P. Bundy and his wife had been close friends of William White and James Rowe, journalists who were similarly close to LBJ. The elder Bundy's children played with White's, while Bill saw LBJ and Lady Bird once or twice a year at dinner with the Whites.

Bill Bundy knew how to talk to Lyndon Johnson, and he was friends with LBJ intimates, including the redoubtable Harry C. McPherson. Thus Bill was both a valued source of advice for Mac Bundy and an alternate channel for communication with the President, when LBJ put Mac in the doghouse. That there were such moments was inevitable given Johnson's essence and style.

Lyndon Johnson delighted in shaking things up, subtly testing his people, serious or teasing by turns. One of LBJ's favorite tests was to receive a staffer in the bathroom as the President performed his personal functions and observe the reaction. Johnson later described the scene to speechwriter Richard N. Goodwin, calling Mac "one of the delicate Kennedyites," recalling that Bundy had tried to stand as far off as he could, and kept turning away so that he could barely be heard. When LBJ asked Bundy to come closer, Mac tried to walk backward toward the President sitting on the toilet, until Johnson thought Mac might fall into his lap. The President told Goodwin it had been "ludicrous" and that it had made him wonder "how that man had made it so far in the world."

But the test was only a test, one Goodwin himself had assertedly passed, not a reflection of LBJ's real opinion of Mac Bundy. Indeed, Goodwin's story is apparently influenced by animosity that grew between himself and Mac, once friends. They had drifted apart during Kennedy's last year, and

Goodwin never forgave Mac a crack made during the Dominican affair. Bundy's humor could be cutting. On the day of decision Goodwin was summoned to the Cabinet Room, shortly after LBJ's orders to intervene. Hurrying down the West Wing steps and up the corridor past the Oval Office, Goodwin ran into Mac, who told him the President had just ordered Marines flown into Santo Domingo. Goodwin was appalled and asked if anything could be done to stop them.

Mac replied, "They're already in the air."

"But why the Marines?" Goodwin then asked. "Why not the Army?"

Bundy said nothing about the Army also having been ordered to the scene. Moments later in the Cabinet Room, Goodwin heard Bundy joke with other participants, "You know what Goodwin says? He wants to know if we can send someone else besides the Marines!"

A couple of weeks later, as Goodwin recounts it, it was Mac who was the butt of a cruelty. According to Goodwin, Bill Moyers called him up at midnight one night and spoke in worried tones of the President's sanity, his weirdness that day, and his apparent inhumanity. It turned out Moyers had entered the Oval Office to find LBJ clutching an item from the press ticker that said Bundy was going to appear in a nationally televised teach-in on the Vietnam War to oppose the views of five other professors and present the administration position.

"I never gave him permission," LBJ thundered. "That's an act of disloyalty. He didn't tell me because he knew I didn't want him to do it."

The President then ordered Moyers to tell Mac that LBJ would be "mighty pleased" to accept his resignation. Moyers ignored Johnson's orders, did nothing, and the following morning LBJ merely grunted when Moyers informed him of the omission.

Bundy, who absented himself from the teach-in, instead sent a long message read to the audience that acknowledged the sincerity of opponents of the war, has admitted that he made the original engagement without checking first with the President. Not only that but Mac had ordered extensive preparatory work by the NSC staff, including negotiations with teach-in organizers, position papers, and lengthy dissections of the views of prominent opponents like Hans J. Morgenthau.

Scholars have found it difficult to believe that Bundy would have taken a step like this on his own. In fact, there are some reasons to suppose it possible. Johnson required his NSC staff to report daily on their contacts with the media, with details of what was said to whom and in what context. The President often included these memoranda in his evening reading. Johnson used the knowledge to shape the face his administration presented to the public. According to senior NSC staffers, LBJ encouraged rather than discouraged such contacts.

Moreover, Johnson was then preparing to make a series of major decisions on Vietnam and needed all the support he could get. Implicit in the invitation to Bundy was an opportunity to try to nip the opposition in the bud. The President apparently thought he could deny credibility to the opposition by refusing to debate it. It was an early illustration of LBJ's failure to comprehend that the antiwar movement was acquiring momentum that only major political accommodation could meet.

Johnson's anger at Bundy was real but, like most of his tantrums, short-lived. Still, it was good that Bill Moyers had been there to deflect the first rush. Without the title, Moyers served LBJ as chief of staff and even press secretary. He had a significant role in national security matters, in particular staff assignments where they impacted upon the larger White House staff, or on matters thought to have political overtones.

In 1954, "Billy Don" had been a sophomore college student studying journalism in Lady Bird Johnson's hometown. He applied for a summer job with Senator Johnson, then the minority leader. First in the basement addressing envelopes, then in the office drafting replies to mail, Moyers impressed LBJ and was soon at his desk listening to the wisdom of the great man. Moyers went on to complete his journalism degree at the University of Texas, did some graduate work at Edinburgh in Scotland, and then, feeling the calling, earned a bachelor's degree with honors from the Southwestern Baptist Bible College in Phoenix. In 1960 he returned to Lyndon as personal assistant during the breathless presidential campaign year, then was rewarded with a primary role in creating the Peace Corps, perhaps the most exciting government initiative of the time.

When Johnson succeeded to the presidency, Moyers was one of the first people brought in as a special assistant. There he had top billing among eight aides holding this title, and was listed as "general assistant to the President on a wide variety of matters with particular emphasis on foreign policy." If anything, these responsibilities only increased during Moyers's time in the West Wing. By early 1965 he was handling sensitive press matters and cooperations with Mac Bundy on the preparation of a State Department white paper justifying the Dominican intervention. The President himself, writing in pencil or crayon in his large script, routed copies of relevant papers to Moyers. Similarly, Moyers worked with Bundy, and General Goodpaster (who was sent to sound out Dwight Eisenhower), on drafting a reply to a Republican white paper on Vietnam. It was finally decided that the Republican paper was so poor that no response was needed.

In 1966, the year of Mac Bundy's departure, Moyers reached full stride in his foreign policy involvement. Johnson ordered that Moyers receive copies of all important memos and cables "which pass to him in the international field." When NSC staffers Chester L. Cooper and James Thomson left, Moyers, though pronouncing himself hesitant to intervene, expressed personal interest in ensuring the high quality of their successors. He similarly prodded Bundy's successor to bring Nathaniel Davis to the staff to cover United Nations and African issues.

Vietnam was and remained a major substantive interest for Billy Don, and would be the final reason for his parting. Walt Rostow consulted him in the summer of 1966 on bombing North Vietnam. Indeed Moyers had been one of the most effective voices arguing for a bombing halt around Christmas of 1965 to explore chances for opening negotiations. At one of those meetings Mac Bundy, referring to LBJ, had turned to Moyers and whispered, "I'll bet you five dollars that he'll never go for it."

An example of Moyers's influence was a dispute over the approved list of bombing targets in North Vietnam. This fight occurred at a Tuesday Lunch and concerned bombing oil facilities. Moyers learned of the agenda item only at the last moment. His assistant discovered a new CIA report on oil targets, concluding that previous bombings of this type had been ineffective. The assistant skimmed the report, noted the key points, and ran from the OEOB to the White House, handing the note to Moyers just as he stepped into the elevator. Moyers prevailed that day and the targets stayed off the approved list.

Moyers's gambit to save Mac Bundy was not the only time he intervened to insulate key staffers from LBJ's ire. There is another story that is told, an earlier one, in which Moyers takes his President by the arm and walks the shouting man completely out of the room saying, "We've had enough of this. You're wasting all of our time." When someone asked Bill how he had had the nerve to do that, Moyers replied, "It's easy—I'd rather be in the Peace Corps!"

As time went on, however, Moyers realized that the Peace Corps was not the place to be. If he really wanted to change conditions for his fellow man, to affect policy, to bring a Christian perspective to power, the place to be was right in the White House. Bill Moyers needed the job that McGeorge Bundy held.

RITES OF PASSAGE

▲▲▲

Nineteen sixty-five was an exhausting year, sparked alternately by Vietnam and the Dominican Republic. Bundy had had a tough time advocating the bombing halt in Vietnam, an occasion on which he had sided with Moyers. There had also been his trip to Vietnam, unexpectedly putting him on the front lines, plus the mediation mission to Santo Domingo. The controversial Dominican intervention put even more pressure on the national security adviser. Two senators on the Foreign Relations Committee led a move that summer to make Bundy testify even though one of them, Republican Wayne Morse of Oregon, "at least knows better than to expect that a White House Staff officer will ever come to a formal Committee hearing." Attempting to forestall any formal confrontation, Mac spoke to some of the interested parties, including committee chairman Bill Fulbright, whom he told that if it was a matter of an "informal talk" he would be at their service. When Bundy reported that to the President, LBJ first intervened with one of the dissident senators, then scribbled on the memo, in his best crayon style: "I would go very slow on this. . . . We are asking for trouble."

Indeed the Dominican affair proved no end of trouble. Gordon Chase, Mac's personal aide, heard as much while on an expedition to Cambridge to arrange details for a teach-in at Harvard. On a Saturday walk, Chase encountered none other than Carl Kaysen on the street. The two chatted for about ten minutes. Kaysen warned that around Cambridge even people who considered themselves Johnson supporters felt the United States' performance in the Dominican Republic to be a "disturbing sign," along with Vietnam, of the President's "impetuosity." When Chase tried to defend the action, Kaysen complained that it had been "horribly mismanaged," and finally came down to the thought that LBJ had been poorly advised by his generals and had sent in too many Marines too quickly.

Johnson relented after the fiasco with the national teach-in, and allowed Mac to debate at the Harvard session. Bundy did all right, or perhaps too well. Soon there were other speaking invitations in addition, including one to appear with Arkansas Democrat Wilbur Mills in his home county. Mac forswore public speaking.

More substantive for Bundy was a quiet meeting at the end of July with Sir Burke Trend, the secretary to the British cabinet, his opposite number in the British governmental system. The British were worried about the international liquidity of their currency, the pound sterling, and wanted American help in the financial markets if a run on the pound occurred. At the same time, Great Britain was refusing to follow the American lead in Vietnam. What Mac wanted to tell Trend, he wrote LBJ, "is that a British Brigade in Vietnam would be worth a billion dollars at the moment of truth for Sterling." Johnson forbade any such pressure tactics, however, and Bundy carefully kept separate his talks with Trend on Vietnam and on the pound.

After two years, Bundy was feeling the absence of a deputy. On September 14, 1965, he recommended Johnson appoint not one but *two* deputies— Bob Komer and Francis Bator. Komer was flourishing, even more so than he had under Kennedy. Bundy called him "a tiger for work" with "a temperament which allows him to bounce back easily when his advice is not taken . . . the kind of staff officer one dreams of and seldom finds." Mac thought Komer one of the handful of men in government on whom LBJ could depend for advice in a crisis. The need for Bator's promotion was less pressing, but Mac felt it desirable to have a deputy for economics. At forty, another Cambridge man (a professor on leave from Harvard with a doctorate from MIT), Bundy considered Bator "probably the best all-around international economist in the Government."

A serious headache that weighed on Bundy was the lack of a China expert at a high enough level in the State Department to be able to speak at NSC meetings. It was especially galling in that the People's Republic of China was in the throes of its Cultural Revolution and spiraling away from the Soviet orbit. Bundy recommended Johnson appoint Edwin O. Reischauer as a senior adviser to Rusk. Reischauer was a Harvard academic then serving as ambassador to Japan, but his appointment was only a partial solution in that he was expert on Japan rather than China.

The lack was less serious on Bundy's staff, which at least had James C. Thomson, Jr., whom some thought one of the country's leading China hands. Thomson had been born in China, of American missionary stock, in 1931. His childhood encompassed some of the most turbulent years in China's history, and he had returned there for the watershed year 1948– 1949, when the communists triumphed and created the People's Republic. Thomson got to the NSC only about a month before the Gulf of Tonkin incidents and the consequent major escalations in Vietnam. He divided his time between Southeast Asia, on which he worked with Chester Cooper, and his first love, China.

Looking for a China watcher was one of Mac Bundy's last tasks on the NSC staff. On November 7, 1965, John McCloy, in the name of Henry Ford and the Ford Foundation, offered Mac the presidency of that institution.

After consultations with Rusk and McNamara, Mac determined to leave the administration at the end of February. By early December, Bundy was quietly feeding LBJ memos on an announcement of his resignation, which was soon to be forthcoming from Moyers. He also gave Rusk a paper outlining the work of the NSC staff and the people comprising it, and met with the President on December 2 to discuss the management of the staff and possible successors. In mid-February, Mac went ahead and designated Bob Komer as interim replacement until Johnson made up his mind on a successor. Bundy was gone to the Ford Foundation on March 1, 1966.

Bundy's departure set up a brief run by the Chicagoan, Robert W. Komer. It easily might not have been. Like Bundy himself, Komer had grown increasingly restless during LBJ's first year. In early 1965 there could have been a change: Robert McNamara wanted Komer to come to the Pentagon as deputy to Assistant Secretary of Defense John McNaughton. Mac was inclined to let Komer switch: Men should move around from time to time, service on his staff was too anonymous given that "unfortunately, the term 'NSC staff' has no real weight in the government." Komer himself scotched the idea of the Pentagon job. Sent to Tel Aviv to do a quiet chore for Lyndon Johnson, on a matter concerning exports of American tanks from West Germany to Israel, Komer did so well that he re-energized himself, and impressed LBJ and Bundy in the bargain.

Bob Komer was ready to be the President's national security adviser and had always relished his work as an expediter on the NSC staff. He had his things moved from the Executive Office Building to Mac's office in the West Wing. He began to take personal care of LBJ's NSC paperwork, and arranged a meeting between Johnson and senior foreign policy advisers no longer in government, the so-called Wise Men, that occurred on March 11. It was a sequel to a session Bundy had arranged in February, and indeed marked Mac's first appearance as a member of the Wise Men.

Komer transacted one very important piece of business in conjunction with General Maxwell Taylor, newly returned to Washington as a consultant to LBJ. The President had put Taylor to work on a scheme for improving coordination of affairs within the bureaucracy, along lines of how ambassadors ran their country teams. The result was a subcabinet committee similar to the Special Group (303 Committee) for intelligence. Taylor prepared and Komer shepherded the directive, NSAM-341. President Johnson signed it on March 2, and brought Taylor to a Cabinet meeting to explain it a couple of days later.

Johnson's order set up a Senior Interdepartmental Group (SIG) under chairmanship of the undersecretary of state. Members were the national security adviser, deputy secretary of defense, Chairman of the JCS, director of central intelligence, and administrator of AID. The chairman would have the right to make actual decisions on issues that came before the SIG, except that members had the right of appeal to the President. The SIG would be the top group, backed up by regional interdepartmental groups at the assistant secretary level. The new structure aimed at reducing the workload for the President, who would not have to deal with the more routine matters that SIG could handle.

What Johnson did not tell his Cabinet when they met with him on March 4, possibly because he may not have realized it himself, was that creation of SIG marked a step back to the more structured NSC of Eisenhower's period. It was an acknowledgment, if one was needed, that the freewheeling Kennedy system required extra work precisely because basic policy was not preset and implementation not formally included.

There could be no better illustration than Vietnam; LBJ had continually felt forced to set up ad hoc groups among the bureaucracy to grease its creaking gears for activity in the field. Simultaneous with NSAM-341, LBJ faced this necessity anew. There had been a succession of groups on Vietnam policy but never a White House office. Lyndon's thoughts turned in that direction, and to Komer, whose crisp style and tremendous energy he felt might be ideal for the task. Without an inkling, Komer sat in his West Wing office doing Bundy's work and expecting to succeed him. President Johnson made Komer a special assistant, but for Vietnam rather than national security affairs. His place would be parallel to but separate from that of the national security adviser. A senior foreign service officer, William K. Leonhart, was drafted to second him.

The national security job suddenly fell vacant for the second time in less than a month. Jack Valenti, a political aide whom Bundy, McNamara, and occasionally Rusk used to communicate during times of difficulty with the President, came through now with the suggestion that LBJ name Brom Smith as caretaker. Brom was so much the manager type, Valenti argued, as clearly not to be in line to be Bundy's successor, and would meanwhile do a crackerjack job on NSC business. Then there was Bill Moyers, a man with a real national security role who aspired to a greater one. Valenti put in a good word for Moyers too, at moments he judged the time ripe, but the President would not have it, snorting that Moyers lacked experience and background for the job.

Lyndon Johnson told Valenti he was leaning toward Walt Rostow as national security adviser. When John Kenneth Galbraith learned of it, he called Valenti for an urgent appointment, then laid out reasons why he felt Walt not appropriate for the NSC slot. Clearly LBJ's choice was going to be a victory for a different kind of bureaucrat, less like such expediters as Komer and more like the keepers of Eisenhower's day, men who took a longer view. At least it seemed that way, for LBJ was choosing from a little unit that fancied itself the State Department complement to the NSC staff, a unit that had been around since Harry Truman's time, something called the Policy Planning Council.

In May 1947 the Policy Planning Staff (PPS) was established under George F. Kennan, the author of "containment" policy and regarded as one of the most brilliant thinkers in the foreign service. The PPS had specific respon-

159

sibility for formulating long-term programs to attain United States foreign policy goals, anticipating problems the State Department could encounter, coordinating planning efforts throughout the department, evaluating current policies, and preparing reports as requested by the NSC.

In practice the PPS had wide-ranging interests in many areas of policy during its early years, including some operational roles. One of the lesser known was handling State Department approval and oversight of CIA covert operations. Another was liaison with senior planners at the Department of Defense on military contingency plans, as well as representing State on the NSC senior staff. Kennan's successor, Paul H. Nitze, had had important roles in such NSC policy papers as NSC-68, NSC-114, and NSC-141, while Kennan himself played a pivotal role in the formalization of containment in the NSC-20 series. The PPS continued to play this role under the Eisenhower administration, during which its director sat with the NSC Planning Board.

John Foster Dulles nevertheless wrought important changes in the PPS, and incurred the lasting wrath of Paul Nitze, dismissing him while telling him all the while how good a job he had done and how there was little with which to disagree in the Truman-Acheson policies, which Foster had attacked vociferously in public.

"As for the work you fellows have been doing," Dulles said, "I think that it is most important work. But I don't think it should be done under the State Department but under the aegis of the National Security Council."

Dulles initially thought he would spend 90 percent of his time at the NSC. The area bureaus at State meanwhile guarded closely their own prerogatives of making and executing policy. That the PPS was not entirely submerged in this flow was a credit to Bobby Cutler and Ike's other keepers, who saw the staff as a useful body for initial drafts of policy papers. Robert R. Bowie, Foster's first PPS director, also helped win back the secretary with a stream of advice during the numerous duels at the brink of that era. Gerard C. Smith succeeded Bowie in 1957 when the latter returned to Harvard.

The Jackson subcommittee was critical of the poor standing of the PPS, which possibly owed something to the fact that Dorothy Fosdick, Jackson's top foreign policy aide, who was then the only woman ever to have worked for PPS, had also been let go during Foster Dulles's first year. When John Kennedy entered office, Rusk replaced Smith with his personal choice, George McGhee, while elevating the unit to the Policy Planning Council (PPC). Walt Rostow, until then deputy national security adviser, became chairman of the council when McGhee moved up to departmental counselor.

Rostow did his best to enhance the standing of the PPC, getting it a military liaison officer from the Joint Chiefs, for the first time, plus certain State perquisites that had been lacking. But the job was a tough one, not least because of Kennedy's preoccupation with daily policy. In particular the new institution of NSAMs, short snappy orders, to replace NSC policy papers removed one of the PPC's main functions—helping to draft extensive statements of American goals and methods of attaining them.

So the PPC remained something of a backwater. Ambitious Foreign Service officers avoided it. A typical example was Rostow's first executive secretary, John W. Ford, who escaped in 1964 to the United States mission at the OAS. But Walt did his best to recruit able, talented staff. On one occasion he brought in a promising fellow, an aide to a senior man, and gave his recruiting pitch. The prospect wanted to know more about the scope of the job. Walt turned to the large globe standing on the floor of his office, gave it a twirl in its frame, and began to speak of America's global responsibilities. It reminded the prospect of nothing so much as the scene in Charlie Chaplin's classic comedy film *The Great Dictator* in which the actor stakes out territorial ambitions of the megalomaniacal dictator. The aide rejected Rostow's job offer.

Nevertheless, over time Rostow built the staff, slowly, painstakingly, with people he had tested and was sure of. It included Bob Johnson, an NSC staffer who'd come with him from the beginning. Later additions were his deputy, Henry Owen; Colonel Robert Ginsburgh, the council's second military detailee; Howard R. Wriggins, an academic expert on South Asia; and Zbigniew Brzezinski, the Columbia University Russian expert whom Walt got to come down on sabbatical. Others moved in and out of the circle as well, but it was noticeable that many of them came from academia rather than the foreign service.

Rostow himself published a paper called "The Planning of Foreign Policy" in October 1963 in the journal *Foreign Affairs*. In it Walt justified his PPC recipe and proposed, as a long-range planning initiative, an effort to determine if détente between the United States and Soviet Union was possible. A 1964 PPC report listed potential responses to forty-four foreseeable crises, and drew attention to the Sino-Soviet split that was becoming increasingly evident.

The PPC's role grew with the advent of Lyndon Johnson, who wanted ideas on foreign policy to match his notions of the Great Society. Generating pithy little think pieces was a Rostow specialty; indeed Walt's desire for work like that had been a major reason he had wanted the PPC job in the first place. The council also developed a larger formal role as a result of NSAM-281, approved by LBJ on February 11, 1964, which provided for comprehensive national policy papers more in the style of the Eisenhower NSC papers. The secretary of state was to be in charge of this process, and Rusk delegated the responsibility to his PPC chairman. Still, this role remained limited since only about twenty national policy papers were approved through the remainder of Johnson's administration.

Rostow had an office near Dean Rusk's but little discernible influence upon the secretary of state. Walt fulminated about the need for more aggressive policy in Laos, then Vietnam, holding forth at long kibbitzing sessions in the evenings after work. For about a year, while he ran one of

LBJ's Vietnam task forces, Mike Forrestal also had a seventh-floor State Department office. Forrestal often joined Walt's sessions to hear him out, not as a sympathizer but to explore the depth of Rostow's commitment.

Rostow was not a man to confine himself to working the fringes of policy. He wanted to be in the thick of the fray, and if the action was not at PPC, he was prepared to insert himself where it was. Thus Rostow forged links with Johnson's speechwriters, working on drafts of foreign policy speeches and passing along a stream of his think pieces. Johnson called upon Walt more and more often, and it was to satisfy this demand for ideas that LBJ appointed Walt W. Rostow his special assistant for national security affairs.

▲ John Kennedy and his military advisers at the White House, January 3, 1962. *Left to right:*
Lyndon Johnson, Kennedy, Robert S. McNamara, Maxwell D. Taylor as special military
representative, Roswell Gilpatric. (Kennedy Library)

▲ The press of national security business: McGeorge Bundy handles urgent papers as President Kennedy walks from his limousine, June 13, 1962. (Kennedy Library)

▲ The advisers in crisis: On the South Portico of the White House at the height of the Cuban Missile Crisis, Bundy converses with a group from the EX COM, October 29, 1962. *Left to right:* Bundy, two unidentified, Maxwell Taylor as chairman of the Joint Chiefs, Robert McNamara partly obscured by column. (Kennedy Library)

▲ The only portrait of the Kennedy National Security Council is one taken during the Cuban crisis on October 29, 1962. President Kennedy sits flanked by Dean Rusk and Robert McNamara. Paul Nitze is at the head of the Cabinet Room conference table. Robert Kennedy and George Ball are visible in front of the vacant easels. (Kennedy Library)

▲ Planning the Vietnam War: President Johnson with his NSC and most of the Joint Chiefs on January 29, 1966. Johnson, McNamara, Cyrus Vance, and, across the table, Hubert H. Humphrey watch intently as Chester Cooper changes the easel display. Dean Rusk reads briefing papers, his head partly obscuring General Earle Wheeler beyond. Bromley Smith and Mac Bundy sit at the far end, and Richard Helms of the CIA at the near end of the Cabinet table. Backbenchers beneath the portrait of Franklin Delano Roosevelt include William Colby of the CIA, Max Taylor, General David C. Jones, Admiral Wesley MacDonald, and General Wallace Greene. (Johnson Library)

▲ President Johnson meets his NSC staff assembled in the Cabinet Room, May 27, 1966. *Clockwise, starting from the end of the table to LBJ's right:* Jim Thomson, Brom Smith, Walt Rostow, LBJ, Francis Bator, Ulric Haynes, obscured staffer watching the President speak, Bill Jorden, partly obscured Hubert Humphrey, Chuck Johnson, Peter Jessup, Howard Wriggins, William Bowdler. *Against the wall, left to right:* Ed Hamilton, Bob Komer, Art McCafferty, Hal Saunders, Don Ropa, and Colonel Robert Bowman. Beyond the Cabinet table the exhibits on the easels are keeping score for LBJ's drive to get his officials to buy U.S. Savings Bonds. (Johnson Library)

▲ The same scene looking the other way: Haynes is now clearly visible; the man at the opposite end of the table is revealed as Henry Rowen. Spurgeon Keeny sits between Bill Jorden and Vice President Humphrey. (Johnson Library)

▲ LBJ makes a point in a meeting with Robert Komer's staff for the "other war" in Vietnam, July 18, 1966. *Left to right:* Komer (facing the president), William Leonhart (also facing LBJ), Norman Getsinger, Colonel Robert Montague, Richard Holbrooke, Robert Nathan (an economist and consultant to Komer), John Sylvester. (Johnson Library)

▲ The President in Council thrashes out issues associated with the Nuclear Non-proliferation Treaty in preparation for the United Nations General Assembly, September 15, 1966. Included in the session were Hubert Humphrey, William C. Foster, Richard Helms, Farris Bryant, George Ball, Arthur Goldberg, Joseph Barr, Leonard Marks, Bill Moyers, Walt Rostow, Brom Smith, George Christian, Joe Sisco. (Johnson Library)

▲ Lyndon Johnson bites the bullet and determines to order a bombing halt, March 27, 1968. LBJ pays rapt attention as General Earle Wheeler makes a point. General Creighton Abrams, MACV deputy commander, sits to Wheeler's left. (Johnson Library)

▲ Dawn of a presidency: Richard Nixon with Henry Kissinger and William P. Rogers at Key Biscayne, February 10, 1969. (Nixon Library Project)

▲ Nixon's first NSC meeting, January 21, 1969. *Left to right:* Henry Kissinger, Andrew J. Goodpaster, David Kennedy, Vice President Spiro Agnew, Brigadier-General George A. Lincoln, Richard Helms, Elliot Richardson, William Rogers, Nixon, Melvin Laird, General Earle Wheeler. (Nixon Library Project)

▲ Getting rid of an old soldier: Nixon with Averell Harriman in the Oval Office, February 20, 1969. (Nixon Library Project)

THE MAN OF IDEAS

▲▲▲

Rostow was born the second son of a Russian-Jewish immigrant family in New York City on October 7, 1916. With an admirable sense of direction, at age seventeen in 1933 Walt Whitman Rostow decided the purpose of his life would be to construct a grand combination of economic theory and history. That purpose he carried across many stages and through many years, and indeed returned to it after the national security years were over. At first, though, he carried his purpose through three years at Yale and then selection, at twenty, as a Rhodes Scholar. Then it was on to Balliol College at Oxford from 1936 to 1938, and a Yale Ph.D. in 1940.

The Oxford years were formative ones for the young Rostow. It could hardly be otherwise in the run up to World War II, in England where Walt had a front seat to witness the rising confrontation. Brought up on the gloomy literature of World War I, works such as *Journey's End* and *What Price Glory,* Rostow was in the thick of the heated British debate over what to do about rising fascism in Adolf Hitler's Germany. He listened to Nancy Astor at Cliveden, arguing that capitalism would inevitably be destroyed if England fought Hitler; to United States ambassador Joseph Kennedy, JFK's father, who also took a cautious view; to pro-German William Joyce (later a Nazi broadcaster known as Lord Haw Haw) describe Nazi doctrine at Carfax. Walt also heard Winston Churchill at the Oxford Union advocate an alliance with the Soviet Union. As his sojourn drew to a close, the British and French agreed with Hitler at Munich upon the dismemberment of Czechoslovakia, and war followed soon afterward. It became an article of faith among much of the World War II generation that accommodation with an adversary ("Munich") was but an invitation to aggression. This doctrine applied without reference to nationalism, social forces, or local issues, and contributed mightily to the following cold war confrontations of the 1950s and 1960s and helped fuel the Vietnam imbroglio. Following Oxford and the 1939–1945 war, Walt Rostow was an almost prototypical exponent of the Munich analogy. In Johnson's administration he would find kindred light in Secretary of State Dean Rusk.

After Pearl Harbor, Walt joined the Office of Strategic Services (OSS), working for its renowned research and analysis branch on studies of the

Soviet economy, demonstrating that the Russians had the wherewithal to stand up to the German invasion of that nation.

A budding intelligence analyst, Rostow was soon seconded to the U.S. Army Air Force, then preparing for a campaign of massive strategic bombing of Germany. One of the great controversies in that bombing campaign centered upon the relative effectiveness of attacks upon German petroleum stocks and refineries, versus such target systems as transportation or war industry. Rostow emerged from the war convinced that if the bombing had only focused sooner on the petroleum targets, Germany's defeat would have been speeded. The World War II bombing controversies would have their echo in the Vietnam conflict.

With the war's end Walt taught American history at Oxford and turned his inaugural lecture into his first publication, *The American Diplomatic Revolution*. He returned to the United States to teach at MIT, and when the CIA provided MIT with funds to establish a Center for International Studies at that institution under economist and former agency analyst Max Millikan, Rostow joined up. He also began consulting for Ike's National Security Council.

The NSC and CIA connections gave Walt a sense of effectiveness, of involvement in policy, of movement and excitement at a perfect pitch. "I don't pose as a philosopher," he told a reporter in 1960. "I'm a working stiff."

But the connections also served as counterweight to troublesome allegations in turbulent times. With loyalty hearings and McCarthyism, a man, like Rostow, who felt social responsibility, could be suspect, as in fact happened to Mac Bundy's brother Bill, who at that time worked for the CIA. Bill Bundy had done no more than contribute some money to causes the McCarthyites considered questionable, Rostow had worked for a real Socialist, Myrdal, and openly consorted with liberal Democrats. Walt had an aunt, Sarah Rosenbaum, of another Russian émigré family that had come to America about 1900, who for a time actually ran a Marxist bookstore in Washington, D.C. In an era of guilt by association it was fortunate the McCarthyites became discredited and their movement ran out of steam before any serious allegations appeared against Rostow.

Rostow joined John Kennedy's brain trust as early as 1957, when Kennedy staffer and former Harvard instructor Fred Holborn asked Walt to contribute ideas for a planned speech on aid to India. The project helped Rostow crystallize his thinking on economic growth and underdevelopment, an area in which he had been interested since the early 1950s. At a conference in Moscow in the spring of 1959 Rostow delivered a lecture on "The Stages of Economic Growth" which he published in the Luce magazine *Fortune* that December and appeared as a book length treatise in 1960. Published by Cambridge University Press, the full length in 1960, *The Stages of Economic Growth*, not only became Rostow's best-known work but supplied Jack Kennedy with the phrase "new frontiers." Perhaps grudging Walt his numerous publications or his ability with wife Elspeth to produce literary stars for their parties, some felt Walt was a social climber. The truth is more complex. Walt was a man of ideas and he gladly shared them with people who might be interested. When people *were* interested, as was John Kennedy in "new frontiers," ideas could lead very far indeed.

So Rostow arrived in Washington on JFK's heels, permanently this time rather than as a consultant. Most of his work on the NSC staff centered on foreign aid, a natural portfolio given his background, and on counter-insurgency, a subject on which Rostow's MIT center had been doing considerable work in the late 1950s. Rostow's visit to Fort Bragg and speech to the Special Forces in the spring of 1961, a sort of combination of stages of growth with guerrilla warfare theory, became famous among Green Beret enthusiasts, but Walt spent at least as much time on foreign aid questions. At State in the early months, George Ball received a constant stream of phone calls from Rostow demanding that more aid be included for this or that worthwhile cause.

Rostow was high in the Andes Mountains, meeting with South American officials on economic matters in February 1966, when he received a summons to join the President in Honolulu, where Johnson had gone for a top-level conference on progress in Vietnam. It was all very subtle—LBJ offered no job, simply felt Rostow out about his work and his ideas about national security policy. On March 31, Bill Moyers, showing no hint of his own disappointment, announced the appointment of Walt Rostow as special assistant for national security affairs.

In keeping with his penchant for ideas, one of Rostow's first acts was to solicit fresh ones from the NSC staff. Different people saw Walt's request differently. Some, such as Don Ropa, a CIA detailee and junior man under Chet Cooper, took the opportunity to propose relatively limited measures. Ropa suggested a division of labor on the staff between Southeast Asia on the one hand, and China plus North Asia on the other. Ropa volunteered to take the former area under the staff's senior Far East man if the proposal was adopted. Instead, Rostow asked him to prepare an analysis of forces at work in the United States relationship with China. Ropa was no China hand; he had served in Vietnam, Laos, and Indonesia and had had temporary postings in four other Southeast Asian cities. One assignment on Taiwan was the full extent of his China experience. Any Ropa report on China would be that of a neophyte, which was exactly what Walt wanted, a fresh look that might generate new ideas.

Others had broader visions of what might be done with the staff. Harold Saunders was one of those. For years since coming to the NSC staff under Kennedy, Hal had worked in the shadow of Bob Komer. He was the solid and capable detail man whose work made Komer's adroit maneuvers possible. Saunders's bottom line, which he communicated to Rostow, was that wherever the staff had two people laboring in the same area, both needed their own contact with the boss and parts of the problem to work on, in essence creating a vertical division of labor rather than a horizontal one. Otherwise, Saunders noted, "the junior member ends up getting only the crumbs that fall from the senior's table." Rostow did not immediately promote Saunders, even though Komer had left the Near East and South Asia section of the staff, but he did give Hal his wish—the new senior man would focus on South Asia while Saunders concentrated on the Middle East.

Saunders's idea of a vertical division of labor was a good one, but it was only part of an even larger concept of the nature and function of the NSC staff that he passed to Walt. Hal argued that members had to be more than "staff" in the pure sense of that role; they had to become advocates and be ready to "wrestle certain decisions into the White House." To do that, "here at the top, planner and operator must become one." The staff had to know the President's thinking, take part in the "town's debate" around Washington, and be in touch with the frontiers of thinking outside the government. That would enable the staff to frame decisions for the President in the broadest perspective, illuminating his real choices and their consequences; to simplify the later choice by injecting the President's viewpoint at an early stage; and to generate new initiatives and concepts so as "to spark the imagination of experts everywhere." The memo was a model statement of roles and missions for the NSC staff, one that Brom Smith laconically marked "Good Memo"; it presented a concept followed by Rostow and every succeeding keeper of the keys.

While Saunders may have had good ideas, he had to wait another year for the senior Near East and South Asia slot on the staff. Rostow instead gave that job to Howard Wriggins, whom he brought over from State.

Wriggins was not the only one to come over from State. Colonel Robert N. Ginsburgh replaced Bowman, the former JCS liaison to the NSC. Chet Cooper, the top Far East man, decided to leave and to replace him Rostow brought in William J. Jorden, author of both State Department white papers on Vietnam. China hand Jim Thomson had also given notice of his intention to leave in the summer. Walt got Rusk to detail Alfred Jenkins to the NSC staff to replace him. Jenkins had first impressed Rostow with his research for a book on China in the early 1950s and was now a foreign service officer commuting from Stockholm to Warsaw for secret informal talks between the United States and People's Republic of China being held in the Polish capital. Thomson was at first very suspicious of Jenkins, and of Rostow too, seeing them as overly swayed by arguments that Chinese expansionists had the upper hand in Peking, and therefore excessively aggressive in meeting that putative Chinese threat. Familiarity changed Thomson's mind, however, and before he left the NSC he came back to Walt and told him that Jenkins was a first-rate staffer.

In the midst of the staff transition Dwight Eisenhower took a hand, causing Lyndon Johnson heartburn. During an interview with journalists toward the end of April 1966, Ike charged that the Johnson administration crippled itself by making little use of its formal NSC machinery. Johnson called Ike to defuse the former President. Since after the tumult of the Bundy resignation, Komer's appointment, and the Rostow transition, the staff was again without a deputy, Ike once more recommended that LBJ turn to Gordon Gray or Andy Goodpaster. Someone was actually asked to sound out Goodpaster on the job, embarrassing Eisenhower, who knew that Andy wished to remain on military duty. Rostow suggested LBJ head off complaints of the obvious disuse of NSC machinery by holding a few meetings.

Walt noted: "My first suggestion is: a formal NSC session on Vietnam at the end of [Ambassador Henry Cabot] Lodge's visit, when all the major issues are settled between us and we can control what matters do and don't get into play." An NSC meeting on Vietnam was duly held on May 10, less than two weeks later, focusing on issues raised by the Lodge visit.

President Johnson, meanwhile, retained his insatiable appetite for ideas. More than once he called in Rostow to say something like, "I want two new ideas by Friday." Within weeks of returning to the NSC staff, Rostow had prepared an explicit program intended to generate new ideas. He planned to have each of State's regional bureaus develop a panel of outside consultants to generate new ideas or consider questions put to them by the bureaus, while NSC staffers "would be instructed to ensure that these consultants were effectively used and their ideas followed up in the bureaucracy."

Lyndon Johnson's style was markedly different from JFK's in that he did not deal directly with his NSC staffers, only through certain senior men, like Rostow, Komer, or Francis Bator and Chet Cooper. Thus he had never met many of the people who worked for him. Walt corrected that, asking the President if he wished to have a meeting with the staff, "an opportunity for you directly to confirm your desire that they . . . use their positions as a means of stimulating and helping formulate new ideas." Johnson approved such a meeting, to be held as a surprise in the Situation Room. The group was large, however, and instead met in the Cabinet Room on May 27, 1966.

Vice President Hubert Humphrey sat opposite LBJ as the NSC staff met its top boss that day. Rostow sat to Johnson's right, and to his right, Brom Smith. Present were Francis Bator, Bill Bowdler, Colonel Bowman, John DeLuca (the junior Far East man), Ulric Haynes and Ed Hamilton (NSC's African staff), Peter Jessup, Charles Johnson, William Jorden, Spurge Keeny, Don Ropa, Hal Saunders, Jim Thomson, and Howard Wriggins. Also present were the Situation Room chief, Art McCafferty, whom Rostow treated as a regular member of the staff, Bob Komer, and domestic political aides Bill Moyers, Douglas Cater, Marvin Watson, Joe Califano, and a few others.

It was, Jim Thomson recalls, "a sort of jawboning session." Johnson did not know who was out there: "If they weren't communists, they might at least be Republicans." It was worth finding out. Once the President had told the staff how important they were, he went around the table and asked each to talk a little about his work. When Thomson's turn came, he spoke about watching China, then about "waifs and strays" like Burma and Cambodia.

"Now Cambodia!" the President suddenly interrupted. "I just don't understand why we can't get along with that little prince," a reference to Cambodian ruler Norodom Sihanouk. "He runs a wonderful country, he's a great little man, little fellow, and I just don't see why we can't find some way to get along with him."

Lyndon banged the table. "I want you to do me a memo on how to get along with that little prince, and I want it here soon."

"Yes, sir," Thomson replied, "I'll be glad to."

Afterward, while other staff were congratulating Thomson on the only order to come of the meeting, Bob Komer came up and gave him a bit of friendly advice: "You better have [the memo] there by two o'clock this afternoon!" Thomson took two days instead, sent it off through Rostow, and it came back with abundant notations and approvals.

But the big meeting with Johnson was only familiarization. There never was another. Rostow's own management device was a morning staff meeting held three times a week. Brom Smith took notes. Francis Bator, to whom Bundy once promised the post of deputy, a promise Rostow honored, served in that capacity until his departure in April 1967. Art McCafferty represented the Situation Room staff. Typically there would be a dozen or so of the senior staff members or more junior ones who were handling the hot issues of the day, plus Komer and a few of the domestic people.

Howard Wriggins considered Jim Thomson wonderfully bright, clever, even a little smart-aleck. Thomson showed it after leaving the staff, when he wrote a satire of a spring 1967 NSC staff meeting:

> Mr. Rostow opened the meeting with a commentary on the latest reports from Vietnam. In general, he felt, the events of the previous day were a wholesome and not unexpected phase. . . . The fall of Saigon to the Vietcong meant that the enemy was now confronted with a challenge of unprecedented proportions for which it was totally unprepared: the administration of a major city. If we could dump rice and airlift pigs at Hue and Danang, the other side would soon cave. He cautioned, however, that this was merely a hunch; "not the kind of smell you can hang your hat on," he said.
>
> Mr. Komer said that Mr. Rostow's views were bullshit; Mr. Rostow had never understood Vietnam and should stop trying. . . .
>
> Mr. Bator said that he had spent the previous day with the German financial mission. . . .
>
> Mr. Rostow commented that the Germans were a fascinating bunch. . . .

Mr. Kintner hoped that Mr. Rostow wouldn't mind his reporting to the staff the President's deep pleasure and pride in Mr. Rostow's performance the previous Thursday on the "What's My Line" Show. . . .

Mr. Wriggins said that the reports of imminent mass starvation in India were more serious than we had expected; a Presidential decision might be required this week.

Mr. Kintner said that it would take a good three weeks to set up and test-run a Harris poll on that kind of question.

Mr. Rostow said he hoped the Indians would take a good hard look at the development of chemical fertilizers. He asked Mr. Wriggins to ride herd on this one.

Mr. Komer noted that neither Mr. Rostow nor Mr. Wriggins knew a goddamn thing about Indian agriculture.

Colonel Bowman explained the previous night's raids on North Vietnam. We had knocked out 78 percent of North Vietnam's [oil] reserves; since we had knocked out 86 percent three days ago, and 92 percent last week, we were doing exceptionally well.

Mr. Bowdler reported the execution by the new Brazilian Government of all the nation's university rectors.

Mr. Rostow commented that the new government had really done its homework in the economic field; the overall curve was very promising. . . .

What fascinated [Mr. Rostow] more than Saigon was the reported purge of the Assistant Managing Editor of the Hankow People's Daily; in writing his book on Communist China in 1953 he had concluded that the assistant managing editors of river-port newspapers were often the key indicators of policy shifts. Did Mr. Jenkins have a comment?

Mr. Jenkins said he would certainly look into this. . . .

Thomson first circulated the satire without his name on it, then added a byline, moved the supposed timing ahead to summer 1967, changed the names of the characters ever so slightly (Rostow became "Herman Melville Breslau"), and published the piece in the *Atlantic Monthly* in May 1967. Walt passed copies of both versions up to LBJ. "Because there is nothing really effective to do about all this," he drily noted, "we will limit our response to pointing out that people have differing ideas about what is 'funny.' "

In the meantime there were the usual housekeeping annoyances. One, which was disturbing because it flowed from LBJ's determination to pursue both the Vietnam War *and* the Great Society, guns and butter, was the campaign he ordered to get the federal bureaucracy to buy U.S. Savings Bonds, as a means of financing expenditures without having to raise taxes or take other inflationary measures. A progress chart was set up on an easel in the Cabinet Room to record the competition in bond purchases, and everyone on the NSC staff was exhorted to buy.

In the summer of 1966, only a few weeks after LBJ met them, the NSC staff lost its only black professional. Thus far in its history the National Security Council had done a poor job of making use of minorities or women in substantive professional positions. Bundy and Rostow both concede they did not put enough thought into this. Bundy did go out and find a man, Clifford A. Alexander, but Johnson stole him away for the White House staff. After some further searching, in 1965 Bundy came up with Ulric St. Clair Haynes, Jr., "the ablest young Negro I have met in ten years of fairly constant looking." Haynes had gone to Yale Law School with Hal Saunders, then worked for the Ford Foundation before joining the Foreign Service. Drafted by Bundy as junior staffer under Bob Komer and Saunders, principally for African affairs, Haynes quickly made several suggestions Mac thought useful. While planning his own move to Ford, Bundy actually warned Rusk, "an intelligent Foundation executive might well try to get him back."

Haynes proved resistant to Mac's blandishments but equally impervious to those of the President, who had the thirty-five-year-old staffer and his wife included at the formal state dinner for an African leader on March 29, 1965. Bundy was considerate and so was Rostow, but Haynes was not satisfied. Referring to a popular television show of the time, Rick remarked to Rostow, "I don't always want to be Tonto. I want to see if I can be the Lone Ranger." He left the NSC staff in June 1966, with Cliff Alexander among the eighteen at a stag luncheon honoring him. Years later Rostow encountered Haynes on the street in New York City. Rick had become a successful entrepreneur.

By refusing to allow anyone to emerge as a strong chief of staff, Johnson maintained open lines to all his special assistants. Rostow took full advantage, feeding Johnson a steady diet of anything he thought necessary. To help him follow up on much of this work, and the side assignments that came back from LBJ, Walt hired a personal assistant, thirty-four-year-old Richard M. Moose. His task evolved from that of gofer to the NSC staff's first congressional and press relations aide.

So there was Rostow, settled in at last. He regularly played tennis on the White House court at seven in the morning on Tuesdays and Thursdays, reaching his office by nine. The President approved this after an incident one morning when he tried to get Walt, whose secretary, the loyal Lois Nivens, stood up to Johnson and refused to let him interrupt. Other days he was in the office early, by six or seven, even though he came from far up on Connecticut Avenue. One morning Walt was in his office reading papers when the President phoned down from the Oval Office. Had Rostow seen *that?* Fulbright had just been on the TV with one more comment that enraged LBJ. But Rostow had no television. Johnson wanted his keeper of the keys to monitor the tube, just as he himself did, with a bank of several sets simultaneously tuned to the different major channels. The President had such a bank of televisions installed in Rostow's office. Rostow judged he could monitor the media perfectly well without succumbing to TV madness; reading the cables was more important. Rostow ignored the televisions. Walt thought he knew when to disobey orders too.

DAYS OF WAR,
DECADES WITHOUT
RESOLUTION

▲▲▲

When Bob Komer went to Tel Aviv in early 1965, it had not been on his own, as some anonymous White House operative. The mission was a quiet one, but Komer was with that old work-horse Averell Harriman. It was a question of Soviet influence in the Middle East versus American arms exports. Jordan's King Hussein had joined a unified command with the United Arab Republic (UAR) and been offered Soviet weapons. Washington wished to keep Hussein out of the Soviet orbit by offering American weapons.

Harriman worked some of the toughest angles, then returned to Washington, leaving the final arrangements in Komer's hands. There could be no better demonstration of the spirit of cooperation that prevailed during the Johnson administration between State and the NSC staff. Israel reluctantly acquiesced in the shipments to Jordan, for which it received the very valuable United States promise to supply the Israel Defense Force (IDF) directly with 210 American tanks of a type previously imported from West Germany. This action for the first time made the United States a major arms supplier to the Middle East. A flow began that was soon augmented by another agreement, to supply forty-eight A-4 Skyhawk jet attack planes.

The arms trade mirrored the general situation in the Middle East: quiescent until about 1965, followed by sharply increasing tensions.

There was a prelude to the 1967 war, a gradually darkening horizon bearing omens of what was to come. Howard Wriggins was one of the first to know. Two years older than Walt, Wriggins was a Quaker from Philadelphia; he had graduated with honors from Dartmouth just before the war, and had spent his junior year abroad in Paris; like Walt in the critical year of 1938–1939. During the big conflict, he held the courage of his convictions and did war relief work, by late 1944 as acting resident in Italy for the Inter-Governmental Committee on Refugees.

Wriggins returned to the United States to complete at Yale a doctorate begun at the University of Chicago before the war. Under a Rockefeller

172

Foundation fellowship, he went to Washington in 1958 as chief of the foreign affairs division of the Legislative Reference Service. It was from there that Rostow had picked up Wriggins for the Policy Planning Council.

While Hal Saunders was on vacation, Wriggins was the NSC staff point man in a delicate and worsening situation. Syrians often took potshots at Israeli tractor drivers, but one exchange had escalated to tanks. Wriggins thought the IDF would have committed aircraft, and that the United States would have heard more, if the exchange had really been serious, so he reassured Rostow, "Thus far there is nothing in this incident to cause unusual alarm."

Wriggins was right, the incident receded. Hal Saunders returned from vacation and resumed the Israeli portfolio. But the situation did not calm down. There were also some clear warning indicators from Arabs. In Egypt the foreign minister told Saunders, "You are working against us everywhere in the Middle East. You have chosen sides." On the West Bank, Palestinians who had lost homes in Israel told him, "Don't make the mistake of thinking that time will solve the refugee problem." It was a message he heard again and again.

The primary question Saunders had tried to keep in mind was why should Lyndon Johnson care about the Middle East. He came back convinced, as he told Rostow, that LBJ had "more than the usual stake in peace" because the President did not want to have to commit American forces in the Middle East while engaged in Vietnam, and because Johnson had invested much in demonstrating that wars of national liberation could not be tolerated.

Saunders had the background necessary to interpret what he heard. He had graduated Phi Beta Kappa from Princeton in 1952, interested in the political and social processes of group interaction, an interest he pursued to a doctorate at Yale in 1956. At twenty-six Saunders entered the Air Force and was sent to Officer Candidate School, then detailed to the CIA. Saunders excited Bob Komer's curiosity and soon became his protégé, brought up through the ranks at both the CIA and the NSC staff. In the Executive Office Building, Saunders was regarded as quiet, almost shy, but highly competent, a perfect foil for his extravagant boss. In terms of personality, Saunders's was actually closer to Komer's successor, the gracious Wriggins. Saunders himself replaced Howard as senior staff for the Middle East on June 1, 1967, just in time to see the region go up in flames.

In actuality, Harold Saunders did not expect the Six Day War. Excepting the claims of an Israeli buildup against Syria, whose veracity cannot be judged, the steps that led to war began on May 15 when Gamal Nasser ordered a military alert around the Egyptian capital Cairo. That seemed of no special significance until that night, when the United States and Israelis learned that UAR troops were moving through Cairo toward the Sinai Peninsula.

Though he did not foresee what was to come, Saunders did no worse than his White House colleagues. President Johnson was at a Tuesday Lunch

173

on May 16. Items up for discussion included the sale of armored personnel carriers to Israel and a prospective visit to Egypt by Hubert Humphrey. Saunders's preparatory memo for Rostow makes clear the Vice President's visit was seen as a matter of general policy, not as a measure designed to prevent an Arab-Israeli war. However, LBJ and his staff reacted swiftly as the affair evolved and improvised an effort to forestall war.

Friday, May 19, Johnson held a second Tuesday Lunch to discuss the situation. Conversation focused on the extent of United States commitments to Israel, on making sure the Arabs knew of them, and on ascertaining the attitudes of major allies like the British and French. Johnson had already cabled a cautionary note to the Israeli prime minister, and wished to focus on action through the UN. He was shocked that U Thant agreed to Nasser's request to withdraw UN troops from Egyptian territory, as indeed were the Egyptians themselves, according to Johnson's account. However, there was no talk at lunch of the obvious alternative of asking Israel to allow stationing of the United Nations Emergency Force (UNEF) on its land. Years later Walt Rostow was unable to answer a researcher who asked why that had not been considered. Such an initiative might have done little more than gain time, however, since Israel had refused to allow the UN on its territory when the force was established in 1957, and there was no particular reason to assume Tel Aviv's attitude had changed.

A decisive move came on Monday, May 22, just as the UNEF left its last positions. Nasser declared that the UAR would bar Israeli ships from the Gulf of Aqaba. In the meantime Egypt began activating reserve military forces and repatriating UAR troops still fighting in Yemen. As far as Israel was concerned, blocking the gulf had cast the die for war.

Nasser's blockade of the Gulf of Aqaba crystallized Washington's thinking on what Harold Saunders believes was its first major decision of the crisis: to attempt to restrain Israel from electing a military solution. President Johnson's effort was complicated by assurances Dwight Eisenhower had given Israel to get her to withdraw after the Suez War. Tel Aviv thought Ike had promised to use force to reopen Aqaba if it were closed, while Washington's interpretation was that it would not oppose an *Israeli* resort to force under those circumstances. Johnson held a further policy lunch on May 23 at which he discussed an approach having two main aspects. One was to warn Egypt of danger of war if it persisted; LBJ issued a statement that day calling the Aqaba action illegal, and also canceled Hubert Humphrey's mission to caution Nasser. The other was to hold back Israel. To that end, LBJ met with Israeli Foreign Minister Abba Eban on the evening of May 26. Johnson now saw the military aid package for Israel—which had been under consideration by the bureaucracy through much of the spring, and included armored personnel carriers, spare parts for the IDF's American-made tanks, and certain other items—as a sop to convince Tel Aviv the military balance would not be changed by any Arab action.

It was nonetheless clear from Eban's talk that the Israelis were contemplating action. The diplomat cited Israeli intelligence reports that the UAR was preparing an invasion, reports that already had been passed along to the CIA station chief in Tel Aviv. On the other hand, the U.S. National Security Agency also had intercepts indicating IDF preparations for a preemptive attack. President Johnson thought he might be able to reassure the Israelis if he had some suitably positive intelligence to present.

Johnson, writing later for history, described how the CIA estimates had held that Israel would win a war in just days, and how he had sent Richard Helms back to recalculate the intelligence because it seemed so unbelievable. The intelligence chief returned with the same conclusion, that the IDF would win, but in an even shorter period of time. In fact, a bit of NSC staff work had preceded this episode. Beginning earlier in May there had been several arguments among staffers at Walt Rostow's early-morning in-house meetings. Given the Soviet arms aid to Egypt, Syria, and Iraq, some people had the opinion that things would be different this time from 1956; Israel might even be driven into the sea. One who disagreed sharply was Bob Ginsburgh. At the time of Suez, Ginsburgh had been a thirty-five-year-old Air Force lieutenant colonel, in Naples, working for NATO's southern flank command.

The subject kept coming up and, once Nasser closed the Gulf of Aqaba, became one whose immediate importance was obvious. No longer faced with some speculative debate on the military balance, Walt asked Bob Ginsburgh for his considered opinion on the subject.

It was perhaps not a good time to go out on a limb, but Ginsburgh did just that with his Arab-Israeli military appreciation. He reached out to the Defense Intelligence Agency (DIA) and got hold of the analysts on its Israeli desk, one a former military attaché at Tel Aviv, the other an air attaché there. They substantiated his intuitive view that the Israelis had the advantage. Armed with more data, Bob went back to the Old Executive Office Building and wrote a paper that observed that the duration of a war, but not the outcome, would depend on who struck first. If the Arabs attacked first, Israel would win, but it would take two or three weeks, no longer than a month. If Israel preempted, the IDF would need only ten days, in any event no longer than two weeks. The DIA analysts actually thought Ginsburgh was being pessimistic; they anticipated an even shorter war, and their view prevailed. When LBJ asked for reconsideration, the intelligence people returned with a prediction very much like Ginsburgh's.

Colonel Ginsburgh gave a copy of his paper to General Earle G. "Bus" Wheeler, Chairman of the Joint Chiefs of Staff. Later, after it had already gone to Rostow, Bus called and completely agreed with Ginsburgh's view, authorizing the military assistant to say his paper represented the JCS Chairman.

The view from Langley was not very different. Richard Helms ordered the data rechecked. As he supposed, LBJ expressed initial doubts. But when the analysts at Langley refined their estimate, Helms came back to report that the CIA believed the Israelis would win in only seven to ten days. Thus LBJ got his intelligence estimate. After the Six Day War, Johnson always included Dick Helms in his Tuesday Lunch group.

Meeting with Abba Eban later, Johnson asked Secretary of Defense McNamara to give the diplomat a summary of United States intelligence findings regarding an Egyptian attack. Bob McNamara reported that three separate groups had examined the evidence and concluded that a UAR attack was not imminent.

"All our intelligence people are unanimous," President Johnson added, "that if the UAR attacks, you will whip hell out of them."

To further reassure the Israelis, LBJ gave them the good news on their military aid package, and spoke of measures to restore freedom of navigation through the Gulf of Aqaba. There could be no automatic resort to force, however. Johnson told Eban he was aware of what previous Presidents had said, "but that is not worth five cents if the people and Congress do not support the President." The British had come up with a plan to assert freedom of navigation with a multilateral naval force positioned in the Red Sea, while Washington intended to make a start by ordering its aircraft carrier *Intrepid* to transit the Suez Canal to the Red Sea. It was a question of awaiting developments.

"The central point, Mr. Minister," Johnson told Eban, "is that your nation not be the one to bear the responsibility for any outbreak of war."

"Israel will not be alone," the President said, then repeated, "unless it decides to go alone."

Eban returned to Tel Aviv and informed the Israeli cabinet that the United States was committed to ensuring freedom of navigation through the gulf. Johnson's play gained only a few days, however.

Much now rode on the prospects for a naval task force, a multilateral undertaking with difficulties similar to those the notorious Suez Canal Users Association had faced in 1956. Insiders dubbed the task force idea the "Red Sea regatta" and it was about that amorphous. The Joint Chiefs of Staff delivered a planning memorandum on May 27. General Wheeler signed the paper, JCSM-301-67, which considered military actions designed to support a probe of the gulf past Sharm al-Sheikh, adverted that additional planning needed to be done, and promised a further study. Commitments to support the regatta came from the British, who had originated the idea, and the Dutch. Australian Prime Minister Harold Holt, visiting Washington, personally promised LBJ he would send two cruisers to join the international flotilla. These commitments formed the subject for a Tuesday Lunch on May 31 and written items on next steps in the Middle East dominated LBJ's evening reading that night.

Hal Saunders was one who had misgivings. He warned Rostow on the morning of May 31 that as long as Washington was planning for contingencies, it should consider what to do if support for an international flotilla dried up, much as had happened with the multilateral Suez Canal users group in 1956. The President and Rostow noted the warning but pressed ahead. Another blow came on June 2, when JCS Chairman Wheeler delivered JCSM-310-67, the Chiefs' follow-up paper. The military judged that it would require more than a month to assemble a balanced flotilla in the Red Sea drawing from the Atlantic Fleet, and that this force would be confined to dangerous narrow seas with tenuous supply lines and would have to be prepared for an Egyptian challenge to its operations; any more rapid action would have to utilize forces already east of Suez, which were of minimal strength.

The basis for any flotilla action was to be an international declaration. By June 4 only eight nations had agreed to be signatories. Except Israel, all were NATO members. The declaration was under active consideration by five other nations but time was fast running out. Action at the United Nations had also, owing to French abstention, failed to attain the required Security Council majority. Finally, Johnson's messages to Soviet Prime Minister Aleksei N. Kosygin elicited conciliatory but insubstantial replies.

The President sent one more letter to Israeli Prime Minister Levi Eshkol on Saturday, June 3, even giving Saunders some last-minute changes in wording over the telephone. The letter reiterated LBJ's words to Eban about Israel being alone if it decided to go alone. Johnson added: "We cannot imagine that it will make this decision." President Johnson was wrong.

The conflict that became known as the Six Day War began, according to Moshe Dayan, the Israeli minister of defense, at 7:14 A.M. (Israeli time) on June 5, when Israeli aircraft began a series of surprise attacks on Arab air bases, first Egyptian, later in the day Syrian and Jordanian, following ineffective attacks upon Israel by warplanes of those countries. Meanwhile, IDF troops crossed the border in the Sinai and began driving toward the Suez Canal in a virtual replay of the 1956 campaign.

Several hours later in Washington, where, because of time differences, it was 2:50 A.M., a long day began for Walt Rostow with a call at home from the Situation Room. Walt asked for confirmation from the National Military Command Center and had it within five minutes. Rostow reached the White House by 3:20 and immediately called Dean Rusk and, at 4:30, the President. LBJ listened to the factual report, based at that time only upon press accounts, and merely said, "Thank you." He got a call from Rusk at 5:09, another from Walt at 6:15, and one from press secretary George Christian at 6:35. Johnson himself called Rostow twice at 6:49 and 6:55, and at 7:50 called United States Ambassador Arthur Goldberg at the United Nations. Meanwhile, both the United States and the Soviet Union moved to open up their direct communications link, the so-called hot line, for an exchange of messages. At 7:47 A.M., Premier Kosygin got off the first of this series reporting the outbreak of war.

One of Johnson's early concerns, in line with warnings to Israel, was ascertaining who had begun the hostilities. Rostow responded by calling Clark Clifford, chairman of the President's Foreign Intelligence Advisory

Board (PFIAB), asking him to come in early and work with Hal Saunders on the available intelligence to make a determination. Harry McPherson, who had just arrived in Israel on the last leg of a trip that had taken him to Vietnam, made similar inquiries on the scene.

Clifford came down to the Executive Office Building, where PFIAB offices, then as now, are located. He received an assignment directly from the national security adviser, unusual in that only the President had the authority to ask Clifford to do anything. But Clark responded with good grace, walked over to the Situation Room to read the latest reports, and went on to the Cabinet Room to report his conclusions. Rostow recalls Clifford's impressions: "It was his judgment . . . that it was a straight Israeli decision to deal with the crisis by initiating war." In Tel Aviv, Harry McPherson's conclusion was the same. Ambassador Walworth Barbour made an appointment with Eshkol for himself and McPherson for later that morning. When the time came, an Israeli general showed up to brief the Americans. He described the UAR buildup of troops in the Sinai that had preceded the war, asserting it had threatened southern Israel and even Tel Aviv. The Americans asked if the Egyptians had attacked. The general answered by enumerating the increases in Egyptian troops and tanks.

The air raid sirens were wailing, so ambassador Barbour suggested they continue in the Foreign Ministry's underground bunker. The Israeli intelligence chief, General Aharon Yariv, quickly assured them they could stay where they were. "If it wasn't necessary," McPherson reasoned, "the Egyptian air force had been destroyed. That could only have happened so quickly if it had been surprised on the ground. We did not need to ask for confirmation, but left at once to cable the news to Washington."

In the United States, LBJ's Situation Room went on twenty-four-hour watch, with senior officers present around the clock, a condition maintained for longer than during any other crisis of the Johnson presidency. Colonel Robert Ginsburgh had the watch that first night of the war, receiving the cables and assembling information to be ready whenever the President wanted an update. Ginsburgh found that the best information in this crisis was coming from the Reuters news ticker rather than the reporting from State, DOD, the NSA, or the CIA.

Ginsburgh was going about his business about nine in the evening when suddenly Hubert Humphrey burst into the Situation Room. The Vice President was in black tie, obviously just back from some reception, looking for the latest developments. Ginsburgh gave Humphrey a fifteen-minute briefing based mostly on the Reuters dispatches, which spoke glowingly of Israeli efficiency in executing their air strike. Vice President Humphrey ended up wondering why the Israelis did so well compared with the U.S. Air Force in Vietnam. Colonel Ginsburgh explained the Israelis were simply using proper concepts for the employment of air power.

Humphrey remained in the Situation Room and continued this discussion. After a time he came back to that question of comparing the Israelis with the United States. Ginsburgh answered the same way. The conversation went on. At length Humphrey repeated his question for a third time. An Air Force officer himself, Colonel Ginsburgh was getting his dander up about Humphrey's needling. Moreover, the Situation Room was becoming crowded as people arrived with messages and papers, for which Ginsburgh could not sign because he could not interrupt the Vice President in that manner. Humphrey had begun playing to this very crowd of onlookers. Enjoying himself, the Vice President came back a fourth time with his disturbing question.

"Well, Mr. Vice President," Ginsburgh shot back, "in Israel the politicians don't try to tell the military how to do their jobs."

That sally pretty much took the wind out of Humphrey's sails, and the Vice President beat a retreat from the Situation Room. The next morning Ginsburgh reported as soon as Rostow arrived for work.

The first item was his encounter with the Vice President. Ginsburgh told Rostow, "Walt, you may find it necessary to fire me some time today." Then he explained what had happened.

Rostow loyally backed his subordinate, ready to take the responsibility and resign himself. When Humphrey arrived to attend a meeting that analyzed Kosygin's first message over the hot line, Rostow took him aside for a rundown on the latest reports, then introduced his military assistant. The Vice President sat down, a big grin on his face, and said, "I've already met Colonel Ginsburgh." The heat was off.

Ginsburgh's second item for Rostow that morning related to his predictions of the war's outcome. "Walt," deadpanned the colonel, "it looks like my estimate was badly off."

Rostow turned pale. "What do you mean?" he asked.

"Looks like the Israelis will be on the Canal by close of business tomorrow night," Ginsburgh replied.

It was Rostow's turn to smile. "Our time or their time?"

The IDF battlefield success brought relief in Washington, partly from the realization that there would not have to be any decision on intervention, partly because the estimates had been accurate. Rostow nevertheless recalled eighteen months later: "President Johnson . . . never believed that this war was anything else than a mistake by the Israelis." According to his watcher, LBJ made that clear to Israeli officials on a number of subsequent occasions.

Meanwhile, McNamara quickly began to press for someone at the White House to coordinate all the work to be done at State, DOD, and the CIA. Naturally that was Rostow's job, but he was busy with Vietnam. Walt had time for a few summary memos to LBJ but not much else. Hal Saunders had the portfolio but not the clout to move bureaucrats. Over at State, Walt's brother, Eugene V. Rostow, who had recently replaced George Ball as undersecretary, still lacked experience and was perceived as a loose manager.

Aware of the problem, Johnson also perceived it had a political overlay. Both Rostows were Jewish, as was UN ambassador Arthur Goldberg.

179

Mac Bundy was one of the first persons to whom the President reached out. Indeed, Mac came in from New York in time for the initial crisis meeting, when Clifford spoke to the group about who started the war. LBJ's thoughts turned toward the Cuban missile crisis and Kennedy's EXCOM. By the afternoon of the first day, Johnson was interested in using a similar device, and he saw Bundy as part of the solution. At a Tuesday Lunch on June 6 the President cleared the idea with Rusk and McNamara. Mac was no longer part of the NSC, while Eugene Rostow was now a very senior official at Foggy Bottom; to preclude ruffled feathers Bundy would be styled the "executive secretary" of the new EXCOM, while Dean Rusk became the official chairman. Johnson announced the move to the full National Security Council on June 7, released the news to the press, and convened the group for the first time that evening.

Mac Bundy went before the press with George Christian early in the afternoon for a brief (eight minutes long) press conference. Asked about the scope of the EXCOM's work, Mac said he didn't want to go beyond the President's statement, which Christian had read and Bundy himself helped draft. Asked to compare the new NSC unit with the Cuban crisis EXCOM, Bundy replied that the two situations were not identical and the new EXCOM was designed to cope with the new situation. Asked what the priorities of the committee would be, Mac shot back that he was only an executive secretary and the EXCOM would tell him what to do. Asked whether the idea of the committee was to stop the war or to resolve the long-term Middle East problem, Bundy repeated his refusal to go beyond LBJ's statement. Asked to evaluate the crisis in terms of United States security, Mac parried once more: "I think it would not be useful for me to engage in evaluations. I am down here on a temporary basis as a staff officer, which is something I have done before. There really isn't much I can add to that."

It was a typical exercise in government public relations, demonstrating that not only on Vietnam was the administration less than forthcoming. Transcripts like this illuminate the frustrations of the working press and suggest reasons why they began to publicize the notion of a "credibility gap" between Johnson's rhetoric and his actions, or between the realities of situations and administration descriptions of them. No subsequent presidency has escaped from this tendency to put a gloss, or "spin" on the facts, which is understandable from a public relations viewpoint, but which endangers public policy at the point when the gloss is deemed more important than the facts.

There was little to be done about press speculation, but an immense load of work was required to cope with the crisis. Mac Bundy moved into an office at the OEOB. For staff assistants he got Hal Saunders plus a couple of people from the Situation Room. Howard Wriggins, who was cleaning out his desk prior to leaving the NSC staff, also had a few talks with Mac and Walt. Wriggins insisted convincingly that the Palestinian refugees had to be accommodated in any settlement. Bundy began to speak of a "Wriggins Doctrine" on refugees while Rostow discussed the refugee problem in his memoranda to the President as something that had to be solved.

President Johnson presided over the first Middle East EXCOM meeting, which occurred that evening at 6:30 P.M. in the Cabinet Room. Belying Bundy's claim to the press that he was a mere executive secretary, it was Hal Saunders who took the notes. Bundy definitely functioned in a substantive role, handing out assignments in a wide-ranging scheme to cope with the crisis. Mac himself would handle information coordination with spokesmen for the White House and departments. Dick Helms from CIA got the intelligence assignment. On security matters, it was decided, there should be a working group from the Pentagon, JCS, and CIA, with representatives of State and the Arms Control and Disarmament Agency. McNamara and Bundy recommended Paul Warnke, Pentagon general counsel, as the DOD member.

Other working groups could handle political developments, arranged between DOD and State; and economic developments should go to a unit that would include representatives of Treasury and State plus Francis Bator of the NSC staff.

The first meeting set the stage for what came later, and also showed the difference between the new EXCOM and its predecessor. Bundy's Middle East EXCOM arranged work for the bureaucracy where the Cuban version formulated policy. Of course in arranging work a policy was formulated, as is implied by Saunders's recollection that the second major Johnson administration decision, to seek a long-term solution to the Middle East problem, seemed to have occurred without much formal consideration.

One thing led to another in a process that was perfectly straightforward. For example, McNamara came to the EXCOM meeting of June 8 worried about arms supplies, quite in line with his responsibilities under the group's division of labor. Bundy interjected that nondelivery of arms could be a major element in a cease-fire and the group agreed to have State generate a talking paper on the subject.

Diplomatic action continued at the United Nations which passed a cease-fire resolution that Israel accepted but Nasser did not. On June 8, Israeli aircraft and torpedo boats suddenly and without provocation attacked the United States intelligence ship *Liberty,* with no less than thirty-four deaths and more than a hundred wounded resulting. The *Liberty* incident caused a flurry of American–Soviet messages on the hot line and a good deal of talk at the NSC special committee on June 9 and later. Late on June 8, Egypt accepted the cease-fire, but by that time the Soviets had introduced a new UN resolution demanding that Israel withdraw to its prewar borders. While discussion of that resolution continued, the IDF completed its conquest of the Sinai (including Sharm al-Sheikh), captured East Jerusalem, and the whole of the West Bank from Jordan, and attacked Syria on the Golan Heights. The war ended with Israel in control of all those places.

The denouement brought a brush involving a near direct confrontation between the United States and Soviet Union. At 8:48 A.M. on June 10, LBJ was told that Soviet leader Kosygin wished him to come to the hot line as quickly as possible. It developed he had sent a message that the Israelis were breaking the cease-fire by continuing to fight Syria. Kosygin thundered it was a "very crucial moment" and threatened independent action. The first rough translation of this cable reached the President at 9:05. Present in the Situation Room were McNamara, Rostow, Bundy, Helms, Clifford, Llewellyn Thompson, and Undersecretary of State Nicholas Katzenbach, who quickly left to put pressure on Tel Aviv to stop fighting once and for all. President Johnson was quite irritated because he thought he had received, six hours earlier, Israeli agreement to the cease-fire. Now, however, the Russians added a new dimension. LBJ believed that the United States could not allow the Russians to strong-arm Israel, so he considered making a naval demonstration with the United States Sixth Fleet in the Mediterranean.

Johnson asked McNamara where the Sixth Fleet was located. The secretary of defense telephoned his Pentagon command center while LBJ had breakfast, then reported the fleet was three hundred miles west of the Syrian coast, about twelve hours away at flank speed. Thompson and Helms agreed that a naval demonstration might work, and the CIA director added that the Soviet submarines that normally monitored United States naval movements would no doubt report it to Moscow the moment the Sixth Fleet changed course for Syria. It was a time when Johnson might have benefited from the wisdom of a larger circle of advisers, men like George Ball, who had served him long and well. In fact, an attempt had been made to get Ball for LBJ—Rostow called him in Chicago on the first day of the war and tried to bring him in for the EXCOM. But Ball had little stomach for giving the White House advice at that moment and begged off. So no voices of caution were raised in the Situation Room for LBJ to hear. Indeed no voices were raised at all—Helms recalled the discussion "was in the lowest voices he had ever heard in a meeting of that kind."

Johnson ordered the Sixth Fleet maneuver. At 9:30 A.M. he sent Kosygin a hot line message of his own reporting Tel Aviv's overnight assurances. Kosygin responded at 9:44 that the fighting was continuing, while an hour later LBJ insisted the cease-fire was taking hold. The men in the Situation Room visibly relaxed during the morning as the war seemed to be ending, particularly after Kosygin's 11:31 hot line message, which looked beyond the war to the next steps toward achieving peace in the Middle East.

It was a subject in which LBJ had vital interest. For several days he'd been talking with Rostow and Bundy about a peacemaking speech he might give. Some of the work Bundy had been assigning to EXCOM subcommittees had been specifically aimed at elements that could quickly be plugged into such a speech. One would be an arms trade freeze, or at least some sort of register. Another, as NSC staffer Nathaniel Davis reported to Brom Smith from the United Nations, where he had been sent to supply daily firsthand reports, would have to be withdrawal to the prewar borders. A third, as Wriggins and Rostow emphasized, would be arrangements for the Palestinians, now an even more serious problem in the wake of the West Bank and Gaza occupation.

Work on the Johnson speech became the main focus for the meeting of the NSC special committee in the days after the June 10 ceasefire went into effect. Walt Rostow submitted two drafts containing points that could be used in the speech, Eugene Rostow supplied another, Bundy prepared at least one, and so did State Department Middle East expert Joseph Sisco. In addition, Bundy suggested to LBJ that Ted Sorensen, though difficult to work with, was the best speechwriter in the United States. Paul Warnke and Raymond Garthoff did a paper on arms control in the Middle East, while Zbigniew Brzezinski supplied thoughts on what the United States posture should be in the light of probable Soviet tactics. It was all boiled down into a speech Johnson gave on June 19 before the National Foreign Policy Conference for Educators.

American diplomatic efforts eventually turned to the United Nations, including a joint United States–Soviet draft resolution prepared in July, which called for withdrawals plus an end to the state of war with Israel. Arab refusal to accept the latter provision scotched this initiative as well. However, both withdrawals and the ending of belligerency, plus LBJ's main points, were included in the document the United Nations finally did approve, Resolution 242, which passed on November 22, 1967.

Two decades later UN Resolution 242 remains at the center of all efforts to achieve Middle East peace. Lyndon Johnson took the long view, and his five points are enshrined in what has become the starting point for peace negotiations, but the struggle to implement Resolution 242 has been blocked by national interests and those of supranational groups such as the Palestine Liberation Organization and its factions. LBJ witnessed just the beginning of this new diplomatic struggle. Leafing through the thick, top-secret loose-leaf notebook containing the newest Mideast policy review, he later asked an aide, "Same old shit, isn't it?"

THE SUMMIT THAT
ALMOST WAS

▲▲▲

I n later years Mac Bundy would evince considerable interest in the arcana of nuclear weapons and arms control, commenting on nuclear doctrine, prospective agreements, and weapons systems. It was an acquired taste, something picked up in his years in the White House. It is also possible that an element of contrition was involved, for it was during Bundy's time, the high years of McNamara at the Pentagon, that the weapons designers were given the liberty to create weapons that have since been the bane of all interested in curbing the arms race.

Decisions were made in 1964 to provide multiple independently target-able reentry vehicle (MIRV) warheads for both the next generation of Min-uteman missiles and for a sea-launched missile to be called Poseidon. President Johnson announced the Poseidon development decision in January 1965, followed it with a deployment decision later that year, and authorized development of the MIRVed Minuteman III in March 1966.

Essentially Johnson would take a stance based on the budgetary impact of the programs; LBJ had no interest in the technical details. When the numbers got too far out of line for the promised payoff in capability, Johnson would bat down a program and take the political heat for it. There were at least four major initiatives LBJ canceled: the Dynasoar aerospace plane; the Manned Orbital Laboratory; a nuclear-powered missile called Rover; and an early cruise missile also intended to be nuclear powered. On the antiballistic missile (ABM), however, there was a lot of political interest; McNamara did LBJ a favor by preventing many of the early recommen-dations for deployment from reaching the White House level. With MIRV the problem was different—the program was "technically sweet" in that an additional increment of expenditure on weapons systems already existing promised a large increase in capability. Moreover, owing to the novelty of the concept that a single intercontinental ballistic missile (ICBM) could be used to strike many different targets, outside the executive there was no entrenched opposition. There was also little understanding anywhere of its arms control implications.

But President Johnson's focus on other issues placed a considerable bur-den, when it came to nuclear matters, on the watchers at his gate. Though he was a quick study, Mac Bundy was not himself expert in the nuclear field and had to depend, in turn, on the lower levels of the NSC staff. In the early days Mac had considered himself fortunate to have Carl Kaysen, who had been around the defense analysis business since the early 1950s, when he had chaired MIT's Project Charles air defense study and been a summer visiting fellow at the RAND Corporation. But Kaysen left in 1963. Mike Forrestal and Bob Komer picked up Kaysen's work on regional issues, but Mac had a problem on the nuclear side. Fortunately presidential science adviser Jerry Wiesner had the solution: Spurgeon M. Keeny, Jr. Familiar with Keeny from exchanges with the President's Science Advisory Committee (PSAC), Bundy tried him out and liked what he found. Soon Keeny was spending half his time on NSC staff business. That remained the case after Donald F. Hornig replaced Wiesner at PSAC. On disarmament and technology, Mac told Dean Rusk, "I get great support" from Keeny.

Superbly equipped for his task on the NSC staff, Spurgeon Keeny had been involved in nuclear matters since student days in New York. Keeny had been an intimate friend of Harold Brown's, a prodigy in nuclear physics; both had gone to Columbia, where Keeny got a B.A. in Russian. When the Air Force drafted Keeny, they learned of his background and made him an analyst of intelligence on Soviet nuclear weapons. He had moved over to PSAC during Eisenhower's administration. Walt Rostow, remarking that "sometimes you need such people," recalls Keeny as "an arms control ideologue." A crusader he certainly was, but Keeny retained a solid grasp of the technical issues and the practical politics.

In addition to his other qualities, Keeny was tremendously energetic, putting in eighteen-hour days when the occasion demanded, for instance, during the 1958 Geneva conference. In effect, as a half-time NSC senior staffer Keeny often did a full-time job. Keeny's greatest drawback seemed to be that he *looked* so young. As Mac put it to Dean Rusk, "If he did not look like an undergraduate, I think [Keeny] would already be emerging into the level of Presidential appointments."

Spurgeon Keeny was not the only half-time professional on the NSC staff. Also coming into that category were the long-serving internal security people, whose importance had diminished steadily since the loyalty hearings of Harry Truman's time and the McCarthyist hysteria of Eisenhower's. J. Patrick Coyne, the most senior member of the security unit, finally had so little work to do that he transferred to the President's Foreign Intelligence Advisory Board (PFIAB) to manage its office. J. Edgar Hoover still liked to spring his surprises, though, and continued to use A. Russell Ash to do it. Formal contact reports had to be made whenever an NSC officer met with anyone from a Soviet bloc country. There was hell to pay when the FBI learned of contacts that had not been reported. Still, no one took it too seriously. Several times Mac Bundy told Ash to run along, or to make sure Hoover learned that NSC staff had to have this kind of contact to do their jobs.

As for the practice of foreign contacts, that was another way in which staff practices changed from Kennedy's time onward. Given their role as expediters of policy, it became necessary to have a certain awareness that could be best conveyed by direct contact with foreign nationals, even though that conflicted with the tradition that the State Department conducted all foreign relations. Soviet and bloc diplomats naturally perceived the NSC staff as a power center and went to pains to develop lines into it, so the process was mutual. This was the stuff of prerogative in official Washington, invitations to cultural evenings, film showings, embassy receptions, private lunches, and dinners. Informal business; relationships cemented.

Bromley Smith tried to regularize the process to some degree. Brom designated an NSC staffer as a sort of official contact point for a lot of this foreign attention.

One of the most capable bloc diplomats was Soviet Ambassador Anatoli Dobrynin. He considered it a part of *his* job to forge relationships with power centers throughout Washington. When LBJ moved Walt to the White House, Dobrynin waited a few months, then called to set up lunch. The first time, Rostow went to the President for approval, saying he would also check with Rusk and Llewellyn Thompson to determine matters he might usefully raise with Dobrynin. Johnson asked Rostow to see him first; Walt did, and got approval for the Dobrynin lunch, afterward carefully supplying the President with a memorandum of what had been said. By 1968 these direct meetings between the national security adviser and a foreign diplomat had achieved a degree of regularity.

Rostow's direct involvement with the Soviet ambassador, like national security advisers taking foreign trips on behalf of the President, raised the apparent power of the keeper of the keys to new heights. It might have raised Rusk's hackles too, except that Walt carefully deferred to the secretary of state, stayed on Lyndon Johnson's good side, and let it be known around town that the job meant nothing to him. Colleagues may or may not have believed Rostow's professions of disinterest, but the keeper's diplomatic contacts replicated themselves with other diplomats—Italians, Israelis, French, and so on. Rostow's successors have not been so scrupulous. The device of private diplomatic contacts was easily abused to create a back channel for the conduct of diplomacy outside the State Department. In the meantime Rostow's meetings with Dobrynin furnished valuable information to Lyndon Johnson for his arms control efforts.

Johnson's arms control efforts were closely related to his military decisions; they were opposite sides of the same coin. The President sought advice on initiatives to prevent proliferation, appointing a study group under former Deputy Secretary of Defense Roswell L. Gilpatric in November 1964. The Gilpatric Committee included such Wise Men as Dean Acheson, John J. McCloy, and George B. Kistiakowski, along with former Gaither Committee members Robert A. Lovett, James A. Perkins, and Herbert F. York. Studies for Gilpatric's committee were organized from the White House by Spurgeon

Keeny. Sparked by the first Chinese nuclear test, which occurred in October 1964, LBJ reportedly told Gilpatric, "Humanity cannot tolerate a step-by-step spread of nuclear weapons."

The Gilpatric Committee met in Room 303 of the Executive Office Building. There were three plenary sessions leading to a final report to LBJ on January 21, 1965. The study group, including staff director Keeny, held a clear preference for a world in which no further spread of nuclear weapons occurred. Only George Kistiakowski, though he favored this "model" world in the long term, thought further proliferation would occur in the short run. Staff specialists supporting the consensus included NSC's Chuck Johnson, PSAC consultant George Rathjens, and State's Ray Garthoff.

Most sensitive among the committee's business was what attitude to take toward a NATO Multilateral Force (MLF), which would give all NATO members at least some access to nuclear weapons. The MLF had been conceived under Kennedy, and, naturally, the Soviets were adamantly opposed. At both the plenary sessions and the meeting with LBJ, John McCloy argued for giving priority to alliance considerations. Some staff think he tried to skew committee opinion in this respect. McCloy got support from James Perkins and General Alfred Gruenther, a former NATO Supreme Commander, but others were irritated at the way McCloy attempted to inject this tangential topic. Johnson received recommendations to negotiate the widest possible agreement on nonproliferation, to use United States influence on nations contemplating nuclear weapons programs, and to set an example by refusal to collaborate in any such programs. A draft NSAM came with the report too. LBJ emphasized avoiding leaks, whereupon Bundy advised restricting the report to the NSC principals.

Johnson planned a major initiative with proposals he would make in a speech in San Francisco on the twentieth anniversary of the founding of the United Nations. The day before the speech, Robert F. Kennedy made some similar remarks in his maiden address as a United States senator. Evidently furious, Johnson, who never relished playing second fiddle to anyone, especially a Kennedy, struck all the nonproliferation passages from his own text. LBJ did issue NSAM-335, on June 28, 1965, responding to the Gilpatric Committee report by directing the Arms Control and Disarmament Agency (ACDA) to include nonproliferation while formulating arms control policy. Glenn T. Seaborg, chairman of the Atomic Energy Commission, later wrote: "I observed no special measures of implementation following the president's directive." That completed the work of the Gilpatric Committee. General Gruenther sent Bundy a note stating that it had been the best advisory committee he had ever sat with, and that the staff work Keeny directed had been "tops," but that he feared the product would not ease the President's job. Keeny himself believes the report actually catalyzed LBJ's thinking, convincing him of the need for purposeful action on nonproliferation.

Meanwhile, the Soviets bounced back from their refusal to honor tacit commitments made before Khrushchev's downfall. The Soviet leadership, now headed by Aleksei Kosygin and Leonid I. Brezhnev, recognized nuclear nonproliferation as being in their own best interests. Indeed the Russians, in a move that contributed to the Sino-Soviet split, had already refused to follow through on their promises to assist the People's Republic of China to acquire its own nuclear capability. Chinese detonation of a first nuclear device in October 1964 underlined the dangers for the Soviets, who subsequently adopted nonproliferation rhetoric. Rusk once told LBJ, at an afternoon meeting, that if the United States was prepared to give up the MLF, he could have a nonproliferation treaty by dinnertime. At the Eighteen Nation Disarmament Committee in Geneva, William C. Foster tabled the first American draft of such a treaty in August 1965, and the Soviets responded that September with a draft of their own. Both LBJ and Soviet Premier Kosygin employed even stronger language in nonproliferation messages to the Geneva group in early 1966.

By then the MLF option was dead, the skids effectively greased by LBJ's former Senate colleague Rhode Island Democrat John O. Pastore, vice-chairman of the Joint Committee on Atomic Energy, who introduced legislation commending Johnson for his nonproliferation efforts. It was just the move to put the President on notice that there was political hay to be made on nonproliferation. The resolution passed by a unanimous 84-0 vote in May 1966. Even had LBJ missed the significance of this, highly unlikely for a figure of his political skill and background, others would surely bring it to his attention. Arthur Goldberg, for example, ambassador to the UN, proposed a dramatic Johnson trip to Geneva to personally lobby for a treaty.

It was at just this time that Walt Rostow became the watcher at Johnson's gate. From his years of policy planning, Walt was known to favor the MLF option. Consequently, instead of going to Rostow, Goldberg worked through Jack Valenti to reach the President. Similarly, Foster and Keeny went to Bill Moyers. The Foster presentation so impressed Moyers that he arranged for the ACDA director to repeat it for Johnson. Not much later, in July 1966, LBJ at a press conference clearly implied he was willing to compromise an MLF to achieve a nonproliferation treaty with the Soviets. It was a green light for serious negotiations.

When done with a paper, this kind of end run around some perceived bureaucratic obstacle is called bootlegging. The practice of end runs had always existed to some degree, but it became common with the inception of the Kennedy-model NSC staff, in which the function of staff professionals was precisely to learn about what was *not* coming up through channels. With staffers working as expediters, bootlegging up to the NSC occurred with some frequency. Bootlegging *around* the NSC staff was not common while Bundy held the top job, if only because Mac, though he might disparage someone's argument in a cover memo, could be depended upon to send it in to the President. With Rostow the bureaucracy was not so sure. Zbigniew Brzezinski, for example, who had actually been *hired* by Rostow, used to bootleg to LBJ through Harry McPherson, John Roche, and Moyers.

Dean Rusk understood the bureaucracy's proclivity for bootlegging and insisted that anyone who was going to do it send a copy of his memo to the secretary of state. An item Brzezinski sent once caught LBJ's fancy to the extent that he picked it up and read it aloud to the NSC. Rusk, who had heard nothing about this from Brzezinski, was incensed. Luckily Brzezinski had put a copy of the memo in the secretary's in-tray that very morning.

Brzezinski claims credit also for a subtle change in Johnson's approach to the Russians that did go through channels. It occurred in the form of a draft speech moderating the tenor of United States policy, reversing the traditional stance on German reunification; to one of insistence that European reconciliation was to be a precondition for reunification rather than a consequence of it. That represented a concession to the Soviets, who had always insisted upon a German peace treaty, an obvious device for European reconciliation. In any case, Brzezinski had worked up the speech draft with PPC director Henry Owen. With Eugene Rostow as Rusk's principal undersecretary there was no obstacle to sending the speech up to Walt and that was done, but then no one knew how to get LBJ to deliver it. Walt and Francis Bator both reworked the draft but could not figure out how to get Johnson to take an interest. Brzezinski did it with a little sleight of hand—he called up one of his friends on the White House political staff and told him Bobby Kennedy was about to deliver a speech sharply critical of LBJ's European policy; Brzezinski said the President ought to be told about the fine speech, full of innovative ideas, sitting at the NSC waiting to be delivered. No doubt believing he was getting sweet revenge for RFK's speech a year before, Lyndon gave the Europe speech that same day.

At about this time Johnson was also moving ahead on the specifics of nonproliferation. In late September, during the annual opening of the UN General Assembly, Rusk was in New York and held private conversations with Soviet Foreign Minister Andrei A. Gromyko. The Soviet diplomat indicated several concessions his country was willing to make. President Johnson called a meeting of senior advisers at Camp David on October 1, continuing the discussions the next day. "Much of the time," Johnson wrote, "we wandered over the paths and through the autumn colored woods." Rusk warned against rushing ahead too quickly, and the President also exhibited Rostow's influence in his refusal to rule out an "Alliance" solution—the MLF option. But LBJ indicated his willingness to go along with a treaty stated in revised language. In effect, the President gave a green light to serious negotiations on arms control.

If the Russians were interested in nonproliferation, Johnson was prepared to take them up on it and also to go for controls on antiballistic missiles (ABMs). To some degree this was a case in which Johnson saw agreement with the adversary as preferable to giving in to pressures in the United States to deploy ballistic missile defenses. The technical advice, from such

officials as McNamara, science adviser Donald Hornig, and others, uniformly ran against deployment. On the other hand, the CIA had evidence
the Soviets were installing an ABM system at Moscow. Not only were
there fears the so-called Moscow system might be extended to other parts
of the Soviet Union, there were some who claimed that the "Tallinn
system," a Soviet surface-to-air missile already deployed nationwide, was
also an ABM. Johnson was under pressure to counter these supposed
threats. In 1966, against administration wishes, Congress appropriated
$160 million for advance preparations to support ABM deployment. There
were signs that the Joint Chiefs of Staff were going to openly advocate such
a step.

The showdown occurred toward the end of 1966. In early November,
McNamara twice visited the President in Texas at the LBJ Ranch, where
they discussed the ABM issue in considerable detail. The system being offered, consisting of both long-range and short-range missiles plus electronic
scan radars, was considerably more advanced than that of the early 1960s
but was still not capable of actually stopping a nuclear attack. The secretary
of defense dates to November LBJ's basic decision *not* to deploy ABMs but
rather to seek arms controls.

McNamara did not have the last word, however. Johnson had to hear
out the Chiefs, and that meeting took place at the federal office building in
Austin, Texas, on December 6, 1966. Rostow recalls that meeting, and not
the November meetings, as the crucial occasion when the JCS challenged
McNamara's case against ABMs. Flying down from Washington, according
to one version, McNamara found General Wheeler reading some unfamiliar
charts. He strode over and grabbed the papers from Bus Wheeler, like a
young schoolboy trying to impress a teacher.

President Johnson was still at the ranch shortly before nine o'clock that
morning, when he was informed that McNamara's plane was about twenty
minutes out of Austin's Bergstrom Air Force Base. Irritated, LBJ ordered
that in the future he be notified when planes left their points of departure,
not when they were about to arrive. Johnson dressed quickly and in only
fifteen minutes was himself bound for Austin on the presidential helicopter.
LBJ set aside an hour for the meeting, and time was tight, for at eleven the
President was due to present the Medal of Honor to a brave young Marine
from Vietnam, Sergeant Robert E. O'Malley.

The big meeting opened promptly at ten. LBJ sat at the head of the table,
McNamara at its foot. Bus Wheeler, who LBJ invariably called "Buz,"
sat to the right of McNamara, and Cy Vance to the right of Johnson.
Walt Rostow was halfway down the table, sandwiched between Air Force
Chief of Staff General John P. McConnell and Chief of Naval Operations
Admiral David L. McDonald. General Wallace M. Greene of the Marines
and General Harold K. Johnson of the Army shared Wheeler's side of
the table. Bus handed out additional copies of the charts McNamara had

taken earlier. He presented the unanimous position of the Joint Chiefs: The United States could not be certain of Soviet security goals and must therefore match Soviet ABMs. In so doing the United States would also hedge against the rapid buildup of Soviet ICBMs that was then reaching stride.

McNamara came back in January with the present and former science advisers and directors of defense research and engineering. The scientists included such leading lights as Jim Killian, George Kistiakowski, Jerry Wiesner, Harold Brown, and Herbert York. All agreed that ABMs would not work as a population defense against a Soviet attack. The Chiefs nevertheless went ahead in February to make their case directly to Congress for a "light" defense of twenty-five cities estimated to cost $10 billion. President Johnson reacted. On January 27, 1967, LBJ sent a letter to Soviet premier Aleksei Kosygin referring explicitly to the pressures he was under to deploy ABMs, offering talks between "some of our highest authorities" at Geneva or another mutually agreeable locale.

In fact, Lyndon Johnson tried repeatedly to extract a concrete commitment that would set a time and place for arms control talks. Kosygin resisted any promises. President Johnson ultimately concluded the Soviet premier lacked authority to make such pledges. He was correct. Kosygin, and a third member of the Soviet troika leadership, Nikolai V. Podgorny, were already being eclipsed by Communist Party General Secretary Leonid Brezhnev. From time to time over the succeeding months, Johnson put out more feelers to check the climate for arms control in Moscow to no avail.

Without negotiations there was no choice except to face the domestic political pressures for ABM deployment. Those pressures intensified as it appeared that the Russian missile defenses continued to increase. The intelligence dispute over the ABM potential of the Tallinn system helped bolster the case made by proponents of missile defense. McNamara sided with the CIA in discounting Tallinn as an ABM weapon, and said as much in his classified statements to Congress on U.S. military posture. The Air Force and Defense Intelligence Agency claimed the Soviet system was a nationwide ABM defense.

Resolving this kind of interagency difference, "integrating" national policy, was the raison d'être of the NSC. Though intelligence disputes are not formal policy matters, as the Tallinn argument vividly demonstrated they have serious policy implications. Moreover, the 1947 National Security Act explicitly charged the NSC with supervision of the intelligence community, and the NSC was the prime consumer for intelligence product. Rostow in fact did try to do a little about the Tallinn dispute. At a session of the Committee of Principals on March 14, 1967, the same one to which Bus Wheeler expounded the JCS view of what arms controls were acceptable, Walt noted that much depended on the nature of Tallinn and that the United States should somehow learn more about it. Richard Helms did not answer directly; the CIA chief expressed doubt regarding the United States' ability to carry out unilateral verification for arms control. It was left to McNamara to suggest an approach to the Soviets with the aim of beginning a dialogue on the superpowers' respective verification capabilities. The secretary of defense thought it could extend as far as an exchange of satellite reconnaissance photographs between the two sides.

In the meantime the Tallinn debate raged within the intelligence community. With his range of contacts there, Spurge Keeny was fully abreast of the esoteric and arcane turns the debate took—radar band widths, scanning mechanisms, decoy discrimination, power ratings—so much that was hardly understood outside a narrow technical community. Rostow and the NSC staff were aware throughout the debate, according to several sources, that some dubious data were being ginned up to support the thesis that Tallinn was something other than an antiaircraft missile. Rostow never quashed the debate because of certainty that a spate of leaks would follow. In the climate that surrounded the decision on ABM deployment, the political cost would be too great.

The administration's ultimate answer was an exercise in political damage limitation. They would deploy a limited ABM system, supposedly not against the Soviets at all, but against the contingency of an ICBM attack from the People's Republic of China or to negate any accidental missile launch. This solution, NSC staffers believe, was brainstormed by McNamara and LBJ together. McNamara announced the decision in a strange way— at the end of a long speech in San Francisco on September 18, 1967, most of which was devoted to postulating reasons why a ballistic missile defense would not work.

At the same time, Lyndon Johnson redoubled his efforts to move the other side of the equation—to get the Soviets to agree to arms control negotiations. He had Bill Foster's deputy, Adrian Fisher, assure the Eighteen Nation Disarmament Committee that McNamara's ABM announcement did not close the door to arms control. To insert a note of urgency, and because development programs were approaching the flight test phase, on December 13 the Pentagon's director of defense research and engineering announced the creation of MIRVs, which were justified specifically as a counter to Soviet ABMs. Johnson himself prodded the Russians several more times through the first half of 1968, starting in January when he raised both the nonproliferation treaty and arms talks in a single letter. It was, Rostow thought, a tacit linkage of the two issues.

Finally, the Soviets seemed to respond, in late May when Deputy Foreign Minister Vasily V. Kuznetsov declared Soviet willingness to agree on practical steps to reduce strategic offensive forces. A month later Kosygin spoke in a letter to LBJ of having a concrete exchange of views. Johnson replied immediately and by the end of June agreed to open talks on both offensive and defensive forces "in the nearest future." Moscow and Washington issued identical statements to that effect on July 1. LBJ's announcement came at the ceremony held for signature of the Treaty on the Nonproliferation of Nuclear Weapons.

At the State Department the same day, Rusk chaired a session of the Committee of Principals for preliminary consideration of the United States position for talks. Clark Clifford, who had succeeded McNamara as secretary of defense, believed the United States should wait to hear what the Russians had to say, not making any concessions at the outset. Clifford, Deputy Secretary of Defense Paul Nitze, and Dick Helms agreed that verification would be a critical issue, and Clifford was not encouraging in his assessment of the adequacy of unilateral intelligence means. At the end, according to Glenn Seaborg, "Rusk . . . made a plea that we not let quibbling over details stand in the way of major accomplishments as we had done in so many previous attempts at arms limitation."

What followed was some high-order bureaucratic politics closely monitored by Spurge Keeny from the Executive Office Building. The Joint Chiefs of Staff had enumerated stiff requirements for agreement and had developed a distrust for the Arms Control and Disarmament Agency (ACDA). It was Butch Fisher of ACDA, on the other hand, who chaired the SIG subcommittee that had responsibility for presentations to the Committee of Principals. In addition, Bus Wheeler harbored animosity for ACDA's Bill Foster after contentious differences during work on a treaty prohibiting nuclear weapons on the ocean floor. The problem was how to formulate a United States bargaining position and get it up through the Committee of Principals.

Even in the Pentagon there were difficulties. Arms control was inimical to John S. Foster, Jr., director of defense research, whose advanced missile systems might be constrained by an agreement. There were other centers of opposition as well. Morton H. Halperin, deputy assistant secretary of defense for policy planning and arms control, carefully finessed the matter. Halperin proposed a working group within his office to coordinate action on arms control. His boss, Paul C. Warnke, assistant secretary of defense for international security affairs, agreed and passed the recommendation along to Clifford, who approved it.

Halperin, a thirty-year-old defense specialist from Harvard, who had come to the Pentagon to work for John McNaughton, had a good sense of what had to be done. He lined up ACDA staffer Jerome Kahan plus Richard H. Ullman, a Harvard friend and academic who was an expert on the Russian civil war. Ullman actually came over to DOD *from* the NSC staff, where he had worked on European and East-West matters under Ed Fried during 1967, so he served as an easy channel of communications to LBJ's expediters.

The DOD working group sought to meet Rusk's admonition by avoiding any "agenda-based" proposal. In practice, that meant avoiding numerical limits on ABMs to keep the JCS on board, plus mollifying Johnny Foster by eschewing constraints on technological improvements, thus permitting MIRV deployment. Consequently the basic proposal would be similar to

LBJ's 1964 verified freeze: a cap on ICBMs (with no MIRV constraints) at twelve hundred, actually permitting slight increases in United States force levels, plus equivalent but unspecified ABM limits. After assembling these elements of a proposal, Halperin sold them to State and to Fisher at ACDA, from whom the formal paper had to come. Conscious of the need to keep ACDA from being completely shut out of the process, Butch Fisher was amenable to circulating the DOD draft treaty outline as his own paper.

Maneuvers to get the Joint Chiefs on board proceeded by means of referring the ACDA proposal first to lower levels, accruing approvals that might carry weight with the Chiefs, and also waiting for the NSC deadline for an agreed arms control position to reach LBJ's desk. As the deadline came closer the pressure to concur built. Wheeler's special arms control representative, Major General Royall B. Allison, played the part of an honest broker and saw nothing amiss in the procedures used to clear the arms control paper.

Harold Brown and Halperin, perhaps as a gambit to make the ACDA paper seem a compromise proposal, pressed for ABM prohibition or at least maximum limits.

A revised paper went before the Committee of Principals on July 31. A freeze on intermediate range ballistic missiles (IRBMs) and lesser missiles, and a ban on mobile missiles further assuaged the Chiefs' sensibilities. General Allison's suggestions helped smooth the way; Rostow thought his role admirable. The United States negotiating position, including a nine-year duration for the agreement, got final approval on August 7. Robert Martin, a specialist at State's political-military office, suggested calling the project the Strategic Arms Limitation Talks, yielding the acronym SALT. Thus was born a generic name for arms negotiations that would endure for over a decade.

While the bureaucrats formulated a United States bargaining position, Johnson set about actually scheduling a summit conference with the Soviets. On August 19, Ambassador Dobrynin called on Rusk and informed him that the Soviets agreed to meet at Leningrad in the first ten days of October. The text of the Soviets' proposed announcement reached LBJ that evening in Detroit, where he had gone to address the Veterans of Foreign Wars. Returning to the nation's capital later that night, LBJ met Rostow and Rusk, and decided to announce the summit on Wednesday, August 21. On the twentieth, aide Tom Johnson actually told reporters to be ready for an interesting announcement the next morning.

Walt Rostow had arranged a Tuesday Lunch for August 20. He usually called around to the regulars to find agenda items for those lunches, but that day Walt took the rare action of selecting a topic himself: Czechoslovakia. That Eastern European nation had been undergoing an experiment in Communist liberalization since the spring of 1968. Tension between Soviets and Czechs had resulted, and it became an open question whether the Russians might send military forces to intervene. LBJ professed to have been aware of the interventionary pressures and to have realized any such Soviet action would, at least temporarily, derail SALT.

Rarely was Rostow so relieved he had taken an action as he was to have scheduled the Czech item for that Tuesday Lunch. As a result, LBJ held a thorough discussion with his NSC principals and most intimate advisers. Suddenly, late that afternoon, the CIA reported that Soviet and other Warsaw Pact troops were flooding across the Czech border.

The phone on Johnson's desk rang at 7:06 P.M. Rostow, who had seen Dobrynin just the previous day to discuss SALT, reported that the Soviet ambassador needed to deliver a message from the highest levels of his government. LBJ saw Dobrynin at eight. The Soviet diplomat nervously read out a long statement assuring Washington that, despite the Czech intervention, nothing should harm United States–Soviet relations.

The President turned around and called an emergency NSC meeting for later that night. Rostow, Wheeler, and Helms summarized what was then known of the Soviet intervention and the group attempted to analyze those tea leaves. Johnson's first instruction to the group was: "We need to give immediate thought to [the] timing of [our] meeting with the Soviets." LBJ posed the twin questions of whether talks could proceed at all, and whether a willingness to talk "would look as though we condone this movement." Rusk was surprised by the Soviets' timing. "This shows they hold the USA in contempt," he said. Clifford remarked that he himself was not clear on the reason the Soviets were taking this action. Leonid Brezhnev soon answered with a speech asserting a Soviet right to intervene in any bloc nation, to prevent that country moving away from socialism. This "Brezhnev Doctrine" coincidentally provided concrete evidence that Brezhnev had attained primacy among the Soviet leadership.

President Johnson canceled the SALT statement scheduled for the next morning. He felt there was no way to proceed with business as usual. The United States fiercely protested the Soviet intervention.

That was not, however, the end of the Leningrad summit. As the days and weeks passed, Johnson felt anew the urgency of SALT. Indeed, the first flight tests of MIRV missiles occurred at that time. Studies seen by the NSC staff already suggested MIRV was going to be a dangerous destabilizing element in the arms race, and if there was going to be a MIRV ban, something had to happen very quickly.

Lyndon Johnson, working in close collaboration with Rusk, almost single-handedly worked to resuscitate the Leningrad summit. It was one of the most closely held activities of his administration—Rostow learned only what *he* needed to know, Spurgeon Keeny heard only in the last stages, Mort Halperin saw very little of anything, and the ACDA people were entirely cut out. On October 16, Undersecretary of State Nicholas Katzenbach told a conference in Europe that dialogue with Moscow had to continue regardless of Czechoslovakia. The Russians responded on November 11, when Kosygin invited Bob McNamara and his wife, visiting Moscow as tourists, to the Kremlin for a three-hour discussion of SALT. The following day a Soviet diplomat told a UN committee that his country was ready for a serious exchange of views without delay.

It was a delicate matter for a lame-duck President. A few days earlier Richard M. Nixon had won the 1968 election and would become President on Inauguration Day. But LBJ felt the urgency and thought the format he had arranged would protect the interests of the President-elect. First the United States and Soviets would exchange papers setting forth their initial bargaining positions. Johnson would then meet the Soviet leaders at the summit to try to agree on broad principles and discuss other world problems. Finally would come the technical negotiations; those Nixon could manage directly.

In the end there would be no summit. President Johnson tried to bring Nixon along on the arrangements, but the President-elect was reluctant. First LBJ suggested that veteran diplomat Robert Murphy represent Nixon's interests. Later the offer was for Nixon himself to come along. Rostow met with newly annointed national security adviser Henry A. Kissinger. He told Henry that LBJ feared MIRV technology was getting out of control—in another year the United States would have them and the Russians would insist on them too. On November 14, Dobrynin told Rostow his government felt it important not to lose momentum in opening SALT. It was the last chance. Clark Clifford, in an eleventh-hour appearance on one of the television news programs on December 15, still advocated the early summit.

But Kissinger and Nixon were not convinced, and were warned off by Robert Murphy. Nixon saw LBJ as making "one last dramatic demonstration of his dedication to peace," and did not believe the Soviets were willing to negotiate seriously on any issue.

Arms control historian John Newhouse quotes a Soviet diplomat and SALT expert: "It's too bad we waited so long. If only we had gone ahead with talks when McNamara was pressing for them. Don't think we weren't studying the problem. It was just too soon. We didn't think we were ready." Nixon and Kissinger would have agreed. Many of Johnson's people thought it tragic that this opportunity was lost. Perhaps the only issue more tragic for Lyndon Johnson was the issue that drove him from office: Vietnam.

▲▲

PART V
▲

VIETNAM: ARROGANCE
TO ADVERSITY

In November 1963, when LBJ entered the Oval Office, Ngo Dinh Diem was three weeks dead and a military junta was in control in Saigon, one the United States had backed, but a junta nonetheless. Diem may not have been very democratic, but the image of the United States fighting for democracy in Southeast Asia was not improved by its support for the military coup. It was the latest of the nagging little anomalies that constantly seemed to blur the image Washington wanted to project; that of a democratic, disinterested protector.

When he was catapulted into office, Johnson saw Vietnam as a problem but could not focus exclusively upon it. He made a short-term decision that turned out to have greater implications than he expected. As Jack Kennedy had once ruminated, it all began with one sip of the drink.

▲▲▲

"WE SEEK AN INDEPENDENT NON-COMMUNIST SOUTH VIETNAM"

▲▲▲

When President Kennedy was shot, Mac Bundy himself had just returned to the capital from Honolulu as the President's team captain in a quiet meeting with Rusk, McNamara, and the entire senior level of the country team from Saigon, headed by Ambassador Henry Cabot Lodge. The object was stocktaking on Indochina, to prepare for the fiscal 1965 appropriations requests. After Honolulu, Lodge also returned to Washington to give the President a firsthand view of the tumultuous days of the overthrow of Diem.

Cabot tried to demonstrate he had no responsibility for the deaths of the Vietnamese leader and his brother. George Ball, who attended this meeting, which occurred on November 24, 1963, felt saddened in retrospect because, in a perfectly rational world, LBJ should have had the opportunity to devote his first weeks to a critical examination of all the assumptions that underlay Vietnam policy. The substitute was instead a meeting of the men who had made the policy—Rusk, McNamara, John McCone, and Mac Bundy. McCone reported that the military leaders in Saigon were having difficulties organizing their junta and that Vietcong activity was increasing.

The new President proved surprisingly critical, but for reasons stemming from a brief visit to Vietnam in 1961. Johnson thought the United States had made a serious mistake in not supporting Diem through the Buddhist crisis and all the rest. In the wake of the coup, he told the group, many were critical of Diem's removal and shocked by his murder. Congressional demands for withdrawal were becoming loud. LBJ also had misgivings about dissension within the country team at the American embassy. Johnson wanted the ambassador to be the sole boss and intended to send fresh people to Saigon to make it happen.

"I told my advisers," LBJ wrote, "that I thought we had spent too much time and energy trying to shape other countries in our own image." The new President rejected so-called nation-building, a primary technique in the counterinsurgency theory favored under Kennedy; his main objective would be to help resist against those using force. "We should not be too critical if they did not become thriving, modern, twentieth-century democracies in a week."

A withdrawal of American troops from Vietnam had already been announced by the White House before JFK's death, and a drawdown of one thousand was planned at the Pentagon. McNamara and Rusk agreed that some military advisers could be brought out before the end of the year and a majority by mid-1965, by which time the Vietnamese could take over all military functions. According to the analysts who wrote the top-secret study of United States decision making now known as the Pentagon Papers, "only the most Macomberesque predictions could have led decision-makers in Washington to believe that the fight against the guerrillas would have clearly turned the corner by FY 65." In fact, McNamara would report after another of his trips to South Vietnam (SVN) in December that the situation was deteriorating, while a Honolulu conference at CINCPAC in March 1964 decided that the real issue was how much of a setback there had been. There was no more talk of withdrawal after that. "It was a reasonably good policy" the Pentagon Papers analyst concludes, that was "overtaken by events."

In the meantime, however, LBJ continued to include withdrawal in the policy paper, NSAM-273, that he approved two days after the initial Vietnam meeting. But the measure lay alongside another provision of the NSAM that called for planning clandestine operations against the Democratic Republic of Vietnam (DRV) and missions up to fifty kilometers deep into Laos. To justify such actions, State was directed to assemble a strong report that could be issued to prove the Vietcong (VC) were controlled, sustained, and supplied by Hanoi. In the same spirit, NSAM-273 gave as the "central objective" of policy to help the government of Vietnam "win their contest against the externally directed and supported communist conspiracy."

According to NSC staffer Chester L. Cooper, soon to become the senior Far East man under Bundy, NSAM-273 was meant as nothing more than a holding action, something to give the bureaucracy its marching orders while the President got essential business out of the way so he could focus on Vietnam. Similarly, George Ball recalls that Johnson seemed "as anxious as Kennedy to avoid an irreversible embroilment." If so, there was little reason for Johnson to include broadened coercion in the NSAM. Evidently LBJ did not clearly understand the option.

Whether or not LBJ had considered its implications, that option went forward from the November conference at Honolulu. At the Pentagon a small group met under General Victor Krulak of the Marines, the JCS special assistant for counterinsurgency and special activities, to devise component measures. The group at Honolulu also ordered the commander of the Military Assistance Command Vietnam (MACV), together with William Colby, the chief of CIA Far Eastern operations, to compile a three-phase plan for a twelve-month-long program of graduated covert pressures against the DRV. The program would include commando raids, covert air missions, psychological operations, naval forays, attempts to implant agents, and anything else that might be useful. Because the plan utilized much CINCPAC work done the previous June for Operations Plan (OPLAN) 34–64, the new plan was called OPLAN 34-A.

Secretary of Defense Robert McNamara returned to Saigon for another of his visits in mid-December. In the course of the trip, he reviewed the OPLAN 34-A concept of operations. In his report to the President on December 21, McNamara noted:

> *Plans for Covert Action into North Vietnam* were prepared as we had requested and were an excellent job. They present a wide variety of sabotage and psychological operations against North Vietnam from which I believe we should aim to select those that provide maximum pressure with minimum risk.

On January 16, 1964, Johnson approved OPLAN 34-A and ordered implementation of its first phase beginning in February.

A few weeks after he took office, LBJ met with a few of his NSC staff. One was Mike Forrestal. LBJ summoned them downstairs, where he was splashing about in the swimming pool, and told them to jump in. Skinny-dipping. It was classic Johnson, a typical test. Forrestal and the others did as bidden but were pretty embarrassed, then equally relieved a few minutes later when LBJ announced, "Let's go to work" and got out of the pool. The group went upstairs and the President began to go around the table, soliciting short reports and summary views. Since the whole thing came as a complete surprise, none of the NSC staffers had very much to say. Then Johnson made a passionate speech extolling the importance to the nation of the work of the NSC staff, urging that none of them leave.

Despite Dean Rusk, a former Army colonel who, when he openly advocated anything, often supported forceful options, and who had lined up solidly behind the NSAM-273 policy, LBJ seemed not to trust State. Meanwhile, the State-chaired Vietnam task force under Paul Kattenburg appeared unable to energize the bureaucracy. Kattenburg finally threw in the towel and went to work for Walt Rostow at Policy Planning. The job of Washington coordinator briefly went to diplomat William H. Sullivan, but in one of his few successes, Forrestal, who opposed the coercive course of OPLAN 34-A, managed to convince LBJ that it was not enough to organize at home, there had to be a counterpart unit in the field. So Sullivan was sent to do that in Saigon. To replace him, LBJ tapped Forrestal, who got an office next to Rusk's but whose salary continued to be paid by the NSC. Forrestal reported directly to the President and initially was supposed to keep an eye on Rusk. After a few months, once Rusk earned LBJ's trust, the function of spy disappeared and Forrestal became a simple coordinator.

The creation of the Sullivan-Forrestal task force removed responsibility from the regional bureau, which became only one of many offices making contributions. Kennedy stalwart Roger Hilsman resigned. Hilsman's enthusiasm for counterinsurgency and roughshod methods had bothered a number of people. Once Bill Bundy took the job, the regional bureau again received formal responsibility and the Vietnam task force reverted to a coordination mechanism.

Reporting from the mission in Vietnam received inordinate attention in Washington. There was literally a deluge of daily reporting cables, commentary, and statistics. To regularize reporting, Mac Bundy sent out Chester Cooper, to whom the flow "evoked visions of the Mississippi River in high-water season." The ambassador began to send weekly summary cables while the embassy expanded its reporting from the provinces. To check its own local reporting, the CIA sent out a special analytical team for an in-depth study.

Still, Cooper would never be entirely satisfied with the official reporting procedures, owing to problems the NSC staff encountered from the President. Originally seconded from the CIA to handle liaison between the NSC staff and the intelligence analysts, Cooper had resigned from the agency after the Cuban missile crisis, though he kept an office at Langley where he spent his afternoons, after mornings in a tight cubicle off the Situation Room. He felt the real problem with the reporting was competition with the press. An official cable coming out of Saigon had to have the approval of hosts of senior people, then had to be encoded, transmitted, decoded, and circulated by messenger in Washington. A reporter simply cabled his copy home to an editor. Since LBJ sat at his desk with a bank of three televisions tuned to the major networks, plus three press service tickers in the Oval Office, he frequently heard a story hours before there was any official cable with which to compare it. Even worse, the daily noontime press briefings also occurred, more often than not, before arrival of the Saigon cables. Prompted by their editors, Washington reporters frequently had questions for which the press secretary had no answers.

It was a "hapless minion," in Cooper's phrase, who got stuck telling LBJ the NSC staff still knew nothing, when he buzzed with a question culled from his TV or the tickers. With Forrestal's departure that minion became Jim Thomson, pulled in from Bill Bundy's regional bureau. Soon enough it would be Cooper himself who, as LBJ moved into the 1964 election campaign, was assigned to coordinate the President's statements and speeches having to do with foreign policy, and who was then made the senior NSC staffer for the Far East, a portfolio that was to a great extent Vietnam, especially as United States involvement deepened.

Chet Cooper had spent fifteen years with the CIA before he was first brought to the White House. There Cooper had handled Chinese economics, then took over the China desk. When the Office of National Estimates was formed in 1950, he became the chief of its Far East staff. By the autumn of 1952, Cooper had witnessed the fall of China, creation of the PRC, the height of the Korean War, and the continuing deterioration in French In-dochina.

Cooper went on to a few more assignments before joining the NSC staff. He attended the 1954 Geneva conference (and the one in 1961–1962 as well) as the top CIA man in the delegation. He spent three years in London as United States representative for exchange of intelligence information. He returned to the Office of National Estimates as its chief, and later became a member of the Board of National Estimates.

His first big moment in Johnson's White House came the very first day, when Cooper was still liaison between the NSC and the CIA's analysts at Langley. LBJ came to Mac's office for his first intelligence briefing and McCone asked Chet to sit in. Afterward Johnson had to cross West Executive Avenue, for during the interregnum he continued to use his vice presidential office in the OEOB. It was cold and raining, and Cooper, who was also leaving for the OEOB, had an umbrella. They crossed together, the staff man holding his umbrella over the President's head. For about a day the corridors buzzed with rumors of Johnson's sudden new regard for Chester Cooper.

Though he became the senior NSC man on what was arguably the single most important national security issue of Johnson's presidency, Cooper would rarely see LBJ alone; he did so maybe six to ten times in almost two and a half years. Even in 1964, when Cooper coordinated candidate LBJ's foreign policy statements, the President remained remote.

As Johnson's coercive policy gathered momentum, it became less possible to avoid war. There is a good case to be made that, given his ambitious domestic plans, LBJ did not want war, but he started out following what he considered were Kennedy's footsteps and then ignored the warning signs. And warning signs there were, from many parts of the far-flung bureaucracy, even from some quite unexpected places.

One of the early warnings came from former NSC staffer Robert H. Johnson, who now toiled for Walt Rostow at policy planning. Walt asked Bob Johnson to assemble a study of the questions that might have to be dealt with in considering a policy of escalation. Rostow did it despite his knowledge that Johnson opposed such a course, for they had been arguing the fine points together since the days when both had been on Kennedy's NSC staff. With a small group drawn entirely from policy planning, Johnson assembled an eighty-page paper that identified all the problems they could think of. In late 1963 or early 1964, Rostow took that paper to Dean Rusk, and came back with orders to conduct an interagency escalation study on a more formal basis. Once again he asked Bob Johnson to head the panel.

Having spent a decade on the NSC staff during Truman's and Ike's administrations, the heyday of Cabinet maneuvers, Bob Johnson was re-luctant to accept Rostow's mandate. He feared his own opposition would become submerged in a panel study that had to reflect the views of the broad bureaucracy. Walt bought him off with the promise that should the final report differ from his own opinions, Johnson could send his own paper on to the recipients of the panel study. But it turned out that Johnson never lost control of the study—the panel included a number of skeptics like himself, time pressures precluded departmental approvals for the views of their representatives, and the same urgency allowed Johnson himself to draft certain vital passages.

The Johnson panel began without any precise deadline, but was soon asked to have a complete report in time for a trip McNamara planned to Honolulu and Vietnam. Thus the crunch. Twenty-six background papers contributed to the study, submitted in combination and individually by all the different components of the bureaucracy. The JCS, for example, provided a list of potential military steps; the CIA and State jointly examined the role of the DRV in the insurgency in South Vietnam. There were papers on negotiations, on legal justifications for escalation, on the path escalation might take, on defining United States objectives. The panel examined three broad policy options: a program of covert pressures against the DRV; overt United States military action elsewhere (such as in SVN); and overt military action, primarily bombing, directly against the DRV.

With no pretense of recommending a policy, the panel attempted an integrated examination of the problems and requirements attached to each of the three options. In the "key problems" paper, of which Bob Johnson prepared the first draft, the first and critical question about any form of escalation was would it work. The study group's bottom line was "probably not." To quote an excerpt Johnson has related: "Probably the most that could be expected would be that the DRV would ultimately slacken and ostensibly cease its support of the VC while pressing for a cease-fire in the South, ordering the VC to regroup and lie low, and covertly preparing to resume the insurrection." There could be no assurance the United States could guarantee the "best circumstances" would obtain, while efforts to achieve them would "considerably" increase the possibility of a direct intervention by the PRC or Soviet Union.

Testing the Johnson panel's conclusions became the object of a series of political-military simulations carried out by a JCS unit called the Joint War Games Agency. These games were called SIGMA-I, held from April 6 to April 9, and SIGMA-II, from September 8 to the 17. Atypically for such exercises, the roster of policy team players read like a list of the top people in the administration. The "Blue" team in SIGMA-I, representing the United States, included Mac Bundy, George Ball, U. Alexis Johnson, John McCone, John McNaughton, plus two members of the Joint Chiefs, Generals Maxwell Taylor and Curtis E. LeMay. The "Red" (North Vietnamese) team included Bill Bundy, General Earle Wheeler, then director of the Joint Staff serving the JCS; General Joseph F. Carroll, director of the Defense Intelligence Agency; and General Rollen H. Anthis, new special assistant to the JCS for

▲

counterinsurgency and special activities. The "Yellow" (Red Chinese) team included Chet Cooper and Michael Forrestal from the NSC staff and William Sullivan, for whom the Johnson study group had done its report.

The game began with a covert bombing campaign, which was exposed with the shooting down and capture of an American aircraft and its pilot at a game date of June 15, 1964. While exploiting the situation for propaganda advantage, the team representing the DRV initially made a move designed to deter United States escalation, then followed by itself escalating the ground war in the south, confident that the PRC would intervene to counter any United States escalation large enough to win the war. William Sullivan, who thought this game played to roughly the same conclusion as an earlier one in which he had participated, believed the experience "produced a very large crop of senior military officers who . . . found the results convincing and sobering."

An exception was Curtis LeMay, who in the earlier game had complained bitterly that the simulation was unrealistic because the control group had given inadequate weight to the ability of air power to interdict DRV supply lines and shatter their operations.

"This is the way we lost Czechoslovakia," LeMay had thundered, waving his cigar in the air for emphasis.

Mac Bundy had retorted, "Curt, I didn't know you ever *had* Czechoslovakia!"

As a result of the war game exercise, Sullivan found himself assigned to develop, in conjunction with Mike Forrestal, a draft text for a joint resolution LBJ could present Congress that would spark a decisive debate which could settle the question whether the public would support a greatly expanded war in Vietnam. Sullivan also headed yet another study, this one to determine whether there were any targets in the DRV whose bombing might make a "strategic difference" on the war in the south if they were destroyed. With a dissent from the Air Force, the study concluded there were none.

In the fall, Washington held SIGMA-II. This time the Army's General Earle Wheeler, recently appointed Chairman of the JCS, led the "Blue" team, which included a senior member of his Joint Staff; General LeMay once more; John McCone of the CIA; and John McNaughton and Cyrus Vance from McNamara's office; and both Bundy brothers. Two more members of the Joint Chiefs, the director of their Joint Staff, CIA deputy director Ray Cline, and senior State officials including Llewellyn Thompson, participated on the "Red" side. With Johnson's top assistants concentrated on the United States side, it is clear that the intent of the simulation was specifically to let them explore the parameters of the upcoming intervention decisions. The intent became explicit in the game scenario, beginning from a game date of April 1965. The scenario assumed NVA troops had entered the south, the Republic of Vietnam (RVN) remained on shaky political ground, the Buddhists were rioting, the Chinese intervening with "volun-

205

teer" air forces, and the United States was continuing to bomb, had mined Haiphong Harbor, and landed a Marine expeditionary force to protect one of the coastal bases.

Wheeler's team followed existing Pentagon contingency plans, sending Army troops in to bolster the Vietnamese around Saigon, mobilizing for war in the United States and escalating the bombing of the DRV. By the end of the third move, the usual duration of these political-military games, "Blue" had resolved its alternatives into three options: a negotiated settlement, an American takeover of the war in the RVN to prop up its government, or "to execute general war plans against Communist China with conventional or nuclear weapons. . . ." As for Curtis Lemay's preference, "the majority of players and Control tended toward belief that industrial and military bombing in the DRV would not quickly cause cessation of the insurgency in South Vietnam." State planner Bob Johnson, who once more served "Blue" as a member of its action group, probably appreciated the conclusion that "the problem of communicating from one team to another a determination not to give in, or of intent to escalate the conflict, was evident in SIGMA-II."

Thus the second war game, like the earlier one, tended to reinforce the cautionary note sounded by the interagency study Bob Johnson had overseen. Johnson remained a skeptic and gathered others around him. Among them were Paul Kattenburg, also in Rostow's shop; William Trueheart, former deputy chief of mission in Saigon; Allen S. Whiting, deputy director for East Asia at State's intelligence bureau; and Carl Salans, Rusk's legal counsel. Kattenburg believes the early skeptics, or at least this group of them, proved ineffective because they did not have the stature of the senior players, because they worked individually rather than as a coherent group, and because they were sufficiently career-oriented not to risk their personal futures on stopping the slide into war. Bob Johnson might have been objecting, but Lyndon Johnson wasn't listening.

As these games were played out in Washington, events in the Republic of Vietnam lurched from one crisis to the next. The RVN certainly did not provide a stable base from which to mount a campaign of coercive diplomacy. The junta of generals who had replaced Ngo Dinh Diem lasted only three months. In early 1964, General Nguyen Khanh overthrew them in another military coup. During that year there were no fewer than *seven* governments of the Republic of Vietnam.

McNamara and Taylor's March 1964 visit to the RVN did much to set the United States course in succeeding months. The secretary and JCS Chairman made their official calls, then took a quick tour of the provinces, all the way from the Mekong Delta to Hue in the north. They sounded out Nguyen Khanh about possible air and naval retaliation against the DRV. "The political-military situation was more serious than I had appreciated in Washington," Taylor wrote later. "The enemy was clearly making the most out of the political turbulence." The Vietcong were stronger than ever, and beginning to use heavy crew-served weapons of Chinese origin. The ARVN, diverted by all the political maneuvering among the generals, were not prosecuting the war effectively. Their desertion rate was high and increasing.

Taylor saw the alternatives as negotiating a settlement at one extreme (President Charles DeGaulle of France was then pushing a formula that might "neutralize" Southeast Asia) to bombing and commando raids against the DRV at the other (Taylor writes of "initiating" these actions as if 34-A did not exist). He notes that Nguyen Khanh himself had seemed unenthusiastic regarding the military option and had raised the problem that political and military conditions in the south did not provide a solid base for action against the north. Sandwiched between the extremes were a long laundry list of half measures. Taylor reports that the secretary of defense rejected both extremes, while he and the Chiefs expressed doubt that the partial measures McNamara recommended could bear fruit in the four to six months he promised.

The President heard them out in his Oval Office on March 16, and broached the topic before a larger group at an NSC meeting the next day. After the discussion, LBJ approved NSAM-288. Following closely McNamara's trip report, the President's directive lifted verbatim the secretary's description of the United States objective: "We seek an independent non-Communist South Vietnam." Although, for the time being, LBJ refused to sanction additional graduated military pressures, the Pentagon Papers analysts conclude that "in enunciating the policies of NSAM-288 we had rhetorically committed ourselves to do whatever was needed to achieve our stated objectives in South Vietnam." Despite Johnson's rejection of increased military pressures, the 34-A naval commando raids began on February 16 and continued at a steady rate, a pace that increased in June and July.

Johnson continued to worry, both about doing enough and about justification for what was being done. He took the occasion of a late May visit to Saigon by Rusk, McNaughton, and others to ask them to meet in Honolulu with the CINCPAC plus Lodge and key embassy officials. Mike Forrestal had sent LBJ a memo warning that it was not at all certain time was working in the United States' favor, that barring some dramatic change in atmosphere, there was an increasing danger of political upheaval or accident. LBJ wanted more advice, and he also wished to reemphasize the rationale for the war. In a public statement regarding the Honolulu meeting, LBJ quoted the October 1954 letter Eisenhower had sent Ngo Dinh Diem, emphasizing America's solid commitment, promising he had no plans to expand the war, saying "that was a good letter then and it is a good letter now, and we feel the same way."

Honolulu began another round of brainstorming among the bureaucracy's brightest minds. Two elements emerged in the thinking of people like John McNaughton, Bill Bundy, Bill Sullivan, and the rest. One was a draft plan for more military pressures; it included lists of bombing targets, the clear notion of "tit for tat" strikes that would retaliate for given provocations, and a time-line scenario to lead from decision through implementation. A second element was a draft congressional resolution, along the lines of the ones Eisenhower had gotten on several occasions, that would authorize the President in advance to undertake unspecified military actions. Forrestal and Sullivan actually wrote the language; Bill Bundy was among its strongest proponents. Lyndon Johnson, who refused to countenance any talk of a declaration of war, seized on the idea of the resolution as a suitable surrogate.

As Washington pondered its options, the situation looked more like war every day. General Paul Harkins retired, to be replaced by William C. Westmoreland, a paratrooper who had fought under Max Taylor's command in World War II. Taylor himself came to Saigon to replace Lodge as the United States ambassador. In late July, LBJ approved a further 5,000-man augmentation in United States advisory strength, which would bring MACV to over 22,000. Not just advisers anymore, Americans were making air strikes, leading units of ethnic minority troops, flying ARVN into battle aboard United States helicopters, and running most South Vietnamese logistics. Nguyen Khanh could easily imply the Americans were included when he, in a late July speech, declared the beginning of a "march north" that would end the insurgency in the south.

Hanoi could hardly avoid feeling pressured, what with Khanh's rhetoric coupled with OPLAN 34-A raids already in progress. Then, on both August 1 and 2, "civilian" aircraft flying from Thai bases to make strikes in Laos bombed the DRV instead. The night of August 1–2 one of the 34-A boat raids went in against NVA radar sites on two offshore islands. In what, it is claimed, was not any part of this provocative activity, the United States destroyer *Maddox* was just then in the Gulf of Tonkin on a mission to collect communications and electronic intelligence on the DRV. On August 2, after the 34-A boat raids, the North Vietnamese sent three torpedo boats to attack the *Maddox*. In a short, sharp naval action the torpedo boats were sunk or driven off by the *Maddox* or naval aircraft that arrived to assist her.

Word of this first incident in the Gulf of Tonkin began to flow into the Situation Room shortly after 4:00 A.M. on August 2. The duty officer sent a summary to LBJ's bedroom as quickly as it could be typed up. By morning Mac Bundy was able to brief Johnson as the President got ready for church. Later LBJ held a meeting with Rusk, George Ball, Cy Vance, new JCS Chairman General Earle Wheeler, and several technical intelligence experts. Johnson decided the engagement must have been a product of DRV miscalculation, reinforced the destroyer patrol with a second ship, and ordered it to resume its mission under strictures to keep farther away from shore.

Privately, according to an eyewitness quoted by Chet Cooper, the President was enraged, both that Hanoi had dared attack an American naval vessel, and that all the attacking forces had not been sunk. Still, the immediate reaction in the West Basement, locale of Bundy's office and the

Situation Room, and of the other Vietnam specialists around Washington, was of mixed "wonder and surprise at the sheer bravado of the North Vietnamese." There was a sense of some relief on August 3, when Cooper recalled the summer air seemed heavier and warmer than usual, though over at State Mike Forrestal fired off a cable to Saigon warning that 34-A activities "are beginning to rattle Hanoi, and *Maddox* incident is directly related to their effort to resist these activities."

Forrestal's voice was quickly drowned out in the cacophony that followed the next day, which began shortly after 9:00 A.M., when McNamara phoned LBJ to report a second incident in the Gulf of Tonkin. The veracity of that second incident remains in doubt to this day: The destroyer commander on the scene filed contradictory reports in the heat of action; the case for the incident rests primarily on communications intercepts, while that against on the lack of physical evidence; and the Tonkin Gulf was known for freak weather conditions affecting electronic mechanisms like radar and sonar. In any case, LBJ used the second incident to justify United States armed action.

"I not only want retaliation," Johnson told Pentagon interlocutors, "I want to go all the way into the shore establishments that support these [torpedo] boats and bomb them out of existence." House Majority Leader Carl Albert (D-Okla.), in the Oval Office that morning to see LBJ, overheard those instructions to DOD.

Johnson also convened the NSC for its 537th meeting shortly after noon. McNamara told the group what DOD thought it knew: Nine or ten torpedoes had been fired, from three to six boats, of which two might have been sunk. Rusk said that he, McNamara, and the JCS were working on recommendations but that they were not yet ready. Mac Bundy warned of the need to consider reactions to the various courses of action that might be adopted. The President instructed that, for the time being, nothing was to be made public.

The President ordered a second NSC session for 6:15 that evening. Between the meetings, however, impatience got the better of him and he directed execution of the retaliatory air strikes of which Carl Albert had heard him speak. In a strike code-named Pierce Arrow, sixty-four Navy planes would bomb five DRV naval bases in a "tit for tat" action. Major Alexander M. Haig, Jr., then an Army aide to McNamara, felt that "President Johnson was engaged much too early, when we just had very fuzzy intelligence reports." Johnson made his actual decision, scheduled a briefing for the leaders of Congress, and a radio and television address to the American people, at a moment when the Joint Chiefs' execute order (JCS 7720) had not yet left the Pentagon. The public address had then to be held up for two and a half hours, until almost midnight, to allow aircraft carriers to reach launch positions for the strikes.

President Johnson's first question at the evening NSC session was "Do they want a war by attacking our ships?"

209

"No," answered John McCone of the CIA. "The North Vietnamese are reacting defensively to our attacks on their off-shore islands. They are responding out of pride and on the basis of defense considerations." This crucial opinion, a judgment reached by many subsequent students of the Tonkin Gulf crisis, was before the President at the very moment of action but made no difference to his decision.

The second critical question was put by Carl Rowan, director of the United States Information Agency. "Do we know for a fact that the North Vietnamese provocation took place," he asked. "Can we nail down exactly what happened?"

"We will know definitely in the morning," McNamara replied.

By the next morning the Pierce Arrow bombing had already taken place and a watershed had been crossed. Thinking of Johnson, Mac Bundy later recalled, "It became very clear that he was in no mood for discussion." Lyndon Johnson himself, speaking to reporters in a more reflective mood a year later, told them, "For all I know, our Navy was shooting at whales out there."

Shooting quickly from the hip, Lyndon Johnson forced his administration into a posture of preemptive denial when doubts arose and in subsequent investigations. That, in turn, contributed mightily to LBJ's credibility gap and to public doubts about the Vietnam War. It was the opposite of what the President had intended in June, when by NSAM-308 he had created an interagency group under Robert Manning to manage public information about Vietnam.

In the immediate aftermath of the Tonkin Gulf incident, Johnson pulled from his pocket the Forrestal-Sullivan draft congressional resolution. LBJ sent Congress a truncated version providing approval and support for his "determination" as commander in chief "to take all necessary measures to repel any armed attack . . . and to prevent further aggression." Thinking themselves in the midst of a traditional crisis, the legislators naturally stood with their President; even Senator Barry Goldwater, LBJ's opponent in the 1964 election, did so. Senator J. William Fulbright actually stage-managed Johnson's resolution in his chamber of Congress. The resolution passed the Senate 88 to 2, the dissenters being Ernest Gruening of Alaska and Wayne Morse of Oregon. Passage in the House of Representatives was unanimous. On August 10 the resolution became law. Bill Fulbright's later staunch opposition to the war related directly to his feeling of having been had in LBJ's scramble for passage of the Tonkin Gulf Resolution.

"PLEIKUS ARE LIKE STREETCARS"

▲▲▲

There would have been no reason to seek such a congressional resolution had LBJ wanted to go ahead with Kennedy's idea of a withdrawal. That option, it can safely be concluded, was dead by the latest at the time of the Tonkin Gulf incident, though no formal decision was ever made to vitiate the instructions conveyed in NSAM-273. Decisions after the incident were to augment United States forces in Southeast Asia with certain naval and air units envisioned in the existing CINC-PAC contingency plan, OPLAN 37-64. While that action opened up additional possibilities, the President did try to dampen initial impulses for action. He ordered a halt to the destroyer patrols up into the gulf, and also in the 34-A covert operations. Additionally, Johnson sided with McNamara in ruling out, for the moment, initiation of air strikes and cross-border operations into the Laotian panhandle, location of the soon-to-be-famous Ho Chi Minh Trail.

In Washington the policy debates continued; some began to look toward overt military pressure, bombing the north, as the very means of restoring stability in the south. Ambassador Taylor reinforced their case on August 18, when he cabled from Saigon attesting to a new belief that the VC could not be defeated by counterinsurgency war in the RVN alone. Max Taylor proposed a bombing campaign aimed at DRV infiltration routes and military targets with a D day of January 1, 1965. A week later, in a memorandum to McNamara, the JCS went on record in support, going so far as to suggest a "provocation strategy" as seen by the Pentagon Papers analysts. John McNaughton took this further in a September 3 examination of the options that proposed several possible means of provocation.

Next to the Situation Room, it was in the West Wing that the United States position on Vietnam was least clear. Mac Bundy sat at the apex of a system serving up an endless stream of proposals for increasingly violent action, plus reports that seemingly justified such a response. In the process of culling the material and passing it along to the President, Mac managed to muddy his own position to the extent that historians have reached diametrically opposite conclusions on Bundy's actual views. To journalist David Halberstam, who received the Pulitzer Prize for his reporting from Vietnam,

Mac had remained disinterested as bureaucratic solutions swirled around him. To longtime Indochina watcher George McTurnan Kahin, Bundy was pressing for greater intervention including, by the fall, commitment of ground troops to the RVN. The record suggests that Mac's preferences fluctuated, sometimes recognizing the pressures for action, sometimes the ambiguity of the situation. In the heat of Tonkin Gulf, for example, Mac's had been one of the few voices of caution.

The biggest cipher of all, Lyndon Baines Johnson, wanted to hear in detail about Taylor's estimates of Saigon's political weakness. He asked the ambassador to return to Washington for a meeting that took place on September 9, its formal subject being whether to resume 34-A operations, destroyer patrols, and several other measures along the lines Taylor had been pressing for. The general-cum-diplomat was now prepared to argue that the South Vietnamese would probably *never* be able to create the kind of solid political base the United States wanted before going north. "We would be faced with the question," Taylor wrote for posterity, "of whether we could wait for the desired stability before taking action. I was inclined to think that we could not wait beyond December 1, as we were playing a losing game that had to be changed." He recalled that senior officials accepted his assessment "with little debate."

McGeorge Bundy's record of this meeting has Max Taylor declaring that the United States could not afford to allow Hanoi to win the war, but not making the statements the ambassador attributes to himself. Rather, Bob McNamara reported that it was the belief of two members of the JCS (Air Force and Marines) that, in addition to the actions LBJ was considering, "it was now necessary . . . to execute extensive U.S. air strikes against North Vietnam." Secretary Rusk felt a decision to go north could be made "at five minutes' notice" but was not yet necessary.

Bus Wheeler, speaking for himself and the other two Chiefs of Staff, declared that they were convinced by *Maxwell Taylor* "that it was important not to overstrain the currently strained GVN [government of Vietnam] by drastic action in the immediate future." Thereupon, "General Taylor repeated that this was indeed his view," though he emphasized that in the *long run* "the current in-country program would not be sufficient." It was an opinion, Taylor said, that he had held for many months and that had only been reinforced by serving in Saigon. In addition, the ambassador thought that "as long as the armed forces are solid, the real power is secure," in other words, that it did not much matter if United States efforts were unsuccessful at strengthening the GVN.

Not only was Taylor's position far from the appeal for emergency measures he recounts, he seemed to side with LBJ in putting brakes on immediate escalation. "As one gloomy opinion followed another," Johnson recalled, "I suddenly asked whether anyone at the table doubted that Vietnam was worth all this effort." He said "what disheartened him" was that "we had our best team out there for sixty days and had lost ground." Already Johnson had observed, "in his judgment the proper answer to those advocating immediate and extensive action against the North was that we should not do this until our side could defend itself in the streets of Saigon."

To make this point one last time, LBJ "indicated that the reason for waiting, then, must be simply that with a weak and wobbly situation it would be unwise to attack until we could stabilize our base."

That had been Taylor's original point. But when the President asked if Vietnam was worth it, it was Max who countered that Hanoi could not be allowed to win. He was seconded by a chorus of voices—General Wheeler saying the JCS believed all Southeast Asia would be lost if South Vietnam fell, John McCone and Dean Rusk concurring. Behind it all stood the Munich analogy.

At the end of the meeting, the President approved NSAM-314, authorizing resumption of destroyer patrols and 34-A covert operations. Two more destroyers were sent up the Gulf of Tonkin on another patrol, and promptly had a nighttime battle with radar phantoms very much like the incident of August 4. Once again LBJ got the news early in the morning, but *this* time he waited until after lunch to meet with McNamara and the DOD people. Johnson decided that the available information simply did not justify a retaliation against the DRV.

One of Lyndon Johnson's more celebrated speeches on Vietnam he gave in Manchester, New Hampshire, as September drew to a close. It was there that LBJ declared, "I have not thought that we are ready for American boys to do the fighting for Asian boys," and also that "we are not going north and drop bombs at this stage of the game." At a Manchester political meeting he further alluded to the problem of the "stable base" in the south.

There are two ways to read the evidence. Johnson was extremely worried about the pressures for escalation and seized on what he could to stymie them, such as the "stable base" argument. This view is held by some former NSC staffers. Another view is that the campaign promises were a charade, intended to defeat Goldwater, a holding action until escalation could be pursued with a new political mandate. Some NSC staff believe LBJ had tendencies in both directions, which is certainly consistent with his desire to carry out an ambitious domestic program. Still, Johnson's proclivity to seek positions reflecting consensus left him especially vulnerable in the Vietnam morass, where the advisers were presenting him with a pessimistic view while overselling the intrinsic importance of the policy problem.

The generals proceeded, as did Bill Bundy at State and John McNaughton at the Pentagon, to elaborate plans for bombing raids, whether "tit for tat" retaliation or a sustained campaign. The JCS soon had an approved target list. McNaughton and Bundy developed rationales and analyses of various options. Bundy was by no means wholly committed to escalation though. He and Mike Forrestal commiserated together when LBJ approved sending B-57 jet bombers out to Vietnam for the covert air unit code-named Farm Gate. Both thought the VC were sure to see these aircraft, the heaviest so far sent to the theater, as provocative. In addition, their presence was a violation of the 1954 Geneva agreement, known to Hanoi if not to the American people. Sure enough, on the night of November 1, Vietcong troops used sampans to move mortars up a stream close to the B-57s at Bien-hoa airfield, then struck the place with a heavy barrage of shells. Five Americans and two Vietnamese were killed and nearly a hundred were injured. Awakened with the news, Max Taylor helicoptered up in the rain to see the devastated base, where six B-57s had been destroyed and twenty more aircraft damaged.

In this case, just forty-eight hours before the 1964 elections, LBJ rejected any retaliation. Washington did ask Taylor to comment on the desirability of bringing in American ground troops to guard the air bases at Bien-hoa, Da Nang, and Nha Trang. Rusk and McNamara had both disagreed with the bid for retaliation. LBJ asked for a policy review by an NSC working group chaired by Bill Bundy. By November 21, Bundy and McNaughton had a paper providing three options for the policy mill: a continuation of covert pressure: a "fast full squeeze," or systematic program of overt military pressure on the DRV; and a "progressive squeeze and talk," or combination of military pressure and negotiations. Taylor came back to Washington for discussions, which began on November 24 with Mac Bundy in the chair. After a long meeting with the President on December 1, the middle option was discarded and the remaining ones became phases one and two of a more extended campaign plan.

Walt Rostow, for one, could be pleased with this result. Rostow had been lobbying for bombing, presenting a thesis on what the effect would be upon Hanoi. In a personal letter to Bob McNamara on November 16, Walt had insisted the important thing was not the damage done by bombing but "the signal we wish to send." Hanoi must learn that it was suffering for its violation of the Geneva agreement, that the United States could go much further than its initial moves, and that it could match any level of escalation the DRV was able to reach. At the same time, Rostow felt a ground troop commitment now necessary before proceeding to the next stage, since withdrawal of those troops could be part of the United States negotiating position.

The President's immediate decision in December ruled out ground troops or reprisal bombing, but Johnson, Bundy, McNaughton, and the rest had accepted the logic and idiom of escalation. Johnson once again resisted reprisal bombing after Christmas Eve, when the Vietcong bombed an officers quarters in Saigon, but, he notes, "I was persuaded increasingly that our forces deserved the support that air strikes against the source of aggression would represent."

The President had not yet made his decision. But some thought it clearly in his mind that the United States ought to go into action in a big way. Mike Forrestal was one who witnessed the change firsthand. Forrestal came up to the White House late one afternoon to speak with Mac. Their business accomplished, Forrestal and Bundy repaired upstairs, where they ran into LBJ. The President invited Forrestal into the Oval Office where they relaxed over bourbons. After a few drinks the talk got a little loose and Vietnam inevitably came up.

"Don't you think," LBJ asked, "the time has come to touch them up a little bit?"

Forrestal denigrated the idea. "Yeah," he replied, "but would it make any difference? It will just make them tougher."

"Well," the President came back, "don't you think if they get tougher, we have to get tougher?"

There was the handwriting on the wall. It was the last substantive conversation Michael Forrestal would ever have with Lyndon Baines Johnson.

Chester Cooper would be the man who was present at the escalation. Soon after LBJ's November 3 election victory, when there were no more foreign policy statements to coordinate, Mac Bundy came to Chet and asked him to join the NSC staff as a full-time senior Asia analyst. Mac warned it would be a difficult, thankless job. Cooper began to appreciate the advice soon afterward, when one of Johnson's secretaries, running into him one day at lunch in the White House Mess, asked in all seriousness why he couldn't arrange a personal encounter between LBJ and Ho Chi Minh.

"The President is so good with people," she said charmingly. "If you could only get the two men alone in one room so that they could reason together!"

There it was. For more than a year Cooper would be inundated, not just with the avalanche of reporting from the field, but with everyone's favorite formula for solving the conflict. Officially anointed when Mac mentioned at a staff meeting, on December 12, that Chet would be the main fellow for Vietnam, Cooper moved across West Executive Avenue to the OEOB, where he got a third-floor office directly above Hubert Humphrey's, with a view of the White House. Though appointed to deal with all Asian matters, Cooper spent 90 percent of his time on Vietnam. Except for emergencies, of which, of course, there were quite a few, Cooper had Jim Thomson spend three quarters of *his* time covering the rest of Asia. Cooper also tried to insulate the junior staff man, Don Ropa, who came on board later, from the hourly flaps so as to have someone who could keep order amid the flood of field reporting.

Cooper at least knew the Saigon political scene, from long observation and a number of trips there. His boss, Mac Bundy, had never been anyplace in Asia much less to Vietnam. Chet had some misgivings about American perceptions of the South Vietnamese leadership. All our knowledge was very subjective, much of it based on the reporting of a handful of individuals who regularly saw the Vietnamese.

The foil to Cooper's doubts was the wonderful conviction Mac Bundy held that General Nguyen Khanh was the right leader for Vietnam at the right time. Bundy's unflagging support for Khanh may have been related more to the idea that the United States should get out of the coup business than to any special regard for the man. But Khanh was one of the most inveterate of the military plotters, and his leadership a poor vehicle on which to hang the adjective "stable." For months Maxwell Taylor tried to convince Washington that Khanh was just not the right fellow to lead the RVN at war.

Hardly a week after Lyndon Johnson's inauguration, the Vietnam policy cauldron boiled over once again. Talk of a new Nguyen Khanh coup led Mac Bundy to propose that LBJ hold a very private discussion of Vietnam policy with only himself and Bob McNamara. Mac's proposition would be that the coups were the symptom not the root cause of the GVN problem. With McNamara's approval Mac wrote a long memorandum for discussion, a copy of which he sent on to Rusk. Bundy reported that he and the secretary of defense were now "pretty well convinced that our current policy can only lead to disastrous defeat." The national security adviser felt this was primarily because anti-Communists in Saigon were in despair—"they feel that we are unwilling to take serious risks." Thus Johnson's keeper of the keys argued there was not going to be a stable government in Saigon *until* the United States took major action, and the only real alternatives were to take the track of negotiations or to "use our military power in the Far East and to force a change of Communist policy." Bundy claimed he and McNamara favored this military course.

There is evidence that Mac Bundy was overreaching, attributing all these views to McNamara. As Mac worked away at his memo, McNamara's aide John McNaughton at the Pentagon was scribbling another set of observations for the secretary of defense. McNaughton talked over the list with McNamara for twenty-five minutes early in the morning of January 27, the day of the private presidential meeting. When McNaughton listed the options—to bomb, negotiate, or "keep plugging"—McNamara made the cryptic comment that that was "drifting." He made his meaning clearer when, after a point specifically on negotiation, the secretary of defense noted "this is better than drifting." McNamara noted the dangers of the "squeeze," overt military pressures: "Dissent. Risk is that U.S. public will not support a squeeze unless results show soon." As for striking the DRV, beginning with reprisals, the comment was "Too narrow. Can use 34-A, Desoto [destroyer patrols] . . . etc. Feel way from there."

If this exchange with McNaughton reflected his actual opinion, McNamara cannot have been in full agreement with Mac Bundy, who was urging strikes on the DRV. What passed between Mac and Lyndon Johnson on January 27 is not known, but subsequently the President, upon Max Taylor's suggestion, decided to send Mac to Saigon himself to report from the field. LBJ continued uncertain—Jim Thomson recalls him "thrashing around" from December through Bundy's trip. Thomson recollected elsewhere that "the sense in the White House was that the President did not want to do this, and this was one reason for the McGeorge Bundy mission—his felt need for a final determination shows his reluctance." Chet Cooper, whom Mac brought along for the festivities, agrees that the administration had been on "dead center."

Mac departed from Andrews Air Force Base on February 2. Even by jet it was a fourteen-hour flight, and that was only the kickoff for the grueling pace of the rest of the trip. Among the papers taken along was a fresh special national intelligence estimate from the CIA that contained the latest thinking on Nguyen Khanh and on the Vietnamese Buddhists. Judging from underlined highlights, which occurred only in the section on the Buddhists, Bundy and his men were pretty complacent about Khanh's leadership. Chester Cooper concedes that Mac did seem to feel confident about Khanh, who was to be overthrown in a month's time, but he emphasizes the underlying mood at the time of the mission—one of uncertainty, frustration, and concern; nothing was going right, the ARVN seemed feckless, the Vietcong appeared able to raise hell at will. And of course, it was an eye-opener for Bundy, who was seeing everything up close for the very first time.

Bundy's mission arrived in the midst of the Vietnamese new year, called Tet. Alongside Cooper, the ranks included Andrew Goodpaster for the Joint Chiefs and John McNaughton for the Pentagon.

Cooper followed through on the intense NSC interest in the Buddhists by arranging a meeting between Mac and Buddhist leader Thich Tri Quang. It took place after the usual round of official discussions with GVN officials; Cooper sat in. There was no meeting of the minds, in fact Mac was "reeling" when he emerged, seemingly dazed from a session that had had aspects of a seance. Quang spoke in vague generalities that oozed past Bundy's logic.

On the last day of the scheduled visit, Bundy and his party were supposed to get up-country, to have a chance to see the "boonies" that would become so familiar to thousands of Americans. Instead, shortly after 2:00 A.M., in what was only one of ten different attacks that day, a Vietcong company struck at the United States helicopter base and advisers' barracks at Pleiku in the Central Highlands.

Although Allen Whiting of State's intelligence bureau claims to have predicted a VC attack against some American base during the Bundy mission, Mac does not recall such a warning. Cooper, who was there, remembers everyone caught by surprise and thinks that was what made the real difference. Bundy was not exactly under fire but it was a good metaphor —he was in a place where in an hour or so, less than two, he could *see* the men who had been hurt. It was not an abstract thing anymore, or some antiseptic question of high policy.

Bundy himself initiated the telephone call to the White House Situation Room, David Halberstam reports, but once Washington was on the line he was hardly able to get off. Both Brom Smith and Cy Vance conferred with Mac on the transpacific phone line.

At the Washington end, LBJ had already convened the NSC, whose 545th meeting was in progress as officials went back and forth to the Situation Room to speak with Bundy. There was an immediate recommendation that United States planes attack three targets in the DRV, and that RVN aircraft attack a fourth; all of the targets were barracks. General Wheeler reported that planes could be over their targets by morning (it was 7:45 P.M. in Washington) if the decision was made in the next two hours. The major NSC concern seemed to be that American dependents be evacuated to preclude any VC revenge against them. Senator Mike Mansfield (D-Montana), whom LBJ had asked to attend this NSC session, probably heartened the President with his comment that "the North Vietnamese attack has opened many eyes. We are not now in a penny ante game."

McNamara stayed at his Pentagon office the night of Pleiku. Walt Rostow, evidently equally excited, visited and spoke with various watch officers at State and DOD. Bundy learned of the retaliation while airborne winging back home across the Pacific. The "tit for tat" bombing, code-named Flaming Dart I, involved 132 U.S. and 22 RVN aircraft. On his own airplane, Mac Bundy worked up a memo recommending a policy of "sustained reprisal" in which "air and naval action against the North is justified by and related to the whole Viet Cong campaign of violence and terror in the South." It would be a "continuous" operation and would accept the possibility that an "air war" might become necessary; indeed Mac conceded that it was "quite possible . . . that this reprisal policy would get us quickly into the level of military activity contemplated in the so called Phase II of our December planning."

Just a few days later the Vietcong struck back, shelling the United States base at Qui Nhon. Twenty-one Americans and seven South Vietnamese were killed and many injured. The American reprisal, Flaming Dart II, which LBJ quickly approved, hit more NVA troop barracks. The JCS ordered four and a half Air Force tactical squadrons to Southeast Asia, thirty B-52 bombers to Guam, aircraft carriers to the area, for an addition of 325 combat aircraft. The President also quickly ordered the first U.S. Marine combat units to Vietnam to help defend some of the critical air bases.

A few days after the inception of the bombing, Mac Bundy was in the White House barber shop about to get a shave when a reporter happened along and took advantage of the opportunity to ask Mac why the United States had not retaliated for earlier provocations.

"Mac," the man wanted to know, "what was the difference between Pleiku and the other incidents?"

After reflecting a moment Bundy replied, "Pleikus are like streetcars."

Had it not been one incident, it would have been another. On February 13, Lyndon Johnson authorized initiation of a regular bombing campaign, Rolling Thunder. It would be an air war the President controlled very closely, beginning with approving attacks on the Hanoi area during the visit of Soviet premier Aleksei Kosygin, an action to which Hubert Humphrey's objections resulted in his virtual exclusion from the inner circle.

President Johnson's Tuesday Lunches became the command post of the air war, and the JCS target list a staple of luncheon discussion. Johnson allowed air operations in one- or two-week increments against specified targets on the JCS list. Some would never be satisfied, such as Oley Sharpe in Honolulu, who writes, "The policy objectives which had been enunciated rather firmly in NSAM-288 and in the Tonkin Gulf Resolution were being emasculated by implementing courses of action that were mostly weak and vacillating." From the NSC staff, Chet Cooper suggests a reason why: There was a policy but no real plan; that is, it was not clear what to do after the first attack, or the first few attacks. Despite the plentiful planning of target lists, and the frequent inclusion of the bombing "option" in policy planning, what was not in the plan was exactly how bombing was supposed to lead to an outcome. At his Tuesday Lunches, LBJ was left to improvise a bombing strategy on a week-to-week basis.

The late-afternoon Tuesday Lunch on April 28, 1965, which got interrupted by the emergency of the Dominican crisis, had actually been scheduled to consider Rolling Thunder 13. Over the succeeding days, as LBJ spent his time on the Dominican Republic, Chet Cooper got relief from the pressure of daily flaps. For the first time he and Bill Bundy and the others got the opportunity for long, calm discussions of where the policy was and where it should go.

Sudden opportunity for calm thought came too late for one man, Mike Forrestal. He felt burned out, and the start of the bombing represented an irrevocable move in a direction opposite to that in which he thought the policy should go. Forrestal left government to go sailing in the Caribbean. Escaping from one crisis, Mike inadvertently almost fell into another. He had planned to sail his twenty-five-foot oceangoing sloop *Belle de Rio* from San Juan, Puerto Rico, about April 1, making stops at a port on the north coast of the Dominican Republic and at Cap Haitien in Haiti, and then to return about May 1. The *Belle de Rio* had no radio aboard, and the Dominican intervention began during the trip. Very upset, LBJ's military aide General Chester V. Clifton arranged for the Coast Guard to keep track of Forrestal during much of his cruise. He was saved from coming to potential harm, as it were, when local police arrested Forrestal on a trumped-up charge at Cap Haitien.

WASHINGTON AT WAR

▲▲▲

Though many of those with doubts about Vietnam were backbenchers, several rungs down the hierarchy, at least one had the stature of a first-team player. He was Undersecretary of State George W. Ball, who managed to preserve remarkable detachment in the heat of the action. At the NSC sessions where LBJ approved the retaliations after Pleiku and Qui Nhon, it had been Ball who raised the only real questions.

Rusk was unavailable the night of Pleiku and Ball was acting in his place at LBJ's meeting.

He raised tactical questions there but he was prepared to fight on strategic grounds too. Having worked for Rusk since Jack Kennedy came to town, Ball had seen the Vietnam commitment deepen and the succession of stratagems that never seemed to work. A Francophile international lawyer, who had commuted monthly to Paris before coming to State, Ball had witnessed France's agony in Vietnam as well. Ball saw a bureaucracy obsessed with "how" questions, starting with how to fight the war. He saw no one asking the "why" question, which he called the "giraffe" question in an allusion to a children's story in which a boy at a zoo, shown a caged animal by his father and told it is a giraffe, asks simply, "Why?"

That fall, months before Pleiku, Ball had begun work on a long memorandum he hoped would highlight the giraffe question. Most of it he dictated into a tape recorder, at home, late at night. He regarded it as highly sensitive, keeping it out of the bureaucracy. Only two or three secretaries and Ball's special assistant, George Springsteen, knew of the sixty-seven-page, single-spaced paper, which he completed on October 5, 1964. Believing that he could trust Mac Bundy to pass on his product, to have his shot at the President, George bided his time to await a propitious moment.

In his presentation of the alternative view, George Ball argued that the burden of proof should be on those who sought greater United States involvement. Vietnam was sui generis; it was *not* Korea, there had been no invasion, and there was no international mandate as Truman had had. Anticipating Mac Bundy's position of January 1965, Ball asserted there was no evidence to prove that bombing the DRV would improve morale in the RVN. He then cited the SIGMA-II war game, which, according to Ball, "revealed that exhausting the 1964 target list presently proposed for air strikes would not cripple Hanoi's capability for increasing its support of the Viet Cong, much less force suspension of present support levels on purely logistical grounds." This Ball followed with a warning that the air campaign alone could not counter ground forces; indeed United States ground troops, at a minimum, would be required to defend the air bases. That act "would necessarily change our relationship to the management of the war."

Ball began by circulating his paper to a tiny circle of NSC principals: Rusk, McNamara, and Mac Bundy. They met and talked it over on November 7, 1964. Ball found them more concerned there should be a leak than over the cogency of his analysis, but regarded him with "benign tolerance." That was when George adopted the tactic of trying to resist piecemeal each new project. "I realized," Ball writes of the moment of Pleiku, "that further frontal opposition would be not only futile but tactically unwise." The only possible filibuster was advising the air strikes be held back until after the Kosygin visit, the same argument pressed by Hubert Humphrey, which received support at later NSC meetings from Mike Mansfield and Llewellyn Thompson.

In preparation for the meeting at which the President actually approved Rolling Thunder, Ball tried to smoke out Mac and McNamara with a paper contrasting their views and his own. Mac phoned before the session to dissociate himself from Ball's construction of his position—the United States could be completely flexible, Bundy now maintained, and did not have to "follow a particular course down the road to a particular result." At the meeting Johnson took Ball's memo, glanced briefly at it, asked George to go through it point by point, then handed it back. Rolling Thunder went forward.

Mac Bundy saw an air campaign as entirely necessary, his phrase "sustained reprisals" being but a euphemism. As Mac put it to LBJ on February 16, "If we limit ourselves to reprisals for spectaculars like Pleiku and Qui Nhon, we leave the initiative in the hands of the Communists, and we can expect no good result." Mac went along with the President's desire to make no "loud public signal" of the decision, but "rightly or wrongly," he noted, "those of us who favor continuing military action against the North do see it as a major watershed decision."

A watershed it was. In the immediate aftermath of Pleiku, LBJ ordered Marine antiaircraft troops to the RVN. A couple of weeks later Rusk recommended he approve dispatching two Marine infantry battalions to guard the air bases. George Ball saw his chance ebbing. On February 24 he managed to have lunch with Bill Moyers and gave the President's assistant his long paper from the previous fall. Moyers handed it to LBJ that afternoon, and on the twenty-sixth the President had a meeting to discuss it. George outlined his position, whereupon McNamara "responded with a pyrotechnic display of facts and statistics to prove I had overstated the difficulties," while Rusk "made a passionate argument about the dangers of not going forward." The two Marine battalions landed in South Vietnam on March 8.

Three weeks later, in a daring car bomb attack in downtown Saigon, the Vietcong blew up the United States embassy. Max Taylor, having returned to Washington for a new round of decisions, escaped the blast which damaged the building, wounded almost 200 Americans and killed 2, along with 17 Vietnamese. Johnson faced swarms of proposals, including one from the military to send two divisions, about 50,000 men when support troops were counted. There was also a twelve-point CIA program and a forty-one-point nonmilitary program advanced by Taylor and Rusk. Though the ambassador continued to advise caution on major ground troop commitments until more field experience was available from the Marines already sent, LBJ approved two additional battalions in NSAM-328, which McGeorge Bundy signed on April 8, 1965. The paper also ordered an increase of 20,000 in United States support troops, acceleration of aircraft and helicopter reinforcements, new parameters for Rolling Thunder, and a search for allied nations willing to send troops to Vietnam alongside those of the United States.

Taking a little of the edge off the NSAM-328 program, the previous evening, in a speech at Johns Hopkins University, Johnson for the first time spoke publicly of negotiations and mentioned the United States requirements for "essential elements" of a just peace: an independent South Vietnam free from "outside interference" with guaranteed security, a member of no alliance. Somewhat disingenuously LBJ declared that the United States was prepared for "unconditional discussions" to resolve the conflict.

Then, on April 20, a conference at Honolulu sharpened the military option by recommending deployment of nine battalions—equivalent to one division—by summer. Together with the advisory forces General Westmoreland already had in MACV, that made eighty thousand troops. The Vietnam War had clearly entered a new phase.

Political master that he was, the President always concerned himself with public relations, the information aspect of policy. During the "tit for tat" period of the summer and fall of 1964, Johnson had ordered the bureaucracy to get busy on some explanatory statements that could be used to justify the war. LBJ wanted something powerful that would draw connections between the insurgency in the south and support from Hanoi. It was, of course, an article of faith in the administration that the Vietcong would collapse without DRV assistance, but no one had attempted to demonstrate that convincingly to the American people.

For once it was perhaps the right man who got assigned the job: William John Jorden, journalist by profession and diplomat perhaps by coincidence. Jorden, born in Montana and raised in Ohio, had picked up a journalism degree from Columbia and spent seven years as correspondent in the Far East for the Associated Press, then *The New York Times*. He covered the Korean War, the signing of the peace treaty with Japan, and the tail end of the Chinese revolution. Following a year on fellowship with the Council on

Foreign Relations, he was off to Moscow in 1956 as *Times* bureau chief, then back in Washington from 1959 to 1961 as diplomatic correspondent covering the State Department. With an eye toward overcoming Jack Kennedy's complaints that diplomats couldn't write, State hired Jorden away from the *Times*.

Averell Harriman, who always had a sharp eye for talent, took one look at Bill Jorden and made him special assistant. Jorden worked for Harriman through the Geneva negotiations on Laos, and "the Crocodile's" time in charge of Far Eastern affairs. There were a half-dozen more trips to Vietnam during this period.

When the President demanded something he could use for justification, State hatched the idea of an official white paper that would detail its charges of aggression from the north. Jorden, forty-one at the time, went around the bureaucracy, collecting impressions, and made another trip to the RVN, where he interviewed prisoners of war who said they had come from North Vietnam. Aware of Jorden's project, the NSC staff supported it fully and Chet Cooper needled the CIA to scrub some intelligence data so it could be included in the white paper. Cooper got a draft of the final product to see what Jorden was doing and if it could be improved.

The final result was Department of State Publication 7839, conveniently released in February 1965, just in time to back up the retaliations after Pleiku and Qui Nhon and the beginning of Rolling Thunder. "The hard core of the Communist forces attacking South Viet-Nam," the white paper argued, "are men trained in North Viet-Nam. They are ordered into the south and remain under the military discipline of the Military High Command in Hanoi." The paper cited annual figures for infiltrators, putting the total at nearly 20,000 since 1959, with possibly another 17,000 "indicated" by "additional information." Jorden then argued that it meant the majority of the hard-core VC were made up of northerners. In a neat reversal of the rule of thumb formula that successful counterinsurgency requires ten soldiers for every guerrilla, the paper claimed that infiltrating 5,000 men from the DRV "is the equivalent of marching perhaps 50,000 regular troops across the border." The white paper described infiltration down the Ho Chi Minh Trail and devoted considerable space to enumerating the supplies found cached near an alleged DRV supply vessel discovered and sunk at Vung Ro Bay, between Qui Nhon and Nha Trang. The paper then argued that the DRV was a "base for conquest of the south," and that the insurgency was organized, directed, and controlled from Hanoi. "The record is conclusive," Jorden wrote. "It establishes beyond question that North Viet-Nam is carrying out a carefully conceived plan of aggression against the south."

The white paper, as Chet Cooper put it, "created ripples of support . . . and tidal waves of opposition." It was not possible to provide sufficient documentary evidence, while some of the intelligence details had to remain classified. The actual findings did not seem that striking: confirmed infiltrators claimed in the paper numbered fewer than the increase in MACV over the same period, the actual numbers of Soviet and Chinese weapons said to have been captured were tiny and hardly justified bombing Hanoi. Journalist I. F. Stone published a classic rejoinder on March 8, the fateful day that U.S. Marines waded ashore for the first time. "That North Viet-Nam supports the guerrillas," Stone countered, "is no more a secret than that the United States supports the South Vietnamese government. . . . The striking thing about the State Department's new white paper is how little support it can prove." Stone showed that the proportion of arms from Communist nations was under 3 percent and that only six of fifteen infiltrators whose case histories were given were actually of North Vietnamese origin. The one-hundred-ton capacity ship at Vung Ro Bay compared to World War II Liberty or Victory ships whose average capacity was more than seven thousand tons. *The New York Times* editorialized that the white paper "merely raises anew the question of whether massive air strikes would accomplish anything except large-scale civilian casualties."

Jorden, who stayed on for some months in Austin to help Johnson after the end of his administration, defended the white paper in a 1969 interview. He argued that such a document for public consumption "can't be eight hundred pages long with fifty-seven footnotes to each chapter," and that "I had to draw a balance between a short ten-page report that stated certain facts or an [enormous] report that stated all the facts as we knew them."

In retrospect, one NSC staffer of that era believes that I. F. Stone was right to lambast the white paper. Chet Cooper, the man who had the NSC Vietnam portfolio, writes forthrightly: "No such publication could have accomplished the ambitious objectives its proponents (including myself) hoped to achieve. It was impossible to provide sufficient documentary evidence of Hanoi's direction and support of the war to convince the confused non-expert or the sophisticated skeptic."

In any case, the white paper was one-sided in dealing only with the DRV and not accounting for the development of United States policy. In his critique Stone mentioned this problem, but it was a former NSC staffer, Marcus Raskin, who focused on it. Raskin wrote a "citizen's white paper," which argued that "the diplomatic policy of the American government by the end of December, 1964, was almost totally militarized." He wrote of American hubris; of the notion the United States was a "policeman" that could dictate an outcome in Southeast Asia; of military involvement that masked real interests and distorted political vision, backing Washington into assuming the "white man's burden" of colonialism. Proponents of negotiation had been so far "eclipsed," Raskin argued, that bombing (to compel negotiation) had become the policy preference of "doves" who *opposed* the war.

Raskin circulated his paper privately in Washington, where he felt it might do some good. The stance was moderate and the themes ones that would become all too familiar in the course of the Vietnam debate. Then the paper leaked and portions were inserted in the *Congressional Record*.

Marc Raskin was identified as a former "White House staff" officer. Mac Bundy went ballistic.

Bundy was not unwitting about the Raskin paper, having presumably seen the copy that had gone to brother Bill. Given the options Mac himself advocated and the decisions actually in train, it is quite possible that the President's gatekeeper was upset by Raskin's description of the broad views of LBJ's advisers, but it was the use of the tag line "White House staff" to which Bundy chose to object. Mac shot off a stinging rebuke to his former staffer: "You know, and I know, where your salary was paid and where the appointment was. You and I also know the kind of advertising purpose that is served by saying 'formerly White House staff.' . . . Finally, you and I know the role that you played in your service here. I must say it never occurred to me that you would choose to capitalize on it in this way later on."

Aside from the heat of Vietnam, on the matter of White House service both Bundy and Raskin had a point. Bundy was correct that Marc Raskin had never been on Kennedy's *personal* White House staff. The question was more ambiguous than that, however. An entity of the Executive Office of the President, the NSC staff certainly belonged to JFK's wider official family. In a parallel case, Henry Kissinger, who had been hired expressly as personal consultant to JFK, had been paid from NSC budget accounts. Moreover, Marc Raskin's identification card read "White House Staff" and served as a White House pass; it carried privileges like exclusive parking and use of the White House Mess. Bob Komer, whom Mac never excoriated on this question, told an interviewer in 1964, before the Raskin affair ever came up, that the "NSC label" was "merely a budgetary device . . . instead of adding people to the White House staff, Bundy carried them all over here. But in fact Kennedy made very clear we were his men, we operated for him, we had direct contact with him." That was precisely what gave NSC staffers the power to command.

Mac Bundy never accepted Marc Raskin's explanation for the tag line used on his article. Raskin's name was mentioned to the NSC staff far more often than people with longer service and usually in a pejorative context. It happened frequently enough that Chet Cooper, for one, gathered the impression that Raskin had been Mac's fair-haired kid gone wrong. The experience also alienated Raskin, who went wholly into opposition, working on a call to resist "illegitimate authority" and helping the antidraft movement in 1967, earning a place on Richard Nixon's notorious "Enemies List."

The white paper was just one part of a public relations offensive, commanded by the interagency group under Robert Manning that the President created in NSAM-308. Another aspect was a program for sending many senior officials on visits to Vietnam, to enable them to comment favorably on progress. A quiet initiative within the White House to generate some favorable commentary on administration decision-making was an invitation to Columbia University history professor Henry A. Graff, a friend of Moyers aide Hayes Redmon's, to interview members of Johnson's inner circle. That resulted in articles in *The New York Times Magazine* and in Graff's book *The Tuesday Cabinet*. Here Bundy launched another gaffe, referring to the United States as the "engine" of the globe and the rest of the world as a "caboose," triggering a frantic scramble to get Graff to suppress the quote and the *Times* to drop an editorial criticizing administration arrogance.

During the summer of 1965 the Manning group tried its hand at a pamphlet, "Why Vietnam?" It was supposed to give the big explanation in easily understandable terms, basing itself on such things as the Eisenhower letter and the alleged obligations of the SEATO treaty. That time a printing error debased a key passage of the text.

Finally came more white paper exercises, both on the Dominican Republic and a second effort on Vietnam. Jorden did his best, the administration pulled out the stops on data, while this time there was much more to report, with the DRV having sent south many regular combat units that had been identified on the battlefield. With much riding on the release, a timing error dissipated some of the impact. Chester Cooper had been instructed to give a background briefing on the paper, after a *Times* reporter approached the NSC and asked for details so that its story could put the new report in perspective.

Cooper spoke with the journalist and allowed him to see a copy of the text, which had been embargoed until a certain time. The reporter managed to go through the paper at some length and either noted or remembered key passages. By that night there was a front-page *Times* story scheduled for the next morning, in advance of the release time. Called for an official reaction, Cooper, who had neglected to use magic words like "off the record," begged to get some items out of the story but was not successful in doing so. The new white paper, in the midst of a war grown much larger, created hardly a stir. The most significant by-product was to earn Bill Jorden a promotion to top State Department press spokesman.

Clark Clifford privately counseled LBJ in 1965 to keep quiet and say little, but the President clearly felt unable to adopt that advice. Instead, the Manning group conducted a whole range of activities that, in substance and content, differed little from the psychological warfare practiced by the Truman-Eisenhower PSB and OCB units. The major distinction was that the target of the NSC spin doctors had become the *American* people, not some foreign population perceived as neutral or an adversary. Seemingly beset with mishaps at every turn, this battle for public opinion was waged so that the war for Vietnam could be fought. Meanwhile, the antiwar protests had begun almost with the first sound of the bombs.

Walt Rostow sent one of his snappy little papers, regarding the possibilities of victory and defeat in guerrilla wars, to Rusk on May 20. Taking issue with LBJ's recent cautious assertion that a military victory was not possible in guerrilla warfare, Walt used postwar examples to argue, to the contrary, that "guerrilla wars have generally been lost or won cleanly." He also observed reassuringly that in all such wars won by "Free World" forces there had been a period when the guerrillas commanded a good portion of the countryside. Now was no time to lose hope.

"They failed to win," Rostow commented, "because all the possible routes to guerrilla victory were closed and, in failing to win, they lost. They finally gave up in discouragement."

Rusk's official thinker asserted that the main task was to convince Hanoi its bargaining position was eroding, a dilemma he thought they well understood and a complete change since Pleiku. Hanoi, Rostow declared, "is staring at quite clear-cut defeat. . . . That readjustment in prospects is painful; and they won't in my view accept its consequences unless they are convinced time has ceased to be their friend. . . . [But] victory . . . is nearer our grasp than we (but not Hanoi) may think."

Mac Bundy focused more on the daily flow of paper, and probably would not have inclined to a claim that the United States was winning already, but he agreed it was within American power to convince Hanoi that time ran against it. Max Taylor, in his last months as ambassador, still felt "it is far from an unmitigated advantage to bring in more U.S. forces." Elsewhere he argued that no amount of bombing would convince the DRV to give up the insurgency. Bundy maintained, along with McNamara, that a program could readily be constructed that pressured Hanoi, satisfied Taylor, *and* ran no unacceptable risks of escalation. Mac favored occasional limited attacks inside the no-bomb zones LBJ had designated surrounding the major DRV cities Hanoi and Haiphong. Mac put some thought into political objectives (arguing the United States needed to refine these in discussion with the GVN) and a possible June bombing pause (for which he summarized pros and cons), but the President's gatekeeper emerged basically as a proponent of force.

This much was clear to George Ball: Somewhere along the line Mac had stopped being referee and become advocate. Ball continued in opposition and had prepared another of his memoranda for the President. It is significant that, like his previous paper, he passed this one through Bill Moyers. Again like his previous paper, though even more directly this time, Ball used the saddle simile a Texan might appreciate, directly quoting Ralph Waldo Emerson: "Things are in the saddle and ride mankind." Ball was nothing if not persistent.

He raised the precedent of the French, whose battle for Vietnam had ended so desperately at Dien Bien Phu a decade before. "Before we commit an endless flow of forces to South Vietnam," Ball maintained, "we must have more evidence than we now have that our troops will not bog down in the jungles or rice paddies—while we slowly blow the country to pieces." The way to maintain control of events was to limit commitments and choose options only on the basis of preselected criteria and established schedules.

The President got Ball's paper on a Friday, just before leaving for a weekend at Camp David. Johnson read it with care; in fact the paper struck a responsive chord. It was *Senator* Lyndon Johnson, a decade before, who had played one of the most central roles in the demise of the option to save the French at Dien Bien Phu with an air strike.

After the Camp David weekend, Moyers reported back to Ball that LBJ agreed with most of what he had written and would have favored only slight changes. LBJ asked Ball to work on what would happen after the monsoon season and informed the diplomat he had told McNamara *not* to assume the President "willing to go overboard on this."

The specter of French Indochina roused McGeorge Bundy. Mac wrote a nine-page memorandum to the President, one of the longest he ever assembled, which he handed to LBJ on June 30, a dozen days after Johnson's sojourn at Camp David. It was a straight effort to reject the analogy on every count. France fought for colonial rule, Mac asserted, using conventional military tactics for a holding action in behalf of a facade of a national government. The United States would have no such interest, *its* forces were "the most significant element of stability and strength" in the RVN. Bundy emphasized that French governments had had to contend with *"concerted and organized domestic opposition"* (Bundy's italics) to a war of acute unpopularity resulting in political instability. As a result France had not been consistent in its prosecution of the war. As for the United States, Mac cited Gallup and Harris poll statistics to show general support for the war, dismissed the opposition as elements of the academic and church communities, "usually a minority within their own groups," making for an analogy of only "superficial" similarity.

Mac rose to the rhetorical conclusion that "the U.S. in 1965 is responding to the call of a people under Communist assault, a people undergoing a non-Communist national revolution; neither our power nor that of our adversaries has been fully engaged as yet. At home we remain politically strong and, in general, politically united. Options, both military and political, remain to us that were no longer available to the French."

Bundy's paper would prove oddly prophetic, though not in the way he imagined, and it contains the essence of a truth for history: The dangers of the war, and of the United States style of managing that war, were *specifically* foreseen *before* the major troop commitment.

Ball followed up with a further paper to the President on July 1 arguing for a compromise solution; Mac forwarded it with the statement that "my hunch is that you will want to listen hard to George Ball and then reject his proposal." In forwarding another Ball think piece, Mac commented, "If and when we wish to shift our course and cut our losses in Vietnam we should do so because of a finding that the Vietnamese themselves are not meeting their obligations." The impossibility of success was not, for Bundy that day, sufficient reason to change course.

On June 7, General Westmoreland reported that the VC seemed to be starting a "summer offensive" and asked for *thirty-four* infantry battalions.

The Joint Chiefs of Staff increased the request to forty-four and added that the United States should mobilize reserves and go on a war footing. Such an increase would bring MACV strength to 200,000 troops. There was no ducking the issue. In fact, along with Ball's proposal for a compromise solution went McNamara's formal statement of the request for forty-four battalions. President Johnson sent McNamara and a group, among whom Bundy included Chet Cooper, for a survey in the field, then scheduled a round of meetings in the third week of July to make his decision.

There is some debate over what exactly was the situation at this juncture of Vietnam decision-making. Some observers believe LBJ had already made up his mind and was essentially staging the events that followed. Others feel the President had genuine doubts. The authors of the Pentagon Papers, plus journalist Stanley Karnow, and historian Larry Berman, relying on a cable from Cy Vance that reached McNamara in Saigon, advance the former interpretation. George Kahin presents extensive excerpts of the meetings that followed to let the record speak for itself.

The record consists of Tuesday Lunches on July 20 and 26, at least six sessions of the NSC or less formal ones of the principals, a meeting of the Wise Men, and a presidential briefing of the congressional leadership. George Ball's day in court came on July 21, when he spoke extensively at a morning session and then was given the floor for the afternoon. Chester Cooper, just back from Saigon with the McNamara party, sat against the wall and felt that Ball reduced his own effectiveness by announcing himself as a devil's advocate. One could refuse to take a devil's advocate seriously, as a mere exercise in debating; if two or three of the major players had joined with Ball, Chet thought, LBJ might have been startled enough to question the whole proposal. As it was, the NSC summaries of discussion show the President asking some pretty tough questions and making certain openings for Ball's arguments. Following the morning session, Cooper himself dashed off a memo to Mac arguing that the forty-four-battalion program should not be accepted without an ancillary special "pacification" program, because the guerrilla problem was too important to leave to the ARVN alone. Jim Thomson, who had opposed Bundy's "sustained reprisal" concept at the time of Pleiku, also had doubts about the big program.

There is also a memo, from Bundy to Johnson, regarding "Vietnam Planning at Close of Business on July 19." Here again the discussion is all about the timing of various events, decisions on reserve call-ups, and a message to the Congress, "really the D-Day for the whole operation," all of which suggests that LBJ's decision was made.

The *outcome* of the 1965 troop decision, however, furnishes the best evidence that Lyndon had not made up his mind. That is, the President *did not* approve the forty-four-battalion program. He refused to mobilize reserves or make a big Vietnam budget request to Congress, probably with the aim, according to biographer Doris Kearns, of avoiding a legislative debate that would sidetrack his cherished Great Society. What Johnson did do was sanction an increase of 50,000 men, a search for more allies to contribute troops, and an understanding that further reinforcements for Westmoreland might be forthcoming later. It is worth noting that the troop decision, arguably the most serious decision of the war, was *not* formalized in an NSAM. In fact, July 1965 marked a new point of departure: Henceforth only *process* would be consecrated by NSAMs; Vietnam *strategy*, including both objectives and troop deployments, went mostly unstated in NSC documents. On one hand, this would bring the ultimate in flexible warfare; on the other, there would be no formal guidance after April 1965 (NSAM-328). To borrow a phrase from the Marines' General Lew Walt, Vietnam would be a "strange war."

President Johnson's attempt to hold the line by giving his generals part of what they wanted effectively opened the door. Westmoreland got the idea that to get some men, he needed to request a whole lot, then fight for the troops. Even before the July decision was made, "Westy" upped his request to 275,000 men (sixty-four battalions), and in December he went to 443,000. In June 1966 came a new request for 542,000 troops, all within a year and without any NSC policy paper. As George Ball feared, it had become an endless flow of forces without any evidence that success was possible. The President found himself swamped in the minutiae of fighting the war, managing the bombing, and seeking negotiations.

A plan for "pacification," for winning the hearts and minds of the Vietnamese, was most urgently necessary if the war was to go anywhere. The conventional thought that pacification could be left to the South Vietnamese foundered in the face of the realities of the situation.

The President puzzled over the twin problems of energizing pacification and stabilizing the Saigon government. Chet Cooper puzzled too, and thought he had some solutions, at least on the pacification side. Cooper pushed the idea of a single manager for all related programs in Vietnam, an individual who would be a deputy ambassador.

President Johnson made the next move, following a January 31, 1966, recommendation from the NSC staff, to hold a summit conference with South Vietnamese leaders on economic and social matters. In his inimitable style, LBJ ordered arrangements and held the conference at Honolulu only a week later.

The Honolulu conference had also a hidden purpose, pursuant to a decision LBJ made privately before going to Hawaii, one directly related to pacification. LBJ had determined to go with Chet Cooper's proposal for a single pacification manager in Saigon. But in their cables home, and in earlier discussions, both the United States embassy and MACV were resistant to the idea. LBJ's hidden purpose was to massage Ambassador Henry Cabot Lodge, now in Saigon for a second tour, and with General William Westmoreland, to obtain acquiescence if not enthusiasm.

To assuage Lodge, who thought existing arrangements were fine, his deputy William J. Porter got the single-manager job. Mac Bundy continued on to Saigon in company with the Vice President, armed with certain powers of negotiation. Bundy set up a back channel using CIA communications facilities, on which he exchanged eyes-only cables with Brom Smith. Mac sent Brom to Rusk and McNamara to get State and DOD approval for certain job offers, including an ambassadorship in Africa for one official and a plum assignment for Lodge's military aide, Colonel Samuel Wilson. Brom got the requisite okays the same day, then cabled back, "You have your two cards to play. . . . Good Luck!" In another gambit earlier that day, Smith had sent Bundy an advance copy of a State cable that would be sent to Lodge.

Mac Bundy succeeded in his task of presiding over the creation of the single pacification manager. Nevertheless, the powers that be were not reconciled. Lodge worried he would be stuck with the humdrum ceremonial chores usually left to deputy ambassadors. Westy carefully kept military pacification resources out of Bill Porter's hands even while gaining a certain say over planning by Porter's new organization, the Office of Civil Operations. Still, it was a start.

Chester Cooper's final contribution on the matter was the idea of a Washington-level single manager. Cooper proposed a "Mr. Vietnam" who would *not* be located at Foggy Bottom (as had Forrestal) but rather be a special assistant "in the White House complex," where "he will not be forced to spend time before Congressional Committees." This was the course Lyndon Johnson adopted for pacification, which was quickly acquiring the nickname "the other war."

Who would be "Mr. Vietnam" was naturally of some importance. Walt Rostow was certainly very interested in Vietnam, but at Honolulu Lyndon quietly took him aside and declared his intention to make Walt national security adviser. The fellow who was dynamic with considerable vision, and who never hesitated to push when he felt it warranted was pipe-toting Robert Komer.

One day in March the President called the Chicagoan into his Oval Office. "Bob, I'm going to put you in charge of the other war in Vietnam."

"What's the other war in Vietnam?" Komer asked. "I thought we had only one!"

"That's part of the problem," Johnson replied. "I want to have a war that will build as well as destroy. . . . Your mandate will be a very extensive one. In fact I wrote it myself."

Komer was probably saddened he had lost out in the sweepstakes for national security adviser, but he threw himself immediately into the new task. In doing so, Robert Komer became the first member of the NSC staff to acquire an *operational*, as distinct from a policy, role. As Bob had told Mac Bundy the previous December, "I enjoy reading history but prefer participating in it." On March 23, Joe Califano circulated a draft NSAM to the agencies specifying Komer's responsibilities. Only minor changes were suggested. President Johnson approved NSAM-343 on March 28, 1966. The NSAM itself designated Komer as "Mr. Vietnam."

It is worth noting that in creating this role, Lyndon Johnson was careful to distinguish it from the NSC staff proper. LBJ made Komer a special assistant to the President, with rank equal to Rostow's. His task was to knock heads together and make things happen: Lodge soon dubbed Komer "Blowtorch Bob." Nevertheless, although he ran a unit parallel to the NSC staff, Komer attended meetings of the staff, dealt with the NSC Southeast Asia people, and spoke frequently with Rostow.

To fulfill his task, the Chicagoan set up a small staff of his own. Tough, and as abrasive as ever, he fought to get things moving in the RVN. He remained optimistic, always encouraging greater effort. In thirteen months as special assistant Komer made six trips to South Vietnam, schemed to get Bill Moyers out there too, expended tremendous energy making Vietnamese national assembly elections demonstrate democratic processes, and spoke innumerable times with journalists in a campaign to generate more favorable press coverage for the war.

Komer's interactions with the press were legion but, like his other activities, cannot be covered in detail here. A few examples will suffice. On one occasion, in September 1966, Bob fielded a call from *Washington Star* reporter Richard Fryklund with questions about CIA counterterror (CT) teams, a program antecedent to the notorious Phoenix project. The Chicagoan reported to Bill Moyers, "He knew his onions so I took the tack of downplaying the CT exercises and suggesting he not raise embarrassing questions to no good purpose." A month later Komer encountered syndicated columnist Rowland Evans who, with partner Robert Novak, had just published a political biography of Lyndon Johnson. They had interviewed Komer for the book and used a couple of the resulting items. Of Evans the Chicagoan reported: "I read him the riot act on his references to me in his book." Another typical example came in February 1967, when Komer reportedly told George Christian of a session with Ward Just, whom he thought the best reporter in Saigon. "I gave him several gems on how we couldn't help but do better on pacification next year ('we had no place to go but up')."

Komer took a hand in trying to formulate a long-term strategy, in December 1966, with a Vietnam strategy directive in the form of a draft NSAM. He sent the draft to Walt Rostow. A fairly comprehensive effort, Komer's draft NSAM ran into LBJ's aversion for approving statements that could later be used to measure performance. The NSAM went nowhere.

Komer was eager to prove his successes. After a February 1967 visit he reported to LBJ, "*I return more optimistic than ever before. The cumulative change . . . is dramatic, if not yet visibly demonstrable in all respects.*" He claimed 1967 would bring "growing momentum . . . on almost every front." How change could be dramatic and yet not visible Komer did not explain.

For all the bluster, however, an immutable basic problem remained: division between the civilian and military sides of pacification robbed the effort of much of its potential. While promoting all types of pacification, Komer realized that MACV resources were much greater, while military foot-dragging on civilian initiatives was a real obstacle. The only solution, finally, was a combined pacification unit called CORDS—Civilian Operations and Revolutionary Development Support. Komer himself negotiated much of the charter for this organization, realizing that the only way to get the military on board was to put them in charge. Thus CORDS became part of MACV and its director a deputy to the MACV commander. Lyndon Johnson sanctioned the operation in one of his process directives, NSAM-362, on May 9, 1967.

Once more the President selected Bob Komer for the job. Komer went out to Saigon and began a sojourn that carried him into the next administration. He began on a typical note by starting an argument over his (civilian) rank—equivalent to a full general's—and how that should be recognized with appropriate symbols and deference when he entered military compounds. Komer knew such pomp was not necessary, but thought that enforcing prerogatives might make the military take pacification more seriously. It was not long before Westmoreland tried to cut him down to size. The issue was back-channel communications, of which Komer had made extensive use in the White House. Westy discovered Bob sending cables to the White House outlining messages he wanted sent back over the President's signature. Thereafter MACV reviewed all cables before Komer was allowed to send them. "The Lord knows," Westmoreland writes, "the President handed me a volatile character in Bob Komer."

BOMB AND TALK,
BOMB AND FIGHT,
BOMB OR TALK

▲▲▲

Rolling Thunder continued with unabated ferocity into December 1965. There were over three thousand attack sorties flown in each of the five preceding months. The administration continued to frame its planning for 1966 deployments and a full budget request, and LBJ met at his ranch on the subject with McNamara, Mac Bundy, and others. The dollar figure for the budget increase required for Vietnam was going to be huge; it imposed dangers of inflation. Mac soon learned the final figure would be greater even than the number discussed at the LBJ Ranch.

Bob McNamara seemed to have lost his earlier boundless optimism. Mac Bundy, who had sided with the advocates of troop commitment in July, was now aware of the growth in Westmoreland's troop requests. In November, Mac and McNamara joined to tell LBJ they had the impression "your mind is settling against a pause," then argued the matter was too important to settle without thorough exploration. Ten days earlier, George Ball had sent a lengthy scenario, with pro-and-con discussion of a bombing pause, and Mac resurrected part to give the President. By December 4, Mac was telling LBJ that a consensus favoring the pause had developed among Rusk, who had previously been opposed, McNamara, Vance, Ball, McNaughton, the Bundy brothers, and Llewellyn Thompson. He argued, "We think this is the best single way of keeping it clear that Johnson is for peace, Ho [Chi Minh] is for war." Resistance came from quarters Bundy predicted—Admiral Sharp, General Westmoreland, Ambassador Lodge, and the Joint Chiefs of Staff. Some, notably Bill Moyers and George Ball, went further than pause advocates and by December 14 were talking with Mac about a full cease-fire.

As he had during the July troop decision, LBJ carefully tallied the views of his advisers in meetings on December 17 and 18. The basic shape of what became the Christmas pause was evident at the very first meeting, which LBJ held in the Cabinet Room with Rusk, McNamara, Bundy, and Ball. Jack Valenti took notes. The President admitted that a pause in the north had "some appeal" for him and asked whether the United States

234

should not "have someone moving throughout the world trying for peace." As with the February 1965 approval of Rolling Thunder, LBJ wanted no public announcements, preferring to use weather as an excuse and Christmas as a factor, but, he said, "anything with bombs is bad for the peace effort. Let's put off bombing until we can talk to others."

President Johnson worried about the military, especially the Joint Chiefs of Staff. "The problem," said LBJ, "is the Chiefs go through the roof when we mention this pause."

"I can take on the Chiefs," McNamara replied. Later he cautioned, "I know exactly what the arguments of the Chiefs are. Before you decide, I cannot deliver. After you decide, I can deliver."

The President went on to an hour-long session with his intimate political adviser Abe Fortas, with whom he then had an even longer dinner. Fortas attended the Cabinet Room discussion that went on all afternoon the next day, where LBJ added Alex Johnson and Clark Clifford to the group from the seventeenth. The President reported he had now had a conversation with JCS Chairman Earle Wheeler, "and I can understand what McNamara is living with." McNamara himself argued the United States had been overoptimistic in previous assessments, that chances of success were only one-in-three or two-in-three. After a suspension, the secretary of defense said, he would recommend bombing Hanoi's fuel stocks, in military parlance "petroleum, oil, lubricants" (POL), and as for mining Haiphong Harbor, "I will suggest this later myself." But the measures would be easier to take after a pause had reinforced Washington's credibility.

Most of the serious objections came from the outsiders, Fortas and Clifford, and from the President himself. LBJ rejected McNamara's assertion that the JCS argument, that a pause would undo all that had been accomplished by the bombing, was "baloney." The President countered, "It is inaccurate to say suspension of bombing carries no military risk."

Nevertheless, Johnson had decided to go ahead with a pause. Already the previous day, in his hour spent with Bus Wheeler, whom LBJ was convinced was a good soldier who would support any decision made by the civilian leadership, the President had mentioned a bombing halt that could last from Christmas through the Vietnamese Tet new year's holiday, a period of more than a month. Even Mac Bundy, thus far, had only been talking of a little more than a week's pause. General Wheeler was about to leave on a visit to the Far East.

In Saigon the ambassador and the MACV commander had the reactions Mac Bundy anticipated, which Wheeler reported as instructed. Andy Goodpaster telephoned Saigon the next day with news that LBJ had decided not to extend a planned thirty-hour Christmas pause, but a day later on Christmas Day came a JCS cable, apparently drafted by Cyrus Vance, extending the stand-down through January 31, 1966. Air Force Chief of Staff John P. McConnell wanted to go to LBJ and protest, but Vance dissuaded him saying the President's mind had been made up.

In fact the President, according to other observers, was rather more uncertain. Chester Cooper was with Mac in the national security adviser's office on December 26, when the President called with Christmas wishes and to ask after Bundy's holiday. LBJ also asked when the air attacks would start again. Mac wasn't sure, and asked Cooper if any execute orders for renewed bombing had gone through the NSC. Chet had not seen any, but they might have been in the "in" basket or on the way over from the JCS. A quick search revealed nothing, so Mac decided to call McNamara.

"Jesus, I don't know," McNamara apparently said, "I haven't seen anything yet."

On the spot, Cooper recalls, Mac and McNamara cooked up a recommendation that the pause be extended further. Bundy met the next afternoon with a selection of the bureaucracy's press spokesmen, all of whom dealt with Vietnam daily. He reported to LBJ, "They all said very strongly, that if the pause goes more than another day or so, it should go long enough to be a real answer to our critics." Mac also reported Bill Moyers's view that the halt ought to be extended at least through New Year's Day, plus a most interesting statement from Max Taylor.

General Taylor, returned from Vietnam, had been brought back by LBJ in a new incarnation as special military adviser. Taylor dropped by Mac's office and volunteered, "Since we have endured three days of pause, we might as well go on for long enough to take the starch out of the idea once and for all."

Orders to extend the bombing halt went out on the night of December 27, while an earlier warning to Saigon had been signed and cleared by Cy Vance but sent as a JCS cable. As for the Chiefs, LBJ had certainly been right on *that* score. They were up in arms. On December 28 members of the JCS complained to Vance they had been cut out of the decision, and of the Goodpaster back channel, isolating them from the priority cables for nine days. Vance assured them that the NSC principals had been advised of the Chiefs' views and let them see the most recent cables. Returning the next day from a long weekend, McNamara held a special conference with the Chiefs and promised continued increases of force in 1966, the mining of Haiphong Harbor by March, bombing escalation, the same kinds of things he had been telling the President at the bombing-halt decision meetings. The halt, McNamara carefully emphasized, would make the escalations easier. The Chiefs were mollified if not reassured.

President Johnson meanwhile began a Christmas peace offensive to accompany the bombing halt. He sent letters and messages himself, sent envoys flying around the world, ordered direct contacts between United States ambassadors and DRV counterparts in Moscow and Rangoon. In the end, the peace offensive finally garnered no result, save that Hanoi used the time to repair its supply routes, and to move troops and supplies to the south. LBJ determined to resume the bombing and did on January 31, 1966, with 132 attack sorties. Henceforth LBJ often scoffed when advisers proposed bombing halts.

*   *   *

An immensely relieved admiral when the bombing resumed, Ulysses S. Grant "Oley" Sharp pitched himself into re-creating the same degree of freedom of action for Rolling Thunder he had had before the pause, a task that took about a month. Admiral Sharp writes of his surprise to learn, in April, of McNamara's strong recommendation to bomb seven of nine DRV oil storage facilities. The President too wished to mount the most effective air threat. Much of this debate quickly boiled down to exchanges over hitting Hanoi's fuel, which everyone was soon calling "POL" after the military acronym.

Strikes on POL had been advocated by CINCPAC and the JCS at least since November 1965, and by the secretary of defense from December. Moreover, Mac Bundy was on his way out the door and his replacement, Walt Rostow, was also an advocate of POL strikes. In this sense there should have been no difficulty moving ahead with a program. During February 1966, however, LBJ's attention was absorbed by Vietnamese political matters, the "other war," and the Honolulu conference. In authorizing resumption during January, LBJ had thought it important to work up to a heavy campaign and not to open at a high crescendo.

Twice in March the Joint Chiefs renewed their call for POL strikes, and got some support both from a CIA special national intelligence estimate and a Pentagon study of measures that might prove militarily effective. Attacks on POL were discussed at the Tuesday Lunch on March 28, a month in which attack sorties over the DRV numbered 4,484. In April, as the POL debate continued, sorties exceeded 5,000 for the first time.

It is still not entirely clear why the POL debate went on as long as it did. President Johnson had McNamara's favorable recommendation by April. Walt Rostow reported similar recommendations from MACV in March. Indications are that opposition emanated from State and Johnson's political staff. Targeting North Vietnamese POL facilities, in cities and populated areas, significantly increased the danger of civilian casualties from the bombing, which would have added to LBJ's political problems.

Johnson's new national security adviser did not hesitate to throw himself into the POL debate. Telling the President that he was "putting an idea into the town as a working colleague," Rostow addressed a memorandum specifically to Rusk and McNamara. In it Walt wrote: "I went through an experience in 1944 which may bear on the decision before us." Noting that the exact same analytical methods had been used measuring the success of the POL campaign against Germany in the big war, Rostow argued that World War II analysts had been mistaken to suppose that the effects of POL attacks would be cushioned by German diversion of fuel from civilian to military uses. It was much more difficult than anticipated for the Germans to reallocate in the face of the general fuel shortage. Thus, "from the moment that serious and systematic oil attacks started, front line single engine fighter strength and tank mobility were affected." With the caveat that attacks had to be "systematic and sustained," Walt argued it would be quite possible that the military effects of POL bombing "may be more prompt and direct than conventional intelligence analysis would suggest."

Within days the arguments were rehearsed at some length at meetings with Henry Cabot Lodge, who had returned to Washington for consultations. Rusk opposed POL attacks, fearing they would greatly heighten international tensions. Max Taylor disagreed. Reporting to LBJ, Rostow remarked that the United States might be in a position where it needed "a softening political-diplomatic track to reduce the noise level." He also believed the United States had "a better chance than ever before of inducing a serious negotiation with Hanoi." Walt started work on a scenario for POL strikes, a letter to Kosygin explaining the attacks, and advised that the attacks, to reduce their political impact, be "hard in a short space of time" rather than spaced out over some interval."

On the President's instructions, Walt acted on June 15 to line up the leadership behind LBJ's new policy, for the decision had been made. The next day, beginning at 6:05 P.M. the National Security Council met for the 559th time. Rostow had failed: UN Ambassador Arthur Goldberg, the NSC discussion notes show, made strenuous objections to POL bombing. As if he had remembered something that had to be done, Lyndon Johnson suddenly stood up and walked out of the meeting, returning more than halfway through Goldberg's remarks.

Ambassador's Goldberg's objections were one of those unfortunate incidents that marred what LBJ had intended as ratification for his POL bombing decision. This session is interesting as an example of just how Johnson structured meetings of this type. The President opened by summarizing the issues that had been under debate for months, disingenuously declaring, "A decision on bombing is not being made now and one is not imminent." Then Rusk began the substantive discussion. McNamara, also somewhat disingenuous, stated that he had *opposed* POL strikes for months but "the situation is now changing and the earlier bombing decision must be reconsidered." General Harold K. Johnson, acting in place of Bus Wheeler, followed up detailing intelligence on the increase of the DRV's use of truck transport and consequent increase in POL imports, then estimated possible U.S. losses from POL strikes. McNamara assessed potential civilian casualties as "very small"—only fifty deaths for the three primary targets—but conceded that if the bombs missed, "we will undoubtedly hurt our cause." In that case, not too unlikely in the era before "smart" bombs, casualties could go as high as twelve thousand, half of them civilians, and half the civilians dead. Repartee among McNamara, Rusk, Rostow, and LBJ underscored the importance of striking the POL sites specifically at Haiphong and Hanoi.

It was Rostow who made clear the rationalization for pretending no decision was being made: "Striking the POL targets is an extension of our bombing program, not a change in our policy."

Assorted comments followed including that of the CIA's Dick Helms, who said, "The petroleum supplies are feeding the meatgrinder in South

Vietnam and this North Vietnamese military effort will continue unless we take out their petroleum supplies."

Bill Moyers commented on the public relations aspect of the decision.

Rostow closed the meeting with the assertion that "the decision is a rational one. Taking out the petroleum supplies sets a ceiling on the capacity of the North Vietnamese to infiltrate men into South Vietnam. A sustained POL offensive will seriously affect the infiltration rate."

One thing that remained an unknown at the time of the NSC meeting was the outcome of a further United States diplomatic feeler, through retired Canadian diplomat Chester A. Ronning, who visited Hanoi from June 14 to 17. Washington soon learned the Ronning mission had gained nothing to speak of. President Johnson followed, on June 22, with a further council meeting including the full Joint Chiefs of Staff. The Chiefs, supported by Dick Helms, recommended mining Haiphong Harbor. There was also talk of hitting the thermal power plant at Hanoi. Even George Ball concurred in the POL strikes, leaving Goldberg the only voice of dissent. Johnson made his formal decision after this meeting and JCS orders went to Admiral Sharp on June 23.

From the beginning Rostow was more engaged than Mac Bundy had been, not only bringing proposals up from the bureaucracy, but taking positions from a very early stage and then fighting the proposals up through the NSC structure. Bundy had begun to do some of this at the end, his concern weighted by the ominous evolution of the war, but Walt started from that point and took the role further.

Political advice, for example, was not beyond Rostow's ken. At the height of the POL debate, after but two months as LBJ's keeper of the keys, Walt weighed in with a proposal that the President go to Notre Dame University and give a short speech on reconciliation that could be "your Gettysburg Address of the Cold War." Johnson rejected that idea out of hand, but less than two weeks later Walt bounced back, with a proposal for a central theme LBJ could highlight during the work-up to the 1966 off-year elections. Starting out with the disclaimer "I have perhaps the least claim to give you political advice," Rostow went on to suggest the theme, "We are on the way to solving great national and international problems; we are making progress; let's stick together and see it through." Walt believed his theme could be applied to race relations, urban problems, the war against poverty, the Alliance for Progress, even Vietnam and China. "Once the theme has been chosen," the adviser wrote, "we could organize quite easily a mass of factual data to back it and get it out to our candidates." The President thought this idea excellent and returned the memorandum to Rostow with the scribbled instruction "Get going!"

Would-be White House chief of staff Robert Kintner felt LBJ thought he could pick on Walt, who "almost had a heart attack every time he buzzed around."

On Vietnam, George Ball recalled, Rostow spent a good deal of time defending his position, not simply managing the paper flow. Ball believes Rostow was a "terrible" influence on the President and thinks others would agree. "He played to Johnson's weaker side," Ball told an interviewer, "always creating an image of Johnson standing against the forces of evil. He used to tell him how Lincoln was abused by everybody when he was at a certain stage of the Civil War, and 'this is the position you are in, Mr. President.' "

Rostow makes no mention of this in his rather extensive treatment of both his Vietnam perspective and the antiwar opposition, in his memoir-cum-history of the postwar era, but it turns out Ball was right to think Rostow was actively bolstering Johnson's beliefs. On February 5, 1966, Henry Owen, then Rostow's deputy at policy planning, completed a memorandum titled "Vietnam," which actually posed the Civil War analogy. It was to 1864, the penultimate year of the Civil War, and had been suggested by a reading of a biography of the great American President. Owen argued that Lincoln had been under pressure for a negotiated peace, as a result of very high casualty rates in General Ulysses S. Grant's campaign against Richmond that year. Standing against those pressures, Lincoln won through to victory. Rostow apparently liked this argument enough that he passed it along to the President.

Ball had been gone from government in March 1967, when Walt forwarded another Owen paper reiterating the analogy. This one argued that the Confederates in 1864 had hoped the presidential elections would save them, then hypothesized Hanoi had the same expectation for the 1968 United States elections. Lincoln was saved, in the 1967 version, by Union victory in the Battle of Atlanta, leading Owen to assert, "The war in Vietnam, too, is being won. The need in the next eighteen months is to find some way of bringing this fact home to our people." Rostow himself put the point on the argument in his covering memo: "In short the analogy would call for our pouring it on in Vietnam so that our people can see clearly the end of the road in 1968, even if the end is not fully achieved by November."

A year later, almost to the day, came a third policy planning paper once again advancing the Civil War analogy. That paper, assembled by Owen and Ralph Clough over a two-week period, was titled "Decision in Vietnam." Intended to put the Civil War analogy in the context of the climactic Tet Offensive, the March 1968 version relied on a different line of argument but arrived at the same prescription. Not even the opening of peace negotiations, the paper argued, would have an effect equivalent to the 1864 victory at Atlanta *unless* talks were "accompanied by military and political progress in South Vietnam." In consequence, "it should be our objective to get such favorable trends in Vietnam under way by late summer." The paper argued this action should precede negotiations, which might be coupled with threats to Hanoi that escalation "remained close at hand." The close timing of these exercises, year after year, suggests these arguments were not being advanced in a merely random fashion.

In another kind of bolstering, Rostow did not shrink from supplying the

President ammunition to use against political opponents who opposed the war. In mid-September 1966, for example, the national security adviser, having heard his brother was making public statements that the Vietnam War was not a civil war, asked Eugene Rostow to write up a sketch of the argument. The elder Rostow took time out from duties as dean of Yale Law School to draft a three-page précis of his claim. Beyond the hyperbole of veiled reference to the Munich analogy and the claim the United States was interested only in peace, the substance of Eugene Rostow's argument came down to the assertion that the 1954 Geneva agreement had created two "states," i.e., nations, from the former Vietnam, a highly debatable proposition. "This is a question of fact," read Rostow's rhetoric, "and not a very complex one." Brother Walt saw the utility of the argument and passed it to LBJ. A couple of months later the President appointed Eugene Rostow undersecretary of state.

Lyndon Johnson liked to invoke the support of symbols and opinion leaders. Rostow could do the same. The CIA, with its pessimistic reporting, was unpopular at the White House from the beginning of the war. Langley did not waver in its position but it did try to make its arguments palatable. In 1966 a study of Hanoi's will to persist in the war went out as a simple thought piece on the CIA letterhead, not even cast as a report or estimate. Agency officials expected a White House blast. Instead LBJ needled them to brief the paper more widely on Capitol Hill. Officials surmised the president was using their report to buttress the latest troop request.

One Saturday the CIA's deputy director for intelligence, Russell Jack Smith, was on duty at Langley when the phone rang on his desk; it was Walt Rostow. The national security adviser explained LBJ was going to make a speech in a few days and wanted a list of gains and accomplishments in Vietnam in recent weeks. Smith took on the assignment, just as he did similar ones from senators and congressmen on the Hill. Turmoil resulted when analysts refused to be a part of helping claim the war a success when the CIA's view was it was a disaster. A deputation visited Jack Smith in his office. To avert revolt, Smith accepted a report on which a list of setbacks and losses was appended. He sent it off to Walt. The CIA official suspected Rostow forwarded the paper without its list of negatives. The incident apparently left a sour taste at Langley.

Meanwhile, bombing policy reared its head as a major issue through 1967. For one thing, more and more figures, some of them quite notable, were coming out against the air war.

The Pentagon, or at least the Office of the Secretary of Defense, came to be regarded as a hotbed of opposition, a cage full of doves nestled at the heart of the war machine. McNamara himself was tired, and had decided to move on. It is perhaps for this reason that he became an open dissenter in the summer of 1967, when he followed the CINCPAC, the JCS, and a variety of others to the witness stand in congressional hearings on the Vietnam bombing. Where the others argued for more bombing, McNamara made the first authoritative argument in public that it was ineffective.

At the apex of the government, Walt Rostow engaged in an effort to limit the damage, as he saw it, of this press for deescalation. In January 1967, Rostow held lengthy conversations with Clark Clifford, on whether LBJ should set up a scientific study group on the bombing similar to Ike's Killian Committee. Walt also forwarded Rolling Thunder recommendations from McNamara and Rusk. Though careful to label his own recommendations as such, Rostow never failed to take a position on a proposal. With Rolling Thunder's fifty-third periodic program, for example, Walt noted: "I believe before we go into any new target system ... you should hear systematic argument on alternative 'northern strategies' so that we decide something more fundamental than merely adding a few targets to the existing list." What Rostow meant became clear that April when, using maps in the Cabinet Room, he argued in detail for a United States invasion of North Vietnam.

Bombing was the third, and key, subject for a late-afternoon Tuesday Lunch on May 19, 1967. Rostow prepped the President with a memo noting objections to bombing of Hanoi and Haiphong by Rusk, McNamara, *and* General Wheeler. Bus actually favored continuation of the strikes, claiming Hanoi would see a stand-down as "an aerial Dien Bien Phu," but he found it tough to make a firm, lucid case. "In a curious way," Walt noted, "all three are arguing negatively." It was both an emotional and technical issue. "So much for sentiments. The question is what kind of scenario can hold our family together in ways that look after the nation's interests and make military sense." Rostow proposed a radical cutback in Hanoi/Haiphong strikes, *after* taking out the thermal power plant. Johnson in fact ordered a twenty-four-hour total bombing halt coupled with a cessation within the Hanoi zone from May 22 to June 9. After new strikes, LBJ renewed the Hanoi zone ban from June 11 to August 9, then again from August 24 to October 23. There could be no room for doubt that Walt W. Rostow had the ear of his President.

Though negotiations seemed unattainable for many years, and in public it appeared the administration was doing little to seek them most of the time, and then too much (as in the Christmas peace offensive) some of the time, the truth was that LBJ tirelessly pursued such leads as seemed to materialize. From 1965 through early 1968 there were over a dozen initiatives, closely held, top-secret ventures with code names like XYZ, Pinta, Sunflower, Buttercup, Ohio, Aspen, Pennsylvania, Packers, and Killy. Johnson relied on emissaries ranging from retired diplomats to leftist writer Norman Cousins, journalists Harry Ashmore and William Baggs, and academic Henry Kissinger.

By comparison with the energy that went into attempts to start talks, Johnson expended a lot less defining a negotiating position for the moment when talks would begin. It was as if the President expected to be able to impose his will once they began. Averell Harriman replaced George Ball as the senior man dealing with peace efforts. Harriman agreed to come on board provided he had his own small staff and full freedom of action. For a deputy Harriman went to Chet Cooper, who by now was at the Institute for Defense Analysis, a think tank run for the government by a consortium of universities.

Meanwhile, Thailand was pressing for an all-Asian peace conference. President Ferdinand Marcos of the Philippines agreed to host the summit, seeing a conference in Manila as a token of international support for his own government, and an opportunity to press certain claims on the Americans. Lyndon Johnson accepted too, seeing it as a chance to assert the legitimacy of the war effort, and press the Thais, the Filipinos, and other Asian allies to increase their respective efforts in South Vietnam.

The Manila conference of October contributed to strengthening the war effort, not the cause of peace. It was notable mostly as the occasion on which Lyndon Johnson, as President of a United States at war in Vietnam, finally made a visit to that beleaguered land. At Manila, Moyers gave Bill Bundy a lesson in quick drafting, once the communiqué the diplomats had painfully worked up proved unacceptable to many. When LBJ rejected it, Bundy thought there was not enough time to draft a new text, whereupon Moyers took the thing and quickly wrote up a text that Johnson not only accepted, but got the other summit nations to accept, in about an hour—record time.

But LBJ's visit to South Vietnam was not the success it could have been. Worried about security on the trip, and about the press, Johnson went to great pains to keep it a deep secret. For security reasons he flew only to Cam Ranh Bay to visit American troops for half a day at the base there. Johnson never visited Saigon. Bui Diem, soon to be appointed South Vietnamese ambassador to the United States, thought his people "felt humiliated by the way this was being handled." He recalled, "Johnson's visit to Cam Ranh was like a slap in the face."

This ham-fisted manner applied also to diplomatic efforts to open negotiations. At the time of Manila, Cooper found both Hanoi and Washington "imbedded [sic] in concrete on the issue of a bombing halt." Pondering the problem, he finally came to the idea that something might be accomplished if both sides could *pretend* things had come out their way; in effect both could declare victory then get on with the talks. Cooper wrote up a working paper before leaving for Manila proposing to separate the parts of the problem: The United States could halt the bombing on the basis of private assurances that soon thereafter Hanoi would stop sending troops down the Ho Chi Minh Trail. In further work that winter this became known as the "Phase A-Phase B" formula.

In London, Prime Minister Harold Wilson proposed mediation and was about to send his foreign minister to Moscow. Wilson's foreign minister, George Brown, had been given a precise presentation of the Phase A-Phase B proposals to relay through Moscow. Henry Cabot Lodge followed up a Polish-Italian channel known as Marigold, which was furthered by Saigon meetings among the three ambassadors.

When the British found out that the Italians were in the same play through

Marigold, they were furious. Harriman sent Cooper, who had known Brown since his days in the 1950s as CIA intelligence liaison in London, to calm the British down. Permitted to tell the British of two other United States initiatives, Cooper demonstrated good faith; one initiative involved face-to-face contacts in Moscow between United States and North Vietnamese diplomats, which began on January 10, 1967.

The NSC staff had always been aware of the various diplomatic maneuvers in progress. In fact, Vietnam staffer Bill Jorden, as a former Harriman intimate, had extra access. Harriman no doubt considered he had a special channel to Rostow and LBJ thereby, but there was no guarantee the diplomats would learn everything that was going on at the OEOB. Since November, Walt had been attracted to the idea of cutting out the middlemen in all these peace negotiations. Rostow sent the President a memorandum arguing that, beyond the problem of getting the DRV to talk, could be that of Hanoi's fears that if it stopped infiltration south, in order to talk, the VC would fall apart and destroy its bargaining position.

Rostow wanted to communicate to Hanoi a solution that took that into account. He wanted to make it credible by making it "a direct U.S.-Hanoi gambit, with no intermediaries," and by making it concrete, with evident seriousness conveyed by a written document that could be transmitted to Hanoi. Walt's idea of an "end position which Hanoi and the Viet Cong can live with" was to offer the VC "a guarantee against slaughter," and a "right to organize politically and to vote." This would be offered only after arms were laid down, infiltration had ceased ("100%"), and North Vietnamese units were marching home both from the RVN and Laos.

Over the ensuing weeks there was some excitement about Marigold, and also the mix-up with the British. There is no telling if LBJ would actually have adopted Walt's suggested settlement, which surely would have been nonnegotiable with Hanoi. But the President *did* pick up on the idea of direct contacts, which he initiated through Moscow, and then, on February 8, in a letter to Ho Chi Minh. In this instance the President's watcher appears to have encouraged an initiative that directly undercut American diplomats in London, for Chet Cooper was then waiting in London, where the British were to talk with Kosygin. Rostow told LBJ on January 14, "I still believe we ought to try a letter from you, before the end of the Tet truce."

Johnson himself, Cooper recounts, indicated a desire to keep his options open when the letter idea was first suggested. Cooper did not know if LBJ approved the idea, but he did not object. Rusk purportedly took a dim view from the start, while the first draft of the letter, Cooper thought, "had the stamp of Walt Rostow's lofty style." The last Cooper saw was an intermediate version, just before his own departure for London.

Rostow and Rusk finally finished the letter, which contained a *different*, more restrictive version of the Phase A-Phase B formula, under which Hanoi would have to stop all infiltration *prior* to a bombing halt. That was not only a step back from the instructions given the British; it was inconsistent with the United States' fourteen points, which Rusk had released to the public only a few days before. When Cooper saw the text as dispatched, he was dumbfounded. Chet called the NSC staff in Washington, to get Rostow on the line. Walt confirmed the language in the letter.

Now Cooper was supposed to get the British to take back the formula they had just advanced, and substitute the more restrictive Johnson letter formula. Understandably, "Brown and Wilson were incredulous and irate." In two decades in diplomacy, Cooper had never seen anyone as angry as Wilson that night.

There was to be one final Wilson-Kosygin session, scheduled for the prime minister's country home, Chequers, on February 12. Cooper was literally to wait in the wings—in the attic room that in 1565 had served as prison for Lady Mary Grey, whose "pathetic graffiti" could still be seen on the walls. Cooper had a direct telephone line to Washington, and got periodic reports that afternoon from Burke Trend, British cabinet secretary and Walt Rostow's counterpart. Trying to salvage something, Cooper and Trend hammered out a modification of the formula, coupled with an extension of the Tet bombing halt that was in effect.

Cooper called Washington and spoke to Ben Read at State. Rusk's executive assistant thought it sounded perfectly okay, but wanted to make sure the White House signed off. Cooper himself, after the Johnson letter, wanted nothing less. Chet made more calls, to Read and Rostow, begging for the word, as the British-Soviet meetings went on downstairs. Wilson could not present the revised formula without sanction. The prime minister kept sending notes upstairs asking for Washington's reply.

Once more Cooper called Rostow. "Now, look," Chet told Walt, "they're having cigars, they're having brandy, for God's sake what do you think of this idea?"

"Well, we're still talking about it, and we'll let you know. See if you can keep everything intact."

Still, Washington could not decide. It seemed to Cooper the Russians were about to leave. He looked out the window and could see the cars turning on their headlights and motorcycles revving up.

Chet called Rostow one more time. "Look," he said, "I'm not kidding you!"

Cooper dangled the telephone receiver out the window, down by its cord, ten feet or so, where it might pick up the sounds of the motorcade. Then he got back on the line.

"They're leaving!"

"Okay, all right," Rostow replied, "not to worry, just make sure that Wilson tells Kosygin that he may have an important message for him some time later on this evening and that Wilson will communicate this message."

Cooper and the United States ambassador, David K. E. Bruce, then got down to the prime minister's London residence, 10 Downing Street, to stand in readiness for the big message. That message was in fact cobbled together by Rostow and Rusk in a midnight drafting session from which such relevant officials as Bill Bundy were excluded. When it came through, the message agreed with Cooper's Phase A-Phase B formula, but only if Hanoi accepted it by 10:00 A.M. the next morning. Since it was already well past midnight, that was patently not possible, indeed Kosygin would be lucky to get a message *to* Hanoi that quickly.

Cooper called Rostow again. "You can't do this," he said this time. "This is impossible. We need more time."

Cooper recalls that Rostow did not sound very friendly. "We've had about enough out of you guys," Walt countered.

This exercise evidently got the British an extra two hours, where they thought they needed at least forty-eight. Harold Wilson talked to Washington himself, and George Brown to Rusk, but neither was able to do any better. Cooper later got enough time to allow Kosygin's return flight to reach Moscow, but that was it. Then Radio Hanoi broadcast a letter from Ho to the pope demanding unconditional cessation of the bombing. The White House was furious that Hanoi took advantage of the Tet truce by moving elements of three divisions into the sector of the Demilitarized Zone. Johnson was in no mood to continue the bombing halt. In Washington later, Cooper discovered that no one at the crucial meetings, where Johnson's more restrictive formulas had been concocted, had had a copy of the original Phase A-Phase B proposal or even remembered its precise wording.

Some other negotiating efforts contrasted favorably with this madness. Project Pennsylvania marked the diplomatic debut of Henry Kissinger. In 1967, Kissinger attended the annual Pugwash conference in Paris. A private symposium on arms control and disarmament created by American industrialist Cyrus Eaton in 1957, Pugwash brings together an international group of distinguished scholars and public servants, including experts from Soviet bloc nations. With the Six Day War and Vietnam such salient conflicts, Pugwash in 1967 included certain discussions on those topics, among them a general description from United States sources of the Phase A-Phase B formula.

At Pugwash, Kissinger met Herbert Marcovich, a biologist with the Pasteur Institute in Paris. The Frenchman mentioned that he had a friend, Raymond Aubrac, an official of the UN Food and Agricultural Organization, who personally knew Ho Chi Minh. With the knowledge and endorsement of the Soviet participant in the Pugwash exchange, Kissinger suggested it might be useful for Aubrac and Marcovich to visit Hanoi and once more present the Phase A-Phase B formula. Kissinger informed Harriman and got a green light to follow this thread wherever it might lead, and the Frenchmen visited Hanoi from July 21 to 26, during which time they had two conversations with Pham Van Dong and one with Ho Chi Minh. Chet Cooper reported the results to Walt Rostow; Harriman, Ben Read, Phil Habib, and Joe Sisco at State; and Paul Warnke at the Pentagon. North Vietnamese officials spoke quite frankly with the Frenchmen and invited them to stay in touch through Hanoi's Paris representative Mai Van Bo.

This began three months of to-ing and fro-ing. On August 11, Lyndon

Johnson deputized Kissinger as presidential emissary by approving an official statement for him to convey through Marcovich and Aubrac. In mid-August, Kissinger met the Frenchmen in Paris and introduced them to Chet Cooper.

Marcovich and Aubrac made another attempt to visit Hanoi but were unable to secure visas. They therefore transmitted the United States proposals through Mai Van Bo. As a sweetener, Kissinger was authorized to pass on news that a bombing pause for the Hanoi vicinity would begin on August 24. The Frenchmen encouraged Bo to meet directly with Kissinger, while the North Vietnamese diplomat countered that he had already asked for authority to do so.

Kissinger stayed in close touch with Marcovich and Aubrac, but Mai Van Bo never agreed to receive the Harvard professor. Kissinger passed along several United States government communications, which, in the absence of Hanoi's reply to its original August 25 proposal, represented attempts to interpret the DRV position. Mai Van Bo kept saying he was awaiting his government's reply. On October 20, Bo refused even to meet with Marcovich or Aubrac, finally ending the initiative.

Again in the absence of any North Vietnamese response, Lyndon Johnson decided to go public himself. On September 29 the President spoke before the National Legislative Conference at San Antonio, Texas. Johnson announced the United States would halt all aerial and naval bombardment "when this will lead promptly to productive discussions," and on the assumption that Hanoi would not "take advantage" of this cessation while negotiations proceeded. This position became known as the San Antonio formula. In substance it was much the same as what Kissinger had presented, so Mai Van Bo would no longer have to ask, as he had once demanded of Marcovich, whether Walt Rostow had approved the United States position. North Vietnamese party newspaper *Nhan Dan* rejected the public San Antonio formula on October 3, while Mai Van Bo delivered a statement on the seventeenth that said the Kissinger proposals were not going to receive a reply on his channel. Bombing in the Hanoi vicinity resumed on October 23.

In actuality there had been some movement in the United States position under the San Antonio formula. The new proposition that Hanoi should not "take advantage" of a halt translated differently from similar language in the old Phase A-Phase B proposal. Where formerly Hanoi had been expected to *stop* its support for the war in the south, now the condition was only that they not increase the level of support. Clark Clifford explained this difference, ambiguous in Johnson's speech itself, to Congress on January 25, 1968, when Clifford appeared at Senate confirmation hearings. Completing the changing of the Pentagon guard, Clifford had been nominated to replace McNamara, who was leaving to become president of the World Bank. It was under Clifford's interpretation of the San Antonio formula that negotiations finally began.

TWILIGHT OF A PRESIDENCY

▲▲▲

Washington being what it is, there were always plenty of people ready to give advice to the President, and plenty more advice than the President had any need or use for. But one piece of advice Lyndon Johnson adopted was the suggestion, contained in the 1967 version of the Civil War analogy, that Washington bring home to the American people the "fact" that the United States was winning the Vietnam War. That amounted to an appeal for a public information program. The President, who had used just such a device in the course of the 1965 troop decisions, understood the method and appreciated its importance.

Walt Rostow was in full agreement with his President on the matter of public information. From his West Wing office Walt watched as the media, reporter by reporter, and outlet by outlet, seemed to turn against the war. Moreover, he could see firsthand the loss of faith within the bureaucracy hidden from the media outside. Rostow sat as a member of Bill Bundy's so-called non-group, an off-the-record drinks and discussion group that met weekly at State and talked only of Vietnam.

President Johnson's solution was the same he had tried in 1965. LBJ created an interagency committee to handle the press. Earlier in the year the President had tried to orchestrate some sympathetic coverage without any special arrangements, calling General Westmoreland home from Vietnam to make a favorable prognosis, but the problem was that there was no lasting impact without constant effort. So the President decided on an interagency press group, not just any group this time, but one headed by Rostow. That unit, called the Vietnam Information Group (VIG), was chaired by Rostow, received staff support from Marshall Wright, an assistant to NSC Far East senior staffer Bill Jorden, and Sven Kraemer, a young conservative recruit. In terms of ability to command resources, always a key indicator of bureaucratic importance, the VIG was able to get William Leonhart, who had replaced Komer as LBJ's special assistant for the "other war," to lend out Thelma Seibert as secretary and administrative assistant. Seibert was one of that small but vital cadre of faithful civil servants who truly make government work, whom Ike had brought into the White House as an NSC secretary a decade before. Leonhart's office, the hottest thing happening in Johnson's White House in 1966, a year later was being raided to benefit the Vietnam Information Group.

Rostow's group was comprehensive and active, meeting weekly in the White House Situation Room. The VIG both organized a program and planned reactions to anticipated events. It required reports from those in the field describing what *they* were doing, and thus encouraged local initiative. In early October 1967, for example, Saigon reported its current projects "to demonstrate to the press and the public that we are making solid progress and are not in a stalemate." Those projects included: preparation of a written comparison with the 1965 situation; extra off-the-record press conferences by Westmoreland, Komer, and Ellsworth Bunker, newly appointed ambassador; release of selected captured VC documents; selection of pacification success stories and unit achievement stories for "detailed briefing of the press"; a new series of MACV intelligence/operations monthly briefings; and "the presentation of concise, hard-hitting briefings designed to allay credibility problems" on a series of "subjects about which the press has doubts." That month the Washington overseers set up a working group on progress indicators, one on information programs for seven foreign nations, and ordered preparation of a special briefing book for Cabinet members and presidential appointees. The VIG also discussed such subjects as possible responses to allegations of differences between McNamara and the JCS, to the CBS television documentary *Mind of the VC*, and to certain congressional hearings. Journalist Don Oberdorfer, in a fine history of this period, cites a long series of "leaks" to the press of data tending to imply progress in the war.

There can be no doubt that much of this press reporting resulted from deliberate releases of information, and that much of it was owed to work of the VIG. For example, at least a month before Westy came home in November 1967, CIA director Richard Helms went to the President to pass on a congressman's suggestion that there be a full-scale TV briefing featuring both Westy and Bunker plus MACV and CIA intelligence people. Johnson seemed interested, and sent Helms to Walt. Similarly, Rostow sent Westmoreland a back-channel message instructing the general to get out and get the word out in public. This use of a back channel was unusual for Rostow, mostly respectful of the chain of command, who avers that in all his time he sent no more than three back-channel cables, one of them congratulations to Ellsworth Bunker in Nepal on the occasion of his marriage.

As for the presumed leaks of specific information, they too resulted from careful preparation. Rostow immediately saw the potential of the charts Westy had used in briefing the President. He ordered that a couple be deleted, and that one on the South Vietnamese presidential elections, in which Nguyen Van Thieu had been made president (with Ky relegated to the vice presidency), be added. The resulting collection was sent out by Art Mc-Cafferty, Situation Room director, to be printed up (three hundred copies) as a little blue booklet. The VIG staff then prepared a letter, over Rostow's signature, that declared that the charts had been compiled "at" MACV headquarters, that they represented "the best data available at this time," and that the progress they implied "is confirmed by captured documents, prisoner interrogations, estimates of field commanders, and by other sources." The booklets and letters were distributed to the press and congressmen by legislative liaison Barefoot Sanders.

With public relations officials from the White House and the agencies, and representatives of the NSC, State, DOD, the CIA, and the USIA, the Vietnam Information Group had the horsepower to move matters forward. Its members included experienced journalists (in private life) like Richard Fryklund, so VIG also had the talent to put together product. An NSC staffer on the VIG is reported to have had the task of arranging a counter, the same day, for every speech critical of the war that appeared in the *Congressional Record.*

There is no mistaking the intent to put a spin on the news. Oberdorfer, who first discussed the activities of this unit in print, spoke with a member in the course of his research who called it the "psychological strategy committee." The journalist noted the name, reporting it as the formal identity of the group, though it is clear that Oberdorfer also had come across the name VIG, which he evidently thought a different unit. Available records contain no reference to a "psychological strategy committee," only to the VIG. It is likely that the reference was by an NSC staffer to Harry Truman's Psychological Strategy Board (PSB); the one member of VIG who had knowledge of the PSB was Walt Rostow. The allusion is further revealing in that, unlike some ordinary information campaign, the PSB reference suggests an intent to mold, even manipulate, opinion.

It is one of the great ironies of Vietnam that the success of the VIG is to be measured by the perception of United States failure in the biggest battle of the war. For the fact was that Hanoi and the Vietcong were preparing a countrywide offensive, their biggest to date. Walt Rostow, and indeed LBJ himself, made the fundamental error of preparing the nation for success when they should have been talking about hard fighting ahead.

The basic error is further compounded because it was witting. There exists a multitude of evidence, from MACV, from the CIA, from the NSC staff, from Johnson himself, that a VC/NVA offensive in early 1968 was anticipated. Westmoreland changed MACV dispositions and requested an acceleration of planned reinforcements to meet it. Johnson spoke of it to the Australian cabinet on a visit there for the funeral of Harold Holt. Rostow singled out the evidence, in the form of captured documents and a CIA assessment, and passed it up to the President. Walt's military aide, General Robert Ginsburgh, clearly remembers Rostow's rising concern, beginning in early December, just a couple of weeks after Westy's claim of victory in sight. Save perhaps for an excess of exuberance, it is inexplicable that the watcher at LBJ's gate did not warn the President against maintaining the victory campaign in the face of what they knew to be coming. Even if LBJ felt uncomfortable warning of coming battle, felt it would make him look a loser, he could at least have kept a low profile until after the battle. The victory campaign, what Oberdorfer calls the "success offensive," was Johnson's greatest gamble, his cosmic roll of the dice.

The most plausible explanation is that Lyndon Johnson expected a great and obvious military victory. Indeed Westmoreland had prepared for one, at Khe Sanh, a mountain plateau position in the northwest corner of the RVN. The signs were many that the NVA intended to attack there, but there was also intelligence indicating their interest in attacks on Vietnamese cities and towns. In Washington, Rostow kept bucking up the President with unremitting optimism, slogans like "Don't mourn. Organize!" Westmoreland was meanwhile predicting Hanoi's attack would come before the Vietnamese new year, Tet.

A week before the anticipated date there was a mean firefight at one of the outlying positions around Khe Sanh. Intelligence data indicated that the NVA had concentrated at least two, possibly three, divisions around Khe Sanh; that was 20,000 to 30,000 men. The firefight engaged only tiny proportions of those forces, and of the United States defenders for that matter, but many in the high command were prepared to think the hill fight confirmed their belief the big battle had begun at Khe Sanh.

Instead, the Tet holiday was disrupted by massive assaults on cities and towns throughout South Vietnam while Khe Sanh remained quiet. The scale and timing of the attacks achieved a tactical surprise. Though most of them were beaten off, the NVA actually gained control of Hue for some weeks, while fighting continued in Saigon almost as long. This was the Tet Offensive. It could not have come at a more inconvenient time for LBJ and Rostow, it seemed, since the White House had been in an uproar for days over the seizure at sea, off the Korean coast, of the United States intelligence ship *Pueblo*.

Early in the morning of January 30, 1968, McCafferty and Ginsburgh, who knew LBJ would soon be up and demanding the latest reports, became concerned that the Situation Room had gotten little since its midnight report. To save time, McCafferty used transpacific phone lines to call the duty officer at MACV for a report. It proved a lucky move—as the call was going through, another phone rang from LBJ's bedroom. McCafferty told the President the Situation Room expected to be in direct contact with MACV shortly. At MACV the call was fielded by a Westmoreland aide, who asked if the White House would not care to speak to the general himself. McCafferty demurred, not wishing to disturb Westy in the midst of critical battle action. The call was then transferred to the MACV combat operations center, but about five minutes later, Westy arrived there too, and the colonel on duty told the Situation Room that the MACV commander wished to speak to the White House. Soon thereafter Westy spoke with General Earle Wheeler, remarking he had been in touch with the White House. Walt soon arrived at the office, to be confronted by an irate Bus Wheeler, outraged that the NSC staff and Situation Room were interrupting his leaders in the heat of the crisis. Rostow went to the Situation Room and established the particulars of the incident, then tried to placate the JCS Chairman with a note explaining what had happened. On Walt's instructions, secretary Lois Nivens ended with a handwritten addition: "I know well that—at a time like now—the field commander is the man at the wheel."

A further Situation Room telephone incident occurred when Phil Habib called the embassy in Saigon for a firsthand report on conditions there. He was told that VC had surrounded the building, inside the compound, but were in turn surrounded on the outside by Marines and military police. Habib called repeatedly, becoming one of the first to learn the embassy had been relieved. Being Bill Bundy's deputy, Habib also called on other occasions seeking specific Foreign Service officers for their perspectives.

The second day of the battle, still seeking information Johnson wanted, Walt observed the chain of command by going first to Wheeler, then having Bus order Westmoreland to call up the White House and ask for Rostow. The national security adviser posed six questions to the MACV commander, then reported Westy's replies to the President. The general stated his belief that the *Pueblo* seizure and Tet attacks were related actions, though taken by different countries, and also felt he was already regaining the initiative. Westmoreland revealed his continuing expectation that Khe Sanh, rather than the city attacks, constituted the central element of NVA strategy with his statement that the NVA were building up to a "third phase" involving a "massive attack" in the northern provinces. "The enemy is now poised for this phase," Westy reported, "which he considers his decisive campaign." Bob Ginsburgh took down Westmoreland's answers.

President Johnson had held a Tuesday Lunch on January 30, at which the talk had been entirely about the *Pueblo* and certain Vietnam negotiating feelers, specifically the Buttercup and Packers initiatives. Another such session followed on Saturday, February 3, and although the *Pueblo* stayed on the agenda, peace talk was entirely supplanted by consideration of moves to strengthen the United States' global military posture. Expecting an attack on Khe Sanh to begin momentarily, the Situation Room shifted to a round-the-clock manning schedule, with Rostow handling the day shifts, and McCafferty and Ginsburgh splitting the nights. It was the first time during Tet that the Situation Room had been manned by senior personnel twenty-four hours a day. With the President constantly pushing for the latest reports, the Situation Room got the CIA to begin a series of spot reports on the northern RVN and Khe Sanh situations similar to the ones it was already sending regarding the Tet Offensive as a whole. Ginsburgh also drafted a memo for the President comparing the huge resources available to the United States for Khe Sanh with the relatively limited capabilities the French had had at Dien Bien Phu, the battle widely taken as analogous.

As the Tet fighting continued, stocktaking became possible. Americans were uncertain, not least of them Walt's wife Elspeth, who on the evening of February 4 asked him to explain what was going on in Vietnam. Both were economists, so Walt had no qualms about sketching graphs to illustrate

his explanation. The top curve on one chart, gradually ascending, represented the allies, Walt said, while the gradually descending curve was the
NVA and VC. That represented the attrition, the slow rate of progress of
1967. Then Walt sketched a second graph, its curves oscillating more wildly,
on the United States side rising gradually at first, then more sharply, and
continuing the rise over the projected future. For Hanoi, the graph depicted
a sudden rise, but then a steep and extended decline. Walt explained that
that was the real shape of the graphs if the perceptions of the sides were
factored in. Rostow presumed to write up this projection in a memorandum
for the President the next morning. The projection, he noted, represented
the eventuality that the cities were cleared up and held, the GVN demonstrated effectiveness, the United States held Khe Sanh, and "we keep U.S.
opinion steady on course."

Of course the last was the real challenge. Members of the VIG, including
Bill Bundy, George Carver of the CIA, and Bill Jorden and Bill Leonhart
from the White House, had worked hard to create the perception of victory.
Nothing undermined it like the Tet Offensive.

A great deal of ink has been spilled in efforts to castigate the American
press for its reporting on Tet. By reporting the setback they saw, the argument runs, the press made Tet a psychological defeat when, because of
the high enemy casualty figures, it should have been a victory. Westy and
his minions harped incessantly on the casualty figures in a manful effort to
"prove" victory. Not only did it not wash, some of the efforts backfired
and convinced important opinion-makers that the United States government
was just not being honest. When Walter Cronkite, anchorman of CBS Evening News and one of the public's most trusted figures, told Americans he
had concluded we were losing the Vietnam War, it made a big difference.

The charges against the press are not nearly so clear-cut, however. In the
first place, the administration *appreciated* the gullibility of the press; the
VIG had used it for its psychological strategy through the fall of 1967.
Without the long run of "victory" rhetoric, the journalists would have seen
Tet much differently. It is significant that both the general, William Westmoreland, and the President, Lyndon Johnson, have admitted error in not
making more efforts to prepare the American public for an enemy offensive
at Tet 1968. LBJ even wrote he should have made it a point in his State of
the Union Address.

The field marshal of the psychological strategy campaign was Walt Rostow. Yes, the journalists ought to have sought more background for their
stories before reporting "defeat" in Vietnam, but faced with the incontro-
vertible evidence of the countrywide Tet Offensive, they cannot be blamed
for their skepticism at what they had been told by United States authorities.

Walt's explanation to Elspeth, a little premature, occurred three days
before the event Lyndon Johnson *had* been awaiting, an evident NVA attack
at Khe Sanh. Hanoi's troops struck at an outlying hill position, and at the
Lang Vei Special Forces camp. Hanoi's psychological victory during Tet

was not some journalistic hocus-pocus, but rather to have gotten the United States high command to fixate on Khe Sanh as the "real" battle. Thus *a week* after the Tet attacks, Rostow was telling Lyndon Johnson of his feeling that Hanoi's objective in attacking the cities was to exhaust the GVN civil and military apparatus and "to force Westy to commit to battle in the cities the reserves he needs to hold Khe Sanh." Concerning that day, the day of Lang Vei, Walt told LBJ, *"This is it!"*

Clark Clifford, Johnson's new secretary of defense, was the man who understood. Westy and Rostow were talking about how Hanoi must have decided to drop "its" attritional strategy and go for broke. Westy was asking for reinforcements again. Johnson was asking how many, and thinking of sending Cyrus Vance on a Fortas-type mission to Saigon to find out. The issue Clifford raised, privately and at the Tuesday Lunch on February 11, was "How do you explain this in terms of past statements of progress?"

Walt suggested a speech, but Clifford had a point. He was perhaps also the right man to make the point, having lined up behind the President and supported him loyally despite initial doubts regarding intervention in Vietnam. So loyal was Clifford that in 1967, when Harriman was supposed to be finding a way out of the war, LBJ commissioned Clifford and Max Taylor to visit America's Pacific allies and solicit increases in *their* Vietnam commitments. Thus, in a way, Clifford represented for LBJ the other alternative, the force option. To have Clark raising questions shocked Lyndon Johnson, and led to a strained relationship between the President and this trusted lieutenant, but that was only one part of the fallout from the Tet Offensive.

To settle his own thoughts LBJ did order a mission to Saigon, but he dropped the idea of asking Vance to make it. Instead, the President turned to Bus Wheeler. It seemed natural to dispatch the Chairman of the JCS to confer with the military commander in the field. Wheeler succeeded in convincing Westmoreland to request a large additional increment of troops. On February 12 the President approved an emergency augmentation of 10,500, but on the twenty-seventh Wheeler reported back MACV's full request for three new divisions and fifteen air squadrons, which, with support forces, totaled 206,000 more soldiers, sailors, airmen, and marines.

Concerned that the emergency reinforcements comprised almost the last combat-ready forces in the United States strategic reserve not committed to NATO, Wheeler actually finagled the MACV troop request in such a way that almost half of it, 97,000 men, were to remain in the continental United States barring exceptional circumstances. This private understanding did not appear in any clear fashion in Bus Wheeler's official report. LBJ went ahead and ordered Clifford, as his first assignment, to supervise a policy review on the troop request, the desire for mobilization measures, and associated issues. The President told Clifford he wanted answers by March 4.

Johnson's request led to frantic activity at the Pentagon. The Joint Chiefs recommended the mobilization of 250,000 and deployment of 200,000. Clifford's final paper to Johnson dropped many early contributions, including a draft NSAM, and recommended mobilization to reconstitute the strategic reserve, but took no position on the actual deployment of new reinforcements beyond a 22,000 post-Tet emergency augmentation.

None too happy with the DOD review, Walt Rostow felt Paul Warnke's paper too pessimistic, and was scandalized that that contribution to the policy review used language drawn from a paper being circulated by Daniel Ellsberg, viewing GVN efforts as ineffective. Walt was also receiving a different stream of advice from military aide Bob Ginsburgh, who looked favorably on JCS requests to escalate against the north. That not only would retaliate for Tet, Ginsburgh thought, it could placate the "hawks," regain credibility with the Soviets and even "indirectly let the North Koreans know that our patience is not inexhaustible." The Joint Chiefs were advocating a series of measures ranging from reducing the no-bomb zones surrounding Hanoi and Haiphong to one third their present size; to accepting greater risks of civilian casualties (though still not bombing populations per se); to mining Haiphong Harbor, mounting an amphibious invasion, and bombing the dikes that held back big rivers in the north. Bombing the dikes would be "beyond the pale," Ginsburgh reasoned, but the invasion option should be preserved; most of the other measures could be implemented right away, while

mining . . . would have the greatest immediate impact—militarily and psychologically. Current weather would not preclude the laying of minefields. It also occurs to me that mining could be a useful bargaining lever. Instead of offering to stop bombing in return for talks a la San Antonio, we could simply say that we would not renew our minefields in return for talks and without making a "not take advantage" assumption.

Ginsburgh in fact went to work on an extensive paper covering many aspects of the mining of Haiphong Harbor, which Rostow passed approvingly to the President in early March.

The JCS proposals clearly involved significant escalation. Clifford's policy review, though not going along with the big troop request, to LBJ's horror contained the dread word "mobilization." A choice LBJ had tried to avoid from the very beginning, it was bound to be controversial. LBJ felt sufficiently uncertain that he readily agreed to seek the views of the Wise Men. He wished to confer anew with the military commanders, and sent his JCS Chairman to sound out Westy at Clark Air Force Base in the Philippines. Wheeler returned bringing MACV deputy commander General Creighton W. Abrams with him.

While these affairs were in progress, the cat got out of the bag on the decision. At a cocktail party a *New York Times* reporter heard that reinforcements were under consideration. He passed the word to two others who, using their own sources, were able to confirm the story. A few days' research added further details and, on March 10, 1968, with a banner headline above the bylines of Neil Sheehan and Hedrick Smith, appeared the number 206,000 and the story of the imminent decision. In conjunction with such large reinforcement requests, the administration claims of victory at Tet rang hollow.

Revelation of the reinforcement request helped turn public opinion decisively against the war, and instantly wiped out any success that had resulted from continuing efforts by the VIG. Moreover, given LBJ's typical attitude, that he would never do anything that appeared in a leak, the story had a profound effect on the troop request itself. Clifford's people, massaging the numbers, got the mobilization request down to 98,000 by mid-March, but LBJ's approval even for that figure was in doubt. Inadvertently, Bus Wheeler backed Westmoreland into a hornet's nest. Neither got what he wanted.

The mobilization choice, and the advocacy of intensified bombing of the north, helped focus the President on the other strand of advice before him, a bombing halt. That began in late 1967 with McNamara, which might have been expected, but also with Harry McPherson, whom LBJ styled his philosopher. McNamara handed the President a paper setting out the case for a halt. Johnson took the paper, had it retyped to eliminate any indication of whence it came, and circulated it for comment, mostly negative. The President himself took the unusual step, almost unheard of for LBJ, of writing a memorandum for the record, indicating the reasons he thought a halt at that time would be a sign of weakness.

A few days earlier Harry McPherson wrote the President privately, laying out his impression that "a lot of Harry McPhersons in private life," centrist Democrats who had supported United States foreign policy since 1948, "have grown increasingly edgy about the bombing program." He supplied ten serious points or objections, then advised a bombing halt everywhere in the DRV except immediately north of the demilitarized zone. At a minimum, McPherson advised, there ought to be a speech to explain the purpose of the bombing. Johnson took up the latter advice, instructing Walt Rostow to join McPherson in drafting such an address. Walt phoned Harry the next day to arrange an appointment, but somehow they never managed to get together.

After Tet a hint of LBJ's new uncertainty was his sudden addition of McPherson to the roster of officials at his Vietnam strategy sessions. Rusk made the issue of a halt more concrete on March 4 with a memo that put a mobilization of troops together with a bombing halt. That theme was followed up at the Tuesday Lunch the next day, arguing that bombing of the DRV could be halted for the current rainy season with little military impact. On March 10, two days after Rostow forwarded the President a detailed analysis of the mining of Haiphong Harbor, Averell Harriman tried out the bombing halt portion of Rusk's suggestion on an Eastern European ambassador, who showed interest but had no immediate response. From the United Nations, Secretary General U Thant passed along reports from France and elsewhere that a halt could lead to negotiations.

American officials soon were staking out positions on a halt. Some had been doing so for weeks or months. At lower levels in the Pentagon, Paul Nitze, Paul Warnke, and Undersecretary of the Air Force Townsend Hoopes all favored the halt option. Ambassador Arthur Goldberg supported it from his UN vantage point. Max Taylor, as part of an analysis of Vietnam alternatives, found that opening negotiations would be a positive development. From Saigon, on the other hand, Ellsworth Bunker opposed any bombing halt, and at the White House Walt Rostow saw benefit in a peace offensive only in the spring, say after May, once the United States had strengthened its hand, even if that entailed additional military measures.

From the day after Tet, Rostow advocated a presidential address in which Johnson could explain what had happened and what he was about. Policy discussions by late March focused on whether LBJ should approve a halt and announce it in the speech. McPherson had been working on drafts since early February. Crucial meetings were Tuesday Lunches on March 20 and 22, at which the President added Mac Bundy and Abe Fortas to his circle.

On Wednesday, March 20, following a discussion of budgetary implications, Rusk brought up the bombing cessation and warned the effect of Tet had been to rob people of hope. Mac Bundy concurred; there had been a "great fall-off in support"; even people who agreed with United States objectives wondered what it would cost. Clifford spoke at length on what those objectives were. He posed the question, "Do we have anything to offer besides new war?" Then Clifford answered his own question: "reasonableness," deescalation, and a bombing halt north of the 20th Parallel. Ambassador Goldberg supported deescalation, and warned against additional troops. Rostow felt bombing had greater impact on world opinion than troop increases. Fortas opposed a halt; LBJ worried it would make the hawks furious. The President concluded the meeting by siding with Abe that putting peace initiatives (a bombing halt) and troop increases in the same speech was too confusing. "Let's make it troops and war," Johnson said. "Later we can revive and extend our peace initiatives."

That Friday, LBJ met the group again, having received a new speech draft in the interval. The speech was put through a wringer; then it came down to brass knuckles. Clifford took a clear line: The military "has not come up with a plan for victory"; people were discouraged; Vietnam had become "a bottomless pit."

"Since the men Westmoreland wants won't get there until summer," said the secretary of defense, "they really aren't going to be of any use to him in the emergency."

Perhaps the United States should call up some reserves, but it should "not commit any troops other than those we had [already] promised." Bus Wheeler could talk it over with Westy at Manila, something the JCS Chairman did do, thereupon returning to Washington, together with MACV deputy Abrams.

Clifford and Rusk agreed on a bombing cessation, while Bill Bundy recalled Ellsworth Bunker's opposition. Rostow marshaled his best argument.

"Hanoi would know full well that we were taking advantage of the bad weather," Walt declared. "It might have some effect on doves and some effect in Europe, but [it] would not succeed and would cause . . . problems."

Mac Bundy thought Clifford's proposal would have a short diplomatic life but he was not against it. On the other hand, Johnson's former keeper of the keys agreed with Rostow that "if you wanted to do more later, it is smarter to do less now."

Rusk summed up, Harry McPherson remembers: "Mr. President, I believe it is the consensus of your advisers that a partial reduction of the bombing would be insufficient to produce talks. . . . [and] the North Vietnamese have given no sign they would not use a total cessation to attack our bases and the cities. Unfortunately that is the situation."

The President shrugged and said, "Okay."

Wheeler returned to Washington on March 24. He and Abrams confirmed the much improved military situation. They met the President for breakfast in the family dining room on the morning of March 26, prior to LBJ's convocation with the Wise Men. Abrams had talked to the senior statesmen the day before, as did George Carver of the CIA, General William DePuy from DOD, and Philip Habib from State. Some of their briefings were cautionary, all generally upbeat, but the Wise Men's verdict dumbfounded Lyndon Johnson.

McGeorge Bundy announced it—reasons for hope in November 1967 had been dashed. Dean Acheson captured the majority feeling in saying, "We can no longer do the job we set out to do in the time we have left and we must begin to take steps to disengage."

Shaken, Lyndon Johnson had the briefers repeat their presentations for him. He had Harry McPherson work up a new speech announcing a partial bombing halt, stopping the bombing north of the 20th Parallel. On the evening of March 31, Johnson presented it on nationwide television. At the end he announced his withdrawal from the 1968 presidential election campaign, a little coda drafted by political aide Horace Busby.

For a time Washington and Hanoi dueled over a site for negotiations, but in May the sides agreed on Paris and held a first full session on the thirteenth. President Johnson insisted on three conditions: that Hanoi respect the demilitarized zone; that it desist from rocket, mortar, or artillery attacks on cities and towns; and that "prompt and serious" talks follow the cessation. At the eleventh secret meeting, a Hanoi delegate asked whether the bombing would stop if the DRV agreed to Saigon's participation. It was the first serious break, but LBJ was napping when the Harriman-Vance ("HARVAN") reporting cable arrived. Rostow and Rusk briefed the President immediately afterward. The following Monday, while the newspapers were reporting a McGeorge Bundy speech at DePauw University, in which Mac proposed an unconditional bombing halt and gradual troop withdrawal, Johnson met his advisers on the Paris developments. There was support for going ahead.

Two weeks of topsy-turvy diplomacy followed. Hanoi wanted to score propaganda points by claiming the pause was "unconditional" although it was accepting the United States conditions. In Saigon, Nguyen Van Thieu was balking. One subplot in all this maneuvering was the United States presidential election, in which Hubert Humphrey faced Richard Nixon, and during which the Republicans were desperately afraid LBJ might pull peace out of a hat at the eleventh hour and hand the election to Humphrey. The President himself tried his best to maneuver between the contending forces.

Johnson also wanted to be sure a bombing halt was acceptable to the United States military. Unlike the 1965–1966 pause, this time the President met with the full Joint Chiefs before taking any action. As for MACV, though General Abrams (with Bunker) had agreed with the proposition in a cable, LBJ wanted his personal advice, and ordered Abrams home for consultations, all on a top-secret basis. The President had been warned the press had already gotten wind of something, first in Saigon, where Ambassador Bunker had gone to see Thieu three times on a single day.

With help from the military and his NSC staff, LBJ managed to pull off a disappearing act. Instructed to go in mufti, Abrams boarded a C-141 jet at Tan Son Nhut that whisked him direct to Washington. The plane landed at Andrews Air Force Base, just outside the capital, and taxied to the dark side of the field, away from the terminal. Waiting there with a car was Rostow's military aide Robert Ginsburgh. It was about two in the morning of October 29. Ginsburgh and Abrams drove downtown. At the White House gate Ginsburgh, also a general, pulled rank to compel a reluctant guard to admit this visitor who lacked any identification. Ginsburgh took General Abrams in through the diplomatic entrance to the West Wing, where they found everything in darkness, total silence, LBJ having ordered this to maintain the facade that nothing was up at the White House that night. Luckily Ginsburgh knew his way around well enough that he could lead Abrams through the darkness to the stairs. Even then, when the pair reached the second floor they felt it necessary to go outside onto the balcony to enter the Cabinet Room from outside, where the light was better.

No flourish here of Washington summoning its proconsul. Press secretary George Christian in fact had been in terror that someone would ask about Abrams. Miraculously Christian got through the day. A White House car picked him up at a friend's house at 2:00 A.M. and he went to Rostow's office, encountering Walt and Clark Clifford followed by LBJ and others. They too went upstairs.

They met in the Cabinet Room. General Abrams sat to the left of the President, Rusk to his right. Everyone else sat down on the opposite side of the table to see better. President Johnson read a background paper that detailed developments at the Paris negotiations and other feelers of that summer. Then Abrams began to describe the military situation. The MACV commander thought the situation well under control; the main threat was no longer in the northern RVN but from the Cambodian border area far to the south. North Vietnamese violations of the Demilitarized Zone posed no danger. Abrams replied confidently in the affirmative when LBJ asked if the situation was good enough to sustain a total halt in the bombing of North Vietnam.

After two and a half hours the President sent Abrams off to bed, telling him to be back at noon for more talk. Johnson actually followed later and talked with the general for over an hour. Following the second Cabinet Room session, Abrams left for Andrews and Vietnam.

President Johnson made his decision, arranged the halt with the North Vietnamese, and announced it in a speech a few days before the election, all for nought. Vietnam's President Nguyen Van Thieu dug in his heels and fought every step along the way. A major issue at Paris became the shape of the negotiating table, as a surrogate for participation by Saigon and the Vietcong. Richard Milhous Nixon won the 1968 election and the petty disputes effectively consumed the time remaining prior to his inauguration on January 20, 1969.

Evidence emerged in later years suggesting that this process of obstruction owed something to political intervention. The Nixon camp, apparently using as intermediary Anna Chennault, widow of general and China lobby stalwart Claire Chennault, encouraged Thieu to believe South Vietnam would get a better deal with Nixon. It was a virtual repeat of the Nixon camp's activities in the area of arms control. Information allowing the Nixon campaign to plan these approaches to Thieu had included fairly detailed updates on Harriman and Vance's progress in Paris. That information may have come from an American academic on the fringes of the negotiating effort, one Henry Kissinger. In a half-dozen transatlantic telephone calls, all from public telephones, Kissinger reportedly passed the information to Nixon foreign policy adviser Richard V. Allen. The Chennault ploy took off from there.

So ended Lyndon Johnson's administration, in disappointment for many participants. Walt Rostow had secured neither victory nor a negotiated settlement in Vietnam, but the national security adviser effectively detached himself from the situation. On the afternoon of January 20, after the Nixon inaugural, Walt worked away at the office, clearing out his desk. That evening Elspeth asked, "You're free of it already, aren't you?"

PART VI

▲

KING RICHARD AND PRINCE HENRY

Inauguration Day brought a new team to Washington, a group carefully selected by a new President, Richard Milhous Nixon. For the NSC a fresh administration meant both a different relationship between President and principals, and a reworking of the NSC machinery. The new arrangements came as a surprise to some, among them Brom Smith. Conservative at heart, Brom applauded Nixon's election and looked forward to serving on the new President's NSC staff. Instead, Smith was one of the first staffers let go.

Nixon knew exactly what he wanted to do with the NSC and its staff. He told an associate it was to be the Eisenhower staff "without the concurrences." Indeed, a paper written by Townsend Hoopes in the Eisenhower transition of 1952–1953 perfectly prefigured the actual Nixon NSC: a strong national security adviser with an expert staff to furnish, in effect, a "little State Department." A key tip-off to Nixon's intentions was insistence on having Andy Goodpaster during the transition at the Hotel Pierre in New York. That was no simple matter, for Goodpaster was now an active-duty general in Saigon, in fact deputy commander of MACV under Creighton Abrams. Nixon nevertheless insisted, and LBJ got the Army to detach Goodpaster for temporary duty with the president-elect.

Advice flowed from Ike's former watchers—Bobby Cutler, Dillon Anderson, and Gordon Gray—as well. Anderson, for example, complained that use of the NSC for "quiet and deliberate" policy formulation had been abandoned, that "too often the NSC is reported as a group hastily assembled to deal with a crisis somewhere, with the lateness of the hour of the meeting roughly indicative of the seriousness of the crisis." Gray told Bobby Cutler that he advocated continuation of PFIAB and of the Special Group overseeing intelligence activities, with the President's keeper of the keys to serve as chairman, but that he had reservations regarding any reconstitution of the Operations Coordinating Board.

Oddly, letters of advice from Anderson and Gray were not made available to Goodpaster, to Nixon's anointed security adviser, Henry Kissinger, or to the man who drafted the actual plans for the NSC reorganization, Morton Halperin.

Mort Halperin played a special role in all of this. Coming off his quiet, but effective, bureaucratic maneuvers from the Pentagon that had forced Washington into a negotiating position for SALT, Halperin was at the apogee of his career in government. He was a respected figure in the circles of international security theorists among whom Kissinger moved. The first part of his task was to prepare a reorganization memorandum for his old friend Kissinger to give the President-elect. The result was an eighteen-page compilation of organization charts, summaries, and recommendations that, the cover memo asserted, was the product of extensive conversations between Kissinger and Andrew Goodpaster.

The paper praised the flexibility and speed of the Johnson NSC system but criticized its lack of staff work and the thinness of the NSAMs, contrasting them with Eisenhower-era NSC policy papers. Neither Kissinger nor Goodpaster, nor Halperin for that matter, had ever attended a Tuesday Lunch, or had the standing to observe that system in operation at close range, so their specific criticisms of that mechanism were far off base. Rather than being inadequately briefed, as claimed in the Hotel Pierre paper, Tuesday Lunch participants themselves proposed and disposed of the agenda items, specifically raising those issues with which they were conversant. Since, to a significant degree they were the *same* issues, like the latest secret peace initiative or Rolling Thunder proposals, that kept coming up at Tuesday Lunches, participants could hardly have avoided familiarity with nuances.

More important than the rationalizations at the Pierre was the intention to combine the best features of the Johnson and Eisenhower NSC systems. Kissinger proposed a hierarchy of units under the council, beginning with an NSC Review Group, somewhat akin to the old Planning Board. This would either buck the issue up to the full council, or down to an NSC Ad Hoc Under Secretary's Committee. This combination would replace LBJ's Senior Interdepartmental Group (SIG), which would be abolished. The subordinate interdepartmental groups, retitled Inter-Agency Regional Groups, which had completed the SIG network, would remain. There would also be ad hoc working groups and outside consultants.

Policy papers would be brought closer to the Eisenhower standard, in which the papers contained justification and discussion of rationales. Policy papers would be called National Security Decision Memoranda (NSDMs). Behind them would be a further collection of interagency studies, termed National Security Study Memoranda (NSSMs), which would collect the bureaucracy's views and advance the policy prescriptions of each player. Though NSSMs would be the product of working groups drawn from all over Washington, the NSC staff alone would be responsible for an annual review of the international situation.

Kissinger proposed an NSC staff proper comprising three categories of professionals. Assistants for programs would be the expediters, getting issues to the NSC in an orderly fashion, developing a strategy to get the work done, and focusing on middle-range goals such as five-year programs. An Operations Staff with about five senior members plus a small number of assistants would divide along regional or functional lines to monitor the bureaucracy in the style of Rostow's staff. Halperin's baby, the Planning Staff, with perhaps three senior and five junior members, would synthesize agency contributions, prepare NSC agendas, undertake specific studies when NSSMs were judged inadequate, and provide backup expertise to the program assistants. Last came the "military assistant," who was to help the national security adviser with papers on military issues, provide military advice, and assist in assembling intelligence materials.

Dr. Kissinger forwarded Halperin's paper to Richard Nixon together with suggestions for the first nine NSSMs. The President-elect quickly approved both the reorganization and the policy reviews. The change upon which Nixon insisted was to exclude the CIA director from the NSC Review Group. Kissinger's discussion of the structure with the President occurred on December 27. Dr. Kissinger recalls himself as an "agnostic" on the question of retaining the SIG, though the Halperin paper suggested that committee was no longer necessary, but Nixon flatly refused to continue the unit. The President-elect then initialed the paper at several points to show his approval. Later that day both men flew to Miami in preparation for an initial session of the designated NSC principals at Nixon's Key Biscayne vacation home. At the meeting, which was supposed to examine Kissinger's proposed NSC machinery, Nixon told the group he had already approved the plan. It was a harbinger of the methods of this new administration.

▲▲▲

▲ Staffwork: preparations for Nixon's first overseas trip to Europe, February 21, 1969. (Nixon Library Project)

▲ Henry makes a joke at a session of the White House staff. John D. Ehrlichman sits to Kissinger's left, Bob Haldeman across the table. With his back to the camera sits Chuck Colson. August 18, 1969. (Nixon Library Project)

▲ Members enter the Cabinet Room before an early session of the NSC on SALT, March 15, 1969. Spurgeon Keeny, soon to be at ACDA, stands next to Al Haig. (Nixon Library Project)

▲ The National Security Council considers SALT on May 13, 1971. Unknown to the principals, Kissinger has been using his back-channel to negotiate in parallel with the Russians. Only one week later Washington and Moscow would announce a breakthrough. (Nixon Library Project)

▲ The President's men watch Nixon's speech announcing the mining of Haiphong Harbor, May 8, 1972. John Connally sits next to Spiro T. Agnew. Among the backbenchers, a younger Caspar Weinberger (third from left) is alongside Alexander Haig. (Nixon Library Project)

▲ Henry Kissinger gestures to Al Haig shortly after Nixon reveals his intention to resign, August 8, 1974. (Nixon Library Project)

▲ Reflecting on the impending fall of South Vietnam: the Cabinet Room, April 24, 1975. Henry Kissinger in the foreground, Air Force General George S. Brown represents the Joint Chiefs, Bill Colby the CIA. President Ford is pensive while Jim Schlesinger, secretary of defense, strikes a typical pose with his pipe. Note that Ford has retained the portrait of Dwight Eisenhower on the wall that Nixon had substituted for that of Thomas Jefferson, which had hung there in LBJ's time. (Ford Library)

▲ Bad to worse in Vietnam: Ford gathers the National Security Council in the Roosevelt Room, April 28, 1975. *Left to right:* William Colby, Robert S. Ingersoll, deputy secretary of state, Kissinger, Ford, Schlesinger, deputy secretary of defense William Clements, Vice President Nelson Rockefeller, and JCS chairman General George Brown (back to camera). (Ford Library)

▲ The evacuation of Saigon: Deputy national security adviser Brent Scowcroft briefs President Ford on the latest developments, April 29, 1975. (Ford Library)

▲ High tension during the *Mayagüez* incident at the 10:40 P.M. NSC session, May, 13, 1975. Kissinger makes a point as acting JCS chairman General David C. Jones looks on. Donald Rumsfeld leans over to examine aerial photographs of Koh Tang island. In the background are NSC staffer Richard Smyser and Scowcroft. In the foreground, back to the camera, sits President Ford. (Ford Library)

▲ The *Mayagüez* incident opens: General David C. Jones briefs the council in the Cabinet Room on the morning of May 13. Jim Schlesinger's broken reading glasses sit on the table in front of him as he holds his pipe. (Ford Library)

▲ Summoned from a state dinner, President Ford and his keepers share as laugh as the Cambodians release the *Mayagüez* and U.S. bombers hit Cambodia, during the night of May 14, 1975. *Left to right:* military assistant Robert C. McFarlane, Donald Rumsfeld, Henry Kissinger, President Ford, national security adviser Brent Scowcroft (back to camera). (Ford Library)

▲ Earlier in the day on May 14 the NSC meets to hear General Jones describe the status of the *Mayagüez* rescue operation. (Ford Library)

▲ Brent Scowcroft whispers to President Ford during a plenary session at the Helsinki conference, July 31, 1975. (Ford Library)

PRINCE HENRY
THE NAVIGATOR

▲▲▲

T he bustle at the Hotel Pierre created the impression of purposeful action. But a good deal of activity, though it may have had a purpose, consisted in working over the same ground. With the proposals for NSC machinery, for example, other NSC principals disregarded Nixon's approval of the Kissinger plan as if there had been no decision. Melvin Laird, secretary of defense-designate, was first off the mark with a series of objections, to the intelligence community's lack of direct access; to the NSC staff's monopoly of authority to initiate interagency studies; and to the availability of the President to other senior officials who would make end runs around the NSC machinery. Laird need not have feared on the last score—there would be no going to Richard Nixon save through Henry Kissinger. The doctor met Laird for dinner at Washington's Sheraton-Carlton Hotel, placating the secretary with gracious agreement to entertain Pentagon requests for studies, plus a promise to reexamine the matter of intelligence advice to the President. Laird had a point there, one that reached as deep as practical politics, for as soon as the public learned the government was acting without benefit of its intelligence apparatus, opponents would have a field day. Nixon relented, with a rearguard action revolving around allowing Richard Helms to attend NSC only for the purpose of briefing.

The State Department was more trouble, if only because it was their SIG system, crafted by U. Alexis Johnson and Max Taylor, that stood to be skewered. Johnson himself, a senior and able diplomat, was being brought back from Japan, where he had been ambassador, to become undersecretary for political affairs, the second-ranking official under Secretary of State-designate William P. Rogers. Both went to the Pierre on January 6, 1969, to meet for fifteen minutes with Kissinger, "long enough," Johnson recalls, "for me to see that some rough roads lay ahead." Johnson subsequently crafted a long explanation of the necessity for the SIG that he sent by a back channel to Nixon adviser Elliot Richardson. He also explained the issues to Rogers, and got all of two minutes to make his case directly to Kissinger, who remained unmoved. In retrospect, Henry recounts, State preeminence was something that "even five minutes' conversation with Nixon could leave no doubt that the President-elect would never tolerate."

So the SIG was abolished. Replacing it proved more difficult than anticipated, however. Instead of one unit like Ike's Planning Board, there evolved a whole series of committees, most chaired by the assistant for national security. This was not immediately apparent, for the new structure developed with events. In February 1969, Kissinger was still talking and corresponding with Gordon Gray about whether the (one) interagency committee's members should carry presidential appointments (Gray thought they should). By that summer there were no fewer than a half-dozen such groups, and no question that members represented anything but their agencies.

An important milestone in the institutional development of the NSC passed unmarked amid all the maneuvering. Richard Nixon wanted to revise the machinery to assist him in making his foreign policy in the White House, to avoid pressures for consensus. He therefore created a White House-centered system of administration in place of an agency-centered one. More than ever before, the NSC staff thereby gained control over the *process* of making policy while the President, as always, held content firmly in his own hands. Nixon no doubt appreciated the advantages this gave him, in terms of marshaling bureaucrats in service of his policy, but the new method saw the bureaucracy as an adversary to be foiled and outplayed, not an ally in the administration of national security.

A corollary of this development was the further frustration of the corporate National Security Council. Lyndon Johnson had relegated the NSC to a briefing function or ratification device, but he had developed a different forum in which to work with the NSC principals. Nixon retained the concept of the NSC as a ratifying board but made no analogue for the Tuesday Lunch. In effect, NSC principals were being put on notice that their advice was for the record only, incidentally to be taken into account in making decisions, but by no means a central element in the process. What emerged was the NSC as theater, an exquisitely choreographed dance between President and principals, the object of which was to elicit certain statements from participants or to avoid others. Kissinger would open each council session with an outline of the issues and Helms would give his intelligence briefing. The principals then had their say. Typically Nixon himself took the floor to end NSC meetings with summaries (that some found brilliant) of the problems and factors that would figure in his decision. A few days later the President's National Security Decision Memorandum would come down giving the result.

With paper there were no face-to-face confrontations, no need to respond directly to serious objections. Moreover, Nixon was an assiduous reader and could be counted on to read even long, convoluted papers. Whatever else might be the case, the NSC staff was very solicitous about getting agency contributions, and very punctilious about full meanings of agency recommendations. But no one in the bureaucracy, NSC principals included, got to see the cover memoranda Kissinger slapped on top of agency papers, or hear the advice he gave Nixon when the two sat down in private.

One early view of the Nixon NSSM-NSDM system, study memoranda followed by decision memoranda, is that it was largely a copybook exercise, that Kissinger assigned all this work to keep the bureaucrats occupied while he busily seized the reins of power. The stream of NSSM demands, the argument runs, created a "bureaucratic logjam" too imposing for officials to disregard, producing documents not sufficiently useful to function as actual decision documents. This view is inaccurate. Former officials, even those with little love for Kissinger, still maintain the NSSMs were useful in distilling the views of the agencies. Their real function was to assist Richard Nixon in choreographing his minuets. In fact, paper became the bureaucracy's final refuge and Richard Nixon liked it enough to assign almost 170 NSSMs during his first term in office.

Nixon's methods put a high premium on a now well-established NSC staff function, monitoring the bureaucracy. That required a top-notch professional staff, and a good deal of time during Kissinger's days at the Hotel Pierre involved a stream of individuals trying to get themselves a piece of the action. One close associate found the atmosphere chaotic because everyone in the world seemed to regard themselves as a close friend of Henry's and all insisted upon immediate access to him. The jockeying for position which began at the Pierre endured through all the White House years and beyond. Not least among the jockeys was Henry Kissinger himself.

Kissinger's grasp for glory began when Nixon offered him the post of national security adviser. Of course Henry had sought advice already. Mac Bundy thought Henry might expect a job like director of policy planning at State. Discovering the real offer, to be assistant for national security Henry was happy to serve, but on *his* conditions. He wanted to set himself apart from his predecessors. Rostow and Mac had been "special assistants" to the President, but there were plenty of top-echelon officials in Washington who had their own special assistants; a special assistant could be anybody. Kissinger insisted on changing the job title to "deputy to the President for national security."

With Nixon's hearty approval, Kissinger's early actions as gatekeeper conformed closely to what he himself advocated before ever connecting with the thirty-seventh President of the United States. In testimony he had published jointly with strategic thinker Bernard Brodie in 1968, Kissinger told interlocutors that a new President, in the areas in which he wanted to effect changes, had to do so within the first four months, and had to "give enough of a shake to the bureaucracy to indicate that he wants a new direction," and be "brutal enough to demonstrate that he means it." The stream of NSDMs and NSSM study directives had precisely that impact, especially combined with Nixon's early activism on the NSC of which there were five sessions within the first month, one of them (on the controversial Middle East problem) on a Saturday.

A perfect illustration of giving the bureaucracy a shake was the story of the first study memorandum, NSSM-1, which dealt with Vietnam. Kissinger had an opinion there, which he set out at some length in the winter of 1968, and which appeared in *Foreign Affairs* in its first issue for 1969. Washington's combination of pragmatism plus bureaucracy, Kissinger argued, resulted in a diplomatic style of rigidity before negotiations followed by "excessive reliance on tactical considerations" once they began. That was the lesson Henry drew from his work in Paris for Johnson, opening contacts with Hanoi. On the other hand, Kissinger thought the North Vietnamese style of communication indirect and devious by American standards, operating in quasi-military phases of reconnaissance and withdrawal. Vietnam, he declared, was an example of a massive breakdown of communications both within the United States government and between Washington and Hanoi. With Vietnam there was the additional problem of the American client state, the RVN, for which "the status of the [Vietcong] cannot be a procedural matter." For Saigon, in fact, "it has been very nearly the central issue of the war."

Kissinger's rendition of the dilemmas of Vietnam diplomacy was accurate. He proceeded to sketch the outlines of a solution and a method for reaching them. The *Foreign Affairs* article lent weight to certain vague promises candidate Richard Nixon had made about a secret plan to end the Vietnam War. Henry's concept was that the United States and Hanoi should negotiate a mutual withdrawal, while Saigon and the Vietcong concentrated on reaching political settlement. There should be an international force that could supervise the withdrawal and whose presence would ensure good faith. While a coalition government was undesirable, Kissinger wrote, he did not rule out a "mixed commission" that could "develop and supervise a political process to reintegrate the country."

If Hanoi did not bargain, if it held out for victory, Kissinger insisted, the fighting must continue; "any other posture would destroy the chances of a settlement and encourage Hanoi to wait us out." In the war, the United States should concentrate on the protection of population, strengthen the South Vietnamese armed forces; the RVN should broaden its political base, and American commanders could permit a gradual withdrawal of forces.

Some commentators fastened on the mention of withdrawals of American troops, or on the hint that the Vietcong could have a role (the "mixed commission") in a postagreement political structure, to declare Nixon's "plan" revealed. Critics pointed to formulas that would clearly be unacceptable to Hanoi to denounce the "secret plan" as a sham and, in fact, a calculated posture to continue the Vietnam War.

The transition team at the Pierre intended a Vietnam review from the beginning. The Halperin paper proposed to list alternative strategies with mutually supporting military and diplomatic actions, and had the nascent NSC staff prepare the study directive before the inauguration. Things were so rushed really, at the Pierre, they needed all the help they could get, and Kissinger contracted with Santa Monica's RAND Corporation for help on his NSC transition.

At RAND there were a variety of opinions about the war, some of them surprisingly negative. Five RAND colleagues in October 1968 had joined in expounding the policy option of "extrication" for the United States. One of them, Daniel Ellsberg, drafted the list of questions for the proposed NSC study, a set of queries deliberately intended to elicit points of difference among the bureaucracy, twenty-eight questions that would have to be answered to the satisfaction of the President. Ellsberg played the role of *enfant terrible* among the small community of American civilian strategic thinkers. Ellsberg was a former Marine officer, a street kid from Detroit and Ph.D. economist from Harvard, like Mac Bundy a member of Harvard's exclusive elite Society of Fellows. Kissinger had known Ellsberg since the late 1950s, when Ellsberg wrote a penetrating analysis of the political value of irrationality demonstrated by Hitler's foreign policy in the last years before World War II. Kissinger admired the work and invited Ellsberg to lecture to his classes. He went to RAND in 1959, where he worked on nuclear force issues—above all the vulnerability of the United States to strategic surprise.

On Vietnam, Ellsberg became an early convert to the importance of the pacification issues, working for the redoubtable John McNaughton from 1964 to 1967. Ellsberg was intimate with Bob Komer, Bill Bundy, Ed Lansdale, and Bernard Fall, and he became a disciple of the well-known John Paul Vann, with whom he shared the experience of staying overnight in Vietnam's small villages, something most people shunned for good security reasons.

In any case, confronted by the unrelenting frustration of the war, the corruption, the seeming inability to make progress, Ellsberg gradually turned against the war. He became one of the stalwart band of defense intellectuals who changed their views even before Tet. After returning to RAND, Ellsberg wrote a paper marshaling his best arguments against the war, using the data he had collected in Vietnam. The Ellsberg paper circulated privately in Washington at just the time Walt Rostow was in high dudgeon with his psychological strategy in the VIG.

There can be little doubt that Kissinger was aware of Dan Ellsberg's views and turned to Dan because of, not despite, them. The thirty-seven-year-old analyst, with two RAND colleagues, flew to New York on Christmas Day, 1968, to discuss the NSSM-1 project with Kissinger at the Pierre. Ellsberg did a fine job with the question list, asking questions that touched on most of the central disputes within the bureaucracy. The NSSM-1 questions included items on the possibilities for negotiations, effectiveness of ARVN, impact of pacification, disputes over the NVA order of battle, the extent of the Vietcong infrastructure, their use of Cambodia for supply purposes, and so on. When the agencies delivered their responses to the NSSM-1 questions, mostly in early February 1969, Ellsberg spent weeks at the NSC summarizing and consolidating them into a study book of over five hundred pages, still half the length of the agency contributions.

"We learned how ignorant we were," Kissinger recalled of the NSSM-1 study.

Ellsberg also did an options paper for Henry, one that framed the discussion for Nixon's first NSC meeting. The one substantive change between the two drafts of the RAND paper was deletion, at Kissinger's request, of the extrication strategy, the option of withdrawal. Ellsberg had included it while not agreeing with it, himself favoring exploration of the outcomes in the Paris negotiations. Kissinger apparently implied to the draftsmen that a senior military adviser to Nixon (quite possibly a reference to Earle Wheeler) refused even to comment on this alternative. In effect, all the withdrawal options Nixon considered became contingent on moves by Hanoi or Saigon, events Washington could by no means count on.

Kissinger possessed a fine knowledge of the essential intractability of the situation. In his *Foreign Affairs* article, the national security adviser noted the divergent aims of Washington and Saigon. American interests, as Henry saw it, were to bring about a staged withdrawal of external forces, both United States and North Vietnamese. The political settlement could and should be left to Saigon. But since, as Kissinger recognized, Saigon would be reluctant to accede to a settlement, there would be built-in problems. The other horn of the dilemma Kissinger perceived was a direct reversal of the formula Walt Rostow had advanced in 1964: As Henry now saw it, "the guerrilla wins if he does not lose; the conventional army loses if it does not win."

Under the circumstances it was inevitable that Washington, to the degree it desired to settle Vietnam, would have to pressure Saigon into a settlement. No outcome acceptable to Hanoi could emerge without reducing the authority of Nguyen Van Thieu. In this respect the Pentagon Papers had reached the useful but disturbing conclusion that U.S. leverage on its minor ally was quite limited at best, the implication being that pressuring Saigon into a settlement could be extremely difficult. Kissinger took the position in *Foreign Affairs* that "there is a point beyond which Saigon cannot be given a veto."

On February 13, with the issuing of NSSM-21, the President created an ad hoc working group under the NSC that became known as the Vietnam Special Studies Group. Its first task, assigned that same day by the NSSM-22 study directive, was to plan for the contingency of a new round of VC attacks on the urban centers as at Tet. Nixon further ordered a plan "to cover proposed U.S. action in the event of the assassination of the President of the Republic of South Vietnam." The NSSM directive specified "this plan should discuss the various South Vietnamese leaders who might come to power, and should include recommendations as to which leader or group the U.S. should be prepared to support." The exercise was valuable as an exploration of what Washington knew of Saigon politics, but may have had more sinister purposes as well. The NSSM-22 study directive has never been disclosed, and the bureaucracy's responses to it remain classified to this day.

Over the following weeks a succession of NSSMs and NSDMs established a structure of policy for the Vietnam War. While the NSSMs proved instructive, there *was* a certain element of diversion associated with them. The study assignments seemed to come precisely at monthly intervals. On March 9, for example, Kissinger promulgated the study directive for NSSM-29 on negotiating strategy and mutual withdrawals; on April 10, it was NSSMs-36 and -37 on Vietnamizing the war and phased withdrawals. There could be no doubt, however, that the NSSMs squarely framed the basic decision Nixon made on Vietnam and its timing. Tetlike fighting had begun in late February. By March 14, when the NSC Review Group received the staff's forty-four-page distillation of the agency responses to NSSM-1, Nixon was back from his first overseas trip as President (to Europe) and ready to take a cut on Vietnam. The NSC had already had, on January 25, a lengthy discussion of the issues based on the RAND options paper Kissinger circulated.

Nixon saw the upsurge in Vietnam fighting as Hanoi's attempt to repeat the political success of Tet. The President determined to be tough in the face of pressure. From the Joint Chiefs and MACV flowed a stream of suggestions that the United States should use its heavy B-52 bombers to wreak havoc with VC/NVA supply lines and staging bases in Cambodia. It was slightly different from bombing North Vietnam, which Melvin Laird opposed from the beginning, but Nixon deferred any decision before his European trip. Afterward, once the first diplomatic feelers sent out by the Nixon administration through Paris and Moscow failed, and once Laird became a strong supporter of the Cambodian bombing, the President ordered that action. Nixon's order came after a two-and-a-half-hour session with Kissinger and the NSC principals on March 16. The bombing began the next day.

The bombing of the North Vietnamese sanctuaries in Cambodia was carried out, in the beginning, with total secrecy. Operation Breakfast was the code name for the initial missions, followed by other meal names, all under the umbrella tag of Menu. Everything was calculated to avoid disclosure, though Kissinger writes that the original intent had been to admit the bombing when the Cambodians or North Vietnamese protested them. Kissinger claims he expected such protests and that the CIA predicted them.

This account fails to explain Nixon's great ire on May 9, 1969, when a story about the Cambodian B-52 bombing appeared on the front page of *The New York Times,* revealed by reporter William Beecher. Just days before, Beecher had received one of the best leaks, about Nixon's decisions during the April EC-121 crisis, in which a United States electronic reconnaissance plane had been shot down near Korea, a virtual replay of the 1968 *Pueblo* incident. Nixon was vulnerable on the EC-121 because he had been raving drunk in the middle of the crisis, according to a careful reconstruction by Kissinger biographer Seymour Hersh.

But beyond the question of Nixon's behavior was his still top-secret decision, of early April, to "Vietnamize" the war. This course, prefigured on April Fool's Day in NSDM-9, represented adoption of Kissinger's *Foreign Affairs* preferred strategy—that the United States should reduce casualties and thus the visibility of the war. That would gain time, move in a direction congruent with LBJ's Vietnam policy, and satisfy Melvin Laird, for whom Vietnamization was the prerequisite for the political support necessary to carry out any coherent national security policy. The problem with American withdrawals is that Nixon wished the initiative to come by request from the South Vietnamese. Nguyen Van Thieu could be expected to take a dim view of the enterprise, and Nixon wanted a personal meeting, a summit, to sanction the strategy. Premature revelation could spoil the delicate maneuvers aimed at eliciting certain words from Saigon.

For whatever reason, Nixon considered the Beecher Cambodia leak the last straw. That day Henry Kissinger spoke four times with FBI director J. Edgar Hoover. Within hours wiretaps were placed on the telephones of National Security Council staffer Morton Halperin. As it happened, Halperin knew nothing of Nixon's drunkenness during the EC-121 incident, and precious little about the Menu bombing, but he was seen as a liberal on the NSC staff, a wolf among the fold, and his presence was protested by, among others, General Earle Wheeler and Senator Barry Goldwater. Nixon eventually got his Vietnamization request from Thieu, at a summit held on Midway Island in June 1969, but the leaks did not stop, and one of the President's own NSC staff was robbed of effectiveness into the bargain.

The forging of Nixon's early Vietnam policy established a sort of norm for the subsequent process. Nixon made quick decisions, often against the recommendations of his advisers, then had to be exposed to new views or data, and given opportunity to revise his initial choices, all the while scared that leaks would reveal what he was about. Invariably actions occurred through the most Byzantine maneuvers. Henry Kissinger, the assistant to the President, remained in the forefront all the way, assuring each of the players of his total confidence. It is worth noting that this Kissinger method relied almost entirely on the tactical considerations academic Kissinger had decried.

What is extraordinary about Kissinger is the extent to which he seemed able to convince contemporary observers that there had been some transformation when he changed from academic to presidential assistant, from "Professor" Kissinger to "Henry." The media constantly employed this professorial image when reporting on Kissinger, although both his immediate predecessors had been academics as well (and from Cambridge too!), and despite the existence of an entire community of defense intellectuals and civilian strategists, men and women who floated seamlessly between government and academia, in and out of one administration after another, of whom Henry was only one. The slightly breathless journalistic pieces reporting Kissinger's appearance on a date with some movie star made great copy but created little understanding.

Henry Alfred Kissinger was a combination of intellect, calculation, ambition, and sensitivity that would succeed brilliantly in the Nixon White House. Henry could be charming or imperious, crafty or careless, solicitous or demanding. Henry Kissinger raised the art of nuance, the delicate shade of meaning, to a new level in Washington. People repeatedly went wrong on Kissinger when they went by literal meanings of words. One example was the Vietnamese ambassador, Bui Diem. He assumed that when Kissinger spoke of "flexibility" for the Vietnamese negotiations, the national security adviser meant that the differences that would become apparent between Saigon and Washington would be merely rhetorical. Mort Halperin, for another, went wrong when he and Kissinger talked of the FBI's investigation of the Cambodia leak. Kissinger proposed ending the suspicion that fell on Halperin by taking Mort out of the paper flow on sensitive subjects. Halperin failed to realize that *all* classified subjects would become "sensitive" ones, and thus his own usefulness would be destroyed.

Early observers, pundits, and commentators seeking to pigeonhole Kissinger searched his academic writings for clues, and saw perhaps too much of the geopolitician or global thinker, too much Metternich in Kissinger. Henry was no academic steeped in the tradition of classical diplomacy; he was a civilian strategist who saw his role as helping form opinions on current policy. Save for his dissertation, published as *A World Restored: Metternich, Castlereagh, and the Problems of Peace 1812–1822*, which appeared in 1957, a piece on Metternich Kissinger published in 1954 in the *American Political Science Review*, and one in *World Politics* on the Congress of Vienna (1956), all of Kissinger's more than thirty articles published before 1969 focused on United States or Western strategy and furnished policy-oriented commentary. In what must have qualified as a witty sally for Kissinger, he once invoked Otto von Bismarck as subject for an essay about continuities in German strategy. As for the historical subject of his dissertation, Kissinger told interviewer Oriana Fallaci, "My only connection with Metternich is a book I wrote."

Dr. Kissinger always sought to speak to men of affairs, to be plugged into the small community of elite opinion makers who, until the Vietnam tragedy, created the national consensus behind American foreign policy. With a gift for facile exposition of convoluted national security policies, Kissinger struck a chord with this community.

For the most part Henry was able to assume and abandon theoretical positions with impunity. His writings are littered with positions expressed with total conviction that are entirely abandoned in later treatments of the same or similar subjects. In *Nuclear Weapons and Foreign Policy,* for example, written in the age of Eisenhower's "New Look" defense policy, Kissinger argued for limited nuclear warfare in Europe. Three years later, in his *The Necessity for Choice,* tactical nuclear weapons had been relegated to the role of deterring escalation of a conventional battle to the nuclear level. In 1960, in parallel with Jack Kennedy's political campaign, Kissinger argued for a buildup of conventional forces. By 1965, when Kissinger published *The Troubled Partnership,* intended as a specific study of the NATO alliance, Henry had evolved a new prescription: Tactical nuclear weapons were to force a halt to the initial enemy offensive, and to inflict enough damage on the adversary to force him into negotiations.

Henry Kissinger was born in Fürth, Germany, a small town near Nürnberg, the son of a middle-class Jewish schoolteacher. Kissinger, named Heinz Alfred, and his brother Walther Bernhardt, began a conventional upbringing that was interrupted by Nazism in Germany. Heinz came to America at fifteen, in 1938, but parents Louis and Paula subsequently explained their emigration by a desire to get the best education for their sons. Henry *had* been denied entry to a gymnasium, forced to attend an all-Jewish school, but Louis had lost his job as instructor in a girls' secondary school.

Louis and Paula settled in New York, in Manhattan, on Washington Heights, a very pleasant, quiet neighborhood, dominated by ethnic Central Europeans. The elder Kissinger found work as bookkeeper and clerk, his wife as a maid. Heinz attended George Washington High School, from which he graduated a straight A student in 1941. Kissinger changed his name to Henry and became a naturalized American citizen. He wanted to be an accountant. He took evening courses at City College of New York, working in the daytime at a factory that made shaving brushes.

Then came Pearl Harbor. The United States entered World War II. In February 1943, Kissinger was drafted, but placed so high on Army proficiency tests that he qualified for a special college program. This education program petered out after a few months and participants were reassigned. Kissinger was sent to the 84th Infantry Division, slated for dispatch to the European Theater. Private Kissinger soon found himself at an Army training camp in Louisiana. There Kissinger went one night to attend a political talk on the war by Fritz Kraemer, an established academic and informal adviser to the division commander. Kissinger thought the talk great, and sent Kraemer a note with some ideas and an offer to help. Thus began a relationship of some importance to both men. Kissinger found in Kraemer a mentor who could advance his own prospects. Kraemer did just that, arranging a job for Kissinger as German translator for the division commander.

The 84th went to Europe and fought its way into Germany. It marched into Krefeld on a weekend day, March 3, 1945. German troops and the Nazi administration had entirely abandoned the place, a large industrial town in the Ruhr. Kissinger was put in charge of the place and within three days had set up a functioning municipal administration. Along the way Sergeant Kissinger took the time to return a birthday cake to an eight-year-old German boy who lost it when his home was taken over by the 84th Division as its headquarters. The boy's misery ended once his nanny picked up the cake; the story got around, assertion of American occupation authority thereby eased.

Such careful personalized touches, the deliberate creation of an atmosphere of intimacy, became a hallmark of Kissinger's technique in the years ahead. Little wonder Fritz Kraemer told Kissinger he had a good political mind. Kraemer worked on young Kissinger, encouraging him to set his sights higher. In the meantime Henry stayed in Germany through March 1946, briefly serving as administrator of Bergstrasse district, then with the 970th Counter-Intelligence Corps (CIC) Detachment.

After the war Kraemer assisted Henry in getting an instructor job at the European Command Intelligence School, teaching new CIC officers how to track down Nazis trying to hide in the chaos of postsurrender Germany. Kraemer's recommendation also helped Kissinger get into Harvard. There followed academic awards and honors, including a Rockefeller award, election to Phi Beta Kappa, and so on. Mentor William Y. Elliott steered Kissinger to a summa cum laude degree with his undergraduate honors thesis. Kissinger finished college in only three years, then went on to earn a master's degree in 1952 and a doctorate two years later. Kissinger's Congress of Vienna dissertation was an award-winning work.

One tie that served Kissinger well was Harvard's Foreign Student Project, a link begun when Henry became its executive director in 1951. From 1952 this program was called the International Seminar. It brings together promising leaders from many different countries—about forty are selected each year to attend. Here Kissinger got unparalleled opportunity to forge links that would serve him in the White House years.

Another important link was that with the Rockefellers. Nelson Rockefeller in those days was a special assistant to the President for cold war matters; in fact he held C. D. Jackson's old psychological strategy job. He was impressed by a speech Kissinger gave, and got Dean Rusk to hire Henry as study director for the Rockefeller Brothers Fund, the beginning of a relationship that lasted more than two decades.

Kissinger began his collaboration with the Nixon campaign organization in September 1968. Richard V. Allen was Nixon's foreign policy coordinator and considered Henry a prize catch, a card-carrying Republican who had written an important book on nuclear strategy. Too conservative himself to be acceptable to moderates and liberals, Allen thought Kissinger qualified and available. "I *was* naive," Allen recounted to Sy Hersh later, "I had my zipper wide open. But I thought, Damn it, we changed the course of history at Miami Beach." Why not?

By 1969, Kissinger had evolved into a significant figure, with connections in several nations. He may have been afflicted with anxieties and insecurities, those of the self-made man, but he appeared always open and charming. As would become apparent, Kissinger's character could be every bit as complex as Richard Nixon's. One of the first to find out was Dick Allen, the man who had thought Kissinger so well qualified that he became "a handmaiden of Henry Kissinger's drive for power."

With Henry as his national security adviser, Nixon also brought Dick Allen onto the NSC staff, with his more sharply conservative view. In the planning for management of the new administration, someone asked Kissinger how he was going to handle Allen. Henry shot back, "Just the way Mac Bundy handled me."

THE CRUCIBLE

▲▲▲

One of Kissinger's big problems turned out to be the hierarchy of the NSC staff. As the weeks passed and Henry got assigned more committee chairmanships, and as he worked late into the nights trying to master the bureaucracy, the need for a deputy with full authority became more and more glaring. Kissinger had to delegate, there was just too much work. That became even more true once Nixon began employing him as personal emissary in very delicate negotiations with Hanoi. Unless the NSC deputy had full powers, the work would just pile up in Dr. Kissinger's absences.

There was precedent both ways for having a deputy national security adviser. Bundy and Rostow had both had deputies, though Walt had allowed the post to remain vacant after Francis Bator returned to Harvard in 1967. Henry's problem was that too many men had claims on the job, and his boss wasn't going to be much help in the selection. Richard Nixon expressly *wanted* to deal through his assistant for national security, so NSC staff got even less access to the President than under Rostow. Early on, within the first two weeks, Nixon had the NSC staff as a group meet with him, much as LBJ had once done for Rostow. The President was clearly uncomfortable at this session, which was run as a reception rather than a meeting. Nixon stood up, made a little speech, shook hands all around, the photographers shot a few pictures. That was the last time most of the NSC staff saw him, unless they were senior people and were later summoned to NSC meetings. Nixon was not going to busy himself with NSC personnel matters, unless it was to put in a good word for his man Richard Allen.

Kissinger told others, who thought they had standing for the appointment, that he was not going to have an NSC deputy, because otherwise the pressure would have been overwhelming to choose Allen.

But a special fate awaited Richard Allen. After appropriate noises about the value of his senior job, about how everyone senior was really a deputy, Allen got an assignment paralleling one of the NSSMs. Kissinger delegated him to produce a global survey of military bases, following up on an interagency report done for LBJ. For Allen the assignment was the "equivalent of being sent on vacation to the Thousand Islands with the requirement of spending a week in each." He left in the autumn.

One man who thought he owned the deputy job was Lawrence S. Eagleburger, a Foreign Service officer sent to the Pierre to help Kissinger with the transition.

Kissinger waylaid Larry Eagleburger upon arrival and Larry soon regarded himself as Henry's senior man, deputy in all but name. In the summer of 1969, soon after the Nixon-Thieu summit at Midway Island, the pace of NSC work brought Eagleburger's demise. Kissinger was meeting in his office with two of Nixon's economic advisers when Larry collapsed unconscious. He was helped to a sofa and an ambulance summoned, which took Eagleburger to Washington Hospital Center. Coming out of his office and learning of Eagleburger's collapse, Kissinger objected that he needed him, then instructed a secretary to get hold of political staffer Pat Buchanan. Henry returned to his office and closed the door.

Later that year Kissinger filled out an efficiency report on Eagleburger by noting he had no organizational ability (wildly inaccurate) though was brilliant and outstanding. Another NSC aide, who had worked under Eagleburger for Dean Acheson, had to conspire with a second staffer to lift the personnel report from Al Haig's desk and rewrite it. Then they smuggled the new report into Henry's paper flow and the national security adviser signed it without noticing. When he recovered from what was diagnosed as a mild heart attack, Eagleburger went to Brussels as chief of the United States mission to NATO.

Morton Halperin was the fellow who seemed to have the inside track. He had, after all, helped Henry conceptualize the Nixon NSC. He was still in place, responsible for the NSSM/NSDM directives, for NSC agendas, and for the flow of advance meeting papers. All agreed more detailed records were necessary, and of course Kissinger wanted to focus on the substance of council sessions. Following one early Vietnam discussion, Haig went to Halperin and asked for help writing an NSDM. Mort, who had been warning Henry of the dangers of meetings without staff presence, took the opportunity to reiterate his point. Haig then broke down, admitting he *had* been at the meeting, had been told not to tell Halperin about it, but needed help to make sense of the NSC talk. After that Halperin, Haig, and an area specialist usually attended council sessions. Exceptions still occurred though; in May, when the NSC considered reports Israel was diverting United States nuclear materials for a weapons program, Kissinger excluded Mort on the grounds he was Jewish.

An outside contender was Helmut Sonnenfeldt, a close friend of Kissinger's. In common with Kissinger, Sonnenfeldt had been born and reared in Germany, was Jewish, and had fled to the United States. Sonnenfeldt had been seen as NSC material as early as 1958, when Eisenhower aide Malcolm Moos suggested him to Gordon Gray for the NSC senior staff, but there were no openings at the time. Kissinger offered him the NSC portfolio for European affairs, but Sonnenfeldt seems not to have inspired much regard from his NSC colleagues. Some thought Hal a social climber and got a kick out of an incident during Nixon's February 1969 European trip, when the

President mistook Hal for one of the host country personnel. Hal could tell Kissinger stories behind Henry's back, but Henry made Sonnenfeldt the butt of many jokes of his own.

It was Nixon's chief of staff, H. R. Haldeman, who ended Sonnenfeldt's hopes to become Henry's deputy. This occurred in mid-October 1970, after an FBI wiretap had picked up a conversation between a diplomat at the Israeli embassy and Richard N. Perle, an aide to Senator Henry Jackson (D-Wash.). Perle discussed classified information given him by an NSC staffer. Sonnenfeldt was known to have close ties to both the Israelis and Perle, and had been investigated for leaks earlier in his career. Kissinger had been shown records of wiretaps on Hal going back to 1960 in an effort to dissuade him from appointing Sonnenfeldt. In any case, Haldeman now asked the FBI to put a new tap on Sonnenfeldt. Little chance remained that Nixon would ever accept Sonnenfeldt as deputy security adviser after that.

The leading contender for deputy, it eventually emerged, was Kissinger's military assistant, Alexander Meigs Haig, Jr. The Army colonel had recently returned from a tour in Vietnam, and came recommended by Kissinger's mentor Fritz Kraemer, who had known him at the Pentagon, as well as others. Initial contact was by Andy Goodpaster on Henry's behalf.

One way to view Haig's rise was to see Haig as a man with the knack for landing plum assignments. Still, choice assignments did not just fall on Al Haig; he fought for everything he got. Born in Philadelphia on December 2, 1924, Alexander was ten years old when his lawyer father died. Altar boy, newspaper delivery boy, post office worker, Alexander helped the family make ends meet. Not sharp enough to get into West Point immediately, Haig used his savings to attend Notre Dame for a year before securing a West Point appointment. His West Point yearbook cited Haig for strong conviction but greater ambition. He graduated in 1947 214th in a class of 310 yet, in 1950, showed up as an assistant at the Tokyo headquarters of proconsul Douglas MacArthur. During the Korean War, Haig served as aide to MacArthur favorite Ned Almond, who got command of the Inchon invasion and hiked up the eastern side of Korea to the Yalu River.

After stints at Columbia University to study business administration, the Naval War College, and Georgetown University, where he received an M.A. in international relations, Haig went to one of McNamara's staff offices early in the Kennedy administration. He dealt with plans and policy for Europe and the Middle East.

Vietnam became the next stop for Lieutenant Colonel Haig, where he commanded the 1st Battalion, 26th Infantry, who called themselves the Blue Spaders. Haig received the Distinguished Service Cross for his role at Ap Gu, along with command of his brigade of the 1st Infantry Division, with which he completed his Vietnam tour, fighting the Vietcong in their tunnel complexes around Cu Chi.

Returning to the United States in June 1967, he received promotion to full colonel and returned to West Point as a cadet regiment commander. There he rose to lead the full cadet brigade and become deputy commander of the military academy. That was where Haig was when Henry Kissinger, organizing his NSC staff, asked former Army General Counsel Joe Califano if he knew some bright officer who could serve as military assistant. Califano, who had worked with Haig under McNamara immediately suggested Al, whom he preferred to a Navy officer he also knew who had similarly been recommended to Henry. Haig moved into this latest plum position and carved out a role.

The NSC staff assignment tested Haig's mettle as a fighter. Having learned the ways of bureaucratic infighting in the top reaches of McNamara's Pentagon, Haig showed himself adept at this brand of warfare also. The NSC organization scheme gave the military assistant only two functions. One was to facilitate the flow of intelligence material to President and council. The other was to give Kissinger military advice. To do this Haig got a cubbyhole office in the West Wing alongside the Situation Room. Haig quickly made himself indispensable to Kissinger, doing anything Henry wanted, working far longer hours than almost anyone else. Haig parlayed the function of facilitating the flow of intelligence material into a more or less formal control over *all* NSC staff paperwork. As Kissinger remarked of Haig, "He disciplined my anarchic tendencies and established coherence and procedure in a National Security Council staff of talented prima donnas."

One by one Haig's competitors fell by the wayside. Haig, incidentally, became Kissinger's representative dealing with the FBI on wiretaps and receiving the transcripts. A number of observers believe this secret role gave Haig an extra advantage in the struggle to become deputy.

However, in the beginning there was no "deputy." Rather, Kissinger maintained his original practice of deputizing two "executive assistants." Haig's final obstacle became Henry's personal assistant, David R. Young, Jr. Another Nelson Rockefeller protégé, and an Oxford scholar who had gone into law and was rising with a Wall Street firm, Young met Kissinger during the 1968 electoral campaign. Henry brought the thirty-year-old, prematurely balding Young in to be a man Friday. Young did all manner of odd jobs for the national security adviser, including buying ties to match his suits and taking care of Kissinger's laundry. Young had the office next door to Haig's.

Haig received promotion to brigadier general only nine months after coming to the NSC staff, but Kissinger was not especially impressed by generals. What seems to have convinced Henry that he had found the right man for deputy was what Haig did to Young. One Sunday, when Haig was working and Young not, the Army man summoned a General Services Administration building crew to the West Wing. Haig had the crew *move the wall* to put half of Young's office inside his own room. Outraged, Young complained to Kissinger, who could hardly stand complaints, and remained unimpressed. When Henry himself moved upstairs, having successfully demanded better quarters and gotten the big corner office, which used to be the press room, Haig took over Kissinger's old basement office. David Young ended up working at a table in the Situation Room, and finally went to counselor John D. Ehrlichman to beg for a job on the domestic side of the White House staff. Haig clearly had the deputy job, and in June 1971, he got the title as well.

Throughout the NSC staff structure, almost no one from the Rostow era survived. The oldest, most experienced staff were among the first let go. Thus Brom Smith's elation at Nixon's election turned to bitter disappointment. Among those who stayed on, Spurgeon Keeny soon discovered how different things were going to be in Henry Kissinger's shop. Keeny had achieved such a position of trust in Rostow's day that he was deputized to stand in for the national security adviser, giving clearances to cables, conducting a full range of business. After the transition to Henry, one could get clearances *only* from Dr. Kissinger, and could go to Henry's office, even late at night, to find a whole line of people, stacked up, all of whom had to see the adviser urgently. The spinning wheels and wasted "rug time" annoyed Keeny, who took the first opportunity to get out, extended by new ACDA chief Gerard C. Smith, who invited Keeny to be his deputy.

A Keeny friend who served briefly on Kissinger's staff was Richard L. Sneider, who had been in East Asian studies at Columbia University during Spurgeon's student years. Kissinger preferred John Holbrooke, a younger Foreign Service officer, but was induced by Halperin and Eagleburger to interview Sneider, and ended up offering him the job. Sneider accepted but was soon disillusioned. He felt discomfited at Kissinger's freewheeling style and Byzantine methods. Very soon he was outraged to learn, from the Indonesian ambassador, of a decision by Nixon to visit that country. Henry had informed the Indonesians without telling his own staff. Colleagues heard that Sneider was not trusted. Then the first big leaks, regarding the EC-121 affair and Cambodia, occurred in his own area of responsibility.

Without his knowledge, Sneider was subjected to FBI wiretaps. So was his assistant Daniel I. Davidson, a younger diplomat who also did some work on the Middle East. Davidson had known Kissinger since 1966 and had recruited himself with a lucky phone call to Henry the day before news of the Kissinger appointment emerged. At the time Davidson was just back from working on the Vietnam negotiations in Paris with Harriman and Vance. Kissinger may have gotten information on the negotiations from Davidson, who, however, denies any campaign political espionage activity.

Another colleague among the group subjected to wiretaps was Richard M. Moose, who, at first, had been Kissinger's staff secretary. Relieved that Nixon did not actually bring back Andy Goodpaster, Kissinger still needed someone to oversee the flow of paper. Moose was a Foreign Service officer with thirteen years' experience. Kissinger intended Moose to be staff secretary without the title, which had not existed since Goodpaster's day, and also without the parallel hierarchy or independent access to the President. Moose left in August 1969.

Another man who enjoyed a brief sojourn on Kissinger's NSC staff was Robert E. Osgood. His best-known book, *Limited War*, published in 1957, had been as influential in its area as Kissinger's study on nuclear policy. There was no question that Osgood was supposed to be a senior man, directing a staff of NSC planners. Instead, he soon discovered that Kissinger's NSC was almost wholly consumed by day-to-day exigencies and paid little attention to long-range planning. Osgood returned to Johns Hopkins once his leave expired. With Osgood perished Nixon's self-conscious effort to emulate the Eisenhower NSC.

Osgood's departure was also significant within the media context of Kissinger's image as the global thinker with a geopolitical concept. Such ideas were Osgood's job and Henry wasn't interested. Bob Osgood simply came to the wrong place. Kissinger's major contributions were dual-track policy implementation and, in Soviet-American relations, the notion of "linkage," an idea that progress in some aspects of relations could be held hostage to that in others. Those contributions were merely tactical even though Hal Sonnenfeldt, who repeatedly encouraged Henry on linkage, made efforts among political scientists to raise linkage to the level of a strategy.

To the degree that some underlying vision infused policy, in fact that vision was Nixon's. The prospective President had been writing and speaking of an opening to China since 1967, an intention that qualified as a strategy. The so-called Nixon Doctrine, which envisaged developing regional alliances with locally strong powers, the theoretical underpinning for Vietnamization, was also a strategic concept. Nixon's campaign promise of a "secret plan" to end the Vietnam War actually did not exist as an intention to seek a political settlement, but was really a strategy to *win*, by convincing Hanoi he would do anything necessary. Nixon put it quite baldly to Haldeman, during a walk on the beach after a hard day of speechwriting: "I call it the Madman Theory, Bob. I want the North Vietnamese to believe I've reached the point where I might do *anything* to stop the war."

Despite departures, Kissinger not only repopulated but expanded the staff; a February 1969 list of 28 professionals represented an establishment as large as Eisenhower's *entire* NSC staff in 1960, administrative personnel included. By September the NSC staff establishment included 114 persons, more than twice the size of the Kennedy-Johnson staff. Those previous administrations had been able to accomplish the routing of memoranda around the NSC staff with a simple rubber stamp listing names, plus the use of tick marks. Kissinger was obliged to use printed forms listing his many staffers. It is not surprising that Nixon's first budget more than doubled, to $1.8 million, the appropriation requested for direct funding of the NSC staff.

Though Kissinger's staff became large enough to sustain departures, the attrition was significant. By September almost 40 percent of the original staff professionals were gone. Working conditions contributed. Henry wanted everything urgently, often required rewrites, was prone to hand out blame when he perceived a setback, and monopolized contact with the President. Those who worked on Soviet-American relations, where Nixon had a personal interest, were lucky. They got to see the top boss fairly frequently. Most others did not. For a time there was a sense of intimacy, as staffers were regaled with stories of the antics of senior officials, but before long staff realized the same kinds of stories were being told about *them.*

Kissinger set the tone at his first meeting with the new NSC staff, held in the Old Executive Office Building soon after the inauguration. Henry entered with Eagleburger, Haig, and Moose, the only ones at that time housed in the West Wing offices. Everyone else inhabited the OEOB third floor.

"I've been in office now for hours and I haven't had a thought yet," Henry quipped. "I took this job to think, and all I've been doing is reading cables, putting out fires, and trying to keep the Department of State from selling us down the river."

Kissinger got laughter, but the mood changed when he told the group the NSC staff would no longer enjoy White House Mess privileges, as had the Rostow staff. According to Kissinger biographer Seymour Hersh, Henry attributed the move to Chief of Staff H. R. Haldeman although it had been his own idea, part of an attempt to isolate the NSC staff from the White House. Sonnenfeldt objected, and Kissinger promised to see what could be done, but nothing was.

Henry's other instruction, that no one was to talk to the press unless on his instruction, that *he* would be the only leaker, proved less successful. Henry did work the press quite assiduously, cultivating certain reporters and columnists, sometimes spending up to half his day talking to the press in his office or on the phone. It was one of the reasons he ran perpetually behind his schedule. It was probably too much to expect that the NSC staff would not follow Henry's example. Former staff members have acknowledged, in fact, that the NSC began to leak in a big way in late 1969 or early the next year.

By 1971 those who remained formed a hard core tested by fire. The whole area of strategic weapons and arms control was a succession of such tests. Rather than following up the contacts LBJ had made for a SALT summit at Leningrad, Nixon's team postponed opening the initial round of negotiations to make a thorough review of arms control policy. Pressing for attention were the proponents of ABM and MIRV deployment. Laird, along with his research and development director, were postulating an unbelievably potent Soviet missile force, potentially capable of crippling America's land-based ICBM force. The Pentagon used this threat to justify reorientation of the ABM program to protect Minuteman bases rather than cities. With a few modifications, the ABM would be deployed at a dozen sites ranging from the missile fields to Washington, D.C., to the euphemistic National Command Authority (NCA). Thinking he was defusing domestic political opposition to ABM deployment, Richard Nixon approved Safeguard, the recommended ABM system, in March 1969.

The Safeguard ABM became a very controversial program, triggering vigorous debate that included numerous congressional hearings and some very heated disagreements. Among the new developments was the unprecedented unanimity of former presidential science advisers and defense research officials (with the exception of the incumbent) in opposing deployment of the planned ABM. At one point, former NSC staffer Carl Kaysen went before a Senate committee to discredit Laird's characterization of the Soviet threat. There were also intense debates about the utility of systems analysis, and about the specifics of calculating the effects of missile attacks. Congress passed the ABM appropriation by the margin of a single vote in August and gave the Vice President, Spiro T. Agnew, a chance to cast his vote in the Senate.

Simultaneously achieving maturity came the MIRV. The land-based Minuteman III was in active flight-testing. The sea-launched ballistic missile (SLBM), called Poseidon, completed flight tests from 1968 to 1970. In the Congress, Massachusetts Republican Senator Edward Brooke spearheaded a drive to get the administration to negotiate a MIRV ban at SALT. Time was running out for achieving this before actual MIRV deployment would remove the incentive for a ban, and greatly complicate verification of any possible accord.

Most of the considerations came together in the preparations for Strategic Arms Limitation Talks (SALT), which consumed a good deal of the bureaucracy in the early months of 1969. Since the subject involved Kissinger's own field of expertise, it is surprising that Henry was so slow off the mark in staking a claim on the arms control process. Not until March 13, *two months* into the administration, was there a study directive for a specific NSSM on SALT. By then there had been four study directives for Vietnam papers and two dealing with the Middle East.

One reason for delay was the immediate focus on assembling the ABM recommendation, but another was the situation with the NSC staff. Kissinger was attempting to cover a lot of territory. His situation was further complicated because two different staffers thought they had the SALT portfolio. Mort Halperin had been immersed from the inception of SALT. The other was Lawrence E. Lynn, Jr., thirty-one-year-old director of the Office of Program Analysis (OPA), a systems analysis shop within the NSC staff, Kissinger's single major organizational innovation upon coming to Washington. A Yale economist, operations researcher, and responsible for most of the draft presidential directives McNamara had sent Lyndon Johnson, Lynn was a Pentagon whiz kid, who in fact got his interview on Halperin's recommendation. Now they engaged in a running battle over responsibility for SALT studies. Sonnenfeldt increasingly became an éminence grise on Soviet policy. His man on Soviet matters, also to become influential, was William G. Hyland.

The SALT study ordered March 13 became NSSM-28, a fateful exercise. There was little coherence in the bureaucracy's response to the study directive. Melvin Laird was on the offensive, declassifying information on threatening weapons, warning of the Soviets' achieving a first-strike capability. The Office of the Secretary of Defense (OSD), however, pulled in several different directions, as different divisions struggled for control of SALT issues within The Building, as the Pentagon is called. Robert Ellsworth, Laird's assistant secretary of defense for intelligence matters, was highly critical of existing verification capabilities. General Earle Wheeler and the Joint Chiefs worked very slowly on preparation of the NSSM-28 study. Up the river, Langley's input also slowed, as the CIA's analysts were in conflict with Laird over the postulated Soviet threat. Moreover, the agency's experts could not but see an NSC verification study as opening a Pandora's box, and NSSM-28 asked the CIA to match possible arms restraints with available verification techniques. According to SALT historian John Newhouse, NSSM-28 was destined to allow the NSC staff to seize control of the issue "by giving inherited procedures their chance to fail."

Following the standard procedures, the ACDA was supposed to chair interagency studies dealing with arms control, so Gerard Smith sat down to wheedle contributions from the laggard agencies. Somehow he actually cobbled together a paper, which went forward for discussion at the NSC. There Bus Wheeler dissociated the JCS from the NSSM, effectively sinking NSSM-28. Wheeler objected that the United States lacked the capability to verify many potential arms control agreements. A MIRV ban was one example, as satellite photographs could not get inside a missile shroud and determine if a given rocket was MIRVed. Eventually the JCS would insist on MIRV exclusion as part of their price for going along on SALT.

In an evolving dispute between the Pentagon and the CIA, Laird and Richard Helms were openly caught feuding during Senate testimony on the presumptive Soviet first-strike threat. Laird's research chief, Dr. John S. Foster, Jr., asserted in Congress that a particular warhead with which the Soviets were testing their heavy SS-9 ICBM was definitely a MIRV. No ACDA initiative on arms control was going far in that climate. In fact, NSC intervention seemed downright warranted.

Henry finally captured SALT by careful work and efforts to discover where some of the skeletons were buried. He got Bill Hyland to assemble the record on Berlin negotiations and crises. Larry Lynn poked around in the MIRV morass, troubled when some at CIA took it personally that the NSC working group was looking into their MIRV estimates. Lynn disliked Henry's centralization of power, his limiting the action to certain people, his secrecy. Halperin too complained that Kissinger seemed to think it necessary to conduct foreign affairs as a conspiracy. "There was a dawning recognition," to cite Lynn, "that this was a frightening place. It was like walking into a room with a bad odor."

To soothe Lynn's qualms, Kissinger used to joke that he had too much integrity. To settle the matter of jurisdiction, at least within the NSC staff, Dr. Kissinger held a breakfast with all the contenders. Halperin, who had invested great energy in the proposal, floated during 1968, tried to sell the same approach to LBJ's successors. Bill Hyland thought Mort "inordinately proud" of the proposal, but concedes that what the Nixon administration came to after great effort was a final position "not far from the Johnson one." Halperin had been down that road and knew how hard it was. Henry lost a little in deciding to reinvent the wheel. Meanwhile, Halperin's fall from grace eventually gave Lawrence Lynn undisputed control over SALT issues.

On July 21 a Verification Panel formed, chaired by Dr. Kissinger, to be supported by an analytical group under Larry Lynn. The Verification Panel would become the main locus for SALT decisions in the Nixon years. It became an NSC subcommittee at the undersecretary level, with members being Kissinger, Elliot Richardson from the State Department, David Packard of DOD, the Chairman of the JCS, Gerard Smith for the ACDA, and the attorney general, John Mitchell, a close adviser to Nixon. Though Mitchell watched Henry for Nixon, Kissinger dominated the SALT bureaucracy through the Verification Panel.

While the bureaucracy had come back with five options in NSSM-28, for NSSM-62 they conjured up nine. One paralleled the 1968 proposal, another a nuclear freeze. Only two of the options left ABMs completely unrestrained, and one permitted mobile ICBMs. Bureaucratic preferences were indicated by the fact that two thirds of the options intended a simple freeze on both land- and sea-based missiles. Five permitted MIRV deployment. In this way a negotiating position was put together by building blocks. The study was massive, its summary over eighty pages, compiled by six different groups of officials. It was the subject at the NSC session on November 11. Afterward Kissinger got a memo from a senior NSC analyst, advocating a passive and exploratory posture for Gerard Smith's SALT delegation. The President approved the delegation's instructions on November 12, in NSDM-33, which were to explore Soviet views and to establish a work program in scheduled talks in Helsinki. There was to be no mention of MIRV without prior express agreement from Washington.

Meanwhile, something happened in Washington that changed the history of arms control. It was the forging of a relationship between Henry Kissinger and the Soviet Union's Ambassador Anatoli Dobrynin. The process began on February 14, 1969, when Dr. Kissinger visited Dobrynin in his apartment. The Soviet ambassador saw the President for the first time several days later, after Nixon had had the opportunity to absorb the results of Henry's preliminary reconnaissance. Nixon emphasized to Dobrynin a desire to estab-

▲

lish a channel of communications between Washington and Moscow through the persons of the ambassador and Kissinger. Henry and Dobrynin became very close, and Dr. Kissinger came to believe the Soviet ambassador an "extraordinary" man. In Kissinger's memoirs in fact, there are more references to Dobrynin than to his deputy Al Haig. Nixon set the tone for the relationship by excluding Secretary of State William P. Rogers from his meeting with Dobrynin.

This was to be the infamous Kissinger back channel.

Before long, Kissinger and Dobrynin had begun negotiations on a variety of subjects from Southeast Asia to the Middle East and Africa. Arms control would not be forgotten. The first word of Soviet agreement to actually attend SALT came through the Dobrynin channel in October. Dobrynin was nobody's fool. Although he customarily took no notes, the Soviet ambassador easily spotted the discrepancies when Kissinger altered the transcript of the October discussion with Nixon, to sharpen certain points for consumption in Moscow. Anatoli smoothly asked Henry which version he wished the Soviet to report home as his official account of the talk. Kissinger told Dobrynin to go by the newly written one.

From that time the Dobrynin channel provided true information; the United States SALT delegation was not authoritative.

The Dobrynin channel became especially active at the end of 1969, and featured exchanges in a number of areas. With a second round of talks coming up at Vienna, SALT was one. Kissinger steadfastly remained very protective of the secrecy of this channel. When Nixon began a public relations ploy of his own, a public foreign policy annual report to Congress, the first of which (ordered as NSSM-80 on October 27, 1969) he released in February 1970, it contained not a word regarding Kissinger's direct participation in negotiations. Few in the bureaucracy, even on the NSC staff, were told of the back channel until much later. Smith and his SALT delegation, along with the ACDA, were kept in the dark until 1971, when events in the front channel drove them to the conclusion that there had to be some such mechanism in operation. Even then, when SALT delegate Paul Nitze came to the NSC to take a look at the record, he was shown only some of the files.

Before the second, Vienna, round of SALT talks, Dobrynin asked Kissinger whether in the back channel they ought to try for a comprehensive or a limited SALT agreement. Henry shot back "the main problem was to get concrete about something." In the front channel, Kissinger staged a succession of NSC meetings to discuss the particulars of the SALT building blocks, even though he knew Nixon's eyes glazed over at such talk, in order to lend credence to anticipated NSDMs. At the council meeting on March 25 there came another acrimonious argument over verification, this time specifically of a MIRV ban. Two days later followed NSDM-49, directing the Verification Panel to assemble four SALT proposals from the collection of building blocks available. Each option was to state how MIRV and ABM programs would be affected, and what specific programs or actions were involved. Henry Kissinger signed this NSDM in place of the President.

The options went to the NSC on April 8, a week before resumption of SALT. That made it difficult for some such as Gerry Smith, who needed to be off for Vienna. Indeed the delegation's instructions came in NSDM-51, issued on April 10. Smith was instructed to offer first a deal under which ABM would be severely restricted but MIRV banned. The MIRV ban was to be accompanied by provisions for intrusive on-site inspections. This the Soviets rejected out of hand. The United States then offered major reductions of both ICBMs and SLBMs, with ABM limited to defense of the capital or banned but MIRV unconstrained. That option got rejected once the Soviets had had enough time to cable Moscow for instructions.

The idea that ABM ought to be for defense of a capital only, Kissinger notes, was one he did not believe in, brought about by bureaucratic politics because it was the only one on which all United States agencies could agree. No matter that Congress would never approve sole defense of Washington, D.C. Dr. Kissinger in retrospect concedes it was "a first-class blunder." He acquiesced despite his "better judgment," in fact, "swayed by bureaucratic and political considerations more than in any other set of decisions in my period in office." Henry argues that he felt honor-bound to stay within the limits of the government consensus because Nixon was leaving him on his own and refused to learn the technical details well enough to make an intelligent choice. "Basically," Kissinger writes, "the security adviser ought not to play this game," but leave the politics to the President and restrict himself to judgment on the merits. Fortunately the Russians rejected the United States proposals.

The first elements of what finally became the SALT I agreements had already gone through the bureaucracy and were bandied about by both sides on occasion. Those were deployment halts for ICBMs and SLBMs, though Kissinger triggered aggravation with his initial back-channel agreement to an offensive freeze that ignored sea-launched missiles. Dobrynin coupled the offensive freeze with an ABM treaty and a broad declaration of superpower concord. Richard Nixon added the condition that such an agreement be reached at a summit and not merely within the SALT negotiations.

In the front channel, when the initial United States proposals foundered, Kissinger and the NSC staff put together on their own the so-called Option E proposal, which became the next United States position. It was promulgated by Nixon when he approved NSDM-69, which he signed on July 4, 1970. It would take until May 1971, however, for the back channel to hand off to the front channel for serious negotiation of the technicalities. By that time the possibilities for a ban on MIRVs were nil.

Lawrence Lynn was gone by the time SALT really began to roll. Another who went with him, one of the few holdovers from Rostow's staff, was Roger Morris. Morris was one of the young, bright ones. A Harvard Ph.D., he had entered government in 1966 as a junior aide to Dean Acheson. When the Six Day War occurred and LBJ brought back Mac Bundy to head an NSC Special Committee, Morris functioned as junior staff person. He impressed Rostow, who asked Rusk to send him back, and Morris took over the portfolio for Africa south of the Sahara in October 1967.

The Biafran civil war began on his watch; the war was born of tribal politics in Nigeria and the failure of an attempted military coup. Nixon had brought up Biafra during the 1968 campaign. A week into the administration Kissinger sent out the study directive for NSSM-11, a policy review of Nigeria. Henry may have felt he needed someone who was already up to speed on Biafra, as he offered the job to Morris despite the latter's known liberalism. Inviting Morris to come along for the ride to the Pentagon, he emphasized that Roger would work for the NSC, *not* Richard Nixon. Kissinger's staff was going to be one pile of good people. Morris went along and soon found himself at work on NSSM-11 and on NSSM-39, a policy review of all southern Africa.

Neither Nixon nor Kissinger had firm, well-considered views on Biafra, nor indeed on South Africa where, Morris believes, Nixon once approved a new policy simply because it was new. The African Bureau at State did have entrenched views and Morris encountered predictable trouble with them. For NSSM-11 there were to be six options. It was decided that one of them could be that the United States might support secessionist Biafra, but only after a marathon nine-hour conclave of the responsible interagency group. On February 9, the NSSM went before the NSC, where only Nixon and Kissinger seemed knowledgeable and interested. When Morris saw the resulting NSDM, a Haig product, it adopted *none* of the NSSM options. Instead, the "new" policy was that the United States would remain neutral in the civil war but try to assume a high profile on refugee relief.

The issue that drove Morris to make a break from the Kissinger NSC was Vietnam. The previous fall Henry had taken Morris aside, along with several of his most trusted aides, for urgent work on a big plan. Not just any Vietnam reassessment, this one was supposed to be a plan to really end the war, by escalating to North Vietnam. Code-named Duck Hook, key planners from several departments worked out a range of escalatory measures from mining Haiphong Harbor to using tactical nuclear weapons.

The origin of Duck Hook remains in dispute. Kissinger traces it to an NSC discussion on September 12. Richard Nixon, on the other hand, says it was in late July that he began to organize an effort to end the war by November 1. Hanoi would be served an ultimatum to settle or face disaster. The form of the Duck Hook idea strongly resembles Dwight Eisenhower's formula for ending the war in Korea, which supports the notion that Nixon first concocted the idea. Ike's threat had involved nuclear weapons, and Nixon has confirmed that Vietnam in the fall of 1969 was one of four occasions on which he thought about using nuclear weaponry.

The Vietnamization strategy must be viewed in this political context. By initiating withdrawals and abandoning the tactic of large-scale military sweep operations, Nixon was effectively reducing American casualties and consequent draft calls. According to official tabulations, American battle deaths in the first half of 1969 totaled 6,340, those in the second six months only 3,074. Instances of combat contact steadily decreased though some battles, like that for the A-Shau Valley, which produced the battle for "Hamburger Hill," continued to sear the public consciousness.

In establishing contact with Hanoi, Nixon adopted the exact arrangement Kissinger advocated in *Foreign Affairs*. At an April 1969 meeting with Dobrynin, Henry showed the Soviet ambassador a paper initialed by Nixon that commented favorably on exploring "avenues other than the existing negotiating framework," separate talks that could arrive at general principles. The Paris negotiators might then work out the details. Nixon underlined the signal by downgrading the United States delegation in Paris, recalling Harriman and, after one last sally to Moscow, Cyrus Vance. The new chief of delegation was William J. Porter, formerly a pacification official in South Vietnam, an able diplomat but not of the stature of Harriman or, for that matter, Henry Kissinger. The national security adviser made it clear that he was available for Hanoi to meet on a private basis. Hanoi responded favorably, and Kissinger borrowed the Paris apartment of his friend Jean Sainteny for the first of a series of secret meetings with the North Vietnamese. It occurred on August 4, 1969. Hanoi's representatives were Xuan Thuy and Mai Van Bo, whom Henry had schemed for months to see in behalf of LBJ a couple of years before. Visiting Paris on the pretext of briefing the French president, Kissinger told Xuan that the United States would like to settle the war by the first anniversary of the start of negotiations—November 1.

Duck Hook turned into a real plan, supported by the full panoply of impedimenta; there was a Joint Chiefs of Staff memo, a Navy operations plan, and a wide variety of parallel preparations. In the Gulf of Tonkin, Navy frogmen reconnoitered the ship channels leading to Haiphong. In Washington, Kissinger tapped Morris along with a trusted group of others to work as a team from the White House Situation Room. Morris, with Anthony Lake and Peter W. Rodman, wrote the speech the President could give while implementing the escalation. The JCS plan included mining Haiphong plus smashing twenty-nine other North Vietnamese targets for four days; after that Hanoi would be bombed in spasms of two or three days' duration if it continued to resist negotiating. Kissinger got Sonnenfeldt to work on the probable Soviet reaction and John Holdridge on the Chinese.

William Watts, the man hired to replace Richard Moose on the paperwork, arrived at the NSC staff in the middle of all this. Relieved to return to national security affairs, Watts was a capable Foreign Service officer who had served in Moscow but had gotten diverted into urban issues by Nelson Rockefeller. Watts found his first day as staff secretary deceptively easy—

Nixon, with Henry and Al Haig, were out in San Clemente. Watts flew to California to join them, and went out to dinner with the group. Things went well enough until, at dinner, someone dropped the words Duck Hook. After that the atmosphere became conspiratorial. As Watts soon discovered, Navy planning documents for Duck Hook were emblazoned with a blue cover featuring the sketch of an attack plane rising from the deck of an aircraft carrier.

Kissinger himself maintains the Duck Hook planning seemed "desultory," so much so that he concluded decisive action from the United States military was "unattainable." Kissinger therefore recommended against going any further on Duck Hook. The same day, October 17, one of Richard Nixon's favorite Vietnam experts, Sir Robert Thompson, also opposed escalation in a conversation with the President. In the end Nixon never sent his ultimatum to Hanoi.

In his memoirs the former President concedes that the antiwar movement in the fall of 1969 ruled out a credible escalation. So Vietnamization continued.

Not having delivered the promised settlement, Nixon made Vietnam his war much as it had previously been Johnson's war. Indeed Nixon's next big move fitted much better his warlike image than that of the peacemaker. Kissinger played a big part, in what became the final crucible for the NSC staff. That was the invasion of Cambodia.

In early 1970, Norodom Sihanouk was overthrown in a bloodless coup. The parliament voted to dissolve the constitutional monarchy and form a "republic," a cloak for a military dictatorship. For Washington policymakers the Cambodian coup could be threat or opportunity. The extent of a United States role, if any, in the Phnom Penh coup remains in dispute.

America's ally and client Nguyen Van Thieu was also involved. He had gained very little from his delaying action in the waning days of the Johnson administration. Instead of rewarding him for helping preserve Nixon's options, the President announced the withdrawal of American troops. A possible way to reverse Nixon's decision might be to embroil the United States in some expansion of the war. In response to a wave of racially motivated murders of Vietnamese residents in Khmer towns and villages, South Vietnam's Vice President Nguyen Cao Ky held meetings with Cambodia's General Lon Nol within days of the Phnom Penh coup. Thieu's military commanders also carried out a series of raids against North Vietnamese base areas across the Cambodian border.

Henry Kissinger's preferred version of history is that Sihanouk was overthrown and the North Vietnamese broke out of their base areas, while the United States did nothing for five weeks, until Nixon began to consider intervention in Cambodia. This version does not square with South Vietnamese actions, including ARVN attacks on March 20, and 27–28. On March 19, the day after the coup, Richard Nixon ordered the CIA to plan an aid program to assist Lon Nol's forces. A few days later, Al Haig met with Dick Helms to further the action, beginning a long dispute over setting up a CIA station in the then tiny (seven-person) American mission in Phnom Penh. Under the direction of its commander, General Creighton W. Abrams, MACV began planning for a large-scale (multidivision) sweep into Cambodia on March 27. Later the Americans approved the South Vietnamese's sending along to Phnom Penh some stocks of infantry weapons and ammunition. Within ten days of the coup there was planning for a major invasion, with a military aid program in motion within two weeks, and a CIA presence to follow shortly.

Concerning the notion that North Vietnamese forces broke out of their base areas, threatening the Phnom Penh regime, some bits of intelligence supported it; others did not. For example, State's Bureau of Intelligence and Research (INR), later decided that the NVA had begun preparation of a move into the interior of Cambodia on March 21. On the other hand, staff at the NSC tried to summarize the evidence of an NVA breakout, but were unable to get the details. Even Kissinger, in his memoirs, does not claim the North Vietnamese left their border sanctuaries until April 3. A more recent inside account by Truong Nhu Tang, then a senior official in the Vietcong's provisional revolutionary government, claims NVA forces moved *away* from the Cambodian capital after the coup.

Newsweek reporter Kevin Buckley chose the weeks immediately after Lon Nol's coup to make an extensive tour of the Cambodian countryside, partly to report the controversial story of pogroms aimed at Vietnamese residents. He had extensive contact with Cambodian army posts and others in the border region and reported that no one was having any trouble with the North Vietnamese.

At the time, Kissinger spoke with North Vietnamese politburo member Le Duc Tho, at a session of their secret negotiations, regarding responsibility for the Cambodian crisis. Dr. Kissinger denied that the United States had anything to do with Lon Nol's machinations. At their next negotiating session, on April 4, the North Vietnamese again complained bitterly, based on participation in the coup by CIA-financed Khmer Serei paramilitary forces. Kissinger then offered to discuss measures to guarantee Cambodian neutrality. Le Duc Tho frankly told his American interlocutor that Hanoi would back Sihanouk's new alliance with Khmer and Chinese Communists.

Not to be overlooked, Thieu made cross-border raids. Kissinger was leaving for a week's vacation at the time, but Al Haig got him first. Henry wanted the raids stopped, at least until after the Le Duc Tho meeting. Ambassador Bunker got orders to get Thieu to agree to restrict attacks to those allowable under United States rules of engagement, which meant only responses to direct attacks from within Cambodia. The necessity for this was squarely attributed to efforts to maintain domestic support for the United States' Vietnam policy. Bunker met with Thieu, who acquiesced, but then Laird heard of the decision and tried to get it reversed. Haig got Henry on the phone, and Kissinger ordered his deputy to stall until after the Paris secret meeting. Nixon countermanded that, however, and allowed ARVN attacks into Cambodia that were not larger than the ones already carried out.

Tensions rose on the NSC staff. William Watts and Larry Lynn both warned Kissinger that attacks into Cambodia were only going to drive the North Vietnamese into the interior, create the threat to Phnom Penh that everyone wanted to avoid.

Anthony Lake also did his part to warn. Lake was a thirty-year-old Foreign Service officer, pressed into service in the emergency of Larry Eagleburger's collapse in the summer of 1969. Henry liked him and kept him on, a useful personal aide who could accomplish chores and had done so for Max Taylor and Henry Cabot Lodge. Lake also had detailed knowledge of Vietnam, where he had served as vice-consul in Hue and Saigon before becoming an ambassador's aide. Lake accompanied Kissinger to his earliest secret negotiations, participated in the Duck Hook planning, and was perhaps the closest staffer to Henry during drafting of the first annual foreign policy report. In October 1969, Lake teamed with Roger Morris to produce a paper advocating a Vietnam cease-fire that would leave the forces of the sides in place, a so-called leopard-spot cease-fire. The United States negotiating position previously had suffered from a demand for full territorial evacuation, a position not likely to spark Hanoi's interest. The Lake-Morris paper failed to spark Kissinger's interest either, and he sent it to Nixon purely for information. For their efforts, Lake and Morris seem to have been written down as troublemakers.

There were also interagency groups meeting on the Cambodia situation. Directly relevant to Kissinger was the Washington Special Action Group (WSAG), which allowed Henry to wear a different hat when working with the undersecretaries on a crisis. There had been a WSAG meeting on March 19, immediately after the coup, but Kissinger maintains this pertained only to Laos. Cambodia was the subject on April 14, after Nixon had separately met Laird and Rogers to demand their cooperation, when the WSAG agreed to send Lon Nol three thousand captured AK-47 assault rifles from South Vietnamese stocks. A further WSAG proposal to funnel $5 million worth of emergency funding to Lon Nol, to be sent through Australia, was approved as well. The following day, April 16, Nixon approved the dispatch of U.S. weapons for the first time, in packs of one thousand the CIA had stashed in warehouses in South Vietnam. At the military level in Vietnam, MACV officers visited the ARVN commander and *handed* him a plan for large ARVN and American forces to invade Cambodia to a depth of twenty kilometers. General Abrams pressed Washington for authority to carry out several kinds of activities related to escalating in Cambodia. Roger Morris saw the President "lurching toward a decision."

First choices condition subsequent ones. The American choice to back

Lon Nol led to five years of a widened Indochina war. The question is how such a decision could be so lightly made—against the advice of quite a few Nixon advisers, including both NSC principals and NSC staff.

Shortly before publication of the first volume of Kissinger's memoirs in 1979, an account of the Cambodian war appeared by journalist William Shawcross that condemned the Nixon-Kissinger Cambodia policy and held it responsible for creating conditions that enabled the murderous Khmer Rouge to triumph five years later. Dr. Kissinger took umbrage at the Shawcross account, and extensively rewrote portions of his narrative shortly after the appearance of the Shawcross book, as documented in some detail by *The New York Times*. A couple of years later, in *The American Spectator*, Peter Rodman went back to the originals of the documents Shawcross had quoted, to charge the writer with selective quotation and overdrawing his case.

This vigorous debate illustrates the continuing controversy surrounding the Cambodian invasion, which began at the time with, among other things, resignations from the National Security Council staff. The event was unprecedented and remains unsurpassed. Perhaps it is not surprising that Henry Kissinger is sensitive about it.

Kissinger insists there was "no consideration" of attacking North Vietnam in Cambodia until April 21, when Dick Helms accompanied Henry to his regular morning meeting with the President. By that time real fighting had begun in Cambodia. Nixon called an NSC session for the next morning. In preparation Kissinger quietly asked Army Chief of Staff General William Westmoreland, for an opinion on the feasibility of ARVN operations into the base areas. Westy thought ARVN attacks could be effective provided they had United States support. Kissinger also sent a cable on a CIA back channel to Ambassador Bunker requesting his and Abrams's judgment. That night Westy followed up with his own cable to Abrams, citing "highest level concern," viewing the situation as one to be exploited to secure a relaxation of operational constraints on MACV. Westy warned Abrams, "We should be prepared to take advantage of the opportunity."

The crucial day was April 22. Early that morning Nixon began bombarding Henry with typewritten notes calling for bold moves to help Lon Nol survive. Dr. Kissinger first met with Ray Cline, State's director of intelligence and research; then Richard Helms accompanied him again on his morning briefing with the President. At 10:00 A.M., Kissinger met with General John W. Vogt, director of operations for the Joint Staff of the JCS. Vogt became Kissinger's top military contact for Cambodia planning. Henry later told Nixon that the Joint Staff and MACV had been working with the assumption the plans would quickly be implemented, while Secretaries Laird and Rogers could be expected to oppose the operations.

In the Cabinet Room the NSC gathered at 2:30 P.M. By then Bunker and Abrams were on record recommending combined MACV-ARVN attacks on the base areas along the border; the return of Sihanouk, argued the proconsuls, would endanger Vietnamization. Kissinger told the NSC Vietnamization was in danger no matter what the North Vietnamese were up to. The options were to do nothing, to attack the sanctuaries with the ARVN only, or to use combined forces. General Westmoreland cautiously opined that attacks entirely by ARVN troops might be sufficient; he was supported by Kissinger. Laird, previously a strong proponent of cross-border operations, opposed the Abrams option for combined attacks, as did Rogers. *Only* Spiro Agnew spoke in favor of MACV-ARVN attacks, which Kissinger believes irked Nixon. That night the President ordered planning for an ARVN assault on the "Parrot's Beak" zone of the Cambodian borderlands. The White House also ordered a new cable distribution restriction—"No Dis Khmer"—which routed Cambodia cables *away* from State's Cambodian experts until after the invasion.

The Washington Special Action Group was scheduled to meet on Thursday, April 23, as State and DOD, or at least the NSC principals who represented those departments, began a rearguard action on Cambodia planning. There were two WSAG sessions that day as the bureaucracy mulled over the options. In a style reminiscent of Eisenhower, Kissinger kept behind a few key officials after the first session, including acting JCS Chairman Admiral Thomas Moorer. Then Henry reported personally to the President. In the evening the WSAG met again, most in black tie en route to a dinner at the Taiwanese embassy, in honor of visiting Vice-Premier Chiang Chingkuo. Kissinger managed a stop at Bill Fulbright's house to update seven key senators. Between 6:30 and 11:00 P.M., Nixon logged ten telephone calls to Kissinger, three while Kissinger was at Fulbright's. Nixon pressed for expanded military operations, hitting more NVA base areas than those in the Parrot's Beak. He ordered a meeting with Admiral Moorer and DCI Helms first thing in the morning, and wanted to see plans for hitting all the sanctuaries. The President was also furious about the leak of a cable to *The New York Times* that told the chargé in Phnom Penh the United States would provide captured weapons to the Cambodian Army.

One who got left behind in the action was General William Westmoreland. The Army Chief of Staff was acting as JCS Chairman one day, when Kissinger turned to him and asked about the effect of using *American* ground troops in Cambodia. Westy advised that Americans would enhance the chances of success. But he was not sure Nixon was prepared to make that political decision. Westy lunched with reporters, who got the faintest whiff of United States government interest in attacking Cambodia. That afternoon Al Haig received a call at the NSC; he tried to dampen speculation by asserting Westy was inclined to hit the panic button. Kissinger also flatly denied the rumors. Laird later admitted that Haig ordered Westmoreland cut out of the communications network on Cambodia decision-making. Westmoreland eventually complained to friends that sometimes things happened so fast the Chiefs were merely debriefed on them after they occurred. Westy was not simply whistling in the wind. The Chiefs, as will be seen, took measures to change that relationship.

First thing the next day, Kissinger ordered Bill Watts to have Admiral Moorer report to the White House in his capacity as the President's "chief" military adviser. Laird and Rogers were to be excluded on the pretext the meeting was a mere military briefing. Helms and Moorer both advocated the option for an expanded invasion. Nixon chose not to make the decision yet, helicoptering up to Camp David for the weekend.

Henry had found Watts that morning at the Jockey Club, a downtown hotel restaurant that Bill favored. Kissinger asked him to collect the documents for the meeting and joked about the President's impulsiveness, the subject of many NSC jests.

"Our peerless leader has flipped out," Henry quipped.

Knowledge of the atmosphere in the Oval Office quickly leaped across West Executive Avenue to the OEOB. A group of three NSC aides, thinking they might yet prevent a disastrous development, went to work on a paper rejecting the invasion option. They were Roger Morris, Anthony Lake, and Winston Lord. Lawrence Lynn worked independently on a systems analysis critique of the military strategy and planning for the invasion. Ironically their arguments served only to convince Kissinger of the wisdom of Nixon's course. The administration would take the same political heat regardless of the size of the Cambodian invasion; Henry followed Agnew in favoring a big operation to do the job right.

Late that afternoon Kissinger met in his office with the dissenters. At the last moment he turned to Watts and asked if he wanted to be included.

"This is my bleeding hearts club," Kissinger said. "Do you consider yourself a bleeding heart?"

Tony Lake looked at Watts and thought Bill was seeing his future pass before his eyes. Then Watts came in to join the impromptu critique.

Impromptu it was: Some of these NSC staff knew Vietnam well, some did not, some knew the details of the planned Cambodia invasion but did not know what parts of that information the others might be cleared for. Talk proceeded as a general critique of a limited invasion to be conducted by the ARVN alone. Tony Lake insisted that extending the war would set a new course, that Washington would not be able to escape once committed. Morris argued the operation would be just one more exercise in futility. All believed the evidence far too murky anyway. Watts argued, more prophetically than he knew, that if it was Cambodia this year, it would be Laos next, and the bombing of Haiphong in two. Larry Lynn's objections are not clearly recorded, while Winston Lord mostly stayed silent. In any event, Kissinger was clearly warned of domestic political difficulties if the Cambodia operation went ahead.

Late that night Kissinger got a telephone call from Camp David. It was

Nixon crony Bebe Rebozo. "The president wants you to know," Rebozo slurred, "that if this doesn't work, it's your ass!"

It would be one of Kissinger's toughest weekends.

At this stage efforts began to get people on board. Laird's objections were collected and Abrams put to work on measures by which MACV could take them into account. Kissinger began Saturday morning with a briefing of the plans to John Ehrlichman, snowing Ehrlichman with more detail than he could handle, leaving him with the impression the decision had already been made. Henry was talking with Lawrence Lynn about improving the plans when Nixon called from Camp David. Dr. Kissinger helicoptered up in time for a hamburger with the President and Bebe Rebozo before going over the plans. Kissinger walked alongside the swimming pool, Nixon paddled in the water. Nixon pushed for expansion of the operation to include renewed bombing of North Vietnam and the mining of Haiphong. Henry dismissed this at the time, as one of Nixon's ploys intended to demonstrate toughness, and Nixon dropped the line after ten minutes, never to raise the subject again. In retrospect Kissinger regrets not taking the President's "musing" more seriously, not making the military strike even bigger.

Kissinger flew back to Washington with Nixon that afternoon, and the President invited his national security adviser aboard the presidential yacht *Sequoia* for a four-hour sunset cruise down the Potomac River to Mount Vernon. Kissinger shared the privilege with Rebozo and Attorney General John Mitchell. Then Nixon invited the group to view the film *Patton* with him, not the first time for Henry, who confessed to friends, "If I have to see that movie one more time, I'll shoot myself."

In the West Wing NSC office, Henry met privately once more with Larry Lynn, who had been sitting with a pad at the Situation Room table, doing his critique of the specific Cambodia planning. Lynn accumulated eighteen solid questions and developed a cost-effectiveness argument that investing a similar amount in South Vietnam would be more useful. It was no use, new arguments could not turn aside the administration.

From available accounts it appears that Kissinger tried to reassure his young NSC staffers. Before seeing Nixon on Saturday, he had told Watts not to worry, that he had seen Nixon and the President would never approve an invasion by Americans. Henry encouraged Watts to become a sort of NSC program manager for Cambodia. Watts may have toyed with the temptation, but on Sunday afternoon, about half an hour before a crucial NSC meeting, Watts informed Kissinger that he would not attend to take notes.

"When I came to work for you," Watts told Henry, "my sense of loyalty was, first, to the American people, secondly to you, and finally to Richard Nixon. I'm against this operation on every count and I'm resigning."

"Your views represent the cowardice of the Eastern Establishment!" Kissinger roared back.

Watts stalked off into the Situation Room, where he told Win Lord what had happened.

Not long after, Al Haig entered looking for Watts, angry. Kissinger was in his office, enraged, reportedly throwing papers around. "What the hell did you say to Henry?" Haig asked. "He's furious."

Watts announced he was leaving the NSC staff, whereupon Haig began to argue too. Watts had no interest in Haig's objections. Then Haig put on his best parade ground voice and thundered, "You've just had an order from your Commander-in-Chief and you can't refuse!"

"Fuck you Al," Watts shot back. "I just have and I've resigned."

Regardless of the chaos on the NSC staff, Nixon went to the council meeting at the appointed time, 4:30 P.M. In preparation Kissinger sent him a memo that noted that Laird and Rogers could be expected to oppose the invasion, and that Laird had not been aware of the likelihood that an invasion with United States troops might be ordered. Kissinger believed Laird and Rogers had worked to scale back even the planned ARVN operation into Parrot's Beak, and in part the NSC session on April 26 was designed to force them into taking positions on the invasion option. Agnew was excluded from this meeting, so the set of statutory members of the NSC continued to be incomplete. Helms gave an intelligence briefing, then Bus Wheeler outlined the invasion plans for both Parrot's Beak and the Fish Hook. Laird and Rogers made no objections at the time, and afterward Nixon called Henry back into the President's family quarters, where with a flourish he signed an NSDM ordering the Cambodia operation.

Nevertheless, ordering the invasion did not turn out to be so easy. More agency objections were voiced at the WSAG. Laird and Rogers demanded to see the President themselves. DOD argued that it was a violation of the statutory chain of command over United States armed forces for an NSDM to assign the WSAG as the "implementing authority" for operations. Determined to move ahead, Nixon revised his NSDM and overruled the objection, made explicitly by an NSC principal, that if he did this the nation's campuses would go up in flames.

Melvin Laird made the inadvertent discovery during these crisis meetings that the White House and MACV *were* in violation of the chain of command: communicating behind his back. Laird deduced as much from the uncanny resemblance between the cables he got from General Creighton Abrams and the arguments he heard in the White House. Laird sent his personal military assistant, Colonel Robert E. Pursley, to Haig with a demand to learn about the back channel. Haig claimed innocence and the two military men got into a shouting match in the West Wing NSC offices. Pursley, a brilliant Air Force officer who was a dove on Vietnam, later found himself victim of FBI national security wiretaps, placed on White House instructions conveyed by Haig. A generally conservative officer, Pursley was not a very likely source for leaks.

Laird and Rogers got their final audience on the morning of April 28.

Nixon did most of the talking, essentially declaring that he had decided for a full invasion, that he had dictated a tape noting their objections. Nixon asserted he was acting to protect Americans in South Vietnam. Meanwhile, Haig met with NSC staffers and assigned Morris and Lake to work on a draft for the President's speech revealing the attack, to be euphemistically termed an "incursion." Morris spurned the request, telling Al he had worked on too many speeches in the last three or four years, but Haig was not to be put off. Morris and Lake then went into an office and, instead of a speech, began drafting a joint letter of resignation.

"We know Henry's very upset and very tense now," Morris told Haig later in the day. "Will you pick a time to give him this? But it's very important to us that we deliver it today prior to what's going to happen. If you want to give it to him after it happens, when things have calmed down, that's fine too."

Haig held on to the resignations for several days, giving them to Kissinger only on Saturday, May 1. By then Nixon had made his speech announcing the invasion.

Nixon did as he planned and got what he bargained for: a national political trauma. Over 500 colleges were forced to close, while 350 were shut down by student strikes; at least 73 reported some degree of violence at demonstrations. The National Guard was called out in 24 instances. At Kent State University in Ohio four students, not all of them protesters, were shot dead by panicky guardsmen. At Jackson State University in Mississippi two more students fell to bullets fired by state police. The resulting outpour left even Richard Nixon in fear, worrying to associates of "incoherent" protesters taking over the Oval Office and urinating on its floor and furnishings.

As isolated as it was, even the Nixon White House had a barometer for the public opinion outside. Henry Kissinger, presiding over the revolt of the NSC staff, could have no illusions about the climate of opinion. The day of the speech was truly tough, when Henry successively had to brief the White House staff, his NSC staff, and the press.

Haldeman gathered the senior staff in the Roosevelt Room of the White House. He distributed a classified list of talking points, which asserted the invasion was an "integral" element of United States operations in Vietnam and had nothing to do with Lon Nol. Kissinger arrived from a last preincursion WSAG meeting, seconded by Haig, who spoke of the need to be tough.

According to an account by speechwriter William Safire, Kissinger was contradictory. Asked about expanding the war, Dr. Kissinger replied, "Look, we're not interested in Cambodia, we're only interested in it not being used as a base." Donald Rumsfeld, then director of the Office of Economic Opportunity, warned it would not be credible not to acknowledge an expansion was occurring. After a mention of the media's revelation that fifty U.S. advisers had entered Cambodia early with some ARVN units, however, Henry took the opposite tack on alleged disinterest. He was personally and "institutionally" impatient, Kissinger rasped; "the North Vietnamese have forty thousand troops marching on the capital of Cambodia, and a lousy fifty U.S. advisers go in last night, and you hear senators say —we're the ones who are escalating!"

"The tone of our questioning shook Kissinger," records Safire. "This was only the White House staff, and two tougher briefings lay ahead."

A briefing for the NSC staff occurred in the Indian Treaty Room of the Old Executive Office Building. Henry appealed to everyone to stand together and behind the President.

"We are all the president's men," Kissinger declared.

One of the staffers present, recalling that the Indian treaties of the nineteenth century had mostly all been broken, thought the selection of that room for the convocation oddly ironic.

Meanwhile, Nixon backed into a credibility gap of his own in his Cambodia speech, citing as one of his objectives capture of the VC and NVA headquarters. Henry had tried to get Nixon to remove the reference after learning from Bill Watts, who had checked with the CIA, that even sophisticated electronic intelligence means were not able to triangulate its location at that time. Laird, who had also warned Nixon against going after the headquarters, was not shown the speech until two hours before Nixon delivered it. Kissinger attempted to limit the damage in advance in his press briefing, claiming there was no expectation of capturing enemy leaders or a functioning command post, but of course there was. The command posts had long since been displaced from border locations to the Cambodian interior.

A few weeks into the offensive the administration suffered considerable embarrassment after a staff report from the Senate Foreign Relations Committee detailed failures to find the reported NVA headquarters. Ironically, one of the two major authors of this report was former Kissinger aide Dick Moose. Equally ironic, or perhaps predictable, Moose became the target of FBI national security wiretaps. So did Anthony Lake, who left the NSC, and Winston Lord, who did not.

The Cambodian invasion racked up impressive statistics for the number of captured weapons and tonnage of supplies destroyed. It became important to claim results from the operation. Kissinger put NSC program analysis to work on a systems analysis study. Lawrence Lynn had had enough; he quit for "personal" reasons. K. Wayne Smith, another whiz kid prominent from the McNamara Pentagon, whom Lynn had brought on earlier in 1970, was assigned the Cambodia study. Smith came to the conclusion that Nixon had gained a year. Once Lynn left, Kissinger selected Wayne Smith to succeed him. Nixon got the NSC to hire Sir Robert Thompson to carry out an independent review. Thompson made a field trip and came back with a prediction of two years' gain. Exactly two years after Cambodia, in fact, Saigon would be tottering at the brink of defeat in the bitterest campaign to date.

Cambodia marked an important rite of passage for the NSC staff as well. The staff became more homogeneous after that, with less concern for employing the best people regardless of political views. Expression of political view became even more guarded. The crisis also brought to the fore Alexander Haig, who increasingly created relationships independent of Kissinger with the President and his chief of staff, H. R. Haldeman. Haig's first solo foreign mission was as emissary to take a firsthand look at Cambodia during the 1970 operations. Soon there would be people saying that Haig had become more than Henry's deputy.

Henry Kissinger burned some bridges in the course of the Cambodian "incursion." The most important of those was with his former colleagues at Harvard. A Harvard faculty group addressed Kissinger with the intention of communicating their views to the President. Historian Ernest May argued the policy was tearing the country apart, which had to be obvious by May 8, the eve of the big Cambodia demonstrations. Kissinger tried to go off the record but the group would not allow it. He then asserted he could not offer an adequate defense without doing so. When the Harvard faculty group finally left, Kissinger sank disconsolately into an armchair in his office.

Kissinger appears to have been shaken. Five years later Nixon told television interviewer David Frost, "Henry came in one day and said, 'You know, I'm not sure that we should have gone into this Cambodian thing, and perhaps now the time has come when we should . . . get out a little sooner.'

" 'Henry,' Nixon recalls himself saying, 'we've done it. . . . Remember Lot's wife. Never look back.' "

Kissinger didn't.

TO THE TOP OF
POLICY HILL

▲▲▲

Destined never to attain complete dominance within the national security bureaucracy, Henry Kissinger still achieved a certain ascendance. Whatever he may have done in the fires of Cambodia, Kissinger passed Nixon's test there, afterward to be given ever increasing responsibilities. One of the first places it became evident was in the Middle East, until then a sacrosanct preserve of the State Department. Kissinger once told Egyptian leader Anwar Sadat that Nixon had initially kept him out of Middle East matters to avoid the specter of favoritism, since Kissinger happened to be Jewish. The appearance and then growth of Kissinger's role on Middle East policy marked a turning point, the decisive defeat of the State Department in the contest for primacy in Washington policy-making.

Secretary of State William Rogers did his best to encourage progress in the Middle East, but used a very light touch, mostly giving the lead to Joseph Sisco, the assistant secretary for the region. Rogers was a close friend of Nixon's—the two had been colleagues in the Eisenhower administration, which Rogers served as attorney general. He knew very little about foreign policy, but knew Nixon's intention to lead from the White House and was comfortable with the role of chief public spokesman for the administration. Recognizing talent, Rogers deferred to Sisco on most diplomatic issues and relied on Joe's extensive prior experience with the Middle East. A perceptive observer himself, Sisco saw the growing White House prerogative in all things and was careful to keep the NSC staff fully informed. A big help to Sisco in building his own line to Kissinger was Hal Saunders, NSC Middle East specialist, who stayed on from the Rostow staff and had thorough confidence in the diplomat.

Rogers and Sisco together held important talks with Soviet Foreign Minister Andrei Gromyko in New York during the UN General Assembly session of 1969. Suddenly there was talk of a "Rogers Plan" for the Middle East. It called for a cease-fire in the increasingly dangerous war of attrition that Israel and Egypt were waging along the Suez Canal. The cease-fire would be followed by negotiations for a peace settlement.

A significant flaw in the policy was the presumption that it would not be undercut by the U.S. arms sales to Israel. Then Washington went ahead to sell Tel Aviv F-4 jet aircraft, which had an especially deleterious effect because they instantly multiplied the range and capacity of Israeli bombing raids into Egypt. For their part the Russians began to send antiaircraft missile units, then more advanced interceptor aircraft piloted by Russians. The Soviet military presence in Egypt grew to more than fifteen thousand; inevitably the day came when American-produced aircraft provided to Israel shot down Soviet-piloted interceptors.

Another Soviet move caused Kissinger great embarrassment in the short run, but in a way opened the door to his becoming involved in Middle East policy. This happened on January 31, 1970, when Ambassador Dobrynin gave Henry a letter for Nixon from Soviet Premier Aleksei Kosygin. The letter gave fair warning that Moscow might feel it necessary to furnish Egypt the means of turning back Israeli bombing raids.

By several accounts Henry Kissinger was loath at first to assert himself fully in Middle East affairs. That changed with the Soviet deployment to the United Arab Republic of air defense troops and fighter interceptors. The Soviet overlay put the war of attrition into the East-West context of super-power arms competition. In all likelihood, however, politics was the primary motivation in Nixon moving in a big way. It was in the middle of the Cambodia crisis when Nixon first gave Kissinger instructions relating to the Middle East. In June 1970, with the nation shell-shocked over Cambodia, it looked like taking charge of foreign policy to be doing something about the war of attrition. After a hiatus of six months, on June 10 and 18 Nixon suddenly called a succession of NSC sessions to discuss the Middle East. Some observers believe the NSC meetings were a pretext for the President to deal himself a hand. Soon after the June 18 meetings Nixon issued NSDM-62, which ordered Secretary Rogers to do pretty much what he was already doing: seek a cease-fire to be followed by negotiations under UN auspices. If Rogers did achieve a cease-fire, Richard Nixon could step forward to claim a measure of the credit for it.

Rogers succeeded in getting the cease-fire a couple of months later, but his comprehensive plan for a Middle East peace fell of its own weight. The UAR used the cessation of bombing to reinforce and advance its antiaircraft missile belt along the Suez Canal. That violation led to widespread recriminations, but in a sense ended the war of attrition, for the Israelis subsequently tried new retaliations and determined the cost was excessive, effectively ending the conflict. In Washington, Rogers, who had signed off on a cease-fire without substantial verification provisions, took the heat of the uproar in public opinion. His failure furnished the White House a full-fledged opportunity to charge into the breach.

Within a month there was a crisis. It was not the one that might have been expected. The Suez remained relatively quiet while Jordan descended into turmoil. A splinter group of the Palestine Liberation Organization (PLO) attempted to hijack several jet airliners on September 6, then another three

303

days later, forcing some planes to fly to an airfield in Jordan, blowing up one of them. The faction, the Popular Front for the Liberation of Palestine (PFLP) led by George Habash, seems to have been trying to provoke a confrontation between the PLO and the Jordanian government of King Hussein. There was also a sizable force of Iraqi troops in Jordan and some question about which side they would support if it came to fighting. Hussein played for time.

The PFLP terrorists attempted to hijack an El Al flight just out of London. An Israeli security agent shot a male hijacker and his female companion was subdued. The El Al plane returned to London where the woman hijacker, Leila Khaled, was arrested. Within a day the PFLP struck back, taking over a British BOAC jet outbound from London on Monday, September 7. It too was forced to fly to Dawson's Field, near the town of Zerqa, Jordan, about twenty-five miles northeast of Amman. Together with the Swissair and TWA planes they already held, the hijackers had three aircraft and 475 hostages. Their demand was that all Palestinians imprisoned in Israel, the United States, West Germany, Switzerland, and Great Britain be released. That included 3,000 prisoners in Israel alone.

Washington had been expecting trouble in Jordan between the government and Palestinians. As early as June the United States embassy in Amman was authorized to send dependents home. Through the WSAG, Kissinger ordered preparation of contingency plans for a crisis in Amman. One paper Kissinger sent the President in July was a Hal Saunders memo warning that greater PLO freedom of action would bring more incidents in the Jordan Valley and compromise the "international credibility" of Hussein's Hashemite monarchy. In August, immediately after the Suez cease-fire violations, Kissinger ordered NSSM-93, a crash study of the implications of giving the Israelis Shrike antiradar missiles to counter the UAR's Soviet-supplied air defenses. There was no Jordan NSSM. When the PFLP hijacked the planes, Nixon privately told Kissinger the crisis should be used as a pretext to crush the PLO in Jordan, then called an ad hoc meeting in his Oval Office. Kissinger activated the WSAG machinery on September 9 for what turned out to be seventeen consecutive days of crisis meetings.

At the first session of the Washington Special Action Group, Kissinger's intention was to signal that the United States had serious intentions in Jordan. Nixon ordered the aircraft carrier *Independence* to a point off the Lebanese coast; a flight of C-130 medium transports moved to Incirlik, in Turkey, in readiness for any evacuation of Americans from Amman. Military readiness was such that it would take forty-eight hours to dispatch a brigade on call in Germany or seventy-two to send the 82nd Airborne Division. Kissinger asked for preliminary alert measures. Naval forces scheduled to sail for the Mediterranean were accelerated, including both a carrier group and a Marine amphibious unit.

Kissinger records that his differences with Bill Rogers came into focus on September 11, when the hijackers released a group of eighty-eight hostages. They were evacuating the planes and wiring them to blow up. Secretary Rogers advised that calming the crisis might help solve it.

Meanwhile, Hussein approached the United States for help and inquired as to the intentions of the Israelis. Kissinger at first refused to speak in their behalf, but a few nights later he would be talking to Israel's Foreign Minister Yitzhak Rabin on behalf of the Jordanians. Kissinger also took the lead, at WSAG on the evening of September 15; when it became known in Washington that Hussein intended to move against the PLO at daybreak, Kissinger help shaped the group consensus in favor of augmenting U.S. forces in the area as rapidly and threateningly as possible. On the sixteenth he ordered detailed planning for the contingencies of military aid to Hussein, intervention solely to conduct an evacuation of Americans, acquiescence in Israeli air or ground strikes, or U.S. air or ground intervention in favor of the Jordanian royal government. Kissinger notes Nixon's preference for the last, forceful option.

Existing accounts of the Jordanian crisis fail to focus enough attention on the role of Richard Nixon. This was the President who, in 1969, had ordered European plumed helmets and dress uniforms for the White House police only to have them quickly laughed out of use.

Nixon's characteristic warlike posturing continued through a weekend at Camp David in which he held out for the most belligerent forms of action. The crisis terminated in a sequence of three NSC meetings held on consecutive days, very unusual for Nixon at this stage of his term. Most extraordinary of all was the President's performance on Sunday evening, September 20, after returning from Camp David. By then Hussein's troops were fighting the PLO while Syrian, not Iraqi, combat units were invading Jordan and an Israeli intervention threatened. Nixon repeatedly ordered military alert measures and even unilateral actions. Speaking for the WSAG consensus, Kissinger would have opposed unilateral action, but the President came around by himself. Nixon did order the WSAG into his Oval Office for a twenty-minute talk about toughness, stressing that Dr. Kissinger would be speaking for him as events unfolded. Two hours later Kissinger and Sisco stumbled through the bowels of the Old Executive Office Building to find the presidential bowling alley, a feature Eisenhower had installed. Kissinger reported on alert measures as the President stood in his shirt sleeves holding a bowling ball.

Twenty minutes later the President strode into Kissinger's own office, sans ball but with his coat *and* tie. That night Kissinger and Sisco repeatedly talked to Yitzhak Rabin, who asked how the United States would react to an Israeli air attack. Nixon agreed to replace any aircraft lost and try to prevent Soviet interference. Kissinger called a midnight WSAG meeting and asked NSC staffers Hal Saunders and Richard Kennedy to make suitable arrangements. By 5:35 the next morning Henry was back on the phone with Nixon, who called to state his approval for an Israeli ground offensive into Jordan. An NSC meeting early in the morning on September 21 qualified that to approval in principle, and attached a few conditions.

Fortunately the question of intervention soon became moot as the Syrian forces halted, then withdrew. Nixon got conclusive intelligence in the afternoon of September 23. Hussein's Jordanian troops bested the PLO, who finally moved their center of operations to Lebanon. The hostages were released. By the end of "Black September," which is what the Palestinians came to call the Jordanian crisis, the secretary of state was being excluded from decisions on the Middle East as he already was from much else.

Just as the pace began to build in the Black September crisis, U-2 pictures of base facilities at the port of Sienfuegos, Cuba, disturbed Washington. Once he had photos in hand, Henry went to see the President. Nixon was in conference on domestic affairs with John Ehrlichman. Henry charged into the office of Chief of Staff Harry Robbins Haldeman and announced he had to see the President *immediately*.

Haldeman looked up; he found Kissinger bearing a thick file that quickly opened on his desk. Kissinger exhibited the Sienfuegos pictures.

"Bob, look at this," Kissinger began. "Well? . . . Well!"

"Well, what?" came the rejoinder.

The photographs showed soccer fields under construction along with other buildings in a supposed base area. Henry had convinced himself, mistakenly, that Cubans were interested only in baseball and do not play soccer.

Kissinger declared, "Those soccer fields could mean war, Bob."

"Why?"

"Cubans play baseball. Russians play soccer."

Nixon was predictably upset, especially on September 18, when careful analysis confirmed the first impressions, as Henry reported to the President in a memo. Nixon's first reaction was to ask Dr. Kissinger to discover what the United States could do to boycott nations dealing with Cuba, what the CIA could do to irritate Castro, and "most important, what actions we can take, covert or overt, to put missiles in Turkey—or a sub base in the Black Sea—anything that will give us some trading stock." The matter came up at the NSC meeting on the morning of September 23. Rogers appeared to champion damping down any Cuban confrontation; he would have gone further than the President, but held back until after the November elections. The State recommendation at WSAG was for Rogers to have a quiet talk with Andrei Gromyko in New York during the next session of the UN General Assembly.

From the NSC meeting came orders for more planning. The contingencies were mining Sienfuegos's harbor, blockade of Cuba, tailing Soviet ships, and removal of all restraints applied to contain the Cuban exile groups in the United States. Siding effectively with Rogers, Nixon readily prevented any action. Kissinger found the options Nixon himself had proposed in an initial note also to be "time-wasting."

Kissinger disagreed and took his dissent to H. R. Haldeman. Kissinger warned that Nixon had not faced the public relations issue of how, when there came a crisis in November, the administration was going to explain what it had done in September.

Nixon overruled the appeal. Dr. Kissinger convened the WSAG in the Situation Room the day after the NSC meeting. The group included U. Alexis Johnson from State, David Packard for the Pentagon, Admiral Thomas Moorer for the Joint Chiefs, and Dick Helms for the CIA. They tried to develop press guidance for the eventuality that the Sienfuegos base might become public while Nixon was away on the European trip. The WSAG decision to say as little as possible was overturned by an error—a DOD press spokesman mistakenly supplied a full description of the Sienfuegos developments when asked about early reports of a problem with Cuba.

Soviet Ambassador Dobrynin returned to Washington at this point, having been on leave for seven weeks. He called in the evening of September 24 for an appointment with Nixon, who refused because he could not see the Russian and remain silent about Cuba. Instead, Kissinger received Dobrynin in the West Wing Map Room the next morning. As they talked the Pentagon spokesman was spilling the beans about Sienfuegos. Seeing the news emerge, Nixon turned tough instantly, ordering Admiral Moorer to send a destroyer to cruise near Sienfuegos, and authorized Kissinger to challenge the Russians publicly.

Kissinger went to the East Room at midafternoon, where he threw down the gauntlet. The United States was watching naval activity in the Caribbean very carefully. Two hours later Dr. Kissinger met Dobrynin again. They had an exploratory exchange after Kissinger started out on the perennial subject of a United States-Soviet summit. Kissinger made his unhappiness quite clear.

Nixon left for his European visit as scheduled. In the interval the pot boiled as the press speculated. When the President returned, Dobrynin was ready with a positive reply on Sienfuegos. On October 9, Henry got back to Dobrynin with a written definition of a "base" worked out with his JCS liaison, Navy Captain Rembrandt C. Robinson. Through State Department channels, Ambassador Jacob D. Beam also made certain inquiries about Sienfuegos in Moscow, answered by a Soviet official release through TASS on October 13. Nixon himself saw Gromyko at the White House on October 22, while Kissinger went up to New York to see Dobrynin at the Soviet UN mission.

In the press of daily business few noticed a significant fact about U.S. actions during the crisis: They had been almost entirely carried out by Henry Kissinger. Both at the level of diplomacy with Soviet officials, and at that of spokesman for American policy, at his background news conferences, the national security adviser acted in place of the secretary of state. Bill Rogers had *no* discernible role in the Sienfuegos crisis.

An equally troublesome aspect of the crisis was confinement of information to a small group selected by Nixon's gatekeeper. For example, "Rem" Robinson showed his service boss, Chief of Naval Operations Elmo R. Zumwalt, a draft paper on Soviet bases in Cuba. Zumwalt got a peek because Kissinger knew from Robinson that the Navy was talking to Laird and to the Chairman of the JCS about not permitting Cuban bases. Zumwalt insisted on this as soon as he saw the U-2 pictures. In any case, Admiral Zumwalt saw the paper, made a few comments, and Captain Robinson left, to return a few days later with a revised paper. The problem was that in the meantime Henry had given the paper to Dobrynin as an aide-mémoire on October 9. The Navy chief believes that there were flaws in the definition of a "base" that was used in the paper.

State had difficulty getting any information at all. No one there had access to the exchange of assurances that had occurred in August. The responsible intelligence officer learned when he read of them in Kissinger's memoirs. So did WSAG members, who last met on this subject on October 6, cleared for Top Secret but kept from knowing some of the things Kissinger wrote for his reading public. In January 1972, Kissinger signed a directive for NSSM-144, an interagency study of Soviet naval deployments to the Caribbean that was to be chaired by the State Department's Soviet expert Raymond Garthoff. Even this official policy review by the responsible departments was not allowed access to the full Sienfuegos record. The NSSM, completed in March, turned into a farce for lack of that critical information.

The ambiguous understandings of the Cuban situation rebounded to the detriment of the United States nine years later, when an arms control treaty was up for ratification before the Senate, and the Soviet submarine visits became for some a reason for opposing it. Had more eyes seen the understandings of 1970, including those of naval persons and professional diplomats, it would have been useful. To the degree this became impossible owing to Kissinger's methods, he bears a share of the responsibility for what happened to détente. Indeed Kissinger's methods would impact upon every issue to come before the Nixon White House.

The Kissinger management technique actually bore a certain resemblance to Lyndon Johnson's, though perhaps LBJ's acts of contrition after his explosions went further than Henry's. Henry had a nicely honed sense of humor; whereas LBJ's humor almost always came at the expense of others, Kissinger could be self-deprecatory. He drew on humor in first establishing relations, not only with the NSC principals but with his own staff and the lower-level interlocutors from other parts of the bureaucracy. With each person, Henry would attempt to create an aura of intimacy, a suggestion they were privy to his innermost thinking. They had no hint they were being told just what Kissinger thought they wanted to hear, or just as much as he thought he could get away with. The way information seemed to flow in Kissinger's time gave him the widest latitude in which to maneuver.

Kissinger's life was made public far more than that of any of his predecessors; indeed here was the direct antithesis of Sidney Souers's advice on the passion for anonymity. Henry worked the press assiduously, on the phone, in his office, at group meetings, in private tête-à-têtes or small dinners. Some of the columnists were like ambassadors of a foreign potentate, favored with regular Kissinger meetings, almost as dependable as Dobrynin's back channel. Kissinger was an Eligible Bachelor who lived in a town house near Rock Creek Park. His fifteen-year marriage to the German-Jewish Ann Fleischer had ended in 1964. Kissinger often visited his children Elizabeth and David and, for the first few months he was in Washington, maintained a pace of visits every weekend to his parents' home on Washington Heights in New York City.

Increasingly Henry was seen on the Washington social circuit. As Nixon spent a great deal of time in California at San Clemente, Kissinger was seen out West too. His dating began to attract notice in society columns and became a recurrent subject of media speculation. On one occasion during the secret Vietnam negotiations, Kissinger used this as a ploy to cover one of his own secret meetings with delegates from Hanoi. Nixon used the attention Henry got to deflect interest from more sensitive issues, though the President was not above envying Kissinger's performance. Nixon once complained to subordinates that in planning the seating at big dinners, Kissinger was too often placed next to the most beautiful woman in the room.

In stark contrast was Kissinger's unavailability to Congress. He occasionally talked on the phone, or privately met, with top legislative leaders, briefed them at pro forma consultations before major military actions or on the occasion of big diplomatic agreements, and once in a while informally briefed larger congressional groups. Kissinger would go to the Hill, incognito as it were, a couple of times a year and might entertain a congressional group in the OEOB maybe once a year. In some of the sessions that did occur the Congress was misinformed on key issues, as will be seen in the cases of the Vietnam peace agreement and the first SALT agreements with the Soviets.

Kissinger's relationship with the White House chief of staff could best be described as prickly. H. R. Haldeman appeared to have little desire for friendship. He insisted on absolute loyalty to the President. He was highly observant, often critical, and would regularly pass on to the President any perception that Kissinger had weakened. On the other hand, Haldeman knew that Nixon had to be protected from some of his wilder orders, and afforded Kissinger access to the Oval Office. Haldeman could also add weight to Henry's views in transmitting them to the President.

Kissinger recognized the importance of a link with Haldeman, but it was Al Haig who exploited it. Haig got as close to Haldeman as anyone could, trading gossip and advice, coming back to the NSC staff with a fund of

West Wing stories to retail. Haldeman's enthusiasm encouraged Nixon to become closer to Haig as well. Though Haldeman had no hankering for a piece of national security turf, he was capable of inflicting annoyances. He needled White House staff endlessly over such issues as the wine and cheese served on official occasions.

John Mitchell, Nixon's attorney general, had been the President's New York law partner in his later pre-White House years. Mitchell's closeness to Nixon seemed unshakable, even in the face of Mitchell's wife, who emerged as a player with press contacts of her own. Nixon used Mitchell, at least as far as Kissinger is concerned, as an observer who would report back with accounts of Kissinger's composure, his resiliency, and the like. Mitchell saw a good deal of Kissinger because Nixon widened Justice Department participation in the NSC subcommittee system, and Kissinger chaired most of those subcommittees.

Officials who succeeded in their dealings with the Nixon-Kissinger NSC apparat, like Joe Sisco or Philip Habib, were men who forged their own links into the White House. Spurgeon Keeny, for example, who often took charge of ACDA policy business because Gerard Smith would be with the SALT delegation, became a very effective player due to his closeness to successive NSC specialists in his field. Best off of all were those with no connection to Bill Rogers.

But Kissinger forged ahead and acquired considerable momentum. In an interview he gave Italian journalist Oriana Fallaci in November 1972, Henry invoked the image of the lone cowboy. "Americans admire that enormously," Kissinger said. "Americans admire the cowboy leading the caravan alone astride his horse, the cowboy entering the village or city alone on his horse. Without even a pistol, maybe, because he doesn't go in for shooting. He acts, that's all; aiming at the right spot at the right time. A Wild West tale, if you like."

One can hardly be surprised, given Henry's stated view, that he ended up in conflict with the bureaucracy. Nixon's eventual solution was to give Henry a concurrent appointment as secretary of state, the only individual ever to combine that post with service as national security adviser. By then James R. Schlesinger was secretary of defense, and was just as implacable a foe of Kissinger as had been Laird. Giving Henry State actually weighed him down in the bureaucratic battle.

The Kissinger NSC staff functioned as a well-oiled mechanism. Area specialists followed the issues in detail, forwarding paperwork to office chiefs who dealt with Kissinger. Nixon consumed the papers, underlining and annotating them, sending them back for action. Cover memos of ten to twenty pages on some arcane NSSM were not unknown. Kissinger saw his NSC function as providing the President with the full range of choices on every matter, ensuring the implementation of his decisions "in the spirit the president intended," and giving the President his advice.

To carry out his functions Kissinger ran a staff of about 100, gradually rising to 150 by the end of his tenure. Approximately a third of this crew were staff professionals, the rest support personnel. Budget allocations rose steadily, to over $2.8 million for Kissinger's last full year.

Not only did the NSC staff grow so big it spilled onto the OEOB fourth floor, its support elements now fully deserved the appellation "secretariat," which had been an exaggeration in Ike's time, used to describe tiny central staff elements of the NSC components. Supervising the secretariat became a full-time function for the NSC executive secretary, who throughout Kissinger's time was Jeanne W. Davis, incidentally the highest-ranking woman on the staff.

After Cambodia the staff was also largely free of dissenters. The exception was "Win" Lord, who had moved over from the Pentagon, ironically enough, on the recommendation of Mort Halperin. Thirty-three at the time, Lord was a fast writer and contributed to the joint paper arguing against the invasion. Just as he took over the job of personal assistant to Kissinger, Lord became embroiled in controversy as it was revealed Americans had been killed in the war in Laos. Lord's postmortem established that the Kissinger staff had failed to coordinate certain key statements between White House and Pentagon spokesmen. Acutely aware also of the anti-war opposition, Winston nevertheless allowed himself to be won over by Kissinger.

Lord stayed with the NSC staff to become Henry's alter ego, the man who kept the schedules and held the documents, who took the notes at all the secret diplomatic encounters. Lord also made sure the lighting was right, the wine appropriate, and so forth. Bill Gulley at the White House Military Office was annoyed by Winston's continuing complaints—about the food at the White House Mess, the music in Kissinger's car, even that the driver didn't comb his hair the right way.

Lord, husband of the novelist Betty Bao Lord, continued to speak his mind, opposing the mining of Haiphong and other enterprises, but only within the confines of the offices of the NSC staff. In many ways Lord became indispensable to Kissinger; he compiled the briefing books for the secret trips to Peking and Moscow, not to mention all the others, and kept track of who on each mission was cleared to know about each aspect of the trip. That was no mean feat: on the secret China trip there were three distinct levels of clearance; on a later expedition there were four. Lord helped Kissinger figure out the hidden meanings behind various Chinese gestures and, with translator Vernon Walters, was the only American with Kissinger at the secret Paris negotiations on Vietnam who possessed complete knowledge of the history of those talks. Henry valued Lord enough that when he became secretary of state, he appointed Win Lord as director of his Policy Planning Staff.

Lord got close enough to Kissinger to do some speechwriting, but the main speechwriter was Henry's own protégé, Peter W. Rodman. As a young student at Harvard College, where Kissinger maintained contact with the undergraduates, Rodman served as research assistant on Henry's NATO book, *The Troubled Partnership*. Rodman wrote what Dr. Kissinger considered one of the outstanding undergraduate theses of his tenure at Harvard. Peter had gone on to Oxford, then law school, then joined Henry on the NSC staff, where he helped organize Kissinger's paper. Colorful where many others on the NSC staff seemed drab, John F. Lehman, Jr., had actually lived a life many dream of: a Philadelphia boy, in childhood acquainted with actor George Kelly and Grace, later to become Princess Grace of Monaco. Though employed as Dick Allen's assistant, Lehman survived Allen's demise, becoming important enough to NSC work that in April 1973, when Lehman had a job offer at the Pentagon, and Henry had just learned from a presidential lawyer how serious was Nixon's involvement in Watergate, the President's gatekeeper refused to let him leave the NSC staff without its congressional liaison.

Lehman was intimately involved in the maneuvers in Congress over passage of the annual defense appropriations, foreign aid bills, and other legislation. The job of congressional liaison was to grease wheels and make things happen, but Lehman acquired a reputation as a hard-nosed fighter ill disposed to compromise.

The Kissinger staff became so large there were many, many more staffers who had minor, but important roles. They included Sven Kraemer, son of the celebrated Fritz. On Southeast Asia and China there were John Holdridge and Dick Smyser, while John D. Negroponte specialized on the Paris negotiations. Walter Slocombe headed the SALT staff, succeeded by Philip Odeen, with such specialists as Barry E. Carter and Jan L. Lodal. Viron P. Vaky handled Latin America, including the negotiations with Panama over revision of the Canal Treaty. Wayne Smith followed Larry Lynn in charge of systems analysis, later to be transmuted into something called net assessment. Economist C. Fred Bergsten held sway over international economics, encouraging Nixon to take the United States dollar off the gold standard. Passing through on special programs were such academics as Wilfrid L. Kohl and Lynn E. Davis, or military men like Marine Lieutenant Colonel Robert C. McFarlane. On Africa was Chester A. Crocker, whom Haig hired after Cambodia without even a perfunctory interview with Henry. Haig also got a friend of many years, retired Colonel Richard T. Kennedy, to replace Halperin with the title deputy assistant to the President for planning. Military aides included Air Force Colonel Jack N. Merritt and Navy Commander Jonathan T. Howe, succeeded late in the administration by Bud McFarlane, back for a real run at an NSC job.

The NSC staff continued to include a mixture of professional talent, about half people hired from outside government, and half detailees from the federal bureaucracy, including military men, diplomats, and intelligence officers. One CIA detailee in 1972, for example, bore the unlikely name Valerie Neveraskas. Dick Smyser was a detailee from State, and Jonathan

Howe one from the Navy. The detailees represented the difference between the size of the NSC staff, even in the expanded Kissinger format, and the real work load Nixon demanded for total control of foreign policy. There was never enough manpower to go around; control always remained imperfect (indeed Nixon continually harped on a succession of snafus in one area or another). Henry could prattle on to the journalists about implementation by the NSC, but in fact one of the favorite notations on NSC staff routing slips was "OBE"—overtaken by events. That notation had not previously figured much in NSC work.

The President set the work load for the Kissinger staff. It was *his* staff, Kissinger worked for him, and so did Haldeman and Ehrlichman and all their minions. Richard Nixon was plenty capable of generating work for anybody, as the annotated texts of his daily news summaries and issue briefings amply attest. Nixon had a voracious appetite for this material, going through dozens of pages of prebriefs before every news conference and hundreds of pages of press summaries every week. Every place that something struck him, Nixon scribbled a note in the margin. Haldeman arranged that when the President finished with each summary, Nixon's notes would be translated into directives for the appropriate officials. A given day's summary might yield a dozen or more of these little missives, many of them for Kissinger. Someday the full record of these annotations will do much to document the Nixon presidency. At one time, when aide Alexander P. Butterfield had the duty of compiling note directives, such orders were familiarly called Butterfieldgrams.

In this space it is impossible to do more than give the flavor of Nixon's summary notations and the kinds of memos distilled from them. This was Nixon actually commenting on the news, telling his men what nuance to evoke. Here the President commented on specific reporters and news media, gave instructions to Haldeman or others for specific actions, or merely made some opaque, cryptic statement that was passed along to the named individual. It could amount to mystification from on high, as in September 1969 when Mac Bundy made a public statement urging Nixon to act unilaterally to slow down nuclear weapons development as a gesture for arms control. Nixon then addressed Kissinger: "K—!! Here we go again."

Nixon's annotations also provide a unique insight into the President's intentions, his private opinions, his means of exhortation with key subordinates, a whole range of issues. A few examples will have to suffice. In March 1969, just after Nixon's decision to build the Safeguard ABM, a Sindlinger survey showed early support for the move. Nixon noted, "Get this to some of the faint hearts!" The same news summary noted a senator's comment that he might vote for ABM if the United States and Soviet Union worked together on a "world shield against accidental missile attack." Nixon's annotation, addressed to Kissinger, was "K— Tell him RN is *for* this."

This summary also reported a leak, that the administration "at the highest levels" was considering air strikes against North Vietnam that would be "designed" to show "the war will take a very tough new direction if the Paris talks collapse." Nixon's comment: *"Good!"*

In a September 1969 summary, press aides reported the Nigerian government was considering a cease-fire in the Biafran war. Nixon's note to Kissinger: "Isn't this the time to move in and get some credit?"

On September 15 the news summary opened with Vietnam and reported Mike Mansfield criticizing the administration on ordering certain B-52 bombing. Nixon first opined, "Bombing of N.V.Nam did not lead to more conciliatory attitude by Hanoi." The President then instructed Henry: "K—A columnist should write this as my conclusion."

Journalist Joe Kraft published a piece on September 16 that discussed resignations from Kissinger's staff, with vague hints that all might not be well. Nixon's note: "K—Did anyone on your staff talk to Kraft on these lines? Allen? Halperin? Check [deputy assistant secretary of defense Robert] Ellsworth."

A structure for arguments to offer both liberals and conservatives on supporting a SALT agreement followed Nixon's note to Al Haig, in the margin of a June 1972 summary. "When Henry gets back tell him," Nixon began the instruction.

On February 5, 1970, the news summary contained an item pertaining to the State Department, an interview describing Bill Rogers in glowing terms. Nixon addressed a remark to Haldeman, Ehrlichman, Kissinger, and others, "McClosky [the State spokesman] is no friend of ours but he does a brilliant job of building up his boss. It is this kind of P.R.-oriented Press man which we simply don't have on our staff."

Typical of presidential exhortations is a marginal comment on the June 20, 1972, summary. By then Vietnam, where the North Vietnamese were conducting a sustained conventional offensive testing Vietnamization, dominated the news. Reacting to assertions that South Vietnamese claims of success were exaggerated, Nixon approvingly underlined a comment that "Thieu made good on his promise to hold An Loc," then wrote Haig: "Al— *This* sounds like propaganda?"

Several of the slim selection of national security documents thus far declassified suggest that Nixon used to annotate his secret documents in the same fashion. Former NSC staff confirm that it was quite common for memos to come back encrusted with presidential marginalia. This source remains an unopened window into the past.

Nixon's direct management of the public relations line was a consequence of his lack of trust in the bureaucracy and desire for personal control of foreign relations. There could be no collegial OCB or dynamic VIG; this President tried to do the work all by himself. The President's secret instructions were hidden, but his fear and hatred of leaks was well known and constantly reiterated, including in a governmentwide order in the fall of 1969, and in at least one NSDM on SALT. Nixon's authority backed FBI national security wiretaps from the spring of 1969; the President himself spent time speculating on who the leakers were, actively suspecting such culprits as Melvin Laird or Mort Halperin. Nixon in a rage ordered polygraphing the entire Washington bureaucracy after one leak he considered egregious, but, as we have seen, he could also coolly compliment the news summaries when he saw his leaks going his way. It was as disingenuous then as in subsequent administrations to blame leaks for paralysis of policy.

Not that there weren't plenty of leaks: Evaluators later tabulated forty national security leaks in 1969, seventy-one in 1970, then eighty-two in just the first half of 1971. In his own memoirs Nixon enumerates ten of the most painful during the spring of 1969. The leaks amplified Nixon's disdain for the press, which attained great heights. In January 1970, Nixon estimated to his senior staff that 65 percent of the press corps began with a negative attitude toward his administration. His theory about reporters, Nixon commented to Haldeman in June 1971, was that "treating them with considerably more contempt is in the long run a more productive policy." Still, for every story that leaked there were three the President put out, and for every leak, as the annotated news summaries demonstrate conclusively, Nixon evolved strategies for countering or measures to limit damage.

In a private note on February 3, 1970, Haldeman recorded the President's thoughts on leaking as really "very sophisticated," even to realizing that sometimes they were not too harmful, or that it was undesirable to run too tight a ship, "which would be necessary to avoid all leaks." Nixon warned he would react by refusing to talk about things that might leak, eventually by eliminating the meetings where those things might be talked about.

Most of this "fresh note," as Haldeman called it, sounded as if he were trying to capture one of Nixon's long monologues. Haldeman ended with an ominous hint: "We are, therefore, treading on very thin ice. If anything leaks there will be no more meetings. The President is perfectly capable of making the decisions alone, and prefers to do so; but he is willing to bring people in and occasionally he recognizes that to see them helps."

Nixon's tendency was inevitably to hold the cards ever closer to his own breast. That was in perfect harmony with Kissinger's own proclivity. Information became a real problem in the Nixon administration, including in its NSC machinery. As in classic theories of bureaucratic politics, maneuvers to affect information came to the fore. The most audacious of them was nothing less than the planting of a spy in the White House. For a time, this espionage was successful in ferreting out the secrets of the Kissinger NSC. The authors of this spy effort were the Joint Chiefs of Staff. They were spying on the President of the United States.

The Joint Chiefs of Staff spy operation unraveled at the end of 1971, revealed in the crisis of the Indian-Pakistani war over the independence of Bangladesh. The administration's public line was that it was neutral, evenhanded, but Nixon privately inclined to favor Pakistan, which had been helping the

United States with the People's Republic of China, as will be seen shortly. In any event, there was a serious discrepancy between the administration's public position and its actual one. In the public posturing, Nixon went so far as to invite NBC News television crews to film part of a December 6 National Security Council meeting. The President and Secretary of State Rogers spoke during the filmed NSC segment.

The public relations appears to have offended the sensibilities of the NSC spy, Charles Radford, already laboring under the burden of his own actions. He had once been attached to the United States mission in India. The man approached syndicated columnist Jack Anderson, explained what he objected to, and provided over a dozen secret documents to back up his charges. The documents included summaries of discussion of relevant WSAG meetings. Anderson met the man in Washington's Chinatown for a restaurant dinner and received four manila envelopes of materials. On December 14 he began publishing a series of columns, including verbatim quotation of some of Kissinger's comments.

When Jack Anderson's column appearing December 14 contained quotations from the WSAG transcripts, Al Haig called Ehrlichman to invite the domestic affairs chief to supervise an investigation into the leak. Conveniently Ehrlichman had created the Plumbers unit that summer to do special investigations. David Young, codirector and former Kissinger aide, was at least familiar with the national security business. Thus Haig brought the Plumbers in to find the leak.

No big investigation proved necessary. The leak was no mystery to Radford's boss Rear Admiral Robert O. Welander, official liaison between the NSC staff and the Joint Chiefs. Radford was often lent to the NSC staff as note taker, and he had been tasked to pass on copies of NSC material he saw to the JCS by Rembrandt Robinson, Welander's predecessor as liaison. Welander instructed him to continue the spying. Over a period of more than a year, by his own count, Radford passed thousands of documents to the Chiefs. The take included notes of Kissinger's secret conversations with leaders in Peking, material on Southeast Asia, and the WSAG India-Pakistan material. Some of the documents, but by no means all of them, later arrived in the regular paper flow from the NSC staff to the JCS liaison office. The Chiefs thus had an extra measure of knowledge about Kissinger, much as Henry did about Secretary of Defense Melvin Laird thanks to the wiretap the FBI placed on Laird's military aide.

When Admiral Welander heard of the Anderson column with its WSAG quotations, he went right away to Radford, who was in effect marched down to see the Plumbers. Polygraphed, Radford admitted to stealing NSC documents. Asked whom he had given them to, the yeoman tearfully admitted they had gone to the Joint Chiefs. There was consternation in the White House, particularly after Welander confirmed the relevant aspects of Radford's story. Ehrlichman and Haldeman made an official report to Nixon on December 21, and the next day Ehrlichman and Young grilled Welander for more details. Kissinger, not told until December 23, promptly fired Welander after trying to appear unconcerned when Ehrlichman informed him of the espionage. Later Kissinger appeared enraged that Nixon refused to take any disciplinary action against Admiral Thomas Moorer, JCS Chairman and presumably the instigator of the entire business.

The Radford affair marked a low in the relations between Nixon and his national security adviser. This time the President wondered about Henry's mood swings. According to Ehrlichman, who spoke to the President on the phone, "Nixon wondered aloud if Henry needed psychiatric care." Al Haig spoke up in Kissinger's favor, trying to convince Ehrlichman the President needed Henry. This moment passed, together with Nixon's halfhearted chop at Kissinger, but it is significant that Haig became closer to the President rather quickly from that day on.

Admiral Rembrandt Robinson came to Ehrlichman's office for interrogation on the morning of December 27, 1971. In full uniform with all his gold braid, Robinson denied everything.

Nixon ordered Yeoman Radford to be sent where he could do no further harm. He was posted to Salem, Oregon. Chief of Naval Operations Elmo Zumwalt thought the yeoman ought to be court-martialed and said so to Tom Moorer, who replied he had recommended that but had been turned down.

Admiral Zumwalt himself does not believe the Radford affair was a JCS spy operation. Zumwalt recalls that Moorer referred to a stream of NSC documents the Chairman received that were not to be shown to Secretary Laird, things necessary for the JCS to do their own jobs. Whatever the truth of that claim, Zumwalt marked the episode down against Henry: "I was all the way up to speed by that time on the way Henry's duplicity left booby traps everywhere."

The Radford affair became public knowledge in January 1974, leading to a hearing before the Senate Committee on Government Operations, one of four times in its first forty years the NSC would be a focus of congressional inquiry. Rembrandt Robinson would not be available to testify. Ironically, only a few days after another NSC-masterminded operation, the May 1972 mining of Haiphong, Robinson was tragically killed in the Gulf of Tonkin. The short, stocky admiral, by then commander of a cruiser-destroyer group in the thick of the action, perished when a helicopter he was riding fell into the sea. As for Henry Kissinger, despite the importance of this affair for his own relations with the President, and despite the official inquiries that flowed from it, the Radford episode receives thirty-eight words among the two thousand eight hundred pages of the keeper's memoirs. Henry Alfred Kissinger stormed the crest of Policy Hill, only to discover precipices on all sides.

THE ILLUSION OF PEACE

▲▲▲

Salvador Allende Gossens, winner of the plurality in the September 1970 election in Chile, was the Socialist leader of the Unidad Popular (UP) popular front movement. Allende had been presidential candidate of the Chilean Left in the 1964 elections as well; then, LBJ had allowed the CIA to intervene, spending more than $3 million to elect Eduardo Frei. Allende's first-round plurality in 1970 proved even more bothersome to Richard Nixon, who was especially vehement in his denunciations of the Chilean Socialist.

Kissinger says he did not focus on Chilean affairs until well into 1970, that in the first year he remained but dimly aware of the danger. His major exposure came through the 40 Committee, the NSC subcommittee Henry chaired that dealt with secret intelligence matters. That unit discussed Chile once in April 1969, then not again until March 1970. Well aware of the run-up to the election, the committee met on a proposal to invest in elections much as had been done in 1964. State's Latin America bureau argued that all money for election finance had to come from within Chile, a bid to respect the tenet of nonintervention in internal affairs. Dr. Kissinger thought that approach might make for a fine college course paper, but for Chile policy it meant running the "kind of unacceptable risk that policymakers are hired to avoid."

Point of entry for the 40 Committee, so named for its creation by means of NSDM-40, was a joint proposal submitted in December 1969 by the embassy and CIA station in Santiago, Chile. The proposed campaign was not going to be the massive kind that had supported Frei in 1964: As early as April 1969 the CIA had warned they needed to get going far in advance to pull major weight in the election, and no decision had been made then. Rather, Ambassador Edward M. Korry and CIA officials were pushing a last-minute "spoiling" operation that might complicate Allende's election but could by no means be decisive. Kissinger accuses the bureaucracy of a conspiracy to keep the problems in Chile from high-level attention, a delicate pact of silence by CIA and State bureaus that knew each other's arguments and preferred not to air them. In fact, it was precisely such a statement of differences that accompanied the "spoiling" operation proposal to the 40 Committee on March 25, 1970. The program called for only $135,000 and it was approved. In June the 40 Committee increased that by $300,000,

318

while another $400,000 went to other CIA covert actions in Chile. The money was funneled to political parties and candidates through prominent Chileans like Augustin Edwards, publisher of *El Mercurio,* a violently anti-Allende daily newspaper that had long been receiving CIA subsidies.

Under Chilean law no absolute majority meant that a final victor for the presidency would be chosen by vote of the legislature after an interval of fifty days. Kissinger describes Nixon after the election as beside himself, the Washington reaction as "stunned surprise." The 40 Committee met September 8 to decide what to do. They decided to ask Ambassador Korry for his assessment of the prospects for a military coup. Two days before the 40 Committee met to consider an action program, Henry cabled Korry on the back channel and asked his recommendations on feasible courses of action. Korry suggested a background news conference by a high Washington official, Kissinger's usual incarnation for the media. Kissinger claims that Ambassador Korry's prognosis was hopeful. Korry denies this.

It happens that Chilean publisher Augustin Edwards was good friends with Donald M. Kendall, chairman of the board of the Pepsi-Cola Corporation. Edwards came to Washington soon after the election to warn of the consequences of an Allende victory in the Chilean congress. Edwards stayed with Kendall. According to Kissinger, it was by chance that Kendall had an appointment with Nixon on September 14, to bring his father for a chat with the President. He took along Edwards, who bombarded Nixon, who summoned Kissinger and the other high priests to meet the next afternoon on Chile. It was mesmerization with a marginal program.

A conversation of less than fifteen minutes early in the afternoon of Tuesday, September 15, resulted in one of Nixon and Kissinger's biggest long-term problems, a problem with political and even legal ramifications. That Tuesday afternoon Nixon was with Kissinger, John Mitchell, and Richard Helms of the CIA, to whom he began a rapid-fire drumbeat of instructions, which Helms translated into scribbled notes on a pad, catching the central phrases or themes. "If I ever carried a marshal's baton out of the Oval Office," the CIA director later testified to a Senate committee, "it was that day."

What were Nixon's orders? Nothing less than to "get" Chile, to "make the economy scream" Helms delicately noted. The CIA was to put its best men on the job; Nixon was not concerned with the risks, was willing to spend $10 million, more if necessary, he only wanted results. The President further told Helms to keep the United States embassy out of it, in effect creating a secret "Track II" policy unknown to those responsible for the official ("Track I") United States policy. According to the Helms testimony, only assassination was ruled out, and that only because he himself put it out of his mind. According to a senior Helms deputy, Track II *did* involve CIA association with assassins, who went on to get weapons from the agency, and indeed went on to kill a top Chilean general. Track II was never revoked, the CIA told Congress; Kissinger claims he ended it a month later, but that "the CIA personnel in Chile apparently thought that the order applied only to [one group of plotters]; they felt they were free to continue."

Actually Nixon went little, if at all, beyond the position of his keeper of the keys. It was Kissinger who presided over three successive sessions of the 40 Committee through the summer and fall planning the Chile "spoiling" operation. Henry, after all, told that group on June 21, "I don't see why we need to stand by and watch a country go Communist due to the irresponsibility of its own people."

It was Kissinger again, in August 1970, who, having begun to distrust polls that showed Allende ahead, put Chile on the NSC Senior Review Group agenda. Henry went on to sign a study directive for NSSM-97, an interagency review of four alternatives ranging from normal relations to a CIA covert campaign to bring about the fall of Allende. The completed NSSM came before the Senior Review Group on October 17, and was the NSC subject for November 6. Kissinger claims that he favored the United States' assuming a "cool but correct" posture; this policy, using precisely those words, expressed in NSDM-93 on November 9, embodied a program of economic warfare against the Allende government, at that moment only *six days* in office.

The Nixon-Kissinger Chile policy attempted to prevent further financial assistance for that country, using United States influence to deny Chile credit, including loans from international financial institutions. While starving the Chilean economy, over the following three years the 40 Committee granted over $7 *million* in covert CIA funding for the anti-Allende opposition. Meanwhile, overtly the Nixon administration *tripled* its level of assistance to the Chilean military. The message at the Chilean political level was unmistakable. Kissinger's affirmation that the United States had nothing to do with the "conception, planning, and execution" of the September 11, 1973, coup by General Augusto Pinochet is true in only the narrowest sense, for Washington created the conditions for the coup.

For several years the Chile plot stewed on the back burner until Allende's end came. After he had become secretary of state, no longer beyond the reach of Congress, Kissinger was questioned under oath about some of these matters. Nixon too was obliged to respond to written interrogatories by a Senate investigating committee in order to avoid a subpoena, and to admit he had sought the downfall of Allende. Helms, who affirmed to the Senate that that had been Nixon's policy, simultaneously negated his own prior sworn testimony. The director of central intelligence ultimately found himself under indictment on charges of perjury and pleaded no contest. As Helms was vulnerable, so was Henry. Another time bomb, as Elmo Zumwalt liked to think of them, had begun to tick.

The friendly and evenhanded, peaceful, public policy toward Chile was an illusion. Indeed illusion became a hallmark of the Nixon-Kissinger technique, wheels within wheels, secret tracks of policy, back channels, silent emissaries. Nixon's first big diplomatic breakthrough, in 1971, featured exactly these techniques, when he sent Henry Kissinger off to make first contact in a gambit to change the course of Sino-American relations. The idea was to end decades of hostility between the United States and the People's Republic of China and forge a new opening with mainland China, Communist or not.

That idea was Nixon's, oddly enough, coming from a man often portrayed as fervidly against all the principles espoused by Peking. During his first trip as President to Europe, in February 1969, Nixon asked the French to convey news of his long-term intentions to Peking. Subtle hints, such as referring to China as the PRC, were inserted into the annual editions of the NSC foreign policy report. In fact, Nixon and Kissinger put their state of the world report to very good use in signaling Peking.

The Chinese sent a few signals of their own, responding relatively mildly to the invasions of Cambodia and Laos. Washington also began private discussions in February 1969 in Warsaw. American Ambassador Walter J. Stoessel ably conducted the informal talks to identify the differences between the two nations. The major ones centered on Taiwan, and the UN, where Peking wanted to assume the seat held by Taiwan.

Kissinger addressed the PRC question as early as February 5, 1969, when his NSSM-14 study directive provided for a paper that would review United States relations with both Chinas, the "nature of the Chinese Communist threat and intentions in Asia," comparison of American policy with those of other interested nations like the British and French, and a menu of alternative options with their costs and risks. Nixon continued to press. He had Kissinger put the bureaucracy to work on a list of actions possible solely on his own authority as President that could ease barriers to trade or other cultural exchanges with Peking. Kissinger divided these into three groups, recommending only the most minor ones be implemented before a Chinese response. In March 1970, Nixon took some of the measures; others he approved a few months later. On April 4, reading in his news summary of reports that Russia had made a compromise and pulled its troops back from the Chinese border, Nixon scribbled a note to Henry: "Possibly we should move up our China move." In October he used a meeting with Pakistani President Yahya Khan, a recipient of Chinese military aid, to activate a secret channel with Peking. A second intermediary was Rumania. On November 19 the NSC staff promulgated study directives for NSSM-106 and NSSM-107, respectively policy papers on China as a whole and on the thorny problem of UN admission. Three days later Nixon dictated a note to Henry ordering the NSC staff by itself to assemble a study of the UN question. Though the bureaucracy already had marching orders for a similar interagency paper, Nixon wanted it cut out of the study, to be done "without any notice to people who might leak."

In March 1971 the United States lifted its ban on travel to China. Coincidentally a national table tennis team was in Nagoya, Japan, playing in the Thirty-first World Table Tennis Championship. Out of the blue on April 6, Chinese officials invited the American team to visit the PRC. The pundits quipped it was "Ping-Pong diplomacy," but though the contacts might be informal they were taken very seriously in the White House. Suddenly, on April 27 the Pakistani ambassador visited Kissinger to deliver a message from Chou En-lai over the private channel. The Chinese premier stated a willingness to publicly receive in Peking a special envoy from the President.

The immediate issue in the White House became whom to send to Peking. Nixon felt that for the initiative to have any chance it had to be completely secret. He and Kissinger considered sending George Bush or Nelson Rockefeller, perhaps accompanied by Al Haig, or else Republican grand old man Thomas Dewey. Kissinger recounts that Bill Rogers's name never came up. Nixon says he himself suggested sending the secretary of state, but that "Kissinger rolled his eyes upward. I knew he would have opposed Rogers on personal grounds regardless, but in this case he had good policy reasons." A visit by the secretary of state could never be kept secret. Within a day or so the President had settled on his solution: Henry would make the trip.

Kissinger brushed up on his Ping-Pong game, practicing with Winston Lord. Not to appear too anxious, the White House delayed its official reply. Nixon and Kissinger got furious on April 29 when Secretary Rogers, who knew nothing of the secret planning, answered negatively in response to a news conference question on the prospects of a Nixon visit to Peking. Kissinger arranged to exchange further back-channel communications with the American ambassador to Pakistan over a Navy channel, through the local naval attaché. Later they switched to a less cumbersome CIA channel. Nixon walked out of a state dinner for Nicaraguan leader Anastasio Somoza Debayle to hear the news when Kissinger finally pinned down Peking on some dates. Nixon took Kissinger to the Lincoln Sitting Room of the White House and toasted the event with brandy.

Everyone went to considerable lengths to make the Peking trip truly secret. Vice President Spiro Agnew and Melvin Laird both wanted to make visits to Taiwan about the same time and had to be talked out of it. Bill Rogers had to be convinced that a mission carried out by the national security adviser would not eclipse the authoritative voice of the State Department. Kissinger, in retrospect, views the reluctance of the secretary of state sympathetically.

"It was painful enough," Kissinger writes, "to see me and the NSC staff dominate the policy process in Washington; it was harder still to accept the proposition that I might begin to intrude on the conduct of foreign policy overseas."

A control plane borrowed from the Tactical Air Command carried Kissinger on a trip across the Pacific to Vietnam, for talks with Nguyen Van Thieu, then on a swing down through Thailand, India, Pakistan, and on to Paris to speak with peace talks envoy David K. E. Bruce, actually the man who had been the first choice of both Nixon and Henry for this very mission but whose selection had been ruled out as too threatening for Peking. The secret portion of the trip began in Pakistan, where Kissinger was spirited onto a Pakistani Boeing and flown off to Peking. His immediate staff consisted of NSC specialists Win Lord, John Holdridge, and Dick Smyser, and Secret Service agents John D. Ready and Gary McLeod. Winston Lord was farthest forward in the jet when it crossed the Chinese border, technically becoming the first American official to enter Red China. Their mission had the codename Polo I. At one point Henry had to borrow shirts from Holdridge. Only subordinates Holdridge and Smyser were able to eat with chopsticks; Henry lost miserably at Ping-Pong when the Chinese set up a match for him, but he brought back the bacon in terms of assurances for Nixon that a Sino-American summit could be held successfully.

Because Henry had had to use a Pakistani plane, he had no communications with the White House while in China. Nixon insisted on an immediate report on Henry's return, which he got at San Clemente twenty minutes after Kissinger touched down at El Toro Marine Air Station. Nixon rewarded Henry with a return engagement, Polo II, a trip back with Colonel Ralph Albertazzie, pilot of *Air Force One,* flying one of his own presidential aircraft. Al Haig got a China trip too, in January 1972, doing an advance job in which they rehearsed every aspect of the summit pageantry.

For Polo II the mission was to work out in advance the agenda as well as the communiqué that would be issued from the summit itself. State's representative on that trip was former NSC staff specialist Al Jenkins, a Rostow veteran gone back to the department. Henry tried to give Jenkins a sense of participating without permitting him to attend key discussions, including drafting of the communiqué.

Richard Nixon made a week-long visit to the PRC from February 21 to 28, 1972. Bill Rogers went along, but was kept busy working on various aspects of protocol. Nixon kept the summitry to himself, attended by Kissinger and, at the staff level, John Holdridge and Win Lord. The summit affirmed that both sides continued to have the same differences they had had before, but it was historic in the symbolic sense; the United States ended the bitterly anti-Chinese legacy of the Korean War era. In the eyes of many observers, not least the media, Nixon chalked up credit for a big diplomatic breakthrough, in the sportive idiom he so favored, a "superplay." In the end the play was not that super. Bilateral trade failed to develop to any great degree, though cultural exchanges made some headway. It was left to Jimmy Carter to normalize relations, and that action was the one that incurred the real political cost of ending the cold war with China.

Kissinger's execution of the China mission shows what had clearly become his standard method. The national security adviser first opened up issues, inserting the wedge himself, pushing against the door, conducting early negotiations personally, then handing the matter on to more normal channels subject to NSC supervision. The President and his gatekeeper went to considerable lengths to structure situations, ensuring that proposals came from the right places, that crises appeared a certain way, and so on. Back channels to subordinates were used to elicit certain requests up the chain of command. The Laos invasion of 1971 is one example. Kissinger favored a dry-season offensive in Laos to demonstrate Vietnamization, from the fall of 1970, but Nixon learned from Cambodia the need for having someone with whom to share the heat of the antiwar opposition. In November 1970, Nixon ordered the bureaucracy to study a full range of options in Indochina. In December, Kissinger sent Al Haig to make a week-long fact-finding tour, during which the concept of an offensive concretized into the notion of a Laotian invasion. Haig's return gave Nixon the opportunity to stage a series of meetings demonstrating successively greater unanimity behind the invasion option. Kissinger and Haig started with the Joint Chiefs Chairman and worked out from there. Before it was over, Melvin Laird was sent out to do his own canvass. The first the Vietnamese Army heard about an invasion of Laos was when MACV commander Creighton Abrams raised the subject with a top ARVN general.

Trying to control everything from the White House had a real disadvantage, in that it ignored the technical background and support afforded by a bureaucracy. In this respect the sharpest illustration comes from the record of Soviet-American relations and the SALT negotiations.

It will be recalled that a regular delegation of United States negotiators under Gerard Smith were laboring on SALT in diplomatic discussions that alternated between Vienna and Helsinki.

But the real negotiations were in Kissinger's back channel with Dobrynin. There, in January 1971, began a new round of SALT exchanges that led to the joint American-Soviet announcement of May 20 that both ABM and offensive forces would be included, and that the agreement would be completed at a summit conference. Chief negotiator Smith learned the news at breakfast with Henry on May 19; Laird was told that afternoon. Henry only talked about ICBM limits, leaving Gerry Smith worried that submarine-based missiles might have been ignored. Smith's fears were confirmed when he saw the negotiating record, meager as it was, and he warned Kissinger that by it the United States might have agreed to exclude SLBMs from the SALT agreement. Henry denied it, thinking the record ambiguous. Soviet Ambassador Dobrynin had in fact raised SLBMs at the very first meeting, and the Soviets had returned to the subject, apparently moving ahead only once they had satisfied themselves that the limits would be applied to land-based forces alone. That was not official United States arms control policy. Smith also thought it unnecessary for Kissinger and Dobrynin to have broached the range of issues. They had simply to arrive at the bilateral declaration. Finally, the ACDA chief discovered that Kissinger had only used Soviet interpreters in his discussions.

Most of the work of fleshing out the SALT agreements was done by Gerard Smith and the delegations at the fifth and sixth rounds of negotiations. It was coming from behind now to get the Russians to agree to include SLBMs after all. The matter went unresolved for months, indeed until the very eve of the planned Moscow summit. By that time the JCS and many others insisted on SLBM limits as part of their price for supporting a SALT agreement. Nixon determined to send Henry to Moscow on one more secret mission.

By now the Kissinger secret missions had become routine to the White House Military Office, which had been taken over by Brigadier General Brent Scowcroft. Presidential aircraft *Air Force One* or its backup flew Kissinger on thirteen clandestine missions during 1970–1971. Chief pilot Albertazzie had a regular contact by then in the United States command in Europe, to run interference for him if anyone should ask too many questions. The contact, made by Albertazzie on his own initiative with a service friend, was made necessary by Kissinger's uncommonly frequent passages through the French military airfield at Avord, the American ones at Stuttgart, Wiesbaden, and Frankfurt, and British fields in the United Kingdom. That someone might recognize Kissinger and compromise the secrecy of negotiations was no longer a remote possibility. Nixon himself revealed the secret negotiations with the Vietnamese in a speech on January 25, 1972. That made arrangements for subsequent trips to Paris much simpler. But the Moscow trip, that April, was kept secret nonetheless.

General Scowcroft's Military Office organized a caper worthy of the CIA, which indeed got confused by it. Departure from Andrews Air Force Base was scheduled late at night. Kissinger stepped away from a Georgetown cocktail party, into a limousine that rushed him to the aircraft. Aboard *Air Force One* were four key NSC aides: Winston Lord, Peter Rodman, Helmut Sonnenfeldt, and John Negroponte. Also aboard was Soviet Ambassador Dobrynin, who was taken to Andrews by a White House station wagon that picked him up on a street corner at midnight, also in Georgetown. Everything went without a hitch until the White House driver realized he was being followed; pandemonium ensued until he could lose the tail and reach the air base. It turned out that the CIA had been trying to follow Dobrynin. Though White House license plate numbers were not supposed to be shared with anyone, the CIA evidently managed to cajole an identification out of the Washington Police Department, only to be deeply chagrined when the trail led directly to Richard Nixon.

When Kissinger arrived in Moscow, Brent Scowcroft was already there, doing advance work for the summit a month hence. Scowcroft was also a bit of cover for Henry—so that he could be identified as the American official in Moscow if anyone caught wind of the Kissinger trip and asked. Kissinger landed at a Soviet military airfield and was immediately taken to a dacha in the Lenin Hills outside Moscow. There was no contact with Scowcroft, who had NSC specialist Bill Hyland with him; in theory the plan was perfect. The United States embassy was kept in ignorance, Henry did not even tell his own SALT specialists, Philip Odeen and Barry Carter. The Kissinger mission took along couriers to keep Henry in touch with the plane and Washington, courtesy of the White House Military Office. A communications failure on the plane, which cut off Kissinger from the President, was the major snafu.

The SLBM constraints Henry discussed with Soviet leader Leonid Brezhnev seemed inadequate to such negotiators as Gerard Smith, Paul Nitze, and others. When Smith saw a record of Kissinger's talks in Moscow he felt acute disappointment. The limit Nixon actually obtained was rather high for the Soviets, and was subject to reinterpretation, as became evident a couple of years later. It was another of Henry's time bombs.

Worst of all was the handling of modernization in the interim agreement. In the absence of a MIRV ban it was certain that both sides would make the transition to MIRV technology as quickly as possible, and the Soviets were known to have a new generation of ICBM missiles already in engineering development. One of them was a very large, so-called heavy ICBM that could lift considerable weight of useful payload. The United States SALT position was to ban or limit heavy ICBMs, several hundred of which had been deployed by the USSR, and which gave the Soviets a large advantage in "throwweight," in effect the tonnage of nuclear warheads that could be hurled in any ultimate holocaust. As Soviet technology improved, miniaturization would enable the Soviets to translate throwweight into huge numbers of warheads. It was a clear technological threat on the horizon.

Kissinger failed to achieve limits on heavy ICBMs, and he actively abetted misunderstanding in his explanations of the SALT agreements, which argued that the Soviets were barred from increasing the size of their missiles. Finally, Kissinger failed to nail down the definition of spatial dimensions, specifically the number of axes covered by a 15 percent cap on increases in missile silo "volume."

Kissinger consulted with his own selection of experts. On the NSC staff he worked most closely with area specialists Hal Sonnenfeldt and Bill Hyland. The NSC technical people on SALT were the whiz kids, the program analysis people, headed by Philip Odeen. They were relatively less involved. Odeen and his subordinate Barry Carter missed both the April secret mission and the May summit. Like the SALT delegation, the NSC technical specialists were left behind. This, as well as Kissinger and Nixon's frequent reliance on Soviet interpreters during their negotiating sessions, contributed to flaws in the agreements.

Still, there was plenty of excitement for those NSC staffers who did go to Moscow. Sonnenfeldt, who had feared the Soviets would cancel the summit (because of American action in Vietnam) was pleasantly surprised to reach Moscow but soon mortified to find himself in an argument with Brezhnev. It happened when the Soviet leader, in the middle of one of the negotiating sessions, saw Sonnenfeldt take off his watch. During the translation of his remarks, Brezhnev turned to Hal and asked for the watch, then put it on. Sonnenfeldt interrupted the translation to ask for his watch back, and he and Leonid Brezhnev argued about it for a few moments. Brezhnev then produced an heirloom, a pocket watch on a chain he said his mother had given him. Brezhnev insisted on taking Sonnenfeldt's watch, giving the American his own, while Hal kept asking for it back, lying that the watch was a gift from his mother-in-law though he had really bought it in a military post exchange.

Kissinger began to kick Sonnenfeldt under the table. "Sonnenfeldt," the national security adviser rasped drily, "you've had enough exposure in the minutes of this meeting."

Win Lord and John Negroponte also had their share of summit adventures. On the third day Brezhnev suddenly bundled Nixon into a limousine for a ride to his dacha in the country. The President's U.S. Secret Service detail promptly took off after them at full speed, and Henry coolly jumped into a KGB chase car belonging to Brezhnev's security detail. Left standing in the road were Lord, holding the briefcase with all of Kissinger's papers in it, and Negroponte, Henry's note taker.

When the President returned he had to sell the arms control measures to the U.S. Congress. Kissinger did his part on June 15, appearing to a large audience of congressmen for a semiformal briefing on the SALT agreements. Kissinger seriously oversold the agreements in what amounted to his one official appearance in behalf of SALT. Fatefully Henry declared, "There are no secret agreements connected to the SALT arrangements."

On Saturday, June 17, four days after the administration submitted the Moscow agreements to Congress for official ratification, Henry Kissinger met with Dobrynin to further clarify the SLBM limitations. Ambiguities in the definition of which forces were covered affected the baseline figure for the treaty limits. Technical specialists on the NSC staff were able to establish the importance of seeking clarification. The first the United States government heard of this further official exchange was in early June 1973, *a year later,* and then from a *Soviet* diplomat at a SALT compliance session mandated by the treaty.

In the ensuing years many of the charges of Soviet noncompliance with the SALT agreements did result from ambiguous definitions. The drumbeat of rhetoric fueled the decline of détente. Some opponents, primarily conservative Jackson-wing Democrats, also took umbrage at what they considered Kissinger's arrogant style.

Attempting in vain to retard the growth of alarm within the United States bureaucracy at Soviet strategic force developments, Kissinger, in October 1972, created a system under which the NSC staff could have a first crack *before* something could be written up in SALT compliance reports. A number of critical intelligence reports were delayed under this system, including reports on the new, larger ICBMs. The information holds made some who knew suspect the worst, and the negotiating ambiguities made it easy for conservatives to tar the Soviets with allegations of violations. In later years Kissinger was forced into the posture of defending SALT, advocating agreements on arms control, and trying to defuse some of the charges being thrown at SALT I. It was incumbent upon him then to step forward and clarify the real basis for the SALT misunderstandings. That was particularly true once Kissinger became secretary of state with an official responsibility for building a constituency for foreign policy. He never did.

In a moment of introspection, Kissinger is recorded as lamenting that he did not, at the time, better think through the implications of MIRV. The generation of bigger Soviet missiles represented a protected pool of ICBM throwweight that could be MIRVed progressively as Russian technology improved. Kissinger tried to compensate with new SLBM and cruise missile programs, and when the Soviets then got interested in SALT limits on cruise missiles, was unable to get Secretary of Defense James Schlesinger to give them up. The Russians first launched an ICBM carrying a MIRV system in 1973, and deployed three new MIRVed missiles the following year. In fact, Kissinger solved his dilemma by joining ranks with SALT critics. In 1975, Kissinger reported in later testimony before the Senate, it began to dawn on him that

> When [the Soviets] continued to push the development of the [ICBMs], and kept working on the accuracy of their missiles and on the throwweight, and when they pushed against at least the spirit of what we had in mind in the 1972 agreement with respect to the conversion of "light" to "heavy" missiles, one really could interpret that only in terms of an intention to achieve a counterforce capability against the United States.

The Foreign Relations Committee heard Kissinger give damningly faint praise to a treaty (SALT II) he had once boasted of negotiating 90 percent of. Nor did Kissinger add that the Soviets had improved their accuracy using precision ball bearings manufactured by equipment whose sale the Nixon administration had authorized.

In his testimony at the SALT II ratification hearings, Dr. Kissinger told the senators that the Moscow agreements focused on launchers because "we were dealing initially with single warhead systems," as if the NSC itself had not ordered up a MIRV Panel to look into this whole question. Similarly, Kissinger "supposed" the problem was "one of the legacies of a period in which technology outran us," as if the question of a MIRV ban had not been squarely posed in 1969.

Kissinger sounded rather better when he still remained secretary of state and a public advocate. Then, one day being hounded by the reporters, Henry had burst out, "One of the questions we have to ask ourselves as a country is: What, in the name of God, is strategic superiority? What is the significance of it, politically, militarily, operationally, at these levels of numbers? What do you do with it?"

The one thing that threatened the Moscow summit, that could have derailed the entire SALT process, was the fact that Vietnam had once more boiled over. Nixon and Kissinger were considering new acts of force in Indochina while, on the secret track, Kissinger continued to meet in Paris with the North Vietnamese. The acts of force were provocative. Hanoi was on the move and Saigon, for a time, on the brink. In Vietnam, 1972 was the Year of the Rat.

The Gulf of Tonkin Resolution had been repealed, while several proposals had begun to float on Capitol Hill to restrict the war powers of the President. Nixon was under political pressure, 1972 being an election year, to declare a final date for withdrawal from the Vietnam War. Nixon chose to answer the critics with a nationally televised speech on January 25. In it he revealed for the first time the secret negotiations between Kissinger and the North Vietnamese.

The day after Nixon's speech the United States asked Hanoi to resume the secret meetings, the last of which had been canceled on three days' notice in November. In mid-February the North Vietnamese accepted, but maneuvering for advantage delayed any actual meeting until April 24. By that time a major NVA offensive was in full swing. Nixon withdrew the American delegation from the regular Paris peace talks after more than 140 weekly plenary sessions. Not a single issue had been resolved. Meanwhile, the urgency of the situation became clear by April 2, when the South Vietnamese Army abandoned all its positions along the DMZ and fell back toward Quang Tri.

Nixon and Kissinger began meeting up to three times a day. Henry quickly activated the WSAG, at first ordering naval and air reinforcements for Indochina, something Nixon had begun doing as early as February. By March there were 800 aircraft in the theater, steadily increasing to over 1,300 by mid-May, including 120 B-52 bombers. Nixon planned to use the forces early on, apparently, for Tom Moorer, as early as April 5, came back to tell the other Chiefs the President was hewing to a strong line that the Easter offensive was an invasion and he wanted all resources set to meet it. Nixon asked Admiral Moorer how long it would take to plan for mining Haiphong Harbor. Moorer had once commanded the Pacific Fleet and told the President he already had the plans.

"But can you do it without leaking?" the President asked.

Moorer replied, "I told him I knew what ship we would use, and, if there were any reporters on board, I would tell them they would be staying on board for an extended period of time."

But, as Moorer recalled it, the "hand wringers" then got busy. It took a full month to orchestrate the option. Al Haig wrote a paper for Henry providing for bombing targets throughout North Vietnam and mining Haiphong Harbor. First preparations for a speech began. Ominously, Kissinger told Dobrynin on April 9, "Anatol, we have been warning you for months that if there were an offensive, we would take drastic measures to end the war once and for all. That situation has now arisen."

In fact, the Navy was well equipped for the mining mission. One of its aircraft carriers in the theater had exactly the right equipment, plus up-to-date mines, while fleet commands held existing operations plans. From April 20 there was daily talk of mining in Admiral Elmo Zumwalt's office, and the Chief of Naval Operations assembled a small private planning unit to update the contingency plans. On April 23 the CNO received a request for authority to mine Haiphong Harbor from CINCPAC Admiral John McCain.

At the end of the month, fortified by a barbecue at John Connally's Picosa Ranch, the President took a tough line. "The North Vietnamese are taking a very great risk if they continue their offensive in the south," Nixon said. "I will just leave it there and they can make their own choice."

Nixon ordered intense B-52 bombing of the Hanoi-Haiphong region. The next morning Al Haig got Elmo Zumwalt on the phone. Zumwalt recollects: "I had said, as a not very subtle hint . . . that if the President got to the verge of deciding to lose the war through unwillingness to mine/ blockade, he should meet with all the Chiefs to hear their professional assessment before making his decision final." Haig told Zumwalt he agreed, and told Richard Nixon that the important thing was to handle the crisis in a way that would permit him to remain in office. Nixon warned Brezhnev of decisions about to be made. He discussed the options with Kissinger and Haig aboard the yacht *Sequoia* on May 2, and in the Lincoln Sitting Room the next evening.

Nixon told television interviewer David Frost in 1977 that both he and Kissinger had initially favored canceling the Moscow summit themselves, saving Brezhnev the pleasure. Nixon credits John Connally with talking him out of it, and reports that Henry began with an estimate of 90 percent probability the Soviets would cancel only to reduce it every succeeding day. Nixon knew everything would be okay, he avers, when Mrs. Dobrynin stayed in touch with Pat Nixon constantly regarding summit incidentals, even as the bombing of North Vietnam resumed and the Haiphong mining occurred. The die was pretty much cast at a midafternoon meeting on May 4, when he decided against meddling with the summit and ordered an NSC meeting for the presumptive day of the mining. Al Haig began telling NSC associates he was 98 percent certain the President would order mining. Zumwalt handed Moorer an actual mining plan on May 5, while Nixon was at Camp David.

Kissinger never told the WSAG for, according to him, to avoid leaks Nixon had ordained there be *no* interagency activity prior to the NSC meeting itself. On Saturday at noon Henry summoned the staff, at least its key people.

"We cannot afford any breast feeding or any flinching," Henry had told the assembled White House staff on April 26. "We are now engaged on a course in which the other side has put all its chips into the pot and in which we have put our chips into the pot."

He began outlining the planned mining operation. The audience included

Al Haig, Hal Sonnenfeldt, Win Lord, Dick Kennedy, NSC Asian specialists John Holdridge, and John Negroponte, plus military aide Commander Jonathan T. Howe. Probably in deference to the dearth of bureaucratic process on this run, Kissinger also invited CIA Vietnam expert George C. Carver. Haig reportedly supported the plan provided it meant a sustained effort over an adequate period. Lord opposed the mining, now dubbed Operation Pocket Money. Sonnenfeldt argued the Soviets would cancel the upcoming summit, Holdridge that the Chinese would freeze all their relations with the United States. Negroponte, the NSC Vietnam man, held the mining could have a dramatic impact on morale in South Vietnam. According to Kissinger, George Carver presented a standard refrain of CIA analysis, that Hanoi would be able to substitute overland transportation for blockaded shipping. Analysts at the working level at the CIA report that Carver actually sided with the NSC staff expert in arguing mining could put considerable pressure on the North Vietnamese leadership. According to Richard Nixon's diary, Kissinger, who summarized the pros and cons at the end of the meeting, reported to the President "all but one of his staff were for the blockade, including his Vietnam expert, who is something of a dove." Henry seemed pleased.

Whatever the danger of leaks, the problem in restricting knowledge to the NSC staff was that a great deal of work needed to be done. Mining, a form of blockade, was illegal in international law except for nations in a state of war, which status the Vietnam conflict did not possess. There had to be research and drafting of a legal-sounding counterargument, consultations with allies, a scenario for informing the United Nations, a declaration of blockade to maritime powers, and a host of other details. Henry compromised by calling in the State Department after all.

The phone rang on the bedside table of Undersecretary U. Alexis Johnson at 6:45 A.M. on Sunday morning. He was told to meet with Kissinger at 9:30. Henry briefed Alex on the mining. Johnson observed that whatever the reaction of the antiwar opposition, he doubted the veracity of Air Force claims that bombing and mining *this time* would work. Kissinger reportedly agreed, declared that he too opposed the mining, and told the diplomat he thought the Russians were sure to cancel the summit. Henry claimed the mining had been dreamed up by Nixon political advisers John Connally and John Mitchell, and said he had to rely upon Secretary Rogers to stay the President's hand at the NSC. Kissinger got Johnson to work on all the diplomatic aspects of Pocket Money. When Johnson met Rogers, returning from a European trip to attend a council session, the secretary of state said he doubted very much whether Kissinger truly opposed the mining. Next morning at the meeting, Rogers refused to be drawn into opposing the plan. Agnew and Connally expressed strong support. Only Melvin Laird opposed Pocket Money, but the secretary of defense learned of it too late to put up much of a fight. Concluded Alex Johnson, "The NSC meeting was obviously a charade to front for the decision already made."

There was no prior consultation with Nguyen Van Thieu, who was simply informed in a letter Bunker delivered that morning in Saigon.

Nixon considered it a "tough, watershed decision," telling Henry in one memo, "I intend to stop at nothing to bring the enemy to his knees." Pocket Money was going to be the real thing. "What distinguishes me from [Lyndon] Johnson," Nixon wrote, "is that I have the will in spades. If we now fail it will be because the bureaucrats . . . will find ways to erode the strong, decisive action I have indicated we are going to take." In fact, the President wished the military and the NSC staff to come up with some ideas to recommend "*action* which is very *strong, threatening* and *effective*" (Nixon's italics).

The administration was by no means out of the woods on the Haiphong mining. Kissinger was blistered by a May 10 protest letter from nine former members of his own staff, but rationalized it on the grounds that most had served on the NSC staff for only a few months, and saw them as trading on the NSC relationship to attract attention. It rang very much like McGeorge Bundy's objections to Marc Raskin. Other gaps still remain in the Haiphong story; to take just one example, U. Alexis Johnson detected a lack of enthusiasm in Admiral Moorer, which he cites as one factor driving him to the private talk with Kissinger where Henry told him he had opposed mining. Kissinger on the other hand reports Moorer as jubilant, while the admiral's own recollections leave no doubt he favored this course.

Particulars of the crisis may be left to detailed study, but the central problem remained the same after Haiphong as before: how to move Hanoi to a peace agreement acceptable to Saigon. That had to be done in a climate in which Richard Nixon's primary concern remained his own image and reelection.

Still, Nixon continued to needle for action. The day after the mining Nixon was berating Henry for the CIA's lack of imagination on psychological warfare, insisting he wanted the agency to put out disinformation reports that whole NVA units had ceased to exist. By mid-month the President spoke of a desire to concentrate all the allied armor in South Vietnam for a surprise offensive. Later there were instructions for Haig to make sure the bombing continued during the Moscow summit.

The administration continued to work against the clock in Vietnam, even with the President's late-June announcement of an additional ten-thousand-man withdrawal. The huge reinforcement of air power in the theater and large-scale bombing was gobbling up money and promised to force Laird to have to ask for a $4-billion to $6-billion supplemental appropriation that would only bring back all the old controversies about the war.

A new negotiating session with Hanoi occurred on September 15. It was the last meeting at Choisy-le-Roi, for reporters succeeded in following Le Duc Tho to the site, 11 rue Darthé. Kissinger adverts the meeting convinced him that Hanoi had begun to waver. Saigon was becoming the bigger problem. Nixon had written a letter to Thieu at the end of August to bring the Vietnamese leader around, claiming many changes had been made in the American position as a result of meetings with Kissinger. Thieu now sent a reply to the Nixon letter, insisting no further concessions be made, charging they were made in an illogical way, only stimulating North Vietnamese intransigence. In a September 20 speech at Hue, Thieu thundered, "No one has a right to negotiate for or accept any solution."

Kissinger nonetheless met the North Vietnamese again on September 26 and 27 at Gif-sur-Yvette, in a home that had once belonged to the abstract painter Fernand Léger, which had been lent by the French Communist party. The snacks included caviar and shrimp flour chips, a token of a change in atmosphere for the better. Le Duc Tho seemed more insistent than ever on early agreement, and made what he called a "final" offer, conceding the anticipated national unity coalition could be merely *advisory* in character. Agreement hinged on meeting a timetable to settle, incidentally before the United States elections.

The negotiations entered their last furlong when Kissinger returned to Paris for a session that began on October 8 and continued, beyond expectations, for more than four days. The North Vietnamese came in with a new comprehensive proposal Kissinger thought might be workable. The negotiations were tough, including a final sixteen-hour marathon discussion. Kissinger demanded but could not obtain a commitment from Hanoi to withdraw its troops from the south. Henry then hurried to Washington to report to the President, who had received only a short reporting cable the first day, and even shorter messages on subsequent days of the talks. Henry left Winston Lord and interpreter David Engel behind to clear up ambiguities in the texts. He and Haig reported to Nixon at his OEOB office on the evening of October 12. By then, significantly, the United States had reestablished the old ten-mile-radius no-bomb zone around Hanoi. Nixon ordered steak and wine to celebrate.

Dr. Kissinger knew all along that securing Saigon's approval would be the final obstacle. Thus the national security adviser now prepared an inducement for the South Vietnamese. This was a rapid replenishment of ARVN equipment losses and buildup in some categories of strength. The program would be called Project Enhance. The very day of Henry's return from Paris, Philip Odeen of the NSC staff was busy making inquiries of the Pentagon of what might be included in Enhance, which had been in planning stages since September. Kissinger knew that Hanoi's timetable called for completion of the agreement by the end of the month, so Melvin Laird planned to complete all deliveries by October 31. Much of the ground forces equipment slated for delivery would have to be airlifted to meet that date. "It appears that this is feasible, but, as you know, will be very expensive," Laird reported to Kissinger on October 15. "This would be an historical [sic] air lift. I am still examining the total costs." Laird authorized delivery of *inoperable* equipment just so that it would be present in South Vietnam and could then be replaced legally under the agreement, including such items as 30 (of 72) M-48 tanks, 96 quadruple .50-caliber machine guns, thirteen 175-millimeter cannon, and 284 (of 424) five-ton trucks. Laird finally calculated the airlift would add about $65 million to the $1-billion cost of the equipment; he issued orders to carry out Enhance on October 20.

Henry Kissinger left Washington before noon on October 16 for what he hoped would be a final, triumphant mission: He stopped at Paris to clear up loose ends with Hanoi, then went on to Saigon to finally sell the agreement to Thieu.

In Paris, Henry met Le Duc Tho again at Gif-sur-Yvette and got the North Vietnamese to agree that military equipment levels could be frozen, to be replaced only on a one-for-one basis with similar equipment. That would give the ARVN a considerable advantage in material if Project Enhance was completed in time, since unserviceable ARVN equipment could then be replaced at leisure.

From Paris, Kissinger flew on to Saigon. Only John Negroponte of his staff, Henry reports, had any doubts Thieu would buy the deal. An Asian expert of Greek-American parentage, Negroponte had been with State for a decade in Hong Kong and South Vietnam, one of relatively few American officials to learn Vietnamese. He had served at the embassy with Max Taylor, Henry Cabot Lodge, and Ellsworth Bunker all, then had gone to Paris to work on the early Vietnam negotiations with Averell Harriman and Cyrus Vance. When he left the NSC staff a year after Kissinger's negotiation, Negroponte's reward would be a dismal posting to Quito, Ecuador.

Nguyen Van Thieu gave no ground in his meeting with Kissinger on October 19. That afternoon Henry, Abrams, and ARVN General Cao Van Vien met to discuss Project Enhance. At that session Dr. Kissinger further increased the offer of equipment to sweeten the bargain for Saigon, adding many more aircraft in a new plan called Project Enhance-Plus. Kissinger writes in his memoirs as if Enhance-Plus had long been intended, but there was no mention of Enhance-Plus prior to October 19, and even more significantly, the character and types of aircraft to be given the Vietnamese Air Force changed dramatically from Enhance to Enhance-Plus. The latter provided Saigon with C-130 medium transports and F-5A jet fighter-bombers, sent with such urgency that planes had to be borrowed from Iran and South Korea.

Thieu pocketed the added military aid without in any sense agreeing to the document, but also without directly objecting to it or to Kissinger's intention to fly on to Hanoi to initial the peace agreement. Only the next day, confronted by lower-ranking Vietnamese officials of Thieu's NSC, did Henry learn of the steadfast opposition to an agreement. He reacted by postponing his projected departure to try to work on the GVN. American embassy aides were also called out to lobby their Vietnamese contacts at all levels; one of them called the effort "Operation Big Lie."

One of the big Vietnamese objections centered on what the United States would do once it had disengaged and Hanoi then violated the agreements. Kissinger insisted the United States would act to enforce the agreements, and claims in his memoirs that this seemed the least controversial of issues. However, according to NSC staffer John Lehman, Henry's own official household had warned him on this very point: Specialist Sven Kraemer, who had been helping with press pointers on the negotiations, was the man. Kraemer warned Kissinger that the strength of antiwar opposition in the United States would preclude any resumption of hostilities once disengagement had occurred. Kraemer had studied with Kissinger at Harvard, begun on the NSC with Rostow's VIG, and was the son of Henry's erstwhile mentor. But his objections were dismissed. A year later, when it had become a matter of telling Saigon that there would not *be* any United States intervention, despite promises to the contrary, Kraemer was rewarded for his pains by being saddled with this dubious mission.

Meanwhile, the deadlock continued over the prospective agreement, complicated by communications difficulties between Kissinger and the White House. Henry began to suspect he was being set up to take the fall, Nixon insisting that no pressure be put on Thieu to accede. Sven Kraemer, along with specialist William L. Stearman and military assistant Jonathan Howe, witnessed a startling scene involving Al Haig, in which the deputy complained that Kissinger was going too far and implied he would take over. Reminiscent of the Cambodia NSC revolt, nothing actually happened, but it was clear Kissinger had no support to force an agreement upon Saigon. The South Vietnamese came up with a list of more than twenty objections, which soon grew to sixty-nine.

Further American-GVN exchanges produced no unity. Then North Vietnamese Premier Pham Van Dong made statements in an interview that allowed the United States to back away from the agreement. On October 26, Radio Hanoi broke the public silence with a long statement reporting that peace was now frustrated. Saigon followed with its own statement issued in Paris, and Henry Kissinger held a news conference in Washington. Henry remained optimistic. "We believe peace is at hand," he told the assembled reporters.

Richard Nixon sent a letter to Thieu on October 29 warning of "the dangerous course which your Government is now pursuing." A week later Nixon sent Al Haig to see Thieu with another letter outlining what the United States would attempt to accomplish in further negotiations. Thieu remained concerned by the presence of NVA troops in the south, but because mutual withdrawal was not negotiable, there was really no way to satisfy him. Nixon said as much in an NSC-drafted letter following the Haig visit: "It is unrealistic to assume that we will be able to secure the absolute assurances which you would hope to have on the troop issue." Three days later Nixon informed Thieu the United States was not prepared to scuttle the agreement or to demand such amendments as would have that result.

How much of this was due to Richard Nixon and how much to his national security adviser still cannot be determined from the available records. One NSC staffer, reportedly involved in the secret negotiations from the beginning, later told an interviewer:

> Nixon hardly focused on the agreement, and we were frankly offended when he would continually say in public that he had been too busy working on peace terms so that he didn't have a moment for domestic politics. Bullshit. He was in there all the time with Haldeman and Ehrlichman talking politics. His only concern was that an agreement be reached. I don't think he even read the GVN's detailed reactions to the draft agreement. After the election Kissinger told me that Nixon had just said to him, "Get this thing signed before the inauguration."

Meanwhile, the price tag for Enhance and Enhance-Plus had grown to about $2 billion. "If we had been giving this aid to the North Vietnamese," one general told the same interviewer, "they could have fought us for the rest of the century."

Kissinger resumed negotiations with Le Duc Tho on November 20, then December 4. Now the DRV also began to drag its feet, becoming almost completely intransigent. After a final sterile effort lasting until December 13 the talks broke off.

According to Nixon, he felt only the most strenuous military action would now suffice to bring around Hanoi, and while Henry agreed on the need for action, the keeper of the keys recommended less forceful options. Nixon decided to hit both Hanoi and Haiphong with B-52 bombers despite their heavy antiaircraft defenses. According to Kissinger, Al Haig favored the B-52 bombing while he himself favored resuming air attacks at the level prevalent in October. Haldeman, Ehrlichman, and Admiral Tom Moorer all reportedly backed the bombing. Certain journalists, however, including some known to have had constant access to Kissinger, reported that Henry *opposed* the air attacks, which soon came to be known as the Christmas Bombing, and triggered a firestorm of public opposition.

Negotiations resumed in January, with Hanoi making more concessions; a revised agreement was achieved and signed in Paris on January 26, 1973, by William Rogers. Nguyen Van Thieu's protection, however, resided in Nixon's assurances during the period of negotiation. In the presidential letter of November 15, 1972, Nixon had said: "You have my absolute assurance that if Hanoi fails to abide by the terms of this agreement it is my intention to take swift and severe retaliatory action." Again, on January 5, 1973, the President signed a letter which stated: "We will respond with full force should the agreement be violated." On January 17 a further missive declared; "The U.S. will respond vigorously to violations of the Agreement." More important than debating the degree of discrimination in the destruction wrought by the Christmas Bombing is the role of that act of force as a token of these very assurances.

Kissinger assured the public, as he had with SALT I, that no secret agreements were associated with the Paris accords. The assurances to Saigon qualified as just this kind of arrangement though, as did an offer of economic aid to *North* Vietnam subsequently revealed by Hanoi. Before the spring was out, it had become clear Hanoi was not going to stop supplying the NVA down the Ho Chi Minh Trail. The promised retaliatory action did not materialize; moreover, political obstacles dictated a steady reduction in United States aid to Saigon. It is said that Nguyen Van Thieu, having met Nixon at a summit in San Clemente that spring, emerged convinced his regime had already been abandoned. Henry Kissinger's denials notwithstanding, there is plentiful evidence that suggests, as CIA Vietnam analyst Frank Snepp concludes, that the policy objective in all this was a "decent interval" between the United States troop withdrawal and the fall of South Vietnam. The illusion here was that Vietnam disengagement represented what Nixon said it was, "peace with honor."

A GATHERING STORM

▲▲▲

A fter his electoral victory in November 1972 the President was more determined than ever to perfect his control over the bureaucracy and make government responsive to his will. Nixon began to talk of a "supercabinet" government that would be controlled by just a few senior officials. In addition, Nixon ordered all presidential appointees, approximately two thousand senior officials, indeed the entire top echelon of the federal government, to submit their resignations.

The latter instruction included Henry Kissinger, then flying high in the last stages of the Paris negotiations on Vietnam. In view of Kissinger's apparent achievements at that time, most people would have thought Nixon loath to part with him, but Henry could not be so sure of Richard Nixon. This President had an insatiable desire for credit and an incredible suspicion of all who surrounded him. Well aware of those tendencies, Henry became greatly alarmed when he learned that *Time* magazine intended to name Nixon *and* Kissinger jointly as its "Men of the Year" for 1973. This annual *Time* cover-story honor had gone to Richard Nixon alone in January 1972. The President's reaction to having to share the limelight with Kissinger was predictable.

What more than anything else probably saved Kissinger's job was Watergate. Kissinger claims he knew nothing about the scandal until later, that when he once asked Haldeman and Ehrlichman about the original break-in, during the summer of 1972, they pleaded ignorance. He claims his first real knowledge came from White House lawyer Leonard Garment on April 14, 1973, when Henry got a briefing on the charges that were about to be investigated by a select committee of the senate forming under Senator Sam Ervin of South Carolina. Kissinger learned the affair involved not only the Watergate break-in itself but a whole range of political intelligence operations. Several of the activities had been orchestrated by the White House "Plumbers," a unit codirected by former Kissinger aide David Young. One was a break-in at the office of a psychiatrist who had been treating Daniel Ellsberg, the Pentagon-whiz-kid-turned-antiwar-activist who had revealed the Pentagon Papers. Kissinger and Haig, not to say Nixon, had been infuriated by this leak. It is not unreasonable to believe that Kissinger may have learned something of Watergate from Young, apart from anything he knew from Garment, but that has never been established.

In any case, Watergate and the related investigations absorbed a growing proportion of Nixon's attention and sapped his political strength. As the domestic scandal overshadowed the President, foreign affairs began to look like the one area where the administration was doing useful work. Thus Henry increasingly became valuable, indeed indispensable, to Nixon.

There could be no doubt that Watergate posed a foreign policy problem for a President who had, in effect, picked a fight with the federal bureaucracy. Once Nixon appeared to be under siege, his authority eroded in every area, not the least of which was national security. In turn the national security adviser circled the wagons and prepared, to elaborate on his cowboy metaphor, to fight off bands of marauding Indians. Thus he refused to allow John Lehman to leave the NSC staff, and the latter stayed on to find that the "fun" had gone out of serving in the White House.

Kissinger claims that he had always intended to leave the administration by the end of 1973. This smacks of an effort to front load the record for historians. First retailed to reporters Marvin and Bernard Kalb who were at work on an early Kissinger biography, there is no direct evidence that Henry ever acted to carry out this supposed intention, nor did Nixon record it either in his memoirs or the Frost interviews. Henry told an interviewer in mid-1972 that he had literally not given the future any thought at all, and made a similar statement in the notorious Fallaci interview, going so far as to say, "we are living in such a revolutionary period that to plan one's life, nowadays, is to revert to a Victorian middle-class mentality."

It seems a lot to believe that Henry was voluntarily about to leave government in 1973, *after* going to the trouble of getting Nixon to reappoint him as security adviser. Moreover, there is a record of Henry Kissinger's threats of resignation to consider—by the President's count, it happened at least a half-dozen times, and Haldeman, Ehrlichman, and Al Haig recall countless more. Those threats were maneuvers, bluffs that Henry must have hoped would never be called. Indeed, the conversations Henry does report on in early 1973, with Melvin Laird and Al Haig, concerned preserving Henry's effectiveness, not easing the transition to a successor. Both colleagues apparently told Henry that if he wished to remain effective he would have to move out of the White House and go to State. Haig even volunteered to take the matter up with Richard Nixon.

Alexander Haig's interceding for Henry Kissinger with the President provided evidence of a subtle shift in relationships within the White House. Nixon had forged a direct relationship with Kissinger's deputy. The President used Haig to pick up the pieces after Kissinger's fiascos, as in Haig's two visits to Nguyen Van Thieu to hammer Saigon into acquiescence to the Paris peace agreements. Nixon valued Haig so much that he engineered Al's entry into the exalted elite of top Army generals, promoting him to two-star rank in the spring of 1972 and then, with unmatched rapidity, to four-star full general only a few months later. Nixon saw himself as grooming Haig for Army Chief of Staff and in fact appointed Al as vice-chief; but for months afterward Haig actually remained at the White House in his NSC staff job.

General Haig finally left the NSC only in January 1973, but even then he remained linked with Nixon over a direct phone line, freely dispensing advice and doing minor chores. That spring, meanwhile, the Watergate charges loomed ever more darkly over the White House. At the end of April, just days after Ehrlichman had dismissed Watergate allegations in talk with Kissinger, both Haldeman and Ehrlichman were forced to resign. At first Nixon thought of being his own chief of staff, but then he allowed Haldeman to convince him otherwise. Both agreed that Haig could be an ideal successor. Nixon saw him as steady, intelligent and tough, and making up in sheer force of personality what he might lack in political experience and organizational finesse. Haig became the President's chief of staff in May 1973.

According to Kissinger, the President had already decided there would have to be a change at the helm of the State Department. Kenneth Rush, a veteran diplomat who had scored a signal success in 1971, when he followed up on certain back-channel exchanges to negotiate an agreement with the Soviets (and East and West Germans) ending disputes over access to Berlin, was mentioned for the job. According to Nixon, in his televised interviews with David Frost, he was sick of the feud between Kissinger and Rogers and the new secretary had to be able to get along with Henry (a point that throws additional light upon Kissinger's supposed intention to leave the administration). Nixon confirmed he had considered John Connally for the post. Kissinger believes the appointment of someone so politically powerful as Connally "would run counter to all Nixon's ideas of how to conduct foreign policy." Henry also insists he had not sought the job, and Nixon had not offered it: "In an undamaged Nixon Presidency, the national security adviser's post was decisive; Nixon had no intention of moving me to the State Department." But, "once Watergate descended, I could not operate effectively as a Presidential staffer."

Al Haig was as good as his word and interceded for Henry. William Rogers at first rejected suggestions he step down, insisting upon a personal request from his old friend Richard Nixon. The President hated these kinds of confrontations and procrastinated for some time, but when he finally bit the bullet and called Rogers in, the secretary of state put a letter of resignation on his desk before Nixon could even open his mouth. Richard Nixon announced the nomination of Henry Alfred Kissinger to be secretary of state on August 22, 1973.

Secretary of State Henry Kissinger occupied a position of unparalleled power within the United States government, for when Nixon offered him the job, the President had said nothing about a new national security adviser. Henry kept that post too, making it pretty easy for him to switch hats, as it were, to order up just about anything he wanted. At the same time, Nixon's growing preoccupation with Watergate prevented his usual close supervision over national security matters. In addition, with Kissinger providing the president *political* support by furnishing luster to an otherwise tarnished image, Henry ended up holding virtually all the cards.

Kissinger achieved this freedom of action just in time to face a new set of international tests, climaxing in another Arab-Israeli war. There was continued movement in U.S. relations with the People's Republic of China, with Henry ultimately to make almost a dozen visits there. On arms control a follow-up SALT agreement was necessary, though Kissinger had great difficulty in getting the Pentagon to serve up a position it felt the United States could live with in a SALT II agreement. On both these issues the to-ing and fro-ing concealed a lack of real achievement that only became gradually apparent. On SALT, for example, there were further Nixon-Brezhnev summits in San Clemente in 1973 and in Moscow in 1974, and it was only as minor understandings and protocols emerged that it became evident that not too much was really happening. Some pundits and journalists even began to see the events as being staged to divert attention from the President's Watergate problems.

In the midst of the hearing to confirm Kissinger as secretary of state, the Chilean military coup that overthrew Salvador Allende occurred. By that time, in an odd throwback to the Johnson-Rostow years, William Jorden had returned to the NSC staff for a second run, now as specialist for Latin America; while the U.S. ambassador in Chile was Nathaniel Davis, also a veteran of the Rostow staff. Jorden, back on the third floor of the OEOB since early 1972, successfully pressed for the United States to take a relatively detached attitude, in particular to delay in recognizing the Chilean military junta under General Augusto Pinochet until other South American and European nations had done so. It was hoped that such a delay would insulate the United States against charges of responsibility for what happened in Chile. Kissinger's flippant denials of any U.S. role at all, beginning at his confirmation hearings, had to be reiterated so often that they finally seemed tired. Kissinger ultimately reacted with anger whenever Chile came up. His denials convinced few. The general tenor of policy on Latin America is aptly illustrated by the simple fact that negotiations for a new Panama Canal treaty were continuing without discernible progress and indeed do not receive a single word in the Kissinger memoirs.

Then there was the "Year of Europe." Having focused so much on the Soviets and Chinese, and on the Vietnam War, U.S. alliance relationships were in disarray. Virtually the only initiative by the United States apparent to the Europeans was Senator Mike Mansfield's effort to force a reduction in American forces assigned to NATO. In late 1972, Western European powers meeting in Paris had called for a new dialogue. Kissinger personally answered with a speech delivered in New York on April 23, 1973, drafted by a small group of NSC specialists without any broader consultation in the administration. As usual the excuse was fear of leaks. Rogers, who was in New York the same day, got no advance notice. Henry made grandiose promises of a Year of Europe and a new Atlantic Charter. "The speech was more hortatory in tone than it might have been," notes Wilfrid L. Kohl, a political scientist who had been European specialist on the NSC staff during 1970–1971, "and the label 'Year of Europe' was presumptuous to say the least." Some desultory negotiations followed, conducted by Helmut Sonnenfeldt and Walter Stoessel, then Arthur Hartman. "Curiously enough," Kohl believes, "the one positive result of the entire exercise was a modest advance, on the European side, of the nascent effort at political cooperation and definition of identity that Kissinger had at the start seemed anxious to head off."

There would be no Year of Europe. What there was was a year of crisis in the Middle East, with the initiative in the hands of the Arab nations, principally the United Arab Republic and Syria. Under the leadership of Anwar el-Sadat, who succeeded Nasser upon his death in 1970, Egypt had startled everyone by expelling its large contingent of Soviet troops and advisers in July 1972. Sadat later decided to launch a war, forcing Israel and the superpowers to take the situation more seriously, and he enlisted the Syrians in the project. On October 6, 1973, just as Israel settled down to its Yom Kippur high holy day, the Arabs struck.

The United States was not quite guilty of ignoring the Middle East before the 1973 war. In February and again in May, Dr. Kissinger met with Sadat's national security adviser, Hafez Ismail. As had become typical of the Kissinger method the meetings were closely guarded secrets. Secretary Rogers found out about the second of them, however, and successfully insisted upon having his own representative there, Deputy Assistant Secretary Alfred L. Atherton. The latter got on well enough with Henry that when the keeper of the keys succeeded Rogers, Atherton remained a trusted lieutenant. Meanwhile, Rogers proposed a new peace plan in May also, one utilizing the two-track technique that was becoming almost de rigueur for U.S. policy. In this case the first track was to publicly seek a broadened Suez Canal agreement while a secret second track encouraged direct negotiations between Egyptians and Israelis.

These American moves represented only a beginning, and not much was accomplished before the October War. Israel resisted talks and harped on the need for more U.S. military aid. The $300 million in credits Tel Aviv obtained for fiscal 1973 represented only slightly more than the preceding year, but raised the total U.S. military aid to Israel to almost $1.3 billion, virtually all awarded by the Nixon administration. Even with the aid, however, Washington did not seem to enjoy very much influence with Israel. Aid did not translate into leverage, a lesson that might have been learned from Vietnam but was not.

Asleep in his suite at the Waldorf Towers in New York, where he was staying during the annual meeting of the United Nations General Assembly, Kissinger first learned of the war when Assistant Secretary Joe Sisco woke him up at 6:15 A.M. on October 6. Sisco still believed quick action could dissuade the belligerents, and there had been a similar incident a couple of weeks before, when Henry had been awakened with news that UAR troops had gone to a very high state of alert. Even before returning to Washington he ordered General Brent Scowcroft, who had succeeded Haig as deputy national security adviser, to call the WSAG into session.

Scowcroft, a cautious and capable watcher, had already taken steps to check out the reports when the NSC staff first learned of the Soviet air evacuation. Peter Rodman took the initiative, but could get no further than the evacuation itself. He suggested to Scowcroft that the CIA be asked for a fresh assessment, but Langley came back with the reassuring but mistaken view that military preparations did not indicate any of the parties had an intention to start a war. Having gotten this misleading report, Scowcroft was left to chair the first WSAG meeting, at 9:00 A.M. the next morning, where Washington shared the erroneous information. Kissinger meanwhile returned to Washington to chair a second WSAG meeting, entering the Situation Room at 7:22 P.M. that night, when a second day of fighting was beginning along the Suez and in the Golan Heights. The only early decision was to order a precautionary concentration of the Sixth Fleet south of Crete. The general atmosphere is suggested by the light banter WSAG members were swapping about the crisis, and the fact that one Cabinet member calmly sat reading comic strips in the local newspaper as Kissinger entered the Situation Room.

On the second day of the war, the United States formally requested the matter be taken up by the UN Security Council. The intent, according to NSC staff specialist William B. Quandt, was to propose a cease-fire with all sides in their prewar positions. That was clearly unacceptable to Sadat, whose troops had succeeded in fording the Suez and capturing or isolating the Israeli defense positions along the canal, but the WSAG expected the Israelis to gain the initiative and recover initial positions. That indeed happened on the Syrian front, but UAR forces could not be dislodged from positions on the east bank of Suez, and in fact a large Israeli Defense Forces (IDF) counterattack met defeat with heavy losses. In succeeding days the IDF made progress against the Syrians and halted further Egyptian attacks. Not until the second *week* of the war, however, did the IDF return to the bank of the Suez and then it was only on a very narrow sector of the front. This was no longer the Egyptian Army of 1967. Israeli officers exploited their success by making a Suez crossing of their own into Egypt.

The IDF sustained substantial tank and aircraft losses. Kissinger quickly told the Israelis aid would be granted and Tel Aviv sent several El Al Boeing 747 jets to pick up the first of it. As IDF losses accumulated, however, the whole aid question loomed increasingly large.

The charge most frequently leveled at Kissinger over the October War is that he obstructed aid and used the aid to manipulate Israel. The national security adviser admits that "from the beginning, I was determined to use the war to start a peace process," but that does not concede the criticism. Henry also admits that "when I had bad news for [the Israeli ambassador], I was not above ascribing it to bureaucratic stalemates or unfortunate decisions by superiors. Neither of us fooled the other . . . he understood that I had not reached eminence by losing too many bureaucratic battles." Again that is not an admission, but it is significant in that the delay has been attributed, by the brothers Kalb following "reliable sources," to resistance by Secretary of Defense James Schlesinger. In his own memoir for this period, Kissinger speaks of "middle levels" at the Pentagon dragging their feet and causing the initial delay.

By October 8, Israeli requests had become formal and urgent. Yet at 5:30 P.M. that afternoon at a WSAG session one participant opined that if the Russians held off resupplying the Arabs the United States ought to do the same with Israel. Already that morning there had been a cable from Brezhnev offering to act in cooperation with the United States. Kissinger's account is completely silent on this WSAG discussion of arms. Immediately afterward Henry met Israeli Ambassador Simcha Dinitz, telling him the shipment via El Al had been cleared for that night (by Scowcroft) while the United States would speed up delivery of *two* F-4 Phantom jets that had already been scheduled for Tel Aviv. Dinitz awakened Henry repeatedly that night with phone calls imploring him to get an aid flow going. At their meeting the previous evening Dinitz had informed Henry of congressmen who had been mobilized to agitate for the resupply. On October 9, Dinitz returned with a military attaché and met with Henry, Scowcroft, and Rodman, telling them of a loss of five hundred tanks and sixty jet aircraft. Skepticism prevailed at the WSAG that day; Kissinger cites Schlesinger's view as concern that meeting Israeli requests might outrage Arab nations —in 1973, Israel was defending her 1967 conquests rather than trying to survive within her pre-1967 borders. Henry believed, he recounts, that "events had gone beyond such fine-tuning."

Nixon met Kissinger in the late afternoon, after two WSAG sessions. Scowcroft, Al Haig, and press secretary Ron Ziegler were also present. "The Israelis must not be allowed to lose," the President declared. That night Henry told Dinitz that IDF tank and aircraft losses would be made good. Immediate deliveries of F-4s, however, were raised from two to only five, with additional aircraft to be scheduled. Many of the tanks were eventually stripped from U.S. Army stocks and even field units committed to NATO.

On October 10, Washington received intelligence that the Soviets had commenced a resupply airlift to both Egypt and Syria. That induced the United States to move faster with supplies, though it soon developed that El Al's seven transports could hardly pick up all the materiel. Kissinger and Schlesinger began to explore using a private air charter instead, involving ten or twenty flights a day. According to Kissinger, two days were then wasted trying to arrange charters. According to NSC staff specialist Bill Quandt, however, "Over the next two days the United States moved slowly on arms for Israel as a form of pressure to induce the Israelis to accept a ceasefire-in-place." The American airlift finally began on October 13, with the first shipments arriving in Israel the next day and the immediate delivery of F-4 Phantoms raised to fourteen jets. After that the airlift assumed truly massive proportions, even greater than Melvin Laird's "historic" airlift for Vietnam's Operation Enhance, delivering more than twenty-two thousand *tons* by air alone over a very short time.

Israel did not await the U.S. airlift before going over to the offensive. Following days of quiescence, Egyptian troops renewed their attacks on October 14 only to be handily defeated. In a closely coordinated riposte, two IDF armored divisions then thrust back to the canal line, smashed Egyptian tank units at an agricultural development called Chinese Farm, and made an assault crossing over the Suez on October 16. Building up strength in "Africa," as the IDF called the canal's west bank, the Israelis lashed out at UAR antiaircraft defenses that had been taking such a toll of their air force, then began a wide turning movement south, *behind* the Egyptian Third Army, still on the east bank of Suez. Meanwhile, on the Syrian front the IDF had pushed down off the Golan Heights and toward the capital, Damascus, stopping within relatively easy striking distance of that objective.

These military moves made a great difference in diplomatic efforts to achieve a cease-fire. The United States started out proposing prewar positions, assuming that the IDF would quickly trounce the Arabs, and was then puzzled when the Arabs showed no interest. The next idea was for a "standstill" cease-fire under which everyone would halt in the positions they occupied, but then the Israelis held back because of their plans for the offensive that took them into Africa. At times, in particular before the defeat of their final attacks on October 14, the Egyptians also resisted the standstill formula. Nevertheless, Kissinger was aware from quiet communications he received from Hafez Ismail over Egyptian UN and other channels, that this kind of formula offered the best prospects of success. It was in the midst of all this maneuvering, in fact during a WSAG meeting, that a news bulletin passed in from the Situation Room informed Henry he and Le Duc Tho had been awarded the Nobel Peace Prize. While some spoke of a cease-fire linked to a comprehensive settlement of Middle East issues, a more acceptable formula finally proved to be a cease-fire linked only with a reference to UN Resolution 242, which had followed the Six Day War. This ultimately proved to be the basis for UN Resolution 338, establishing the October War cease-fire. First ensued a lengthy dispute Kissinger had not expected, in which Golda Meir's government tried to reject any linkage to Resolution 242.

These diplomatic exchanges introduced the development that most directly damaged United States and Western European security, an Arab oil embargo, which triggered inflation, recessions, and an energy crisis that crippled most Western economies through the rest of the decade. A group of Arab foreign ministers met with Kissinger and Nixon, and the Saudis sent a letter protesting the American airlift to Israel. Nixon promised to do his best to work within Resolution 242 but could not guarantee returning Israel to her 1967 borders. On October 17 the Arabs announced a huge price hike for oil, monthly production cutbacks to enforce it, to continue until Israel withdrew to the 1967 boundaries. Given this context, Kissinger's account fails to mention his own advocacy of an equally huge military aid request for Israel, up to $3 billion, that is documented by staff specialist Bill Quandt. Administration interest in exploiting the situation for its own ends is illustrated by the tacking on to this project of $500 million for aid to Cambodia and other nations, where United States involvement had been terminated in August by executive-legislative agreement. Nixon sent forward a bill for $2.2 billion in aid to Israel on October 19. On October 20 the Saudis declared a total embargo on oil exports to the United States.

At the instant the oil crisis began, Henry Kissinger was airborne, en route to Moscow to discuss arrangements for a cease-fire. Again Henry's trip was secret, although he did inform Ambassador Dinitz, who was shocked. To calm him, according to an Israeli account so authoritative that the government took the unprecedented step of censoring an entire book to conceal it, Henry tried to calm Dinitz by telling him no agreement could be reached in Moscow but that going would gain the IDF a few more days and prevent the Kremlin's hardening its position. Kissinger recounts that he accepted the Soviet invitation too quickly: "Possibly I could have delayed my departure another twenty-four hours—and strengthened Israel's military position even further." Then came a further disaster—Nixon accorded Henry full powers to negotiate! As a factor in his delaying tactics Henry had wanted to be in the position of having to forward Soviet proposals to Washington for agreement. "History will not record that I resisted many grants of authority," Henry drily reflects. "This one I resented bitterly." Henry not only protested in cables to Scowcroft, he telephoned Al Haig to activate another channel.

"Will you get off my back?" Haig said testily. "I have troubles of my own."

"What troubles can you possibly have in Washington on a Saturday night?"

"The president has just fired Cox. Richardson and Ruckelshaus have resigned and all hell has broken loose," Haig shot back. Kissinger went back to the Russians and agreed to their latest cease-fire proposals, or, more accurately, the Soviets accepted the draft Henry and Joe Sisco put forward in order to avoid negotiations based upon a Soviet text.

United States crisis management during the October War can be distinguished by the almost complete absence of the President. Nixon was preoccupied with handling the fallout from the resignation of Vice President Spiro

Agnew, the selection of Gerald R. Ford to succeed him, and the President's own legal difficulties. Not a single meeting of the NSC occurred during the October War, which was handled entirely by Kissinger and the WSAG. Nixon held several small meetings with his national security adviser and senior associates, had the WSAG in for one pep talk, and met with the Arab foreign ministers and Kissinger; he issued the orders in principle for the airlift, but otherwise the President's mind was elsewhere. Nixon was attempting to prevent the release of tapes recording his Oval Office conversations to Special Prosecutor Archibald Cox. Once he lost that legal battle, Nixon tried to compel Cox's resignation and, failing that, fired him. Attorney General Elliot Richardson resigned rather than implement the order, as did deputy William D. Ruckelshaus. Solicitor general Robert H. Bork finally carried out the order, news of which ignited public opinion and probably cost Nixon his last vestiges of political support.

Kissinger was still in Moscow, crippled by communications failures that frustrated him but left State aide Larry Eagleburger standing in the middle of the room "with smoke issuing from nose, eyes, and ears." Of the twenty to thirty diplomats and NSC people in the room, only Winston Lord stayed through the ensuing fireworks. The communications breakdown lessened the notice that could be given Tel Aviv, leaving Golda Meir shocked and furious. The UN resolution passed at 12:52 A.M. New York time on October 22. Kissinger decided to stop in Israel on his way back from Moscow.

"I presume she is wild with anger at me," Henry whispered to Foreign Minister Abba Eban, according to the Israeli account by journalist Matti Golan. Eban could only nod in agreement. Kissinger explained his technical difficulties to the Israeli cabinet and mentioned the possibility of a multilateral Geneva conference on the Middle East, strenuously resisted by the Israelis. Golda Meir, in subtle acknowledgment of Henry's diplomatic style, pressed him repeatedly on whether there were any secret agreements to impose on Israel the 1967 borders or any other ones. The moment of the cease-fire found the IDF on the brink of completing the encirclement of the Egyptian Third Army in the southern sector along the Suez. Kissinger asked how long it would take to complete the operation, and made remarks about cease-fire supervision that "Israelis could not help but interpret . . . as an indication that he would not be so unhappy if for some reason the fighting went on past the ceasefire deadline." Henry was told the IDF would need only two or three days to finish the job.

"Two or three days?" Golan quotes Kissinger. "That's all? Well, in Vietnam the ceasefire did not go into effect at the exact time that was agreed on."

Kissinger's memoirs make no mention of those remarks. Henry does record the Israeli need for two or three days more, but attributes it to a cable received from Ambassador Kenneth Keating after his return and says it was never communicated to him *in Moscow.*

In any case, by the time Henry returned to Washington, got a little rest at home, and reached the office, the IDF was again at full stride attacking in Africa to complete the encirclement. Egypt's President Anwar Sadat called on the Soviets and Americans to enforce the cease-fire, and on the night of October 24 Dobrynin called Kissinger to convey a message from Brezhnev, talking about joint measures, then saying, "If you find it impossible to act jointly with us in this matter, we should be faced with the necessity urgently to consider the question of taking appropriate steps unilaterally." These were the makings of a superpower crisis, triggered by the end of a war, not its beginning.

Kissinger immediately convened the WSAG for a late-night session. The consensus favored a conciliatory but strong reply combined with some noticeable U.S. action. At 11:41 P.M., Schlesinger and Admiral Moorer dispatched orders for American nuclear forces to assume an alert posture. It was extended to the 82nd Airborne Division when Washington received intelligence indications that Soviet air transports might be en route to Egypt with Russian paratroopers aboard. The reply to Brezhnev that WSAG crafted was given to Dobrynin by Scowcroft, in Nixon's name, at 5:40 A.M.

Nixon himself tries to present this episode as an illustration of himself in control, writing that "*I* sent a letter to the Soviet embassy," although other accounts indicate that the President slept through the entire episode and was informed of it only the next morning. The Soviets backed away, the cease-fire took hold, and Israeli and Egyptian military representatives began meetings at a tent site at Kilometer 101 along the Suez Canal to arrange for supplies to the Third Army, which remained in place, encircled, on the east bank of Suez.

The October War marked an important turning point for Kissinger because it convinced him that the Middle East could no longer be avoided. Already he had received feelers from Egypt and even quieter ones from the Palestine Liberation Organization (PLO), but Washington had lacked any sense of urgency or commitment. The war put everyone on notice to the volatility of the situation while the oil embargo revealed beyond doubt that such distant events could have immediate impact on U.S. security. Both Kissinger and Nixon agree that at the beginning of the 1973 war they decided to try for a broader settlement at the end of it. Kissinger's strategy was to avoid any attempt at a comprehensive settlement that could be blocked by one or more of the parties. Instead, he would practice step-by-step diplomacy, focusing first on easing the tense cease-fire, then on disengagement, perhaps later on a political settlement. He believed that because of the close relationship between Washington and Tel Aviv, only the United States could deliver an Israeli agreement, so that consequently the Arab states would be obliged to deal with Washington too. Kissinger's beliefs led him into a series of mediation attempts that took Henry from capital to capital, a process that came to be called shuttle diplomacy.

The jet airplane made possible Henry's frequent calls at Middle Eastern capitals; modern communications enabled Kissinger to pass along messages and also to conduct the more ordinary business of a secretary of state. For *this* secretary, who was simultaneously the President's watcher, a loyal staff and a new style of Washington organization freed him for the task in the Middle East.

With the President largely out of play and Kissinger wearing a Cabinet-rank hat, a new arrangement became necessary for the WSAG. Kissinger now found it useful to create a "principal's" WSAG at which he would act as chairman, be represented by his State deputy, and be matched on the Pentagon side by the secretary of defense. It was this amplified WSAG that largely established U.S. policy during the October War and was now to backstop Henry's shuttle effort.

At the White House and OEOB, Henry's move to State also transformed the NSC staff. Brent Scowcroft, a West Point classmate of Al Haig's who had transferred to the Air Force, had done such good work at the White House Military Office that once Haig moved on Henry recommended him as replacement. Richard Nixon duly made the appointment. Since Kissinger mostly worked either out of his Foggy Bottom office or was completely absent on one of his global jaunts, the coordination work of the national security adviser now fell to Scowcroft. Assisting him by keeping track of NSC items, and still Henry's most prominent speechwriter, was Peter Rodman. Some of Henry's increasingly numerous public appearances were being advanced by State people, others by the White House staff. White House advance men were under instructions that Kissinger should never be scheduled to appear with another White House staff member, and never for any type of fund-raising event or any activity where fund-raising would occur.

At the working level the most prominent holdover among NSC staff specialists was Harold Saunders, the Middle East man, by now the longest serving expert on the OEOB third floor. Saunders spent a good deal of the next couple of years on Kissinger's airplane in the thick of Henry's shuttle diplomacy. A new crop of staff specialists were also on the rise, such men as Jan M. Lodal on SALT, William Stearman on military issues, Charles E. Neuhauser for intelligence, Robert B. Oakley to back up Saunders, and Charles Cooper on economics. The staff had grown so large that some of the less sensitive offices, like that for international economics, had spilled up onto the fourth floor. Budget expenditures rose to $2.6 million for fiscal year 1974. To consolidate offices and improve security, the staff wanted to trade in its space on the fourth floor for more on the third. Al Haig, now White House chief of staff, turned them down.

It was at Foggy Bottom that Kissinger gathered many of the familiar faces of his past. Hard-liner Helmut Sonnenfeldt moved over as counselor, with a general hunting license on Soviet-American relations. Hal's friend William Hyland was installed as director of State's intelligence unit, the Bureau of Intelligence and Research, where Kissinger opponent Ray Cline handed in his resignation soon after Henry's appointment. Winston Lord came to take the Policy Planning Staff, which suddenly got authority to screen most cables before dispatch. Foreign Service officer and former NSC staffer Larry Eagleburger also now appeared as Henry's deputy undersecretary for management. Among other Foreign Service veterans, Kenneth Rush stayed on as Henry's deputy. Joe Sisco as the assistant secretary for the Middle East, and Alfred "Roy" Atherton as his deputy. Atherton and Sisco from State and Saunders from the NSC accompanied Henry on most of the shuttle trips, Sonnenfeldt on many of them, and Lord and Eagleburger on some. These officials constituted a small action group surrounding Kissinger.

Within the next months, Kissinger became entrenched at Foggy Bottom, ducking over to the NSC offices when he wished to escape, much as Nixon had a hideaway at the OEOB. Most NSC staff business Kissinger conducted over the telephone or at interagency meetings, where Henry almost always wore his national security adviser hat, bringing in others to represent State. Ken Rush, Nixon's old teacher, his own route to the top blocked by the ascendance of Kissinger, left the department in 1974. Henry promoted Joe Sisco to replace him. Roy Atherton thereupon moved up to assistant secretary and, after thirteen years on the NSC staff, Hal Saunders became deputy assistant secretary for the Near East and South Asia.

Henry gradually admitted a few more people to his inner circle, or brought along extra or different ones depending upon the object of a particular trip, but he basically maintained personal control. The rationale for Win Lord at Policy Planning approving outgoing cables was to ensure they remained consistent with policy, no doubt because Lord would know exactly what was acceptable to Henry and what was not. This notion of personal control seems quite similar to the formula Henry attempted to implement in his early years as national security adviser. Several administrations later, when James Baker served George Bush as secretary of state, *his* attempts to control the department through a small circle of intimates led journalists to call this method of administration the "Kissinger model."

Agreements between Israel and Egypt came finally in January and March of 1974 and September 1975, and between Israel and Syria in May 1974. The disengagements Kissinger achieved were just that and no more. They firmed up the October War cease-fire and got the forces out of contact. Israeli troops returned to the east bank of Suez, then withdrew further into the Sinai, with an international observer force to monitor developments. The UAR accepted limits on the numbers and types of troops it could station east of the canal. The Syrian disengagement was similar. The step-by-step diplomacy failed to broaden into any peace process.

This outcome was unfortunate given that Kissinger and Nixon, by their own accounts, had explicitly set out to forge peace in the aftermath of the war. It may be that Israel was not ready for peace in 1973–1974, but Kissinger's view was that peace might take decades. In consequence he set his aims rather narrowly. If ever there was a time for an attempt at comprehensive negotiation, however, it was at this instant, after the October War had shaken the image of Israeli invincibility.

Hungry for a share of this credit, Richard Nixon conceived the idea of a triumphal tour through the Middle East, to suggest he was still delivering the diplomatic superplays. Kissinger returned to Washington to prepare Nixon for the trip, incidentally holding his first news conference in the wake of the Syrian-Israeli agreement. But the press was more interested in Watergate, one facet of which was those FBI "national security" wiretaps, a matter that involved Kissinger, regarding which, it had been leaked, the House Judiciary Committee was considering new evidence. In his confirmation hearings, Henry denied having any real role. Now one of the reporters asked Kissinger if he had retained a lawyer to defend him against perjury charges.

"I am not conducting my office as if it were a conspiracy." Kissinger retorted.

Another reporter promptly pointed out that this inability to recall and evasion of questions was characteristic of Watergate and asked Henry to answer the direct question of whether he had had a role in initiating the wiretaps.

Kissinger walked away from the news conference having learned just how debilitating the scandal could be. It has been widely reported that Henry afterward threw a tantrum, threatening resignation once more if the press did not stop its attacks. But the media was only reflecting popular suspicions. Columnist John Osborne, for example, who sided with Henry in believing these questions had been off base, nevertheless reported: "My judgment is that Kissinger has been obscuring and unduly minimizing his role in the wiretaps and his knowledge of the plumbers operation ever since the rumors of his involvement began to plague him last year."

Days later the Nixon party left for the Middle East tour, stopping at Salzburg en route to Cairo. There, on June 11, Henry held another news conference. Nixon reports he tried through Haig to dissuade Kissinger. Haig, Eagleburger, and Scowcroft all advised Henry against it. Exhausted after thirty-three days on his most recent shuttle, Henry was in no mood to listen, and a *New York Times* editorial that day set Kissinger off by advocating a perjury investigation. At Salzburg, Henry went public with his threat to resign if the attacks did not cease. But where instrumental threats had some value in the White House, with the public they merely made Kissinger a laughingstock. Afterward, Nixon refused even to talk to Henry, as did press secretary Ron Ziegler. He describes their response as "churlish."

As Henry's step-by-step diplomacy inched forward in the Middle East, the option of trying for a more comprehensive agreement remained open. Kissinger summoned the Wise Men in the course of this effort. Two group meetings ensued. The larger one included Averell Harriman, Mac Bundy, Dean Rusk, Robert McNamara, George Ball, John J. McCloy, C. Douglas

Dillon, David K. E. Bruce, David Rockefeller, and others. As was his wont, George Ball was among the most forthright, advising a return to Geneva and a multilateral approach as the only feasible path. A smaller group of academics met directly with Kissinger as well. They included Stanley Hoffman and Nadav Safran of Harvard and Zbigniew Brzezinski of Columbia. The seminar-style convocation, observed by *New York Times* reporter Edward Sheehan, commissioned to do another of those inside accounts Henry seemed to favor, quickly identified the three possible options. They were to seek a comprehensive settlement, to seek a full peace agreement covering only part of the region (such as Egypt), or to revive step-by-step diplomacy. Sheehan reports that the rough consensus favored the first option. Kissinger was noncommittal. When the reporter asked how Henry planned to deal with the issue of the dispossessed Palestinian population, Kissinger shot back, in an apparent reference to American Jewish opinion, "Do you want to start a revolution in the United States?"

Within a year of Kissinger's departure from office, Egypt's President Anwar Sadat began making exactly the sort of bold move Henry had resisted. One of the themes Sadat stressed was the necessity of dealing with the Palestinian question. Kissinger confesses in his memoirs that Sadat's actions startled him.

Meanwhile, Richard Nixon was gone. At the time of Kissinger's Salzburg statement, Nixon had already begun his Watergate end game, appointing Gerald Ford Vice President, continuing to resist investigation. With their stream of revelations of sordid action at the heart of government, the White House tapes progressively undermined Nixon's protestations of innocence.

Some aspects of Watergate struck close to the NSC and its staff, but Kissinger was ultimately very lucky. Henry had had nothing to do with the White House "enemies" list, which turned out to include former Bundy-era NSC staffer Marcus Raskin, an administration critic at the Institute for Policy Studies, an enemy in the world of ideas, but hardly a dangerous man. Kissinger also had nothing to do with talk of firebombing the Brookings Institution, another Washington think tank, where Mort Halperin had gone after leaving the NSC staff. On the other hand, Henry was rather more involved with the FBI wiretap on Halperin, and along with Nixon would be made a defendant in a civil damage suit brought by the former staffer, in which Kissinger and Nixon were ultimately found at fault. No perjury charge was brought against Kissinger on the wiretaps at congressional impeachment proceedings, and a feeling that foreign policy matters should be excluded led the House Judiciary Committee to reject an impeachment count that would have indicted Nixon for the secret bombing of Cambodia.

Nixon announced his resignation in a speech on the evening of August 8, 1974. He handed a one-sentence letter of resignation to Al Haig, who delivered it shortly before noon the next day. At about that time Nixon made some farewell comments on the White House lawn and departed for *Air Force One* and his last flight as President to San Clemente. The disgraced President recalls advising Gerald Ford that the one man who would be indispensable to him would be Henry Kissinger. To Kissinger he recalls saying, "You must stay here and carry on for Jerry the things that you and I have begun." Resignation brought an end to a national political trauma.

A FORD NOT A NIXON

▲▲▲

P resident Gerald R. Ford had no difficulty taking Richard Nixon's advice to heart. One of his first acts was to have Kissinger in for a lengthy review of the world situation in the course of which he insisted that Henry stay on. Ford's transition team quickly recommended that Kissinger be relieved of his post as national security adviser, but Jerry would have none of that. Instead he replied affirmatively to a series of Kissinger questions on whether he wished to continue with Nixon's policies on arms control, Soviet-American relations, the Middle East, and so forth.

The next morning, with Ford not yet twenty-four hours in office, he confronted his first significant national security decision when Kissinger, Brent Scowcroft, Secretary of Defense James Schlesinger, and CIA director William E. Colby came to him for final authority to complete an intelligence operation already in progress. It was an attempt to recover portions of a Soviet ballistic missile submarine sunk in the Pacific Ocean years earlier. President Ford agreed and the project, to retrieve portions of the wreck along with significant intelligence information, went ahead.

Immediately after meeting privately with this group of NSC principals, Ford went on to preside over his first session of the NSC. Unlike his predecessor, Ford had no interest in any big push during his first weeks. It was a month before another council meeting, although then there were a brace of sessions on September 9 and 14. High on the agenda were the Middle East and the Soviet Union. Ford first received Soviet Ambassador Anatoli Dobrynin on August 14, and Foreign Minister Andrei Gromyko on September 20.

Before the end of his second week Ford settled into a routine he maintained through the remainder of his presidency. He would get up about 5:15 A.M., then go through that day's *New York Times, Washington Post,* press shop news summary, and CIA intelligence summary. After that, Ford would shower, dress, breakfast, and be at the Oval Office by about 7:30. First into the office was Brent Scowcroft, who matched the President minute for minute, often working past midnight and always at his office before seven in the morning. Scowcroft would appear alone or with David Peterson of the CIA, who could field the President's questions on the daily brief. Al Haig, whom Ford kept to symbolize continuity, appeared with the schedule and a list of decisions to be made that day. Before long Haig was succeeded by Donald H. Rumsfeld, who did the same work. "Rummie" was from Ford's home state, Michigan, had been a wrestler at college, congressman, Nixon appointee, and ambassador to NATO. Next would normally be political adviser Jack Marsh, who had been Vice President Ford's national security aide. Henry Kissinger would usually appear between nine and ten in the morning and stay an hour or more, first reviewing urgent matters, then discussing philosophical points.

Ford's primary interests turned out to be domestic, so his national security people got a good deal of freedom of action. That was especially true for Kissinger, who had such stature at the time that Ford consulted him even on domestic matters. It was true of Ford's September 1974 decision to pardon Richard Nixon, before the disgraced President had yet been charged with a crime; and Henry was sworn to secrecy. President Ford tried to balance the political impact of a pardon with a simultaneous amnesty for Vietnam War draft resisters he announced in a speech in Chicago before the Veterans of Foreign Wars convention.

Arms control was the most immediate issue in foreign policy at the time. There had been desultory exchanges within the administration, peppered by the growing animosity between Kissinger and Defense Secretary Schlesinger, and further complicated by Senator Henry Jackson. An economist and former RAND Corporation whiz kid, Jim Schlesinger had become a Nixon favorite as the result of his work on a budget study of the intelligence community, and had been made director of central intelligence, then secretary of defense. In that job he matched Henry in Cabinet rank, as well as Kissinger's knowledge of the finer points of nuclear strategy and weapons, and had the Pentagon under his authority. A struggle between the two had been growing, owing to their differences over the October War, arms control, and the development of nuclear cruise missiles; where Schlesinger sided with the military, who had little interest in the program. In late 1973, in Henry's capacity as chairman of one of the NSC subcommittees, the Defense Program Review Committee, Kissinger issued a directive for DOD to get cracking on the cruise; Schlesinger promptly quashed the order.

The specific problem areas with SALT were the old question of MIRV limits and a new one of offensive force reductions. The first SALT agreement had been a simple freeze, which left the Russians with substantially more ICBMs, though offset by American MIRVs and much higher numbers of bombers. To get a handle on the Soviet throwweight advantage, which in the long term could translate into a MIRV lead, there was great interest in a new limit, preferably a reduction, on "heavy" ICBMs like the Soviet SS-9 and SS-18. The appearance of the latter during 1973 made it mathematically predictable, according to Kissinger, that United States land-based missiles would become vulnerable to a Soviet strike by the mid-1980s at the latest. Kissinger wished to use SALT to delay the emergence of that threat.

Senator Jackson, assisted by conservative colleagues and such able staffers as Richard Perle and Dorothy Fosdick, attached a condition to congressional approval of the SALT agreements that future ones had to provide for "equality" between the sides. Schlesinger played to the equality condition, in turn, maintaining it required equal limits for the two sides for every category of weapons, even if that meant accepting large Soviet ICBMs that could not be matched by any American missile program. The Pentagon came back with the idea of equal MIRVed throwweight, not realistic in Henry's view because the United States would be giving up nothing and so the Russians would never agree. The Joint Chiefs finally offered a little hope by proposing "equal aggregates," which meant equal overall numbers of nuclear delivery vehicles, and implied a freedom to choose which forces would make up the aggregate.

The suggestion went up to Ford's NSC meeting on September 13, 1974, and received further airing at the council on October 7 and 18, prior to another Kissinger mission to Moscow. Those meetings considered five to eight building-block-style options for a United States proposal developed by the Verification Panel, DOD, and State. Agreement was now a matter of urgency since SALT negotiations had *already* resumed. Alex Johnson had had to leave without *any* instructions, much less an agreed-upon proposal. Johnson had left a paper describing the instructions he wanted, and that too contributed to the October deliberations. President Ford selected a hybrid of two options providing for equal aggregates and for a separate sublimit on MIRVs. Ford insisted he wanted a strong push for an agreement, while ACDA director Fred Iklé was ambiguous and Pentagon and JCS representatives seemed torn between limiting the Russians and preserving their own flexibility to deploy fresh nuclear forces.

Henry Kissinger went to Moscow with the latest offer. By now he no longer had the freedom of action he once enjoyed. In September, Kissinger had testified before the Senate Foreign Relations Committee, defending the desirability of détente in general and SALT in particular. He described Soviet-American relations as a balance of risks and incentives, but was reduced to arguing against linkage, a tactic he himself had championed— because Senator Jackson had effectively imposed it in connecting Soviet emigration policy with trade concessions and SALT. Over the summer Jackson had also used the resignation in protest of Paul Nitze from the SALT delegation to bring out the case of the unusual "clarifications" of the SLBM limits. Henry had sought those *after* the Moscow summit, which some contended made them secret agreements. The diplomats could not but be aware of Kissinger's out-of-channels bargaining, since John Newhouse's inside account of SALT I, according to Alex Johnson, contained details the SALT delegation itself did not know. Newhouse apparently confirmed to Nitze that the NSC had been the source of his information. Questioned about Newhouse's sources at his own confirmation hearings, Kissinger denied any knowledge. Finally, the public had become aware of the mutual

suspicion between the JCS and Kissinger when the Radford affair was revealed at the outset of 1974. Kissinger maintained his back channels, but
using them acquired a political cost. With steering, backstopping, and monitoring groups, an entire bureaucracy was being created around the issue
of arms control, going beyond Kissinger's ability to dominate through the
Verification Panel. The Joint Chiefs already had official representation
on the SALT delegation, but by now everyone was aware that might not
be the true locus of negotiation. Impelled by the Schlesinger-Kissinger
schism, the Pentagon was now agitating for direct representation on Henry's
diplomatic missions.

Kissinger seemed depressed when he met with Alex Johnson just before
the Moscow mission, but the atmosphere in the Russian capital was busi-
nesslike and cordial. Henry presented the American proposal, a preview of
which he had passed on through Dobrynin. Brezhnev countered with an
offer that would give the Soviets a higher aggregate number but allowed
the United States an advantage in MIRVed missiles. When the United States
insisted upon equal limits, Brezhnev replied he could go either way. The
state of play sounded fine to Jerry Ford, who quickly arranged a "mini-
summit" with Brezhnev in the Soviet Far East, to be added on to a scheduled
November visit to Japan and South Korea. The idea was to complete a
comprehensive SALT II agreement whose details could then be fleshed out
by the regular SALT negotiations.

This summit took place at a military sanatorium outside Vladivostok
named Okeanskaya. Arrangements were primitive by summit standards.
President Ford thought it looked like "an abandoned YMCA camp in the
Catskills." He greeted Brezhnev and Gromyko, who had traveled by train
to meet at a military airfield near Vladivostok. Ford and Brezhnev got on
well, exchanging small talk regarding their early athletic endeavors, respectively in football and soccer. The train took an hour and a half to get
from the airfield to the summit site.

At the first session, Brezhnev launched into a typical diatribe. Kissinger
had prepared Ford for that, advising him to be tough and give no ground,
predicting the Soviet leader would be speaking primarily for domestic consumption and soon would bargain more seriously. The Soviets offered to
agree to equal aggregates or lower force numbers but not both. They gave
up their insistence on limiting American forward-based nuclear forces, and
on "compensation" for the nuclear forces of other minor powers and for
its supposedly more vulnerable geographic position. The Russians agreed
to equal aggregate limits of 2,400 for the total number of nuclear delivery
vehicles and 1,320 for MIRVed ones. "Vehicles" included both missiles and
bombers.

During the negotiations a couple of senior Soviet generals assisted Brezhnev, and would pass notes up whenever the discussion came around to
technical matters. Ford, whose party included a total of 140 persons, did
not have official Pentagon representation, although Brent Scowcroft was

present as deputy national security adviser and he was a general. That became significant because of the particular concessions the United States made at Vladivostok: It agreed to exclude a type of Soviet supersonic medium bomber that carried the NATO designation Backfire. It happened that the Backfire was the first really capable Soviet aircraft, and the U.S. military was set on constraining the plane through a SALT agreement. Pentagon representatives on the Ford delegation would certainly have apprised the President of what they thought, at a minimum preventing him from passing lightly over this decision.

Kissinger evidently thought DOD opposition on Backfire could be finessed with the prospect of a comprehensive agreement. In Washington after the summit, when Henry held a background press conference, one of the reporters asked him about the Backfire issue and Kissinger apparently admitted it had been excluded. When the Pentagon refused to abandon its opposition, Henry's answer proved a source of embarrassment and was deleted when a text of the press conference was released. The Backfire issue would prove to be so contentious it provoked an intelligence dispute among the Air Force, Defense Intelligence Agency, and CIA, contributing considerably to blocking SALT II through the remainder of Ford's administration.

President Ford thought the decision he made at Vladivostok was one between equal aggregates or the "offsetting asymmetry" of an agreement featuring a higher U.S. MIRV limit. Since the Soviets rejected constraints on their "heavy" ICBMs, the latter option offered the only means of holding Soviet MIRV development in check. Since there was really nowhere for the Americans to caucus privately, at about 1:00 A.M. Ford went outside for a walk in the snow with his advisers. He was accompanied by Kissinger, Scowcroft, Hal Sonnenfeldt, Bill Hyland, and NSC staffer Jan Lodal. Mindful perhaps of the Jackson forces in Congress, Ford returned to the bargaining table and accepted equal aggregates to be embodied in a ten-year treaty. The details would be finalized elsewhere and expressed in an aide-mémoire to be negotiated in a few days. President Ford and Leonid Brezhnev parted on warm terms thinking they had an agreement.

When the Soviet draft of the aide-mémoire came through, it specified that air-to-surface missiles with a certain range (above 600 kilometers) counted against the vehicle limits. At Vladivostok the United States had agreed to include some air-launched missiles, but cleverly thought it had restricted the category to *ballistic* ones, which was essentially meaningless since neither side had an air-launched ballistic missile or any plans to create one. The Russians thought they were getting a handle on cruise missiles by this means, and Russian interest in restricting them is what finally led the Pentagon to take cruise missiles seriously. Acrimonious dispute over the wording of this part of the aide-mémoire lasted so long the administration was unable to brief Congress on what had been agreed for a suspiciously long time. On December 10 the American side abandoned its insistence on including the word "ballistic" just in order to complete the document and begin the congressional briefings. As Soviet expert Raymond Garthoff has noted, the simple phrase "air-to-surface missiles" without any modifiers "certainly favored the Soviet position."

Once an issue had been made of cruise missiles, the Pentagon happily added them, along with the Backfire bomber, to the list of items in dispute on the U.S. arms control position. For over a year Kissinger tried out, on both the Soviets and the U.S. government, a succession of formulas for accommodating everyone's preferences on the Backfire and cruise missiles, all the while telling anyone who would listen that the agreement was 90 percent complete and needed only a few more details resolved. The process was accompanied by a plethora of leaks, some as damaging as any of those during Nixon's time. Henry's relationship with the upper reaches of the Pentagon remained delicate, and with the Joint Chiefs it was only slightly less touchy.

Ford and Kissinger saw Brezhnev again at Helsinki in mid-1975. They met bilaterally at a big European summit that adopted measures on human rights, trade, and other issues. That time the intelligence dispute over the Backfire bomber led Ford into heated argument with the Soviet leader, both of them insisting they were relying upon the best military advice. The argument brought progress to a halt, while the cruise missile problem remained equally intractable. Kissinger experienced momentary elation in the fall, when he heard Schlesinger at an NSC session concede that the Backfire really was not so important after all; but a change of leadership at the Pentagon took him back to square one.

Kissinger tried a last push at the end of 1975 and beginning of 1976, with Gerald Ford going into an election year and hoping to show an agreement with the Russians as a central foreign policy achievement. After some jockeying among State, the ACDA, the Pentagon, and the Russians, at a January 1976 NSC meeting the military proposed an option with a new formula that would include Backfire, but would count bombers with cruise missiles as MIRV carriers and ban cruise missiles on submarines. Henry took the formula to Moscow, where he made a few final concessions on deployment of cruise missiles aboard surface ships. He cabled the results home, and Ford had Scowcroft call an NSC session for final consideration of the SALT II package. Instead, Fred Iklé of ACDA and Admiral James Holloway, acting JCS Chairman, opposed agreement. At a follow-up council meeting, the representative of the secretary of defense joined them. John Lehman, who had by then moved to ACDA as deputy to Iklé, recalls Kissinger, Scowcroft, and Ford knocking heads together to try to force the bureaucracy into supporting the package.

There was one final council meeting on SALT. This time Lehman deputized for Iklé, who happened to be traveling in Europe. It was late February and the atmosphere matched the weather outside. Ford frowned when Lehman launched into the litany of ACDA's objections.

"What I'd like to know," the President asked Lehman in a very unfriendly tone, "is why the *Arms Control and Disarmament Agency* is here supporting the Pentagon against an arms control agreement."

"Mr. President, because a bad agreement is worse for arms control than no agreement, and giving up Tomahawk [cruise missiles] and leaving out Backfire is a bad deal."

Lehman recounts that he was not again invited to an NSC meeting. Brezhnev rejected last-ditch compromise as a step backward, and Ford concluded that no agreement was attainable before the election. It was the end of arms control in the Ford administration.

As it had for a series of Presidents before him, Vietnam became one of Gerald Ford's more delicate problems. The Paris agreements of 1972 began to unravel quite quickly, starting with the operating difficulties experienced by the assorted bilateral and multilateral bodies created by the accords. Most important was the international control commission supposed to monitor the cease-fire, whose inspection teams were prevented from exercising their full functions. The Vietnamese quasi-government entity, the "commission" for national reconciliation and concord, also proved moribund. Its North Vietnamese and Vietcong members seemed more interested in putting out propaganda, while South Vietnamese officials did their utmost to ensure the body accomplished nothing of a concrete nature.

A second problem grew out of the character of the cease-fire, in which the respective sides got to control the territory they held. That immediately led to a "war of the flags" wherein both sides tried to stake out claims on territory. The land grabbing gradually turned into a pattern of regular military operations. In fact, the ARVN suffered some 12,778 killed in action for 1973, a level of casualties comparable to that sustained during 1967 (12,178).

Thieu desired to force a North Vietnamese withdrawal from the south, but Hanoi refused. The agreements were entirely silent on the subject of withdrawal, leaving Hanoi under no compulsion to do so, while the Enhance project furnished it a reason to counter the ARVN buildup with reinforcements of its own. Since the exact size and composition of North Vietnamese forces in the south had long been in dispute, and since the Paris agreements provided for "one for one" replacement, it was extremely difficult to show that violations had occurred.

By mid-April 1973, United States authorities were claiming that aerial reconnaissance of the Ho Chi Minh Trail revealed the infiltration of thirty-five thousand fresh North Vietnamese Army (NVA) troops, and by the end of the year the figure was put at seventy thousand soldiers, backed by over two hundred NVA guns and plenty of tanks.

If Washington's intent had been to establish evidence for a clear case of aggression from the north it probably would have been better to have gone without Operation Enhance. Hanoi would then have lacked strong reason to reinforce, while such a reinforcement would have permitted the administration to argue that Saigon could not meet it alone, creating a case for renewed U.S. intervention. By artificially inflating the ARVN, moreover, Enhance performed a disservice because the South Vietnamese could not maintain or operate all of the extra equipment, and the attempt to do so soaked up much of the available military aid money. The same funds, devoted to more lavish support with such items as ammunition, would have left Saigon much better off. In addition, the large amounts of equipment furnished the ARVN provided a false impression on Capitol Hill that Saigon had been well taken care of. When the South Vietnamese position thereafter deteriorated, a number of lawmakers drew the conclusion that seemed appropriate—the ARVN just would not fight.

Washington made its charges, as did Saigon, but the whole Vietnam issue was so murky that nothing stuck. Henry Kissinger favored air strikes on the Ho Chi Minh Trail, and there were WSAG sessions devoted to the issue in April 1973, but the JCS did not believe Laos could be bombed without eliminating NVA antiaircraft positions in northern South Vietnam, while Nixon was not prepared to order such action. Kissinger returned to Paris in May and June for new meetings with Le Duc Tho, who simply rejected all charges. Henry believes the failure of the negotiations contributed to demoralization in Saigon. Soon thereafter Washington's hands were tied by passage of the War Powers Act (Public Law 93–148) limiting a President's ability to use military force without congressional authorization. Vehemently opposed by Kissinger and Nixon both, as well as by some liberals who feared the law extended certain powers to the President he had *not* had under the Constitution, Nixon went on to veto the bill. On November 7, 1973, mindful of all the executive arrogance that had led to the Vietnam War, Congress overrode the presidential veto. Nixon's strong promises to Thieu prior to the Paris agreements were worth less than the paper they were written on.

One final aspect of the Paris accords that needs mention is the side deal with Hanoi for economic aid. The evidence suggests that Kissinger did not in fact expect the Paris accords to be self-enforcing. Rather the promises to Thieu were a stick to hold over Hanoi while a promise of economic aid constituted a carrot. In connection with this, on February 1, 1973, Nixon sent a letter to DRV Premier Pham Van Dong informing him that U.S. "preliminary" studies indicated an appropriate contribution of $3.25 billion in grant aid over five years for reconstruction, plus humanitarian and commodity aid in the range of $1 billion to $1.5 billion. About a week earlier, at his news conference explaining the accords, Kissinger had explicitly denied that any secret understandings existed under the Paris accords.

When a few years later legislators were investigating whether Hanoi had returned all American prisoners, they met with Kissinger and were told all relevant documents had been given to Congress. Then, in Hanoi, they learned from a North Vietnamese diplomat of the February 1973 Nixon letter. It was the first they had heard of it. Returning to Washington the congressmen held a further meeting with Kissinger on March 12, 1976. Henry reverted to a defense of the substance of his actions, claiming even his most severe congressional critics would have been proud of the way he handled the matter, and that the Nixon letter was not an unconditional commitment. Philip Habib, Henry's assistant secretary for East Asia, declared in testimony that no agreement existed, that the letter was merely to inform Hanoi of the preliminary U.S. financial assessments. At the White House, on the grounds of executive privilege, Brent Scowcroft initially refused to provide a copy of the correspondence.

The Nixon letter turned out to be a time bomb. It cast further doubt upon Kissinger's credibility at a moment when it was crucial for the evolution of arms control negotiations and other matters. Indeed, had there been an arms control agreement in 1976, a price would have been exacted in congressional ratification proceedings as a result of this unrelated episode. Moreover, because of the fashion in which the story emerged, the press drew the worst conclusions and reported the Nixon letter as a secret agreement after all.

Both North and South Vietnam dispensed with the pretense that the Paris agreement meant anything at all. Perhaps it began sooner for Hanoi, in the fall of 1973 when Le Duc Tho refused to accept the Nobel Prize he was supposed to share with Kissinger, and when it became clear there was nothing to the economic aid promises. Saigon did not believe in the accords either, as symbolized by Nguyen Van Thieu's campaign of the "Four No's," which amounted to rejecting critical elements of the settlement. Saigon did pretend to observe the accords, however, in order to maximize its chances for military aid appropriations in the U.S. Congress.

The hope was an idle one. Whatever their merits or lack thereof, Operations Enhance and Enhance-Plus exhausted the $2.7-billion ceiling placed on military aid for the U.S. fiscal year 1973 (July 1, 1972 to June 30, 1973). For fiscal 1974 the administration asked for a $1.6-billion ceiling but Congress approved only $1.126 billion to cover both South Vietnam and Laos.

During 1974 a similar exercise occurred in connection with the budget for fiscal year 1975. President Ford requested a ceiling of $1.45 billion; Congress approved about $1.0 billion and then appropriated only $722 million. At that level there could be no replacement of major equipment, fuel supplies would be cut by almost two thirds and ammunition by over a third, training would have to be cut back, some aircraft grounded, contract flying hours reduced 30 percent, communications would become ineffective, and so forth. Ominously, however, the Defense Attaché Office's (DAO) own study showed that *no* level of funding that could be expected would endow ARVN with an offensive capability. Congress stood its ground and delayed action on Ford's supplementary request for $500 million, seemingly intent on cutting U.S. losses even if the administration was not.

Ominous signs accumulated rapidly. Previously, the ARVN had held its own, but at the beginning of 1975 the NVA won a clear victory ejecting Saigon's forces from Phuoc Long Province. In March, at the foot of the Central Highlands, major ARVN units were routed at the provincial capital of Darlac, Banmethuot. Serious though they were, those events were but the prelude to a full-scale offensive. That was unleashed days later in the highlands and the northern provinces. Over a matter of a few days the South Vietnamese Army began to disintegrate.

Washington had expected a North Vietnamese offensive since 1974. Bill Hyland was confronted with the prediction when he moved over from the NSC staff to take charge of State's Bureau of Intelligence and Research. Other intelligence chiefs, Bill Colby at the CIA and General Daniel O. Graham at the DIA, did not seem especially concerned, however. Hyland limited himself to writing up a summary for Kissinger. In the late winter came new evidence of NVA preparations for an offensive and the estimate began to appear accurate, but the intelligence consensus was that the offensive would be a limited action. Frank Snepp, for example, the CIA's chief analyst in Saigon, initially believed the NVA purpose was to position Hanoi for a further round of negotiations.

The disaster in Phuoc Long greatly impressed Hyland, who had visited it in 1966, when he had been working on Vietnam for the CIA; he drew the conclusion that South Vietnam's situation was unraveling and a rout would be only a matter of time. He made that clear to Dr. Kissinger and to Phil Habib. Ambassador Graham Martin, who had replaced Ellsworth Bunker, was recovering from dental surgery at home in North Carolina when he heard of this new prediction and he came to Washington to try to knock it down with claims that Thieu had a viable strategy. Beliefs were so strongly held that a shouting match ensued in front of Kissinger between Martin and Hyland plus Habib.

Martin returned to his post in Saigon, where he continued to put all developments in the most optimistic light imaginable. But there was no disguising the fact that the ARVN troops were being driven back into coastal enclaves, or the request the GVN made for American ships to pick up the ARVN troops and move them south to the region around Saigon. Enemy artillery began shelling Da Nang on the morning of March 25.

President Ford held a meeting in the Oval Office with senior advisers somewhat later, on the afternoon of March 25 (Washington time). Present were Secretary Kissinger, Ambassador Martin, Brent Scowcroft, and Army Chief of Staff General Frederick C. Weyand. What became abundantly clear was the lack of adequate information. Ford resolved to dispatch General Weyand to Saigon to conduct a fact-finding mission. Given only a week to complete the assignment, Weyand had to leave as quickly as possible.

White House photographer David Kennerly had been in the Oval Office recording part of the meeting. Kennerly had previously won a Pulitzer Prize for his photographs from Vietnam. After the meeting he went up to Ford.

"Vietnam is falling to pieces," he said. "I've spent two and a half years there as a Time-Life photographer, and I've just got to go back. I have to see for myself what's going on."

"Fine," Ford replied. "Do it. Tell Scowcroft to take care of the arrangements."

Weyand's plane was leaving at dawn. Kennerly left to pack, then realized he had no money. When the President asked if Kennerly had everything he needed, Dave mentioned that he couldn't get any cash. Nonplussed, Ford finally pulled out his billfold and gave the photographer forty-seven dollars—everything that was in it. As Kennerly took his leave of First Lady Betty Ford, the President pulled a quarter from his pocket, flipping it to the photographer.

"Here. You might as well clean me out."

Another man who hustled to go along on the Weyand mission was Kenneth Quinn, the NSC staff specialist for Vietnam, deputized as staff aide to Weyand. A Foreign Service officer on loan to the NSC, Quinn had spent years in the Mekong Delta working with one of the Vietnamese religious minorities, the Hoa Hao. He knew plenty of people still serving in-country and thought he could get a solid perspective. One of his contacts told Quinn they might have until August before the end, but most agreed South Vietnam was on its last legs.

Quinn took a good look at general evacuation arrangements and was able to see how inadequate they were. The embassy and DAO, for example, had revised the standing evacuation plan as recently as February. It provided for the evacuation of some sixty-eight hundred persons, the vast majority of whom would have to be Americans. Quinn encouraged colleagues at the United States embassy to begin thinking in somewhat grander terms.

Also along on the Weyand mission was Eric Von Marbod, the Pentagon official charged with overseeing the supply of equipment to South Vietnam. Von Marbod had been coming to Saigon since 1973 and had a good feel for the limitations of the United States programs. "Vietnamization," he once said, "was like getting nine women pregnant in order to have a baby in one month." Vietnamese interlocutors were now counting on the promises contained in those letters Nixon had sent Thieu at the time of the Paris accords. The letters implied a powerful response like B-52 bombing. Thieu's officials briefed General Weyand on the letters, giving him copies of some of them, and showing them to Von Marbod. The Americans seemed impressed but could not promise anything.

The reality was that a new American intervention seemed impossible, both politically and legally. President Ford was now confined by the War Powers Act in a way his predecessors had never been. He did authorize United States military aircraft and money for an early passage from Saigon of orphaned Vietnamese children in what was called Operation Babylift.

More momentous decisions hinged on the Weyand report. Weyand recommended $722 million in new military aid in his report, and stated: "The use of United States military airpower . . . would offer both a material and psychological assist to [the] GVN and provide a much needed battlefield pause." Privately the general managed in a brief moment to show Ford the Nixon letters, while at the briefing, Von Marbod claims to have made the case for air strikes. "If you do that," he recalls Kissinger objecting, "the American people will take to the streets again."

In Washington the situation sharpened in several ways. Defense Secretary Schlesinger remarked at a news conference that South Vietnam was of little intrinsic importance and that its fall would not affect the world balance of military power. The comment reportedly enraged Kissinger, who thereafter made little effort to ensure Pentagon participation in decisions on Vietnam. Schlesinger also followed Weyand's recommendations privately, however, in pressing for an early start to evacuating the six thousand Americans who remained in South Vietnam. Kissinger opposed such a move as detrimental to GVN morale. Then Senator Henry Jackson, known to have a good working relationship with Schlesinger, charged publicly that the United States had secret agreements with Saigon of which Ford had learned only recently. Kissinger made no direct comment but a State spokesman denied any legal commitment to aid the GVN acknowledging only that a moral commitment did exist. Interviewed later, Ford maintained he knew of the Nixon-Thieu correspondence at the time he succeeded to the presidency, but had not actually read the letters, even though on his first day in office Kissinger had presented him for signing a further letter to Thieu that promised reassuringly that all Nixon's commitments would be kept.

On April 8 and 9, Kissinger convened the WSAG and Ford the National Security Council to discuss appropriate action for Vietnam. This rapidly resolved itself into the $722-million aid request. In the WSAG and NSC deliberations, support for beginning withdrawal came from General George Brown, JCS Chairman; Director of Central Intelligence William Colby; and Schlesinger. Kissinger kept arguing immediate evacuation was unnecessary and would just weaken Saigon. According to CIA analyst Frank Snepp, some got the impression Henry had never been so inflexible on so many issues. Though the secretary of state temporarily carried the day, relying upon Martin's rosy cables from Saigon, NSC staffer Ken Quinn began to make sure the latest and most alarming intelligence reports were put at the front of the President's daily briefing book.

NVA troops were advancing rapidly and began to fight for the town of Xuan Loc on April 9. Xuan Loc was a mere thirty-eight miles northeast of Saigon. At this late date the ARVN suddenly buckled down and fought hard, holding out at Xuan Loc a good two weeks. This tough resistance eventually made a large-scale evacuation possible.

Ford's immediate problem was the aid request resulting from Weyand's report. The President decided to take it to Congress with a speech to a joint session in place of the usual state of the world report. Kissinger remained combative, supplying a speech draft that claimed the Congress was solely to blame for the debacle. Some would continue to push this interpretation of the fall of South Vietnam, ignoring all the many command decisions along the way, but Ford judged the time not ripe for open confrontation. Kissinger was already under fire with the latest secret agreement charges and segments of the media, beginning with the Long Island daily newspaper *Newsday,* were calling anew for his resignation. Ford restricted himself to calling for the aid, asking for an additional $250 million in economic aid for good measure. Two Democratic congressmen walked out on his speech. Senator Henry Jackson told the press the aid request was dead.

On April 18, Kissinger cabled Martin that after "a very sober interagency meeting today" he had to impose an accelerated departure schedule, to get remaining Americans down to under two thousand within four days, and to consult with Thieu about evacuating Vietnamese who were closely associated with the United States.

Next to the passage where Kissinger promised to make available whatever was necessary to accomplish the evacuation, an irreverent aide scribbled: "1 magic wand."

Within twenty-four hours Kissinger had to order, "despite your best efforts and my own instincts," a reduction to eleven hundred Americans by the same deadline. Martin cabled accusing everyone in Washington of engaging in a bureaucratic "cover your ass" exercise. Henry cabled back insisting his ass was not covered: "I can assure you that I will be hanging several yards higher than you when this is all over."

An eyes-only cable from Kissinger to Martin on April 20, according to the secretary of state's text, did something he never had before—revealed details of his negotiations. Henry had gone to the Soviets on the Vietnam matter, and they had gone to Hanoi and then returned to report North Vietnam's statement that it would do nothing to impede an American evacuation. Kissinger now advised that "there is a great deal to be said for trickling Americans out slowly" after that day in order to prolong the evacuation and save the greatest number of South Vietnamese. By April 21 the evacuation was proceeding around the clock by aircraft from Tan Son Nhut. Henry included the text of the Soviet reply in his cable to the ambassador.

Washington clearly seemed to be getting more serious about evacuation. A good deal of the credit belongs to a loose coalition of men who were staff assistants to the WSAG members. The staffers had taken to having lunchtime meetings at State's cafeteria, where they would coordinate maneuvers to get their principals on the move. The group included Ken Quinn, the NSC staff specialist; Lionel Rosenblatt, an assistant to the undersecretary of state; Al Adams, special assistant to Kissinger; Jim Bullington, State's Vietnam desk officer; Frank Wisner of the public affairs office; L. Craig Johnstone from Kissinger's secretariat; and USIA staffers Ev Baumgardner and Frank Scotton. Rosenblatt and Johnstone even went further and, taking annual leave time and their own money, went out to Saigon to help organize the rescue of friends, associates, and other Vietnamese. Irate superiors ordered them back to Washington when it was discovered, but the staff cabal sidetracked the orders so they never reached Ambassador Martin.

With the NVA closing in on Saigon, Admiral Donald Whitmire's Task Force 76 provided ships to pick up anyone who could get to sea, as Ford ordered compliance with the War Powers Act. Whitmire's task force provided helicopters and Marine security detachments, fourteen platoon-size units drawn from various elements of the 3rd Marine Division, together amounting to perhaps 750 combat troops. These forces executed the final heliborne lift from Saigon, called Operation Frequent Wind, on April 29, 1975.

One important command post for Frequent Wind was the White House Situation Room some eight thousand miles away. Brent Scowcroft held sway there for a long, exhausting day of one emergency after another. In the thick of it with him were NSC staffer Ken Quinn and military assistant Lieutenant Colonel Robert C. McFarlane. The latter had come through the White House on a presidential fellowship in Nixon's time, when Scowcroft headed the White House Military Office. McFarlane had impressed Scowcroft but moved on, and was a student at Quantico when Captain Jonathan Howe returned to the Navy. By that time Scowcroft had become deputy national security adviser and, with Kissinger mostly at Foggy Bottom, practically ran the NSC shop. It seemed logical to give Brent his choice for military assistant and he had wanted McFarlane. Scowcroft called the Marine at Quantico and invited him back to Washington; "Bud" McFarlane was happy to return. Frequent Wind would be a poignant moment for McFarlane, who had commanded one of the first Marine artillery units sent to Vietnam at the dawn of the U.S. war.

An Air Force general and former pilot, Scowcroft was well equipped to ride herd on the Vietnam evacuation. On the final day, however, the NVA were closing on Tan Son Nhut and that airfield came under fire. Continued use of large transport aircraft seemed too dangerous. McFarlane was better versed in helicopters, providing Scowcroft able assistance. Scowcroft was also able to knock heads together at CINCPAC and with the fleet commanders when critical bottlenecks showed up. At one point, with Saigon demanding more large helicopter flights, Scowcroft made sure they got them, then cabled the word to Martin. The crisis continued some nineteen hours straight, until at 7:46 P.M. Washington time the last helicopter lifted off from the very roof of the U.S. embassy. Some 1,400 Americans and 5,600 Vietnamese and other nationals were evacuated in the helicopter lift. Marine Major James Kean, chief of the embassy guard, held on until the last moment to get out as many as possible. Another 5,300 Americans and 39,000 Vietnamese came out by other means, including some 6,000 by barge convoy down the Mekong River, organized by Americans at Can Tho. Some 14,000 left by air in the days before the final emergency, and an estimated 65,000 Vietnamese got out on their own in the aftermath or during the first two years of Communist rule. America's Vietnam War had ended.

*   *   *

The final days in Vietnam, searing and tragic as they were, left many bitter and not a little breathless. It was the worst possible time for another incident and yet one promptly occurred.

The incident concerned the S.S. *Mayaguez,* a 10,766-ton container ship belonging to Sea-Land Service of Menlo Park, New Jersey. The ship played a bit part in the last days of Saigon, hauling away vans loaded with records and equipment, reportedly from the U.S. embassy or CIA station, and with such urgency that local Sea-Land employees had been left to find other means of escape. Master of the ship Charles T. Miller had sailed it to Hong Kong, then begun a voyage with general cargo from there to Sattahip, port of entry for most American supplies used at the American bases in Thailand. The ship's route took her up the Gulf of Siam near Poulo Wai, an island seventy miles west southwest of the Cambodian coast.

The exact location of the *Mayaguez* and whether it entered territorial waters was disputed by members of the thirty-eight-man crew, who later sued Sea-Land and the ship's captain. In the chaotic aftermath of the Vietnam War, however, the skipper did not know that Poulo Wai and Koh Tang, another island between it and the Cambodian coast, were being claimed by both Cambodia and Vietnam. In what was probably an effort to enforce the Cambodian territorial claim, patrol boats in the gulf had fired on or briefly detained as many as twenty-five ships or fishing boats in this area over a period of ten days. The action was taken without announcement or public claim; indeed the Hydrographic Office of the U.S. Defense Mapping Service, which usually issued warnings to mariners in circumstances of this sort, had not done so this time. Nor had the State Department.

In any case, the *Mayaguez* was under way at 2:20 P.M. local time, on May 12, 1975, when a gunboat appeared and fired machine guns and a rocket across her bow.

The news caused unhappiness in Washington. Just nineteen days before, Gerald Ford had given a speech at Tulane University that had been widely taken as a eulogy for Vietnam. Now the *Mayaguez* incident had the potential to rekindle the war.

This crisis began as a relatively routine matter. President Ford finished his normal half hour's morning exercises, then went to work in the West Wing. General Scowcroft stepped in at 7:40 A.M. for his national security briefing and told the President there were reports Cambodians had seized an American merchant ship in international waters and were towing it toward the Cambodian port of Kompong Som. Ford ordered a lunchtime NSC meeting.

At Foggy Bottom, Bill Hyland came in early to read the cable traffic in preparation for Kissinger's morning staff meeting. He noticed several items about a merchant vessel, mistakenly identifying it as Filipino. The incident had occurred hours earlier, the reporting was fuzzy, and Hyland assumed Phil Habib was on top of the matter. At the meeting, alluding to the report the *Mayaguez* was under tow, Hyland casually remarked that the Cambodians must have their captured vessel in port by now. Consternation ensued. Henry asked if the President had been called; he had not, Scowcroft was just then learning the same news himself.

Across the Potomac the Pentagon was caught unaware. Press spokesman Joseph Laitin reached his office about 7:00 A.M. to find a copy of a warning from Djakarta, and simply assumed Jim Schlesinger had seen the same thing. He recommended nothing be said until the report could be confirmed. About 9:35 A.M., Ford met with White House staff. "I think we have a little problem," the President told them. "I have some bad news."

The NSC session was held at noon. Stressing the need to respond to the challenge, Kissinger emotionally insisted upon drawing a line lest the United States be perceived as a pitiful, weak giant. He felt what was at stake went far beyond the simple seizure of the *Mayaguez*. Bill Colby told the group what was known so far about the incident itself. All agreed there had to be a response, but Schlesinger and Air Force Chief of Staff General David C. Jones, substituting for the JCS Chairman, pointed out that there were no forces positioned in the Gulf of Siam at that moment.

Ford instructed Kissinger to make diplomatic representations to Cambodia through the Chinese, insisting Phnom Penh release *Mayaguez* and its crew. The specter of LBJ's *Pueblo* incident in 1968 hung over everyone. In Washington, Undersecretary of State Robert Ingersoll gave a note to the senior Chinese diplomat. In Peking, George Bush, then chief of the U.S. Liaison Office, interrupted a picnic at the Ming Dynasty tombs to present a similar note. The episode goes completely unmentioned in Bush's memoir *Looking Forward,* possibly because it ended abortively the next day, when the Chinese returned the note, as they did also in Washington.

Kissinger and Schlesinger, according to the account given one of the major weekly newsmagazines, argued over how much force to use in the situation. The secretary of defense held out for a measured response; Henry argued for "enough force to give the operation broad political impact in Asia." Ford ordered forces into position without any immediate decision. The aircraft carrier *Coral Sea* and her task force were diverted from a ceremonial cruise to Australia. Marines moved from Okinawa and Subic Bay to Sattahip to be in position for a rescue mission. At about 9:35 P.M. that night a P-3 aircraft of the Navy's Patrol Squadron 4, flying out of Thailand, sighted the *Mayaguez* and two Cambodian gunboats anchored off Poulo Wai. Brent Scowcroft called the President with the information an hour later when the news reached Washington. Three hours after Scowcroft called again with an erroneous report the ship had almost reached Kompong Som, but by 2:30 A.M. it had been established the *Mayaguez* was anchored off Koh Tang, where it remained. The President spoke with Schlesinger on the phone for over an hour at 5:52 A.M., reviewing the military preparations.

Ford convened the NSC at 10:22 A.M. It was the 880th session. Henry Kissinger had to hustle to be there, having gone to Missouri immediately following the previous day's meeting, drumming up political support for the administration's foreign policy. The President now ordered deployment of the Marines to Thailand and another carrier to reinforce the *Coral Sea*. Aircraft based in Thailand were to prevent Cambodian boats moving between Koh Tang and the mainland. As a result of this order, the *Mayaguez* crew was strafed and teargassed by American planes that were supposed to be helping save them. Ford ordered a halt to air attacks on one "gunboat" later that day when the pilot saw Caucasian faces peering up from it and requested instructions. A late-night NSC session went over the ground once more; Marines were now in place and two United States destroyers rapidly approaching Koh Tang. The Thai government was seriously disturbed at events and had ordered the Marines out by May 14.

On May 13, faced with imminent loss of the Marine intervention capability, Ford held a final NSC session before ordering in the Marines at 4:45 P.M. *Coral Sea* was almost in place and would shortly be close enough to offer air cover. At the council meeting, Kissinger favored mounting B-52 strikes on the mainland; Schlesinger wished to confine action to the ship rescue itself. Ford overruled his secretary of defense; with the *Coral Sea* arriving, he ordered limited strikes on the mainland from the aircraft carrier.

This council meeting featured an intervention by David Kennerly, the White House photographer who had gone along on the Weyand mission to Vietnam. As the NSC members fell silent, Kennerly spoke up:

> "Has anyone considered," he asked, "that this might be the act of a local Cambodian commander who has just taken it into his own hands to halt any ship that comes by? Has anyone stopped to think that he might not have gotten his orders from Phnom Penh? If that's what has happened, you know, you can blow the whole place away and it's not gonna make any difference. Everyone here has been talking about Cambodia as if it were a traditional government. Like France. We have trouble with France, we just pick up the telephone and call. We know who to talk to. But I was in Cambodia just two weeks ago, and it's not that kind of government at all. We don't even know who the leadership is. Has anyone considered that?"

President Ford reports he was glad to hear Kennerly's point of view, though others at the meeting seemed stunned the photographer had spoken up.

Ford felt air strikes by B-52s would be overkill. In this he differed with Vice President Rockefeller, who favored them, and with Schlesinger, who wished to avoid any strikes at all. The JCS Chairman, General George Brown, wished to hit the mainland but rejected using B-52s. Scowcroft and Kissinger united in favoring strong action, but preferred using carrier planes if available. The President ordered carrier strikes plus a Marine assault on Koh Tang.

The assault was the most problematic aspect of the affair. Intelligence about the Khmer Rouge on Koh Tang was incorrect and had no idea of the whereabouts of the *Mayaguez* crew. The Marines went in anyway, encountering fierce resistance from 150 to 200 defenders, as big a force as their own. Three assault helicopters were shot down landing, two more disabled. Of 110 Marines who finally landed, 15 ended up dead, 50 wounded, and 3 missing in action.

That night, about fifteen minutes before another party of Marines boarded the *Mayaguez* herself from the destroyer *Harold E. Holt*, Scowcroft told Ford that a local Phnom Penh radio station had just broadcast that Cambodia was willing to return the ship. The statement said nothing about the crew, and for that reason Ford told the deputy national security adviser to go ahead with the air strike. At about 10:45 P.M., with Ford, Kissinger, and many others at a state dinner for the visiting Dutch prime minister, a Thai fishing craft approached another U.S. destroyer and transferred the crew. Ford, Kissinger, Scowcroft, still in black tie from the dinner, met in the Oval Office for a jovial late-night session. In the corner, straining to seem amused, sat military assistant Bud McFarlane.

Henry Kissinger thought no one would argue with success, but he was mistaken. Columnists rounded on him for the idea of renewed B-52 strikes, evidently first revealed to reporters on Henry's plane during one of his trips. At a news conference he was asked why no State warning had reached the *Mayaguez*. Shooting from the hip, Kissinger replied that a routine notification had gone to the insurance companies that insured ships like the *Mayaguez*. In the court case that flowed from the incident, however, the State Department was forced into an official admission that no records could be found anywhere which supported this contention. Other press snafus occurred at the White House, such as with the timing of the initial announcement by spokesman Ron Nessen. Scowcroft's press liaison, NSC staffer Margaret Vanderhye, was able to clear up some confusions but questions still remained.

For its part, Congress was unhappy with the timing and extent of Ford's consultations under the War Powers Act, and had its doubts about the propriety of the operations themselves. The General Accounting Office (GAO) was asked to do a study of the incident after the *Mayaguez* crew reported they had been released about one hour *before* the Marine attack on Koh Tang. The GAO, working under comptroller Elmer B. Staats, former Eisenhower NSC and OCB official, was no radical hotbed. The GAO report on the *Mayaguez* concluded the attacks had been conducted prematurely, before exhaustion of diplomatic options. When the report was completed in 1976, it was classified by direction of the National Security Council. Negotiations between the NSC and a congressional committee resulted in a watered-down public version of the report, which Ford attacked as an effort to affect the presidential campaign. The GAO report further contained a State Department letter by Lawrence Eagleburger accusing it of "attempts to second-guess the actions of officials acting under the constraints of time."

Someday the documentary record may reveal whether the attacks during this incident were instrumental or punitive in nature, but it can already be said that whatever the time constraints, the administration was certainly deliberating before it acted. In fact, Gerald Ford held more NSC deliberations in the seventy-two hours of the *Mayaguez* incident than he had during the six-week denouement of the Vietnam War.

Unlike many of his predecessors and successors, Gerald Ford benefited from a quiet tenure marked by a relative dearth of crises. The fall of Saigon had been painful but was preferable to managing the war another four years. Ford's most prominent exposure to crisis came in the Middle East. *There,* no doubt, crisis *was* inevitable, and this one occurred in Lebanon, the product of civil war in that unfortunate land.

The crisis was Beirut's, not Gerald Ford's. It involved the Lebanese Maronite Christians, the Druze, and Shiite Muslims, and now had an overlay of Palestinians and PLO factions in the wake of Black September. There had been outbreaks of violence in 1970, 1973, and 1974, but civil war began in earnest in April 1975 when Phalangist militia halted a bus loaded with Palestinians and massacred everyone on board. After that fighting proceeded in an on-again, off-again fashion, with dozens of cease-fires that began hopefully, only to be broken when one faction or another considered itself betrayed, thought it could gain an advantage, or felt the butt of provocation.

Middle Eastern regional powers also sought to gain advantage from the struggle in Lebanon, carefully positioning themselves in the civil war, attempting to manipulate the factions. The Israelis quietly encouraged the Phalange, growing closer and closer until they forged a quasi-alliance with the Gemayels, powerful Phalangist leaders. The Syrians backed certain factions of the PLO, which fought all comers, not only Phalange, for example, but other groups within the PLO.

For many months the United States attempted to remain neutral amid the factional strife. At the end of March 1976 the United States launched an effort to mediate among the factions, sending Ambassador L. Dean Brown, who met with the political rivals. Without much to show, Brown left Beirut on April 23, flying to London where he reported to Kissinger. In the guise of imposing a true cease-fire, the Syrians invaded Lebanon on June 1. A week later, attempting to put a better face on the Lebanese situation, Arab League foreign ministers met and agreed to assemble an Arab peace-keeping force in Lebanon to replace the Syrians.

For Washington an important issue in all this was the safety of approximately fourteen hundred American residents in Lebanon. Periodically updated, the embassy evacuation plan provided several options, including evacuation by ships from an amphibious task force off the Lebanese coast, or by overland road convoy to Damascus, Syria.

On June 16, U.S. Ambassador Francis E. Meloy, Jr., and his economic counselor, Robert O. Waring, together with their Lebanese driver, disappeared while driving through Beirut on official business.

This startled Washington. President Ford called his advisers into session. In contrast to the *Mayaguez* incident, however, he did *not* summon the NSC. They reviewed the information from Beirut CIA station chief Clair E. George but it was fragmentary and uncertain. Brent Scowcroft had had a personal exposure to Middle Eastern uncertainties and he was not about to overreact this time. That had been in 1974, during Richard Nixon's Middle Eastern trip, when Soviet-built MiG jets had closed in on the presidential aircraft as it approached Damascus. The question had been whether the Syrian Air Force jets had been an escort or an ambush and there had been a few tense moments. Everything had turned out all right then, and it possibly would do so again in 1976. But Meloy and Waring were found dead. The question became what to do about other Americans in Beirut.

Ford held another session with a group consisting of Scowcroft, Kissinger, special envoy Dean Brown, George Bush (now CIA director), Deputy Secretary of Defense William C. Clements, JCS Chairman General George Brown, and the White House chief of staff, by then Dick Cheney. Bush placed a large map of Beirut on the conference table and briefed the group. On Friday, June 18, Ford held more private meetings with the same officials, making the decision to conduct an evacuation of those Americans who wished to leave Beirut. The move would be by overland convoy to Damascus the next morning. Though Ford canceled a campaign trip to monitor the situation, had the Beirut map put on an easel in Scowcroft's office, and stayed up until 3:30 A.M. to follow the action, only about a hundred Americans showed up for the convoy, which was finally canceled anyway owing to fighting along the Beirut–Damascus highway.

Huddling with Scowcroft, Bill Hyland, and NSC staffer Robert Oakley, the President now decided to switch to a seaborne evacuation using the amphibious ship U.S.S. *Spiegel Grove*. The vessel received orders to send landing craft to the Beirut quays to pick up evacuees. The situation of potential hostilities and use of a naval vessel brought questions about the War Powers Act; Scowcroft and Ford puzzled over whether the landing craft crews should be allowed to carry weapons. Finally, they authorized standard sidearms. The night of June 20, Ford returned to Scowcroft's office and stayed from 1:55 until 5:16 A.M. as the evacuation progressed. The only shots fired, it turned out, were by PLO guards in the area who fired into the air to keep newsmen away. Despite Washington's crisis atmosphere, however, only 116 Americans and 147 third-country nationals chose to be evacuated.

Though internal discussions considered the provisions of the War Powers Act, the armament of the American sailors and circumstances of the evacuations were such that no formal reports to Congress were required. Kissinger, appearing at a House of Representatives committee hearing on unrelated matters during the episode, restricted himself to giving a general outline of options open to the administration and the time frame in which a decision would be made. Having made his decision in an orderly fashion, Gerald Ford turned his attention back to American presidential politics, for 1976 was an election year.

Focused on politics as he remained, President Ford could not avoid seeing the deleterious effects of the continuing reports of divisions among his senior advisers. Ford himself became less enamored of the style and manner of some Cabinet officers, in particular Secretary of Defense James Schlesinger. Ford's relationship with Schlesinger declined to the point that it seemed reminiscent of Harry Truman's struggles with Louis Johnson more than two decades before. As had the earlier confrontation, this one could end in only one way, and it did, with Schlesinger's resignation.

Henry Kissinger was seen as part of the problem. As Ford professes to have viewed it, the constant feuding between Henry and the secretary of defense made every task harder. Kissinger's post as national security adviser made things worse by inserting Henry between the President and Schlesinger, creating even more opportunities for bickering. Ford had never taken action on the recommendation of his transition team that Kissinger be relieved of the NSC staff job, but in the fall of 1975 the President began to reconsider.

By no means was Kissinger the source of all Jim Schlesinger's problems. Gerald Ford himself had growing doubts about the defense secretary. Ford and Schlesinger had gotten off to a bad start, when there were certain leaks to the press about Pentagon activities during the period of Richard Nixon's resignation. The President suspected Schlesinger as the source, and reports that in at least one instance he actually discussed the leak problem with his secretary of defense, to find them disappear for a while afterward. In any case, the leaks incensed Ford, and there were more on the occasion of the *Mayaguez* affair.

Probably President Ford's biggest single political problem during 1975 was the congressional investigations of the CIA and other elements of the U.S. intelligence community. That too had a Schlesinger angle. The most controversial aspects of intelligence activity were domestic ones, evidence of harassment of political opponents and the like, charges against which the administration had difficulty defending itself after the excesses of the Nixon years. Many of the charges flowed from evidence contained in a compendium of allegations collected within the CIA. This document, notorious to fans of Watergate lore as "the family jewels," had been ordered by Schlesinger during a brief term as director of central intelligence.

To add to the rest, Schlesinger affected a detached style, tended to lecture at meetings, frequently losing the President, who preferred direct exchanges. Ford considered himself a conservative, finding Schlesinger too dovish, a surprising objection given the latter's public image as a hawk. A year into his own administration, Jerry Ford reasoned, it was high time to put his own crew at the top.

374

Having decided to sever the relationship with Schlesinger, Ford turned to thinking about other changes he would like to see. He decided to change the head of the CIA; Bill Colby had faced the succession of investigators gamely, but it had all gone on too long. Ford probably felt that changing the CIA director now would dampen enthusiasm for continuing lengthy, detailed congressional investigations.

An additional motivation for what came to be known as the Halloween Massacre came from rivalries between Kissinger and other members of Ford's White House entourage. Donald Rumsfeld had been the President's "coordinator" (Ford refused to name a chief of staff), but the boss's door had always been open for an appeal. Rumsfeld presided over the White House staff establishment, so was also the supervisor over press secretary Ron Nessen, who had had some real difficulties with Kissinger. During the last days in South Vietnam, the *Mayaguez* incident, and the summer's big détente festival at Helsinki, Nessen felt he was being cut out of the loop, deprived of such key information as access to briefing books before the conference. Ford speechwriters also reported that they encountered difficulties and delay in securing NSC contributions to scheduled speeches. Kissinger insisted such complaints were without foundation.

In 1975 at a NATO conference at Brussels a tiff followed Rumsfeld's attempt to have Ford alone conduct the press conferences and, apparently, cut Kissinger out of group pictures. The Helsinki byplay included a delicate moment between White House and NSC staffs over Ford's speeches. For Ford's departing remarks, the speechwriting staff apparently refused even to give the NSC staff a copy of the draft. Fearing Ford's remarks might put Helsinki in too negative a light, Brent Scowcroft went ahead and submitted an NSC draft text for the departure speech, listing his reservations to Ford in a cover memo. Ford used the NSC text in the comments he finally delivered on that occasion.

At the Helsinki conference itself Gerald Ford chose the words of his speechwriters. They were trying to project the image that Ford was *in control* of national security policy, which included intimating *differences* between the President and Kissinger for the purpose of demonstrating that Ford's foreign policy thinking was different from Henry's. Gerald Ford recounts that this effort by Robert T. Hartman and the other speechwriters was well-meaning but misguided.

In late October, on a Saturday morning the President had Don Rumsfeld, then Henry Kissinger, in to discuss their futures in the administration. Ford had decided to make Rumsfeld the new secretary of defense, while Henry would revert to simply being secretary of state. Bill Colby would be replaced by George Bush, who wanted to be director of central intelligence and promised to still his presidential ambitions for 1976 if he was in that job. When part of the realignment leaked the following weekend, Ford realized he could delay no longer, and held a series of meetings in the Oval Office early on Sunday morning, November 2. Bill Colby came in at 8:00 A.M., to be asked to submit his resignation. Following him were Schlesinger and Kissinger. Henry considered resignation upon being deprived of his NSC position, but decided against it, and ultimately found that he had put down an encumbrance in losing the NSC job. The manner in which Ford handled this "Halloween Massacre" was held against him in the 1976 electoral season, not least because it had involved the simultaneous scuttling of Nelson Rockefeller, his hopes of a place on the 1976 GOP ticket dashed to serve those of Ford.

The Halloween Massacre brought a new era to the National Security Council and its staff. The NSC principals suddenly regained their customary primacy and the full council became the primary decision-making body of government once more. For the NSC staff came the somewhat brash realization that there was life after Kissinger.

It helped the transition that Brent Scowcroft was simply moving up to assume the title that corresponded to the work he had been doing since about the end of 1973. Scowcroft had only to move his desk photos across to the West Wing. The general was a rock of stability for the NSC staff at a moment that could have been quite traumatic. It also helped to have a solid deputy in the general's old slot, and Scowcroft asked Henry to give up William Hyland and send him back from State.

The accession of Scowcroft as national security adviser ushered in a period of consolidation for the NSC staff. Scowcroft streamlined the staff slightly, trimming back to about forty-five professionals, with salary and expenses requested for fiscal year 1976 at $2.9 million, only about 20 percent the size of the request for the White House Office. More women professionals appeared, including Rosemary Niehuss and Mary Brownell for Latin America under Bill Jorden. For the most part the staff ran smoothly, moving forward the succession of NSSMs and NSDMs, which topped out at 318 at the end of Ford's administration.

Scowcroft's capacity for work became legendary, adding to an already notable record of lifetime accomplishment. Fifty years old when he became Gerald Ford's watcher, Brent Scowcroft was not only an Air Force general and former fighter pilot, but a Slavic specialist who spoke both Russian and Serbo-Croatian and had worked as a military attaché in Eastern European nations. He had absolute determination, having rehabilitated himself after serious injury in a plane crash. Scowcroft held a Ph.D. in international relations from Columbia University earned under W.T.R. Fox, the academic who originated the concept of "superpowers" in describing the capabilities of nation-states.

The methods of the new keeper were pragmatic but direct. Scowcroft tried to divide up the work so that either he or Bill Hyland would be with the President's party at all times; Scowcroft, for example, accompanied Ford to the 1976 Republican political convention. The NSC staff was a happier one, with a boss who rarely blew his stack, hardly drank more than a glass of wine, and believed that people who felt good would work harder. In addition, the relationship between national security adviser and his Cabinet-level interlocutors, the NSC principals, suddenly became considerably less turbulent. Scowcroft got the work done, ran a tight ship, did so without controversies between the NSC staff and Defense or State, just when the pundits were convincing themselves that conflict at that level of government had become inevitable. Several NSC staff veterans cite Brent Scowcroft's practice as the model for management of national security staffs.

Through the remainder of Gerald Ford's term the NSC system functioned smoothly, and did as well as it ever had during emergencies, as illustrated in the Lebanon evacuation decisions. There were more troubles in Cyprus, a problem at least as old as Lebanon, and with Turkey; Henry Kissinger began to show an interest in southern Africa, making some effort to mediate in Zimbabwe (then called Rhodesia), and with leaders of the white minority in the Republic of South Africa. The NSC monitored these efforts, something of a turnaround from the year before, when CIA covert action staffs had interpreted Kissinger's grunt in conversation as an order to intervene along-side white South Africa in Angola.

Truly critical changes occurred in NSC machinery during the Kissinger era. Mac Bundy and Rostow had been the President's lieutenants, supported by a well-informed NSC staff, operating the very informal *system* they had developed; Henry Kissinger became the President's agent just out there *operating*. Following Kissinger, the NSC staff acquired an eminence it had not previously had either. Al Haig, Winston Lord, Hal Sonnenfeldt, Sven Kraemer, and others, all carried out independent missions on the Kissinger staff and were proud of their accomplishments. Peter Rodman still wrote his joke memos, but all of them had changed, become more powerful, without their even knowing it. Just how powerful remained to be demonstrated by a subsequent five-star lieutenant colonel, but the trend had been set in motion. Bob Komer, the Chicagoan, by then immersed in the world of the think tanks, would have recognized it.

The quiet passage at the Old Executive Office Building was marked publicly, not by Bob Komer, but Bob Johnson, who preceded Komer and worked on the staff for Truman, Eisenhower, and Kennedy. In an article in the summer of 1969, Johnson wrote that "the Special Assistant and his staff seem to be using the NSC and Review Board mechanisms as fulcrums with which to pry information and policy perspectives." It was a case of emphasizing White House and NSC staffs over the NSC principals. "The evidence suggests that the balance has already tipped toward a system in which the Special Assistant and NSC staff, rather than the NSC, form the key element." Although government operations became less Byzantine under Gerald Ford, and recovered to relative normality after the Halloween Massacre, the pattern of NSC operations retained the newer dynamic. Bob Johnson's observation was deadly accurate.

At the time, Kissinger probably believed he was facilitating delicate operations with all the secrecy. Over time, however, the secrecy created great resentment. Inertia gradually increased in the bureaucracy *against* anything Henry might be *for,* substantially increasing the effort necessary to conduct routine business.

One frequent feature of the NSC-conducted operations of Kissinger's era was use of a dual-track policy. At a minimum the result was much wasted motion in the front channel; at worst the danger included missed signals or treaty loopholes that did much to seal the fate of détente. For Kissinger himself, just conducting all the diplomatic missions was a strain, and detracted from his work as national security adviser. The agreements that resulted did not rise above the flaws in their creation, but the techniques resorted to in the process cheapened the coin of American credibility and forthrightness.

▲▲▲

PART VII

▲

BETWEEN POWER AND PRINCIPLE

America had had too much of the Kissinger style in foreign policy. At least that was what Jimmy Carter decided, and he thought he could do something about it. Carter was running as Democratic candidate for President of the United States. In the summer of 1976, Carter made a speech critical of "Lone Ranger" diplomacy, which became one rallying cry of the political campaign. Carter asserted, "As far as foreign policy goes, Mr. Kissinger has been the President of this country." It was a good line, Carter's advisers believed firmly; those advisers included experts well versed in the ways of Washington, like former officials Cyrus Vance and Paul Warnke; Kissinger-era NSC specialist Anthony Lake; and Columbia University colleagues of Zbigniew Brzezinski, Marshall Shulman, Richard N. Gardner, and Lynn E. Davis. Many of them claimed contributions to Carter's "Lone Ranger" speech and criticism. At intervals during the campaign Carter held weekend brainstorming sessions for which the advisers trooped down to Plains, Georgia, where James Earl Carter had his peanut farm.

Carter seemed about as different from his predecessors as it was possible to be. Not even a national figure really, until his emergence as Democrat front-runner, Carter's strengths were his sound basic instincts and the fervor of his appeals. Insisting everyone call him "Jimmy," Carter gained a populist image. Unlike Ford, Carter could not be seen as an establishment politician; unlike Nixon, he was no foreign policy expert. When Carter proved the victor, suddenly the problem changed from one of winning an election to one of running the government.

Jimmy Carter did not know how different were the two problems. Nor could he imagine that running the federal bureaucracy would be much different from that of the state of Georgia, of which he had been governor. Carter had little awareness of the political cost left to be paid from the diplomatic "superplays" of the Nixon-Ford years. These factors would weigh heavily in determining the fate of Carter's presidency.

▲ ▲ ▲

"I HAVE GOT
EXCELLENT ADVISERS!"

▲▲▲

Some accused Zbigniew Brzezinski of having "selected" Jimmy Carter. That is, years before the 1976 election Zbig, as he was familiarly known, had identified Carter as a potential presidential front-runner and built a relationship with the former governor. What seems to be the truth is more prosaic, if equally revealing. Promoting his own views on international relations, Brzezinski's outreach efforts touched Carter and drew him in, with the Polish-American professor ending up perfectly positioned to leap ahead later when Carter emerged as a national figure. The Carter-Brzezinski relationship represented no mere shot in the dark; Zbig had long practice at giving advice to political candidates. Those he had assisted included Hubert Humphrey, JFK, Birch Bayh, Edward M. Kennedy, Henry Jackson, and Walter Mondale.

There was another aspect to this, one not so evident to the pundits, or at least one to which they paid little heed. Brzezinski wanted to be active and engaged; he undoubtedly saw in aiding politicians a means to that end, and the demand for his services as a measure of his relevance. That word "relevance" was perhaps the key—a much overused word of the epoch, not least by Brzezinski. Zbig's explanation for the rise of opposition to the Vietnam War hinged on the leadership role of elements that realized "consciously or unconsciously" that "there was no role for them in the newly emerging society." In a 1968 article in *The New Republic*, Brzezinski called the antiwar movement "the death rattle of historical irrelevants." The aim of the academic community, Brzezinski told *Newsweek* a year later, was "dispassionate scholarship relevant to society." Zbig saw the more radical elements as recognizing they were "becoming historically obsolescent to American society."

For himself Zbig tried to remain the epitome of relevance, moving back and forth between government and academia constantly absorbing information and giving advice. Whether working at Columbia University or on policy planning at State, Zbig's objective was to be provocative but right in step with the national security consensus. Thus in May 1965, when the issue was Vietnam and the forum the big televised national teach-in, the one LBJ refused to let Mac Bundy attend, Brzezinski showed up to argue the government's case for intervention. A withdrawal from South Vietnam, Zbig insisted, would abandon Southeast Asia to the Chinese Communists. Reaching for the kinds of precedents favored in the Munich analogy, Brzezinski compared the situation to that of Germany or Japan in 1940, or of the Soviet Union at the outset of the cold war. In 1966, at Policy Planning under Henry Owen, relevance was Brzezinski coining the term "peaceful engagement" as slogan for a liberalization of contacts with the Soviets. At Columbia the push for relevance was evident in the way Brzezinski's institute switched names amid the shifting winds of interest in national security and political science. Originally a kind of Eastern European complement to Columbia's Russian Institute, to which it seemed a poor sister, Zbig's shop was created as the Research Institute on Communist Affairs. In the Nixon era the name changed to Research Institute on International Communism and then, in the mid-1970s, to Research Institute on International Change.

That final mutation was a perfect illustration of Brzezinski's drive for relevance. It came at a time when political science, always responsive to trendy theoretical advances, had just discovered multinational corporations and rediscovered political economy. In particular relations between the industrial West and the less developed world, "North-South" relations as they became known, were attracting considerably greater attention as the process of decolonization rapidly increased the size of the community of nations. Newly independent, ideologically nonaligned countries were the majority in the United Nations and other international bodies to a degree that would have made John Foster Dulles blanch.

Coping with these changes became a central problem for international relations theorists like Brzezinski, as well as for national security specialists in government. "World order" politics were conceived in response to this systemic transformation. In this vision the industrialized, wealthy nations of the "First World," and the Communist countries of the "Second," in order to ensure international stability, had a special responsibility for the poor, less developed "Third World." The crippling impact of Third World international debts on economic development was but one example of the new foci for analysis.

Polish-American that he was, Zbigniew Kazimierz Brzezinski's traditional academic interests lay far from the field of world order politics. An impressionable teenager at the time of the Communist takeover of Poland in 1945, Brzezinski was old enough to have some idea of what things had been like in the old days. Coming from the Polish elite, with relatives in high legal and political-party positions and a father in the Polish diplomatic service, his family clearly lost heavily in the takeover. By then his father was Poland's consul general in Canada, and the family remained there instead of returning to Europe. Zbigniew, educated by private tutors in Poland, France, and Germany, then in Canadian schools after 1938, matriculated for college at Montreal's McGill University in 1945. He earned an undergraduate degree in economics with honors, then went to Harvard for doctoral study. There he worked in political science, writing a dissertation to demonstrate that dramatic purges in Stalinist Russia constituted the political system and not an aberration of it. Much of Zbig's subsequent work continued in that vein. He coauthored books comparing political power in America and Russia, and on totalitarian dictatorship and autocracy; edited volumes on political control of the Soviet military and on Africa in the Communist world; and wrote major studies of ideology and power in Soviet politics and of the Soviet bloc. Zbig remained a hard-nosed cold warrior, very competitive, steadfastly convinced that Moscow could be forced to recede or disintegrate. The economic backwardness, the nationalities problem, disparities among ethnic groups in population growth rates, the general dearth of resources, were sure to impose limits on Soviet power.

In Brzezinski's worldview the limits would become apparent in the course of superpower competition. As he looked toward the 1970s, during his days supporting Hubert Humphrey, Brzezinski thought the end of the Vietnam War plus the gradual but steady growth of Soviet military capability would lead to a situation where the superpowers would have "overlapping" global military postures and conflicting global policies in "a dynamic setting of Third World instability." Referring to an African colonial crisis of the 1880s, which nearly drove the European great powers to war, Zbig argued, "at the minimum, at least one 'Fashoda' is to be expected." Zbig's aim was to position the United States so that, when "Fashoda" occurred, the Soviets could be trounced and their inherent limitations brought into play.

In all this Brzezinski was not far different from Henry Kissinger. They were compared with what must have been for Zbig annoying frequency, down to their accented English.

Brzezinski's response to the trendy transnational focus of 1970s political science was to try to stay relevant by adopting some of its perspectives, grafting them upon his older worldview. He attempted a work of theoretical synthesis in *Between Two Ages,* published in 1970, postulating a "technetronic era" conditioned by the flow of information, extensive in the industrial countries, sparse in the Third World. Less developed lands remained passive participants in the Brzezinski schema, for he saw the Third World as a "victim of the technetronic revolution." The essential features of that world, to Brzezinski's mind, were that the First World had entered a post-industrial age while the Third had yet to enter the Industrial Revolution and the Second (Communist) remained mired somewhere in the middle of it. Brzezinski built upon the theories of Canadian communications theorist Marshall McLuhan, integrating them with an international relations perspective.

Zbig's theory book got mixed reviews. Some thought it original, others tendentious. It did not help that Brzezinski had chosen to expatiate on a number of subjects. "Compelling ideologies," he wrote, "thus are giving way to compulsive ideas, but without the eschatology that characterized other historical eras." He indulged himself in rhetoric directed at the student antiwar movement, arguing that the younger generation were reacting to threatened economic obsolescence, like the Luddites who destroyed machinery in England at the dawn of the Industrial Revolution. Their attraction to poetry, to lyricism, was a clash between "emotion and necessity." The student generation was not a true revolutionary class because it had failed to master techniques for social organization. Brzezinski argued that the New Left would be succeeded by a "Violent Left," and speculated positively about its suppression though, as Zbig put it, "organized coercion would require the introduction of a variety of controls over the individual," and though he recognized the nation would necessarily move to the right in the course of such a campaign.

It is the vehemence of Brzezinski's view that is striking, even more so in retrospect, for *Between Two Ages* is generally remembered as a mildly innovative study of international media with a genuflection toward "global problems of human growth and nourishment." The book marked Brzezinski's passage into support for a partnership among the United States, Western Europe, and Japan to help answer the problems of the Third World. In fact Brzezinski ended his book with an appeal for the formation of a supranational First World club to address foreign-aid and economic issues and to improve "North-South" relations.

Taking his own advice, Brzezinski attracted the attention of Chase Manhattan Bank chairman David Rockefeller, himself concerned about international economic trends. Organizing committees of like-minded individuals in Europe and Japan, American proponents soon christened what they called the Trilateral Commission, composed of prominent figures from politics, business, and academia. Former SALT negotiator Gerard C. Smith became the North American chairman of the Trilateral Commission, Brzezinski its director. Among North American members of its executive committee were Robert McNamara, Pentagon officials Harold Brown and Paul Warnke, Rockefeller, and Japan expert Edwin O. Reischauer. The commission held meetings and informational events, published a newsletter, and assembled a series of quarterly analytical reports intended to highlight "trilateral"-type issues.

Enter Jimmy Carter. Brzezinski originally sought out the Georgia politician in a gambit to add to the luster of the Trilateral Commission. Trilateralist and *Time* magazine editor Hedley Donovan suggested Carter might be appropriate and Zbig took it from there. Jimmy Carter, who needed a means of building his knowledge of foreign affairs to be a credible presidential candidate, proved most amenable.

Zbig learned in 1974 that Carter would declare for the presidency and needed a source of regular foreign policy advice. Brzezinski signed on. Carter acknowledged the tie in a handwritten note that New Year's Eve. Zbig sent Jimmy a steady stream of memoranda on issues of the moment, interspersed with copies of his articles and speeches. The relationship blossomed through 1975. For Brzezinski the moment of real commitment came that summer, at a Trilateral Commission meeting in Kyoto, Japan, where Carter made an eloquent plea for a fair settlement in the Middle East. When Zbig told his wife Muška how impressed he was, she encouraged him to pitch in and help the Carter campaign more actively. By the end of the year he had emerged as principal adviser to Carter on foreign affairs.

After the election Carter made Brzezinski chief of the transition team for national security. According to Zbig, as late as his breakfast with Carter on the morning of the first debate with Gerald Ford, he did not know Jimmy well. Brzezinski denied to reporters that summer any expectations of a Carter administration job, and continues to assert in his memoir that, as far as he himself was concerned, he would say nothing about jobs to President-elect Carter. For national security adviser he suggested Harold Brown, Henry Owen, or Richard Gardner. For secretary of state he favored Cyrus Vance over George Ball or Paul Warnke.

Carter indeed chose Vance for secretary of state, and the advice helped convince Jimmy that Zbig could work well with Vance if he too was in the new administration. On the evening of Pearl Harbor Day, Carter invited Brzezinski to come to Atlanta to discuss positions in the administration. The two men talked of the positions of deputy secretary of state and assistant for national security affairs. Brzezinski preferred the latter.

Attending a friend's Christmas party some days later, Brzezinski was interrupted to take a telephone call from Carter, who teasingly offered the NSC job.

"Zbig, I want you to do me a favor. . . . I would like you to be my national security adviser."

"That's no favor—that is an honor," Brzezinski replied. "And I hope and feel confident that you won't regret your decision."

"Actually," Jimmy drawled cheerfully, "I knew as of some months ago that you were my choice, but I had to go through all these processes of selection. But I knew all along."

During the transition Brzezinski never hesitated to express his views regarding prospective appointees, even though Anthony Lake was the chief of Carter's personnel task force. Brzezinski notes his belief that George Ball was a poor organizer, too much an Atlanticist, and had controversial views on the Middle East. Elsewhere he writes that Ball had been the source of much "anti-Kissinger" agitation that reached Carter's ear before the "Lone Ranger" speech. Paul Warnke was perceived publicly, Zbig thought, as too "soft" on Soviet-American relations. Zbig was also uneasy about the policy orientation of the second rank of officials Carter chose, fearing that Carter "would not be obtaining, especially from the State Department, the kind of realistic and hard-nosed advice which should balance his more idealistic views."

Brzezinski's concern is puzzling, and must have been especially so to his Trilateralist colleagues of the time. The one clear thread that runs through

Carter's early appointments is definitely the Trilateral one. Vice President Walter F. Mondale was a Trilateralist. Others included Cyrus Vance; Harold Brown, whom Carter chose for secretary of defense; Paul Warnke, selected to direct the ACDA and be chief SALT negotiator; Warren Christopher, deputy secretary of state; Richard Gardner, ambassador to Italy. Anthony Lake, who had stood on principle in resigning from Kissinger's NSC staff during the Cambodia revolt, had worked on papers for the Trilateralists. He took over the Policy Planning Staff under Vance. Leslie Gelb, director of the Political-Military Bureau at State, had also been a Trilateral author. Richard Holbrooke, who became assistant secretary for East Asian and Pacific affairs, was a Trilateralist who had been managing editor of *Foreign Policy*.

Perhaps Brzezinski objected to the smattering of talent recycled from previous Washington administrations. Brown and Vance typified this crew, but they could only be described as top-notch. Others included Brown's boyhood Manhattan friends, Spurgeon Keeny, and more NSC staff veterans like Robert Komer and Richard Moose; even Larry Eagleburger was kept in government with an ambassadorial slot (to Yugoslavia).

Not to be satisfied, nine days *before* Carter's inauguration Brzezinski noted in his diary: "I will try to sensitize [Carter] to the need to have somewhat more tough-minded a group in security and arms control-oriented areas. I have a slight sense that perhaps too homogenous a group is emerging."

While worrying about the ideological toughness of Carter's bureaucracy, Brzezinski himself went out of his way to appear open to the concerns of the post-Vietnam liberal consensus, and to recruit a staff with a wide range of perspectives. Zbig divided his NSC staff into "clusters" that had regional or functional specialties, a few of which had additional substaffs. Trilateral interests were clearly to the fore in Brzezinski's creation of a "North-South" cluster. World order concerns found expression in the functional "global issues" cluster, which handled arms transfers, security assistance, chemical warfare, nonproliferation, refugees, and human rights.

Initially pared back to a pre-Kissinger size, the Brzezinski staff started with two dozen professional specialists, two consultants, plus Zbig, his deputy, and a support staff. Kept over from the Scowcroft staff were Bill Hyland, directing the Soviet-Eastern European cluster, and seven other staff specialists, plus some support people. Among Zbig's additions were onetime coauthor Sam Huntington, his former boss Henry Owen, given a supergrade position as special representative for economic summits, and fellow academic Robert Hunter, who handled European affairs. These men held views similar to Brzezinski's. Paul Henze, first chief of the intelligence cluster, was even more conservative. So was Brzezinski's military assistant, Army Colonel William E. Odom.

Brzezinski's deputy was David L. Aaron, formerly a top aide to Walter Mondale as a senator, and Mondale's personal designee to the Church

Committee investigating United States intelligence abuses. Church Committee work actually seems to have been a significant qualification considered by the Carter administration in its initial personnel selections, including Karl Inderfurth, Zbig's special assistant; Gregory Treverton, a staff specialist on Western Europe; Richard K. Betts, NSC consultant; and Lynn Davis, who, though she went to the Pentagon, had been author of the initial draft of the chapter of the Church Committee's report that dealt with the National Security Council. Given that the Church investigation aroused acute resentment in certain quarters at the CIA and Pentagon, people elsewhere in Washington worried about Zbig's staff in much the same way he worried about Carter's appointments.

Also on the liberal side among the Brzezinski staff were his Global Issues director, Jessica Tuchman. A thirty-one-year-old, she was a former issues director for the presidential primary campaign of progressive Arizona Democrat Morris K. Udall. Bill Quandt, heading the Middle East cluster, had been brought back by Brzezinski for another stint on the NSC staff after leaving Scowcroft's employ. Some considered Quandt an Arabist who favored accommodating the Palestinians in a Middle East solution. Then there was the NSC China specialist, Michel Oksenberg, long a colleague of Brzezinski's at Columbia, who had just moved to the University of Michigan and whom Zbig brought with him to Washington. A virtually unknown quantity on the staff was Zbig's Latin America specialist, Robert Pastor, who defended his dissertation for a Ph.D. at Harvard the day before joining the NSC. Finally, there was the defense cluster chief, Victor Utgoff, whose views were decidedly more liberal than Zbig's.

Brzezinski's private criticism of Carter's appointments could be applied to Zbig's own staff. In fact, Richard Burt, a moderately conservative *New York Times* reporter, would term Brzezinski's NSC staff a "floating seminar." Naturally, coordinating national security policy had nothing to do with academia or seminars.

Though comparisons with Kissinger were annoying, Zbig in some ways encouraged them. Probably thinking he was distinguishing himself from Henry, Zbig insisted upon having a different job title. Carter agreed. Early news stories invariably noted the change and made another Brzezinski-Kissinger comparison.

In at least one respect the actual machinery of Carter's NSC stood in contrast to that of his predecessors. Nixon and Ford had employed a panoply of NSC subcommittees, from the WSAG to the 40 Committee to the Verification Panel, through which Kissinger exercised leadership over the bureaucracy. President Carter changed that, but not at Brzezinski's instigation. Zbig actually proposed a structure similar to the old one, merely reducing the scope of the national security adviser by reducing his chairmanships to three among the seven NSC subcommittees. Carter objected to the number of committees and ordered Zbig to come up with a simpler, cleaner structure. Brzezinski came back with a scheme to carry out all business with but two interagency bodies: the Special Coordination Committee (SCC); and the Policy Review Committee (PRC). The arrangement was formalized after a preinauguration meeting Carter held with Brzezinski and other advisers at St. Simons Island off the Georgia coast.

On January 20, 1977, followed Carter's presidential directive creating his national security machinery. A separate order established Presidential Directives (PD/NSC) to replace NSDMs and Presidential Review Memoranda (PRM/NSC) supplanted NSSMs. Thus Carter retained that feature of the Nixon-Ford NSC system. Under the newly revised NSC system, the full council met only when it had to. Otherwise the SCC and PRC would conduct most business, while Carter kept his finger on the pulse of the bureaucracy through weekly Friday morning breakfasts akin to LBJ's Tuesday Lunches. Brzezinski followed matters up himself at weekly lunches with Vance and Harold Brown.

"I don't envisage my job as a policymaking job," Zbig told reporters when Carter announced the appointment and introduced him. "I see my job essentially as heading the operational staff of the President, helping him to integrate policy, but above all helping him to facilitate the process of decision-making in which he will consult closely with his principal Cabinet members." Things turned out much differently in practice, and this statement is nowhere to be found in the Brzezinski memoir, but it is worth noting that Zbig seemingly accepted Carter's "Lone Ranger" critique, at least initially. Nor did Brzezinski object to Jimmy Carter's public statements that he intended to have a strong secretary of state.

Had one cared to look closely, however, a few straws could already be seen in the wind. One was the fact that Zbig established a press office for the NSC staff, not just a designated staff person to work in tandem with the presidential press secretary, but a full-scale operation. Brzezinski put a *Time* magazine reporter, Jerrold L. Schecter, in charge of it. At the very same press conference he pledged not to make policy, Zbig entertained and answered in some detail a long series of reporters' questions on Carter administration policy on a range of issues. At his own introductory news conference earlier, Cy Vance had *refused* to take policy questions on the grounds the new team had yet to study them.

Jimmy Carter was smart and he could be tough. The President did not mind, indeed encouraged, strong-willed advisers with contrary views. A few months after coming to the White House he exclaimed to a national newsweekly, "I have got excellent advisers!"

Carter wanted to be the judge, to choose from the range of viewpoints. This augured well for decisions, in Carter's scheme of things. But the President underestimated the degree to which differences would become evident, and also the extent of political damage the appearance of a divided administration might cause. It was a lesson learned only in retrospect, and some of the sharpest conflicts would concern the role of the national security adviser.

DÉTENTE TO
CONFRONTATION

▲▲▲

he arms race was one thing Jimmy Carter was serious about. He talked of agreements during the campaign and came to office determined to get moving on SALT II. In fact, Jimmy was willing to go a lot further than the existing agreement. The bureaucracy, even the arms controllers, understood the SALT regime as stabilizing the nuclear balance more or less where it stood. Vladivostok, so the line went, had put a "cap" on the arms race. At one of his early military briefings Carter startled participants by asking them to describe the consequences if the sides *reduced* to very low levels of force, say only two hundred missiles to a side. The military started a crash study of the strategic balance as a result. One of the earliest Presidential Review Memoranda, PRM-2, concerned the effect deep SALT cuts might have on the nuclear balance.

The arms control proposal on the table continued to be Ford's Vladivostok agreement. Carter wanted to explore something more ambitious. Brzezinski too wanted something new, if only to distinguish the administration from its predecessors. The arms control community, inside and outside government, were ambivalent about Vladivostok, especially after the aide-mémoire dispute, and were not averse to having another try at an agreement. The JCS, who had lost out on Vladivostok, getting neither Backfire constraints nor limits on Soviet large ICBMs, welcomed a new effort, especially after Carter approved negotiating instructions that contained a sublimit of 150 on "heavy" ICBMs, requiring the Soviets to dismantle more than half their force of these MIRVed missiles. In mid-February, Carter received a letter from Senator Henry Jackson critical of the Vladivostok accord for not going further. Carter figured from that that a more extensive SALT proposal might also gain some favor from the traditional SALT opposition.

Washington's SALT decision-making now proceeded within the NSC Special Coordination Committee, the interagency unit Brzezinski chaired. The Carter administration SCC held its first session in the White House Situation Room on the morning of February 3, 1977. Having given some thought to the symbolism of the occasion, Brzezinski asked the President to initiate the first session. Carter made a general statement of satisfaction with the national security arrangements he had prescribed, then turned things over to Zbig and left. President Carter's only statement of substance was to reiterate his commitment to a SALT proposal containing deep cuts.

Zbig proceeded quite methodically to build the SALT options decision. The SCC discussed several alternatives, and set up ad hoc working groups to develop packages for each alternative. At the SCC sessions, Brzezinski deliberately tried to balance the hards and the softs by the order in which he called on them to speak. Zbig reserved the final say for Cy Vance, then summarized and reported the SCC deliberations to the President. Carter followed up directly at his breakfasts with Vance, Mondale, and Zbig. Harold Brown was only later admitted to the foreign policy breakfasts as were Hamilton Jordan, Jody Powell, and special counsel Hedley Donovan.

By early March the SALT II options were beginning to crystallize. Deputy National Security Adviser David Aaron had been a technical negotiator on SALT I, while NSC staff specialist Roger Molander was highly knowledgeable on the subject; he had authored a highly classified history of the SALT negotiations Brzezinski circulated only to Jimmy Carter, Cyrus Vance, and Harold Brown. Victor A. Utgoff, who had come from the Center for Naval Analysis to be the NSC staff systems analyst, pointed out the merits of ICBM flight test limits, and the CIA soon produced an estimate that the Soviets would require at least fifteen flight tests to perfect the accuracy of their new MIRVed ICBMs. Flight tests fit right into Molander's concept of a ban on ICBM modernization. David Aaron suggested including this and other ambitious items in what came to be called the "comprehensive package." This discussion, at the SCC meeting on March 10, was one of those Zbig thought he had guided most effectively, getting Paul Warnke relaxed with jokes about his recent (disturbingly narrow) confirmation as chief SALT negotiator and ACDA director, then drawing him out, followed by Harold Brown, then the JCS Chairman, and finally Vance.

On March 11 the national security adviser sent Carter a memorandum outlining four alternative proposals for SALT: the Vladivostok agreement; that agreement minus the issues that had fallen into contention; modest cuts to about two thousand strategic nuclear delivery systems; or deep cuts below that level. Brzezinski claims he favored moderate cuts; in his memoirs he rejects reports that he, alone or together with Harold Brown, pressed for the deeper reductions. On March 12 came a principals-only meeting of the SCC, attended also by Carter and Mondale. In the midst of a more general discussion of foreign policy, Carter reiterated his desire for "real arms control" and distaste for "merely staying within the Vladivostok framework." Brzezinski, who saw his role at this stage as assuring that military concerns were fully guarded, so that an eventual treaty would get full support of the services, spoke in favor of the more radical ban on ICBM modernization, which might still be exploited to impede deployment of the new Russian MIRVs.

Carter listened closely, asked a few questions, then said, "Good, let's do that."

After the meeting, never intended to be a formal NSC session, Brzezinski and Aaron called in Bill Hyland, asking him to turn the President's short instruction into a SALT position. Recalling the endless debates under Scowcroft and Kissinger, Hyland was amazed that the new administration seemed to be uniting so easily around the deep-cuts option. That position got further consideration at top-level meetings with the President on March 19 and 22, just days before Vance was to leave for Moscow to negotiate the deal. After final approval, Hyland, *not* anyone from Vance's staff, got the job of guarding the delegation's written instructions until the moment they were on the way.

This was an unusual procedure for a crowd of bureaucrats supposed to be so collegial, but not if the object was to prevent last-minute appeals to the President.

The draft Presidential Directive Zbig prepared for the President placed the comprehensive package elements within the moderate-cuts option. It included the modernization freeze favored by the NSC staff, cuts in Soviet heavy ICBMs to placate the Joint Chiefs, even limits on cruise missiles to mollify the Russians. The PD nevertheless awarded first place to the so-called deferral option, an agreement based upon Vladivostok minus the disputed issues, Backfire and cruise missiles. A third option represented a compromise between the others and was to be the fallback position. Vance and Warnke commented on the draft PD in a joint memo on March 18, in which they embraced Carter's desire for significant reductions in SALT, reversing the initial State/ACDA preference for an agreement based upon Vladivostok.

The critical discussion came at a foreign policy breakfast Carter held on Saturday, March 19. Brzezinski, again in the interest of "balancing" a meeting (this time the *President's,* not his own SCC), included Harold Brown at the last moment. Vance represented both State and the ACDA. Carter himself and Fritz Mondale made up the rest of the group. Carter not only accepted the comprehensive package but ordered the force reductions it envisioned be increased to provide for an overall limit of only 1,800–2,000 delivery systems with a MIRV ceiling of 1,100 (as against 2,400 and 1,320 respectively in the Vladivostok accord). Further, the President reversed the order of preference in the PD—the United States should present the comprehensive package first before presenting the deferral option. That order became the basis for PD-7, which Carter approved after a further full NSC meeting on March 22, at which he steered a careful course between the JCS and State, in a largely successful attempt to keep all his Indians on the reservation. Carter gave Vance a personal handwritten note for Soviet leader Leonid Brezhnev. It was a token of the President's realization of the far-reaching nature of his SALT proposals.

There can be no doubt that a SALT treaty based upon the comprehensive package would have significantly affected the arms race. The ICBM freeze would have halted the relentless pace of technological improvements. Missile flight test limits in particular would have retarded improvements in accuracy, postponing the evolution of a Soviet threat to the survivability of American ICBMs. A *cessation* of flight tests would eventually shake confidence in the continued reliability of the missiles themselves. No comparable opportunity had existed at SALT since the MIRV ban fiasco of 1969. Now an American administration was actually united in a move for "comprehensive" arms control.

The opportunity of March 1977 was dashed owing to a combination of Brezhnev's lack of vision, Jimmy Carter's inept diplomacy, and the new administration's simultaneous move to establish human rights as a central concern of international relations. Carter succeeded in the human rights effort, succeeded wildly, to the extent that three subsequent administrations have proved unable to dethrone this public concern, but he paid a price at the time in arms control.

The one thing wrong with the United States comprehensive package was that it had nothing to do with Soviet expectations. The Russians expected to complete the Vladivostok accord, argue about Backfire, and insist that cruise missiles were included in the SALT totals, not air-launched *ballistic* missiles, which Henry Kissinger continued to insist were the only type to whose inclusion he had agreed. They did not expect the American package, which tied up a lot of things awfully fast, and gave Moscow the briefest of intervals in which to analyze the proposal. Vance said later the Russians got a preview a week ahead of time, which would have been virtually simultaneous with Carter's March 19 meeting or even before it.

The comprehensive package was not without merit for Moscow. Had Brezhnev agreed, the United States could have been bound to stringent constraints on air-launched cruise missiles, while the furious creativity of American weaponeers would have been restrained. Accuracy improvement, which threatened to make American SLBMs the equivalent of Soviet land-based missiles, could have been slowed or stopped. The United States would also have forgone its MX ICBM program, an effort designed to create an American version of a heavy ICBM. The alarms began to go off when the Soviets saw the Carter deep-cuts package, which would have required dismantling over half the force of Soviet heavy missiles, and could have stopped or substantially slowed Soviet MIRV deployment. To meet the deep-cuts missile numbers, Russia would have had to take down a quarter of its overall force of strategic nuclear missiles. Into the bargain, the United States wanted them to count the Backfire bombers against the overall-force numbers for an extra reduction. That seemed like a blatant effort to use arms control to constrain theater forces. Many in Moscow concluded the comprehensive package was an American attempt to seek unilateral advantage. Foreign

Minister Andrei Gromyko used exactly those words at a rather angry news conference held following the Vance mission.

Because the Soviets reacted so angrily, they never fully explored the United States bargaining position. According to NSC staffer Bill Hyland, keeper of the delegation's secret instructions, Vance had sweeteners in his hip pocket that included cancellation of the B-1 bomber and Trident submarine programs, the American efforts most threatening to Moscow at that time.

Jimmy Carter's first mistake was to assure Moscow, both through a private letter to Brezhnev and in a news conference, that the United States would move ahead on the "deferral" (Vladivostok) agreement. Carter created this expectation, then came in with an entirely different proposal. Adding to his mistake, Carter did not await presentation of the SALT plan to the Russians before detailing its general features in a UN speech. The President also permitted Brzezinski to give the press some background. Reporters were writing knowledgeably of something the Russians were just learning. Moscow felt slighted.

Vance's first meeting with the Soviets occurred the morning after his arrival, when he met Brezhnev in the Politburo conference room. Cy hoped to get immediately into SALT, but Brezhnev instead opened with a lengthy condemnation of human rights practices in the United States. Feeling vulnerable to questions of nationalities, dissidents, and Jewish emigration, Brezhnev made a preemptive attack on Carter's human rights vision. Late in the afternoon of March 28, Vance presented both the comprehensive package and the deferral proposal, emphasizing American desire for the first.

After a day of official silence, Vance met again with Brezhnev on the evening of March 30. He expected a series of objections to specific points in the SALT plan. Instead, Brezhnev's objection was summary and brutal. The United States offer was "unconstructive and one-sided," he insisted; it would be "harmful to Soviet security."

As quickly as he could, Vance cabled for authority to present the American fallback position. Brzezinski and Fritz Mondale believed strongly the United States should stand on the proposals it had tendered. Carter's instructions followed that line. That left Vance very little to talk about. With the Vance team, Bill Hyland felt regret since, except for their hard line on human rights, it seemed the Soviets were really interested in arms control agreements. It was baffling also, the NSC man thought, that Vance seemed to believe he could not bring any concession into play without first referring back to Washington. "This gave the affair a surreal quality," recalls Hyland, who had accompanied Kissinger on many similar occasions.

Denouement of the comprehensive package fiasco was a sharp exchange in public. Brzezinski gave a press conference on April 1, his first on the record in office.

"I truly believe," Brzezinski declared, "that this proposal, if accepted, or when accepted, could serve as a driving wedge, as a historical driving wedge, for a more stable and eventually more cooperative American and Soviet relationship."

So far, so good. But Brzezinski was asked elliptically about the Vladivostok aide-mémoire dispute. He shot back, "I don't want to engage here in a critique of the Soviet position because, as I said . . . I am really not going to engage in recriminations."

At another point, however, Brzezinski went so far as to say, "We made our damnedest effort to produce a package which, within the limits of our own intelligence—and by intelligence, I not only mean information, I also mean what is in our heads—we could say was reasonably equitable for both sides."

That must have grated in Moscow.

Asked if the outcome had been a surprise or a miscalculation, Zbig resorted to pure obfuscation: "If I wasn't [surprised], then it couldn't be a miscalculation. It would be a miscalculation if I was." In his memoirs Zbig blames the press, plus Vance's admissions, for any impression of a miscalculation. The furthest he goes is to admit *with the benefit of hindsight,* it seems to me that our side perhaps did make the mistake of discussing too publicly its proposals."

While still in Europe Hyland had talked to Brzezinski, who decided to have his press conference, then asked Bill to draft some remarks he might use. Hyland did as asked, only then realizing the new administration had *no back channel,* so he could not cable the White House without upsetting his State colleagues. That night in London, he got an embassy friend out of bed and got his cable to Zbig. This reappearance of the back channel, ad hoc though it was, occurred barely two months after the inauguration.

"Looking back on this episode," NSC staffer Bill Hyland comments, "I have no doubt that it was badly handled by everyone. As the one with the most experience, I had been far too sanguine. I doubt that I could have changed the course of events very much, but both Marshall Shulman and I blamed ourselves for not advising Vance of the potential for considerable Soviet hostility." Hyland felt so bad that, as *Air Force One* flew the Vance delegation home, Hyland called ahead to Brzezinski, recommending the President meet the plane at Andrews. Carter did just that.

Picking up the pieces on SALT began in mid-April when a measure of Soviet-American contact resumed. Warnke met with Soviet diplomats on technical questions. Brzezinski, then the President, received Anatoli Dobrynin, who was given private communications for the Kremlin. Vance went to Geneva that May, where both sides showed more flexibility but narrowed the scope of their goals.

The eventual SALT II Treaty had a ceiling for all nuclear delivery vehicles

(2,250), then sub-ceilings for MIRVed missiles plus air-launched cruise missile carriers together (1,320), for MIRVed missiles alone (1,200), and finally one for MIRVed land-based missiles (820). The last amounted to the total of the Soviet MIRVed ICBMs. Protocols banned air-launched cruise missiles and mobile ICBMs until 1981. The Soviets never accepted direct constraints on their Backfire bomber, but they did eventually provide certain assurances that could reduce the Backfire's availability for intercontinental attack and preclude increases in production.

By and large the numbers had been agreed by the spring of 1978. It was the definitions, protocols, and discussions about verification that took another year. Paul Warnke turned out to be an able and discreet negotiator, not at all in the "Mr. Softee" mold his detractors had cast him during the confirmation process. On the United States side, Brzezinski was an active player, backed by Hyland until the fall of 1977, when Reginald Bartholomew, former director of the Policy Planning Staff, picked up the Soviet portfolio.

Bartholomew was a suave thirty-five-year-old who was an expert on French conservative political parties in the postwar era, not a Soviet specialist. From 1972 to 1974, he had served as director of the Pentagon's task force for Warsaw Pact-NATO conventional negotiations on the balance of forces in Europe. One of Bartholomew's new jobs for Zbig was to accompany the United States delegation at the successive rounds of SALT. Once, in a Kremlin meeting room, Bartholomew picked up a curious-looking object on the table. It turned out to be an electronic gavel that emitted a loud, clanging sound, startling everyone at the negotiation.

"Well, there goes Washington!" cracked Georgi Kornienko, Gromyko's usually dour deputy.

Not to be outdone, Anatoli Dobrynin quipped, "Quick! Quick! Call Zbig and tell him it was a mistake!"

Vance and Warnke worked well as a team. Warnke had been reluctant to take the ACDA job. He did so with the proviso that he would return to his law firm once SALT was on the tracks again. With homes in Washington and on Martha's Vineyard and three sons in college at a time of high inflation, Warnke could not make ends meet on the $58,000-a-year salary of ACDA director. In October 1978 he resigned, although he remained a consultant to Vance.

Warnke's departure occurred against the backdrop of Jimmy Carter's concern for presenting the smallest possible target for anti-SALT conservatives during Senate ratification of the SALT II Treaty. The resignation met with quiet approval, Brzezinski claims, from Ham Jordan and Jody Powell, the President's top Georgia cohorts, and no doubt from Zbig himself.

Hot skirmishing followed over Warnke's successor. Warnke recommended his deputy, Ralph Earle II. Vance wavered between Warnke's recommendation and two others, Matthew Nimitz, Vance's counselor, or

Leslie Gelb, director of the Political-Military Bureau, who was also current on SALT. With an eye to Senate ratification, the White House favored a director who would focus more on selling SALT than on its technical detail.

Jimmy Carter split Warnke's job. For chief SALT delegate he selected Earle. But the job of ACDA director was offered elsewhere. Brzezinski says he recommended George M. Seignious II, who, it turned out, was a member of the Coalition for Peace Through Strength, the anti-SALT lobby of the American Security Council. Seignious took the ACDA job anyway. A retired lieutenant general and president of The Citadel, a well-known military college in Charleston, South Carolina, Seignious turned out to be relatively inoffensive and a good spokesman for the administration.

Seignious and Warnke too, by then in his capacity as consultant, missed one of the high dramas of SALT II a couple of months later, when both decided to skip the last day of a Vance-Gromyko round at Geneva on Friday, December 22, to get an early start home for Christmas with the families. Both expected Vance and Gromyko to announce agreement on a Carter-Brezhnev summit. Since the summit had been made contingent upon the completion of SALT II, announcement of it would signal arms control progress. By the next morning in Geneva, the whole thing had broken down.

The big stumbling block this time was verification. At first everything looked great. The Russians made a reluctant concession on cruise missiles. The United States proposed language specifying that encryption (concealment by encoding) of test missile telemetry would be banned wherever it impeded verification. The Soviets had previously resisted any provisions on telemetry encryption; now they suddenly accepted, with the proviso that SALT II also specify encryption *was* permitted where it did *not* interfere. In Geneva, Vance had instructions to raise the example of the Soviet use of encryption in a test of their SS-18 the previous summer. The instruction acquired particular urgency when the Russians repeated the practice for another SS-18 flight test on December 21, just the day before. During SALT discussions Vance said the SS-18 encryption was an example of the type that would be prohibited after the treaty entered force. Gromyko said nothing.

Secretary Vance thought he might be on the verge of a breakthrough. The delegation agreed. They dispatched a cable recommending the most recent proposal on encryption be accepted. Concurring were Earle, Les Gelb, Walt Slocombe for DOD, even Reggie Bartholomew from Brzezinski's staff. Vance believed that to reject the Soviet compromise at this stage might jeopardize the negotiation.

Hitting Washington at early evening, the Vance cable demanded immediate reply. Zbig Brzezinski and David Aaron were due at the British ambassador's for a Christmas party, their wives waiting outside the Situation Room in evening dress. In what became a rump SCC meeting, they were joined by Harold Brown, Stansfield Turner, Warren Christopher, and Spurgeon Keeny, returned to government as deputy director of the ACDA. The West Wing skull session went until nearly midnight.

Stansfield Turner came to the fore on this issue. Admiral Turner, director of central intelligence, had a strong proprietary concern over what SALT II said about encryption, and was already concerned over the United States failure to achieve a *total ban*. According to Brzezinski, Secretary Brown was also adamant. Turner eventually acquiesced in the compromise, *provided* that Vance go back to Gromyko and get the Soviet diplomat to say explicitly that encryption to the degree of the summer SS-18 test would be prohibited. Warren Christopher, Vance's deputy, warned in his cautious, lawyerly way that using an example as a benchmark for legality could create new difficulties. Roger Molander of the NSC staff thought inserting the example was bound to blow the White House plan for Carter to announce the summit on national TV, for which the networks had already been told to stand ready.

Zbig finished up by telephoning Jimmy Carter, then at home in Plains, Georgia. Carter authorized a modified form of the compromise, in which the United States would be satisfied if Gromyko did not contradict a certain formula Vance presented. The White House Communications Agency sent the reply at about midnight. Vance, who had gone to bed in Geneva with optimistic reports of Washington approval, was infuriated when he saw the cable. He was being asked to repeat the discussion he had had with Gromyko the previous day, as had Ralph Earle with a lower-rank Soviet official. Usually not one to question his instructions, Vance got on the secure phone to Brzezinski. Zbig then held a conference call with Stan Turner and Harold Brown, after which he called Plains. It was 4:00 A.M. Brzezinski consulted briefly with Jody Powell, who decided to awaken the President, the second time that night. Brzezinski reports that he had gone along with the midnight compromise, but in the early-morning call he sided with Turner and Brown. President Carter agreed, instructing Zbig to so inform the secretary of state.

By that time Cyrus Vance was closeted with Gromyko *at the Soviet mission* in Geneva, engaged in the next session of negotiations. When Brzezinski's telephone call got through, Marshall Shulman came on the line: "Do you know where you've reached us, Zbig?" he asked. "Do you still want to talk to Cy?"

"Considering the circumstances, yes," replied the national security adviser.

In his nasal, accented English, over a Soviet phone, Brzezinski told Vance the bad news, using double-talk to try to prevent the Soviets, who were certainly listening in, from discovering what was up.

Vance did as he was told. The Soviets were not happy, and there is also some evidence they misinterpreted the Brzezinski-Vance phone conversation, thinking it about a subject other than encryption. In any case, Gromyko countered by making it clear that no date could be set for the anticipated summit until *all* issues were resolved. Cy Vance was left to pick up the pieces.

Brzezinski's comment on the Christmas fiasco is to argue that Moscow eventually gave way on encryption, and that anything less would have been no good in the U.S. Senate. Brzezinski's defense is slightly inaccurate in asserting that only the Soviets gave way on encryption: Article XV, Paragraph 3 of the SALT II Treaty contains the relevant provision, which does ban encryption as a means of "deliberate denial of telemetric information . . . whenever such denial impedes verification." The very same article also states, however, "Each party is free to use various means of transmitting telemetric information during testing, *including its encryption*." That sounds very much like the December 1978 Gromyko-Vance compromise. Senators at the ratification hearings had no need to discover this point of controversy because Lieutenant General Edward L. Rowny, the Joint Chiefs' representative on the SALT delegation, resigned from the service following completion of the treaty and gave hostile testimony on it, including raising the question of the specific content of the encryption ban.

Encryption, the Backfire bomber, the baseline figure for the number of warheads permitted on an ICBM, plus other details on modernization provisions remained in dispute into 1979. Vance began a series of private sessions with Dobrynin at which they tried to thrash out the issues, meeting over two dozen times before SALT II reached its end. On May 7, Vance and Shulman left one such meeting convinced an acceptable treaty was finally at hand. Ralph Earle and Victor Karpov, his Soviet opposite number, continued putting touches on the treaty into June. At the Vienna summit itself, Brezhnev made the final concession, agreeing to extra assurances about the Backfire. President Carter and Soviet President Leonid Brezhnev signed the SALT II Treaty on June 18, 1979.

Hard though it had been reaching agreement with the Russians, that was as nothing compared with the White House's problem with the U.S. Senate. Carter had had the ratification problem in mind for some time, as illustrated by his choice of a replacement for Paul Warnke. Preparations commenced in earnest in the late spring of 1979, when it became pretty clear the treaty would be signed. Brzezinski planned scenarios for SALT II ratification; Cy Vance carefully considered the presentation he would give Congress on the treaty. Jimmy Carter appointed a special counsel, sixty-two-year-old Washington lawyer Lloyd N. Cutler, specifically to help him shepherd the treaty through the Senate. Carter also asked *Time* magazine editor Hedley Donovan to become a special adviser on public opinion. Carter included both in his national security inner sanctum, the foreign policy breakfast.

On Capitol Hill the administration's SALT outreach took the form of testifying at hearings. There were twelve appearances from 1977 to 1979, five by Warnke, six by Vance, plus one by CIA officials. There were also five executive sessions with State, Pentagon, or CIA officials once it became clear the treaty was going to become a reality. The administration also took the novel course of setting aside places on the regular SALT delegation just for legislators. By May 1979 forty-six members of the House of Representatives and twenty-six of the Senate had worked on the SALT delegation.

Since Senate ratification of the treaty required a two-thirds majority vote, marshaling opposition to the treaty was relatively simple. Jackson and like-minded opponents had only to keep together the constellation of forces that had opposed Paul Warnke's appointment as SALT negotiator, totaling forty votes, to reach their magic number thirty-four.

The arithmetic could be read without much difficulty, both by the administration and outside it. The hard-core opposition to SALT, Jackson aide Richard Perle told the New York Arms Control Seminar in April 1978, amounted to some *thirty-two* senators. That was a year before the treaty was even completed. Perle, in a perfect place to judge, estimated that if the treaty followed the expected lines (and it did) *fifty-one* votes could be mustered against it.

When SALT finally came before the Senate, the opposition redoubled its efforts. Bipartisanship took a beating as Ford administration stalwarts came bearing faint praise for SALT II. Gerald Ford capped the point himself, in late September, alleging an "air of unreality" in the debate.

"Some suggest," Ford thundered in a speech, "that they are *for* the treaty on the *assumption* that the necessary defense spending decisions *will be made*. That is not my position. My position is that I am *against* the treaty *unless* the necessary defense spending decisions have been made and *written into law*."

Zbig Brzezinski defended the administration at a gathering of alumni of international affairs schools at Washington's Cosmos Club the evening of September 27. Zbig made the obvious point that the Ford people had negotiated "much of the foundation of this agreement." Ford had prepared a "sound framework" and Carter had built on it. "It is a simple fact," Brzezinski declared, "that an issue-by-issue comparison between the SALT II Treaty and the last SALT proposal of the Ford Administration shows that on essentially every issue the treaty is on the same track or better."

Then, just when it seemed that not another morsel would fit on Carter's plate, the administration inflicted itself with a needless and largely senseless crisis that SALT opponents used to attack Soviet trustworthiness and impeach the treaty. The place was Cuba, again. This time Zbigniew Brzezinski had a good deal to do with the embarrassing interlude.

"There's nothing like starting in your own end zone," Lloyd Cutler quipped when reacting for reporters upon his appointment. He did not know, then, just how true that was. The new Cuban crisis would be instructive.

National Security Adviser Brzezinski lit the powder that led to the keg of what came to be called the "brigade crisis" by a simple request to the intelligence community. The President's watcher suspected that the Soviet presence in Cuba might be growing. Brzezinski wanted an estimate and asked for one in the spring of 1979, before SALT II went to the Senate. That exercise triggered the brigade crisis, so-called to distinguish it from Cienfuegos, or from the historic Cuban missile crisis.

Brzezinski's request, not out of the ordinary, was the latest illustration of a sensitivity regarding Cuba that made it an exception to the Trilateral vision of "North-South" accommodation. Zbig saw Cuba strictly in the East-West context. In that, he went further than Jimmy Carter, whose inclination was to emphasize human rights and make improvement of Cuban-American relations contingent upon it alone.

One of Zbig's earliest sallies threw a monkey wrench into developing United States-Cuban contacts. At a background briefing for reporters in mid-November 1977, Brzezinski announced that new CIA studies revealed a Cuban military buildup in Angola since the summer, and claimed that the United States had protested through diplomatic channels. The State Department went into an uproar. The regional assistant secretary, Terence Todman, was furious at the Cuba desk officer for approving the national security adviser's statement, until he learned the country director had known nothing about it either. When State checked with the NSC staff, the specialist for Latin America lamely replied that there had been no need to coordinate because the statement contained nothing "new." Desk officer Wayne Smith's further investigation, with the relevant analysts at CIA, determined that the agency "study" Brzezinski had referred to was no more than an information item consisting of a map of Africa plus a list of the number of Cubans in various countries. The alleged buildup in Angola was merely a revision of the standing estimate based on reevaluation of evidence.

After publication of the charges came a protest from the Cuban chargé d'affaires that the United States had *never raised* in diplomatic channels, as Brzezinski claimed it had, the charges Zbig was now making. Moreover, airing the allegations provoked inevitable press inquiries at State, and the NSC staff provided no guidelines on how to handle *them*. Wayne Smith finally concluded, "I never felt the Carter White House, particularly the NSC [staff], understood the nature of the problem or how to address it." Brzezinski, in his view, "tended to interpret most political and military events in terms of some Soviet blueprint for world conquest."

This was certainly the case with the Horn of Africa, where the conflict situation was entirely transformed on Zbig's watch. There the American ally, Emperor Haile Selassie, was overthrown by a Marxist military faction. The United States soon stopped all aid to Ethiopia, and lost its military bases in that country, including important communications and electronic intelligence facilities. Meanwhile, neighboring Somalia, a *Soviet* ally, decided to invade Ethiopia, with whom it had a territorial dispute over the Ogaden desert region. Convinced that the Somalis had had promises of U.S. aid, the Soviets severed their ties with that nation and helped Ethiopia, also afflicted with a guerrilla war against nationalist guerrillas in Tigre and Eritrea provinces. The United States did go on to aid Somalia. In effect the two sides simply switched local proxies. Cuban troops went to Ethiopia to back the government in December 1977, and there were fifteen thousand by February 1978.

The strong inclination of Carter's administration was to stay out of these local squabbles and pursue the main issues, particularly SALT, which had acquired strong momentum of its own. But Brzezinski saw the Horn of Africa as a potential superpower conflict, and wanted to send an aircraft carrier task force to lie offshore. On that occasion the President sided with Vance, who resisted such military moves as extreme. There was a renewed farce about military aid to the Yemen. Brzezinski meanwhile, at one of his press conferences, observed that although the United States did not use the tactic of linkage, the Soviets might "impose" linkage through their own actions. The remark was heavy-handed and plainly aimed at Soviet policy in the Horn. It was Cuba's misfortune to form a component of that policy.

With instability in the Horn a continuing problem, there was then a rerun of the Shaba crisis, in Zaire, where local instabilities were trumpeted as superpower gambits. Almost immediately Fidel Castro privately summoned the American chargé d'affaires to declare that Cuba not only did not support the invasion but had tried to prevent it. The cable reporting Castro's position leaked to the press, inducing Brzezinski to lash back with charges putting the matter of Katanga, from bygone Congo days, squarely into the East-West context. There was a Soviet challenge in Africa, Brzezinski seemed to believe, of which the alleged Cuban backing for the Shaba invaders was the latest manifestation. Carter made similar charges the very day Vance was meeting with a top Cuban official, which could only poison the atmosphere at those talks. Startlingly, once again the NSC staff failed to supply Secretary Vance with the draft language it had prepared for the President.

Castro's solicitude during the second Shaba incident no doubt related to his most secret gambit: back channel talks with the United States. They were kept secret from operating levels of the State Department and even from the Cuban desk officers. Castro had made the preliminary contact through a Cuban exile banker who had gone straight to the White House. Brzezinski sent him on to Vance, but put Dave Aaron on the United States team formed to conduct the secret talks. Zbig's deputy was to guard the President's interests and provide an eyewitness account of the discussions.

It was in this kind of international maneuvering that David Aaron truly shone. First Zbig sent Aaron to Addis Ababa, the Ethiopian capital, to insist upon an end to the Ogaden war. For the Cuban affair, Aaron accompanied David Newsom, Vance's undersecretary. There were several rounds of talks, in New York, Atlanta, Havana, and Mexico. Aaron made at least one trip to New York with Brzezinski's personal aide Bob Gates, who reportedly went wired for sound, wearing a special vest provided by the FBI that recorded the conversations. The thirty-nine-year-old Aaron opted for a nice

French restaurant in a hotel off Fifth Avenue. It was in character for him, a natty dresser and California boy, indeed a graduate of Hollywood High. Aaron's career had been mostly in the Foreign Service. His special interests included East Asia and arms control, and he had been a member of the American SALT delegation from 1969 through 1974, serving on the technical but critical ABM working panel, and on temporary assignment to the Kissinger NSC staff. Cuba was not exactly Aaron's forte.

The most significant round of the secret talks with Cuba took place in Atlanta in August 1978. It was the first time the United States had agreed to entertain agenda items other than its grievances against Havana. When the sides managed to agree on a special release of Cuban political prisoners and their emigration to the United States, the NSC staff refused to allow the American government to admit it had had any role in the matter. That might send the wrong signal to those nations whose support the United States sought in its effort to get the Cubans out of Africa. Later, when Washington determined to downgrade the U.S.-Cuban talks, Aaron and Newsom were taken out of play. A less prestigious team then became NSC staffer Robert Pastor and State's Executive Secretary Peter Tarnoff.

Pastor and Tarnoff were preparing to go to Havana when it became known in Washington that Cuba had received some MiG-23 aircraft from the Soviets. Though most models of this plane function as interceptors, there is one type equipped as an attack aircraft, and the Americans became very concerned as to which MiG-23 model the Cubans had. Brzezinski went to Carter for permission to use SR-71 spy planes to collect the intelligence. The sonic booms as these planes broke the sound barrier north of Cuba were plainly audible in Havana. In one instance they occurred as the American chargé stood in the Cuban Foreign Ministry talking with his official counterpart.

In addition, the United States chose this moment to hold a large bilateral naval maneuver in conjunction with the Royal Navy, including carrier task forces and air operations, directly off the north coast of Cuba. The Cubans learned of them only when warplanes showed up on their radar scopes. Washington had approved the maneuver as a matter of routine, with DOD and the NSC staff assuming that if State had any objection they would speak up.

"If State objected," Bob Pastor asked Wayne Smith in a quick conversation in a West Wing hallway, "why didn't someone over there say so before the thing got going?"

When Pastor and Tarnoff visited Havana in December they got nothing, not even four American prisoners languishing in Cuban prisons, whose release in connection with this round of the secret talks had been expected.

The MiG incident rose to the level of Vance and Dobrynin, who assured the secretary of state during one of their direct meetings that the MiG-23s in Cuba were of the same "class"—interceptors—as the aircraft long present in the Cuban Air Force.

This spiral toward hostility occurred before Zbigniew Brzezinski made his request for an estimate on Soviet activities in Cuba. His request led to more enmity as a result of an intelligence error.

Combat troop units had been present in Cuba ever since the missile crisis, when five regiment-sized combined arms teams formed part of the Soviets' forty-two-thousand-man deployment. President Kennedy's NSC EXCOM had discussed the combat troops in December 1962, while JFK himself referred to them at a press conference in early 1963.

This knowledge seems to have been lost to the institutional memory of the intelligence community by mid-1978, when the CIA got information from a human source that the Soviets were rotating one or two battalions of combat troops through Cuba in addition to their twenty-five-hundred-man advisory group. Partial corroboration from satellites led the November 1978 SR-71 flights to collect intelligence on this as well. Before the end of that year the consensus was that organized Soviet troop activities were taking place in Cuba.

Brzezinski's March request led the intelligence community to reevaluate its holdings on Soviet troops in Cuba. At the National Security Agency (NSA), material that had been recorded, but never broken out for analysis, was now decrypted, while older intercepts were examined. An NSA analyst found references to a "*brigada*," the Spanish word for a brigade, as far back as 1976. Reportedly, the White House was informed in April of a growing consensus that the Soviets had apparently stationed combat units in Cuba on a permanent basis. By June the NSA had a report claiming the existence of a Soviet combat brigade. Army intelligence agreed but the CIA and other U.S. intelligence agencies did not. Brzezinski admits seeing the first reports the Soviets might have a unit in Cuba in late July, telling the President on July 24, observing that such an eventuality could have serious implications for SALT.

If this recounting is accurate, the President's watcher had fallen behind the pace of developments. In fact, CIA director Stansfield Turner reports that a copy of the original NSA report quickly leaked to Florida Democratic Senator Richard Stone, who began asking sharp questions about Cuba at the SALT ratification hearings. On July 11 he felt out the Joint Chiefs. Six days later he caught Harold Brown in an assertion that the Pentagon knew nothing of Soviet combat troops in Cuba, a denial Cy Vance reinforced in a later official letter. Brown's assertion, at an executive session of the Senate Foreign Relations Committee, leaked almost immediately. Senator Stone also went public with charges of Soviet military activity in Cuba, charges he pursued with both Brown and Vance in later open SALT testimony. Stone, who faced reelection in 1980, was attempting to build an image for his conservative Florida constituents, who took a dim view of Stone's having voted for ratification of the Panama Canal Treaty.

It was in this rarefied political atmosphere that the intelligence consensus on the Soviet brigade fell into place. On August 14, Zbig briefed Carter and reported Soviet plans to conduct maneuvers. American intelligence assets observed these maneuvers, getting both pictures and intercepts. Shortly thereafter the CIA completed an analysis that agreed a Soviet brigade was in Cuba. An item to that effect appeared in the top-secret *National Intelligence Daily* on August 27. Two days later Clarence Robinson, an editor for *Aviation Week and Space Technology* magazine, called an aide of David Newsom's to check out reports of a Soviet troop unit in Cuba. The flap began immediately once it became clear the journalist had the brigade story, which the CIA had specifically cleared with the NSC staff before publishing.

This was the moment for a reminder that the Soviet troops had been in Cuba since 1962, that there was nothing new in all this. Instead, Brzezinski convinced himself and the President that this development was serious enough to throw SALT ratification into jeopardy. Treated like a crisis, the brigade issue rapidly became one.

It was August and everyone was on vacation. Jimmy Carter was on his way down the Mississippi River aboard the luxury riverboat *Delta Queen*. Cy Vance was in Martha's Vineyard, while Brzezinski vacationed in Vermont. Brown was also away. In their absence David Aaron convened the mini-SCC to decide how to handle the brigade issue. State was for confronting the Soviets, but Aaron objected, wanting to prevent the Soviets' prematurely committing themselves to a position. Afterward Aaron called Brzezinski, who wanted to avoid any action at all before his return from vacation around Labor Day.

Unfortunately, the defense media already had wind of the story. Newsom was more realistic, asking Cyrus Vance for permission to begin briefing senior members of Congress. Though *Aviation Week* would not appear before Labor Day, it was quite possible they would spread the story themselves, or that other media might learn of the item in the *National Intelligence Daily*. Vance instructed Newsom to raise the issue with the Soviets, and the next day he informed key congressional leaders, "to my amazement" notes Brzezinski. Senator Frank Church, chairman of the Foreign Relations Committee, who faced an uphill reelection effort as did Richard Stone, was the first to go public with the exact information about the brigade.

Now the fat was in the fire; the Soviet brigade seemed to break the administration's assurances to Congress that there were no "significant" Soviet ground forces in Cuba. One could debate whether the brigade itself was significant, with fewer than three thousand troops and only forty tanks, but SALT opponents seized on the discovery to claim it showed that the Soviets would be able to evade monitoring under the treaty. Carter found himself thrown into a situation in which he was required to hang tough over a minor issue that had become a symbol of his leadership.

Brzezinski returned to Washington on September 4, met with Carter, and then went on to a session of the NSC Policy Review Committee chaired by Vance. It was the only crisis of Carter's presidency handled by the PRC as opposed to Zbig's SCC. Vance initially took a hard line, seconded by Lloyd

Cutler, but softened over succeeding days. Brzezinski notes that he countered by bringing in Donovan "who had a distinctly more hawkish outlook." Another time, encountering a PRC session he thought Vance had stacked with colleagues Zbig considered dovish, such as Marshall Shulman and David Newsom, Brzezinski got Carter himself to attend, automatically converting the PRC into a regular NSC meeting and forcing lesser-ranking officials to leave. As Brzezinski put it in one of his weekly memos to the President on September 13:

> You may not want to hear this, but I think that the increasingly pervasive perception here and abroad is that in U.S.-Soviet relations, the Soviets are increasingly assertive and the U.S. more acquiescent. State's handling of the Soviet brigade negotiations is a case in point. I recommend that in the future we will have to work for greater White House control.

Carter's marginal note read: "Good!"

Vance held a series of meetings with Soviet Ambassador Dobrynin at which the Russian tried to reassure the United States, but would make no concessions, since the Soviets considered the entire crisis to have been trumped up in the first place.

Hedley Donovan and Lloyd Cutler backed the President when Carter threw out the idea of calling in a body of senior statesmen akin to LBJ's Wise Men group. Brzezinski thought it a poor idea, and objected strongly, insisting that Truman, Kennedy, and Nixon had never resorted to such groups. Carter held the convocation despite this advice, on Friday and Saturday, September 28 and 29. First a group of the Wise Men began with a morning session at Langley where they familiarized themselves with the intelligence. From seven the group swelled to sixteen when it moved down to the White House for its deliberations, an informal lunch with the President, and finally their session with him.

According to Hedley Donovan the group decided that the crisis had been blown out of all proportion and that there had probably been a Soviet brigade in Cuba all along. Only Henry Kissinger remained adamant: No such Soviet unit had been in Cuba during *his* time in office. Comprising the consensus were Mac Bundy, Brent Scowcroft, Bill Rogers, Dean Rusk, Roswell Gilpatric, George Ball, John McCone, Sol M. Linowitz, and chairman of the study group Clark Clifford. "The group did meet," writes Brzezinski, "and then widely circulated reports of the Administration's alleged disarray."

After listening to the Wise Men, Carter determined to make a television speech on the general problem.

Carter could not be drawn out in the direction Brzezinski wanted. "My fellow Americans," the President declared in his speech, "the greatest danger to American security tonight is certainly not the two or three thousand

Soviet troops in Cuba. The greatest danger to all the nations of the world
—including the United States and the Soviet Union—is the breakdown of
the common effort to preserve the peace."

Brzezinski, with some support from Donovan, had wanted a tougher
speech hitting at the Soviets more globally. Following the speech there was
a small champagne party to celebrate Carter's birthday. Brzezinski and
Donovan stayed away.

Zbigniew Brzezinski records that he thought seriously of resignation in
the wake of the brigade crisis, the only time he ever did so. "The most
disagreeable comments I ever made to the President," Zbig recorded on
Thursday, October 4. The United States had finally told Russia its activities
in several regions of the world were unacceptable, complained Brzezinski,
then did nothing about it, which could be a dangerous move inducing the
Soviets to miscalculate later. "The President looked quite furious, and told
me he had no intention of going to war over the Soviet brigade in Cuba."

In his formal postmortem Brzezinski struck once more at the State Department, alleging that their briefings had precipitated the crisis, and that
the handling of subsequent events by the Policy Review Committee had
been flawed by changing membership and repetitive discussions. Zbig also
objected once more to resorting to the Wise Men panel. In retrospect, in
his memoirs, Zbig blames himself for allowing the PRC to hold sway. The
more significant realization, however, was another one. "I should have
judged more accurately the extent of the President's concern for SALT,"
Brzezinski writes, "and I might have served the President's interests better
if I had concentrated my efforts on dampening down the whole issue." If
only hindsight were foresight!

PAYING THE PIPER

▲▲▲

O ne thing as important for the administration as arms control was military planning. Jimmy Carter came to office pledging more rational "zero-base" budgeting and some discipline in defense spending. Carter ordered a review of military posture. The study directive also asked for a net assessment, what Zbig calls a "broadly gauged review of the U.S.-Soviet strategic balance." Though first discussed at St. Simons before the inaugural, such attention was given to the scope and terms of reference of the review that the study directive did not go out until February 18, long after those for sixteen other Presidential Review Memoranda (PRM/NSC). The consultants Brzezinski brought on to the NSC staff were employed on this project, numbered PRM-10.

Carter's policy review was a truly massive affair, of the same order as Dwight Eisenhower's "New Look" NSC paper or his Project Solarium. Almost a dozen interagency groups worked on PRM-10, which contained studies of regional issues, intelligence, and military matters. Most of the panels were chaired by State Department representatives, but most of the leaks and media attention that eventually surrounded PRM-10 focused on the contributions from the panel chaired by Deputy Assistant Secretary of Defense Lynn Davis. Net assessment work was done by Andrew Marshall, also from DOD, though certain "contingency assessments" were supposed to be compiled under Victor Utgoff of the NSC staff. The eleven task force reports were summarized, expanded upon, and analyzed by a four-person executive staff under Sam Huntington. Across the Potomac at the Pentagon, the PRM-10 executive group were called the Gang of Four, the term the Red Chinese were then using for Mao Tse-tung's wife and her closest associates, who were on trial for dissidence in Peking.

Zbigniew Brzezinski's major innovation in the NSC policy review procedure was the way in which the interagency studies were processed on their way up to the President. The executive panel group did not merely outline the agency contributions in a memorandum of a few pages, Brzezinski wanted evaluations of Soviet military, political, economic, and even ideological, performance, far broader an analytical problem than a "mere" military net assessment. Brzezinski saw it as a "more sophisticated appraisal." It was the way he and Huntington had written their book *Political Power: U.S.A./USSR*. Still, Huntington had able assistants, including Rich-

407

ard Betts, Catherine Kelleher, and George Lawton. Together this "Gang of Four" wrote an executive summary of over three hundred pages, probably about as much material as there was in the task force reports.

The leaks began immediately after presentation of PRM-10 at a Cabinet Room meeting in early July 1977. Many of the leaks accused the administration of planning for the demise of Western Europe, of assuming in PRM-10 that West Germany could not be defended successfully. In actuality the paper did point up some glaring NATO weaknesses in the face of a short-warning attack, and a comprehensive package of NATO initiatives was adopted thereafter, many of them implemented by General Alexander M. Haig, until 1979 the Supreme Allied Commander in Europe.

The policy review was important in other ways as well. Brzezinski credits PRM-10 with identifying the Persian Gulf as an endangered region and, with its economic and political judgments, providing intellectual support for "my own predisposition in favor of an activist, assertive, and historically optimistic policy of détente."

Bureaucratic fires burned hottest over that portion of PRM-10, called Annex C, that concerned strategic forces, put together by the panel under Lynn Davis. The JCS stalled, dribbling out the data Davis's panel needed. Davis aide Joel Resnick had to invoke the authority of the secretary of defense to pry the information loose. The whole exercise left both sides embittered and Davis out on a limb in pursuing her particular interests.

It happened that Lynn Davis was a proponent of what she called "limited nuclear options," a subject on which she had recently written an Adelphi Paper for the International Institute for Strategic Studies. The idea was to get away from the traditional doctrine of mutual assured destruction, which required plans for massive nuclear attacks. Limited options provided an extra rung in the escalation ladder. Annex C of PRM-10 treated the subject from the standpoint of targeting Soviet strategic forces, other Soviet military forces, command and intelligence headquarters, and economic recovery assets, classes of targets that had been set by NSDM-242 in Gerald Ford's time, when limited options were first bruited about and called the Schlesinger Doctrine. The treatment in PRM-10 followed these standard lines.

When this portion of the policy review came up for discussion at an NSC session, it was Brzezinski who brought the briefers to a halt. "Where are the criteria for killing Russians?" Zbig wanted to know.

Following his own predilections the national security adviser was projecting his knowledge of Soviet nationalities problems into the U.S. nuclear war plans. His briefers misunderstood and began to talk about levels of exchanges and population fatality rates.

"I mean *Russian* Russians!" Brzezinski interjected.

Ethnic or nationality targeting was something that had been talked about in the very early days of the cold war, before the era of nuclear plenty, when there were not enough nuclear weapons to hit all of Russia. It had been seen as a way to introduce political instability in the Soviet Union.

Such fine distinctions were no longer made once the United States had attained ample target coverage, making Brzezinski's sudden objection novel if not startling.

President Carter answered the policy review with his own order, PD/NSC-18, which he signed on August 24. The directive confirmed NATO's forward defense strategy, called for creation of a force of light divisions rapidly deployable to global hot spots, and adopted a nuclear policy of strategic equivalence. But Brzezinski's questions about nationalities options were only early sallies in an administration debate that subsumed PD-18 and endured well into 1980, with Brzezinski pushing for "assertive" détente and others wanting to limit United States strategic forces to those necessary for assured destruction, while reducing troop levels in Europe and Korea. Carter may have inclined to side with the latter group, but time and again maneuvers plus external developments led the President into Zbig's camp.

In one instance Carter attempted to withdraw some American forces from South Korea, only to encounter leaks about North Korean ability to cross secretly into the south through tunnels. After that Major General John K. Singlaub, highly decorated chief of staff of the Korea command, resigned under duress after publicly criticizing the President's decision. Carter let Singlaub visit him in the Oval Office, enforcing the resignation, but he halted the withdrawal from Korea.

Fortified after the PRM-10 exercise, Brzezinski thought he had even more arguments against allowing the Soviets a role in Middle East peacemaking, plus more points he could use advocating rapprochement between the United States and the People's Republic of China, in effect fulfilling Richard Nixon's promises of the Shanghai Communiqué. Cy Vance strenuously opposed any approach that was not evenhanded between the two Communist superpowers, and threatened to resign if the United States began to make military sales to the PRC. This dispute between a powerful NSC principal and the national security adviser began to sharpen even as Brzezinski acquired his public persona about a year into the administration.

Brzezinski continued to hammer away at the Soviets and Cubans in Africa. He got the President to agree to give a tougher speech and put Sam Huntington to work on a draft. Carter eventually made the speech on March 17, 1978, at Wake Forest University in Winston-Salem, North Carolina. He spoke of "an ominous inclination on the part of the Soviet Union to use its military power to intervene in local conflicts." The President referred to the "recently" completed strategic policy review and declared the United States would match Soviet power, work closely with its NATO allies, and develop forces to counter threats to allies or vital interests in Asia, the Middle East, or elsewhere. Pleased with the speech, Brzezinski became furious when he learned later that Marshall Shulman had been around to the Soviet embassy to tell the Russians the Wake Forest speech ought to be regarded as primarily for United States internal consumption. Two years later, in March 1980, Zbig in his daily journal traced the subsequent downfall of détente, including the "Soviet brigade fiasco" (Brzezinski's term) and withdrawal of the SALT II Treaty (following the Soviet intervention in Afghanistan), to the simple failure to be tougher on the Horn of Africa. "That is why," Brzezinski writes, "I have occassionally used the phrase 'SALT lies buried in the sands of the Ogaden.' "

Brzezinski's diary remark, and its inclusion in a memoir three years later, show the national security adviser's bulldoglike tactics in debate. As Hodding Carter, Vance's assistant secretary for public affairs, put it in a retrospective look at the administration, Brzezinski "never accepted a defeat as final or a policy as decided if it did not please him." The keeper of the keys was "like a rat terrier," who would "shake himself off after a losing encounter and begin nipping at Vance's ankles."

The quintessential illustration of Zbig's bulldog tactics may be the question of the limited nuclear options in which PRM-10 had become mired. In PRM-10, Sam Huntington had sided with Harvard colleague Richard Pipes who argued, most prominently in the magazine *Commentary* in the summer of 1977, that the Soviets thought they could fight and win a nuclear war, that they did not accept the doctrine of mutual assured destruction. President Carter's answering directive, PD-18, ordered a study of the nuclear war plan. The orders went to Harold Brown and much talk followed of who might chair a working group for such a panel. Brown went to his assistant secretary, Walter Slocombe, and to Andrew Marshall, for advice. Eventually Brown settled upon a group under Leon Sloss, a figure from the same mold as Paul Nitze. The study explored seven different ways of revising the war plans, using existing and projected forces. Lynn Davis and the PRM-10 analysts were cut completely out of the action.

One cannot say what the "Nuclear Targeting Policy Review," as it was known to the bureaucracy, concluded with respect to Brzezinski's notion of nationalities targeting because the study remains highly classified. After the Sloss study, however, intellectuals in the defense community began to bubble with talk of selecting the Soviet *political leadership* as a target, a group dominated by the Russian nationality in the USSR. There was so much of this that the jargon term "decapitation" was coined to connote that kind of a nuclear strike plan. Finished in November, the Sloss study went to the NSC staff the following month.

On the Brzezinski staff, defense business was split between that functional cluster in the OEOB, and his own military assistant. Zbig's man for this job was Army Colonel William Odom, a hard charger who was also bright, and had taken the time to learn Russian. Odom's language and Soviet area studies had been at Columbia University, where he studied under Brzezinski. A forty-six-year-old Tennessean, he was called by some "Brzezinski's Brzezinski." With no formal NSC staff assignment other than being crisis coordinator, Odom nevertheless managed to carve out significant roles for himself on issues such as terrorism, civil defense, MX missile development, and Afghanistan. He once described himself to reporter Charles Mohr as

"Brzezinski's poacher." Asked what that meant, Odom responded, "I can poach in a variety of policy fields." The nuclear weapons employment doctrine became one of Odom's most important involvements.

Brzezinski writes approvingly of how he strengthened the military affairs cluster on his NSC staff in 1978 and 1979. Though Vic Utgoff remained throughout the administration, he was supplemented by additional specialists: Fritz W. Ermarth, a Young Turk conservative Soviet specialist from the CIA, and Major General Jasper A. Welch, Jr., a Berkeley Ph.D. in physics who had worked in the nuclear weapons labs in Eisenhower's day, and was now chief of the Air Force's unit for systems analysis. Though the political coloration of his defense cluster swung sharply to the right, Brzezinski notes, "I acquired a team of collaborators with considerable expertise and capacity for doctrinal innovation."

The defense staff cluster plus Odom worked closely with Harold Brown's staff in the Pentagon, exerting a significant influence on people like Walt Slocombe and Robert Komer who returned to government in the Carter years in a Pentagon policy-making position. Harold Brown also took greater interest in the revision of nuclear doctrine. Brown began to speak in his annual reports to the Congress of "countervailing" strategic power that would balance the Russians'. Brzezinski noted approvingly in his diary, in the late spring of 1979: "Harold Brown has now become much more interested in greater flexibility and is clearly moving away from a rigid deterrence posture." At one meeting on May 15, Zbig argued the time had come for a formal directive on nuclear weapons doctrine. Brown sided with him though both were opposed by State representative Warren Christopher.

State Department opposition continued to stall the project for a time, but early in 1980 Brzezinski advised the President that the nuclear doctrine directive should go forward. Carter agreed. Brzezinski assigned Bill Odom and Jasper Welch to draft the order. Once the text was ready it went to Harold Brown for DOD revisions. A process of give-and-take resulted in a text acceptable to all, and Jimmy Carter signed PD/NSC-59 on July 25, 1980. Before the end of the year a nuclear war plan based on the new doctrine was in process at Strategic Air Command headquarters.

There were two flaps that occurred once PD-59 became known. One concerned the apparent intention of the United States under this doctrine to think in terms of fighting nuclear wars rather than preventing them. Carter lost moderate and left political support that cost him dearly in the November elections. Zbig was not known to shy away from injecting political considerations into national security discussions; one wonders if he warned Carter of the potential political hazards of the new nuclear doctrine.

The second flap of the PD-59 affair, very much like the Cuban brigade crisis, was entirely avoidable. While the document was in draft, Cyrus Vance finally resigned, as we shall see shortly. Former Senator Edmund S. Muskie succeeded him. No one told Muskie anything about PD-59, and when its existence was revealed he spoke up to that effect, leaving the public impression that Brzezinski was pulling end runs on the new secretary of state. As the national security adviser himself explains the matter, when the PD came up for signature he asked Carter for an NSC meeting that would ventilate the final draft and give everyone an opportunity for a last say. Instead, the President chose to receive a briefing on PD-59 with only Vice President Mondale in attendance, and to have Muskie separately informed. Circumstances delayed Muskie's briefing, Brzezinski avers. Walt Slocombe traveled up to Kennebunk, Maine, to brief Muskie on August 11, the day news of PD-59 broke in the form of the leak of a United States message to the NATO Nuclear Planning Group. Muskie learned of the policy from the newspaper, even though he had been with Jimmy Carter at one of the President's foreign policy breakfasts the morning Carter signed PD-59.

Fortunately Cy Vance came to the administration's defense, confirming that the State Department *had* known of the evolution of the new nuclear doctrine. Without the media's image of a bureaucratic war between the national security adviser and the secretary of state the dominant perception by 1980, the entire policy might have been received much differently.

First of Kissinger's Debits to fall due was that for the Panama Canal. It had been a long time coming, since the 1964 riots in fact, and Carter was the fourth United States President to grapple with the tar baby of sovereignty versus settlement. Cyrus Vance *knew*—he had been there at the beginning, sent by LBJ while the smoke was still in the air. Vance recalls: "The anti-American events of 1964 led me to the conclusion that almost all Panamanians regarded exclusive U.S. authority over the canal and zone as an affront to their national dignity and sovereignty." In this, Vance was among the mainstream of elite opinion on foreign policy. Sol Linowitz had just led a blue-ribbon commission of prominent citizens whose report argued that failure to agree with Panama on a new treaty was the single factor most damaging to United States policy interests in Latin America.

President Carter asked Linowitz to become his special representative to the Panama Canal negotiations. Linowitz refused unless Ellsworth Bunker was kept on as co-negotiator, and in any case only for a period of six months. Carter met with the negotiators in his first week in office and gave them free rein to explore solutions. Carter also made Panama the subject of his very first policy review, PRM-1, and Brzezinski gave the bureaucracy only three days to produce the report. It was in turn discussed at the initial meeting of the NSC Policy Review Committee on January 27, 1977. Only a few minutes into the meeting there was a broad consensus in favor of resuming negotiations with Panama on the basis of the so-called Kissinger-Tack principles, which Bunker had agreed on with the Panamanians during 1974. Vance made a public statement reaffirming the principles on January 31.

Brzezinski meanwhile ordered a second PRM, broadening the focus to all Latin America, as soon as PRM-1 came in on January 24. The follow-up study, PRM-17, was the subject for the Policy Review Committee on March 24, when Warren Christopher sat in as chairman for Vance, who had just left on his abortive Moscow mission. Years into these negotiations, the United States had yet to propose an acceptable duration for the treaty, while Panama resisted assurances of the canal's continued neutrality or accepting a posttreaty United States residual right in the defense of the canal.

Negotiations with Panama went through several rounds in the spring of 1977, alternating between Washington and Panama City. Despite Zbig's crustiness, Panamanian leader General Omar Torrijos was beginning to give on the issues of neutrality and defense rights. Crucial moves came from the White House as much as anywhere else. At one of the last roadblocks Carter had both teams of negotiators in to see him together. The Panamanians told the President that only direct communication with Torrijos could dissolve the sticking point. President Carter made a phone call. Brzezinski records that agreement in principle was made on August 10. Treaty texts were completed on August 29, to be signed at a Washington ceremony on September 7.

As he did with SALT II, Jimmy Carter planned elaborate efforts to lobby for Senate ratification of the two treaties, one governing neutrality, the other the operation and defense of the Panama Canal. President Carter had his negotiators, Bunker and Linowitz, meet with interested congressmen regularly, sometimes once or twice a week. Brzezinski made many trips to the Hill, while the President himself kept a notepad on his desk, recording every day the latest rumors on how senators were leaning, and organizing efforts to keep them in the fold, including personal meetings with wavering legislators. On one especially bad day, with Vance and Christopher already up on the Hill lobbying, Carter ordered in Harold Brown and the entire Joint Chiefs of Staff to reinforce them! The intense effort paid off on March 16, 1978, when the Neutrality Treaty was adopted by a vote of 68 to 32, and in April when the second treaty received conditional approval by an identical margin. The Panamanians actually agreed to renegotiate, accepting amendments inserted by the U.S. Congress. Torrijos and Jimmy Carter signed the revised Panama Canal treaties as all of Panama seemingly looked on, on June 16, 1978.

President Carter remains convinced of the value of the canal treaties. He believes the cession of sovereignty to be equitable and the arrangements to afford the United States ample rights for operation and defense of the canal plus a role in any future sea-level canal project. But the former President also notes: "If I could have foreseen early in 1977 the terrible battle we would face in Congress, it would have been a great temptation for me to avoid the issue—at least during my first term. The struggle left deep and serious political wounds that have never healed." Jimmy Carter paid the price for solving the canal dispute and deserves honor for it.

*　　*　　*

President Carter meant exactly what he said when he talked about human rights, but it was a vision shared with only a sprinkling of idealists in government. The bureaucrats, old-line diplomats, generals, and a lot of other people were uncomfortable with Carter's approach, fearing it would obstruct traditional diplomacy. Much of the bureaucracy would pay lip service to these objectives, then conduct their business in the traditional fashion.

In the preinauguration dream days, Brzezinski formed a Global Issues cluster on his NSC staff, while the State Department established a Human Rights Bureau. Zbig's Global Issues cluster handled human rights, but it also did nuclear nonproliferation, chemical warfare, refugees, security assistance and arms sales. Directing the cluster was Jessica Tuchman Matthews, daughter of historian Barbara Tuchman. Matthews had a Ph.D. in microbiology from MIT and was Brzezinski's expert on the nuclear fuel cycle. Helping her was Air Force Colonel Leslie G. Denend, who went on to become Zbig's last special assistant.

Global Issues became a miasma, not least because it was buffeted by contradictory impulses. Arms sales to certain countries might be objectionable on human rights grounds. Global Issues would be expected to make that case, but also the one for the sale. In fact, arms sales were a particular problem for Brzezinski because the President, with great fanfare, promulgated a new policy of cutting back United States overseas arms sales. In an era of rampant inflation and very high oil prices, arms sales were one of the few positive factors in the American balance of payments. It was not long before the policy of arms sales reductions bumped into a prospect of selling advanced F-15 jet fighters to Saudi Arabia, one of the major oil producers. The deal would break the quota for reduced arms sales. It was the policy that got scuttled instead. Brzezinski favored the F-15 sale, which went ahead regardless of opposition from the ACDA and American Jewish groups. Morale suffered at Global Issues. In mid-1979 Brzezinski reached into the cluster to transfer Jessica Tuchman's assistant without consulting her. Tuchman resigned.

At the interagency level the senior human rights unit was a working group that met under Warren Christopher, undersecretary of state, a lawyer who had been Vance's staff director during his investigation of the 1967 Detroit urban riots for Lyndon Johnson. Christopher and Vance divided up the work of State to cover all areas as best they could.

State's formal interests were represented by its Human Rights Bureau, which danced rather delicately among the department's regional bureaus, who had the main responsibility for affairs. Human Rights was the bailiwick of one of Carter's political appointees, forty-seven-year-old former civil rights activist Patt Derian; she was tough, blunt, and ready to be as abrasive for human rights worldwide as she had been for black civil rights in Mississippi. Derian was seconded by a former aide to Senator Edward Kennedy, Mark Schneider, as well as Stephen Cohen, a political activist from the

Vietnam antiwar movement and Eugene McCarthy's 1968 presidential campaign.

The most enduring change the Carter administration made was to enshrine human rights, establishing what has, at least rhetorically, been a centerpiece of American foreign policy ever since. A fervent supporter of human rights, Carter believed in taking it into account in foreign policy, fitting with his vision of a new order of morality in foreign affairs and his Baptist religion. Knowledge of the President's support became an important factor preventing the skeptical bureaucracy from completely throttling the fledgling policy and its State Department manifestation. Wittingly or not, Jimmy Carter popularized an ideal so compelling it acquired force and momentum of its own in foreign relations. In Harry Truman's day, the Psychological Strategy Board experts would have picked it up right away.

As Patt Derian soon discovered, however, the momentum behind human rights opposed the inertia of realpolitik. Brzezinski showed in Africa how easy it was to substitute the East-West axis for the North-South one. Even within Foggy Bottom it was sometimes hard to get a hearing for human rights issues. Richard M. Moose, assistant secretary of state for African affairs, recommended Derian for her job, and gave her the easiest entrée. Richard M. Holbrooke, like Moose a onetime NSC staffer, had independent ties to Carter as an early Trilateralist, and tried to keep Derian out of Far Eastern affairs. Their struggle has been chronicled in a detached account of United States relations with the Philippines by Raymond Bonner, *Waltzing with a Dictator*.

In Latin America, what happened with Nicaragua showed the prevalence of realpolitik thinking at the center of government. Nicaragua (and Iran) began as countries viewed primarily in the context of human rights concerns. As events evolved, the security dimension loomed larger. The national security adviser exhibited a predilection for absorbing issues whenever they acquired intensity, substituting his Special Coordination Committee for the NSC Policy Review Committee whose operation, as we have seen, Zbig derided in the case of the brigade crisis.

At the outset the battle lines were drawn between the Human Rights Bureau and the Latin American Bureau's Office for Central American Affairs over the concept of "dissociation" from human rights offenders. Nicaraguan dictator Anastasio Somoza Debayle fell in that category, although the State desk officer for the region, Wade Matthews, felt the policy was a cosmetic effort, something to make one "feel good" about the United States rather than answering the real problems of Nicaragua. Patt Derian and her people naturally felt otherwise. One bloody bureaucratic skirmish was fought over whether the United States would supply rifle sling swivels to Somoza's National Guard, the Nicaraguan armed force, a simple item but one Mark Schneider of Human Rights bitterly opposed. Matthews outflanked Schneider by waiting for a weekend when he was out of town, then getting Derian's approval on a paper that stated the views of both bureaus, afterward taking the thing to Philip Habib, who ruled in favor of the Latin American Bureau. Furious when he found out, Schneider immediately appealed to Warren Christopher, who reversed Habib's decision. The denial leaked very quickly to Congressman Charles Wilson of Texas, who scored points among conservatives denouncing the administration's refusal of such a minor item on human rights grounds.

Nestled within the NSC staff's North-South cluster was its tiny Latin American section under Robert Pastor, which occupied the OEOB office directly next door to the space made infamous by Ollie North. Pastor was part of that graduate seminar that a few journalists thought they saw in the Brzezinski staff. An organizer of Vietnam antiwar demonstrations during his junior year abroad, in England, Bob Pastor joined the Peace Corps and served in Malaysia. Later, looking for material for a paper about Guatemala, he shipped on a banana boat running between Tampa and Bluefields, Nicaragua, the most dangerous job he ever held because of the snakes that usually came aboard among the bananas.

The firsthand look at Nicaragua would serve Pastor better than he could have thought. He started out researching Latin America for the Congressional Research Service, did some work for the Murphy Commission, a study of government organization, and agreed to write a few papers for Sol Linowitz's commission, of which Pastor ended up as staff director. He pursued his Harvard Ph.D. on the side. Trilateralist Richard Gardner encountered Pastor with Linowitz, recruiting him for Jimmy Carter's presidential campaign in 1975. Brzezinski liked him and took the twenty-nine-year-old Pastor along for the NSC staff.

Pastor was not above playing bureaucratic politics. Information about meetings, bootleg memoranda, private understandings, Pastor used all the tools of the back-alley bureaucrat. Because of this, perhaps, Pastor was not held in high regard by Terence Todman, his opposite number at Foggy Bottom, the assistant secretary for Latin America. Pastor really warmed up when Viron "Pete" Vaky succeeded Todman as assistant secretary. A former member of the Kissinger NSC staff, Vaky had a far superior understanding of the range of White House interests. Pastor believed his relations with State improved immeasurably with Pete Vaky in the State Department job.

One place Vaky differed with Pastor was in their assessment of Nicaragua. An old-line Latin Americanist, like William Bowdler or Wayne Smith, Vaky was interested in avoiding a Batistalike collapse in Nicaragua, and he thought Somoza's chances to survive in power until 1981, the end of the constitutional term of office, were poor. Pastor did not initially see Nicaragua's situation in such stark terms. His opposition to sanctions against Somoza was in line with that of State's desk officer, Wade Matthews. Favoring such measures as "distancing" from Somoza were the Human Rights Bureau and Richard Feinberg, Latin America specialist of the Policy Planning Staff, which exercised a prominent role in the Vance State Department.

A wild card landed on the table on January 10, 1978, when opposition

416

editor Pedro Joaquin Chamorro was gunned down in the streets of Managua, capital of Nicaragua. Within a few days the police arrested a man who admitted to the murder but claimed he had been hired to so do the deed by a Cuban-American doctor who owned blood banks in Nicaragua and Haiti and had been criticized in Chamorro's paper *La Prensa*. The explanation, it was widely believed, had been concocted to disguise Somoza's hand in the Chamorro killing. President Carlos Andres Perez of Venezuela, who happened to be a longtime friend of Chamorro's, sent a letter to Jimmy Carter demanding action against Somoza.

Meanwhile, President Carter determined to consult with Latin American leaders on measures that he could take about Cubans in Africa. President Perez was among those Carter sent letters on this subject. Bob Pastor could not interest Brzezinski in the issues raised by the Venezuelan letter. Zbig merely asked what Perez had answered on Carter's letter. Pastor finally put through a phone call to Pete Vaky, only to find out the Venezuelans refused either to meet with Vaky or accept Jimmy Carter's letter until the United States replied to the Venezuelan letter of January 31, 1978. Suddenly Brzezinski was interested. A Carter reply went back on February 17, duly reviewed by Warren Christopher's committee. Jimmy Carter promised to work closely with Perez on human rights issues and try to get Somoza to accept a visit by the Inter-American Human Rights Commission (IAHRC).

President Carter did not concern himself further with Nicaragua until June 20, when he happened to read in his daily Situation Room summary that Somoza had agreed to talk to the IAHRC. Carter mentioned to Zbig that a positive letter might encourage Somoza. Brzezinski sent a memo to Pastor on June 21, 1978, telling him to get to work on a letter for Somoza that would be cleared by State and to report back by the close of business the next day.

Pastor recounts he felt uncomfortable. There was a good chance Somoza would seize upon such a letter as a token of presidential support by the United States, in the face of the rising tide of social discontent in Nicaragua. But when Pastor tried to make this point to the national security adviser, Brzezinski cut him off.

"Write it," Zbig said. "Put your concerns in a memo to the President and clear it with State."

Somoza, in fact, did use Carter's letter as evidence of United States support for his leadership. It came as Somoza's power was ebbing. An unmistakable signal of Somoza's vulnerability, the takeover of the National Palace in Managua with fifteen hundred people in it on August 22, resulted from a commando action of rebels from the Frente Sandinista de Liberación Nacional (FSLN), the Sandinista National Liberation Front. The Sandinistas at the time were one of several opposition groups that drew strength from different sectors of Nicaraguan society.

On September 4, David Aaron chaired a mini-SCC meeting on Nicaragua. It was the first time the White House side of the NSC machinery had been convened on the subject. Originally intended to be a PRC session at State, Brzezinski recast the meeting once he learned of it, to produce, at Carter's request, a recommendation. David Newsom and Tony Lake attended for State. The department argued that the United States had the influence to help remove Somoza and would gain credit for doing so. Pastor disagreed. The mini-SCC met a week later to ventilate the issue again. At length the group decided to try to get Latin Americans to mediate the departure of Somoza rather than attempting it directly. The United States also decided to send Bill Bowdler on a consultation mission to Central American states other than Nicaragua.

What does not seem to have been clear in Washington was the extent of support for the Sandinista resistance. Aaron chaired his third mini-SCC session the day Omar Torrijos told Bowdler that he was already considering direct action in concert with Venezuela's President Perez. On September 22 rumors the Panamanian Air Force was about to bomb Managua induced Brzezinski to call an urgent meeting in his office with Harold Brown and Warren Christopher, plus Vaky, Aaron, Pastor, and others. President Carter managed to convince Torrijos by telephone to abandon the plan. Meanwhile, the situation within Nicaragua escalated to full-scale civil war, during the first month of which six cities were devastated with an estimated 1,500 to 3,000 persons killed.

For the next few months attempts at mediation bounced between the Organization of the American States (OAS) and American diplomats, principally Bowdler. He got Dominican diplomats to take the lead in the mediation mission. The choice of Dominicans was inspired by the 1965 Dominican crisis, when it had been Bowdler sitting on Bob Pastor's NSC staff hot seat. By January 26, 1979, when Bowdler reviewed the mediation for a session of the PRC, Somoza had perfected tactics of seeming to make concessions while playing for time. He had received the IAHRC, offered to hold a plebiscite on his rule, and taken other minor measures to encourage the impression he was making reforms. Harold Brown commented that the Pentagon's impression was the longer Somoza stayed on, the greater was the likelihood of a radical turnover.

Brown's statement had to be a red flag for the NSC principals, but there was just too much going on, with the fall of the Shah plus the fighting between China and Vietnam. The United States decided to end the mediation, which it did on February 8, 1979, imposing sanctions on Nicaragua thereafter. Somoza had received new arms shipments during the period of the mediation, however, and took the field with an even stronger National Guard. However, he had been losing popular support during the interval, with the Sandinistas steadily emerging as the most popular opposition front.

Brzezinski ordered a Presidential Review Memorandum.

Begun during February, the PRM had been completed by early June and became the subject of a PRC meeting Christopher chaired on June 11. By now the Sandinistas had the capacity for a winning offensive. At the PRC,

Brzezinski took the lead proposing a formula that would stop the civil war by halting arms supplies to both sides and inserting an OAS peace force. Mention of an OAS peace force hinted of crisis management rather than accommodation to Nicaraguan realities. Pete Vaky, however, was not averse to a peace force provided it was linked to Somoza's actual resignation and departure. David Newsom pointed out the United States would have to make the major contribution to any such force.

"Yes, the peso stops here!" David Aaron quipped.

Brzezinski convened the Special Coordination Committee on June 19, immediately after returning from the Vienna SALT II summit. The State Department was proposing an OAS meeting, if not yet a peace force. Brzezinski warned that Nicaragua would have an impact on political support for SALT II and on the President's standing in southern and western states. Vance presented a five-point plan, excluding any peace force. Nevertheless, consulting with Latin governments on a peace force emerged as a decision from the SCC session, which Pastor describes as "decisive." The next day one of Somoza's National Guardsmen in Managua, on camera, callously murdered ABC television correspondent Bill Stewart. That event shocked many Americans and destroyed what United States support was left for the dictatorship.

Thus began a month of frenzied activity in the United States government. With time out for a trip to Japan with Carter, Brzezinski chaired eight meetings of the SCC while David Aaron held two mini-SCCs. President Carter put Nicaragua on the agenda for his foreign policy breakfast on June 22. Brzezinski forcefully made the case for U.S. intervention, warning of major domestic and international implications of a "Castro-ite" takeover in Nicaragua. Though Carter had approved Zbig's inserting warnings to Cuba within the text of a Vance speech, the President did not seem very impressed with the case for intervention. Then Vance reported that talks with OAS members were very negative on a peace force.

Subsequently both Vance and Harold Brown went on record opposing any unilateral U.S. intervention.

Later, in Tokyo, Zbig got the impression from Aaron's phone calls and cables that the Nicaragua situation was deteriorating. In fact, at a mini-SCC on June 29, Pete Vaky argued that the question in Nicaragua had become how to stop the fighting. It was "the first time in a year," Bob Pastor notes, "that anyone had suggested the central U.S. objective was anything other than preventing a Sandinista victory."

Zbig tried to take the reins when he returned to Washington, but events had outrun him. He sent Pastor on at least one special mission to visit Omar Torrijos, who had taken a role as one of the most active mediators, very pro-Sandinista, a man Jimmy Carter could not deny. Pastor tells us Zbig knew the President did not agree with him on the crisis. The NSC staffer also notes: "Brzezinski's anxiety had caused him to abandon his forward-looking vision of the region in favor of a traditional 'spheres of influence' approach." Thereafter Zbig began and ended almost every meeting with remarks critical of the U.S. government for standing passively by as historical changes rippled through Central America. At the SCC session on July 13, for example, Brzezinski lamented his view "of the baton being passed from the United States to Cuba" in Central America, worrying "it fills me with unease."

By then the FSLN had begun its offensive from Costa Rica, while less well organized bands were capturing cities to the north and nearing Managua. The National Guard, several months on the defensive, began to crumble and melt away. Ambassador Lawrence A. Pezullo, just dispatched to Nicaragua, and Bill Bowdler, the old hand, were still working on Somoza, who could not bring himself to relinquish power. Finally he did, leaving on July 17, to be followed only forty-three hours later by the parliamentarian who initially succeeded him. The Sandinistas formed a junta of nine, which became the Nicaraguan government on July 19, 1979.

Jimmy Carter met with Daniel Ortega Saavedra, spokesman of the Nicaraguan junta, in September 1979. A small amount of economic aid, a token of what could be a lot more, became the carrot to tempt Managua toward Washington. Pastor became convinced the Sandinistas were assisting a similar guerrilla resistance movement in neighboring El Salvador and became instrumental in securing military aid for the Salvadoran government, over State and ambassadorial objections concerning human rights practices. Only when three American missionary nuns and a lay worker in El Salvador were raped and murdered by army troops on December 2, 1980, could the practitioners of realpolitik in Washington be made to sit up and take notice. By then Ronald Reagan was on his way into the White House and military aid quickly resumed.

At the time, in June 1979, Pete Vaky recalled one senior official saying, "It's too bad the Shah isn't the head of Nicaragua and Somoza of Iran!"

By then, both Nicaragua and Iran had escaped from the purview of the Human Rights Bureau. Patt Derian and her associates were left to think about resigning. They had stuck to their guns throughout the Carter years. Their tenacity contributed to a number of important achievements, including the strong public support that has evolved for human rights policies. But in Nicaragua and Iran, and in most other places where power seemed important, national security considerations prevailed.

Nixon's problem with China was Carter's too: the China lobby. All of those years of an aggressively pursued cold war, of hurling charges about who lost China, had pumped a balloon full of resentment waiting to burst upon whoever declared the end of the cold war with China. Nixon realized that better than anyone, and it was precisely for that reason that he and Kissinger concocted the so-called two-Chinas policy, acknowledging the PRC while continuing to aid Taiwan. Peking's position was naturally that there was but *one* China and that was the PRC. If Washington wanted an ambassador in Peking, it would have to halt aid to Taiwan.

The embassies the sides had in Peking and Washington were styled people's liaison bureaus. Foreign Service officers assigned there were in an administrative limbo, officially representing their people rather than their government.

Jimmy Carter had determined to change all that. China was one of the subjects he pressed Henry Kissinger most closely on during their transition meetings. Privately Carter, Mondale, Vance, and Brzezinski all agreed normalization of relations was a desirable objective. In a detailed compilation of administration goals Brzezinski wrote just for the NSC principals, he notes, the objective for China was to achieve normalization by 1979.

For Carter the issue was complicated by the question of postwar relations with Vietnam. There too the case could be made for normalization, which Richard Holbrooke, assistant secretary of state for East Asian and Pacific affairs, did. Though not well liked by colleagues or subordinates, Holbrooke definitely knew what he was talking about on Vietnam, where he had known Ed Lansdale intimately, worked under both Henry Cabot Lodge and Max Taylor, roomed with John Negroponte, and worked with Bob Komer on LBJ's "other war" White House staff, not to mention with Averell Harriman and Vance on the Paris negotiations in 1968. An assistant secretary of state at thirty-five, reportedly the youngest in forty years, Holbrooke was especially close to Vance.

Before the inauguration Zbig had put Holbrooke to work on a policy paper in conjunction with Michel Oksenberg of the NSC and other State experts. Once they had a draft, it seemed a more ambitious interagency effort had become appropriate and Brzezinski ordered PRM/NSC-24. Late in August, Vance made the administration's first expedition to Peking, but Carter got cold feet about normalizing relations just as the Panama treaties were completed, Brezezinski reports, and gave Vance no leeway to bargain on the two-Chinas policy.

For the record, it should be noted that during this identical period Holbrooke was meeting with Vietnamese diplomats about normalization of relations with their country. The Vietnamese angered Washington by assuming the United States was bound to carry out the promises of postwar aid they alleged had been made by Kissinger. Kissinger flatly denied what the documents said; he had promised nothing except vague "studies." It was rather similar to his equally determined denials that there was any substance to the concession the Soviets claimed Henry had made at Vladivostok.

A second factor complicating the Vietnam normalization question was the issue of American servicemen missing in action (MIA) in Southeast Asia during the war. Veterans organizations and associations of families demanded that all missing persons be accounted for before any normalization of relations with Hanoi.

Holbrooke was seriously set back as MIA politics developed and accounting for the missing acquired importance in the United States negotiating position. He was told that the China normalization project was as much as could be done at one time, and the Vietnamese track was deemphasized. The road to normalization with the PRC was a carefully choreographed succession of overtures and flattery. Prime mover on the NSC staff was Mike Oksenberg, the snappy and knowledgeable China expert whom Zbig brought with him. Oksenberg complemented Brzezinski; with edges a little smoother, he was more gracious and not quite as impulsive. The son of Belgian Jews who left Antwerp as soon as World War II began, he had become a naturalized American citizen in 1945 when he was seven years old. A political scientist trained at Swarthmore and Columbia, Oksenberg taught at Columbia, then achieved a tenured position at the University of Michigan.

Brzezinski knew nothing about China, but he knew who did, and there was never much question that Oksenberg would go with him. Not initially much concerned about the PRC, Brzezinski began to get interested toward the end of 1977, after he was invited to a special dinner at the Chinese liaison mission. The question became who would go to Peking finally to negotiate normalization terms; Brzezinski wanted very much to go. He got Mike Oksenberg to drop hints in the right places, and the result in November 1977 was an invitation extended directly to Brzezinski by Chinese diplomats during a lunch with Walter Mondale.

Cyrus Vance resolutely opposed a Brzezinski visit to China. He feared it would become a mark of the resuscitation of "Lone Ranger" diplomacy. Mondale also opposed the Brzezinski visit and wanted to make the trip himself. At a critical moment Zbig apparently convinced the Vice President to switch sides. President Carter recounts that he finally decided to send Vance to Moscow in a parallel visit to demonstrate evenhandedness. Vance reluctantly acquiesced; Zbig promised to be a good emissary.

Brzezinski went to China with the twofold purpose of continuing consultations under the Shanghai Communiqué, and reassuring Peking the United States was serious about normalization. Brzezinski planned to tantalize the Chinese with intelligence briefings on the Soviet threat, and also describe Jimmy Carter's own private views that the United States and PRC had a common interest in "opposition to global or regional hegemony by any single power." That was significant because this phrase was virtually a Peking code word then being used to attack perceived Soviet social imperialism and Vietnamese expansionism. The list of places Peking was to be told it could make positive contributions included the Horn of Africa, southern Africa, Israel, India, and Cambodia. To a great degree it was Brzezinski's agenda, not Vance's. As a matter of fact, Brzezinski apparently succeeded in excluding Dick Holbrooke, Vance's senior man on the delegation, from his most sensitive sessions with the Chinese.

Upon his return, a tad exuberant, Zbig went on the television interview show *Meet the Press* to make vexing remarks about Soviet actions in Africa violating the "code of détente." Brzezinski did little to discourage press interpretations that viewed Brzezinski as playing a China card in the game of international relations.

"You're not just a professor," Jimmy Carter told Zbig the next morning. "You speak for me. And I think you went too far in your statements. You put all of this responsibility on the Soviets."

The President worried Brzezinski's remarks might damage détente.

There would be more trips after Brzezinski's. Walter Mondale got his chance the following summer, in one of the most successful visits to China by any American official, during which Peking agreed to a number of collaborative measures, including some very sensitive ones such as intelligence-gathering facilities. Harold Brown was to make the journey during 1980. Jimmy Carter himself never reached Peking until he had become once more a private citizen. Finally, the Chinese returned the visits. A military delegation saw American defense industry and visited military bases. Then, at the beginning of 1979, came a state visit by Chinese leader Teng Hsiao-ping.

The Teng visit completed the process of normalization. Washington withdrew its diplomats from Taiwan and upgraded the embassy in Peking to official status effective January 1, 1979.

In the meantime the situation regarding relations with Vietnam completely reversed itself. A further round of quiet negotiations occurred in New York. Once again the United States team was headed by Dick Holbrooke and Mike Oksenberg. Meetings were held in apartments, Oksenberg and others arriving in separate cabs to avoid attracting attention. Holbrooke was excited and thought Hanoi about to abandon its insistence on American postwar recovery aid. By September 1978 there was such optimism that Holbrooke set a group to work planning for an American embassy in Hanoi. Ken Quinn, now Holbrooke's special assistant, advised that no one with a Vietnamese wife (as Quinn had) should be sent back to Vietnam. The Vietnamese would be in New York for a month, there was time for a decision in Washington. In fact, Zbig told *Far Eastern Economic Review* reporter Nayan Chanda in 1981, he took a dim view of the State Department's trying to insert Vietnam into the Sino-American normalization process, seeing the Southeast Asian nation as peripheral and a mere Soviet proxy. Brzezinski boasted of having shot down the attempt. Hanoi's diplomats left New York empty-handed.

In the meantime Vietnam was experiencing increasing difficulties with the Pol Pot regime in Cambodia, and conflict sharpened into an active border war. Hanoi made plans to invade Cambodia and did so in December. Reportedly that came as no surprise in Washington, where the CIA's responsible national intelligence officer, John Holdridge, the Kissinger NSC staffer, predicted the attack. Holdridge apparently also found indications that Peking had determined to teach Vietnam a lesson and was assembling forces for an attack in support of the Khmer Rouge, whom it favored in Cambodia.

Brzezinski brought up the question of an attack on Vietnam with Chinese interlocutors when Teng Hsiao-ping came to Washington. The official United States position was not to support any such effort, but Zbig worked on Jimmy Carter, telling the President it was important "for us *not* to convey any excessive U.S. alarm," thus passing up an opportunity to dissuade the Chinese from this show of force. Brzezinski worried the United States would seem a "paper tiger" in opposing the attack, and concedes he felt the PRC was acting in parallel with American interests. Instead, early in the Chinese military action, Brzezinski warned Anatoli Dobrynin at one of their periodic meetings against any Soviet action to support Vietnam.

In effect, though there was no American commitment to Peking, and though the administration protested loudly any assertion it was playing a China card, United States action during the border fighting between China and Vietnam followed the lines one would expect from a power fulfilling an alliance delegation.

Meanwhile, the Vietnamese forces in the north of the country, mostly militia and reserve units, fought the vaunted People's Liberation Army to a standstill. Humiliated, Peking funded a Pol Pot guerrilla war against the pro-Vietnamese successor regime in Phnom Penh. It marked the beginning of *another* decade of war in Southeast Asia, with Washington eventually coming under pressure to intervene again, *on the side of the Pol Pot Khmer Rouge*. Carter administration Asian policy suffered grievously from taking Vietnam to be a Soviet satrapy rather than treating it as a sovereign nation with security and economic concerns in its own right.

TRIUMPH AND TRAGEDY

▲▲▲

Jimmy Carter first visited Israel a few months before the October War. The Georgian was mightily impressed. Then the fourth Arab-Israeli war shook the world when the Arabs' oil weapon jarred the global economy. The lesson seemed clear; the world, especially the developed countries, could not afford another Middle East war. Promoting peace in the Middle East was not just another point in the goals paper Brzezinski prepared before the inauguration, but a central element in Carter's policy, one on which Zbigniew Brzezinski and Cyrus Vance agreed.

Zbigniew Brzezinski made his visit to Israel in the summer of 1976. He was given the full treatment with extensive official briefings, a trip to the Golan Heights, and so forth. Zbig was at dinner at the home of Shimon Peres, then Israeli defense minister, the night Israeli paratroopers mounted a daring commando raid at Entebbe, Uganda, to free from terrorists an El Al plane with a hundred passengers.

"My trip to the Golan and my travels within the country," Brzezinski writes, "convinced me of the futility of seeking security through the acquisition of territory. It became clear . . . that Israel could never acquire enough territory to compensate for Arab hostility."

Among the second echelon of the bureaucracy Roy Atherton, followed by Hal Saunders, were the assistant secretaries of state for the region. Warren Christopher, David Newsom, and Philip Habib, the undersecretaries and the deputy secretary, agreed with Vance that only progress toward peace would avert another war. The responsible NSC staff analyst was Bill Quandt, who had learned the trade under Hal Saunders in Kissinger's NSC. Toward the end of Carter's administration, Quandt was replaced by Robert Hunter, who moved over from the NSC European portfolio. The change to Hunter, who was philosophically closer to Brzezinski than the pragmatic Quandt, symbolized the progressive narrowing of the Brzezinski staff.

At the outset there was substantial agreement within the United States government to make a Middle East initiative. The major disagreement was tactical. In line with most mainstream foreign policy advocates, Vance was thinking in terms of a Geneva conference on the Middle East, reactivating a mechanism of which the United States and Soviet Union were cochairmen. Thinking it desirable to limit Soviet influence in the Middle East, Brzezinski preferred to avoid this kind of multilateral device. He did not, however, try to create obstacles for the exploration of this path to a settlement.

The administration got its own house in order by means of a series of detailed discussions. First came an informal session on January 30, 1977, among Carter, Vance, Andrew Young, and Brzezinski. On February 4 there followed a meeting of the NSC Policy Review Committee, the first held under Vance's chairmanship. Cy was quite collegial about it, and sat back to allow Zbig to take the lead defining the issue. At this point Brzezinski saw the ideal was to settle as much as possible before any Geneva conference. Zbig wanted to use the prospect of a conference as a tool to influence both Israelis and Arabs.

There was a full-dress NSC meeting on February 23, a clue to the gravity with which Jimmy Carter saw the situation, for this President found less reason to assemble his council than anyone since Harry Truman. Vance reported differences among Arab nations regarding details of their participation at Geneva, but all agreed to attend. The situation seemed hopeful.

The perspective changed somewhat as Jimmy Carter's days stretched into weeks and then months. Carter began to meet the Middle Eastern leaders to take their measure and engage them more directly. In April, for Carter, President Anwar Sadat of Egypt was "a shining light burst." On the other hand, Jimmy found Israel's Prime Minister Yitzhak Rabin cold and distant, and Syria's President Hafez Assad someone who would try to block a Geneva settlement. The setback with Rabin proved less consequential than feared because two months later his Labor party lost the election in Israel. Its cabinet was replaced by a right-wing–religious coalition under Menachem Begin. A Washington visit for Begin was then arranged for July 1977.

Preparing for the Begin visit, Carter ordered a further series of Policy Review Committee deliberations. These considered proposed arms sales to Saudi Arabia, Egypt, and Israel too. Brzezinski used the discussions to underline the utility of arms assistance as positive incentives for agreement. Privately Bill Quandt had begun to argue to Brzezinski that a Geneva conference did not look so good anymore. Another time Quandt asked whether the United States ought to encourage secret meetings between Begin and Sadat. By October, Carter had met both Begin and his foreign minister, Moshe Dayan, and it was evident difficult obstacles now blocked the way to Geneva.

In a handwritten letter, on October 21, Carter reminded Sadat of his pledge to lend support at a crucial moment, then said, "We have reached such a moment, and I need your help."

Sadat later told three Israeli journalists, Eitan Huber, Zeev Schiff and Ehud Yaari, whose account remains one of the best of this period, that Carter's letter had made him stand back and look at the deadlock in a new way. On November 9, speaking before an audience that included PLO leader Yasir Arafat, Sadat declared he would go to Jerusalem and argue with the Knesset if necessary to achieve peace in the Middle East. Privately Sadat had told Carter in a letter ten days before that he would propose a conference in East Jerusalem. Just like Carter's message to him, Sadat handwrote his reply, sealing it with wax and a signet.

Sadat did travel to Jerusalem. He met Begin there, and as promised addressed the Knesset. It was a dramatic moment, but costly to Egypt as other Arab nations, fearful the UAR was deserting the common front against Israel, ostracized her. Sadat, sincerely believing he was standing for the interests of the Palestinian people as well as Egypt, persisted. But Begin made no concessions, and Sadat finally had to give up. For a time, in early 1978, it seemed as if Sadat's initiative had gone for nothing.

Carter's frustration rose when the Israelis presented a proposal for Palestinian autonomy on the West Bank and Gaza that was clearly not negotiable. By January 1978, Brzezinski thought the issue of a Palestinian homeland had been introduced too soon and without adequate political care. Because he thought Sadat's initiative had led into a new phase, Zbig seemed anxious to preserve the sense of momentum. In spite of Bill Quandt's opinion that the United States should not attempt to paper over the differences between Sadat and the Israelis, Brzezinski prepared suggestions to turn Begin's West Bank autonomy plan into a more acceptable transitional administration. Zbig's alternative moved ahead in the tactical vacuum that existed because Carter had adopted general principles for Middle East policy but never a specific strategy.

The President himself put considerable thought into this matter of a strategy. Before leaving for a fishing weekend at St. Simons Island, Carter had a long talk with Zbig about the options. On Sunday morning, in the middle of the trip, Carter called the national security adviser and ordered him to set up a larger group for the next day to include both Fritz Mondale and Cy Vance. It was on that occasion that Carter broached inviting both Sadat and Begin to Camp David for mediated negotiations. At first hearing Vance spoke against the idea and so did Brzezinski who, along with Quandt, preferred colluding with Sadat in order to put pressure on Tel Aviv. President Carter went over the issues again at a foreign policy breakfast on February 3, just prior to a Sadat visit to Washington. The President complained of the slow progress and inferior quality of the recommendations he was getting, whereupon Zbig presented Carter a ten-point proposal for revision of the Begin autonomy plan. Carter recalled the session in his diary as "quite an argument," with Mondale, Vance, Brzezinski, and Chief of Staff Hamilton Jordan all ranged against him. The President approved Zbig's idea of trying to make the Begin plan more palatable. Over the next several days Carter then held talks with Anwar Sadat, and reached a special understanding. There can be little doubt that Sadat had an intense faith in his relationship with President Carter.

Meanwhile, Washington came to a decision on weapons sales to the Middle East. Carter decided to go ahead, not only with F-15 sales to the Saudis, but with advanced F-16s and F-15s to Israel and F-5s to Egypt.

427

American Jewish interest groups opposed the Saudi and Egyptian sales. The arms sale debate brought an escalation in rhetoric regarding Brzezinski himself, who had previously antagonized the Jewish groups with off-the-cuff remarks at his press conferences. Carter felt obliged to defend his national security adviser in a June 1978 speech before a civic group in Fort Worth. It was almost two years to the day since Carter's "Lone Ranger" critique of Henry Kissinger. Ironically, Kissinger had called Brzezinski to warn him of the coming Jewish-American onslaught before things began to get really bad.

Zbig consoled himself that such political attacks were partly a reflection of disapproval of the President. Carter may have wavered on many things, but he stuck by Brzezinski *and* held out on the Middle East. Through the good offices of Great Britain, Vance was able to get Dayan and the Egyptian foreign minister, Mohammed Kamel, together at Leeds Castle in the Surrey countryside. Once more the sides failed to reach an agreement. On July 30, Carter decided to invite Sadat and Begin to Camp David and a week later Vance traveled to the Middle East to extend the invitations personally. That set the stage for the grueling summit that occurred at Camp David between September 5 and 17, previewed by Carter at a full NSC meeting on September 1. To prepare the briefing book, Vance, Saunders, Atherton, and Quandt traveled to Middleburg, West Virginia, where Averell Harriman lent them his country estate.

At the NSC meeting the President conceded that the Israelis saw him and Brzezinski with some suspicion, while they viewed Vance as objective and liked Vice President Mondale. Carter did not wish to pressure either side, and thought a week sufficient for the talks. After the meeting the President left for Camp David with his briefing books, there to spend a last quiet weekend before his visitors arrived. Brzezinski helicoptered up after lunch on September 5, the first day of the summit. He shared a small cabin with Hamilton Jordan, whose foreign policy role increased during 1978, when the President ordered he be informed of important national security documents in order to advise on their political dimensions.

At Camp David, Carter found Begin preoccupied with the meanings of words, and willing to exploit the least loophole. Sadat considered that he had made a series of concessions already in coming to Camp David and waited to hear of answering Israeli ones. Begin's autonomy proposals had changed but slightly since Brzezinski's attempt to reform them, while the Israelis now chose to make an issue of the reversion of Sinai to Egypt, in particular three major air bases Tel Aviv had established in the years since the Six Day War.

Carter thought it important to get the Israelis an unambiguous message by a channel they trusted implicitly. That was Walter Mondale, whom the President called in on September 14. The next morning Mondale conveyed to both Begin and Sadat Carter's personal message that he intended to wind up the conference in forty-eight hours and then make a joint statement to the assembled press.

That day Sadat threatened to walk out of the conference. Vance came back to Carter, his face ashen. "Sadat is leaving," the secretary announced. "He and his aides are already packed. He asked me to order him a helicopter!"

Carter was stunned. He had never seen Vance look so grave, nor had he looked so grave himself, the President recounted to Brzezinski. What could be done? President Carter went to Sadat's lodge, where the Egyptian explained he felt the Israelis did not want peace. Dayan had told him they would sign no agreement. Carter somehow persuaded Sadat to go back for one more try, perhaps as they sat watching the world heavyweight boxing championship that night, a prize fight between Muhammad Ali and Leon Spinks. Carter and Sadat agreed on an exchange of letters in which the United States would go on record in certain ways critical of Israel. Begin balked at first but finally went along with the form of what became the Camp David accords, signed in Washington on September 17, 1978. In what many still recall as Carter's finest achievement, the accords permitted a disengagement between at least two of the belligerents of the Arab-Israeli wars. Camp David has been less successful in securing Palestinian rights, however, and much of the succeeding decade of Middle Eastern affairs was taken up in working to induce Tel Aviv, then Jerusalem, to implement the accords. That began just a month later, in October, when there were talks at Blair House on a tripartite basis. Later there were talks Carter again came into, plus a round in Israel when the President stayed at the King David Hotel. Along the way came a Brzezinski special mission, when Zbig went to Sadat with the last round of language changes for what became the Egyptian-Israeli Peace Treaty, signed on March 26, 1979.

Billy Carter, the President's brother, became involved in representing Libya's business interests in America. In September 1978, Billy traveled to Libya with assistant Henry R. Coleman and other Georgia businessmen. Later they showed some Libyans around Georgia.

Billy Carter's commercial activities ran into national security areas from the beginning. He went to the White House through appointments secretary Philip Wise for NSC staff briefings on Libya prior to the original trip. Fresh from the Camp David triumph, Bill Quandt and Rick Inderfurth, Zbig's special assistant, fielded the questions thrown at them by Henry Coleman. Billy himself came on the line during part of one conversation. Some months later Coleman contacted official sources in behalf of the Libyans to ask why they were not receiving delivery of some C-130–type planes and parts the Libyans had purchased from Lockheed.

President Carter found Billy's association with the Libyans a political embarrassment and publicly disassociated himself from Billy's activities in

January 1979. The very next day the Justice Department wrote Billy Carter asking for details about his Libyan contacts and whether he was receiving money from them, advising that if so, he would have to register as a foreign agent under the Foreign Agents Registration Act. Billy Carter ignored the letter and one that followed. In April the Justice Department announced it had begun an investigation. Billy confirmed that Libya had paid for his September 1978 trip, but insisted that he had no business dealings with Muammar Qaddafi. Only much later was it revealed that Jimmy Carter had gotten the embassy cable traffic concerning his brother's visit, discussing it with Billy on an undisclosed occasion.

In August 1979, Billy Carter took up with Charter Oil Company of Jacksonville, Florida, in a scheme to market Libyan oil in the United States. Billy's Arab contacts proved useful during the Iranian hostage crisis, when Rosalynn Carter and Zbigniew Brzezinski convinced him to set up a meeting he then sat in on with the chief Libyan diplomat in the United States, Ali el-Houdari. Brzezinski met with Houdari on November 27, 1979. Five days later Carter received him as well. President Carter thanked Libya for the message Qaddafi had sent Ayatollah Ruhollah Khomeini in the interval, requesting Iran to release the American hostages.

In January 1980 the foreign agents registration unit at the Justice Department, under Joel S. Lisker, began an active investigation of Billy Carter. After them came the Internal Revenue Service and Congress. Allegations that followed included that the President had given his brother copies of classified cables concerning his visit to Libya, that the President had received Libyan money, or had interfered in the Justice Department investigation of his brother. There were other allegations that Billy Carter used improper influence with the government on aircraft sales. The President relates that every allegation was eventually refuted; but it took the administration several weeks to assemble a report presenting the relevant material.

Meanwhile, because there *had* been contacts between the Brzezinski staff and Billy Carter, the NSC rapidly became one focus of investigation. A subcommittee of the Senate under Indiana Democrat Birch Bayh pursued the leads to the NSC, which set the stage for an ugly standoff between Carter and Congress over executive privilege. Brzezinski was dragged back in on June 10, when Billy Carter asked for a meeting in order to ascertain whether there were national security objections to his answering certain questions the Justice Department had put. When Zbig heard the subject, he asked Carter counsel Lloyd Cutler to attend also. Cutler was instrumental in helping Billy Carter get legal representation afterward.

"The Libyan mess," President Carter recalls, "which was dominating the news, was wreaking havoc with our efforts to deal with anything else on the political scene or in Congress, and I wanted to resolve it as soon as possible."

It was about the time Jimmy Carter was making his final preparations for the Democratic National Convention that he completed the report on the so-called Billygate affair. President Carter's hour-long news conference of August 4, 1980, concerned Libya and Billy almost entirely. That same day Brzezinski submitted a statement to the Bayh subcommittee on NSC staff involvement in the affair.

Carter hoped he could leave it at that. There had been demands he himself testify before the Senate but Carter had convinced his advisers it was a poor idea. The President proved less able to resist demands for an appearance by Brzezinski. The gatekeeper was already under some pressure from Congress where, in the Senate, a bill had been introduced that would provide for congressional confirmation for the President's national security adviser. Maverick Nebraska Democrat Edward J. Zorinsky proposed the bill, which the administration had been able to knock down in 1979. The President ultimately sent Brzezinski up to Capitol Hill to give sworn testimony on September 17, 1980.

Witnessing the event for *The New York Times,* reporter David E. Rosenbaum wrote: "Brzezinski seemed to seethe under the criticism, his eyes narrow and his lips clinched. He maintained his composure overall, but it seemed to require every bit of his diplomatic experience."

"We're trying to get the truth," intoned Strom Thurmond at one point in Zbig's testimony, "but we're not sure you're telling it."

"Excuse me, Senator," Brzezinski shot back. "You may not be sure. I *know* I'm telling the truth."

The administration made much of the supposed fact that it was the first time a national security adviser was giving sworn testimony to Congress. Evidently Brzezinski's researchers were unaware that under Dwight Eisenhower national security advisers had repeatedly appeared before Congress to justify the NSC's own budget requests. Under appropriations committee rules these executive branch witnesses were under oath. The precedent Jimmy Carter thought he had been defending, and which he finally waived, did not exist.

This historical curiosity illustrates the hidden tragedy of the Billygate affair—Congress could not be interested in legislating executive branch organizational and management issues, as Zorinsky had proposed in his bill, but only in investigating hints of political scandal. It is also a tragedy for American democracy and public administration that the investigative impulse Congress had gained from Watergate was exhausted at this time. The Billygate business diverted whatever interest there was. Unlike the Zorinsky hearings, moreover, the Brzezinski staff took this investigation seriously. Robert M. Kimmitt, then NSC staff legal counsel, corresponded with Zbig about what degree of latitude to allow congressional requests for NSC documents. Anxious to preclude fishing expeditions, they decided on very narrow criteria.

The search for relevant NSC files was treated as a broad-based request for all documents, whether of NSC or White House origin, including relevant appointment and telephone logs. To avoid surrendering the actual documents the NSC secretariat created a new excerpt document listing the times and dates of relevant meetings and telephone conferences. President Carter also declassified the cables related to the Billy Carter Libya trip, which were basically innocuous, authorized a White House public statement released in July, and allowed the Brzezinski September testimony.

Such effort was wasted on the salacious but empty Billy Carter affair. Much more productive would have been a policy review of government machinery for national security, the administration of which bore little resemblance to the structure stipulated in the National Security Act. The Brzezinski staff, at first cut back, had by now burgeoned to seventy-two with a $3.5-million budget. It was almost two decades since Scoop Jackson's investigation of Eisenhower's NSC. Congress had looked at the presidency in Watergate, the intelligence community through the Church Committee, Pentagon organization for weapons procurement, but seemingly could not be made to pay attention to the level where policy all came together.

Inside government such an effort actually *was* undertaken, under the auspices of a presidential reorganization project. Philip Odeen, who had worked on the NSC staff for Kissinger and Scowcroft, headed the group looking at Brzezinski's staff. The players were distracted by current events, however, in particular Iran, and had little time for an NSC management study. There were snickers at NSC staff meetings. Odeen was not let in on anything too vital.

The Odeen report, despite or perhaps because of its inception, was not very favorable toward the Brzezinski staff. It found that there were too many meetings of the SCC and PRC, that these often lacked clear focus, that preparatory papers were mostly uncoordinated products by a single agency, that NSC analyses were uneven and did not help facilitate decisions. There was the usual conclusion that the NSC was not monitoring implementation, and the report added its belief that the Brzezinski staff was not adequately communicating the rationales for presidential decisions to the bureaucracy. Odeen was specifically critical of Bill Odom's function in concluding procedures for interagency crisis planning were inadequate. Odeen's bottom line was that the NSC institutional performance lagged because of a preoccupation with advising the President.

The Odeen effort received little attention outside government. Inside, it was buried as quickly as possible. It proved easier to dispense with the report on national security policy integration than deal with the problems it had identified.

In the Third World, Zbig was still expecting some Fashoda. When the Soviets intervened in Afghanistan in December 1979, the national security adviser may very well have thought he had it. By this time, late in the administration, Zbig had done it all, attaining Cabinet-level status. His zest for competition undimmed, Brzezinski had begun with the Horn of Africa, only to start talking of an "arc of crisis" as Iran entered its revolution and the insurgency built in Afghanistan. Large-scale Soviet intervention seemed just the vehicle on which to hang a wholesale change in direction for administration policy, paraded as the "Carter Doctrine."

Zbig soon found himself deputized to help complete arrangements for a covert operation to support anti-Soviet Afghan resistance groups. Everything went well until he reached Pakistan, where he narrowly escaped personal tragedy.

In the course of his Pakistan visit, Zbig went to the Khyber Pass, a stop not unusual for distinguished visitors, but especially symbolic in the first weeks after the Soviet invasion. Brzezinski went to a small guard outpost overlooking Afghanistan, about four miles from the tree line that designated the border. The outpost was built in such a fashion that one entered from the top and had to climb ladders, which could be retracted, to get in. Accompanied by Pakistani General Fazle Haq, Zbig went with a retinue of Pakistani and American officials, and a slice of reporters covering Brzezinski's exotic mission to the Orient. All these people crowded into the small outpost in addition to its regular garrison.

Brzezinski inspected the post, gazed into the distance at Afghanistan. Asking how near the Russians had come, he was told not closer than Jelalabad, sixty miles distant. Then there was a weapons demonstration, a fitting climax to an afternoon begun with lunch at the mess of the Khyber Rifles. General Haq asked if Zbig had ever seen a weapon of the kind with which his men were armed—they had old Soviet-type submachine guns. The Pakistani pointed out the gun's features, then handed Zbig the weapon. Brzezinski took it and briefly sighted the weapon as flashbulbs went off and the press took photographs.

The general asked Brzezinski if he wanted to fire a few rounds. Zbig thought a moment, then demurred.

General Haq handed the submachine gun to its owner, a young soldier, whom he told to shoot the weapon. The nervous trooper began to fire out the gun port but the weapon jammed after only a few rounds, after which a sergeant came over and cleared the man's gun.

The soldier then neglected to assume proper firing position, and as he began to fire the automatic weapon, lost control of it. Recoil forced him up onto the balls of his feet, drove him backward as the gun barrel began to shift upward. Within seconds bullets would be spraying throughout the crowded fort on the Khyber Pass.

Fortunately the Pakistani sergeant kept his head, jumped the soldier, and batted down his gun barrel. Otherwise there might have been a bloodbath. Brzezinski could have been killed.

General Haq quickly decided the party had had enough of the fort and led everyone outside.

The incident made no dent in Brzezinski, who continued to use stark rhetoric during this trip. He referred to the pre-World War II period, in a subtle invocation of the Munich analogy, by asking whether Pakistan was going to respond as Poland had, or as Czechoslovakia.

Through an interpreter the national security adviser-cum-emissary had an emotional exchange with a group of the Afghan resistance.

"It's a fact that people who are determined to fight for their own freedom end up winning the respect and sympathy and something more than that from the rest of the world," Brzezinski told them. "That's a historical fact, not a statement of policy."

Anyone listening to Brzezinski's rendition of the "fact" would immediately realize what was the policy, however. This trip in the spring of 1980 set the stage for years of guerrilla warfare pursued equally zestfully by Brzezinski's successors.

Zbig's antics on the Khyber Pass seemed deliberately intended to signal a counteroffensive stance. Most suggestive was when Zbig, trying to get General Haq to pose with him for a picture, urged, "It'll be a historic photo. Three weeks before the march on Kabul!" Who was this to play the Great Game? Afghanistan, at war a couple of years already, would be rent by conflict for more than a decade.

Revolution toppled the Iranian government aligned with the United States, substituting a vitriolic theocracy. The United States initially faced the crisis of the revolution, then the derivative hostage crisis. The wave of Islamic furor that ensued consumed Jimmy Carter's presidency and reverberates still in our time.

The Iranian crisis developed at a time when the backstage conflict between Zbigniew Brzezinski and Cyrus Vance had crystallized over the Brzezinski mission to China. There was no constellation of forces in Washington that could have prevented the Iranian revolution, but a different one might have read the signs better, acted sooner, been more successful with the Islamic successor government, and averted the hostage crisis. At a critical moment, the NSC-State Department competition weakened the United States government's ability to discern a course of action on Iran. Brzezinski's subsequent effort to hold open a particular option delayed the entire American response when the decision finally neared.

Surely the Carter administration expected no such crisis in Iran. If anything the Iranians were being built up as a regional ally, a local power that could help dominate the Indian Ocean. Any worries about the Shah were reflected through a prism of self-interest. For the Carter administration, at least initially, Iran policy was one of those issues squarely in contention between the human rights advocates and the regional bureau at State. When a sale of destroyers to the Iranians threatened the arms sales ceilings Carter had established in PD/NSC-13, Brzezinski was in the forefront of those working to finagle the sale or the ceilings.

In the decade since the Iranian crisis some observers put the blame squarely on the intelligence community and argue the CIA avoided contact with the Iranian opposition and was thus unable to predict the threat to the Shah. Like most simple explanations, that is only partly true. The CIA reflected the general desire to deal only with the Iranian government, whose goodwill was necessary to permit the continued use of some United States intelligence facilities that were very sensitive indeed. The State Department, of course, had a natural counterpart in the Iranian government, as did the military.

When the Shah came to see Carter in Washington in November 1977, Zbig was with them both on the White House lawn when, during a welcoming ceremony gone awry, police used tear gas to disperse anti-Shah demonstrators from Lafayette Park, across Pennsylvania Avenue. The wind changed direction, befouling the Shah's ceremony with the gas. It was a bad omen but an accurate one.

Zbig also did not object when Carter made a gaffe that had the human rights people fainting. On a presidential Middle East trip early in the new year, a difficult itinerary led to the last-moment inclusion of an overnight stopover in Teheran. At the state dinner, Carter praised the Shah as "an island of stability in a turbulent corner of the world." This language was not in the text of the toast initially prepared aboard *Air Force One*. According to NSC Middle East specialist Gary Sick, it was added in the executive suite of the aircraft somewhere between a stop at Warsaw and arrival in Teheran.

Only a few days later riots broke out in the city of Qom, a religious center, after an article ridiculing the Islamic Shiite leader Ruhollah Khomeini, a highly respected holy man, or ayatollah. Iranian security forces fired on the rioters, killing several students. Forty days later, following the prescribed Shiite period of mourning, there were renewed demonstrations, each seemingly more serious than the last.

In January 1978 there were State Department morning summaries on two occasions on the unrest in Iran. Starting in February there were a stream of field reports from such diplomats as Michael Metrinko, a consul who spoke Farsi and had seven years' experience in the country in different capacities. He reported, for example, that the merchants of the bazaars had begun financing opposition to the Shah, and that Iranians with ties to the Shah were secretly moving money out of the country.

At that time the United States ambassador in Teheran was William H. Sullivan. Sullivan had served as American proconsul in Laos running a secret war, and he afterward continued to hold senior positions in the Foreign Service. When Jimmy Carter came to Teheran, Sullivan had been at the post long enough to put out his diplomatic tentacles.

Michael Metrinko's reporting struck a note at Foggy Bottom but it may have had trouble in Teheran. According to one source, Sullivan advised Metrinko to sample a wider range of opinions before filing his reports.

However, State's chief South Asia analyst at its Bureau of Intelligence and Research became concerned enough that he convened a staff meeting to review the data. Few senior people attended. In June the NSC staff ordered a national intelligence estimate on Iran and the Shah, a paper prepared with the speed of molasses that was not published until August. Its notorious conclusion read that Iran "is not in a revolutionary, or even in a prerevolutionary situation." Robert R. Bowie, returned to government in Carter's administration as director of the CIA's National Foreign Assessment Center, a unit with a primary role in putting together the NIE, believes the intelligence community did a reasonable job under the circumstances. Eight years later Bowie told a group of diplomatic historians that a whole series of factors were involved in the intelligence failure. The question of the data from Iran was only a small piece to the puzzle. How could you predict, Bowie asked, which opposition elements would come together and what weight they would have when they did? Bowie was one of the Americans Jimmy Carter sent to Teheran during 1978, to take the Shah's temperature, so to speak, and so was among those with the best basis to judge.

In the State Department itself there were also some who were very concerned. Stephen B. Cohen, one of Patt Derian's deputies, and Theodore Moran, a political officer who had written an earlier report critical of the Shah, got the idea for a "zero-base" assessment of United States relations with Iran, a novel format for foreign policy assessment. A member of the Policy Planning Staff, Moran took the idea to his boss, Anthony Lake, who liked it and told them to go ahead. Before Moran could get very far, however, Lake called and said the project had been ruled out higher up.

This was another check for Moran, who got the impression he was viewed as bizarre for even questioning the stability of Iran. A memo he had written to that effect at the time of the Shah's Washington visit could not get past Vance's office. Moran, it happened, had written his doctoral dissertation at Harvard under Samuel Huntington. The policy planner tried an end run to the NSC staff, where Huntington worked with Brzezinski on PRM-10, the Wake Forest speech, and other matters. Huntington met with Moran but did not agree to pass his concerns to Zbig.

Instead, the advocates of arms sales gained full control of the policy by the summer of 1978. The Human Rights Bureau lost out over approvals for shipments of tear gas to Iran. David Aaron cut off the bureau's protests with a crack about Carter and the Shah teargassed on the White House lawn; the United States could hardly deny Iran things allowed Washington police. Following a rearguard action delaying authorization, the cable went out on September 8. That was the day of the Jaleh Square massacre, known as Black Friday among the opposition, in which security forces opened fire resulting in hundreds killed and thousands of total casualties in Teheran.

After Black Friday, Bill Sullivan noted an immediate change in the Shah. He became listless, devoid of hope or determination. It took the remainder of September and October, however, to convince Washington. "Strange as it may seem," writes NSC specialist Gary Sick, "by the end of October

436

1978, after some ten months of civil disturbance in Iran, there had still been not a single high-level policy meeting in Washington on this subject." Brzezinski convened the first one, a session of the Special Coordination Committee (SCC) at 6:00 P.M. on November 2.

Once Brzezinski began to move, he became an activist on Iran. Zbig's contact with Iran's Ambassador Zahedi was a solo move. Gary Sick, Zbig's staffer in charge of the area, first learned of the Brzezinski-Zahedi channel when the Iranian ambassador went home for consultations and left a message outlining how he would resume contacts when he returned. A naval officer by trade and a small-town Kansas boy by origin, Commander Sick was not about to question actions of his superiors, but Zahedi had not lived at home for five years, had considerable interests vested in the Shah, and represented the official position of the Iranian government. Zbig mentioned Zahedi at the November 2 SCC session that focused on instructing Ambassador Sullivan, who was requesting new instructions for the first time since his arrival in Teheran.

The next morning Brzezinski spoke directly to the Shah in the first of a series of long-distance telephone talks. Zbig assured the Shah of U.S. support no matter what course he chose, and announced that the United States did not favor any particular solution to the growing crisis. On November 6, Cy Vance chaired a Policy Review Committee session on Iran, the first and last that occurred. After that Brzezinski monopolized the crisis with his SCC. Beginning November 21, David Aaron then followed up with the first of a series of mini-SCCs.

In one instance David Newsom sent several analysts recently returned from Iran to the OEOB to share their impressions with the NSC staff. Their briefing at the OEOB resulted in a clash between Aaron and Henry Precht, State's Iran desk officer.

Aaron kept talking as if there was a small group of dissidents causing all the trouble, a minority that could be mollified or eradicated. Precht swung into a detailed rundown on the opposition. After an hour of this, David Aaron finally cut in, "Tell me, Henry, exactly who is the opposition?"

"The people, David, the people," Precht shot back.

The forty-six-year-old Precht was another of those responsible diplomats who made themselves unpopular at the OEOB. Zbigniew Brzezinski thought Henry Precht "motivated by doctrinal dislike of the Shah and simply wanted him out of power altogether." Gary Sick happened to be an old friend of Precht's, for he had been assistant naval attaché in Egypt from 1965 to 1967, when Precht had served as a consular official in Alexandria. Their friendship did not survive Sick's NSC staff service, however. After about the third phone call in which Precht lectured him on the faults of United States policy for Iran, Sick began to bypass him in favor of boss Hal Saunders.

Complacency could not be fueled much longer after November 9. That was the day Bill Sullivan sent in a now famous long cable bearing the title "Thinking the Unthinkable," which discussed a post-Shah Iran, identifying the key elements as the mullahs and the military. In Washington there was a White House meeting to acquaint Treasury Secretary Michael Blumenthal with the situation prior to departure for yet another survey visit to Teheran. For Bill Sullivan it must have seemed more like Saigon every day.

Brzezinski meanwhile hit upon the idea of seeking one more opinion on the condition of the Shah, and arranged for an American businessman to see him. The businessman knew the Shah personally and had extensive knowledge of Iran because he was a former CIA officer and station chief in Teheran. After seeing the Shah on November 14, the man reported back the Shah seemed to be doubting his own judgment, trusting no one, finding the situation baffling and incomprehensible, almost overwhelming. A few days later Iran's Ambassador Zahedi decided to go home to see if he could help the Shah. Zbig went to the President to argue that the quality of intelligence simply wasn't good enough, convincing Carter to issue an order on November 11 which said:

> To Cy, Zbig, Stan—
> I am not satisfied with the quality of our political intelligence. Assess our assets and, as soon as possible, give me a report concerning our abilities in the most important areas of the world. Make a joint recommendation on what we should do to improve your ability to give me political information and advice.

The directive was couched as a letter to Vance, Brzezinski, and Turner, in order to avoid the implication that this was a CIA intelligence failure.

Director of Central Intelligence Stansfield Turner immediately assumed the missive *was* a criticism aimed at the CIA. What is more, he decided Brzezinski, who had already restricted Stan Turner's access to the President, was behind it. Just a week before, Turner relates in his own account of the incident, Jimmy Carter had complimented him on the excellent work of the intelligence community.

Treasury Secretary Blumenthal saw the Shah on November 21. He returned to paint a picture gloomier than ever, and told Brzezinski of the need for a comprehensive policy review. Blumenthal suggested an independent review by someone outside the administration and mentioned George Ball, with whom Blumenthal was friends and had just rehearsed the findings he was presenting to Jimmy Carter.

Brzezinski therefore went to the President to propose "a bureaucratic initiative which I later came to regret." President Carter agreed. The phone rang in Gary Sick's office at the OEOB on November 30; Zbig asked the staffer to come over to the West Wing immediately. On the short walk over, Sick went over the things he thought Zbig might be agitated about.

With his future passing before his eyes, as it were, Sick reached the West Wing and ascended the narrow stairway to Zbig's second-floor office. Brzezinski's elaborate casualness tipped Sick off that something was definitely up. Zbig's eyes narrowed after they talked a couple of minutes about some routine report.

"Oh, by the way, there is one other thing," Brzezinski said, "George Ball is coming down to Washington to take over the Iran business for a while. You ought to be thinking about finding him a place to work."

Startled, Gary Sick nevertheless recovered quickly and offered his own room on the third floor, and suggested an advance briefing. Zbig deputized him for the job. The next morning found Sick in Ball's Wall Street office, where they had a four-hour marathon, which Sick recalls as "the most far-ranging discussion of the Iranian crisis I had had with anyone inside or outside the government."

Commander Sick then found himself assigned to Ball as a staff assistant with loyalties divided between the national security adviser and the outside consultant. Determined to make the best of it, Sick found Ball full of energy and an experienced political operator, willing to go to anyone who might have wisdom to share. The NSC staffer observes: "Wisdom may be more than an open mind, a zest for the truth, a lively intelligence, and the absence of pomposity, but that is a very good start. Those were the qualities I came to appreciate in George Ball during those hectic two weeks."

Ball amazed everyone by *not* running off to Teheran to meet with the Shah. "I had learned from our Vietnam experience," Ball recounts, "how dangerous it can be when travel is substituted for thought." Instead, Ball stayed in Washington digging into opinions, examining facts, asking the giraffe questions, as he called them. Brzezinski warned Ball not to talk to Henry Precht because he leaked, but George promptly disregarded the advice. Ball talked to the CIA, to the Pentagon, to everyone else as well. He came to the conclusion that the Shah's regime was on the verge of collapse and the problem was to somehow accomplish a transfer of power to an entity that would not automatically be discredited. Ball suggested a council of notable citizens who could be caretakers during a transition to a government of the moderate opposition.

George Ball completed his report, which went to Carter on December 11. Over Brzezinski's objections he also had it circulated to the Pentagon, State, the Treasury, the JCS, and the CIA. A day or two later (accounts differ) the paper framed the discussion at the SCC, which Zbig describes as developing into a debate between himself and Ball. While policy change might be desirable, Zbig argued, this time a military government might be the best solution. Ball's alternative would merely be giving the power to the other side. Brzezinski was forced into the ironic position of citing cables from Bill Sullivan, with whom he was now at odds, against Ball's propositions. That afternoon Jimmy Carter told Ball he felt compelled to support the Shah as long as he remained in Iran. It was time, the President said, for Brzezinski to go speak to the Shah.

"With all due respect," Ball responded to the President, it was "the worst idea I ever heard."

The visit would become known immediately, it would only further im-mobilize the Shah, and *whatever* the Shah did afterward, it would be said he was acting on Carter's orders.

The President gave up the idea of a Brzezinski mission. That was all George Ball got for his hard work.

Ball retired to his Florida vacation home, where Cy Vance called him on December 17 or 18 to say he had found the report very useful. George Ball then told Cy, "as an old friend," that he had found the NSC situation most disturbing, with Brzezinski doing everything possible to exclude State, even from knowledge of his communications on a back channel with Ardeshir Zahedi.

Back channel? Vance recounts that this conversation plus his own in-quiries first established for him that, after Zahedi returned to Teheran, Zbig had not only stayed in touch but carried out actual negotiations, of which he said nothing to Foggy Bottom. Vance went immediately to see Brzezinski and told him of the information "from an impeccable source" that he was communicating directly with the Iranians and that this was intolerable. Brzezinski denied it. Vance replied he believed otherwise and insisted both go immediately to see the President.

Vance related his story to Jimmy Carter, who turned to Brzezinski and asked if it was true. Zbig denied it a second time. Carter then asked to see copies of any and all communications between the White House and Tehe-ran. The back-channel traffic then stopped.

"This was, to say the least," Vance recalls, "a painful experience."

In fact, this matter is quite a significant one, because a major element in Zbigniew Brzezinski's explanation for the failure in Iran is that Washington was confusing the Shah with different signals on the different channels. Vance himself writes: "This, I believe, contributed to the shah's confusion about where he stood and his inability to decide what to do." By repeatedly dangling the forceful alternative Brzezinski thought he was holding open the option for the Shah to stay in Teheran but in actuality the delays were diminishing the Shah's ability to implement any option at all. The missing piece to the puzzle, for the NSC, State, and the CIA, was that the Shah was suffering from cancer that had reached an advanced state, and which helped mightily to sap his strength.

Over at Foggy Bottom, Henry Precht decided he could take it no longer, and compiled a six-page memo arguing the cosmetic reforms the Iranians were still talking about at that point would be too little and too late. Precht took the paper to Hal Saunders on December 19, but the assistant secretary disagreed, reportedly believing that time was on the Shah's side in Teheran. Precht took his dissent to the Policy Planning Staff and talked to Tony Lake. Precht also spoke with Vance's senior executive assistant, Arnold Raphel, a diplomat with Iran experience of his own.

Sympathetic, Raphel cautioned Precht that his paper seemed too emo-tional and that emotional appeals never succeeded with Vance.

440

Brzezinski concludes his account of the Ball report lamenting he had not paid more attention to Vance, an unusual admission from Zbig, for Cy had been unenthusiastic about an outside report from the beginning. Zbig believed Ball's participation in the policy meetings sharpened the existing disagreements "while delaying basic choices by wasting some two weeks," Most revealingly, Zbig writes: "In selecting Ball I violated a basic rule of bureaucratic tactics: One should never obtain the services of an 'impartial' outside consultant regarding an issue that one feels strongly about without first making certain in advance that one knows the likely contents of his advice."

Note the implicit suggestion that in the midst of a major crisis, a key national security planning exercise to support the President be operated purely for tactical advantage among the bureaucracy. When Brzezinski argues that the Ball report *delayed* decision and "wasted" two weeks, it seems like an attempt to lay off some of the crucial period of indecision on Ball. The truth is that over a week *later,* during the NSC staff Christmas party, the decision had not been made when a cable arrived that made Gary Sick think the crisis had reached a turning point. Sick drew Brzezinski aside to show it to him. By December 28, *a week after that,* a decision had *still* not been made when there were contingency decisions to get an aircraft carrier task force moving from the Far East to the waters of the Arabian Sea.

By that time, Brzezinski had posed the Iran policy question as whether to back an "iron fist" policy, and on December 28, with backing from Harold Brown, Brzezinski thought he had hammered down the last objections. He went to Carter and got a cable to that effect dispatched by that afternoon. In the first days of 1979 the Shah himself told Sullivan an iron fist would not work. Brzezinski's victory had been Pyrrhic.

Nevertheless, the United States dispatched a senior military officer to Iran, General Robert E. Huyser, deputy commander of American forces in Europe, to hold the hands of the Iranian generals. On January 15, with Huyser already in Teheran over ten days, Brzezinski learned from his secure call that Iranian military plans for a show of force were poorly developed and the option still considered a marginal one. The next day the Shah left Teheran forever.

There was brief talk of a military coup but it never got off the ground. General Huyser was asked about the Iranian military virtually every night. Almost every day they seemed less determined and capable. The cabinet the Shah had left in place lasted only a week past the triumphal return of the Ayatollah Khomeini to Teheran on January 31, 1979. A few days later Huyser left, and was invited back to Washington to meet with President Carter and the NSC principals. The further maneuvers of Carter and Brzezinski, however, did nothing to save either the Shah or the successor regime he left in place. For the Islamic republic, the next Iranian government, Khomeini's first prime minister was Mehdi Bazargan, ironically, a figure Henry Precht had favored, and with whom Brzezinski had resisted dealing.

Once the Shah was on the move—a "flying Dutchman" Henry Kissinger called him in a speech on April 9, 1979—the White House came under considerable pressure to take the lead in admitting the Shah to the United States. Kissinger and David Rockefeller were among the most ardent lobbyists. Brzezinski recounts that "Kissinger in his subtle fashion linked his willingness to support us on SALT to a more forthcoming attitude on our part regarding the Shah." A sharp discussion occurred on July 27 at a foreign policy breakfast, when the President complained about the lobbying.

"Zbig bugged me on it every day," Carter said.

Brzezinski interrupted, "No, sir!"

Jimmy Carter softened. "Not every day but very often," President Carter said. Zbig argued that American traditions and national honor were at stake, that Iranian statements were the threats of a third-rate regime. President Carter and Cy Vance were angry that day, and the issue of the Shah's admission went nowhere until October, when a Rockefeller emissary brought medical evidence of the Shah's condition. Vance had a doctor fly to Mexico and look at the man, and he too recommended certain American hospitals. Carter made the formal decision at Camp David on October 20, with the Shah flying to New York several days afterward. The moderate Iranian government made four protests over the next week, and Ayatollah Khomeini an ominous radio speech from Qom on November 1.

On Sunday, November 4, a mob of Iranian student demonstrators seized the American embassy along with sixty-three hostages. There will be long debate over whether the United States was prepared adequately—after all the embassy had been seized once already, chargé d'affaires L. Bruce Laingen had asked that the staff there be reduced, and the Americans had asked the Iranian government to provide protection for their embassy, clearly anticipating demonstrations at least. To no avail.

This hostage crisis became the extended and exhausting denouement to the fall of the Shah, punctuated by repeated bouts of euphoria and despair as new channels opened up, seemed to produce results, then went dry. Days before the embassy seizure Brzezinski spoke with Iranian officials in Algiers; during the succeeding months Jimmy Carter would dispatch as emissaries not only Zbig, but Hamilton Jordan and Warren Christopher.

In April 1980 a heavy exclamation point punctuating the crisis was Operation Eagle Claw, a commando raid that attempted to extract the hostages. A combination of bad weather, bad luck, and inadequate material preparations aborted the mission at a desert staging base hundreds of miles from Teheran. Brzezinski, who had led the secret planning group for the raid, making his own handwritten notes on their twice-weekly meetings, claims his original preference had been to execute the raid under the cover of punitive air attacks. That way, whatever the raid's outcome, the United States could claim a forceful action. President Carter ruled out the bombing option the day before the raid.

Going into the longest day of his White House years, Zbigniew Brzezinski recorded in his diary: "The first critical phase of the operation will begin fourteen hours from now. I feel good about it. I realize that if it fails I will probably be blamed more than anybody else, but I am quite prepared to accept that. If it is a success, it will give the United States a shot in the arm, which it has badly needed for twenty years."

The Eagle Claw rescue mission was not quite Fashoda; Brzezinski had to make do with a climactic crisis in the Third World that he could not blame on the Russians.

Six Americans died.

Afterward, an even bigger hostage rescue operation was prepared, code-name Honey Badger, but never carried out. Sunday morning, April 26, Zbig called Gary Sick and Bill Odom into his office and declared he had obtained the President's approval to begin plans for a new mission. Just as Brzezinski wore combat boots to play soccer, Honey Badger would be weighty enough to smash its way into Teheran. Odom and Sick were to do the first options paper.

Gary Sick knew he was not giving Zbig what the adviser wanted, but the memo he wrote pointed out the second mission had to succeed or it would go very bad on the hostages, while the difficulties were immensely complicated by the lack of reliable information on the location and circumstances of the hostages, who had been dispersed immediately after failure of the first rescue attempt.

Sick never heard anything more about his memo or the operation. Brzezinski simply cut him out of the action. But Honey Badger went on. Colonel Richard V. Secord, an Air Force special operations officer who was chief intelligence planner for Honey Badger later learned through postmortem debriefings with the hostages that the information upon which the plan was based was entirely incorrect.

Meanwhile the abortive rescue mission also led to the final break between Cyrus Vance and the administration. The critical NSC meeting where Carter gave final approval for the raid was held while Cy and his wife Grace weekended in Florida. State was represented at the council meeting by Warren Christopher, who was aware of Vance's opposition to the rescue mission, and reserved the department's position in the discussion. Brzezinski lays this crucial timing of the NSC session at Jimmy Carter's feet, remarking also that Carter seemed to think Vance burned out and looking for a reason to quit. In any case, when Vance returned he was furious, but proved unable to sway anyone with his argument that the Iranians would merely seize other Americans as hostages, such as the many journalists in Teheran covering the crisis, if the United States freed the ones at the embassy. Vance declared he would resign if the operation was carried out; then he did so. His successor as secretary of state was Edmund Muskie, who served through the remainder of Carter's term in office.

In the midst of all this, Brzezinski almost got his Fashoda after all. In August 1980 the United States intercepted communications and gathered other intelligence indicating a Soviet military buildup north of Iran. Some twenty-eight Soviet divisions, usually at a low state of readiness, were brought up to strength and roughly 350 fighter-bombers concentrated in the area for what turned out to be an extensive maneuver that appeared to simulate an invasion of Iran. Washington worried the invasion was real, which would have left Carter in the odd situation of having to intervene to save the Khomeini regime. Meeting at the Pentagon the JCS concluded the United States would have no practicable means of halting an invasion other than use of nuclear weapons. The Soviet moves were soon discovered to be an exercise, but Carter nonetheless sent Moscow a strong warning and consulted with his NATO allies. The incident accelerated American creation of a rapid deployment force.

In his memoir of Carter administration service, Brzezinski argues that there are only two ways the necessary job of coordination can be done in government. One is the "presidential" mode of making policy, the other the "secretarial" one. Brzezinski believes the presidential mode is the only one suitable for modern conditions, and that that dictates according primacy to the national security adviser. He would accept a requirement for Senate confirmation for the national security adviser *if* that meant the gatekeeper's primacy had been institutionalized.

This former national security adviser argues the secretarial-type system cannot be made to work efficiently, especially as America moves into the twenty-first century. The secretary of state would have to be given primacy in the NSC subcommittee system, and could not be a successful coordinator, Zbig writes, "since coordination also means subordination." He further argues that political and international realities will make less possible operation of nonpresidential systems, and that the President's main advisers are, after all, themselves located at the White House. Brzezinski goes on to relate that he attempted at first to exclude Carter's domestic advisers from national security matters but ultimately found it more useful to forge alliances with them.

By Brzezinski's definition, there could never be NSC excesses because anything a national security staff might do could only be in extension of the President's objectives. This arrangement would give the national security adviser a wide latitude to interpret the President's goals, as Bill Odom might put it, a broad charter to poach. The record of the Carter administration reveals numerous instances in which Brzezinski, following his own agenda, extended the President's meaning, halted initiatives in which Carter had indeed been interested, or worked to hold open options in hopes the President might be induced to change his mind later. That was the presidential system at work—Brzezinski the advocate. Such strong advocacy must create obstacles to coordination just as surely as any system based upon the secretary of state, a difficulty for which Brzezinski suggests no solution.

It might have been a different story if the national security adviser, or, to give him his correct title, the assistant to the President for national security, had provided an administrative system, one parallel to the chain of advice. Harry Truman and Dwight Eisenhower had had such a dual-track system, with the keeper of the keys as the adviser and operative and the NSC executive secretary as the person focused on coordination. This kind of machinery went out with Mac Bundy, however, and Zbigniew Brzezinski in his time further downgraded the executive secretary post, relegated to a sort of glorified office manager with the title staff secretary, as Andrew Goodpaster had had. Zbig's staff secretary, Christine Dodson, was no Andy Goodpaster. She was Zbig's longtime secretary from Columbia University, who had stayed with him through several institutes and book manuscripts, from *The Soviet Bloc* right on. Amiable and efficient, Dodson could function as an executive assistant but not an operative.

So policy bumbled on, blown to and fro by the arguments and maneuvers of characters from Zbigniew Brzezinski to Henry Precht. The cost to American foreign policy was high, but not all of it should be attributed to the President or Brzezinski or their lieutenants. The record of the administration has been distorted by the lens of the Iranian crisis, while the extent to which Carter was paying bills for his predecessors has been generally overlooked. As time goes on and the documentary record becomes more ample, it is quite likely that Carter's foreign policy achievements will be reevaluated.

The American electorate is not known for picking Presidents for their national security experience. It was no different in Carter's case and the choice told, for Jimmy became a victim of his own ignorance. With a dearth of knowledge about the critical issues he was suddenly managing, Carter had not the depth to detect when his advisers were trying to run circles around him. Carter learned a tremendous amount in his years in Washington. A voracious reader and a quick study, Jimmy soon knew better about a lot of things, but nuances escaped him. Nevertheless, Jimmy Carter, with Zbigniew Brzezinski at his side, *managed* his affairs. Ronald Reagan's experience would show what could happen with a powerful NSC staff when a President did not or would not do so.

PART VIII

▲

THE YEARS
THE LOCUSTS ATE

Ronald Reagan knew the score when he came to office as the forty-first President of the United States. Like each of the others, Reagan availed himself fully of his ability to appoint cohorts to high office throughout the federal government. Wearing a conservative mantle, Reagan had pledged to strengthen defense, reject SALT II ratification, and balance the budget. Like Jimmy Carter before him, Reagan promised reforms in the NSC, in an October 1980 television speech in which he promised to bring coherence to American foreign policy, once more by restoring the primacy of the secretary of state.

President Reagan used his inaugural address to warn terrorists the United States would never deal with them, sentiments echoed by the secretary of state at his first news conference. The rhetoric quickly mushroomed into a policy of attempting to counter terrorism, but ultimately degenerated into the very opposite of Ronald Reagan's earnest intention of 1981. The history of the Reagan NSC unfortunately figures prominently in the process by which policy was thus perverted.

Following an initial period of reform, the NSC staff resumed its activist role during the Reagan years. It began with an emergency in Lebanon, led through the Middle East to a renewed hostage crisis, and from there to a scandal in which the NSC staff played a central role. Along the way there was a good deal of mischief, and more

447

than a little grief, as a succession of national security advisers tried to put things right.

Conventional foreign policy in many respects would grind to a virtual halt in the Reagan years. Instead, the system brought forth a new class of bureaucratic entrepreneurs, men and women who held strong personal beliefs and were willing to fight for them. Much of what passed for foreign policy represented personal agendas in action, compatible by and large with the President's goals, but personal agendas nonetheless. Developments in the Reagan NSC system permitted this style of bureaucratic play to arise and dominate.

▲▲▲

NO VICAR FOR
FOREIGN POLICY

▲▲▲

During his transition Ronald Reagan appointed Richard Allen as national security adviser. It seemed a little unreal because just a few weeks before, Dick Allen had been forced to resign from the Reagan campaign. Allen, it emerged, had arranged certain contacts with Nixon administration officials for fugitive financier Robert Vesco or his representatives. Resignation robbed Dick Allen of the chance to be at Reagan's side down to the wire, but the President-elect swiftly brought him back once the votes were cast.

Dick Allen sold off his consulting business and began to work at transition headquarters. For him to become national security adviser was the fulfillment of a dream. Allen had worked his way through several presidential campaigns only to see the good jobs handed out to others. He had gotten a place from Nixon on Kissinger's initial NSC staff, but been frozen out of the action. What better revenge than to return as national security adviser?

Better? Not quite. Allen returned to an NSC staff the President-elect was cutting down to size. Perhaps it was fulfilling to be returning to dismantle the *Kissinger*-style NSC staff, perhaps not. Allen never seemed the least perturbed, and repeatedly claimed to support the successive moves narrowing the scope of the President's keeper of the keys. "The policy-formulation function of the national security adviser," Allen told a reporter during the transition, "should be offloaded to the secretary of state." The keeper, Allen felt, ought to have "a clear-cut staff function," and he supported reducing the degree of contact between President and national security adviser.

Once the Reagan White House had been set up, it became clear the national security adviser was not even going to be in the same league as the President's other key men. Dick Allen acknowledged the change symbolically, relinquishing the West Wing office Kissinger had won and moving downstairs to the basement again. Allen did not report to the President, but to the counselor to the President, Edwin Meese. Since Meese effectively constituted one of a triumvirate of senior Reagan staff, the others being Chief of Staff James A. Baker and his deputy Michael K. Deaver, Allen actually had to convince three people if he wished to bring a national security matter to Reagan.

Allen also appears to have put in a good word for the man who beat him out on the Kissinger NSC staff, Alexander Haig. The general had retired after a tour as NATO commander in chief. It was Richard Allen who was the first to call and ask Haig about jobs. The general recounts that Allen initially mentioned secretary of defense, until the general reminded him of the restriction that a military man cannot hold that office until at least ten years after his service. Then discussion focused more on becoming secretary of state.

Another candidate was in the running too, George Shultz, then heading the Bechtel Corporation, the global construction concern. Shultz had plenty of Cabinet experience under Nixon and was known to be interested. Reagan actually called Shultz to offer him the secretary of state position, but the conversation became confused and Shultz thought the President-elect was talking about secretary of the treasury. Shultz had had that job before and didn't want it again. He rejected it.

That was when Reagan called Al Haig. Their talk went easily. They argued about whether there should be a draft but disagreed on little else.

"You know my feeling about the secretary of state," Reagan told Haig, "He would be *the* spokesman. I won't have a repeat of the Kissinger-Rogers situation. I'll look to you, Al." Richard Allen would work exclusively as a staff coordinator. Haig accepted, and went on to some rancorous confirmation hearings before the Senate Foreign Relations Committee, which grilled Haig in some detail about his own work on Cambodia, Chile, Watergate, and the Nixon pardon. Zbigniew Brzezinski helped Haig by refusing senatorial requests for relevant NSC documents, once more relying upon arguments of executive privilege. Still, the predominant mood was to let Ronald Reagan have his chosen advisers.

Al Haig took to heart Reagan's promise of primacy. He worked up a set of talking points for the scheduled ninety-minute preparatory NSC meeting of January 6, 1981. (The talking paper leaked and appeared somewhat later in the press.) Haig argued that Cabinet government in foreign affairs "requires that the Secretary of State be your Vicar for the community of Departments having an interest in the several dimensions of foreign policy." Haig saw himself as exercising the coordinating role. When he addressed the NSC staff, Haig revealingly sought two strictures: that all contact with foreign officials be conducted at State, and that the national security adviser have no independent press contact.

At his very first news conference as secretary of state, Al Haig reused the term "vicar," only to hear it played back disparagingly by the media, lampooning the pretensions of the self-styled "vicar of foreign policy." In fact, Haig had gotten no response to his proposed arrangements, and got none either to an official memorandum he presented the President just moments after the inaugural ceremony. That paper went into Ed Meese's briefcase, which turned out to be bottomless. A second copy Haig gave Meese later also disappeared. Deciding he must have stumbled into a turf fight, Haig backed off and went to Caspar Weinberger, now secretary of defense, and the two together worked out a new version. When the Haig-Weinberger joint paper went forward to Meese, it too disappeared. Haig's repeated efforts to get an approved paper defining the NSC machinery failed. The failure prevented Al Haig from establishing himself as a "vicar," but it also meant *no* formally defined NSC machinery *for the first year of the administration.*

Over time Haig might have built trust among his colleagues, especially the White House triumvirate of Baker, Deaver, and Meese. Instead, a notorious incident that occurred on March 30, 1981, put an end to Haig's possibilities. That was the day Ronald Reagan was shot by would-be assassin John W. Hinckley, Jr. Lucky and robust, the President survived the bullet, but Al Haig's reputation became a casualty of the aftermath.

Mike Deaver happened to be with Reagan at the time. Baker and Meese left for the hospital soon after they learned the news. Haig, as soon as *he* heard the news, rushed to the White House, convening available staff ad hoc in the Situation Room. Vice President George Bush was making speeches in Texas and would be back by nightfall. Richard Allen stayed in the Situation Room as chief staff person and note taker. Allen proceeded efficiently for the first hour or so, but the tension was great. Some noted Haig seemed to be wearing a bulldog look; then someone heard him comment, "The helm is right here in this chair."

The observation suggests Haig's line of thinking shortly before he appeared in the White House press room, where reporters were pressing deputy press secretary Larry Speakes to tell them just who was in charge of the government.

This scene was being broadcast live on television, and it was being watched, among other places, in the Situation Room. Haig wanted to go quiet the reporters. Richard Allen considered trying to talk Haig out of it, but decided not to. The secretary of state bolted out of his chair rasping, "We've got to straighten this out."

Al Haig charged into the press room just as Speakes made his way back to the Situation Room for instructions. Haig stood before the reporters. "I was standing right next to him, prepared to catch him," Allen recalls. "I thought that he was going to collapse. His legs were shaking as if they were gelatinous. It was extraordinary, absolutely extraordinary."

Looking pasty and drawn, Haig faced the cameras, then recited an erroneous rendition of the line of succession to the presidency. With Bush still returning to the capital Haig was the senior official present. "As of now," he said, "I am in control here."

On television Al Haig seemed pretty wild, *out* of control, not in charge at all.

Al proved to be his own worst enemy, suspicious of his colleagues, and with vaguely authoritarian demands to be the administration's *only* spokesman on foreign policy. On at least one occasion, when he heard of a foreign policy pronouncement he did not like, Haig tried to "countermand" it. To countermand is to issue an order nullifying a previous order, a military practice not seen in foreign policy. Such fractured syntax soon became known as Haigspeak. The magazine *Armed Forces Journal* to this day gives out awards named for Haig that criticize tortured jargon and language.

Not only did Haig receive no approval for his NSC machinery proposals, the White House announced creation of a special Crisis Management Group within the NSC to be chaired by the Vice President. Crisis management provisions had been one of the major features of the Haig proposal. The first the secretary of state heard of the new NSC device was when he read the announcement in *The Washington Post*. Haig phoned Ronald Reagan, who simply replied, "Al, I want you to know that you are my foreign policy guy."

The evidence indicates, in fact, that the NSC Crisis Management Group evolved specifically to shut Haig out of that field of play. The group held a formative meeting, never to be convened again, while a later device, the Special Situations Group, (also chaired by Bush) met only a few times. Eight years later, asked if he would be placing his own Vice President in charge of crisis management, George Bush replied, "The crisis management job really was substituting for the president when he did not attend the NSC meeting. That's all it was."

The most concrete thing to come out of the crisis project was a plan for what would, in effect, be a second White House Situation Room. The old one was cramped and lacked the latest computers and display technology. But the new one would be located in the OEOB. The center had its own budget and staff lines separate from NSC staff allocations, and so became a convenient source for extra NSC staff manpower. Allen's military aide, Rear Admiral John M. Poindexter, and his senior director for military affairs, Major General Robert L. Schweitzer, combined to push installation of new computers. A minor skirmish occurred in the press a couple of years later when it discovered that David Aaron's new novel *State Scarlet* ridiculed the Crisis Management Center as "Allen's Folly."

Although Alexander Haig lost his battle for control of Reagan's NSC machinery, and though he was to leave in frustration in June 1982, in important ways Haig was far more influential, or perhaps he was much closer to Ronald Reagan's real thinking, than is usually perceived. The issues Haig pushed, to a considerable degree, became Reagan's issues, including substitution of counterterrorism for human rights, along with Cuba, Nicaragua, Afghanistan, and more. Haig showed the same propensity as Reagan for dispensing with facts that did not suit his theses; the secretary of state made claims about Soviet support for terrorism, and alleged Soviet use of poison gas, neither of which could be supported with the facts available. Even Haig's advocacy of arms control and insistence upon retaining the SALT II regime—things that made Haig liberal in relation to other members of Reagan's original Cabinet—were causes President Reagan embraced in his second term. Al Haig's fate was the result of having played too hard, peaked too soon, and lost the confidence of his colleagues.

Others among Ronald Reagan's advisers seemed as vulnerable as Haig or more so. One of them was William J. Casey, the director of central intelligence, statutory adviser to the NSC. Casey was a man who had wanted Al Haig's job and as Reagan's campaign manager through the last weeks of the campaign, was thought to have an inside track. At length Casey accepted the CIA directorship, though he successfully enhanced the position by having Reagan give the DCI Cabinet status plus his own office at the OEOB.

Actually Bill Casey's credentials for secretary of state or defense were rather thin, but he seemed a classic candidate for director of central intelligence. Casey's main claim to national security expertise resided in his role funding and directing a conservative think tank named the National Strategy Information Center, which he had helped set up during the mid-1960s. What Casey had been, and still was, was a lawyer, a tax lawyer at that, with Park Avenue offices in New York City. He represented large corporations and even foreign governments, but he was no diplomat and never had been. He *was* a voracious reader quick to assimilate arguments, but could seldom be moved off a position once he had adopted it. Casey's mumbling style of talk, his fiddling with his socks or chewing his tie, concealed a clever and determined bureaucratic infighter who long outlasted Haig in the Reagan administration.

Casey had been one of the original covert warriors of World War II. With a naval reserve commission the young Casey, thirty years old, joined the Office of Strategic Services (OSS) in 1943. He ended the war with the OSS in Europe, where he ran the United States program to infiltrate intelligence agents into Nazi Germany. Gerald Ford appointed Casey to the President's Foreign Intelligence Advisory Board (PFIAB), on which he served a year before Jimmy Carter abolished it. Active in associations of former intelligence officers and OSS people, Bill Casey kept open his links with that world, even while working as chairman of the Securities and Exchange Commission or president of the Export-Import Bank, things he did in the 1970s.

The sure thing turned into controversy, however, which seemed to dog Casey in Ronald Reagan's administration. It began on Capitol Hill, where the Senate consented to Casey's nomination only to mount an investigation of him later. Casey's financial disclosure forms had failed to mention $250,000 in investments, nearly $500,000 in debts, and the names of seventy of his clients, including two foreign governments. Claiming innocence, Casey asserted he had misread the instructions on the disclosure form. But it took him two amendments of his paperwork, and it also emerged that Bill had represented Indonesia without registering as a foreign agent. The inquiry ended with faint praise for the CIA director, concluding it had found no reason Casey was unfit to serve in the Reagan administration.

Then there was Casey's stock portfolio, which the CIA director continued to manage himself in spite of his access to secret information. In 1982, a year of sharp increases in the market, Casey traded over $1.5 million in stock. Several years later it was reported he owned stock in companies that held contracts with the Central Intelligence Agency. Only repeated controversy finally induced Casey to put his stock in trust.

In 1983 the matter of documents purloined from Jimmy Carter became a major problem for Casey. A purloined Carter foreign policy briefing book had been kept in William Joseph Casey's safe at Reagan campaign headquarters. Chief of Staff James Baker and Budget Director David Stockman acknowledged using the document and admitted they had gotten it from Casey. The CIA director denied everything, in statements, an affidavit to a House inquiry panel, and an interview with *The New York Times*. Casey denied ever seeing any Carter papers, said he wouldn't have touched them with a ten-foot pole, had no recollection of how those papers happened to be in his safe. After a ten-month investigation, the House subcommittee found that "the better evidence indicates that Carter debate briefing material . . . entered the Reagan-Bush campaign through its director, Casey. This conclusion is not lightly reached but seems appropriate."

A survivor, Casey rode out the "Debategate" storm. He was never held accountable, although Ronald Reagan at one point promised that anyone found involved in political espionage activities would be appropriately disciplined. Debategate was some fairly serious business; if Reagan was not willing to enforce discipline on that, it is no wonder that in 1984, when Casey became embroiled in open defiance of the CIA's congressional overseers, no discipline was imposed either. Ronald Reagan was being a nice guy, but the signal he was sending was wrong, a virtual green light for those officials who became the policy entrepreneurs, among them the CIA director.

There would be many entrepreneurs in Ronald Reagan's administration, but one man who never rose to that level was Richard Vincent Allen, the President's keeper of the keys. Only too well aware of the intent to cut the NSC staff down to size, Allen had also already planted the seeds of his own destruction, arranging an interview for three Japanese journalists with Nancy Reagan. There had been nothing improper in the interview, or in Allen's scheduling it. But, following Japanese custom, the journalists gave Allen an envelope for Mrs. Reagan that contained ten crisp new $100 bills. It was inappropriate to give her the money, and Allen stuck the envelope in his safe. That proved to be his undoing.

Forgetting the envelope, Dick Allen went off about the business of organizing his NSC staff. Like many previous keepers of the keys, Allen thought the staff organization needed revamping, so he rearranged the NSC staff to have four major clusters, political affairs, defense policy, intelligence, plus policy planning and evaluation. Staffers for regions and functional subjects were assigned to the different clusters. An NSC secretariat furnished support. There were about a hundred support people, with some thirty-five professional staff during Reagan's first months. The fiscal year 1982 budget request was for $3.8 million, but the Reagan NSC reforms shaved about $400,000 off the request for the next year. After that, however, expenditures increased steadily.

"If you're looking for action in terms of day to day operations, sending out cables and circulating memos," Allen told his prospective staffers, "this is not the place for you—you should be out in the operating agencies. But if you are interested in seeing the policy-making machinery mesh in a coherent and intelligent fashion and you want to be at the crossroads of policy-making, then this is the place for you." The national security adviser claimed Gordon Gray as his model, an excellent choice but one based on an inadequate understanding of Gray's scope. Asked if he was going to chair interagency committees, Allen shot back, "Not if I can avoid it. The best system is to have those committees chaired from the outside."

Dick Allen's implication was that the NSC staff would be concerned with policy planning, perhaps in more direct competition with the State Department's unit for this. If so, it is curious that the only NSC staff cluster for which Allen held off selecting a director was the one for policy planning and evaluation. Moreover, unlike earlier administrations, quickly off the mark with their policy reviews, in fact using the policy reviews to help gain control of the bureaucracy, the Reagan administration was notably flaccid about its effort in this area. In April 1981, Allen told a reporter that policy reviews were in progress on the Middle East, Soviet-American relations, and Asian policy. Nothing more was heard of them. In fact, for the next eight years there would be hardly any leaks about National Security Study Documents (NSSDs), the administration's equivalent to PRMs and NSSMs. In an administration that leaked everywhere, that suggests less frequent NSC policy reviews. In part the policy review function merged with the bureaucratic maneuvers over the National Security Decision Documents (NSDDs), Ronald Reagan's vehicle for presidential directives.

President Reagan got much of his information from his daily national security briefings. They also accounted for much of his contact with national security adviser Allen. The morning briefings came complete with a CIA report, the President's Daily Bulletin (PDB), to which Reagan's watcher added anything that seemed necessary, such as matters coming up from the bureaucracy, or comments on the latest leaks in the press. Allen would leave the PDB behind after the briefing; then a messenger would pick it up once the President had finished with it. Over time, NSC, State, and Pentagon papers came to be added to the PDB in hopes the President would see them.

Haig felt the White House triumvirate was attempting to monopolize the President, with all of them careful to attend every meeting where a decision might conceivably be made. This included the national security briefings. Being no slouch himself, Alexander Haig made it a point to go too, or to send his deputy William P. Clark, one of Reagan's Californians. Also there were Vice President George Bush and his chief of staff, Admiral Daniel J. Murphy. The national security briefings got to be quite large, sort of rump NSC meetings where not much happened, except that Haig was getting extra time with Ronald Reagan.

In the summer of 1981, still without an NSDD defining the national security machinery, Reagan formed a unit he called the National Security Planning Group (NSPG), in essence the NSC plus extra advisers Reagan added, chaired by George Bush. It became the real crisis management unit, had final authority for covert operations by the CIA, plus a host of other national security minutiae. President Reagan attended NSPG meetings himself; his schedulers reportedly budgeted time for three NSC or NSPG meetings a week.

Once the NSPG was in place, a decision came down to stop the daily national security briefings. Instead, Dick Allen was to restrict himself to submitting the PDB to which he could add a written report with items from all the agencies, or flag things he considered important. The national security adviser would then attend the first five minutes of the President's regularly scheduled White House staff meeting.

"We are trying to make better use of the president's time," Allen told a reporter. "I'm altogether enthusiastic about the new schedule."

Narrowing of his job was good, Allen argued, because it would focus the NSC staff better on its policy reviews.

Sometimes you have to wonder.

If Richard Allen thought something was urgent he had to convince Ed Meese then the triumvirate once Meese convened it in person or by phone. One practical demonstration of the absurdity of all this occurred in April 1981, when there was an incident between U.S. Navy and Libyan aircraft over the Mediterranean while the President slept at his California ranch. The triumvirate decided against awakening Reagan. Second thoughts came later when the White House realized the *image* cast was one in which the president *had not been in control*. Because Reagan had been an actor before turning to politics, such arguments about the President resonated naturally, even though the almost seventy-year-old Reagan appreciated his sleep and could often be found in pajamas after 6:00 P.M.

Concern over image turned out to be significant for the subsequent history of the NSC. Never before had image makers been so prominent among policymakers. The NSPG, for example, included unprecedented numbers of White House staff. In the Reagan system, where anyone who threw out a proposal was likely to have it approved, this amounted to a greater role for political advisers. During the tenure of Richard Allen, Reagan's political staff predominated.

In Jimmy Carter's time, when the President made his unfortunate stopover to visit the Shah in Iran, White House advance men could still become embittered at the restrictions set for them by NSC staff specialists. During Ronald Reagan's years the embitterment ran the other way, as it no doubt did when the image makers produced the Bitburg fiasco, in 1985, making Reagan seem to honor Nazi war dead by visiting a cemetery in which some SS veterans' bodies lay.

In any case the isolation of Richard Allen's NSC staff and the general predominance of the image makers, had a pronounced effect on the ability of the national security system to produce a foreign policy. It was much worse than Allen made it out in his friendly sessions with reporters. Reagan's administration did not produce a proposal for arms control for well over a year, introduced proposals strictly for propaganda value then, and did not manage much in other areas either. One of the most active early policy issues was an effort to induce Western Europeans not to sell the Soviet Union material for pipelines that would deliver energy to Western Europe. Other issues arose over claims about so-called yellow rain or Soviet support to terrorism. The two things in common among almost all the administration's evident concerns was that they were information themes, not foreign policies, and that they carried an anti-Soviet bent. There was no sense that the policy aimed at attainable goals or used sustainable means.

It was the job of the national security machinery to ensure the quality of policy, its "integration" in the term of the 1947 act. The keeper of the keys and his NSC staff were to impose coherence, in effect discipline the anarchic tendencies of the agencies and departments. Because of his isolation Richard Allen could not do that. Al Haig put it best: "To live on this kind of sufferance defeats efficiency. By definition Allen was not a member of the inner circle. According to the remorseless standards of judgment that apply in such cases, Allen was therefore regarded by his colleagues as irrelevant. In time, I am sorry to say, I came to regard him in that light, too."

In the Brzezinski era the bureaucracy had lived in dread of the NSC cover memo, the first document the President would see, in which the security adviser could set the stage lights for a matter coming to the President. The bureaucracy almost never saw the cover memos and could only rely on what it was told about them. That did not happen with Allen's NSC staff. Major General Robert Schweitzer, who headed Allen's defense policy staff cluster, made sure copies of his draft memos went to the departments and that they got the chance to comment. If there wasn't time to do it in writing, he would take comments on the phone. If the action were one initiated by the bureaucracy, Schweitzer would also see they received a copy of his final cover memo.

"I would feel that, in the forty year history, there was always a clearly defined purpose for the National Security Council, until we came to that first year of the Reagan administration and the clearly defined purpose did not exist," Schweitzer recalls. "Not because Richard Allen didn't know what it was or want to define it in the traditional sense . . . but the way the government was being run by a troika and the way the government was being run through a cabinet system." Nonetheless, Allen remained faithful to the concept. "He believed," Schweitzer says, "that eventually all this would work its way out and we would come back to the traditional way of doing things in the National Security Council staff."

General Schweitzer went on to argue that exactly this finally happened, but it would not be on Richard Allen's watch. Instead, the safe containing cash in an envelope was reassigned for use of several temporary duty officers brought to the NSC staff to help lobbying Capitol Hill for approval of a sale of advanced radar aircraft to Saudi Arabia. The officers worked out of the Crisis Management Center and were carried on its roster, but they had been hired by General Schweitzer. An Army officer named Allan Myer found the envelope and called security, after which NSC security officer Jerry Jennings took custody of the thing. Allen quickly admitted the provenance of the money and his story held up to subsequent investigation, but the affair left Washington abuzz. Controversy grew when it was alleged Allen had accepted gifts, expensive watches, from former clients, and when questions were asked regarding Allen's sale of his consulting firm upon entering the administration.

This played into the hands of the Reagan political staff, some of whom felt Richard Allen had to go. As early as mid-July the subject of getting rid of the national security adviser had been discussed at the beach house of presidential secretary Helene von Damm in Beach Haven Crest on the Jersey shore. A New Jersey boy, Dick Allen had a beach house of his own a few miles away. Ironically, he had been relaxing there that weekend.

Helene von Damm claims the subject arose incidentally, during a long series of ruminations among friends over the state of affairs in Washington. Present at the time were White House sparkplug Mike Deaver plus Von Damm's close friends Bill and Joan Clark. Bill Clark, Haig's deputy, had already clashed a few times with Allen despite their long intimacy in Reagan's service. Now Clark rated Allen ineffective and a poor manager.

Von Damm, who liked Allen, interjected, "But who would you get to replace Dick?"

Deaver looked at Clark. "How about it, Bill?"

"If that's what the president wants," Clark replied.

Deaver himself recalls he made the judgment that Allen's future effectiveness would be impaired at the time the allegations regarding accepting gifts emerged. He then urged Ronald Reagan to replace Allen, who went on administrative leave around Thanksgiving to await results of the inquiries. He never returned. Instead, Allen was informed the President wished his resignation. Insisting he wanted to hear it from the President's own lips, Dick Allen saw President Reagan on January 4, 1982. It must have been a painful encounter.

Richard Allen lasted only eleven months as national security adviser.

Unbelievable as it may seem, Ronald Reagan would employ a keeper of the keys for an even shorter time, plus five others, one of whom served about the same term as Dick Allen. The turbulent years had come.

The rise and fall of Bob Schweitzer and Richard Pipes typified Reagan's national security system in practice. This President offered an open playing field but, more important, *no rules*! Most chilling of all, it was sudden-death elimination from the White House game, based on little more than the visceral feelings of the image makers. Schweitzer and Pipes came to the NSC staff from different directions, a military man and a professor, one ordered to the OEOB, the other a passionate advocate invited to join the staff. Both were well in tune with Richard Allen and the dominant conservative philosophy of the Reagan administration.

Robert Schweitzer was a war hero, a man who had enlisted in the Army to fight in Korea, won a battlefield commission, and rose to be a general. He held the Distinguished Service Cross and *seven* Purple Hearts, decorations awarded for combat wounds, which had cost the general an eye, a kidney, lung injuries, and orthopedic ones.

Typically, Schweitzer had wanted to return to the troops, not work for the NSC. He felt he'd already spent too much time on staffs, as chief of a NATO policy staff for five years under Supreme Allied Commander Alexander Haig, and then as director of strategy, plans, and policy under the Army's deputy chief of staff for operations.

Called to NSC staff offices for an interview, General Schweitzer told his interlocutors that he had no desire for the job. "It turned out that was exactly the wrong thing to say over there," he recalled. "If I had expressed a salivating desire to serve on the NSC [staff] I might have escaped the assignment." So Schweitzer found himself at the OEOB, along with Rear Admiral James W. Nance, Allen's deputy security adviser, who had also worked at NATO under Haig. The media interpreted the presence of both Schweitzer and Nance on the NSC staff as evidence of Al Haig's supposed ascendency as the "vicar" of foreign policy.

Schweitzer came to grief with the image makers, but before his demise had time to introduce a few of the characters who would become crucial in the history of Reagan's administration. One was Oliver Laurence North, a Marine major brought in to help lobbying for the Saudi arms sale. Another was Dick Allen's military assistant, a slot that went unfilled at the outset of the administration. The designee was a naval officer at Pensacola, the chief of staff to the chief for naval training and education, a man with five sons in Florida public schools. An immediate move to Washington would have meant enormous disruption for Rear Admiral John Poindexter, so Schweitzer volunteered to stand in for him until the end of the school year, holding open the White House post. Poindexter duly arrived that summer. Schweitzer also takes credit for arranging a soft landing for General William

Odom, Brzezinski's former military assistant at the NSC, who had stepped on a lot of toes during his White House years but now managed to be selected for director of the National Security Agency.

No one stood in for Schweitzer when he came under fire. The general gave a speech before the Army Association in which he was quoted as saying that the United States was "in the greatest danger that the republic has ever faced since its founding days." The Russians were "on the move," intoned Schweitzer; "they are going to strike." The bottom line, according to this NSC staffer, was that there was "a drift toward war."

The speech, especially that last quote, was picked up and widely reported in the press. With the audience Schweitzer had joked that his last contact with the political side of government had been as the smallest constituency imaginable—"Army colonels for McGovern at Harvard." But this was no joke. Schweitzer later recalled in a deposition that press reports were "deemed that morning in the White House Mess to be unfavorable by the troika that then decided everything." He was to be fired. Al Haig interceded immediately with President Reagan, only to report back that it was too late, the press releases had already gone out.

When the dust cleared, the general, who had never wanted his NSC staff job and was getting his wish to be returned to the Army, was *still* laboring at the OEOB. Bob Schweitzer passed back under Army command only in mid-November, almost a month after the speech, and the Army kept him on White House detail until January 1982, even after the press discovered the general still at the NSC and reported it. When Schweitzer did leave, Ronald Reagan held a little ceremony to mark his passage.

Ranged along the same philosophical axis as Schweitzer, but at the opposite extreme on passion to get the NSC staff job, Richard Pipes became the Harvard NSC man of Reagan's administration. Like Brzezinski and Kissinger, Pipes was a naturalized American, born in 1923 in Cieszyn, Poland. Like them, he got his doctorate at Harvard, was recognized for brilliance, and more. A force in creation of Harvard's Russian Institute, Pipes surpassed his colleagues in academic accomplishment. At the OEOB, however, he never did better than senior director and was very quickly muzzled by the troika.

Encouraging fears of the Soviets, Pipes selected quotations from Russian military literature to argue the Soviets thought they could fight and win a nuclear war. He continued to believe this during his NSC staff tenure. Richard Allen's first public appearance after taking over as national security adviser occurred on March 21, 1981. Just a few days later Pipes gave an interview in which he declared that there was bound to be a war between the superpowers unless the Soviets changed their system. After that, Pipes was told to keep quiet, and get permission for future interviews, permission he was not given for a *year*. By then it was clear that ultraconservative Reaganauts throughout the administration were being stalemated as the

President compromised in an effort to govern. Pipes finished out his two-year leave of absence from Harvard, then returned to academia.

Men like Bob Schweitzer and Dick Pipes were not going against the grain of the President. They must have thought they represented him. President Reagan confirmed it by a gaffe that occurred during preparations for one of his weekly radio speeches, in which, doing a voice-level test for broadcasters, he joked about sending nuclear bombers to hit Russia. Publicly, the President talked of the Soviet Union as an "evil empire." In fact, the signs of hostility, both overt and covert, so frazzled the Russians that Moscow feared the United States might really be seeking war. Yet the image makers prevailed over Reagan's loyalty to his crew. The brave new world was an illusion.

INTO THE LAND OF
THE BLIND

▲▲▲

T he departure of Richard Allen brought a new broom to the West Wing NSC offices. William Patrick Clark, Judge Clark, one of Reagan's Californians, restored a measure of coherence to the NSC process, but also presided over the first of a series of instances in which the NSC staff shifted from its traditional focus on policy and became embroiled in operations. Unlike the special missions Eisenhower allotted to Goodpaster, or the tasks LBJ assigned Mac Bundy, Ave Harriman, or Bob Komer, Clark's NSC staff would engage in sustained activities in the field. Even some of its traditional NSC staff work took new forms, increasingly activist ones, as the national security adviser and his junior staff showed up in unexpected places as lobbyists, facilitators, and monitors.

Clark had absolutely no background in national security save what he acquired as Al Haig's deputy during 1981, but he was the one Reagan loyalist getting foreign policy experience most directly during that first year. Clark had other attributes even more attractive to the President. From a traditionally Democratic family, he had been an early Reagan-for-governor man, recruiter of Edwin Meese and Michael Deaver. In Sacramento, Clark had been central to Reagan's success as governor, devising the "short memo," a new administrative art form that compressed every decision into four easy paragraphs for a busy governor. When Clark tired of the strain of acting as Reagan's chief of staff, a grateful governor appointed him to a succession of state judicial posts, culminating in justice of the state supreme court in 1972.

That was heady stuff for someone who had completed neither college nor law school. Son of a wealthy cattleman and police chief of Oxnard, California, this fifth-generation Californian worked to support himself from an early age as ranch hand, waiter, house painter, and athletic coach. After attending Stanford for a while, the Catholic Clark had enrolled as a novice in the Augustinian order, only to give it up after a year and return to Stanford, which he eventually left for good. Clark continued his college studies at the University of Santa Clara but never completed his degree. He was nevertheless allowed to enter Loyola Law School. In December 1953 the Army drafted him and he spent two years in Germany in the counterintelligence corps. Later he resumed law school at night, working as an insurance adjuster in the daytime. In 1957 he left Loyola and doggedly finished his law studies on his own, and though he failed the bar once, in 1958 he passed, and then hung out his shingle, forming the Oxnard law firm Clark, Cole & Fairfield.

Clark's original appointment as deputy to Haig was like Casey's to the CIA: the best left after the choicest plums were gone. Once Reagan had nominated him, Larry Eagleburger set up a crash course to prep Clark for the Senate Foreign Relations Committee with indifferent success. At the witness table he was unable to define "détente" or "Third World," unable to name the leaders of Zimbabwe or South Africa, or to discuss developments in the British Labor party. Clark had no opinion to give on the dangers of nuclear proliferation. Elsewhere he once joked that his foreign affairs experience consisted of "seventy-two hours in Santiago [Chile]." On the arguments that the new President was entitled to his picked team, and that Clark was really to be Reagan's eyes and ears at State, Bill Clark managed to attain confirmation.

At the White House, Clark inevitably moved into the President's orbit. As one of the Californians, Judge (that was what he liked to be called) Clark worked under far better conditions than had Richard Allen. The national security adviser regained his direct relationship with the President, taking Ed Meese out of the paper flow. Judge Clark also resumed morning briefings for the President and Vice President, often bringing with him NSC staffers or other principals depending on the topic of the day. Judge Clark might show up with Bill Casey or Cap Weinberger, or it might be Middle East senior director Geof Kemp. Contact with the big boss boosted morale of the staffers in the trenches. Clark did not pretend to be the national security expert. As the Judge put it, he did not intend to "become a heavy on the substance, other than to recognize an issue when I see it."

Clark tried to reenergize the policy reviews by bringing in a friend, Thomas C. Reed, Jr., a former secretary of the Air Force and defense industry official, as consultant to run a big defense policy review called NSSD-1. Later offered a full-time NSC staff job as a special assistant to the President, Reed left the administration under a cloud with allegations of improprieties having to do with 1978 stock transactions. The policy review, meanwhile, had been swept away by the pace of daily events.

An area in which the new security adviser enjoyed some success was policy machinery, codified in NSDD-2. Interestingly enough, NSDD-2 recognized the existing system of senior interagency groups (SIGs) but made no provision for the National Security Planning Group the President himself had established. The directive specifically authorized three SIGs, one each for foreign policy, defense policy, and intelligence, each to be supported as required by working groups. The device would ultimately be overused by Reagan's administration, with a bloated structure of some twenty-two SIG-level groups among two hundred interagency committees, some formed for a single project, many of which never met more than once. The NSC structure at first looked better organized, then badly cluttered, finally hopelessly snarled. In areas where policy did move forward, as in Central America, it frequently happened under an entrepreneur with his own agenda who had mastered the interagency system. Zbigniew Brzezinski later penned a critique of NSC practice during the Reagan era he called "The NSC's Mid-Life Crisis."

At the same time, Clark had a penchant for activity. As he got the machinery oiled, he began to nudge on the system of presidential directives. More than twice as many NSDDs appeared during Clark's first year as had in Allen's. The NSDDs also became more substantive, beginning to cover such subjects as basic strategy (NSDD-32), national space policy (NSDD-44), and strategy with respect to the Soviet Union and covert operations (NSDD-75).

A notable hot potato in the summer of 1982 was the Nofziger affair, which erupted later when it was discovered that former Reagan political aide Lyn C. Nofziger had lobbied the White House in behalf of defense contractor Fairchild Republic Corporation. The contractor employed five thousand workers, and wanted Reagan to reinstate a budget item of $350 million for twenty Fairchild A-10 planes that Congress had deleted. The problem seemed important to at least five New York congressmen, who worked behind the scenes to save the A-10 appropriation. President Reagan needed support for a tax bill on which the voting was expected to be very close. Reagan won. On August 22, 1982, he signed a directive ordering the Defense Department to find ways to continue producing the A-10. There was a White House meeting on the A-10 on September 8, followed up on September 24 when Nofziger and another Fairchild lobbyist met with NSC staffers Richard Levine and Horace Russell. The encounter occurred in the White House Situation Room. Russell, an Air Force brigadier general, had replaced Schweitzer as senior director of the military group on the NSC staff. After the meeting Levine and Russell wrote a memo to Clark advising him to discuss the A-10 matter with Cap Weinberger.

Reagan's image makers took particular interest in information and propaganda programs. Significantly, Clark revived the post of NSC press spokesman, giving the job to former *Washington Star* reporter Jeremiah O'Leary. As NSC staffer Walt Raymond put it: "Mr. Clark, on behalf of the president, was very, very anxious to see to it that it was a sharply focused public diplomacy effort."

Ronald Reagan, it happens, gave a speech in England, at Westminster, during the summer of 1982 in which he spoke of the power of the idea of democracy, expressed by free nations, lofty stuff but also standard cold war rhetoric. For months afterward Walter Raymond, Jr., a CIA propaganda specialist on detail to run the intelligence cluster of the NSC staff, kept bending Clark's ear about the need for a concrete program. There had also been an article by Kenneth Adelman published in *Foreign Affairs* in 1980.

Then CIA director Bill Casey got the ball rolling on December 21, 1982, when he wrote Clark suggesting "more effective governmental instrumentalities to deal with public diplomacy."

President Reagan's answer was NSDD-77, "Management of Public Diplomacy Relative to National Security," which he signed on January 14, 1983. The directive created a Special Planning Group (SPG), at first chaired by White House communications director David Gergen, to provide guidance for all government efforts in this area. Under the SPG were established four coordinating groups, one each for public affairs, international political matters, international broadcasting, and international information.

With Bill Clark's backing, such precedents as Harry Truman's Psychological Strategy Board and Ike's Operations Coordinating Board were considered. At length, Clark chose to form a new Office of Public Diplomacy (OPD) on the NSC staff to support the Special Planning Group and its subcommittees. Clark moved Walt Raymond over from the intelligence cluster to take charge, even though for a time the former CIA man, who retired to take the OPD job, had to continue handling covert operations for the intelligence staff. Raymond was appointed senior director and, as part of a reorganization in which Clark also created a political-military staff section, became one of six newly minted special assistants to the President on the NSC staff. That made ten men on the NSC staff with rank equal to or greater than that which Mac Bundy had held, intensifying the fight for such perquisites as limousines and parking spaces.

The Office of Public Diplomacy supervised agency activities and provided the staff support for the Special Planning Group. Raymond himself chaired the subcommittee on international broadcasting, which worked on modernization for the Voice of America and Radio Free Europe, the creation of the anti-Cuban Radio Marti, and the use of direct satellite transmitting by the White House. Steve Steiner ran an intensified public diplomacy campaign on arms control. A couple more assistants followed. By 1987, four years after formation of OPD, its staff still numbered only three. The OPD's principal action agency, at least for Latin America, would become a new unit for Latin Public Diplomacy (S/LPD) formed within the office of the secretary of state.

Western Europe was one of the biggest problems at the beginning of the "public diplomacy" program. This dated from the outset of the administration, when the United States agitated to keep the Europeans from cooperating with the Soviet Union on a natural gas pipeline. Coming off the energy crisis of the 1970s, there was no way the Europeans were going to be dissuaded. Al Haig saw this, trying to moderate the more extreme ideologues, but by 1982 there were Reaganauts who wanted to impose economic sanctions on America's European allies. Siding with the more extreme protagonists, Clark gave the President only the most aggressive options paper, then scheduled a crucial NSC session for a time he knew Haig would be meeting Andrei Gromyko in New York. Excessive rhetoric outraged the

Europeans, but then the issue became submerged in the even more controversial question of NATO nuclear modernization, for which the United States proposed to deploy new nuclear missiles in seven NATO nations. Massive antinuclear demonstrations took place in several NATO countries and in France, which was not any longer even a member of the military branch of the alliance.

The public diplomacy experts sought to counter the European opposition with a propaganda campaign of their own. For this initial effort Peter Daily, the United States ambassador to Ireland, was recalled from his post to spend several months actively setting up the campaign, which sought to paint the antinuclear opposition as manipulated by Soviet disinformation efforts.

Early in 1983, meanwhile, the President appointed former Senator Richard Stone as special envoy for public diplomacy in an attempt to show the administration was moving on NSDD-77. But Reagan soon reappointed Stone as envoy to Central America, leaving the public diplomacy post vacant. Walt Raymond recommended Otto J. Reich of the Agency for International Development for the job, and suggested a regular office be formed for the activity under the NSC. There is some evidence that Reich was appointed despite opposition from the secretary of state, but Reich's S/LPD materialized at Foggy Bottom and not under the NSC directly, although it took general guidance from the Special Planning Group.

As far as propaganda operations are concerned, the chance of a lifetime came on the night of August 31, 1983, when Soviet interceptor aircraft sent to find an intruder into Russian airspace shot down Korean Air Lines Flight 007, a Boeing 747 jetliner with 269 persons aboard. It will never be known definitively whether the plane simply wandered off course or if it had more sinister motives, but the OPD went into action.

The image makers had the usual problem of how to cast Reagan. He was at Rancho Cielo, his California ranch, at the moment of crisis. The immediate question became whether the President should return to the capital and convene the NSC. Reagan's initial reaction was to wait and see, asking for more information. Larry Speakes made a brief press statement in that spirit, before political aides got to the President and convinced him to cut short his vacation two days.

Before the President returned to Washington, the NSC staff were already busy. John Lenczowski, an NSC Soviet specialist hired by Dick Pipes, favored a strong response and discussed alternatives ranging from attacking Cuba to hitting the Soviets in Eastern Europe. He assembled this menu into a formal options paper that he got Clark to append to the paper prepared for the NSC principals.

Reagan returned to Washington on the evening of Friday, September 2, to an NSC session that began only forty minutes after *Air Force One* touched down at Andrews. Still wearing vacation clothes, Reagan listened quietly for over an hour as the options were debated. After that Reagan spoke up but did not in fact select any of the options prepared for him. Right after the meeting officials of the USIA first learned, in Walt Raymond's office, that an American intelligence-collection plane had been aloft in that area that night and could have contributed to the Soviets' confusion.

President Reagan approved an alternative in NSDD-102, issued the following Monday, September 5. It called for maximum public condemnation of the Soviet Union at the United Nations and, among other things, for a "major public diplomatic effort to keep international and domestic attention focused on the Soviet action." The resulting campaign, with Walt Raymond watching closely from the OEOB, included use of selectively edited translations of tapes of the voice radio traffic from the Russian interceptors, and the suppression of early conclusions by United States intelligence authorities that the Russians had made a genuine error.

The KAL incident came as the swan song for Judge Clark, who began to take aggressive stances on Central America and the Middle East. These brought him into conflict with the State Department, and there were other conflicts, such as between CIA and State on covert operations, or between the Pentagon and State on arms control. Reportedly the fall of 1983 was a period in which the President himself could not be induced to attend the NSC. It all added up to frustration for Bill Clark.

That fall Judge Clark learned that James Watt, secretary of the interior, was about to leave his job. Clark volunteered to replace him, setting off a scramble for a new national security adviser. Chief of Staff James Baker decided he wanted to be the President's keeper of the keys, and together with Mike Deaver almost pulled it off, in the face of Bill Casey and others, who put up presidential favorite Jeane J. Kirkpatrick as a more conservative choice. Clark foiled the Baker-Deaver ploy in one of his last actions as keeper.

In all it was a close thing. Clark found out about Baker only as the President was about to go down to the press room to announce the appointment. He followed Reagan into the West Wing elevator, then pulled the President into the Situation Room where Clark and others convinced him not to give the job to Baker. President Reagan did not approve any of the other candidates either, however. Instead he gave the job to Deputy National Security Adviser Robert McFarlane. The appointment was announced on October 17, 1983. It was mere days before the work McFarlane had just been doing would, quite literally, blow up in his face. The setting for this tragedy would be Lebanon.

One trouble with the grueling twelve-hour days of work for the NSC staff was that it was too easy to get completely caught up in immediate affairs, whether of national security or West Wing corridor gossip. Geoffrey Kemp was one area specialist who undoubtedly lamented Bill Clark's departure, and he might have done so even more had he not been so taken up with events in the Middle East, where the Judge had allowed his staff to go operational. Besides, Clark cooked a mean turkey, as he had shown at a

Christmas party the previous year, which Judge Clark had arranged to hold at Blair House. Clark hoped to use the occasion to settle some of the differences emerging among himself, George Shultz, Caspar Weinberger, and Bill Casey, but instead it turned into another awkward argument added to a growing list. Geof Kemp could appreciate the importance of Clark's gesture, for his area was one of those most affected by the divisions. Kemp also appreciated Clark's openness in taking him along fairly often on his morning briefings with the President.

Actually Kemp saw much of Ronald Reagan primarily because the Middle East continued in such turmoil. The summer of 1981 brought the Israeli bombing of Baghdad, intended to prevent Iraq from developing nuclear weapons research facilities. Lebanon had gotten worse and worse, with Israeli military raids into the southern part of the country, and a virtual crisis over the Syrian presence and SAM missile sites in the Bekaa Valley. Then 1982 brought a full-scale Israeli invasion of Lebanon, leading to the battle for Beirut. When Bill Clark left the White House, Geoffrey Kemp had his hands full.

Kemp became another of the newly minted special assistants to the President. An academic and an Englishman, he had not come to the United States until 1967, to get his Ph.D. at MIT. A student at Oxford and researcher at the International Institute for Strategic Studies, Kemp had co-authored a prescient paper studying the American presence in Iran. Unlike some on Reagan's NSC staff, Kemp, who became a naturalized American citizen in 1974, was very much the pragmatist.

In the administration's first days, Al Haig's Middle East policy had been pragmatic too, engaging Israel by broadening the American-Israeli strategic relationship and putting it on a more formal basis. Haig thought that would give the Israelis reason to pay more attention to Washington's advice, but the Israelis tried to play the relationship the other way, making Washington acquiesce in Israeli actions.

The Israeli bombing of Baghdad on June 7, 1981, was a notable example of this process. The IDF bombing utilized sixteen American planes, F-15s and F-16s, which under the military aid agreements were supposed to be used only for defensive purposes. The Baghdad raid could be construed as defensive only in the vaguest rhetorical sense: A Sunday morning surprise attack on a target in a civilian area, it was more like Pearl Harbor. Washington delayed delivery of the next four F-16s due to be shipped to Israel for three weeks. Cap Weinberger demanded stronger sanctions, but the President overruled him at a series of NSC meetings a few days after the bombing. It has since become clear that the Israelis considered they had reached such an entente with Haig that later in 1981, they went ahead with covert shipments of American weapons and military spare parts to Iran, a project that reportedly received Haig's approval. As for the President himself, a week after the bombing Reagan approved an intensified lobbying effort on behalf of a Middle East arms sale package that included *more* advanced aircraft for Israel.

Throughout this period tension sharpened over Lebanon where the Israelis repeatedly bombed targets to retaliate for terrorist incidents. The bombings were brutal enough that in July 1981 the United States felt compelled to officially protest them. In view of the strategic alignment proceeding simultaneously, the Israelis dismissed American protests as strictly pro forma.

Exactly one year after the Baghdad bombing affair, using the apparently unrelated attempted assassination of an Israeli diplomat as the pretext, Israel launched a major invasion of Lebanon with the object of wiping out the PLO and setting back the Syrians in the Bekaa Valley. The initial Israeli assault happened while Reagan attended a Western economic summit at Versailles. Along on the trip, Haig noticed that Judge Clark seemed to have his own communications channels, so active he appeared to be "conducting a second foreign policy." In fact, Clark was in touch with George Bush's NSC Special Situations Group back in Washington. Once the presidential party returned, the secretary of state asked what the national security adviser was up to.

"You've won a lot of battles in this administration, Al," Clark shot back, "but you'd better understand that from now on it's going to be the *President's* foreign policy."

With Habib already en route on a shuttle, Haig submitted draft instructions to Bill Clark. The document was faxed to the President at Camp David. Clark reported back that Reagan had not approved it and wanted to examine the issue at an NSC session scheduled for June 14. Haig then called Reagan personally to reiterate the need for immediate instructions, only to receive the impression the President had no idea what he was talking about. Haig then sent out the instructions on his own authority, which drove the detached President to chew him out. Haig bristled. A few days later he struck back with two papers giving chapter and verse on occasions he had felt upstaged by the White House, asking for clear orders that would set the chain of authority. When Al asked what the President had decided, Reagan handed him an unsealed envelope containing a one-line note to the effect that Haig's resignation had been accepted.

During much of this summer of 1982 the NSC remained a beehive of activity. Haig recounts that the Bush group once advised going along with an anti-Israel resolution at the United Nations, though that would trigger a break with the Israelis. Haig torpedoed the move with just moments to get the orders to Ambassador Jeane Kirkpatrick. Habib plodded ahead. At the OEOB there was work to spare for Geoffrey Kemp's staff section, including area director Howard J. Teicher, augmented by Marine officer Oliver L. North.

"For weeks I sat there and listened," Deaver recalls, "as the National Security Council briefers kept telling Reagan Israel could win, *he* could win, by letting Sharon's tanks and infantry clean out the terrorists once and for all, in the process driving Syria back across its own borders." Deaver feared escalation to a superpower war, and he dreaded the nightly news broadcasts, with their film footage of apartment buildings collapsing under the bombs or bodies lying in the streets.

It happens that Mike Deaver's office was the small room off the Oval Office, used by LBJ as a hideaway office and Jack Kennedy for a small bedroom. There was a connecting door that led Deaver straight to the President; he could walk in at any time without even passing a secretary. Thinking of Beirut, Deaver walked in one day in August after a national security briefing.

"Mr. President, I have to leave," Deaver records himself as saying.

"What do you mean?" Reagan looked startled.

"I can't be a part of this anymore," Mike replied. "The bombings, the killing of children. It's wrong. And you're the one person on the face of the earth right now who can stop it. All you have to do is tell Begin you want it stopped."

President Reagan buzzed his secretary and asked her to get Israeli Prime Minister Menachem Begin on the phone. Hearing something was up, George Shultz rushed over and supported Deaver. As a result Reagan was tough on Begin, warning him Israel was in danger of losing moral support among Americans, ending up, "It has gone too far. You must stop it."

Begin called back within twenty minutes to report he had just issued appropriate orders to Defense Minister Ariel Sharon. Impressed, Reagan afterward turned to Deaver and said seriously, "I didn't know I had that kind of power."

In fact, Israel was in the same bind it had been with the Baghdad bombing—its American weapons were not supposed to be used offensively. The Israel Defense Force invasion of Lebanon would not have been possible without U.S. arms and equipment and there were even particular problems with some weapons, such as cluster bombs, which were subject to special restriction.

Every day that passed weakened Israel's diplomatic position while bringing no military solution. Israel needed to end the war, but to save face it insisted on tangible achievements, finally expressed as the disarming of the PLO and its removal from Lebanon. Yasir Arafat resisted such an outcome, but Sharon could up the level of violence at will with the IDF's artillery, gunboats, and air power. Had the Israelis been driven to it, their actual assault on Beirut would have been devastating for the PLO. Arafat's real problem was to salvage as much prestige as he could from the defense of the city, then get out before the Israelis could attack. Encouraged by Syria, Arafat finally acquiesced in the disarming of the PLO and its evacuation to Tunisia in return for guarantees of the safety of the Palestinian refugee camps around Beirut. The terms of a cease-fire began to solidify in early August. French troops were the first on the scene, setting up a Multi-National

Force (MNF) to oversee the PLO evacuation. The American Marines arrived four days later, secured a perimeter around the port of Beirut, continuing the evacuation at a greater pace.

By early September the rudiments of order seemed to have returned to Lebanon. The MNF withdrew in its turn by September 10. Four days later a car bomb assassinated Bashir Gemayel and many close associates at their headquarters. Then the Christian militia broke into the Palestinian refugee camps Sabra and Shatilla for a two-day orgy of massacre and wanton violence. At least seven hundred Palestinians perished. That brought back the MNF, not to evacuate the city as before, but to separate the belligerents in ethnic warfare.

The changed mission would be important to those Marines who served with the MNF, who were sent in harm's way without adequate direction from superiors. The Marines operated under standard peacetime rules of engagement plus further restrictions set by the European Command. Owing to his own reluctance to invoke the War Powers Act, Reagan was obliged to pretend that conditions in Beirut were other than they were. There were intelligence problems for the MNF Marines that should be noted but cannot be discussed here in detail. The MNF had an amorphous mission in Beirut, while Joint Chiefs of Staff assumptions underlying the orders were never reviewed. Original MNF planning assumed a duration of no more than two months and that the population would be friendly.

As assumptions grow outdated, most administrations review them periodically, but Reagan's never did. Yet its own actions changed those assumptions, and the NSC staff came to be the center of that process. Reagan chose to throw his weight behind a government whose legitimacy was questioned. Bill Clark succumbed to the notion he was an expert, while George Shultz, who took over the helm at State at the height of this crisis, went along with the general consensus. Cap Weinberger is supposed to have had misgivings, but he never undertook to rectify the policy vacuum at the NSC level. American policy also took no account of the growing militance of Islamic fundamentalists in Lebanon, especially Shia factions, which would have fateful implications for a brand-new set of American hostages; it would be Iran all over again.

In the beginning was Lebanon writ large: A proposal was discussed in the National Security Council for a huge MNF, bigger than Ike's in 1958, many *divisions* of troops, with ultimatums to Israel and Syria. Geoffrey Kemp pushed this option: Arguing the time had come to be bold, he saw the chance to use Beirut as a fulcrum to attain a new balance in the Middle East. Bill Clark and Bud McFarlane liked the idea, as did the President, but Weinberger objected. That was in the fall of 1982. By the next spring Weinberger was being bypassed in Lebanese matters.

Philip Habib's mission came to an end in the spring of 1983, though he had been fairly confident he might be able to negotiate a Syrian withdrawal from Lebanon. Here was another point at which the administration could have taken stock of its stake in Lebanon and its limited ability to influence events there. Instead, the White House rushed to replace Habib and used the occasion to seize control of Lebanon policy for the NSC staff. Who became the new special envoy to the Middle East? Robert McFarlane. Back-stopping him were Geof Kemp and Howard Teicher of the NSC staff, Richard Fairbanks of State, plus military aides and technical people.

No stranger to the Kissinger method of personal diplomacy, McFarlane made a secret visit to Damascus to explore the parameters of the problem. "I shouldn't even have gone if I had any sense," he later told reporters. "The only hope was a naive one that we could get the Syrians and the Israelis out and let the Lebanese duke it out among themselves, and I clung to that."

McFarlane regretted it later because the underlying situation was that the Israelis had no intention of compromising with Syria, and Syria had a major interest in preventing any other power, in particular Israel, from dominating Lebanese politics. The United States not only had little assurance of its ability to deliver an agreement, *it developed no plan or policy to do so.* The very reason for McFarlane's designation as special envoy was to avoid an NSC policy fight between George Shultz, who essentially followed Haig in believing the United States ought to align itself with Israel, and Cap Weinberger, who regarded any alliance with Israel as a liability. In the absence of a solution to this policy conflict it was foolish for Washington to become embroiled in a Lebanon mediation.

Obstacles notwithstanding, McFarlane took on the job, established his base in Rome, and began to move in and out of Beirut at the beginning of August 1983. He had a direct connection with the White House Situation Room and Judge Clark by means of a satellite communications link. This innovation in technology had an important impact on the making of policy; it permitted Bill Clark to run a back channel to McFarlane that bypassed the entire bureaucracy. Moreover, since Bud was deputy national security adviser, the chain of command ran naturally to Clark; there was no problem with cross-cutting loyalty to any other department. It was Lebanon, not the later Iran-Contra excesses, that became the first instance of the NSC staff going operational. "On the ground in Beirut, we figured out how to move the bureaucracy," Teicher later said.

Barely having finished his initial meetings with the principals in Beirut, McFarlane was visiting the MNF Marines, by this time the 24th Marine Amphibious Unit (MAU), when they suffered their first clearly deliberate shelling, by rockets and mortars on the headquarters building, on August 10. Himself a former Marine artillery officer, McFarlane could see the vulnerability of the Marine positions around Beirut International Airport. That day marked the first time 24th MAU fired weapons in Beirut, although it was only mortar illumination rounds subtly telling the Lebanese the Marines knew which were the batteries firing on them.

On August 28, Marines returned fire for the first time. They first employed artillery the next day. Things became so tense the Marines stopped all patrolling as of August 31. That day, following JCS orders, the Marines gave some of their own small arms ammunition to the Lebanese military. In Washington the administration continued to insist the War Powers Act did not apply to Beirut both because hostilities were not imminent, an increasingly tenuous argument, and because "peacekeeping" forces should not be subject to the act. Meanwhile, special envoy McFarlane began advocating that the Marines send some officers into the Shuf Mountains as observers to assist the Lebanese armed forces.

Behind McFarlane, Howard Teicher and naval aide Captain Philip Dur suggested bringing up the battleship *New Jersey,* greatly augmenting United States firepower if a naval bombardment ensued. Weinberger and the JCS went along with the naval buildup, adding the 31st Marine Amphibious Unit, which sailed from Hawaii on September 2. Three days later, when shells were fired at MNF positions, U.S. Navy ships offshore opened fire for the first time, to support Lebanese armed forces operations. Washington's claims to neutrality lay in tatters. Moreover, by incompetence or design, Lebanese armed forces sources providing targets for United States fire got the Americans engaged against both Druze and Shiite militias.

On September 9 the Lebanese military commander went to McFarlane to request American forces provide fire support for his army in the Shuf, fighting rather ineffectively at a place called Suq al-Gharb. Bud sent Major Gatanas to survey the battle site, but he inclined to feel the government of Amin Gemayel might fall if it lost the Shuf battle. Geof Kemp believed the United States had exercised great self-restraint already and might as well demonstrate its force. Teicher had favored greater use of force all along. Richard Fairbanks, senior State official, acquiesced. McFarlane drafted and sent what David Martin and John Walcott, historians of the Reagan effort to counterterrorism, call the "sky is falling" cable, on September 11 in the middle of a Washington weekend. Judge Clark and George Shultz backed Bud's panicked interpretation, at the White House meeting sparked by the cable, arguing the United States should fire artillery support for the Lebanese military, that is, Gemayel's Christians. President Reagan signed an NSDD on September 12 that authorized the artillery fire, but left it to the discretion of the commander on the scene. That led to several heated arguments between McFarlane and the local Marine commander, Colonel Timothy Geraghty, who saw that if he were to open fire his Marines would be extremely vulnerable in their low-lying positions around the airport.

Despite his satellite communications, Bud McFarlane proved unable to get anyone in Washington to order Geraghty to *ask* for naval gunfire supporting the Lebanese, or to get the commander replaced by someone willing to make the request. At the same time Clark and others fumed that Bud did not seem to be getting results.

When an Army officer, probably Major Gatanas, reported the Druze massing tanks near Suq al-Gharb, Geraghty filed the request. Three United

States warships initiated the first bombardment solely to support Gemayel's army on September 19. By early October, American tanks and armored personnel carriers began arriving as military aid. The battleship *New Jersey* and the reinforcing MAU also made their appearance off the coast, to see a cease-fire declared on September 26. Initial optimism that this would hold masked the change in the terms of the conflict from conventional warfare to terrorist violence.

McFarlane returned temporarily to Rome. The Marines shifted uneasily in their positions around the airport. From the beginning they had had intelligence reports that a terrorist threat existed, hundreds in fact over the long summer of 1983. On Sunday, October 23, at 6:22 in the morning, a yellow Mercedes truck entered the Marine compound and sped past two guard posts and through a barbed-wire barrier to crash into the headquarters building. The truck was wired as a bomb with the equivalent of twelve thousand pounds of explosives. The building was destroyed, hours after NSC staffer Howard Teicher had passed through on one of McFarlane's errands. Rescuers found the bodies of 243 dead Marines in the ruins. Another bomb destroyed French MNF headquarters.

Presiding over this disaster from Washington where, just six days before, his appointment as national security adviser had been announced, was Bud McFarlane. The Marines clung to their precarious positions for a few more months, the devastated MAU replaced by a new unit, but ultimately withdrew in frustration. As they left, the battleship *New Jersey* carried out a massive naval bombardment of the Shuf with no visible result. Geoffrey Kemp thought Weinberger silly to sanction such a useless bombardment after months of resisting NSC calls to action.

It had all been disturbingly reminiscent of Vietnam. In Lebanon there was the same failure to take a hard look at the stakes in the beginning, a proud refusal to question the utility and purpose of action whenever it was suggested, a failure to plan a way from the starting point to an attainable goal. In short, a mess. Typically, Reagan rewarded Bud McFarlane for it.

A SPLENDID LITTLE WAR

▲▲▲

Bad news from Beirut arrived at the White House as the National Security Council staff struggled to cope with its most ambitious adventure yet, Operation Urgent Fury: the invasion of Grenada. A somnolent island in the West Indies, Grenada achieved independence in 1974, becoming a member of the British Commonwealth, which maintained a "governor" on the island who had ceremonial functions. Power went to Prime Minister Eric Gairy, whose authoritarian style fit the classic mold of Latin American dictators, while his expressed belief in flying saucers strained credulity. On March 13, 1979, while Gairy was on a trip to New York, a popular revolt toppled his government in the name of the New Jewel Movement of British-educated lawyer Maurice Bishop. Fearing Gairy would be able to mount a countercoup using mercenaries, about a month later Bishop announced he would seek arms and aid from Cuba.

In the spring of 1983, Reagan complained of "Soviet-Cuban militarization" of Grenada. The President mentioned Grenada and showed an aerial photo of Point Salines in his extraordinary address to a joint session of Congress on the Strategic Defense Initiative. The Chief of Naval Operations supported Reagan with a claim that Russia planned to use Grenada as a base for air and sea surveillance of the Caribbean, in conjunction with naval patrols out of Angola.

Proving a negative is always difficult, but Maurice Bishop had a hell of a time trying to tell the United States his airport was *not* a military base. The United States did its best to isolate the island, using its voting power in international financial institutions as Nixon had done with Chile. Washington was not interested in talk. Dessima Williams, Grenadian ambassador to the United States, had little success reaching even junior State Department officials. Bishop was humiliated in June 1983, when he visited Washington and no senior United States official would agree to meet him.

The Americans relented at the last moment during the Bishop trip, and Judge Clark plus Kenneth Dam from State met with him. The documents that purport to be talking points for, and notes of, a Clark-Bishop meeting on June 7 are among a collection of materials later captured by United States forces, then assembled and disseminated by the S/LPD public diplomacy operatives. Handwritten, unsigned, undated papers, anyone could have inserted these into the Grenada collection. The notes show Bill Clark agreeing to secret negotiations with the Grenadians, being breezily conciliatory and telling Bishop to "expect change in criticisms in future." Moreover, the national security adviser, according to these notes, mouthed a perfect public diplomacy line in his "hope that we return to basic form of government rather than [the] model of E [astern] Eur[ope]." Finally, Clark is quoted as discussing the need to move a school, presumably the St. George's University Medical School, attended by many American students. The last item casts suspicion on the authenticity of the notes because the United States government is not known to have shown any such solicitousness for the American medical students in Grenada, and definitely not prior to the coup by the ultra-Left that overthrew Bishop. On the other hand, these particular documents read like exactly what the Reagan administration would have wanted, *after the invasion,* to help create an image that Grenada was not an act of opportunism.

Such evidence as exists on Point Salines airport also shows a far more complex situation than the stark images portrayed in Washington. Grenadians had been interested in an international airport for many years and repeated studies had been done of one beginning in 1969. Bishop was the man who did something about it, contracting a Miami company to design an airport and the British firm Plessey to instrument it. Cuba donated labor and materials for the largest share of the $73-million project, but other donors included European Common Market countries, through their development fund; a consortium of four Arab nations (Algeria, Libya, Syria, and Iraq) recruited by the Common Market fund; and Grenada's neighbor Venezuela. Journalists who visited the site found no trace of the strict security measures usually associated with military construction. Administration hacks were reduced to claims that the presence of fuel tanks at Grenada's airport proved its military intent. The British decided that was excessive, and an official spokesman for the Royal Air Force countered that any large airport has need of fuel tanks.

On October 12, 1983, meanwhile, ultraleft elements of the New Jewel Movement mounted a putsch that ousted Bishop, arresting him, his pregnant wife, and other close supporters. Mass demonstrations (by Grenadian standards) freed Bishop from house arrest a week later. Soldiers closed in as a smaller group of demonstrators tarried with Bishop at Fort Rupert, where Bishop and several of his ministers were gunned down. This "Fort Rupert Massacre" became the proximate cause of the American invasion once the Grenadian military leader General Hudson Austin imposed a twenty-four-hour curfew.

Helping the invasion option along to approval was a critical development—the struggle over the NSC replacement for Clark. The fight over the succession diverted the attention of the top-level players for several days. With the appointment of Bud McFarlane the options game could continue, although the new national security adviser occupied a much less exalted place in the firmament of Reagan's advisers.

McFarlane's newness and his recent preoccupation with Lebanon played in favor of the policy entrepreneurs, in particular NSC staffer Constantine Menges. A Reaganaut and protégé of Bill Casey, Menges saw the opportunity to stage a rescue mission that would, incidentally, overthrow the Grenadian government. The initial paper for what became the invasion option Menges fit into a single page on October 13, the morning after the putsch. That afternoon he was called to the Roosevelt Room of the West Wing, but it was to hear Judge Clark announce he would be leaving.

As the big boys fought it out over the succession, Menges circulated his preliminary rescue plan to two other NSC staffers, intelligence senior director Kenneth de Graffenreid and political-military staffer Oliver North. Menges told them it was a personal idea, but asked each to think about requirements in his area. Ollie North had had a good deal of contact with Langley, where Bill Casey had employed Menges until a mere four days before, and where the NSC senior director was lampooned with the nickname Constant Menace. North seemed skeptical of the Menges rescue plan. A top Pentagon official also warned Menges against suggesting his plan to the new national security adviser. Once Menges learned the new keeper would be Robert McFarlane, he became even more perturbed, for he had had a fair amount of contact with Bud in 1981–1982 when at the CIA while McFarlane had been at State. Menges tarred McFarlane as wishy-washy, lacking the steel nerves to be a real national security adviser.

On October 19, State held its first meeting to consider the contingency of a rescue. Menges reported that he was not invited, cut out as Bob Schweitzer and Roger Fontaine had been when they were the NSC Latin America men. Still, the knowledge others were also interested impelled Menges to recommend that McFarlane convene the Crisis Pre-Planning Group (CPPG). Bud could do this on his own authority in a situation requiring the use of force that would involve presidential action. McFarlane agreed. Admiral Poindexter assembled the CPPG in the new crisis management center at 9:00 A.M. on October 20. Menges had held private conversations by secure telephone before the meeting with Bill Middendorf, and with the Pentagon's Fred Iklé. At the CPPG meeting Menges suddenly raised the specter of nuclear weapons, warning that if the United States carried out the rescue *without* toppling the New Jewel Movement, the Grenadians might be so angry they would offer territory as a base for Soviet bloc forces, "which could include nuclear weapons." Middendorf and then Iklé declared a belief that the invasion could be carried out with regional international support.

Menges was assigned to write an options paper that Vice President Bush would use for his Special Situations Group. Menges and Ollie North split up the legwork. Constantine handled the State and CIA angles, Ollie the Pentagon and Joint Chiefs of Staff. Bush held an hour-long NSC session that evening (Reagan was traveling) that could not have come off better for Menges, who ended up with instructions to draft an NSDD the President could sign to order the invasion, now code-named Urgent Fury. Menges did so following a huddle with McFarlane, Poindexter, and North after the Situation Room meeting. The next day brought sessions of the CPPG and the Restricted Interagency Group (RIG) in preparation for another Bush crisis meeting on the morning of Saturday, October 22. It was only now that State sent diplomats to Grenada, and it was not until *after* the key Bush meeting that there were any reports regarding the American medical students.

Menges had expected Bush, McFarlane, and Shultz to oppose an invasion. Instead, however, McFarlane did not flinch a muscle through the preparations, and then Bush came through for the NSC principals. The phenomenon was disturbingly like what Japan encountered in its decade before World War II, during which middle-level officers repeatedly confronted seniors with militaristic choices, and seniors acquiesced owing to a desire to preserve their image and save face. The Reagan NSC operated similarly. Actual decisions were made in an increasingly rarefied atmosphere. Bush's October 22 NSPG met at Room 208 of the OEOB, where it could be hooked in by secure mobile phone with Ronald Reagan and George Shultz, who happened to be playing golf in Augusta, Georgia. Menges was now confident because the appeal of the Organization of Eastern Caribbean States (OECS) had come in on a unanimous vote. Reagan made some characteristic cracks, asked a few questions. The NSPG expressed the consensus that Urgent Fury should be carried out on October 25. By afternoon of the twenty-second, Menges had completed the final draft of the NSDD. McFarlane would get the President's signature on the document the next day. Ollie North reportedly carried the paper out of the Oval Office.

From then on, it was a matter of observing the forms and keeping things quiet until the moment of action. Thus Poindexter's subsequent misleading of the press. At another moment, Menges reports, he had to inform the admiral that Hudson Austin had agreed to reopen the airport, permit flights to enter, and talk to the United States.

"Constantine," Poindexter replied in a mock-serious voice, "tell the State Department to inform Grenada that we will send some people to talk, and that they will arrive early next week."

It was one of the few times Menges ever heard the admiral joke.

Menges busied himself on the minutiae of intervention, like a draft for the President's announcement of the action, a fact sheet on Grenada, and others on supporting subjects, such as the OECS which was almost completely unknown. Oliver North served as White House contact point for the JCS, and among the many stories told about North is one that he tried to get the Joint Chiefs to allow the Navy and Marines to carry out the invasion all by themselves. North may have raised the suggestion in jest, but it is improbable Lieutenant Colonel North tried to make the Joint Chiefs do *anything*. Given the prevailing interservice environment among the military and the operation of the JCS system, it was guaranteed Urgent Fury would be a combined service operation. North was very much the disciplined action officer at this point in his career.

Having returned from George Shultz's invitational golf tournament, Ronald Reagan convened the NSC for formal meetings on October 24. The first NSC session concerned Lebanon. The Grenada group waited in McFarlane's office while the NSC principals commiserated with each other about the disaster at the Marine barracks. Menges sat with Fred Iklé, Larry Eagleburger, and the others waiting their turn up. Constantine decided to use the time to outline what he thought ought to be done in conjunction with the invasion: The United States should send Michael Ledeen to Europe to help explain the action; the United States should argue it had been a correct and necessary action; the United States should ensure the "humane deinstitutionalization" of the Grenadian "communist dictatorship." Intelligence interrogations of all prisoners would identify the key leaders, of whom only the most important need be held in prison. It would, of course, be important to give them a fair trial using British legal procedures. Fred Iklé chimed in to talk about postinvasion civil government. Larry Eagleburger said practically nothing. Langhorne Motley, according to Menges, "seemed not to grasp what I meant by 'humane deinstitutionalization' of the dictatorship."

The military plan was based on the fact that a Marine amphibious unit (MAU) had just sailed for the Eastern Mediterranean, eventually to replace the MAU at Beirut. Customary practice with Mediterranean deployments was to pass by Puerto Rico to practice amphibious landings at the Vieques Island facility. The Marine 22nd MAU, fresh from this rehearsal, could then execute Operation Urgent Fury. The Joint Chiefs divided Grenada in two operating zones, giving the southern area to the Army and Air Force, who would take St. George's and Point Salines.

The official version of events began to unravel beginning with the landing, When the Marines hit the beach and the Army rangers and paratroopers, not to say Special Forces started to land from the air, it became instantly apparent the White House had directly lied to the press. Bill Plante, a reporter for CBS, had gone to Reagan spokesman Larry Speakes the day before to inquire about reports the network had received indicating action had begun or was imminent. "Are we going to invade Grenada tomorrow morning?" Plante asked Speakes.

Speakes took the question to Rear Admiral John Poindexter, deputy national security adviser, just promoted from military assistant. Robert Sims, NSC press officer, relayed the inquiry. Speakes came back with the word: "Preposterous!" Poindexter had said, and added, "Knock it down hard!"

Deputy press secretary Speakes took that answer to Plante. When Urgent Fury began only hours later, the manipulation became transparent, while the Pentagon compounded it by refusing to permit the press to cover combat operations. According to Speakes, "Poindexter had hung me out to dry, and I didn't even know it." The spokesman got a warning from Jim Baker that night, then learned the truth from him in the White House mess at 5:45 A.M. the morning of Urgent Fury, when troops were already on the ground.

The details of the invasion itself need not detain us long. American forces were massive—up to 4,700 on the first day and a peak of about 6,000. The Grenadian Army hardly fought. Cuban engineer units that Washington public relations built up into the biggest obstacle to Urgent Fury, turned out to be much overestimated. Those Cubans who did fight gave a good account of themselves, however, and came close to beating a detachment of the Army's Delta Force commandos. An effort by the Army to conceal casualties among its Special Forces followed the operation, ultimately to the detriment of administration credibility. Also controversial were the large number of medals awarded (8,612), communications foul-ups among the services, the presence and activities of special operations helicopters, Navy bombing of a mental hospital, and Delta Force difficulties. Measurable direct costs for Urgent Fury totaled $75.5 million above routine operating expenses. American casualties were 19 killed or dead of wounds, 115 wounded, and 23 nonbattle casualties.

Washington's coffers opened up and gave Grenada $57 million in foreign aid during the first year after the intervention. Much of the money went to American contractors to resume work on the Point Salines airport. Aid fell to little more than half that amount the second year, then to a trickle of perhaps $10 million a year. By 1988, Grenada had received $110 million in United States aid. That amount was strikingly close to the amount, $100 million, of the total Grenadian damage claims filed against the United States in the wake of Urgent Fury.

▲ President Ford negotiates with the Russians at Helsinki, August 2, 1975. The American delegation sits at the right-hand side of the table. *Left to right:* State interpreter Alexander Akalovsky, Helmut Sonnenfeldt, President Ford, assistant secretary of state Arthur A. Hartman, Brent Scowcroft. Backbenchers are William G. Hyland, then working under Kissinger at State, and NSC staffer Jan Lodal. Soviet leader Leonid Brezhnev, hand to mouth, sits opposite Ford. Kissinger, obscured, sits between Ford and Sonnenfeldt. (Ford Library)

▲ George Bush, then CIA director, briefs the National Security Council, using aerial photographs, on the situation in Beirut, shortly before President Ford decides upon an evacuation of Americans. *Clockwise from left foreground:* General George Brown, JCS chairman, Bush, Brent Scowcroft, L. Dean Brown, special emissary to Lebanon, Vice President Rockefeller, Henry Kissinger, and Ford, June 17, 1976. (Ford Library)

▲ Carter administration National Security Council invitees gather in the White House Situation Room just prior to the first meeting of the NSC Special Coordination Committee, February 3, 1977. (Carter Library)

▲ The President being briefed in Scowcroft's office on June 19. Deputy national security adviser William G. Hyland stands to his right and Scowcroft behind him. The display behind Scowcroft contains the general's rank badges and medals. (Ford Library)

▲ Scowcroft stands with his deputy Bill Hyland, confirming the latest word on Beirut, June 19, 1976. (Ford Library)

▲ President Ford's late-night vigil in Brent Scowcroft's office, June 19, 1976. The President ponders a mounted map of Beirut. (Ford Library)

▲ President Jimmy Carter makes introductory remarks before turning the Special Coordinating Committee over to Zbigniew Brzezinski, February 3, 1977. Brzezinski, sitting between Carter and Vice President Walter Mondale, reviews his own notes for the meeting. Among other NSC staffers present are David Aaron, sitting against the curtain at the back, and Bill Hyland, second from right. (Carter Library)

▲ National security adviser Zbigniew Brzezinski meets with the President in the Oval Office, April 19, 1977. (Carter Library)

▲ In the heat of the Iran crisis President Carter instructs Brzezinski he means business,
November 20, 1979. (Carter Library)

▲ Carter restricts the Iran meeting to the circle of his NSC principals. *From left:* secretary of defense Harold Brown, secretary of state Cyrus Vance, Carter, Brzezinski, November 20, 1979. (Carter Library)

▲ Waiting for the President: Special counsel Lloyd Cutler talks with David Aaron as Brzezinski sits prior to NSC on January 2, 1980. (Carter Library)

▲ President Carter's NSC mulls over its response to the twin crises of Iran and Afghanistan, January 2, 1980. Lloyd Cutler and David Aaron are mostly out of the picture to Brzezinski's right. Joint Chiefs chairman General David C. Jones sits in his customary place, obscuring Frank C. Carlucci, who is attending in place of Stansfield Turner. Carter sits between Cy Vance and Harold Brown, who is obscured in this picture. Note that Carter has put a portrait of Harry Truman on the wall in place of that of Dwight Eisenhower. (Carter Library)

"SOMETHING WRONG WITH THE WAY THIS COUNTRY MAKES FOREIGN POLICY"

▲▲▲

Bud McFarlane had no choice but to hit the ground running. In fact, he did a good job coordinating the myriad details necessary to bring forward the Grenada invasion in minimum time. In actuality, the administration was remarkably united on Grenada.

Below the surface, however, intrigues continued to roil. Menges would find fault with his boss soon enough, on Nicaragua if not Grenada. So would other NSC principals. The balance of forces was no secret either: Within two weeks of Bud's appointment there appeared an item in one of the national newsweeklies stating, "One of Robert McFarlane's first tasks ... will be to convince ... Weinberger and ... Casey that he is not a 'captive' of the State Department."

Such opposition as existed to McFarlane's appointment came from neo-conservative ranks, circles that disliked Henry Kissinger and tried to minimize his influence. Those circles saw Robert McFarlane as a surrogate for the man who had moved on to form the consulting firm of Kissinger Associates and range the world for his clients. McFarlane had gotten his start under Henry, it is true, but he was no Kissinger. Guarded, taciturn, frightfully ambiguous, McFarlane lacked the intellectual stature of Kissinger and had no pretension of attaining it. On the other hand, Bud was easier to work for than Henry had been, and as lobbyist on Capitol Hill even surpassed Kissinger.

It was McFarlane's fate to be seconded to a President who allowed his administration to become paralyzed by the policies and egos of NSC principals. Rather than playing arbiter for the knights at his round table, Reagan sat back and agreed with all of them. The key became being the last to see him before the moment of decision. Many of the President's keepers developed their own techniques for that. The triumvirate controlled Reagan's schedule, an enormous advantage, and had the most constant access to him.

Judge Clark reestablished the national security adviser's "walk-in" privilege of direct access to the President. George Bush had weekly luncheons with Reagan, and made it a point to attend the morning national security briefings. George Shultz insisted on two-hour private meetings weekly. Caspar Weinberger stayed in close touch to judge when decisions were at hand, then tried to meet with Reagan right away. Bill Casey got himself a hideaway office at the OEOB, where he could stalk the corridors and establish a presence at the White House no other agency head matched.

In a celebrated article in *Fortune* magazine toward the end of McFarlane's tenure, President Reagan described his management style as highly successful, attributing this to an ability to select subordinates carefully, then leave it to them to do the work. There can be little doubt therefore that Ronald Reagan understood what he was doing. The problem was a matter of discipline at the top. Every bureaucrat could create national policy, provided he could be astute enough to move the issue to a presidential level. The dynamics of NSC machinery created a new class of these policy entrepreneurs. Like Menges, many of the NSC staff became entrepreneurs themselves, not least Walter Raymond, Kenneth de Graffenreid, and Oliver North. In a system where the President has no fixed agenda and a limited interest in national security, this might be a reasonable way to generate options, but without discipline at the top the result was chaos. The easiest way around the approval of a competitor's proposal seemed to be to get approval for additional initiatives that modified or canceled the original plan. Thus it became typical of the administration that it would carry out the SALT II agreements despite Reagan's denunciation of them in the 1980 campaign, or that it would swear to uphold the ABM Treaty while unilaterally defining it out of existence.

At the beginning Bud did just like the others. In the Watergate idiom it was a "modified limited hangout"—each issue was to be approached tactically until assessed as a threat and a strategy defined for dealing with it. McFarlane's basic problem stemmed from Reagan's initial NSC reforms: The keeper of the keys had less institutional stature in a Cabinet government. Bill Clark had had a personal relationship with the President to compensate, but Bud McFarlane, a compromise candidate, had been everybody's second choice. Reportedly admired by Nancy Reagan for his soldierly bearing, "he wasn't a member of the million dollar club," Dave Gergen later recalled. "My own credibility with the president seemed to be rather modest," McFarlane himself told a reporter. "He was looking to others for ideas and results."

So McFarlane fell back to the function of coordination, that "integration" of policy so central to the National Security Act. But not being a major player limited McFarlane's ability to compel action from the NSC principals, who had policy as well as ideological interests of their own. McFarlane personally felt closer to George Shultz and often supported him. Other NSC staffers opposed that policy stance and *deliberately undercut their boss.*

Little wonder then that Bud became frustrated. "Many people have come to think there is something wrong with the way this country makes foreign policy," McFarlane intoned before the joint congressional committee investigating Iran-Contra. "They probably don't know how wrong." That was not a view Bud had kept to himself. A year earlier, before the Iran-Contra excesses had even been revealed, the former national security adviser expressed himself almost identically to *The Washington Post:*

> You have two very, very fundamentally opposed individuals—Cap and George—both men of good will . . . each believing that they are expressing what the president wants. Now this cannot be . . . leads basically to paralysis for as long as the decision-making model is a cabinet government. . . . when it became a matter of each of those opinions going laterally to the president in a very chaotic fashion, that's dysfunctional . . . There was growing disorder.

This national security adviser seems to have been strangely inarticulate for a man of such exalted place and advanced degrees. With two coauthors he had published a book on international crises in 1979, and he had written a few articles. He had taught at the National Defense University and held a master's degree from the Institut des Hautes Études in Geneva. McFarlane's stilted manner and labored syntax obscured ideas that could be penetrating, but sometimes collapsed into a hopeless muddle.

Bud McFarlane was a native, that rarity among a city of itinerant residents. He was also the son of a congressman, three-term New Deal Democrat William Doddridge McFarlane. Dividing his childhood between Texas and Washington, Bud graduated from the capital's fine Wilson High School, went to Annapolis, from which he was graduated with a solid, not brilliant record, and entered the Marines. Vietnam framed McFarlane's experience, as it did for many Marines in the Pacific. He led a battery in one of the first Marine artillery battalions to land at Da Nang in 1965, when the war still seemed fresh and bands played to greet the arriving troops. He was on a second tour in 'Nam when the North Vietnamese struck at Tet. McFarlane won a Bronze Star coordinating artillery fire around Con Thien. He arrived at the White House a thirty-four-year-old Marine major on a fellowship program, to work with Nixon political aide Bill Timmons, but moved on to work for Kissinger in 1973.

McFarlane returned to the Marine Corps when Jimmy Carter came to town, but soon decided his future lay elsewhere. Bud got a job on the staff of the Senate Armed Services Committee, hired by powerful Senator John Tower of Texas. Al Haig had invited McFarlane into the Reagan administration as counselor.

There was one aide who went with McFarlane to State, and again when he returned to the White House. She did much to make Robert Carl McFarlane effective, functioning as his personal assistant. She had first met Bud when he was a White House fellow and she was secretary to Kissinger deputy Alexander Haig. Wilma Gray Hall was among that dedicated body of anonymous civil servants who furnish government an institutional memory. Mrs. Hall was good, very good; Henry Kissinger soon used her also. After them she had continued working for national security advisers and their deputies, first Scowcroft and Hyland, then Brzezinski and Aaron, then Richard Allen. Wilma actually left the White House for Foggy Bottom to work for the far less exalted McFarlane, though she ended up coming back before very long, and even became secretary to a national security adviser once again, when Reagan promoted Bud to the job.

Back at the White House, Wilma settled in, keeping Bud McFarlane's schedule, monitoring his paperwork, seeing the visitors he could not make the time for. Five months after her arrival the Pentagon detailed Wilma's daughter, Fawn Hall, to serve with the NSC staff. Until then, Fawn had been a secretary in the office of the Chief of Naval Operations. The NSC staff secretariat assigned Fawn Hall to work for one of the McFarlane protégés, Colonel Oliver North. The explosive results would rock Reagan's administration to its core.

If there was an area with which McFarlane felt his prior experience and interest equipped him to play a role, it was nuclear weapons and arms control. McFarlane contributed significantly here in 1982–1983 while deputy national security adviser, before succeeding Judge Clark. Bud subscribed to the orthodox view prevalent since Lyndon Johnson's administration—that sound agreements should be pursued and would be useful to national security. It is ironic therefore that Bud's contribution to nuclear policy helped undermine the existing ABM Treaty, one of the strongest arms control measures in effect.

The Reagan administration's major achievement in its first year of arms control policy-making was a change in acronym from the well-worn SALT to the new START, for Strategic Arms Reduction Talks. It did not commence actual negotiations until June 1982. Reagan resumed procurement of the B-1 bomber, which Jimmy Carter had canceled, deployment of the MX and Trident II missiles, plus large expenditures for new communications facilities to enable the Pentagon to plan for a "protracted" nuclear war. At a December 1982 meeting between President Reagan and the Joint Chiefs of Staff, the President suddenly asked, "What if we begin to move away from our total reliance on offense to deter a nuclear attack and moved toward a relatively greater reliance on defense?"

Apparently it was only later that the JCS realized what that question meant. After the meeting one of the Chiefs called Judge Clark.

"Did we just get orders to take a hard look at missile defense?"

The keeper of the keys said simply, "Yes!"

Bill Clark not only interpreted Reagan to the Joint Chiefs, he pushed his deputy, Bud McFarlane, into the center of the fray. Reagan's question to the JCS, along with the whole direction of the nation's ICBM effort, were matters of intense controversy.

As Bud McFarlane approached the matter, tactically, the "charged political climate" promised "continued paralysis." The solution? Reagan appointed a Bipartisan Commission on Strategic Forces, selecting Brent Scowcroft to direct it (Henry Kissinger was a member). In April 1983 the Scowcroft Commission recommended the United States deploy both the MX *and* a small Midgetman ICBM still to be designed and built, and that it further pursue arms control with the Soviets. With the latter sop thrown to the growing strength of the nuclear freeze movement, the commission tried to build a moderate argument for continued nuclear modernization.

The image makers planned for a nationally televised speech Reagan could use to rally support for his expensive defense program, countering revelations of extravagance in defense procurement such as $8,000 coffee makers and $700 hammers. On February 11, 1983, President Reagan had another meeting with the Joint Chiefs. This time the JCS brought their answer to Reagan's questions. The JCS were evidently uncertain how to take their mandate, because they did not just look at missile defense, they brought back all kinds of alternatives, including defending the missiles by moving them to sea aboard new SLBM submarines. There did not seem to be a single solution all the Chiefs clearly preferred.

The Chief of Naval Operations, Admiral James D. Watkins, brought up the possibility of a missile defense. According to one account, he had been in touch with McFarlane before the meeting through NSC military aide Poindexter. Watkins had also lunched a couple of weeks earlier with physicist Edward Teller to hear his arguments for a laser missile defense. Watkins had adopted a proposal for forward strategic defense and argued it for the Chiefs at the meeting with the President.

Other Chiefs were lukewarm but no one openly opposed taking a new look at missile defense.

"Wait a minute," Bud interjected at the presidential session, setting the stage for the record. "Are you saying that you think it possible, not probable but possible, that we might be able to develop an effective defense against ballistic missiles?"

Once the admiral affirmed his view, Bud immediately marked the point for the President: Missile defense would transform America's nuclear dilemma.

President Reagan instantly queried the other Chiefs: "Do you all feel that way?"

The Roosevelt Room went very quiet.

"We should protect the American people and our allies, not just avenge them." Admiral Watkins said at one point.

"Don't lose those words," Ronald Reagan replied.

Words made images, and the image of a functional ABM defense captured the President's mind during preparations for the defense speech, finally scheduled for March 23. Over at the Pentagon, Richard Perle tried to fight inclusion of a completely undefined program in the speech, but all he could achieve was a twenty-four-hour delay in its timing. Secretary of State George Shultz was shown the prepared text just two days before the occasion. He was furious but powerless. Weinberger was at a NATO meeting and barely got advance warning to brief his colleagues. To prevent leaks the prepared text came in two parts, the larger of which was a conventional appeal to support MX deployment. The missile defense portion was in an addendum personally drafted by McFarlane on his own typewriter and circulated only at the last moment.

President Reagan's exposition in his address of March 23, 1983, conceded at the outset that missile defense was a dream, but he redirected American technological resources to attain it. Calling the effort his Strategic Defense Initiative (SDI), Ronald Reagan made it a centerpiece of his defense policy. For the first year or so the military did not take SDI seriously. Edward Teller's claims that a working X-ray laser capable of destroying the entire Soviet ICBM force could be fit into a satellite the size of a desk may have been attainable in the ideal realm of theoretical physics, but the immense requirement for power generation would put the reality far into the future. None of the defense advocates had been able to demonstrate that an SDI defense could work, or why SDI would matter even if it did, since there were no defenses capable of stopping the adversary's nuclear bombers and cruise missiles. Almost a decade later, the United States has scaled back the technology and the object of the system to mere defense of retaliatory forces, and has little to show beyond experiments.

Resumption of production of the B-1, continued efforts to deploy the MX in spite of the explosion of its latest preferred basing mode, the "Dense Pack," engineering development of the high-accuracy SLBM Trident II— to Moscow all the activity could hardly look like anything other than an attempt to gain a new strategic superiority. The SDI program reinforced that perception because it looked like a good candidate to enhance the *first-strike* capability of existing forces. Added to the weapons programs was Washington's harsh language. As early as 1981, Al Haig sounded quite bellicose about opposing Cuba, and later he refused to rule out American first use of nuclear weapons in a crisis in Europe. President Reagan joked about sending the bombers over Russia "in five minutes."

The Soviets themselves were confronting tough domestic problems: The continuing stagnation of the economy had sharpened competition for resources; the nationalities were increasingly restive, with demographic trends that actually favored them; the Soviet leadership was ossified in Brezhnev's last years, then in flux through the truncated tenures of Konstantin Chernenko and Yuri Andropov.

One of the most intriguing mysteries of this period is whether Moscow experienced a war scare similar to what the United States endured at the dawn of the cold war. Scattered evidence suggests such an event may have occurred. According to press reports that have been embroidered but never denied, British intelligence succeeded in recruiting a senior KGB officer as a spy, and in running him for many years before his forced defection in 1986. The man rose to become KGB chief of station in London. Through this British double agent, named Oleg Gordiyevsky, the West learned in late 1981 that the KGB had sent out a global warning to be alert for signs of impending war, and again in late 1983, when on November 8 and 9 NATO happened to have scheduled a command post exercise code-named Able Archer. Gordiyevsky warned the British that relations were entering a danger zone. This was also, of course, during the immediate aftermath of the KAL-007 airliner incident, when Washington rhetoric was especially vituperative. Moscow walked out of arms control talks, preventing progress on START or INF for over a year. Gregory Romanov, a high Soviet Communist party official, actually declared on November 7, 1983, "The international situation is white hot." In February 1986, Soviet leader Mikhail Gorbachev told another audience, "Never, perhaps, in the postwar decades, has the situation in the world been as explosive and hence, more difficult and unfavorable, as in the first half of the '80s."

American intelligence detected the Soviets systematically testing the procedures and communications circuits necessary to operate its own nuclear forces. At Langley the national intelligence officer responsible for warning, very concerned, reportedly took the matter to the President. In any event intelligence officials talked to Reagan, cautioning him about the delicacy of the situation. Anxiety spread so widely that on New Year's Day, 1984, former national security adviser Averell Harriman published an extensive op-ed piece in *The New York Times* titled "If the Reagan Pattern Continues, America May Face Nuclear War."

Only two weeks later Ronald Reagan made a speech that reflected remarkable dilution of his administration's previous tone. "Harsh words have led some to speak of heightened uncertainty and an increased danger of conflict," the President declared, using the softer backdrop of the White House East Room. "This is understandable but profoundly mistaken. . . . we should always remember that we do have common interests. And the foremost among them is to avoid war and reduce the level of arms." Cautioning that differences between the superpowers could not be wished away, Reagan said he hoped to base his solution on realism, strength, and dialogue. On another occasion the President made a considered statement that he thought nuclear war could not be won and thus must never be fought.

Reagan's new rhetoric owed something to 1984 electoral politics, but there was something there too of changed image. It was the same kind of changed image, the ending of war, the settling of conflict, that Reagan attempted to evoke in his European tour of the spring, participating in

487

elaborate ceremonies commemorating the Normandy invasion, ending with conciliatory gestures alluding to resolution of conflict. Image maker Michael Deaver masterminded the trip.

Despite atmospheric improvements it was some time before the administration had any arms control achievements to which it could point. For one thing there was plenty of well-entrenched opposition, some of it from the old Committee on the Present Danger crowd, and also from the new policy entrepreneurs. Plotting got to be so Byzantine it was unbelievable. For instance, because Haig once banished Soviet Ambassador Anatoli Dobrynin from Foggy Bottom, a device signaling to Moscow the old cooperation was over, Bill Clark had taken a dislike to this sophisticated, amiable Soviet Diplomat. A typical plot was one hatched by George Shultz and Mike Deaver to smuggle Dobrynin into the Oval Office for an hour-long chat with the President. Such infighting, along with Nancy Reagan's criticisms of him, encouraged Judge Clark to leave his headaches to Bud McFarlane.

McFarlane's fate was to become mired in the intricacies of arms control and the seemingly endless ramifications of the proposals thrown around by the policy entrepreneurs. The NSC arms control machinery was a unit called the Special Arms Control Policy Group (SACPG), an acronym with the unfortunate pronunciation "sack-pig," later changed for obvious reasons to the more innocuous Senior Arms Control Group (SAC-G). McFarlane chaired the group, which included Fred Iklé and Richard Perle representing the Pentagon, and Paul Nitze, INF negotiator and special adviser to the President. Richard Burt represented State early on, with a surprisingly free hand as George Shultz proved much less interested in arms control than usually supposed. Perle engaged Burt very quickly in a bureaucratic battle, which had much to do with the administration's inability to present a START proposal for seventeen months at a key point in Soviet-American relations. Burt eventually lost, being shunted over to Western European relations, and later made ambassador to Bonn. Perle remained, seconded by such like-minded assistants as Frank J. Gaffney, Jr., and Douglas J. Feith. Perle, Gaffney, and Feith, not to mention Fred Iklé, were all veterans of the staff of the Senate Armed Services Committee, the tool of Scoop Jackson and John Tower. Bud McFarlane, also an alumnus of that very same Senate staff, found the battle frustrated his own desire to get on with START negotiations.

McFarlane's other great disappointment lay in the speed with which the Strategic Defense Initiative became a touchstone of administration policy. *Because* it was Ronald Reagan's dream, the policy entrepreneurs eventually realized their support for SDI gained them credibility with the President. Suddenly SDI became sacrosanct, the program to be protected at all costs. McFarlane's motive in encouraging SDI apparently had been to create a bargaining chip that could break the START deadlock, but like Kissinger with the cruise missile, once the Pentagon got serious about SDI the bargaining chip became nonnegotiable.

488

The ultimate irony is how the existence of SDI, even as a *potential* weapon, inexorably led to an attempt to eviscerate the ABM Treaty. A good case can be made that the logic of the entrepreneurial policy system contributed to this senseless and wholly self-inflicted debate. Because SDI, familiarly known as Star Wars, had an ABM function it would either have to be deployed within the treaty or the treaty scrapped. The solution the Reagan administration finally arrived at, characteristic of what passed for innovation in this period, was to attempt to redefine the restrictions of the ABM Treaty. This effort, thirteen years after the fact, and in the face of senatorial understanding plus prior practice of all administrations including Reagan's, was bound to be controversial.

In January 1985, T. K. Jones, one of the entrepreneurs over at the Pentagon, commissioned the first studies, both classified and unclassified, of "alternative interpretations" of the ABM Treaty. The fifty-eight-page classified study was conducted at the Systems Planning Corporation, a defense think tank, by Sidney N. Graybeal and Colonel Charles L. Fitzgerald, both former SALT negotiators. The unclassified study, prepared in half the time by RAND Corporation analyst William R. Harris, found "no binding commitment" in the ABM Treaty. Harris recommended the ABM Treaty be reinterpreted. A couple of months later, an issue paper from the conservative Heritage Foundation argued that the ABM Treaty restricted neither the development nor deployment of SDI. In July 1985 a DOD research official was asked about the meaning of the ABM Treaty, affording an opportunity to follow up with a clarification.

The Pentagon's ABM Treaty review was conducted by Philip H. Kunsberg, a lawyer in its general counsel's office who had been an assistant district attorney in New York, fighting mafiosi and street crime, never dealing in international law or interpreting treaties. Interviewing no one, not studying the ratification process, only the documents in the negotiating record, Kunsberg concluded that the United States had made an effort to prohibit all "exotic" ABMs, but that the Soviets had never agreed to it. Richard Perle later said that when he heard the results he "almost fell out of [his] chair."

On September 17, Perle chaired a session of the interagency working group under the SAC-G to discuss the ABM clarification that would be given the Senate. Paul Nitze presented the standard interpretation of the treaty the United States had taken, but he had to leave early. After he left Perle tabled the Kunsberg paper. Faced with dissent from the Pentagon, Secretary of State George Shultz asked Abraham Sofaer, his own general counsel, for an official view on the matter. Sofaer at least spoke to Nitze before rendering his opinion, but based on several nights with the treaty and negotiating record, he too came back to advise that the ABM Treaty did not limit SDI. In the vociferous debate that has followed, the Sofaer-Kunsberg view has come to be called the broad interpretation, while the traditional view is often termed the narrow interpretation.

Aware of what was percolating in the NSC machinery, Bud McFarlane said on one of the Sunday-morning television news shows on September 22 that the ABM Treaty "was written in 1972" and did not "encompass" things that "can be done in the way of research or testing of many kinds of systems."

The Sofaer reinterpretation of the ABM Treaty took the form of a memorandum he addressed to George Shultz and Paul Nitze on October 3. Sofaer, it is worth noting, was like Kunsberg in that he had little international experience; he had been a federal district court judge in New York. The convoluted argument he eventually developed leaned heavily on such devices as investing unilateral statements with legal force equal to treaty language, and insisting the operative meaning of sentences is to be drawn from such words as "and" or "the." It is also worth noting that other reinterpretation studies, which supported the narrow interpretation, were advanced by Pentagon assistant general counsel John H. McNeill and by the ACDA general counsel Thomas Graham, Jr.

In any case, on October 4 McFarlane chaired the SAC-G meeting as the Sofaer paper came up for discussion. The consensus favored reinterpretation, a recommendation that went to the President at a National Security Planning Group Session on October 11. Later congressional testimony by a key Sofaer aide indicates that DOD and ACDA papers arguing the narrow interpretation were provided to members only immediately prior to the NSPG meeting. Reagan characteristically decided to have his cake and eat it too: On October 12 he approved NSDD-192, which stated as policy that the broad interpretation was fully justified although the administration would continue to observe the narrow definition in practice. Once more McFarlane telegraphed the outcome in advance of the final NSPG decision, again on a television news show, asserting that research and testing of SDI were "approved and authorized" by the existing ABM Treaty.

Bud McFarlane went public to an inordinate degree in the late months of 1985 and many of the national security adviser's appearances related to arms control. But the administration was retreating in this area of Bud's interest, while he himself was increasingly embattled by the NSC principals and especially at odds with a new White House chief of staff, Donald Regan. McFarlane felt exhausted. He stayed on just long enough to conduct President Reagan to his first summit with Soviet leader Gorbachev in November 1985, a summit permitted even though there were no agreements to seal. Bud had had it by then. Arms control would figure among his disappointments.

Concerned about America's ability to achieve results over the period remaining to Ronald Reagan as President, McFarlane went to some trouble to plan for the second term in office. A Brzezinski or a Kissinger might have ordered up an interagency study; Bud McFarlane exchanged memos with his deputy, Admiral John Poindexter. He then took a revised paper to the

President, highlighting about a dozen goals that might be attainable in the time remaining. McFarlane's notion was that the President would rank his preferences, thus giving priorities to the bureaucracy. The incident took place aboard *Air Force One,* while Reagan winged to California for another break from the capital.

Reagan took the goals paper and scanned it awhile, then handed it back. He indicated it looked fine.

When McFarlane asked which were his preferences, Ronald Reagan replied he liked *all* the goals.

Besides adding to our knowledge of the administration's inability to choose between the desirable and the possible, this incident is important for another reason: Bud McFarlane *did not* go outside his own shop for the recommendations. This was a closed system. In fact, one of the few passages declassified from the Poindexter goals memorandum reads: "Withhold true objectives from staffs." That referred to Central America, in which the United States ought to "continue active negotiations but agree on no treaty," and "work out some way to support the Contras either directly or indirectly."

McFarlane's major tool for coordination was the Family Group Luncheon (FGL), which brought him together with the secretaries of state and defense and the director of central intelligence. Cap Weinberger kept close to Bill Casey and they had weekly informal sessions. Quiet dinners were preferred by George Shultz, McFarlane, and their wives. Bud held the reins in his own shop with daily meetings with his staff chiefs, dubbed ODSMs by an acronym-happy bureaucracy, for office director staff meetings.

All the players viewed one another with mutual suspicion. Attempting in 1987 to explain the failure of the administration's Nicaragua policy to the congressional committee investigating the Iran-Contra affair, McFarlane told the senators and congressmen that the United States had not chosen the right instrument.

"Where I went wrong," the former national security adviser testified, "was not having the guts to stand up and tell the President that." The ideological traps were many, and implicit, and built into the decisions. "To tell you the truth," McFarlane went on, "if I had done that Bill Casey, Jeane Kirkpatrick and Cap Weinberger would have said I was some kind of a commie."

The keeper of Reagan's keys would be cut down by *ad hominem* attack. Rumors linked McFarlane romantically with an ABC television reporter, and with NSC press spokeswoman Karna Small, a former television weathercaster from southern California. But the kind of personal attack McFarlane *said* he feared *was* in fact made on Paul Nitze, who lost credibility with the President after being quoted as believing Soviet-American differences in arms control could be worked out. When Nitze went on to produce with his Soviet opposite number a formula for agreement on INF missiles, their "walk in the woods" initiative got rejected out of hand. Nitze suffered derision as an inveterate problem solver. When experienced diplomat Phil Habib went out on a limb in 1985 to deliver Nicaraguan agreement to a Central American peace accord the United States had declared it would support, he too would be cut off.

Information, the having of it, keeping of it, and manipulation of it became even more central to the operation of the NSC machinery. Now you had NSC staff people on mission, at the end of satellite communications links, in places like Lebanon or New York, fairly regularly. *Using* information, exploiting it, figured as the primary job for the Public Diplomacy office. Controlling others' information, and their access to media had been Judge Clark's objective in 1982, when he almost got an executive order allowing polygraphing in leak investigations up to the level of the Vice President. George Shultz effectively scotched the decision with a public threat to resign if ever asked to take such a test.

Technology of all kinds was brought into the offices of the keepers of the keys in unprecedented fashion in the Reagan years. The two main elements were the crisis center and the introduction of desktop computers netted with a mainframe operated by the White House Communications Agency.

As regards the crisis center, the effective precedent was probably the operations center of Ronald Reagan's 1980 political campaign. At times that had operated on a twenty-four-hour basis like a military headquarters, making efforts to predict the likely impact of events on voters as they unfolded. Simulation of voter behavior was an important part of the job, much of it done by Reagan's pollster Richard Wirthlin, assisted by Richard S. Beal, a computer expert who had taught at Brigham Young University. Beal proposed to computerize the National Security Council. It took four years and $10 million in computer equipment. A hallowed room of the Old Executive Office Building, one occupied by secretaries of state until the department moved to Foggy Bottom, became the NSC conference room.

Equipped with three VAX computers, the formally titled Special Situations Support Facility had the audiovisual equipment to call up data on file in many federal departments and agencies, plus the most modern communications. Most NSC principals saw the crisis center for the first time only during the Grenada conflict, when they had a long-distance teleconference with the President and George Shultz on a golf course in Augusta, Georgia. Some NSC subcommittees used OEOB Room 208 more regularly, units to a significant degree dominated by the NSC staff. Admiral John Poindexter, computer whiz and nuclear physicist, chaired the Crisis Pre-Planning Group (CPPG) that constituted the working-level backup to the Vice President's crisis unit. Later he received the added responsibility for the Terrorist Incident Working Group, and the Planning and Coordination Group, sometimes called the 208 Committee, which ran the administration's "Reagan Doctrine" secret wars. More than most, John Poindexter became the denizen of the crisis center.

Poindexter achieved greatness in the other aspect of the mechanization of the NSC; the computers. He supervised their introduction, then devised software to compartmentalize data and segregate knowledge. The basic operating system, the IBM Professional Office System (PROFS) was flexible with electronic mail and bulletin board features, where the national security advisers felt they needed restrictions. Executive secretary Robert M. Kimmitt, friend of James Baker and a holdover from the Brzezinski staff, wanted to preserve the old formal system in which all papers to the national security adviser went through him first. But something had to be done, the days when Brom Smith could route an NSC memo simply by stamping the corner of the document and ticking off a box were gone. The NSC staff under McFarlane hit a peak of 185, about a third of whom did most of the work. Routing slips on the papers this staff sent were printed forms with boxes or space for four dozen addressees.

One response was to segregate data and documents to reflect secrecy and sensitivity. Previous national security staffs had *filed* documents in ways that allowed them to be handled with special sensitivity, but no one had applied such handling concepts to documents from the instant of their creation. The NSC secretariat, in particular Brian Merchant, the White House Communications Agency, and Poindexter, cooperated on the details. Internal NSC documents, for example on administrative matters or travel vouchers, were grouped in System-I. By and large, these were files that could be kept in OEOB offices. Sensitive material of the traditional variety existed as System-II and was held by a secretariat vault open from 9:30 A.M. to 9:00 P.M., though often someone was still there for an hour afterward. System-IV documents were originally those originating within the NSC intelligence directorate, but later expanded to include other highly sensitive matters, which could be given this status simply by getting the custodian to assign a number for the document. A computerized log recorded the fact each time a document was withdrawn, moved to another office, approved, and so on. This record could only be made or changed by the NSC secretariat, the security adviser or his deputy, or the executive secretary. The document log allowed subordinate NSC staff to check the status of their projects and memos without taking up the time of the small rump of NSC staff who worked in the West Wing of the White House.

The System-IV documents were maintained separately from the NSC vault, in the safe of a special custodian in the OEOB offices of the NSC intelligence cluster. His files surpassed fifteen hundred documents for the first time in 1985, when the System-IV set had to be broken up, with the last two and a half years retained and earlier material sent to the vault. The active System-IV document set took up about two and a half file drawers inside a walk-in safe. Custodian of the System-IV records, and assigner of document numbers throughout Bud McFarlane's tenure, was James R. Radzimski, a Navy petty officer on detail to the NSC staff since the summer of 1983. The System-IV restrictions became crucial during the Iran-Contra affair, when an effort was apparently made to falsify some of the documents on record.

Tight restrictions on physical documents were replicated when it came to the communications channels allowed by the PROFS computer system. The national security adviser and executive secretary could communicate to any terminal on the system, but NSC staff had to go through Bob Kimmitt, then, after January 1985, William F. Martin. Admiral Poindexter went outside the formal system to arrange direct links to David Majors, NSC director for counterintelligence, and Colonel Oliver North, the latter channel dubbed Private Blank Check.

As had Judge Clark's, the McFarlane national security staff tried to promulgate regulations for information security widely seen as draconian. In this case, Poindexter spearheaded the effort to impose new standards for computerized and other information that would allow *un*classified and public record data, in certain circumstances, to be regarded as secret. The attempt reached the NSDD stage, only to be vitiated by implementation instructions that contradicted the directive. Though the specific effort failed, the tendency toward secrecy is clear.

At the apex of the structure stood President Ronald Reagan, the man all the elaborate machinery was supposed to assist. Instead, maneuvers to affect the President's information were the fiercest of all. That should have surprised no one. Blood had long been shed over which issues should reach the President's attention or topics be set for the National Security Council for debate.

In national security the lack of a firm presidential agenda invited the entrepreneurs to fight and refight policy battles. Many of the battles hinged on the very stuff of the information reaching the President. The major instrument for transmitting national security data in McFarlane and Poindexter's time, as before, was the President's Daily Brief (PDB) and the morning national security briefing.

The morning briefings returned to their usual time of 9:30 when Bill Clark reestablished them in 1982. Bud McFarlane maintained his contact with the President, including a secure direct telephone link from the West Wing to Camp David. For the time that Baker, Deaver, and Meese constituted the triumvirate, as many as seven people were at the morning briefs, including Ronald Reagan with his top people, George Bush with his chief of staff, plus the national security adviser and deputy. As McFarlane briefed the most important items of the PDB, Poindexter sat taking notes, rarely speaking unless questions were specifically addressed to him. Bud took no notes, but did list significant decisions as reminders to himself for subsequent action. He would go through the lists, marking out items as he dealt with them, then crossing out the page and putting it in his out-box. His assistant Wilma Hall treated those papers as material for shredding or burning. Once Poindexter succeeded McFarlane he stopped taking notes of sessions, though he continued making checklists. The admiral's secretary Florence Gantt collected the daily lists in something Poindexter called his 9:30 File.

Each day the report came up to Reagan adorned with extra material as the gatekeeper saw fit. Properly the PDB was a loose-leaf binder that included a CIA review, reflecting current events and the highlights of long-range estimates or monographs. For most of this period the Langley official producing the PDB was Richard D. Kovar. An NSC staff digest plus entries from the State and Defense departments completed the PDB, which averaged twenty to twenty-five pages in length. In addition, inside the PDB the national security adviser often added a file folder of documents. Donald Regan, who came over from the Treasury Department to be chief of staff, succeeding the triumvirate during Reagan's second term, was jealous of his prerogatives and thought he should see every paper going to Reagan. He was not allowed into the folders inside the daily briefs, so Regan reportedly struck back by doing away with McFarlane's direct phone link to Camp David.

Regan clashed more often with Bud over the degree of his control over NSC employees, giving rise to confusion later as claims were made of a national security role for the chief of staff. Regan really blew his top on the occasion of the death of Soviet leader Konstantin Chernenko in March 1985.

The next morning Regan encountered the President. "Gosh," President Reagan innocently remarked, "I didn't get much sleep thinking about [Chernenko] after I was told last night."

It was the first Regan had heard that anyone had woken up the President. The chief of staff asked Reagan when he had been informed and discovered it was at two-thirty or three-thirty in the morning. "I had words with Mr. McFarlane," Regan later told investigators. "If something untoward happened that would involve [movement] of the President, for the Chief of Staff to still remain in his bed asleep was most inappropriate so I wanted to be notified."

After that McFarlane consulted Regan first if he thought President Reagan needed to be told something late at night. Another time, in the summer of 1985 when Reagan went into the hospital, Regan prevented McFarlane from seeing the President at all for an interval of five days. Then Bud got twenty-three minutes with his President. According to McFarlane, Ronald Reagan's initial consent for arms deals with Iran occurred during that frantic conversation. Regan made it a point to attend the 9:30 A.M. national security briefings unless circumstances made that impossible, which typically happened once or twice a month.

Despite Regan's desire to be on top of everything, like the President himself, the chief of staff had neither time nor inclination to become closely involved in national security matters. Instead, Regan wanted to construct an image for the President, greatly restricting access to him. He clashed with McFarlane at or after council or NSPG meetings.

As Donald Regan took up his White House duties, Michael Deaver was phasing out of his. Deaver's last act before leaving was a publicity stunt that turned into a public relations disaster. Responding to a request from West German leaders, the idea was for the President to make a ceremonial visit to a German historical site. Michael Deaver simply missed out on the fact that Bitburg, the site selected for the honor of Reagan's visit, was a military cemetery some of whose graves contained the remains of Nazi SS troopers. Those particular graves had been covered by snow when Deaver had made his advance visit.

This error would never have been permitted by Henry Kissinger, Al Haig, or Zbig Brzezinski. The inability of the McFarlane staff to contribute to this function provides further evidence of its decline relative to earlier national security staffs.

Nor would McFarlane's predecessors have tolerated what was done to him in the name of "proper" functioning of the NSC machinery. Middle-level officials of the staff were prepared to fight their bosses in the name of some purist conception of Reagan's philosophy. Some subordinates judged seniors against their concept of the conservative ideal. Finding McFarlane wanting, these NSC subordinates thought nothing of going outside the NSC staff, trying to activate such players as Jeane Kirkpatrick or Bill Casey. No wonder Bud McFarlane feared he would be called "some kind of a commie."

An early paradigm of private agendas on the NSC staff was the Central America policy of Constantine Menges. An academic polemicist before joining Bill Casey's CIA, Menges was variously seen as a stalking horse for the director of central intelligence or a brash Reaganaut with a mind of his own in high-earth orbit. Menges was OSC also, yet one more of those naturalized American citizens who seem to figure so prominently in national security history; he was born in Istanbul, Turkey, on September 1, 1939. Recognized for his brilliance, Menges attended Columbia College, where he was a classmate of Mort Halperin. As a student, Menges became research assistant to Alexander Dallin, a Sovietologist known for a much more careful and thorough method than the strong prose and bold claims which predominated in Menges's writing.

Menges often tried to document cases where, he supposed, George Shultz's State Department was trying to make end runs around the President's policy. As NSC senior director for Latin America, Menges retaliated with some end runs of his own. In October 1984, for example, he succeeded almost single-handedly in shooting down a prospective Central American peace plan that might have been agreed upon on the eve of the election. He did it by getting copies of the text to Kirkpatrick and Casey, who predictably considered it heretical. On another occasion Menges drew up a twelve-page letter direct to the President telling Reagan that McFarlane and Poindexter were not "permitting" the NSC to function the way it was supposed to and were at times actively keeping Reagan in the dark. On yet another occasion the errant NSC staffer conveyed much the same message to a senator known to be close to the President.

Each of the entrepreneurs had an interest; for Menges that was Latin

America. The Grenada invasion had been a perfect debut but things went downhill quickly after that. Somewhat controversial in his previous incarnation at the CIA, when Menges arrived at the OEOB John Poindexter made a point of telling him the NSC staff's goal was to get along with the bureaucracy. Soon into the new year the CIA's secret plan to mine the harbors of Nicaragua turned sour, considerably complicating Reagan's problems in an election year.

After the mining fiasco, Menges learned that George Shultz was putting together a program for a compromise peace with Nicaragua under the rubric of the "Contadora" nations, Central and Latin American countries standing for peace in the region. Menges and much of the rest of the bureaucracy opposed any success by the Contadora countries. He held that the position Shultz was preparing contained concessions contrary to agreed policy. According to Menges, Bud McFarlane resisted scheduling an NSC meeting on Central America until he threatened to take the problem to NSC principals—Bill Casey, Cap Weinberger, and Jeane Kirkpatrick.

The council session of June 25 was the stormiest Menges ever saw. It lasted a full hour past schedule, something unheard of in Reagan's administration. However, the summary of discussion at that meeting, which was declassified in the course of the later trial of Oliver North, reveals very little talk of negotiations. Rather the council focused upon where to find money to make up for CIA aid to Nicaraguan rebels, which Congress terminated after the CIA harbor mining.

George Bush told the group he did not see "how anyone could object" to the United States "encouraging third parties to help." Bill Casey brought the opinion of the CIA general counsel that United States solicitation of money for the rebels was legal. Secretary of State Shultz went against the consensus, opposing solicitation, reporting that Jim Baker held similar views. "If we go out and try to get money from third countries," Shultz had said, "it is an impeachable offense."

Bud McFarlane summarized the sense of the meeting that there be no authority to solicit until more information was obtained. Bud said nothing of the solicitation that had already occurred, for several nights before the national security adviser had personally made the key pitch to Saudi Arabian diplomats. McFarlane ended up, "I certainly hope none of this discussion will be made public in any way."

Ronald Reagan seconded that, and got in the last word. "If such a story gets out," the President said, "we'll all be hanging by our thumbs in front of the White House until we find out who did it."

Even as the NSC met in Washington, American special presidential envoy Harry Shlaudeman was opening bilateral talks in Manzanillo, Mexico, with Nicaragua's Deputy Foreign Minister Victor Hugo Tinoco. Among Shlaudeman's retinue, to keep an eye on him for the NSC staff, was Ray Burghardt, Menges's assistant since the spring. Washington and Manzanillo had arranged a telephone code that might or might not allow Shlaudeman to present the United States compromise plan. The approval never came. Instead, Reagan's decision against any concessions was expressed in an NSDD sent out only two hours after the NSC meeting itself.

The decision did not stick. State replied to the NSDD with a memo giving lip service to the Reagan policy while advising it wished to use the Shultz peace plan as one means of achieving Reagan's goals. Another NSC session was therefore necessary toward the end of July. This included a scene involving George Shultz and Cap Weinberger, in which the secretary of state seemed to Menges to want to bar the President himself from leaving the room.

Afterward Menges dropped by John Poindexter's West Wing office on NSC business. The admiral looked up from his lunch tray. "You are causing all this trouble!" Poindexter shouted. "It's your job to see that these problems don't come to the president. You're not doing your job!" Menges was astonished at this outburst from the normally placid deputy national security adviser.

Admiral Poindexter told Menges to forget about drafting any Nicaragua NSDDs; he would put Ollie North on it instead.

Menges also managed to trigger an eruption from super-controlled Robert McFarlane. That came in mid-October, when Shultz was attempting to deliver a Contadora treaty on the eve of the United States elections, and indeed Managua pulled out the stops and seemed to agree to every United States stipulation. Menges torpedoed the option, again by going through the NSC principals. When Menges began his morning update at the senior director's staff meeting on October 15, McFarlane suddenly broke in.

"Constantine, your actions in this matter have been *subversive!*" Bud roared. "You talked to the press, and you've talked to Congress! Your actions are entirely out of line!"

McFarlane never spoke to Menges again, except for official exchanges. Embattled, Menges was reduced to producing memoranda defending himself and his effectiveness. In August 1985, McFarlane, afraid to fire Menges for fear he might go public, moved him over to the Office of Public Diplomacy (OPD). Ray Burghardt took over Central America, but never caught up with Colonel Oliver North, who by then began to assume a critical role.

At Public Diplomacy, Menges was under Walt Raymond, though the chain of command became sticky because Constantine retained his rank of special assistant to the President. McFarlane and Poindexter, however, no longer permitted him to attend the office director staff meetings. Raymond represented Public Diplomacy, Burghardt Latin America, and Oliver North the portfolio for the Nicaraguan rebels, *contras* as they were called. The product of twenty months' work handling the NSC Latin America account was 800 memos, 290 of them from the period before Menges had anyone to help him. Constantine had worked closely with certain individuals who kept him in touch with internal matters at State and Defense.

Elliott Abrams came in as assistant secretary of state for Latin America just as Menges was giving up the portfolio. Menges recalls trying to warn Abrams about Ollie North, not to trust anything North might say without checking it out with other sources first. Menges and subordinate staffer Jacqueline Tillman had caught North forging their initials for concurrence on his memos to the national security adviser. Menges felt North's boasting went too far, crossing into the substance of matters, and that he held the classic military staff notion of boxing in superiors to predetermine their decisions. Abrams did not seem interested in the warning, conveyed under a tree on the White House lawn, in the midst of a staff picnic in the July heat. Abrams also apparently did little with an instruction George Shultz gave him directly to "monitor Ollie." North and Abrams sat on the interagency SIG for Latin America, while Abrams also included North in the more exclusive Restricted Interagency Group (RIG) setting policy on Central America. North proved useful in Elliott Abrams's own effort to win a role as an entrepreneur.

Constantine Menges came to the Office of Public Diplomacy at the time it was perhaps most in vogue, coming off the perceived success of Radio Marti broadcasting into Cuba, and the success of its Nicaraguan information programs. In one case, that of the campaign against Nicaraguan MiGs, a wild rumor had been fanned into a minicrisis on the very eve of the American election. Walt Raymond's outfit and its operating arm, the Latin Public Diplomacy (S/LPD) unit, employed consultants who could suggest propaganda themes, write appropriate copy for releases and op-ed pieces, and do media appearances. Reserve officer, military consultant, and historian John F. Guilmartin published an op-ed piece in *The Wall Street Journal* that used government information and was written under government contract, but carried no indication of the affiliation.

The Guilmartin caper was among five similar cases of recent work that Jonathan Miller, deputy director of the S/LPD unit, offered as examples of recent achievements in a March 13, 1985, memorandum. Miller specifically called the projects "white propaganda." Ambassador Otto Reich was out of the country when the Miller memo was sent to the White House, and insists he would have stopped it had he been at the office. Reich calls the claim an exaggeration, insisting that military officers temporarily assigned to public diplomacy were researching case studies on Latin insurgencies, not planning propaganda campaigns.

S/LPD, among its other activities, awarded classified contracts for the care and feeding of Latin defectors to a company called International Business Communications (IBC). IBC also served as conduit for funds raised in behalf of the Nicaraguan rebels by the Channel Group of charities.

Otto Reich's office grew and grew, from himself alone to about twenty staff by the time he moved on to become ambassador to Venezuela. In 1986, LPD moved from the secretary's office within the State Department to that of the assistant secretary for Latin America. Instead of reporting to Kenneth Dam, Reich began to see Elliott Abrams.

By that time Constantine Menges and other Reaganaut staffers were bitter that their access was being cut off, that they were simply being used to give the NSC staff a conservative veneer. Bud McFarlane was indeed trying to work around these people, and had let go some eight senior staff when he came in with Judge Clark. By 1985, with Bud the gatekeeper and the laconic Poindexter his deputy, the Reaganauts felt quite isolated. Menges and like-minded cohorts banded together to express their estrangement. One time they met in the White House mess, another in Constantine's office; the press spoke of a "Madison Group," named for a meeting room in a downtown hotel. Among them were Christopher Lehman, eclipsed as legislative liaison by McFarlane's personal efforts; Gaston Sigur, top Asian specialist; Roger Robinson, exposed by questionable dealings with Israel about an Iraqi pipeline; and Kenneth de Graffenreid, senior director for intelligence. Writing from inside sources, columnists soon commented that only two of the original Allen staff still remained with the NSC.

Menges too could see the coming end. Friends told him NSC executive secretary Rodney McDaniel planned a breakfast where he would request Constantine's resignation. Instead all he got was a brief note from McDaniel. Menges's last act for the OPD was to accompany Elliott Abrams up to lobby Capitol Hill one day. He found Ollie North with Fawn Hall already there. After one briefing Poindexter's office asked him to desist.

BEST LAID PLANS

▲▲▲

A preoccupation with terrorism became probably the single most obvious defining characteristic of Reagan foreign policy. The irony is that it was Alexander Haig who had first raised the antiterrorism banner in those barely remembered days at the dawn of Reagan's presidency. This was another of those places where the erstwhile "vicar," run out of town for his presumption, was more successful than he knew. Unfortunately the policy path led Ronald Reagan to pretend that selling arms was foreign policy and that ransoming hostages was *not* dealing with terrorists, or that no arms had been exchanged for the hostages. At the end, after all the arms, all the money, *and* all the rest of the Iran-Contra activities, there were *still* American hostages in Lebanon, a problem Reagan bequeathed to his successor. President Reagan had been no more successful than Jimmy Carter, while the tactics to which he resorted considerably cheapened American credibility, skirting the very edge of legality.

Seven Americans were seized in various kidnappings in Beirut between March 7, 1984, and June 9 of the following year. On June 14, 1985, Shiite Lebanese hijacked TWA Flight 847 out of Athens, beginning a two-week odyssey across the Mediterranean, from Algiers to Beirut and back, and an experiment in mass hostage taking. Presidential advisers this time were determined that hostage takers were not to be seen as influencing the United States. No one argued that Reagan should return to Washington for the crisis. John Poindexter nonetheless convened the CPPG in Room 208. Two days into the crisis there came a moment of elation as the hijackers released sixty-four of the hostages, but thirty-nine Americans, plus the TWA air crew, remained. The military moved forward detachments of their Delta Force commandos but could not do anything with them.

Before Haig left government there was a directive on the books, NSDD-30, that awarded the State Department the primary role for formulating policy against terrorism. The CIA gained greater responsibilities in NSDD-138, which vaguely hinted at retaliation for acts of terrorism and even preemptive attacks. But no part of this directive was ever implemented; it fell victim to the fierce differences between George Shultz and Cap Weinberger. In addition, the cautious CIA deputy director, John McMahon, had found Ollie North, who was doing the NSC drafting on the directive, to be using language that might take the CIA across the bounds in the eyes of its congressional overseers.

George Shultz would have agreed with Ollie North about preemption and retaliation against terrorists. At about the time of the NSDD-138 imbroglio, the secretary of state gave a speech publicly calling for retaliation to terror, even recognizing that sometimes the perpetrators are not known for certain. Shultz's speech was a sort of public reply to Weinberger, who in a speech of his own had set down a list of conditions that needed to be met before using military power.

The fine points of antiterror doctrine lost meaning in the TWA 847 affair, when the commandos moved to the front but there was no possibility of using them. President Reagan conceded as much in public statements on June 18 and 23. Eleven days into the crisis, on June 25, Reagan met for the first time with his National Security Planning Group. McFarlane favored threatening a blockade of Beirut, something all the factions would have suffered from, perhaps inducing them to cooperate to stop the terrorists. Hints of a new use of force actually brought Lebanese Amal militia leader Nabih Berri to intervene with the hijackers, taking custody of the hostages, who were released on June 27. The hijackers themselves disappeared into the shadows of Beirut's nether world.

During its last few days the Americans had played the TWA 847 affair for all it was worth, increasing their demands for release of *all* hostages held in Beirut, i.e., those seven other Americans, a librarian here, a priest there, who had literally been snatched from the streets of the city. Most embarrassing of them all was the kidnapping of William Buckley, CIA station chief. Buckley was interrogated at length after being made a hostage on March 16, 1984, and died in captivity.

As he had done in ordering a Middle East directive only after the Marine bombing, it was after the TWA 847 episode that Reagan decided he wanted a policy review on measures to counter terrorism. The President declared formation of a Task Force on Combatting Terrorism, and on July 20 he signed NSDD-179 with instructions for the study group. Vice President George Bush was put in charge, with Admiral James L. Holloway, former Chief of Naval Operations, as staff director.

Bush appears to have been assiduous in tracking down reports, getting the official word on the operation of units ranging from the Delta commandos to Team Six of Navy special warfare people. Even Constantine Menges, by now almost cut off from policy input at the NSC, got a call from Bush when the Vice President heard, through his brother, that Menges had worked out an analysis of the terrorism problem and had some practical suggestions for steps to take.

Menges saw little reflection of his ideas in the unclassified version of Bush's final report, at first requested for the end of the year but actually rendered a couple of months later. The classified version was said to be so closely held almost no one knew what it said. The version Reagan released expressed confidence that existing antiterror programs were on the right track and endorsed anew the assertion that the United States would never "deal" with terrorists. The United States would engage in "judicious" retaliation. Vice President Bush held a news conference as his report was released.

"I think we should reiterate the willingness of our administration to retaliate and retaliate swiftly," Bush declared, "when we feel we can punish those who were directly responsible."

In fact, retaliation happened to be already in motion, though it was not called that and it was not aimed at terrorist groups at all, but at a sovereign state, Libya. The retaliation started as a naval maneuver of the Sixth Fleet in the western Mediterranean, designed to assert freedom of navigation in the Gulf of Sidra, which the Libyans claimed as territorial waters. It was the fourth of these challenges in the gulf, which the Navy had come to give an acronym, OVL for "operations in the vicinity of Libya." Previous operations had repeatedly triggered reactions from the Libyans, ranging from denunciation to encounters with the Libyan Air Force. In the very first OVL maneuver, American aircraft shot down a Libyan interceptor, leading to an early NSC dilemma over waking the President.

The 1986 OVL, code-named Prairie Fire, was planned to be provocative from the beginning. The original rules of engagement for this maneuver stated that the President was likely to order raids on five Libyan targets if there were *any sign* of hostile action. It was part of Reagan's program of graduated escalation against Qaddafi's Libya, which intensified after a Christmas 1985 incident—machine-gun attacks on the ticket counters of El Al airlines at the airports in Rome and Vienna. The terrorist incidents were eventually attributed to Abu Nidal's terrorist group, which had links to both Syria and Libya. Washington focused on Qaddafi, however, and Reagan imposed complete economic sanctions on January 7, 1986, the day after an NSPG meeting that also approved the OVL rules of engagement. A briefing memo for the meeting prepared by Oliver North, Howard Teicher, and military staff specialist James Stark, who was a captain in the Navy, suggested the United States would be able to attack Libya with impunity if cruise missiles were used. The Navy was left to its own devices, however, and preferred to use manned aircraft from its Sixth Fleet carriers.

Even more secret than the OVL planning was the work being done on the contingency of attacks on Libya directly after terrorist incidents, and United States efforts to entice Egypt into some kind of joint effort to "redraw the map of North Africa," as CIA intelligence director Robert Gates put it. The CIA had already attempted covertly to overthrow Qaddafi by engineering a revolt; now the Reagan administration was moving to consideration of even more ambitious gambits. The OVL maneuvers, and the retaliatory bombing and joint anti-Libyan action plans, were like three tracks of policy—the Reagan NSC had done Henry Kissinger one better.

At the Pentagon, Weinberger and the Joint Chiefs of Staff wanted no

503

part of any invasion or occupation of Libya, which was implied by the joint action proposal. They provided the White House an estimate of the forces necessary to subdue Libya: ninety thousand men in six divisions, consuming all United States strategic reserves and probably many NATO committed forces. Even then there was no guarantee that American forces would not become tied down in a long campaign against guerrilla resistance. In their opposition to the joint action option, reportedly code-named Flower, the Chiefs may have seen the other policy tracks as less objectionable and encouraged them.

Across the Potomac the White House appeared to be pushing the Flower planning. Soon after the conclusion of the TWA 847 affair, Bud McFarlane told the President that stronger measures were necessary to stop Libyan support for terrorism. Bill Casey promised to do a target analysis, while the CIA produced a special estimate on the Libyan challenge to the United States, plus the Bob Gates paper on action in concert with Egypt. At the end of August, Admiral Poindexter, staffer Donald Fortier, and a senior CIA official made a secret trip to Egypt where they tried to enthuse the Egyptians on Flower. Egyptian and Libyan intrigues conflicted in the Sudan and elsewhere, and Qaddafi had made attempts at assassination in Egypt.

"Look Admiral," Egyptian President Hosni Mubarak interrupted, before Poindexter could even get through his prepared remarks, "when we decide to attack Libya it will be our decision and on our timetable."

Within two months of the *Achille Lauro* incident, John Poindexter succeeded McFarlane as national security adviser. Don Fortier moved up to principal deputy. Thus the keeper of the keys and his chief acolyte were both well aware of the Flower project and supported it. Reagan also approved augmentation of the existing CIA covert program against Libya in a presidential finding toward the end of 1985. The CIA component of the Flower project was reportedly called Tulip, the military side Rose. An abortive coup attempt against Qaddafi actually took place in late November.

As part of the continuing relationship with Egypt, the Joint Chiefs planned to send a mission of their own, the chief of plans and policy on their Joint Staff, Lieutenant General Dale A. Vesser, to Cairo. It was an attempt to involve Mubarak in the appearance of joint planning if not the fact. *The Washington Post* got wind of the story and was going to print it on January 24. At 5:00 P.M. on January 23 who should show up in the *Post* newsroom but Admiral John Poindexter. The national security adviser went to editor Ben Bradlee and argued against publication of this story and others on espionage. These were national security matters; Poindexter insisted there was nothing going on with Libya; publication of the Vesser story would foreclose the President's options. Bradlee went along to the extent of cutting the story back to a vague reference in a different article. Poindexter protested even that much of a story. He also delayed General Vesser's trip to Cairo. No one caught the mention in *The Washington Post*.

Meanwhile, in the front channel the national security advisers worked up to the Navy's OVL maneuver. President Reagan gave final approval on March 14, when he signed an NSDD after a session of the National Security Planning Group. The aggressive rules of engagement were definitely intended. At the subordinate Crisis Pre-Planning Group (CPPG) the keepers of the keys clashed with the JCS on the question. Don Fortier, chairing the meeting that day, asked General John H. Moellering, representing the Chiefs, to describe how the rules of engagement would operate.

Moellering described it in a word: "Proportionality."

Fortier suddenly erupted, an edge in his voice, like an angry teacher with a recalcitrant student, "They should be *disproportionate!*"

Washington anticipated the Sidra patrol with relish, clearly expecting combat. The rules of engagement permitted the Navy to fire first if it decided an adversary had "hostile intent." The night of the penetration, much of the top brass gathered at command centers at the Pentagon, Langley, and the White House, to listen to the front line action. For Navy Secretary John Lehman it was almost a festive occasion.

The naval forces managed to get into action famously. Several Libyan naval craft at sea were deemed hostile and sunk. After the Libyans fired SAM missiles at American aircraft the task force went back and bombed the Libyan antiaircraft sites. President Reagan felt the raids a resounding success. Then the OVL operation was halted at about 1:30 P.M. of March 26, Washington time.

That morning's *Washington Post* had a story by investigative reporter Bob Woodward revealing the existence of the Flower project and some details, including the secret mission to Egypt by Poindexter and Fortier. That afternoon an NSC staffer, speaking for the keepers, told Woodward, "You've got to know, there is such unhappiness over here." Fortier was described as more upset than he had ever been.

Poindexter phoned Ben Bradlee two days later to protest the Woodward story personally. According to Woodward's account, presumably from Bradlee, the admiral was most upset about their names appearing in the paper. "When it's in the paper, it focuses their thinking," the admiral said, then confirmed he meant terrorists focusing on him as a target.

Bradlee thought it sad the national security adviser was making these protests to the *Post*. There was just no meeting of the minds. In January, when Poindexter proved more successful with the *Post*, Bradlee could not understand how a story on Libya breached national security if nothing was going on, as the admiral assured him. Many previous national security advisers had tried to stop, or protest, countless stories in the past. Poindexter's ineptness sowed distrust neither he nor the National Security Council could afford.

Actually Poindexter had not long to wait for a terrorist strike, but it was not against himself. Instead, a bomb exploded at La Belle, a dance club in Berlin popular with American soldiers, at 1:49 A.M. on April 5. Two Americans and a Turkish woman were killed and 229 persons were injured, including 78 more American troops. Communications intercepts reportedly show Libyan connections to the bombing. The West Germans remained cool to this interpretation, perhaps owing to the fact that the brother of the suspected bomber, picked up in a different terrorist action, proved to be linked to *Syrian* intelligence. Attribution to Libya of the La Belle discotheque bombing may or may not have been accurate but it was a rush to judgment: Washington hastened to activate its second policy track, the retaliatory bombing contingency.

Howard Teicher completed a discussion paper for the NSC by April 7, while the Pentagon updated its January plans. Poindexter immediately convened regular sessions of the CPPG. United States ambassador to the United Nations, Vernon Walters, traveled to Europe to attempt lining up support for American action. Margaret Thatcher agreed to allow the F-111s stationed in England to be used in the bombing mission, but France refused to allow overflights of its territory, forcing the Air Force to fly down and around Gibraltar lengthening the flight route by a thousand miles.

President Reagan held meetings at the White House on April 12 and 13, giving final approval at the second. The operation, called El Dorado Canyon, was closely monitored by Rodney McDaniel, NSC executive secretary, who began to host the CPPG in his own office. The NSC staff role was carried by Teicher, Oliver North, and the Navy's Captain James Stark.

On April 14 the Navy and Air Force carried out the bombing. Targets included the base housing one of Qaddafi's residences, plus commando schools, intelligence facilities, air bases, and so on. It remains in dispute whether the death of Qaddafi was a goal of the mission. Qaddafi himself escaped, though one of his daughters died under the bombs and other relatives were wounded. The planes got into the exact target areas planned, but the results were less surgical than the Americans wanted. Damage included the French embassy in Tripoli. One Air Force F-111 was lost in the mission with its crew of two. The Navy suffered no losses. Admiral Poindexter probably thought it was his finest hour.

Everyone's description of John Marlan Poindexter was "technocrat," which described both his function and personality. He was distant, introspective, not just cold but air-conditioned. Tough too; that was probably the admiral's image of a ship's captain at sea. "You learn to be cool," Poindexter once told Bob Woodward, reflecting that it made him a better national security adviser. Holding his pipe, the admiral told the reporter, "Naval officers are better equipped because of command at sea. You have to make decisions; you learn there is nobody else out there in a pinch." The NSC staff became the ship and he was the captain; *he* made the decisions. Poindexter made that clear in his outburst against Connie Menges: The problem *had gotten to* the President, Menges was *not* doing his job. But when Poindexter reached his pinnacle of command at the NSC, he lacked the resources to move the bureaucracy. Having kept away from the President, he was forced to invoke Reagan's name to get anything done, only to have to explain later why Ronald Reagan did not know all about those things that had been done in his name.

Actually Poindexter had made his way in the Navy more as staff aide than a commander at sea. He had commanded the missile cruiser *England* from 1974 to 1976, and had later commanded a cruiser-destroyer squadron. He had served in the Atlantic, western Pacific, and Indian oceans. On the other hand, Poindexter had been an aide for three years in the McNamara Pentagon, then again for three years under Navy Secretary John Warner. Poindexter thought it permanent enough duty to buy a house in Rockville, Maryland, in 1971.

Poindexter had a problem solver's mentality. In his first duty assignment, to a destroyer in the Atlantic, he found he did not know enough about electronics, so he went to the California Institute of Technology and got a Ph.D. in physics under Nobel laureate Rudolph Mössbauer, where he wrote a solid dissertation on electronic shielding, a subject important to intelligence work and nuclear warfare analysis.

Poindexter was the son of Marlan Poindexter, owner of the only bank in Odon, Indiana. He had been first in his class (1958) at Annapolis and also midshipman brigade commander, a double distinction that otherwise is held only by Douglas MacArthur.

In the Navy, Poindexter received outstanding fitness reports, citing him for brilliance, for a photographic memory, for knowing how to recognize which were significant problems and which were not. Later at the NSC some accused Poindexter of having an engineer's mind, difficult to bring to see things in new ways, fastening on details rather than looking at the big picture. Brent Scowcroft is said to have warned McFarlane that Poindexter was out of his depth and should be sent back to active duty.

"Poindexter improperly took a military man's view of the job," Scowcroft affirms in retrospect. The admiral saw a chain of command to the President and the President *commanded*. It was the same mistake as that of the Reagan ideologues, who believed the President *ruled*. Both lost sight of the reality of the political presidency, governing by balancing delicate interests and nodes of power.

The opposite of McFarlane, who had liked working with the politicians, Poindexter saw such activities as a waste of time. The most the admiral would do was make a few calls a week to key legislators. Only for a *contra* humanitarian aid vote in the spring of 1986 did Poindexter become significantly involved in the legislative liaison work. The task devolved upon Ronald K. Sable, the NSC staff specialist for that area.

Things might have gone better for the admiral but for the departure of Don Fortier. One of those Jackson Democrats, who had gotten a master's under Albert Wohlstetter at the University of Chicago, Fortier had come to the NSC staff after a stint as deputy director of the Policy Planning Staff for Al Haig. He handled arms sales, overseas training and exercises, and many items that had a congressional angle; Bud McFarlane, who had known Don on the Hill, used him increasingly on these tasks.

When Poindexter moved up to national security adviser, Fortier was promoted to deputy, and the admiral continued to use him to advantage on Capitol Hill. But Don Fortier had to leave owing to deteriorating health.

The loss of Fortier robbed Admiral Poindexter of his political antennae, a senior person who could be attuned to the most important nuances. Poindexter compounded the loss by *not replacing* Fortier, either as political factotum or as deputy national security adviser.

With the NSC executive secretary, Rod McDaniel, and the adviser's military assistant, Commander Paul B. Thompson, also Navy men, it meant that all the top NSC posts were in the hands of the military. Grumbling even started about a "Navy mafia" at the top. Poindexter bit the bullet and brought in Alton G. Keel, Jr., onetime Air Force official who had been an adviser to David Stockman and most recently executive director of the presidential commission investigating the fatal accident in January 1986 of the space shuttle *Challenger*. Keel had a Ph.D. in engineering, though he had at least worked on the staff of the Senate Armed Services Committee. It was not until September 1986, however, that Keel arrived to take up some of the load.

Admiral Poindexter marched ahead, his narrow focus unchallenged. Thus, when Mike Deaver eventually went on trial for trading on his White House access, Poindexter could testify he had seen nothing improper in Deaver's lobbying efforts for South Korea, Puerto Rico, or Rockwell International. Conversely, despite the absence of any clear legal grounds, when Bill Casey and National Security Agency director William Odom, Brzezinski's former aide, became frustrated in May and June 1986 with press reporting on espionage trials, Poindexter blithely went along with the suggestion the media be threatened with prosecution under the espionage laws.

This was the national security adviser who had answered "Maybe" when reporters asked him, on the occasion of his appointment, whether they would see him again. As it turned out, the media saw a lot more of Poindexter than anyone imagined. It also turned out that the internal operation of Poindexter's NSC staff became every bit as closed as his relationship with the press. The admiral saw the secrecy and compartmentalization as giving him room to move in Washington. Others saw Poindexter's role in a more sinister light, fearing the national security adviser, in effect, had become a disinformation agent.

As the dust settled after the April bombing of Libya, Poindexter faced a new situation. No one had agreed on what to do next. Two givens were that the Libyans had learned of Project Flower from press disclosure and that Washington had unprecedented amounts of naval capability in the western Mediterranean. With 3 carriers and 122 other ships, the Sixth Fleet was larger than it had been in many a year. Tempted to use force against

Qaddafi, Washington canvassed its options. In working-level groups Oliver North reportedly suggested mining Libyan harbors, but after the fiasco with mining in Nicaragua, there was little enthusiasm for that idea. The Libyans, in addition, were thought to be the perpetrators of the covert mining that had occurred in the Red Sea in 1982 and 1983. Use of this weapon might tempt Qaddafi to reply in kind.

On July 30, Rodney McDaniel met the Crisis Pre-Planning Group in his office. After some desultory talk, State was told to do a paper. With the paper in hand, a week later there was another CPPG session, which forwarded a plan to the NSC. The State paper in fact outlined a disinformation campaign—the paper itself used that word—designed to create instability in Libya and encourage the overthrow of Qaddafi. William Safire's version is that this idea was concocted at the CIA and sanctioned by its appearance as a State document. "Can you imagine a bureaucratic wimp like Poindexter," Safire writes, "opposing a policy originated by Casey and approved by Shultz?"

Actually George Shultz was quite capable of proposing such a policy all on his own. At the secretary of state's first press conference after the April bombing, he urged an end to Qaddafi's rule and presumably would have approved actions to reach that goal. In any event the State planning memo had been written by Richard Clarke of the Bureau of Intelligence and Research (INR), plus Arnold Raphel and Michael Ussery of the Near East Bureau. The plan called for creating a "three-ring circus" of contending threats within Libya by a program of "foreign media placements" and background news events for domestic press. It was public diplomacy writ large. An accompanying INR assessment called for the combination of "real and illusory events."

Around the time the paper circulated, Richard Kerr, the CIA's deputy director for intelligence, and Thomas Tweeten, the agency's top Middle East operations officer, visited the White House to provide details of the things Langley could do to put psychological pressure on Qaddafi.

The real event to give substance to the psychological pressure was an old-fashioned deception. The Sixth Fleet would again concentrate its surface forces off the Libyan coast, after an exercise in which one of its carrier battle groups maneuvered in conjunction with the Egyptians, suggesting collusion in that direction as well. The Navy would re-create the dispositions that had existed for the April bombing. Also, just as before the bombing, Ambassador Vernon Walters would be sent on a trip to rally the Europeans behind United States actions. Finally, a senior officer working for the JCS and visiting Chad, just to the south of Libya, could help create the impression that the United States had cooked up something with France to assist Chad's resistance to Libyan encroachments. With the right spin, the events might look like another El Dorado Canyon; Qaddafi wouldn't know where to turn next.

This plan received the CPPG imprimatur on August 7. The responsible

NSC staffers were covert action specialist Vince Cannistraro, a CIA officer who had previously headed Langley's own Libya task force, and political-military man Howard Teicher. Both of them supported the Libya disinformation plan. Teicher returned to his OEOB office to write a cover memo that would prepare NSC members for discussion of the State plan.

That summer of 1986 was definitely Howie Teicher's greatest moment on the NSC staff. In February the admiral had offered Teicher senior directorship over the political-military cluster. Meanwhile, Teicher's own Middle East senior director, James P. "Jock" Covey, returned to the State Department, making Howard the acting senior director until Dennis Ross arrived in May. In that time he was among the inner circle on Libya, a steadfast advocate of action. To celebrate the big bombing, Teicher invited his NSC colleagues out to dinner. Then came his thirty-second birthday and elevation to one of the top dozen jobs in one of the most select organizations in the nation.

In truth, Teicher had made a lucky connection with Bud McFarlane. That was after forging a link with Foggy Bottom during a summer internship in 1977. When McFarlane needed a sharp young fellow for special assistant in the summer of 1981, a few words sent him to Howard Teicher. The aide moved on with Bud to the NSC, where he settled into the Middle East cluster, later accompanying McFarlane on the Lebanese mission, and still later on the one to Teheran.

Faced with the State disinformation plan, Teicher had no doubt the United States should do that and more. The briefing memorandum for NSC members put a gloss on the Libya plan, with Teicher never using the word "disinformation" and collapsing into one the very different activities of planting stories in foreign periodicals and influencing domestic media.

Elaine Morton was a Foreign Service officer assigned to work on the NSC staff under Dennis Ross. A former Libya desk officer at State, Morton worried that the disinformation plan could backfire. She assembled a different memo, for Poindexter to send the President, which went over the details of the plan in such a way as to underline its dangers. This paper described the plan as intended to keep Qaddafi preoccupied and off-balance, and to paint him as "paranoid and ineffective" by means of "a series of closely coordinated events involving covert, diplomatic, military, and public actions." Morton was mistaken to hope explicit mention of some features of the plan would warn off Reagan.

Another man who worried was Vice Admiral Arthur S. Moreau, commander of naval forces in Europe, the immediate superior of the Sixth Fleet commander. Moreau's previous duty post had been assistant to the Chairman of the Joint Chiefs of Staff for NSC matters. In that capacity he had seen the NSC system at work in Lebanon and Grenada, and had sat with Ollie North through countless sessions of the Central America Restricted Interagency Group. Moreau worried the Libya plan could escalate into a real crisis and made his points to the JCS Chairman, Admiral William J. Crowe.

Admiral Poindexter welcomed Crowe and the others at the critical NSPG meeting of August 14 with warm approval of the military's performance in El Dorado Canyon. The time had come to follow up, Poindexter declared, and the State plan represented the best way to do it. Then the Joint Chiefs Chairman spoke up, "visibly disturbed" according to Bob Woodward, who made the original revelations of this affair in *The Washington Post,* and describes the NSPG scene in his book *Veil.* Admiral Crowe questioned whether this represented a proper use for military resources, warning that staging the Sixth Fleet and then doing nothing might in fact weaken the lesson supposedly taught by the April bombing.

According to Woodward, the President cracked, "Why not invite Qaddafi to San Francisco, he likes to dress up so much."

"Why don't we give him AIDS," George Shultz came back.

That repartee framed the discussion: Reagan appeared to have reached his decision already. In the corner Howard Teicher sat furiously scribbling notes for the record.

Two days later Ronald Reagan signed an NSDD authorizing the disinformation campaign, directing it be carried out under an existing presidential finding on Libya.

On August 25, *The Wall Street Journal* carried a story whose lead declared the United States and Libya were on a "collision course," and which then went on to talk about American military preparations and alleged Libyan plans for new acts of terror. Coming on top of the bombing, the story of impending crisis was too much to resist and both the print and broadcast media pursued it, reporting additional details over succeeding days. The official reaction from Reagan spokesman Larry Speakes was that the story was "not authorized but is highly authoritative." Admiral Poindexter quietly put out that he "felt it was a good thing to lay it all out."

The Libya story built for a few days, but the advertised crisis did not materialize. Cooler heads, advising caution at the height of the disinformation effort, now began to question the pattern of the leaks and what the motive might have been. Then a *real* leak occurred that fatally damaged the whole disinformation operation—Poindexter's August 12 memo to the President plus other papers. After spending a couple of weeks assembling and checking the story, Bob Woodward wrote it up and Ben Bradlee published it in the October 2 edition of *The Washington Post.* The result was pandemonium.

Had John Poindexter had better relations with the *Post,* this would have been a prime story to try stopping on national security grounds. Bill Casey had known for at least a week in advance that Woodward had the Poindexter disinformation memo. Howard Teicher spoke to Woodward but insisted the reporter already had the story. At the White House, Ronald Reagan denounced the "veracity of that entire story" but went on to admit that documents mentioned in the news report gave the *Post* "something to hang it on." Ten days later Poindexter was reduced to assuring all he "had no intention and did not plan or conspire to mislead the American press," while simultaneously insisting that deception should "be a tool that the government can use."

It was a lame apology for a sordid episode forgotten only because it was swiftly surpassed by even wilder tales of mayhem. In fact, the threads of secrecy still obscuring those tales were already unraveling, beginning on October 5 when a *contra* supply plane was shot down deep inside Nicaragua. That plane had been flying to targets furnished by NSC staffer Ollie North and belonged to private operators acting on North's instructions. The Reagan National Security Council staff had begun to look like a wild place indeed!

Howard Teicher had a central role in Iran policy in addition to Libya, primarily owing to the luck of the draw. Geof Kemp was at full stride in the summer of 1984, and Iran had been one of Kemp's primary interests. It was Kemp who wrote up the study directive for the administration's Iran policy review, NSSD-5-84, which Robert McFarlane signed on August 31, 1984. Late that year the State Department completed a draft NSDD for Reagan that would provide the first authoritative guidance for the administration on Iran policy. By then Kemp was phasing out, exhausted by the constant state of emergency that characterized NSC staff life. Teicher took the draft presidential directive to Don Fortier and John Poindexter, both of whom had trouble with it. The draft disappeared, Teicher told Iran-Contra investigators, because it had no official standing.

Such was the auspicious beginning of the Iran policy, which stumbled on from one Band-Aid solution to the next. In January 1985, Bud McFarlane approved an exploratory trip to Europe by consultant Michael Ledeen, and in May he sent Ledeen to Israel. Teicher and Don Fortier prepared a new directive on Iran, one presumably more acceptable to the President. This version drew on the original, so agencies would be able to recognize their original contributions, but it had a whole new slant more in line with the thinking of Teicher and allies like Graham Fuller at the CIA, national intelligence officer for the Middle East. In May, Fuller wrote a thoughtful memo suggesting several directions that might be taken, while several days later the CIA released a formal special national intelligence estimate (SNIE) on prospects for Iran after Khomeini. Both Teicher's NSDD and the Fuller memo speculated on the possibility of selling quantities of arms. That was when Ledeen returned to report there was interest in Israel in selling arms to Iran.

"I also think the Israeli option is one we have to pursue," Don Fortier told McFarlane in a note on May 28, "even though we may have to pay a certain price for the help."

In June, when the draft NSDD was ready, Fortier and Teicher told Bud the paper was so sensitive it should be circulated only on an eyes-only basis to Weinberger and Shultz. Weinberger's actual reaction to receiving the NSDD, by his own account, was to write "absurd" in the margin of his copy, though DOD's official reply on July 16 was couched more diplomatically. George Shultz also had choice words for the quality of this proposal. Only Bill Casey backed the policy and that was not enough, not on Iran, not after what the CIA had done and lost there. The 1985 presidential directive sank without a trace, just as had the one drafted the year before.

In an administration most often paralyzed by the conflicts between George Shultz and Cap Weinberger, it is particularly poignant that on Iran, *where the secretaries of state and defense agreed on something,* the policy went on despite them and left them behind. Before it was all over, the NSC staff would cut off the secretary of defense from intelligence ordered from defense agencies; and the staff would order the secretary of state kept in ignorance of business the White House conducted directly through the U.S. ambassador in Lebanon.

How could that happen? In two words, McFarlane and Poindexter. In essence, middle-level NSC staffers seized effective control of the policy, thinking they were carrying out the will of the President, ignoring the little games the President played with his political supporters. The NSC staff got so far in spite of its weak chiefs, not because of them, and primarily because the staff had acquired, by 1985, the kind of institutional power never before exercised by personal staffs.

In any case, the NSC principals heard little about Iran from the NSDD debacle of the summer to December 1985. Instead, the action moved directly into the NSC staff at its most senior level, with McFarlane. Early in August, Bud met with certain Israeli officials and arms dealers, who informed him the Iranians wanted to know if the United States would supply them with military hardware. They also told the national security adviser there was a prospect of getting the American hostages in Beirut freed. In some brief form, McFarlane claims, in early August the keeper took this proposal to the President at Walter Reed Hospital, where Reagan had just had cancer surgery. President Reagan agreed, according to McFarlane. Don Regan remembers the President only approving vague political contacts. Ronald Reagan had no recollection of the incident. On August 8 a National Security Planning Group meeting was held specially in the White House residence so the President, just returned from Walter Reed, could hear discussion on Israeli sale of antitank missiles to Iran. McFarlane has testified that Reagan approved the deal after the meeting. According to the plan, four of the American hostages would be freed in the bargain. According to testimony by Attorney General Edwin Meese, the President's decision constituted an "oral finding" that satisfied the requirements in law for authorization of covert operations.

There was a first shipment by the Israelis; supposed to be 100 antitank missiles, it was shorted at 96. Then another followed with the balance plus

400 more. In September, Ledeen informed McFarlane that the Israelis expected the United States to replenish their own stocks of the weapons sold, and they held out for the latest models too. Then, in November, came a delivery of antiaircraft missiles the Israelis routed through Portugal and botched badly, neglecting proper shipping documents for the transit, mistiming departure of the aircraft (during a Jewish holy day), then throwing the whole thing into the laps of the Americans.

Bud McFarlane was in Geneva when he learned about *this* headache. Bud was in the middle of the first Reagan-Gorbachev summit, with almost every minute prescheduled by the image makers. The national security adviser tried a quick stab at a solution—calling a senior Portuguese official late at night to intercede—when that didn't work McFarlane got North on a secure transatlantic phone link and told him to take over.

Once more into the breach went the Marines, or at least Marine Lieutenant Colonel Oliver North, whose intervention in the shipment of the antiaircraft missiles was his introduction to Middle East arms trading. North went to the CIA, which at least knew how to run an airlift, and the agency found planes and made arrangements to move the cargo to Teheran. When the plane delivered the missiles, the Iranians impounded them in order to return them later. The equipment was not of the exact type the Iranians thought they were buying, and there were only eighteen missiles against the eighty promised. The other side released only one hostage. To top it all off, John McMahon, the deputy director of central intelligence, who represented Bill Casey's good side, noticed that no presidential finding supported the CIA moves in Portugal to free up these arms and hire the contract air carrier that moved them onward.

Under Stanley Sporkin, the CIA general counsel's office labored to come up with a presidential finding that would retroactively authorize the CIA actions with regard to the November 1985 missile shipment. Everyone focused on the "retrospective" aspect of this authority. A suitable document went to John Poindexter, one of whose earliest acts in office was to take this finding to the President, apparently not concerned that the document explicitly authorized a trade of arms for hostages. President Reagan for his part approved the policy despite an NSPG session on December 6 where both George Shultz and Cap Weinberger and, according to some accounts, George Bush, all opposed the recommended action. Poindexter locked the finding away in his desk, not even putting it into the System-IV document flow. Later, when the affair became controversial, he destroyed it in front of military aide Paul Thompson, who happened to be the admiral's NSC lawyer on the side.

Poindexter also started the ball rolling for another presidential finding designed to bring private agents into the arms traffic between the United States and Iran. After the fiasco of the missile shipment, these private agents would supplant the Israelis. Introduced to the CIA general counsel and other key officials just before signature of this second presidential finding was

Richard V. Secord, a retired Air Force general and North lieutenant in *contra* operations. The President signed the revised finding on January 17, 1986.

Through almost a year General Secord and his associates organized several further United States arms deals. They carried over fifteen hundred antitank missiles to Teheran in addition to arranging for the aircraft and associated services. One more American hostage went free in Beirut. But Ollie North complicated the field there by mounting a competing effort to free hostages by ransoming them out. North asked Texas billionaire H. Ross Perot, a member of the President's Foreign Intelligence Advisory Board, to contribute cash to be used in the attempt. The end result was not much because, although two were freed, terrorists in Beirut kidnapped four more, *plus* the widely respected British hostage negotiator Terry Waite.

The maneuvering began with a new plan Ollie North put together early in December, followed by a meeting in London. Bud McFarlane went even though he had just resigned, met North there, and conversed with General Secord, Israeli official Yaacov Nimrodi, and the Iranian intermediary. The Iranian was Manucher Ghorbanifar, a man thought unreliable by the CIA and who would indeed fail more CIA lie detector tests when asked to take them. McFarlane did not think much of Ghorbanifar either, as he presumably made clear when he personally reported on the trip at an Oval Office meeting with the President on December 10. That did not slay the dragon, however, and Bud's consternation rose in succeeding months as North and Poindexter continued to deal with Ghorbanifar. Secord and North had extensive talks with Ghorbanifar and a representative of the Iranian government in Frankfurt, Germany, in February 1986, conversations supposed to be followed up by a second round with a delegation of Americans who were more official.

That was the start of the Teheran mission, for which North once again devised a plan anticipating release of all the American hostages as a sequence of arms shipments arrived for the Iranians. McFarlane, whom Poindexter retained as consultant to deal with the Iran matter, finally agreed to undertake the mission on behalf of the national security adviser. Bud would be billed as an emissary from the President. Howard Teicher was brought in because McFarlane trusted him and he could work on the terms of reference. Colonel North would be among the group, so he initiated an assistant, another Marine, Lieutenant Colonel Robert L. Earl. From the CIA, Bill Casey contributed an interpreter, George Cave, and a communications man. Once again McFarlane would take along the gear necessary for a satellite communications link through the Situation Room.

Rodney McDaniel's notes affirm that Ronald Reagan listened to a discussion of the hostages and the McFarlane trip at his daily briefing on May 12 and that he approved instructions three days later. Afterward Poindexter got Bud to drop by for a final orientation on the four-page instructions. When McFarlane asked the admiral whether Shultz and Weinberger were on board, Poindexter seemed reluctant to admit they were not. Instead, he attempted to imply approval, by telling the mission leader that both officials had participated in approval of the terms of reference. McFarlane was also unaware that the aircraft carrying his mission to Teheran would itself transport a pallet of the missile spare parts involved in the latest arms deal. The mission leader did not learn that until he arrived at Ben Gurion Airport outside Tel Aviv to board the plane, arranged for by Richard Secord, who remained in Israel coordinating the Teheran mission throughout. The final delegation consisted of McFarlane, North, Teicher, George Cave, Amiram Nir, who was terrorism adviser to the Israeli prime minister, and a CIA communications specialist. Also aboard was a chocolate cake, baked in the form of a key, from a Tel Aviv bakery, and a fine old edition of the Bible personally inscribed by Ronald Reagan.

McFarlane's plane arrived in Teheran on the morning of Sunday, May 25. There were difficulties immediately, at the airport, where no one seemed to be expecting them. Iranian guards made fun of the chocolate cake. McFarlane was undoubtedly steaming by the time his party was taken to the Independence Hotel where they were installed in a penthouse suite. Over the next several days there were desultory conversations at the hotel, formerly the Teheran Hilton, between the delegation and Ghorbanifar plus officials of the Iranian prime minister's office. McFarlane concluded the Iranians were not really going to get the Lebanese Shiites to release the American hostages, so he finally refused to release the weapons shipment. He did try to be conciliatory on questions of establishing a longer-term relationship. The Americans stressed, perhaps excessively, the putative *Soviet* threat to Iran. Embroiled in a life-and-death war with the Iraqis, that was not what Teheran wanted to hear. North, who had given the Iranians some Iraqi intelligence as a sample, did not volunteer any more. The Iranians tried a last-minute compromise under which they would take the weapons and release two hostages. McFarlane rejected the proposal.

"You are not keeping the agreement," McFarlane snapped. "We are leaving."

The Americans left the Independence Hotel about 8:00 A.M. on May 28. Fifty-five minutes later their Boeing 707 was airborne en route to Tel Aviv. McFarlane had had a second plane, with the weapons shipment aboard, turn around in mid-flight to abort the hostage transaction.

In all the Teheran mission was a desperate measure. McFarlane, North, and Teicher were three of the most knowledgeable current and former officials of the United States government. With the precedent of William Buckley before them, they had flown into the center of fundamentalist Islam. It was a brave but foolhardy effort that should never have been permitted, on security grounds alone, irrespective of the propriety of trading arms for hostages.

McFarlane subsequently explained his agreement to undertake this mission as being intended to demonstrate once and for all the uselessness of Iranian intermediary Manucher Ghorbanifar. But he still looked dejected as the plane flew back from Teheran. He would be mortified later to learn that North, Secord, and other associates went on trying to deal with the Iranians through a different intermediary.

When their plane landed at Ben Gurion once more, McFarlane's communicator lost no time setting up his dish antenna to transmit an early report to the President.

"Don't be too downhearted," Bud recalls North telling him on the tarmac. "The one bright spot is that the government is availing itself of part of the money for application to Central America."

There are other, more colorful versions of what Ollie North said to Bud that morning on the tarmac. But the crux of the matter is that North devised a structure to support the Nicaraguan *contras* that extended itself to the Iranian arms deals and the hostage bargaining in Lebanon. It was, according to North's sworn testimony before a joint congressional investigating committee, to be a private "off-the-shelf" apparatus created at the direction of William Casey. Casey, who died in 1987, cannot answer such claims. Admiral John Poindexter insists everything was perfectly aboveboard. Robert McFarlane declares he never gave instructions to North to run an activity, and indeed avers he *did* make clear to NSC staff they were to consider themselves bound by the Boland Amendment, a provision of law restricting United States assistance to the *contras*. Poindexter and North, not to mention Gaston Sigur and other staff, admit no recollection of McFarlane giving such orders at the daily NSC staff meetings. McFarlane also insists he explicitly instructed North *not* to make any solicitations whatsoever on behalf of the Nicaraguan rebels. North denies he made such solicitations. Amid the welter of claims and counterclaims surrounding the Iran-Contra affair, a few undisputed facts can be distilled. They show NSC staff clearly conducting field operations for the United States government. Poindexter took over a situation in which Colonel North already had the *contra* account. The admiral saw little reason to change the arrangements. It was Poindexter, after all, who gave North direct access to his computer, the password he called "Private Blank Check."

Ironically, there is another "Private Blank Check" in the history of the National Security Council, and it also had to do with operations. That was the title assigned to a file of back-channel communications from the Chicagoan, Bob Komer, on aspects of pacification in Vietnam. Komer had known how to invoke a President's name, and he had been a talented bureaucratic infighter who would yield to no one. Ollie North knew how to invoke his President too, and retailed a fund of apparent tall tales placing himself at the center of actions with Ronald Reagan and virtually every other senior figure of the administration.

Without the growth in the NSC staff's institutional power, Oliver North could never have accomplished so much. *Never,* because his colleagues had seen North in action: CIA Central America task force chief Alan Fiers told investigators he had seen Ollie play fast and loose with facts; Elliott Abrams had his warning to monitor Ollie; NSC Latin America colleagues Constantine Menges and Jacqueline Tillman actually caught North forging *their* initials on memoranda to NSC higher-ups. Joint Chiefs Chairman Admiral William Crowe denies a North story that had the Marine lieutenant colonel arguing with the JCS Chairman about appropriate tactics for the Libya bombing. Donald Regan reports that White House records make clear that Oliver North *never* saw the President or chief of staff alone, and only once spoke to Regan on the telephone, in contrast with another North tale. Yet another story North retailed, in which he argued strenuously with Reagan communications director Pat Buchanan about whether the President should go ahead with a misleading speech that helped deepen the scandal, has been denied as well. So have stories North told such journalist friends as David Halevy and Neil Livingstone.

Not all these instances were discovered by the subsequent investigations. Some were known at the time. Nothing revealed thus far suggests that North was disciplined for going beyond facts, any more than was Mike Ledeen for deliberately mistranslating the President's remarks to the prime minister of Italy, or Larry Speakes for inventing quotes for the President, or indeed John Poindexter for misrepresentations on the occasion of Grenada. The only possible conclusion is that such tactics were accepted practice in the Reagan administration.

In what can most charitably be described as an excess of zeal, Lieutenant Colonel Oliver North took it upon himself to do whatever was necessary to ensure continued support for the Nicaraguan *contras*. Where Bud McFarlane saw the mission as holding the rebels' hands, North interpreted it liberally. In this he apparently also went beyond colleague Don Fortier, who had the political side of the Nicaragua account until his tragic death.

The matter was important because of the Boland Amendment, but also because this kind of support implied operational activity on the part of NSC staff. McFarlane yielded that point in 1984, in the immediate aftermath of the harbor mining fiasco. Then Ronald Lehman and North accompanied CIA chieftain Dewey Clarridge on a trip to Honduras in which they were introduced to the rebel leaders as the new United States focal point, the NSC staff. The pudgy Lehman and the cigar-chomping North made an odd contrast in "Tegu," colloquial for the Honduran capital Tegucigalpa. Though Lehman merely stood in for Fortier and the legislative liaison people, North became a key figure in *contra* military operations for the next two years. McFarlane made the two big solicitations of money, from the Saudis, but there is evidence North spoke with representatives of several foreign countries, one of which donated a couple of million dollars to the *contras*.

One area where Ollie North was especially good was outreach, public information. A tough Marine, decorated Vietnam veteran and former instructor, Lieutenant Colonel Oliver North developed a standard Nicaragua briefing with slides he could present on demand, a talk he gave over a hundred times just for Faith Ryan Whittlesley's White House Office of Public Liaison. Other North talks were to groups of potential donors to the *contras*, assembled by conservative fund-raiser Carl Channell. On one occasion Bill Casey joked with North about donating a million dollars of his own, while on another occasion the CIA director sent donor Joseph Coors on to North to find out what he could buy for the Nicaraguan rebels.

It is worth noting that Channell's groups of donors were treated to situation briefings by Elliott Abrams and photo opportunities with President Reagan. Assistant Secretary of State Abrams also took time out from official duties to critique the story boards for pro*contra* advertisements the Channell Group planned as part of a media campaign.

Abrams and North sat together on the administration's Restricted Interagency Group on Central America. The RIG was another of the myriad elements of Reagan's NSC machinery, and probably a good illustration of how the policy entrepreneurs compelled the bureaucracy to act in ways that were atomized and incoherent. Abrams, like North, had a keen appreciation for RIG's potential as an entrepreneurial tool. Where Langhorne Motley, Abrams's predecessor, had begun to move in this direction, the RIG became much more exclusive under Abrams. Complaining of large, unwieldy meetings, Abrams held smaller sessions of a core group of RIG members. Often excluded were the State Department's own Bureau of Intelligence and Research and such critical implementing agencies as the Nicaraguan Humanitarian Assistance Office (NHAO), charged with delivering nonlethal aid to the *contras*.

The assistant secretary of state now excluded subordinates from RIG meetings too. Whereas previously Jackie Tillman, who held the NSC Central America account from early 1984, occasionally was invited, under Abrams she was not welcome. Even Ollie North's aide, Bob Earl, was denied entry when substituting for his senior director. That happened despite North's political-military cluster having responsibility for reporting on the RIG to the national security adviser. Still there was little to choose between Abrams and Colonel North. Jackie Tillman repeatedly found North taking her for granted, even retailing as a personal experience a story *she* had told him. When Tillman called him on it, Ollie argued for over twenty minutes that it *really was* his own experience. In fact, Tillman had originally heard the story from a third person altogether.

The straw that broke Tillman's back was an incident in the fall of 1984, toward the end of the rainy season in El Salvador. The United States had started to get intelligence suggesting Salvadoran guerrillas could be preparing a big offensive. Bud McFarlane used one of his television appearances to warn of a coming "Tet" in El Salvador. Jackie Tillman saw the intelligence and believed it, but even so came away feeling Colonel North was overstating the case. North was selling a project to counter the offensive with a series of covert operations Tillman thought very poorly conceived. The project might not work, disclosure seemed probable, and it would cause controversy in the middle of the reelection campaign.

Admiral Poindexter scheduled a Crisis Pre-Planning Group meeting to thrash out the proposal. In preparation, Tillman went to the Vice President's national security people, and to Ray Burghardt, whom she badgered until he agreed to talk to Poindexter. Tillman also went to Bill Casey, whom she had previously known while serving Jeane Kirkpatrick as executive assistant. When Tillman tried to get a look at North's memo for the CPPG, to see if it merited a dissent from the Latin American cluster, she could not get access. This was not some hostile implementing agency but a fellow NSC staffer. Furious, Tillman stalked out of North's office and headed for the West Wing to complain directly to Poindexter. By the time she got across the short street, North had called and gotten the admiral on the phone. Poindexter refused to see Jackie Tillman, who made her complaint to Commander Paul Thompson instead.

"His body language was more eloquent than what he actually said," Tillman later recalled. "He just sort of threw his hands up in the air."

A bitter taste in her mouth, Jackie arranged to switch assignments with Ray Burghardt, who would now handle Central America while Tillman took the South American continent.

Tillman was a Reaganaut, Burghardt a conventional Foreign Service officer, albeit one who had been friends with John Negroponte since Vietnam days. He had just finished a tour in Honduras as counselor to Ambassador Negroponte, widely perceived as a proconsul over the Reagan administration *contra* operation. Burghardt had seen Reaganauts before, indeed his first NSC boss had been Connie Menges, and he knew bureaucratic politics. It was not difficult to see Ollie North's ascendancy. There was more to be gained from playing along with North than from bucking him. Burghardt played along.

The power of operations was seductive. Moreover, as the CIA found with its own covert operations, there was a danger of either going native, transferring operatives' loyalties to the local ally, or becoming a "loose cannon" or "cowboy," not following the proper chain of command. There were recognized procedures the CIA would follow when that kind of thing happened under its control. The NSC staff, on the other hand, was answerable to no one save the President. With Admiral John Poindexter's view of his job as keeping contentious issues away from the President, some policy disaster was probably inevitable.

Poindexter's "vague recollection" is that before McFarlane first talked to the Saudis, Ollie was asked to do some kind of a cost estimate for what it would take to keep the *contras* in the field. Days afterward an NSPG meeting set the marching orders. By then North had already recruited a go-between who could serve as courier, Robert W. Owen, formerly of the Senate staff of Dan Quayle, who used the *nom de guerre* "Armando." He was paid first by *contra* leader Adolfo Calero and later as a consultant to the NHAO aid office. By July 2, 1984, Owen was sending North letters discussing weapons requirements using the shallow euphemism "firecracker costs." Later that month North attended the Republican National Convention in Dallas, where he held direct meetings with Calero and where wealthy widow Ellen Garwood was convinced to put up the money for the *contras* to buy a new helicopter. In August, North himself made a trip to Central America. Approving the travel voucher, Bud McFarlane instructed the NSC staffer, "Exercise absolute stealth."

Over the winter of 1984–1985, Colonel North involved himself supplying packets of intelligence for the *contras,* some of them pertaining to specific targets and plans. Rob Owen carried three packages of this material to Honduras from December to April. Ollie also met with a senior Red Chinese general to discuss antiaircraft missiles and tried to get McFarlane to intercede with the British to permit Chile to export Blowpipe antiaircraft missiles to the *contras.* The NSC Marine helped Calero look for a British soldier of fortune who might be willing to carry out commando missions inside Nicaragua. David Walker, a veteran of the Special Air Service, eventually was hired and made scouting trips into the country. North also got NSC colleague Gaston Sigur to introduce him to Nationalist Chinese representatives. There appears to have been some effort here to follow up private solicitations made by retired Army General John Singlaub. Taiwanese sources contributed $2 million to the *contra* cause.

The most important initiative taken that winter was formation of an entity that had paramilitary capabilities, enabling the *contras* to step up their military campaign inside Nicaragua. At Langley they would have called this a proprietary. Poindexter later told investigators he could understand how people could think the NSC entity was a proprietary, but it wasn't. Former Air Force Major General Richard Secord, the key operator in the NSC proprietary, has testified that he was asked to do the job, and that he himself recruited Iranian-American business associate Albert A. Hakim, who set up a corporation called Energy Resources, which made its first registered transaction in November 1984. The Secord-Hakim group started out selling arms to Calero's *contra* forces. General Secord was first introduced to Calero by Oliver North in his OEOB office. Later the same evening Secord picked up the Nicaraguan for their first direct talks.

Oliver North's role deepened as he facilitated the activities of Secord, Singlaub, and other "private benefactors" helping the *contras.* In February 1985 he recommended pirating a Nicaraguan ship on the high seas to divert its suspected cargo of North Korean weapons to the *contras.* In June, when NSC colleague Lewis Tambs, who had been made ambassador to Costa Rica, was leaving for his station, North told him the primary mission would be to help open up a second front against the Sandinista government forces. The colonel cited RIG as his authority for the instructions, which Elliott Abrams would later deny. In July, North presided over a *contra* council of war, a late-night affair in a conference room of the hotel at Miami International Airport. Running late, Ollie finally made it, only to face a gloomy recitation of *contra* military failure attributed to scarce supplies in the field. The group made the key decision to ask Secord to set up an airlift. That in turn committed North to an unprecedented degree of *contra* support work. On August 31, 1985, John Poindexter gave Ollie the "Private Blank Check" link to his computer.

All of this would have strained the capacity of an ample staff much less a single forty-two-year-old Marine officer. Organizing a military-style operation was second nature to Ollie, who had been a training battalion operations officer from 1978 to 1980, but he had not exercised the responsibilities of command since September 1974, when he gave up leadership of a training detachment on Okinawa, and he then spent four years as a policy analyst at Marine Corps headquarters. By the time of Nicaragua, or Project Democracy as he liked to call the operation, North could draw on a decade of experience as a staffer.

Commissioned a Marine lieutenant, Oliver North's combat experience and troop command occurred in Vietnam, where he led an infantry platoon and company in Quang Tri Province. North won Silver Star and Bronze Star medals, along with two Purple Hearts for combat wounds. One man whose life North saved by getting him to an aid station in time became a lifelong associate. When North had to develop a network for the Secord airlift operation, he brought in his Vietnam buddy, who assumed the name "Frederick Olmsted."

With Ollie North stretched so thin, inquiries were inevitable. Bud McFarlane got one from Lee Hamilton, chairman of the House Intelligence Committee, and another from Democrat Congressman Michael D. Barnes of Maryland. Bud's solution was to supply assurances in letters drafted by North. To base the responses on something solid, Bud had Paul Thompson and Brenda S. Reger of the NSC secretariat conduct a document search somewhat more limited than that during the Billy Carter affair. Reger, who had been a fresh gofer in the documents during the earlier search, had a good idea of what was required. The search did turn up a number of documents, in particular a half-dozen System-IV items, referring to activities by North that might be questionable under the Boland provisions. Mc-Farlane made a list of the document numbers, then held talks with Commander Thompson and Colonel North. Bud rationalized away North's work on behalf of the *contras,* including the activities outlined already. That was enough to support a letter to Congressman Hamilton denying a whole series of charges.

The Barnes inquiry was more complicated because he asked for documents and access to material to make an independent determination. The national security adviser solved that crisis by refusing access to anyone on Barnes's staff, giving the congressman personal assurances at a meeting deliberately kept too short for detailed examination, then offering Barnes himself an opportunity to look at documents, which contained North's problem memos but among a tall stack of other material. Barnes chose to accept the verbal guarantees. A letter followed to reiterate them. McFarlane later pled guilty to criminal charges based in part upon these obfuscations, and North was convicted by a trial jury of criminal counts embodying them.

What Bud McFarlane did was warn North to lower his profile. Bud counseled Ollie that it might be time to move on and attend the National War College. Dick Secord also advised Ollie to take the ticket, which would have taken him away from the *contras* but might have reopened the path to troop command. Ollie North had already twice extended his tour on the NSC staff, with dispensation by the Marine commandant. Still determined to see it to the end, North dismissed the idea. Instead, he took McFarlane's list of System-IV problem memos and taped it to the side of his computer.

Ollie North's steadily increasing status, further embellished by a December 1985 Poindexter whirlwind tour of Central America, received symbolic recognition in early 1986 when he was moved to OEOB Room 302, an office suite, and given two subordinate staff members. Both new staffers were brought into the NSC by way of the Crisis Management Center, and both had just completed work for the Vice President's task force on terrorism. North used Marine Lieutenant Colonel Robert Earl mostly for *contra* matters, and Coast Guard Commander Craig Coy mostly on terrorism. In January 1986, North became chairman of the Operations Sub-Group of the Terrorist Incidents Working Group.

But it was outside the machinery, with the Secord enterprise (that had no acronym) that the real work was being done. In the summer and fall of 1985, North helped induce the Costa Ricans to agree to an emergency airstrip on their territory. Olmsted and Rob Owen, along with Costa Rican CIA station chief Joseph Fernandez, surveyed the alternative sites. Santa Elena, near the Costa Rican Pacific coast, was selected. In September, North recruited former CIA contract officer Felix Rodriguez to assist Secord dealing with the Salvadorans at their main air base at Ilopango, where the ex-CIA man was on close terms with senior Salvadoran Air Force officers.

Colonel North supplied his far-flung Central American network with National Security Agency encryption machines, KL-43s, plus associated tapes, to permit secure communications. With the exception of North himself and Joe Fernandez, none of the participants had up-to-date security clearances of the type required for the on-line encoders. It was a calculated risk, involving poor judgment, for North to have supplied the top-secret code machines. The NSA official responsible for giving North the machines upon request lost *his* job over the incident.

By the spring of 1986 the *contra* airlift would be poised for action. The Secord enterprise had a base at Ilopango, plus a warehouse crammed full of equipment for delivery to Calero's *contras*. In conjunction with their chief pilot, a former CIA proprietary flier, Secord and Hakim bought two twin-engine C-123K transports and two smaller twin-engine C-7s. There were also several light planes whose ownership some apparently dispute. Secord hired a just-retiring Air Force special warfare expert as his program manager, and assembled a contingent of about twenty mechanics and air crew, again mostly CIA veterans. Early supply flights were not very successful, however, until a big battle occurred with the Sandinistas right along the Honduran border in March 1986. Quite close to the *contra* base camps, the battle simplified support considerably and the airlift became a real lifeline. After that supply became problematic once more as action moved into the interior of Nicaragua. Mechanical problems with the old planes, poor weather conditions, and relatively primitive navigational equipment continually frustrated the airlift.

A separate problem was the United States' preoccupation with creating a "southern front," a force of *contras* attacking the Sandinistas from the south, from Costa Rica rather than Honduras. In the CIA days of the Nicaraguan war, before the mining fiasco, there had been a nascent anti-Sandinista movement in Costa Rica, but key leader Eden Pastora dropped out after an assassination attempt probably resulting from *contra* internal machinations. In the effort to motivate factions to replace Pastora, Ollie North dispatched Rob Owen on repeated visits to Costa Rica, and made cash payments to *contra* political figures. This money appears to have been separate from the $600,000 that Secord's enterprise spent on the southern front effort.

Of the various monies contributed to the *contra* cause, Adolfo Calero converted about $3 million into unsigned traveler's checks. Some $90,000 worth of the unsigned checks went to Oliver North, kept in his safe at the OEOB, dispensed to *contra* leaders through Rob Owen or Public Diplomacy official Jonathan Miller. In one instance, on a rainy night in April 1986, Owen picked up a quantity of money at North's office and handed it through the window of a car that pulled up at the curb outside. Owen further testified to moving quantities of cash on several occasions from New York to Washington. North himself used $2,440 of the traveler's checks for such sundries as groceries and snow tires, gave $1,000 to Rob Owen as a wedding present, and once lent $60 of *contra* money to secretary Fawn Hall for a beach weekend. North made operational use of the *contra* money, with Calero's express approval, using about $25,000 in Cyprus and Lebanon for hostage ransom deals that never seemed to crystallize.

Major activity surrounded the creation of the airlift to the *contras*. In spite of many problems, by September Secord and airlift manager Robert Dutton, at least, had become confident. Successful air drops to southern rebels had not yet opened up a true "front," but it was felt that the main operational difficulties had been overcome. Secord and Hakim were also confident of their Iranian activities, in which they and North were developing a new "second channel" into Teheran that bypassed Ghorbanifar. The single

524

major problem that loomed, one Ollie North was handling, remained the question of security.

The obvious security problem concerned Felix Rodriguez, enterprise base manager in El Salvador, whom North had recruited toward the end of 1985. Rodriguez had become convinced the arms sales to the *contras* and the airlift involved corruption and were being exploited by renegade former CIA officers. Previously an agency contract man himself, Rodriguez had good connections to the Vice President's national security adviser, Donald Gregg, who had been Felix's CIA superior in Vietnam.

Felix Rodriguez may have taken his story to Gregg in May 1986—the evidence on that remains in dispute—but he definitely did so in August, following a final confrontation with Ollie North.

"Colonel, I have learned that people are stealing here," Felix told Ollie. It was "going to be worse than Watergate," Rodriguez warned. "This could destroy the president of the United States!"

Ollie North seems to have imagined that by stilling a few voices of complaint, such as Felix Rodriguez's, he could preserve the secrecy of his Project Democracy airlift. Actually Felix proved dependable, made his complaints more or less through channels, then got out of the way and kept quiet. Secrecy was compromised far more by the regular operations in Central America and the movements of agents like Rob Owen, self-styled courier "Armando." Exposure was inevitable. The shootdown of the airplane on October 5, the so-called Hasenfus plane incident, made the truth abundantly clear.

Ironically it was through Rodriguez that Oliver North got his first news of the loss of the Hasenfus plane. When Felix got the word, he passed it along to Don Gregg, who relayed it to Bob Earl in Room 302. As too frequently was the case, Ollie was off on a mission somewhere.

ALL THE KING'S HORSES

▲▲▲

When Eugene Hasenfus's plane went down, it was difficult enough explaining the loss of several Americans deep inside Nicaragua; it became even more complicated when Hasenfus was captured alive and told the Sandinistas he had been employed by the CIA. Lending credence to the claim, the aircraft wreckage yielded flight logs and other documents linking the plane to Southern Air Transport.

On Thursday, October 9, President Reagan, Admiral Poindexter, George Shultz, and a good part of the administration's senior national security echelon flew off to Reykjavík for a summit with the Soviets, using the NATO northern base at Keflavík as their main access. President Reagan's first session with Mikhail Gorbachev occurred on Saturday morning, after Reagan had had a full day of rest.

It is said that Hofdi House, where the talks took place, is haunted. That drawback did not prevent selection of the site for the summit talks, but it is not clear whether the ghost, Nancy Reagan's astrologer, or some other influence is to be credited for what happened over the next two days. An administration that took eighteen months to make its first steps on arms control, one in which neither President nor secretary of state had heretofore possessed a strong commitment to the concept, almost negotiated the abolition of nuclear weapons inside of forty-eight hours.

Briefly, what happened was that Mikhail Gorbachev arrived aiming at some achievements in restraining the Strategic Defense Initiative (SDI). In exchange for that the Soviets were willing to go a long way toward meeting American preferences in a number of other arms control areas including a zero-option-type agreement on INF forces, deep reductions in ICBMs, and concessions on testing. What the Soviets insisted upon was that the sides agree on a fifteen-year nonabrogation clause for the ABM Treaty.

One of those along on the U.S. delegation was Richard Perle, the man who had invented the "zero-option" ploy and labored to defeat most arms initiatives since. Perle's usual disarming tactic was to agree and then set such draconian stipulations that others would not. Often he managed to out-arms-control the arms controllers. This worked well enough in Washington infighting, but at Reykjavík outdoing the Russians suddenly meant offering an even bolder proposal. Perle did not object when someone suggested the United States *accept* Gorbachev's offer but stipulate a reduced

526

interval for preserving the ABM Treaty plus the total elimination of ballistic missiles, a goal that had been sanctioned by an NSDD in the summer of 1986.

Forced to improvise, Perle joined with NSC staffer Robert E. Linhard during night-long sessions of the summit negotiators, working out new formulas for the American side. The Soviets offered to come down on the ABM Treaty from fifteen years to ten, but that was rock bottom. Perle and Linhard countered by working the same time frame into the suggestion that ballistic missiles be eliminated.

Ronald Reagan was not completely asleep. He did explicitly ask Perle whether the United States *itself* could afford to eliminate all ballistic missiles. Perle affirmed he thought so.

Perle and Linhard worked up some of their compromise language on their knees on the floor of a bathroom at Hofdi House, using a board placed over the tub as a desk. Without a copy machine, the Americans were also unable to reproduce their proposal papers. The Soviets had brought carbon paper, which the Americans finally had to borrow. There was no papering over the differences, however, especially once Reagan refused to be locked into the ABM Treaty for more than seven and a half years. The stand remains perplexing in that there was no prospect of a viable SDI for deployment within the decade. Even the longer duration the Soviets initially proposed could probably have been accepted almost without qualms.

In a further attempt at diplomatic one-upmanship, Gorbachev countered the U.S. proposal on ballistic missiles with an offer to eliminate "all nuclear arms."

Ronald Reagan thought he had what he wanted. The President offered Gorbachev a summit in Washington. "If we agree," Reagan had said, "that by the end of the ten year period, all nuclear arms are to be eliminated, we can refer this to our delegations to prepare an agreement that you could sign during your visit to the United States." Later, however, the President again refused to budge on the ABM Treaty, and Reykjavík ended in complete failure. There was no conference communiqué and both Reagan and George Shultz cast the summit somberly in news conferences before their departure.

As *Air Force One* winged back across the Atlantic, the image makers perceived the summit as a great disaster. Larry Speakes attributed the perception to sheer exhaustion on the part of Reagan and Shultz. Speakes and Don Regan put together a media blitz of television and radio appearances and op-ed pieces designed to project Reykjavík as a success instead. Speakes wrote up the plan on a piece of *Air Force One* stationery. As a result Admiral John Poindexter appeared for an hour and forty minutes in the back of the presidential plane, and the President gave a speech defending U.S. proposals as "the most sweeping and generous" in history.

Reykjavík proved very embarrassing because the United States tried to deny Reagan's acceptance of the principle of eliminating all nuclear weapons. Speakes and other spokesmen maintained it was a misunderstanding, then claimed the President had spoken only of ballistic missiles. Western European allies were miffed at Washington for going far out on a limb, since eliminating NATO nuclear weapons would leave the Soviets with superior conventional forces in Europe. The policy professionals in the U.S. bureaucracy were horrified that Reagan would have allowed himself to be drawn so far. Soviet statements on Reykjavík mentioned the nuclear weapons ban, the United States denied it, and charges went back and forth for some days until the Russians released the transcript of the Reagan-Gorbachev discussion, with the exact words of the President already quoted.

Washington relapsed with a waspish statement that revealing diplomatic secrets impeded relations between the powers.

Donald Regan quipped, in a remark that has become notorious, "Some of us were like a shovel brigade that follows a parade down Main Street, cleaning up."

Bob Linhard would go on from the summit to finish with the Reagan administration, virtually the only NSC staffer to go the distance, conflicted so much he ate compulsively and swelled up. Ollie North did not survive much past the Hasenfus plane. What made the difference? Linhard, an Air Force colonel capable of some creative ideas, kept himself to the narrow and technical. Ollie North tried to superimpose his own vision of events but lost, the day his vision went out of sync with the needs of the image makers.

The Hasenfus affair was handled about as poorly as can be imagined, from the beginning the image making went awry. Like the Watergate break-in, it lit the fuse for major scandal. The State Department quickly claimed that there was no connection whatever between the U.S. government and the downed aircraft. A suggestion that retired General John Singlaub was behind the airlift sent the media down a false trail. Singlaub was traveling to the Philippines at the time. When confronted with the U.S. government claim he denied it vehemently. Already annoyed at Elliott Abrams, who had obstructed his efforts to enlarge the southern front, Singlaub now turned the reporters right back toward Foggy Bottom. In Managua, State was of little help to captured American Eugene Hasenfus, and did not want to ship the bodies of the deceased pilots until prepaid for expenses.

The original Hasenfus story did not hold up very long. The Secord enterprise was not a CIA operation. Under questioning Hasenfus talked about a "Max Gomez" who supervised them in El Salvador and claimed to be a close friend of the Vice President. That claim quickly checked out, and Max proved to be none other than Felix Rodriguez. Many people knew Max, had Max stories, or had heard him boast. Max was well known at Ilopango, his connections to George Bush quietly rumored. Reporters soon established that Max Gomez had received certain help from the U.S. embassy. Ambassador Thomas Pickering denied knowing him, but was later reduced to the claim he had no idea Felix was calling himself "Max Gomez." Telephone records for Felix's office, and the Escalona district houses of the other Americans disclosed frequent phone calls to Richard Secord, both at home and at the office, as well as calls to the *unlisted White House number* assigned to Oliver North. Just before that news came out, Elliott Abrams and a senior CIA official had gone before a congressional committee under oath to repeat their litany of no American connections to the "private benefactors."

Actually Abrams had his hands tied to some degree by Ollie North. In August, Admiral Poindexter had permitted North to submit to questioning by members of the House intelligence committee, including its chairman Lee Hamilton. North's tactics were to split the hairs of questions to avoid telling the truth without actually lying. Poindexter awarded Ollie the naval accolade "Well done!" for the performance, but as a result the government position became restricted to maintaining it was aware of the "private benefactors" without knowing anything about them. In many quarters that argument seemed ludicrous.

Meanwhile, the tail number of the plane plus documents aboard led to the enterprise houses in El Salvador and to Southern Air Transport in Miami. The Customs Service and FBI opened investigations. North intervened to halt or delay the investigations, enlisting Admiral Poindexter to help with a call to a senior official. There were also efforts to interfere with FBI investigations and law enforcement efforts in Florida against suspected drug traffickers.

On November 5 a story appeared that ignited the firestorm—revelation of Bud McFarlane's secret mission to Teheran. Of all places, the story first surfaced in Beirut, in *Al Shir'aa,* a Lebanese political magazine. The story reported that the United States had supplied arms to Teheran. American media reported this two days later and within twenty-four hours it became a major press feature.

Alarmed, George Shultz cabled Poindexter that the United States had better put out that the Iran thing had been a special one-shot initiative based purely upon humanitarian concerns. Here was Shultz, who had opposed the operation and made clear he did not want to know the details, offering suggestions to meet the crisis.

John Poindexter decided that the buck stopped with him. The admiral thought the White House could ride out public opinion. On the day the story broke, Poindexter was concerned because the most recent weapons deal had freed another Beirut hostage—David G. Jacobsen—on November 2. The President's watcher hoped for more hostage releases. He called McFarlane as soon as he heard of the *Al Shir'aa* piece, but told Bud the NSC would take the position of refusing to comment on the story. Poindexter hoped Bud would similarly refrain. McFarlane agreed. The admiral then told the former national security adviser that the NSC staff would begin assembling a narrative of events of the Iran venture. Admiral Poindexter said President Reagan had ordered the report.

Meanwhile Poindexter reassured the President. Don Regan recalls the admiral telling Reagan, "It will blow over." Regan himself advised the President that the administration would have to come out with some sort of explanation. The White House could not stonewall.

The chronology began as a device to establish what the record was, so the President could act to put the issue behind him. The paper went through numerous changes, additions and subtractions, with contributions from outsiders such as McFarlane, Mike Ledeen, CIA lawyers, and others. Ollie North took charge of the project, with help from Bob Earl and Craig Coy. At least a dozen drafts were written, plus a presidential speech, and input into testimony William J. Casey planned to give under oath to a congressional committee. Some of the chronologies and the Casey testimony contained false statements.

President Reagan held a meeting of his top advisers first thing Monday, November 10. Notes of the meeting were made at the time by Don Regan and by Alton Keel, while Weinberger wrote a memorandum recording it and George Shultz dictated recollections to his executive secretary. According to the official report of the joint congressional committee investigating the affair, there are no material differences among these accounts of the November 10 strategy meeting.

President Reagan opened with a frank admission that some statement about the Iran allegations had become a necessity but he wanted it to be as general as possible. Admiral Poindexter then took over the meeting for a briefing that was misleading or false in at least five respects, including concocting a story about an Israeli warehouse in Europe, halving the number of antitank missiles shipped in the transactions, and declaring that the initial transactions had been by Israel without U.S. permission. Not mentioned at all were the presidential finding of December 1985, the one authorizing a straight arms-for-hostages trade and the one awarding retrospective approval, which lay in John Poindexter's office safe. Contrary to his President, Poindexter went on to argue that the Iran news story had already peaked and that no statement was really needed.

"In the presence of the president and senior Cabinet officers," the congressional report concludes, "Poindexter either was confused or purposely dissembled."

Admiral Poindexter maintained the same position for the next two weeks. During this interval Poindexter appeared before the congressional intelligence committees, conducted an official briefing for congressional leaders, briefed at sessions of the NSC and NSPG, and did backgrounders with reporters. The time Poindexter had spent with reporters after Reykjavík had been his first on-the-record sally with the press. Now Iran-Contra refused to leave him alone, and sucked the admiral in deeper with every passing day.

A central theme of the widening scandal would be deliberate destruction of evidence. Admiral Poindexter by his own admission participated. When Colonel North reported back to the admiral, mortified at the downing of the Hasenfus plane, Poindexter lambasted the hapless Ollie because the enterprise airplane had carried so much identifying information on it. He may have said something to North about his own files. Bill Casey is also said to have warned North to destroy the ledger in which he had kept track of his payments of *contra* traveler's checks.

Then there was the matter of the old problem memos. The same papers that had bothered Bud McFarlane in 1985 still lay, secure, in the NSC's System-IV files. The papers linked North with various activities on behalf of the *contras*. If Poindexter had any inclination to forget them, he was reminded, by NSC intelligence staff chief Ken de Graffenreid. The admiral did not remember the August 1985 inquiry, he later recalled in a deposition, but he did remember that there had been a series of papers from North to McFarlane that discussed the status of funding and logistics.

De Graffenreid warned the admiral that those papers could be damaging to the administration. Ken also seemed, to Poindexter, concerned at the exposure of North, a pretty close friend with whom De Graffenreid often worked. "The clear intent of de Graffenreid's visit," Poindexter told investigators, "was to figure out a way to get rid of those memos."

"Go talk to Colonel North," Poindexter told him, "see what you can work out."

De Graffenreid's own deposition account is that the meeting with Poindexter occurred at "a quiet time in the evening." The staffer dates it sometime in November, after the Iran side of the affair began to emerge. The date is important because of the major conflicts between De Graffenreid and other key NSC players on what happened afterward. Poindexter's clear recollection was that the conversation occurred in October. De Graffenreid says he volunteered, asking how he could be of help, but that Poindexter had gracefully declined, telling De Graffenreid it was better that he stay out. It was then, De Graffenreid recalls, that he asked how Ollie stood, and told the admiral, "Well, Ollie's asked to look at some documents."

The senior director of the NSC's intelligence staff could not remember whether Poindexter's response was to nod, say fine, or say okay.

Room 300 of the OEOB was the suite housing the intelligence office, where the System-IV files reposed in custody of Jim Radzimski. The custodian was well known to De Graffenreid, whom he helped with administrative matters. Radzimski's father had died the previous fall so the Navy yeoman put in for twenty-year retirement. That was coming up for him when the Iran-Contra affair began to break.

Radzimski's memory is that in August or September Ken de Graffenreid had come up to him with a request to pull a number of documents. Radzimski recognized some of the document numbers as the same ones involved in the Barnes inquiry. Feeling very uneasy, Radzimski never complied, pretending always to be too busy, even when De Graffenreid asked a couple of times what had happened to the request.

After the second or third time, Radzimski recalls, the intelligence senior director asked him into the inner office, then asked why he was too busy to pull the papers. The Navy yeoman hesitated, then said, "I replied to him that I would not pull those documents. I said—I told him that I just do not feel right and I cannot pull them." De Graffenreid seemed startled and surprised.

"I would never ask you to do anything improper or illegal," Radzimski recalls De Graffenreid telling him. "If you feel that there may be that particular type of attachment to this request, then thank you."

De Graffenreid never mentioned it again.

This sworn testimony by Radzimski is in major conflict with Ken de Graffenreid's story. The NSC staffer denies any recollection of the incidents, and maintained this stance through a surprise confrontation with Radzimski, arranged by the Iran-Contra investigators. The System-IV records custodian could have been a devastating witness at the congressional hearings but he was never called. Evidently the joint committee members grew doubts about Radzimski after the yeoman's claim that he had seen two documents in 1985 that referred to the diversion of money from Iran arms sales to the *contras,* and that the diversion document the investigators had found was something else again. No trace of these papers could be found.

It is a matter of public record, however, in admissions by both Robert McFarlane and Paul Thompson, that at the time of the Barnes inquiry the national security adviser had a conversation with his legal aide regarding the propriety and feasibility of altering file documents. Radzimski's recollections therefore provide evidence of continuity in high-level NSC interest in the North problem documents.

Radzimski was phasing out his NSC staff work by November 1986, but with an office right next door to North, ran into Ollie one morning in the hallway. Ollie asked if he had been following what was in the newspapers. When he replied in the affirmative, Radzimski recalls, North hung his head in mock chagrin and quipped, "All those System-IV documents!"

The yeoman's replacement, Brian T. Merchant, was a senior NSC secretariat official with fourteen years' experience. In the late morning of November 21, 1986, De Graffenreid's secretary, June Bartlett, asked him to pull a number of System-IV documents. The list was of a half-dozen items and it was in Bud McFarlane's handwriting. He found five of them, passed them on, and got back a note that they were checked out to Ollie North. Later that afternoon they came back to the custodian, to be refiled and found later by investigators. North met with Poindexter in the afternoon at 1:30 and again at 2:25 P.M. The refiled System-IV documents were found to have been altered, shortened, in one case from four pages to one. The new versions were easy to spot, however, for the NSC and White House had changed stationery since the documents were first created. The altered documents appeared on the new stationery. All the documents on McFarlane's problem list were altered with the exception of one originated in December 1984. That happened to correspond neatly to the fact that System-

IV files from 1984 and earlier were housed in the vault, not De Graffenreid's office.

The panic that necessitated attempts to falsify documents resulted from Reagan's belated determination to manage the burgeoning affair. A first gambit, a televised speech on November 13, admitted that arms deals had taken place but stuck to Poindexter's fiction that it was an Israeli operation the United States had not approved. Poindexter also supplied the President with the vivid but false claim that all the weapons shipped would have fit into a single airplane with plenty of room to spare. A news conference on November 19 degenerated into complete disaster, with Reagan losing himself, continuing denials already surpassed by the evidence, and making such egregious errors of fact that NSC and State had to issue statements taking back his remarks. Don Regan felt President Reagan had heard so many different views on what to say and not say that he had become thoroughly confused. The following day the President had a heated exchange with Secretary of State Shultz, who complained Poindexter was providing the President with poor data. It was at 11:30 A.M. on Friday the twenty-first that Reagan met with Poindexter, Regan, and Meese and asked the latter to make an inquiry over the weekend to find out what had actually happened. Only later that afternoon, at about 3:00 P.M., did Meese get around to phoning Poindexter to ask the admiral to set aside documents.

The Meese phone call apparently led to wholesale destruction of documents and other records. Admiral Poindexter called Commander Thompson into his office to witness him tearing up the December 1985 presidential finding. Poindexter also destroyed some other documents stored with the finding and purged his computer records of 5,062 messages, often called PROFS notes for the IBM operating system the machines used. That morning the admiral had presented misleading briefings to both House and Senate intelligence committees and Bill Casey gave false testimony to the same groups.

Lieutenant Colonel Oliver North separately told Bud McFarlane and Michael Ledeen that afternoon that a shredding party had become necessary. Ledeen could not have gotten the news directly from Poindexter because the two were hardly on speaking terms. That evening, assisted by Fawn Hall and Bob Earl, Ollie went to work shredding the damaging documents, including North's phone logs, the *contra* money ledger, and a file of the most sensitive material, which he had given Earl for safekeeping before leaving on the Teheran mission that summer. The amount of material shredded has been estimated as the equivalent of a pile of paper eighteen inches high—that would be 3,000 or 4,000 pages. There was so much the shredder jammed from the clog. The next morning, when a party of Justice Department lawyers arrived to examine North's papers, Ollie was so worried about the documents still left that he took enormous risks, ducking out the back door to carry papers to the crisis center and shred them there. North also purged the PROFS notes from his computer, and must have spent most of that weekend doing it. White House Communications Agency personnel established that Ollie's machine had had 737 messages on memory as of November 22, but just 1 a week later. The operating system of the computer required the messages be deleted one by one. North's office was sealed and not accessible after Tuesday, November 25.

Wholesale destruction of records also occurred at the offices of the Secord-Hakim company, a northern Virginia firm called Stanford Technology Trading Group International (STTGI). It was STTGI that exercised control of the actual assets of the *contra* airlift activity. This company destroyed its phone logs and much other documentation. In Swiss courts the company contested U.S. government efforts to gain access to bank records.

Despite all the shredding, Justice Department lawyers in North's office came across a document that discussed making available Iran arms sale funds for the *contra* rebels. This evidence of a diversion suddenly gave the investigation legal and even criminal implications it had not previously had, though some subordinates at Justice had worried about criminal implications as soon as there was evidence North had participated in preparation of false testimony.

Not much that is good can be said about the Meese inquiry. Even if intended merely as a personal inquiry on behalf of the President, it was conducted in lackadaisical fashion with little attention to detail. Meese failed to question key figures soon enough, to press them hard enough, and kept no notes of key conversations. He also kept out the criminal division of the Justice Department, even after discovery of the diversion memo. Once there were criminal implications, he failed to seal North's office immediately. Meese walked out of one of his own interviews to pick up his wife at the airport.

On Monday morning, never mind the cursory investigation, Edwin Meese faced the obligation of telling the President of a diversion. The first thing he did was call Don Regan and say he had to see the President. Meese came over a little after eleven and he and Regan entered the Oval Office at 11:13 A.M.

"It's a terrible mess," Meese told Ronald Reagan. "I have a few things to button up and then I'll give you a full report. But it's going to be bad news."

Apparently Meese had not the heart to tell the president there had been a possible diversion of funds in the Iran sales, something he had already told Don Regan, which phrase made the chief of staff's blood run cold.

The group arranged to meet again at 4:15 that afternoon, after an NSC session. Meese arrived seven minutes late, to inform Reagan that it appeared there was an $18-million difference between the amount the Iranians had paid for weapons and what the United States had been given for providing the materiel. In addition, said the attorney general, Colonel North had admitted over the weekend that some proceeds had been diverted to the *contras*.

Meese had just been to see Admiral John Poindexter. The national security adviser had seen a diversion memorandum on the morning of November 24. He had been surprised to see it. The attorney general asked Poindexter directly if he had known about the diversion.

Poindexter admitted he had.

Meese asked what the admiral had done about it.

Admiral Poindexter had not wanted to know. "Ollie has given me enough hints about this so that I generally knew, but I did nothing to follow up or stop it," he had said.

Poindexter understood he would have to resign and said he would leave the timing to Meese. The admiral apparently assumed Ollie North would be accorded the same privilege.

At the meeting with the President, Don Regan insisted on the resignation and he got it the next morning. He further advised that Reagan should appear to be in charge. The President should take the lead in briefing key congressional leaders, then introduce Meese at a press conference that would disclose the diversion. That would be done the next day, making Monday, November 24, a priceless gift of time for all those trying to escape the consequences of this affair.

Don Regan found the admiral in his office at 7:40 A.M. Tuesday morning. "John, what the hell happened? What went on here? What did you know about all this?"

Poindexter was eating breakfast, cool as ever. He put down his knife and fork, then repeated for Regan's benefit what he had told Ed Meese.

"I felt sorry for the *contras,*" Regan recalls the admiral telling him. "I was so damned mad at Tip O'Neill for the way he was dragging the *contras* around that I didn't want to know what, if anything, was going on."

Again Poindexter said nothing of his detailed knowledge of numerous machinations by Project Democracy. Ollie North has testified he sent Poindexter as many as five papers regarding the diversion aspect alone.

The denouement came at the morning national security briefing. To Regan, Poindexter had still seemed his unflappable self earlier and now entered purposeful, unblinking, with a firm voice, "I'm sorry it's come to this, Mr. President."

They did not shake hands when Poindexter left.

The National Security Planning Group met soon afterward, and there was strong pressure for a blue-ribbon commission that would investigate the diversion. Then there was a session with key congressional leaders followed by the Meese press conference at noon. Pandemonium broke out after that.

President Reagan planned to spend Thanksgiving at his Rancho Cielo in California. He left as quickly as possible in view of the new developments. Late in the afternoon Don Regan convened a group of senior advisers to consider candidates for the investigating commission. They came up with former Senator John Tower, Brent Scowcroft, and former Senator Edmund Muskie. A Texas Republican, Tower was a military expert and a U.S. START negotiator; Scowcroft was a former keeper of the keys; a former secretary of state, Muskie gave the board a bipartisan composition.

"What we're trying to find out is what the procedures are," Scowcroft told the reporters, "what happened so that we can make recommendations as to any changes that ought to be made in the system." At another point he reminded the audience that "all the executive branch apparatus serves . . . the President. . . . He's the decision maker, and that's what the whole process is designed to do." Senator John Tower became chairman of the group, subsequently known as the Tower Board. They were to make a final report within sixty days.

To assist him in the fight for public opinion, Reagan brought in as an aide David Abshire, director of the Center for Strategic and International Studies, a conservative Washington think tank. Abshire shepherded the President through a very delicate series of encounters with his investigating board. There was immense public demand to get to the bottom of Iran-Contra.

Discussing Ollie North's charter a reporter had asked, "Wouldn't that necessarily follow then that you're going to have to trace where that charter came from no matter [how] high up it went?"

"I think you can be sure we will," Scowcroft replied.

The form as well as the substance of presidential cooperation and Ronald Reagan's memories became issues. The President refused to allow the board to use his authority as Commander in Chief to compel testimony from John Poindexter and Oliver North. Meanwhile, Reagan had diary notes of his own, and refused to allow access until after review by his own lawyer Peter Wallison. The Tower Board built up a staff of twenty-three under Rhett Dawson, a partner in the McNair law firm, who had gained his early national security experience as an investigator for the Church Committee inquiry of 1975. Evidence was taken from fifty-three witnesses, and others were interviewed by staff. The principal authors of the final report were lawyers Stephen Hadley and Nicholas Rostow.

Ronald Reagan also ran into a problem of testimony. In an initial interview on January 26, 1987, he cited as accurate McFarlane testimony before the House intelligence committee that he had approved the August 1985 arms sale. Don Regan, however, had testified that there was no approval for that transaction. This was one of those time bombs in the tradition of Henry Kissinger. It seems to have resulted from Poindexter's misleading cover story attributing the early moves to the Israelis. Not willing to permit this conflict in testimony to stand, Regan then persuaded the President in February 1987 to revise his account, giving testimony that he truly did not remember giving any approval.

It was in mid-February, moreover, that the Tower Board's staff got access to PROFS messages sent in the period after November 8, the earliest date central memory backup files contained at the time the board was formed.

Once Rostow and Hadley completed the text, there were some further difficulties declassifying it. The final Tower Board report was presented on February 26, 1987. It contained a wealth of factual detail on the Iran arms deals, and less but significant material concerning *contra* operations. The board did not quite do the job some claimed for it: Tower talked about how they had considered the use of the NSC over time and used specific case studies of the NSC system from Eisenhower's time to the present. In fact, though considerable time was expended listening to former officials, including Presidents Nixon, Ford, and Carter, plus keepers of the keys Walt Rostow, Kissinger, and Brzezinski, virtually no use was made of this material in the report. Similarly, when historians inquired later about the case studies, they were informed no case studies had actually been done by the board, which had simply made use of the case series of the Kennedy School of Government at Harvard, good academic work but hardly authoritative.

"What happened in this case is that the system did not compensate for the management style of the President," Brent Scowcroft told the reporters. The investigation had been difficult for him, as mentor for Bud McFarlane, but especially wrenching for Bud, who took the responsibility upon himself. Scowcroft noted there really had been little choice: "[The President] did not perhaps ask enough questions, but it was incumbent upon other participants in the system to insure [*sic*] that the president was absolutely clear about what was going on. There should have been bells ringing, lights flashing and so on."

Toward the end of the investigation the conflicted McFarlane made an inept attempt at suicide, swallowing a whole pile of Valium tablets after scribbling notes to his wife Jonda and others. (Valium is rarely fatal even in extremely large doses.) Explaining himself later McFarlane referred to oriental concepts of responsibility, such as hara-kiri, ritual suicide once practiced in Japan. It was a striking reference because the truth about the Reagan NSC was that the entrepreneurial policy system had made things work very much like the Japanese government in its imperialist days before World War II. There was not even a hint of this in the Tower Report, which concluded that any errors were not of process but rather mere mistakes by individuals.

The NSC model suggested by the Tower Board as its principal recommendation was pretty standard stuff: a more responsible national security adviser with a small staff. The major change suggested was the addition of a regular legal office to the NSC staff. Ronald Reagan adopted the board's recommendations in NSDD-266 of March 31, 1987, and NSDD-276 of June 9. Instructively, the staff did not in fact get much smaller, though the political-military cluster was eliminated. The former Crisis Pre-Planning Group also gave way to a Policy Review Committee under the deputy national security adviser, in effect the same wine in a new bottle.

This is not the place for detailed review of the several further Iran-Contra investigations carried out by House and Senate intelligence committees and by the joint congressional committee. Those investigations, depositions, and hearings went on through much of 1987, finally to be supplanted by *further* investigation by an Iran-Contra special prosecutor. The point worth noting is that those investigations, just as the Tower Board, pulled back from criticism of process. Again the NSC machinery escaped. The joint congressional committee recommended that the job of national security adviser not be given to military men, the closest it came to zeroing in on the NSC. That advice was laughable. Reagan had already selected another military man, as did George Bush, forty-second President of the United States, when the occasion came to appoint the next keeper.

"The root cause of the United States' foreign policy difficulties is not the strength but the weakness of the national security adviser's staff." Henry Kissinger pronounced this opinion relatively early in the Iran-Contra controversy. Kissinger, however, was assuming the NSC's goal was to develop realistic options for a President and his NSC principals. The entrepreneurs of the Reagan era hewed to a new standard: how close one came to the President's goals despite all the obstacles. That placed a premium on circumventing perceived obstacles, whether rooted in laws or in the dug-in heels of an entrenched bureaucracy. Under this standard, NSC staff operations were seen as superior to grinding the policy wheels. At least in the Poindexter era, operations was the way to keep the delicate issues away from the President. Ronald Reagan accepted responsibility for his errors in a relatively thoughtful speech on March 4, 1987, in which he responded publicly to the Tower Board report calling it "honest, convincing, and highly critical."

"When it came to managing the NSC staff," Reagan admitted, "let's face it, my style didn't match its previous track record."

Under the circumstances the question of who would replace Poindexter as national security adviser assumed critical importance. President Reagan made his decision during his Thanksgiving sojourn in California at the very outset of the affair. The decision was also kept within a very narrow circle, excluding both the NSC staff and the presidential chief of staff, with staff work on the appointment carried out directly from Santa Barbara. Selections that followed suggest that Cap Weinberger played a key role in the presidential decision. Returning to Washington after the holidays, Ronald Reagan announced his appointment of Frank Carlucci as national security adviser. Lieutenant General Colin L. Powell of the Army would be deputy. Carlucci had been associated with Caspar Weinberger for a decade and a half while Colin Powell happened to be Cap's military assistant.

The new team took over with a charter to reform the NSC staff, to which the President soon added implementation of the Tower Board recommendations. In many ways the Carlucci-Powell team was ideal for President Reagan, who needed to restore the image of the NSC as a responsible,

responsive mechanism, and to begin the rehabilitation of the national security adviser.

It fell to Ronald Reagan to celebrate two key milestones of National
Security Council history, the one-thousandth meeting of the NSC and the
fortieth anniversary of the National Security Act of 1947. For one of the occasions there was a toast and brief observance before the session; for the other,
a midsummer picnic. To a considerable degree it was due to Carlucci and
Powell that when those occasions came there was anything to celebrate.

Frank Charles Carlucci was a quintessential survivor who rose about as
high as a man could go and still stay out of politics. From Scranton, Pennsylvania, the fifty-seven-year-old Carlucci had been both deputy secretary
of defense and deputy director of central intelligence, in both Democratic
and Republican administrations. Conservative but not ideological, he had
had a little trouble with the Jesse Helms wing of the Republican party at
the beginning of Reagan's administration. Attempts to block Carlucci's
nomination faltered, however, when Cap Weinberger went to Reagan and
told the President he would not serve in the Cabinet unless he had a free
hand to pick his subordinates. Reagan insisted and the conservative Republicans backed off.

Carlucci graduated from Princeton in 1952. He wrestled on the Princeton
team with Don Rumsfeld and was classmates with future triumvir James
Baker and NSC staffer Robert Oakley. Frank went into the Navy after
college, then tried business for a year, as a management trainee in Portland,
Oregon, for Jantzen, the swimsuit company. Unhappy with that, Carlucci
took the Foreign Service exam and also applied to Harvard Business School.
Accepted at Harvard, Frank went in 1956 but then was offered a Foreign
Service posting, vice-consul and economic officer in Johannesburg, South
Africa. He never looked back.

Dispatched to the Congo, to what became Kinshasa of Zaire, Carlucci
served as second secretary from 1960 to 1962, key years of U.S. involvement,
including a crisis that established Carlucci among Foreign Service professionals. When Carlucci returned to Washington, it was as officer in charge
of Congolese affairs, the position he held from 1962 to 1964. Next he
served as consul general in Zanzibar, and then in Brazil, as embassy counselor for four years.

The Nixon years established Carlucci as a senior player in Washington.
He succeeded Rumsfeld in charge of the Office of Equal Opportunity, held
top posts in the Office of Management and Budget, became undersecretary
of HEW, and ambassador to Portugal from 1975 to 1978. Carlucci met
Caspar Weinberger during his OEO stint. Cap was then finance chief for
Governor Ronald Reagan of California, and Reagan, to put the agency out
of business there, was refusing to spend money the OEO had granted to
California. Carlucci talked Weinberger into accepting the money to keep
local OEO offices open while mounting an investigation of their operations.

Weinberger thought it a capital solution, and when Cap came to Washington in 1973 to head HEW, he brought Carlucci in as undersecretary.

Carlucci was ambassador in Lisbon at a turbulent moment in Portuguese history, but maintained friendly relations with Portugal despite the leftward shift of that government and the ire of Henry Kissinger. Jimmy Carter considered it a good enough performance to nominate Carlucci later as second-in-command to Stansfield Turner at the CIA.

Carlucci talked of the span of a national security adviser's control, then implied he might cut back the NSC staff by a unit or two. In fact, he abolished the political-military staff and North's special office. The bureaucratic span for the national security adviser to control changed very little, for the keeper soon added a regular legal counsel office. Tower Board lawyer Nicholas Rostow was brought in to head the office. With Rostow's appointment NSC history passed another milestone. Nick Rostow was son of Eugene Rostow and nephew of the illustrious Walt. As special assistant to the President, moreover, Nick held a title identical to his uncle's.

Under Carlucci, reforming the NSC did not take the staff entirely out of operations. Orders soon came from the President prohibiting NSC staff from *covert* operations; special mission work stayed on the platter. In Central America, where the appropriation for CIA aid once more ran out, relegating the administration to "humanitarian" assistance, the national security problem appeared to fall through the seams between State, the Pentagon, the CIA, and other operating departments. The NSC staff assumed increasing prominence, beginning with an early Carlucci visit to the area to assess the *contras*. Most particularly, Elliott Abrams's ascendancy in setting policy was supplanted by Colin Powell, Carlucci's deputy, who personally chaired a new Policy Review Group (PRG) and worked on this subject. Powell's committee replaced Poindexter's old CPPG and gave the NSC a sharper long-range focus on issues. Carlucci also hired another Jeane Kirkpatrick aide, Jose S. Sorzano, to take up the Central America portfolio within the NSC staff.

As a whole Carlucci regenerated the NSC staff by inserting new blood. About half the professional staff were replaced during Frank's first hundred days. Some old-timers, most prominently Howard Teicher, found their time drastically cut short. That Middle East staffer realized early on that Iran-Contra would force him to resign. When he did, Teicher thought he had worked out a deal whereby he could stay on winding things up for a couple more months. Instead, the afternoon of the day the Tower Board report appeared, security came by to change the locks on Teicher's office door. The staffer was told to clean out his desk immediately. Others swept away included most of Poindexter's "Navy mafia," from Rodney McDaniel to Paul Thompson. Carlucci brought in retired Army General Grant S. Green, Jr., as NSC executive secretary, and hired Alison Brenner Fortier, widow of the deceased NSC aide, as legislative liaison director. Then Frank asked Princeton classmate Bob Oakley to be senior director for the Middle East.

Having been a staff specialist for the Middle East under Kissinger, it would be Oakley's second tour on the NSC staff. Longtime factotum Peter Rodman got the title "counselor" to the keeper of the keys.

Congressional liaison continued to be an important function of the Carlucci staff. Alison Fortier cooperated with David Abshire in handling the fallout of the Iran-Contra affair. She also confronted a House of Representatives inquiry into the National Security Decision Document (NSDD) series. The Government Operations Committee of the House asked that detailed data about five categories of the NSDDs be provided. Note the request was for information, not for the decision documents themselves. A month later Carlucci replied that the request was without precedent and "involves the broadest possible range of classified subjects." Reagan's administration was satisfied with its practice of providing briefings on, or selective access to, NSDDs for particular congressional committees on subjects within their direct jurisdiction. On May 15, 1987, Carlucci formally replied that the House request had necessitated "a thorough review of the legal authorities that would govern application of the doctrine of executive privilege." Carlucci cited an amorphous "necessity" to protect information "when disclosure would be inconsistent with the President's performance of his constitutional duties." In his interim letter the national security adviser had invoked John Kennedy; now he resorted to George Washington.

The administration decided to provide only a list of unclassified directives, plus a collection of press releases about NSDDs that had been made at various times. In cases where documents *were* declassified, retyped plain paper versions were substituted for copies of the originals.

On July 5, 1987, in one of the more lurid reports of the Iran-Contra period, allegations appeared that Ollie North had helped prepare NSDDs that provided executive authority to suspend the Constitution, not just for nuclear war but in the event of widespread internal dissent. On July 8, Speaker of the House Jim Wright followed up the earlier inquiry and demanded access to the full set of NSDDs and implementing directives. On August 7, Carlucci replied that "it is not altogether clear what legislative purpose you foresee being served by such access," but promised further reply. No such communication is recorded. Carlucci confined himself to assurances that no plans like those described had been proposed or approved by the United States government at any time, but insisted the national security machinery could continue to plan for contingencies.

In July 1988, Congressman Jack Brooks of Texas, chairman of the House Government Operations Committee, tabled a bill for a "Presidential Directives and Records Accountability Act" (H.R. 5092). He scheduled hearings on the bill about a week later and invited the national security adviser to testify.

Frank Carlucci did not have to respond. He had been called away in the fall of 1987 to replace Caspar Weinberger at the Pentagon, for Cap had had enough as secretary of defense. It was Carlucci's last save for Cap, and an appointment that restored a measure of mobility to administration policy. Soon afterward the ice broke on arms negotiations, leading to a December summit in Washington and signing of a treaty for the elimination of INF missiles. Prominent at the summit was a new keeper of the keys, Colin Powell. For the third time in eight years the President had selected his national security adviser merely by promoting the deputy. Powell was a sophisticated operator, very much in the Carlucci mold, well equipped to handle the tentative inquiries about Reagan's NSDDs.

On August 3, 1988, the day of the committee hearing on the NSDD bill, which would have required copies of such documents to be filed with the House, Senate, and Federal Register, Powell sent a letter of reply to Jack Brooks. The national security adviser claimed the NSC staff had become aware of the hearing only on August 1, when committee staff members asked NSC officials to pick up their invitation letter, actually dated July 26. Powell declined the request. "In accordance with the doctrines of separation of powers," the national security adviser argued, "members of the President's personal staff who participate in the deliberative process . . . traditionally have not testified before Congress."

Colin Powell's treatment of the NSDD inquiry was authoritative, befitting his experience as a lieutenant general in the Army. Like Poindexter, the fifty-one-year-old general remained on active service with the forces while he served in the White House. Powell once explained he couldn't afford to retire, and was on record as favoring a civilian in the post of national security adviser, but the question was what did the President want, and Ronald Reagan had asked Powell to serve. He would protect the prerogatives of the President.

Loyalty to the chain of command was ingrained in Colin Luther Powell, the first African-American to become national security adviser and a sharp military officer who would one day be jumped over thirty more senior generals and admirals to become Chairman of the Joint Chiefs of Staff. Born in Harlem, reared in the South Bronx, Powell's parents were immigrants from Jamaica, his father a shipping foreman, mother a seamstress. Though only an average student, Colin persevered through high school and went on to City University of New York. At college he found something that truly enthused him—the Army. Powell joined ROTC and became upon graduation in 1958, a fresh second lieutenant in the Army.

Colin Powell did the things that young Army officers usually do—a tour in Germany as commander of a platoon, then a rifle company, a tour in Massachusetts, at Fort Devens. As military adviser in South Vietnam, Powell earned an Air Medal by pulling injured men from a burning helicopter, and a Purple Heart up near the Laotian border when he stepped on a pungi stick booby-trap set by the Vietcong. After a stint as a trainer at Fort Benning he did a second Vietnam tour, as executive officer of an infantry battalion, then operations staff officer for the Americal Division.

Major Powell began the 1970s with higher education—an M.B.A. from

George Washington University. After that he applied for the prestigious White House Fellows program and was accepted, one of seven lucky candidates from among fifteen hundred applicants. Major Powell got assigned to the Office of Management and Budget. There he worked under Frank Carlucci. That began the beginning of a long relationship.

Powell breezed through Iran-Contra without pausing to doubt. As far as he was concerned, he carried out legal orders in a straightforward fashion. General Powell sat in Cap Weinberger's office one morning in the summer of 1985 when Bud McFarlane came to the Pentagon to give the secretary of defense a private rundown on a contemplated Iran initiative. Cap asked a few questions, then was caustic about the draft Iran NSDD once it came up to him. "This is almost too absurd to comment on," Weinberger told Powell about the Iran NSDD. "Like asking Qaddafi to Washington for a cozy chat." For one of the arms deals, Powell helped identify suitable anti-tank missiles that could be shipped from the arsenal at Red River, Arkansas. Later he passed along to Poindexter without comment the protests of the Defense Security Assistance Agency, which was being ordered to give antitank missiles to the CIA outside the usual channels.

While he was at the Pentagon, Powell more or less ran Cap Weinberger's outer office. Colin did the same when he went to the NSC as Carlucci's deputy. When Frank went into the job, he found the NSC bloated with support people. He asked why the staff needed so many secretaries, to be told it was because they worked in shifts over the weekends.

"The hell we do!" Carlucci shot back.

After that the national security adviser went home most days by six o'clock, though during his ten-month stewardship there were still two or three intense weekends. Carlucci made a point of leaving the door to his office open, but while he set the tone it fell to Powell to make the system work.

For Colin the regimen was actually easier than it had been across the Potomac. Pentagon colleagues had noticed that Powell would be in the office by 5:30 A.M., fresh as a daisy. At the NSC, particularly once he became gatekeeper in his own right, General Powell usually arrived at the office an hour later. He would review the overnight business for a half hour, participate in breakfasts or other early-morning functions until about nine, then have a last half hour for phone calls and priority business before the President's daily national security briefing.

"It was a heck of a homework quiz," Powell said of the national security briefings. "I would go in and plop down on that sofa directly across from the President. I would give him warning of what was coming our way, or sometimes just philosophize: For example, what was happening in the Soviet Union or how Congress was reacting to a particular issue. It was a challenge, but it becomes a natural one because you're doing it every day."

Major vehicles for Powell on administrative action regarding national security, for which the keeper of the keys has had formal responsibility beginning with NSDD-276, were the Policy Review Group chaired by the deputy adviser, and the keeper's own activity at the NSC, NSPG, and directly with the President. Colin Powell, unlike such predecessors as Kissinger or Brzezinski, kept very much in mind that he worked for *all* the NSC principals, not just the President. Policy would be the common denominator the agencies could all agree upon. Reaganaut visions of conservative utopia perished.

Symptomatic of the new process was the 1987–1988 Persian Gulf crisis that began during Carlucci's tenure and lasted through the end of the Iran-Iraq war. An adjunct to that conflict was the so-called tanker war in the Persian Gulf, where the belligerents attacked each other's oil exports. The Iraqis used their capable air force. The Iranians used mine warfare, small boats, a few air strikes, and later they got shore-based antiship missiles.

The United States intervened in this tanker war in 1987, after it had been going on for five years. Why then? There had been better opportunities. In January 1986 the Iranian Navy halted an American merchant vessel in international waters outside the Persian Gulf to inspect for war materials. Washington had made *no* response. A year later the situation was simply that Kuwait, one of the gulf nations most affected by the war, asked the Soviet Union to take over some of its tanker fleet so those ships would enjoy naval protection in the gulf war. The idea of "reflagging" ships to give them protection attracted Washington, so the United States made an offer to forestall Kuwait's accepting Soviet protection.

President Reagan made the basic decision after a breakfast meeting on March 4, 1987, with the NSC principals: Shultz, Weinberger, and Carlucci. The State Department strongly supported reflagging and carried the day. It was not regarded as that important. But then a stream of consequent decisions followed: whether to convoy; to sweep for mines; what to do about the Iranian flyboats; whether to use a barge base; and especially the old Beirut question, what were to be the rules of engagement. Those questions crowded subsequent PRG and NSPG agendas. Washington wandered through the decision tree with no clear objective. The reflagging decision went through both the PRG and NSPG and at both, according to Colin Powell, "the risks of inaction were judged to be greater."

Action soon proved to have a cost in human lives. On the night of May 17 an Iraqi aircraft attacked the frigate U.S.S. *Stark* with antiship missiles that inflicted heavy damage and left thirty-five dead. Whether the Iraqis intended to attack an American warship remains in dispute, but the attempt to interdict any vessel at sea appears quite deliberate. The next day in Washington there was an NSPG session to sort out just what had happened. Reagan approved changes in the rules of engagement and augmentation of the forces. In particular the Navy wanted to get some of its newest, most powerful radar equipment on station in the gulf. Those were on AEGIS-equipped cruisers like the *Yorktown* or *Vincennes*. The President allowed the reinforcements. At the same time he held the line against Congress maintaining that the War Powers Act did not apply to the actions in the Persian Gulf.

The Navy got orders to convoy merchant ships in July, something it had been doing for its own supply vessels for over two years. In the first convoy the large supertanker *Bridgeton* was mined. There were other merchantman casualties over succeeding months, and the U.S. frigate *Samuel B. Roberts* was also mined with loss of life. In all, the Navy would escort seventy convoys up the gulf before the service terminated in late 1988. The incremental cost in 1987 alone was $120 million, excluding costs of repairs and casualties.

In October 1987 the Iranians succeeded in getting their imported anti-ship missiles to hit one of the reflagged American tankers. By now Colin Powell was in command of the NSC staff. His new deputy handled most of the action in the Policy Review Group, which held three meetings for every NSPG session. The PRG approved retaliatory strikes on Iranian offshore oil platforms the United States claimed had been used for radar surveillance of the convoys. After the frigate *Roberts* was mined in April 1988 the NSPG convened again, initiating a series of several PRG sessions that worked up a military retaliation plan. The United States struck at selected Iranian targets on the gulf littoral. Chairman of the PRG through this period was John Negroponte, Powell's deputy security adviser, veteran of the Vietnam backroom wars, lately proconsul in Honduras of the Nicaragua secret war. Once approved, Negroponte's PRG plan was executed in the Persian Gulf. When Iranian flyboats and larger naval vessels appeared to react to the strikes, American helicopters and ships sank or damaged a number of them.

Through this long involvement the vague United States objective hardly improved. Secretary of the Navy James H. Webb resigned from the administration out of concern at the seemingly open-ended requirements of the gulf neutrality patrols. On July 3, 1988, the *Vincennes,* one of the Navy's sophisticated radar guided missile cruisers, mistook Iran Air Flight 655, with 290 passengers on board, for an attacking aircraft and shot it down. Ronald Reagan's policy had led full circle: from KAL 007, with the Russians cast as murderers of the innocent, to Iran Air 655, with America itself in that unenviable role. The Public Diplomacy mavens had a hard time once the shoe was on the opposite foot. Had administration policy been somewhat less anti-Soviet in the first instance, the path forward could have been much smoother.

Central America continued to pose its particular problems during Powell's time as national security adviser. Here General Powell probably involved himself more than the "honest broker" image suggests. American officials in Reagan's time always seemed to think they could understand Latin problems with a two-day visit to six or eight countries. General Powell did that too, early on in his national security stewardship. Powell worked closely as a team with Negroponte, who had a primary interest in the field. So strong was Negroponte that he conflicted with area specialist Jose Sorzano and eventually drove the senior director to resign. Powell went to Capitol Hill himself to lobby for a certain compromise on a *contra* "humanitarian" aid package, and he remained involved in the issue as chairman of the Policy Coordinating Group, the administration's new name for the

NSC unit that supervises covert operations. In a retrospective interview at Christmas, 1988, a "ranking White House official" who was probably Powell conceded to *The New York Times* that in Nicaragua "we weren't able to do what we wanted to do," and that it was the one area where Congress had really had an impact on Ronald Reagan.

Panama was probably the policy area on which the administration was most divided at this period. Panamanian politics degenerated in February 1988 when military strongman General Manuel Noriega ousted the civilian government of his country and held elections widely perceived as a sham before installing the government of his choice. Washington tried to support the toppled civilian president. Abrams advocated using force if necessary to overthrow Noriega. General Powell and Frank Carlucci argued that propping up Eric Delvalle, the deposed Panamanian president, would merely be seen as "Yankee imperialism" in Latin America. Indeed that was precisely the argument Noriega used to good effect once the fact of Washington's deliberations became known.

At the Pentagon members of the Joint Chiefs were also pessimistic. Vice Admiral Jonathan Howe, top aide to CJCS Admiral William Crowe went to his boss to argue against the delusion Noriega could be easily removed from power. Crowe took up the theme and became an important voice against the intervention schemes. Jonathan Howe had known General Powell in his last duty post before the White House, when for six months he had been a corps commander for NATO and Howe served at NATO headquarters. Interestingly enough, when General Powell was appointed Chairman of the Joint Chiefs in 1989, his candidate for deputy was Jonathan Howe.

President Reagan decided to limit United States action to sanctions against Panama and refused to recognize the government Noriega installed. But the Treasury Department made many exceptions to the sanctions rules. A coup was attempted against Noriega and failed miserably, vividly demonstrating the extent of Noriega's power.

Colin Powell has been recorded as regretting that he had not acted at an early date to block the grand jury investigation of Noriega for drugs. The indictments, in the security adviser's opinion, turned up the heat on the Panama issue just when going very quietly might have enabled the United States to accomplish something.

In a related instance Colin Powell did block investigation. That was in restricting government cooperation with the investigation of drugs, law enforcement, and foreign policy by a panel of the Senate's Foreign Relations Committee. The subcommittee, headed by Massachusetts Democrat John Kerry, was seen by some in the administration as politically motivated. Both Noriega and *contra* drug angles were being pursued by the investigation, and both had NSC aspects. At one point in the spring of 1988, Kerry asked the General Accounting Office to do an official inquiry into the covert operations links of the drug traffickers.

On May 23, NSC legal counsel Nicholas Rostow learned of the GAO inquiry but said he wanted to think about it before scheduling a meeting. Then other officials began to refuse to cooperate with investigators, citing NSC orders. On June 6, GAO officials met with Dan Levin, Rostow's deputy, who told the GAO that henceforth the NSC staff would be its point of contact on this investigation, and that he was not sure what access would be permitted. Levin and his assistant, Jonathan Scharfman, continued to deny access until July 18, when Nicholas Rostow complained the GAO had not chosen to narrow its inquiry. On July 22 the NSC circulated guidance to the bureaucracy prohibiting cooperation with the GAO. The NSC staff stood fast through the remainder of Reagan's term. National security had clearly impinged on the national interest in halting the flow of drugs. That was the one prominent blemish on Colin Powell's October 1988 declaration that he had made the NSC staff once more a "moral" operation. It was the second congressional investigation sidestepped during the tenure of Colin Powell.

Of course General Powell acted as the President's lieutenant in rejecting congressional oversight. In this he was no different from John Poindexter, Robert McFarlane, Zbig Brzezinski, Henry Kissinger, Mac Bundy, and Gordon Gray, all of whom had rejected congressional invitations in the past. Still, the precedent many former national security staffers defend, sometimes ferociously, lost its value long ago. National security advisers and NSC executive secretaries, at the very dawn of the age, made regular budget presentations to Congress. The range of informal contacts grew to be broader, up to full-court lobbying in the last administration. *Subordinate* NSC staffers *have* testified before Congress, while *former* national security advisers' testimony is *frequently* sought and given. Kissinger's testimony was important to Carter for SALT II ratification, then again to Reagan during ratification of the INF Treaty. In the cases of John Poindexter and Robert McFarlane, the legislature has effectively compelled testimony by keepers of the keys about their own *recent* activities, while a sitting national security adviser, Zbigniew Brzezinski, felt obliged to testify on matters of current and continuing import.

Colin Powell was perhaps most successful in the arena of Soviet-American relations. He worked hard on the Washington summit Gorbachev and Reagan held in December 1987, and became the top summit planner for their return engagement in Moscow six months later. The Moscow summit of May 1988 won regard as the smoothest event of that magnitude yet. By dint of tremendous lobbying effort, Reagan was able to present Gorbachev with the instrument of ratification for the INF Treaty as the main event of the visit. General Powell coasted out of office on the strength of that performance. The Army then appointed him to head its Forces Command, in charge of all troops within the United States. Like his NATO corps command, which had been V Corps in Frankfurt, West Germany, the Army assignment lasted for just a few months. *President* George Bush reached down to nominate the general to the nation's most prestigious military post, Chairman of the Joint Chiefs of Staff.

ANOTHER NEW BEGINNING

▲▲▲

Unparalleled among Presidents in the degree of his national security experience prior to taking office, George Bush had been Vice President, director of central intelligence, ambassador to the United Nations, emissary to China, had done chores for several Presidents. Bush had observed in action most of the figures in the national security business, and participated in the councils of several administrations. President Bush made hardly any changes in NSC machinery; his selection of people to handle national security affairs met with wide public approval.

Bush administration organization for national security remains virtually identical to that provided by NSDD-276. The Policy Review Group has been enlarged to become a committee, the Deputies Committee, which remains under the chairmanship of the deputy national security adviser. There is a Principals Committee the keeper of the keys chairs that raises questions to the NSC level and implements presidential decisions. The NSC subcommittee supervising covert operations is also chaired by the national security adviser. Beneath this apex is a network of eight Policy Coordinating Committees (PCCs) that have regional or functional specialties. These working groups clear the rafters of the debris of interagency groups that so cluttered the Reagan years. Policy reviews have been rechristened National Security Review (NSR) papers and presidential directives are now National Security Decisions (NSDs). These distinctions the new President established with NSD-1 on Inauguration Day.

As newly inaugurated Presidents have done since Richard Nixon's time, Bush swiftly put in orders for a number of policy reviews. Such reviews serve to signal shifts in the distribution of support for given policies among the myriad islands of power and interest that make up government. George Bush announced there would be policy reviews at the same time he named his keeper of the keys, on November 23, 1988, two months before Inauguration Day.

"We're going to take whatever time is necessary for a thorough review and analysis on our policy initiatives," Bush declared. "Then [we'll] come out with our own strategic objectives, and then move this country forward."

It was a tall order. With the hiatus in staffing and changeover at senior levels typical of the change in administrations, too many key posts stood vacant. A few top officials forged ahead to get business done. Rozanne Ridgway, a diplomat who had already put in for retirement, spent her last months running several Bush-style PCCs that drafted policy reviews. The most notable was NSR-3, a review of Soviet-American relations that went before the Bush NSC in April 1989. The option selected has been reported as status quo-plus, an approach only slightly warmer than that of the Reagan administration.

This seemed the pattern in arms control, the subject of NSR-14, late getting started because of the late arrival on the NSC staff of the man who chaired the study, RAND Corporation political scientist Arnold Kanter, who is a moderate on technical issues. The Bush administration refused to react to Soviet overtures before the inauguration. Then Bush nominated Richard Burt as chief arms negotiator. Burt, the entrepreneur who had lost out against Richard Perle in the Reagan years, made it to the top after all; it had just taken eight extra years, lost time, years the locusts had eaten.

When the next round of formal START negotiations convened, in Geneva in June 1989, Bush proposed further experiments in intrusive verification *prior* to concluding an arms reduction agreement. Bush also seems to be resisting the agreement achieved by his predecessor. That is probably related to Bush's interest in mobile deployment of ICBMs, and in preserving the SDI option and interpreting the ABM Treaty. Problems also persist with formulas for counting weapons and air-launched cruise missiles.

The idea for the mobile ICBM deployments actually originated during Reagan's administration, the product of a blue-ribbon commission headed by General Brent Scowcroft. The former keeper of the keys opposed a mobile ban in the START treaty, but Reagan had been more concerned with trying to prohibit Soviet missiles from assuming the mobile configuration. This wheel too came full circle, for George Bush selected Brent Scowcroft as his national security adviser.

"I realized on day one of the 1988 campaign," James Baker recalled, "that George would probably like to have him as NSC adviser." This came from a close Bush associate, the man George made secretary of state, who had once almost convinced Ronald Reagan to name him keeper of the keys. Jim Baker knew what he was talking about. Bush had seen Scowcroft in action in the last year of Jerry Ford's presidency, when Bush directed the CIA and Brent ran the NSC staff; then again, when the Vice President observed the Tower Board, of which Scowcroft was a member. The appointment became the second time in NSC history that an individual got the call for a return engagement as keeper of the keys.

The appointment did draw some flak from conservative circles suspicious of Henry Kissinger (Scowcroft had consulted for Henry Kissinger's firm and eventually became its president), particularly when other Bush appointments went to old Kissinger cadres. Larry Eagleburger became undersecretary of state and Richard H. Solomon assistant secretary for East Asia and the

Pacific. At the NSC, Kissinger-era veterans start with Peter Rodman and include Robert Blackwill, senior specialist for Soviet affairs. Pentagon colleagues include Henry Rowen and now Jonathan Howe.

Still, seeing cabals is often too easy. Kissinger actually dissociated himself from early efforts by Secretary of State James Baker to invoke his support on Eastern European policy. More to the point, the staff is Scowcroft's, not Henry Kissinger's. Those who focus overly on the Kissinger legacy in United States national security could miss the very real and present Scowcroft connection. Robert Gates is the key Scowcroft man in the new NSC. A career CIA officer, Gates had been Scowcroft's Soviet specialist in the Ford administration. In corridors at Langley it is whispered that Gates is a creation of the NSC system, a bright and brash Kansas boy, but one of an army of talented mid-level (GS-13) analysts at Langley. *From* the Ford NSC, Gates returned to supergrade executive jobs at the CIA, assisting the national intelligence officer for the Soviet Union, holding that position himself, and that of executive assistant to the director of central intelligence and then to the national security adviser.

Bob Gates flourished in the Reagan administration, in which Bill Casey made him the CIA's chief analyst, then promoted him to deputy director for central intelligence, the second top job in the entire intelligence community. Gates acted in Casey's stead from December 1986, when the old spymaster was stricken with a brain tumor. Reagan nominated Gates to succeed Casey, but it seems he had been a shade too close to several events in the Iran-Contra period, in particular the preparation of false testimony for Bill Casey. Gates sat through nomination hearings but eventually withdrew himself from consideration for the post.

Now Brent Scowcroft has brought Bob Gates back to the NSC as deputy security adviser. This forty-five-year-old Sovietologist with a Ph.D. from Georgetown holds a presidential appointment to a job that has often featured action. Gates also chairs the NSC Deputies Committee and is a major collaborator with Scowcroft on oversight of CIA covert operations. It is his third NSC staff assignment.

Actually the new national security adviser has staffed his Soviet section carefully. Bob Blackwill impressed Scowcroft, although not Kissinger, in his earlier NSC tour. Condoleeza Rice, a bright, young, African-American policy professional, formerly an academic at Stanford University, got Scowcroft's attention during a seminar at the Aspen Institute. Counselor Peter Rodman of course grew close to Brent during their Ford administration NSC days. Also of note is Stephen Hadley, who has gone to the Pentagon as assistant secretary for policy, Dick Perle's old job. Hadley not only worked for Scowcroft on Ford's NSC staff but came back with Brent as a principal investigator for the Tower Board. Blackwill lasted through the fall of 1990 but then left Scowcroft's staff. Both he and Rice had favored a stronger line toward the Soviet Union than the administration in fact adopted.

Brent Scowcroft's style as assistant to the President for national security is to function as éminence grise to his President. This keeper is an informal adviser in deed as well as theory, spending many hours a day closeted with Bush in the Oval Office. Scowcroft advises upon whatever may be the business of the moment, without regard to whether they happen to be at an NSC meeting. President Bush appears much taken with his keeper, joking in early 1990 about a "Scowcroft Award" his press secretary deserved. There have nevertheless been rumors in Washington that Scowcroft might move over to become director of central intelligence.

With the Scowcroft method paperwork must be done in the early hours, before the daily briefing when the kitchen cabinet goes into session. Otherwise papers await the evening or the snippets of time during which the President takes care of political or ceremonial functions. There are no extra opportunities during presidential trips because either Scowcroft or his deputy accompany Bush. In practice this enhances Bob Gates's role as deputy, since throughout most of the day he is the senior NSC staff official available. Gates is even more formidable as his Deputies Committee is already the focal point for the NSC policy papers, and because Gates has been Bush's most frequent emissary.

George Bush refused to react when Soviet leader Mikhail Gorbachev came to the United States in December 1988, while Bush remained President-elect, to declare unilateral troop reductions, including substantial cutbacks in Soviet forces stationed in Eastern Europe. Instead, Bush repeated his formula about awaiting the results of his policy reviews. The Russians continued to elaborate their proposals, adding a further layer of reductions they proposed be mutual, and for the first time releasing official figures tabulating Warsaw Pact and NATO strength in various categories of military equipment.

By spring 1989, with a NATO summit conference approaching at Brussels, the United States seemed oddly out of step with its alliance partners, except for Great Britain. Most of the others called for a more positive response to the Soviet overtures. In particular the West Germans favored concessions on tactical nuclear weapons Washington opposed. Ministerial talks failed to break the impasse. It began to look as if the Brussels summit might bring about an open split among NATO allies.

In Washington, alliance policy questions were on hold owing to the policy reviews Bush had ordered. A paper called NSR-12 was to establish fresh guidelines for basic national security policy. In charge of the PCC working group drafting the paper was Paul D. Wolfowitz, back from a short tour as ambassador to Indonesia. Highly conservative, Wolfowitz had been one of eight on the notorious B Team panel in 1976, later being purged by Paul Warnke from an ACDA verification job. Most influential in Haig's Foggy Bottom, where he headed the Policy Planning Staff, Wolfowitz encountered foot-dragging on the policy review for Bush. Whatever the reason, his PCC had continued very slowly with NSR-12. According to one account, by early May 1989 only a preliminary draft of the policy paper was ready, according to another just a single section of the paper had been completed, and that Scowcroft had returned as inadequate.

Aware of the impending NATO summit, President Bush needed quick decisions; he could no longer wait for the results of NSR-12. Brent Scowcroft took the lead in fashioning a conventional arms control proposal the President could announce at Brussels. It was a complete reversal of the gatekeeper's attitude of three months earlier, when he had said, "I'm very relaxed about the time we're taking."

The national security adviser, the secretary of state, and a few associates assembled a plan for "asymmetrical" reductions in NATO and Warsaw Pact forces. Then they circulated their option for comment. It is said the JCS price for supporting the bid was big cuts in the numbers of U.S. forces that would be affected, from 75,000 down to about 30,000. Deliberations proceeded at the Bush summer home at Kennebunkport, Maine. President Bush bought the option, then presented the proposal at Brussels to good reviews. He asked the Russians to reduce by more than a quarter of a million men, to agree to the plan in a single year, and to implement it in a wonderfully short two-year period. A treaty would be achieved in 1990, a year later than Bush had proposed, without the U.S. initial proposal ever having changed to meet circumstances as Eastern Europe became transformed.

So far the most frequent criticism of Bush national security policy is that it has been too slow getting into gear. *Aviation Week and Space Technology* called it "The Strategy Morass." *The Washington Post* headlined one story, MILITARY BUDGET TO PRECEDE STRATEGIC REVIEW. Perhaps the real world is getting too complex for the policy papers, or maybe the papers need better focus on what is truly long-term.

"I believe the president is not trying to make quick headlines," Scowcroft told the reporters. "What he is trying is to put into place a foreign and a national security policy which will look forward . . . toward the end of the century."

That was in February 1989. By June nothing more was to be heard about the strategy review, declared to be at an end with no significant changes. In the interim the early revelations about the Bush NSC system, the NSRs and NSDs, occurred in an orchestrated fashion that bears the earmarks of a deliberate White House effort, likely intended to show the administration getting its work done.

In the meantime the first serious crisis, like Lyndon Johnson's, came in Panama. During his presidential campaign George Bush had gone along with the Reagan administration rhetoric against Panamanian General Manuel Noriega. Bush even survived a momentary flap over whether he had had early knowledge of Noriega drug trafficking links. In office, Bush openly invited the Panamanian military to overthrow the errant dictator. That was in May 1989. Yet five months later, when Panamanian officers tried to do just that, Washington was revealed to be in disarray.

As it happened, it was not a case of being taken unawares. Major Moisés Giroldi Vega, who was commander of the guard battalion at Panama Defense Forces (PDF) headquarters, wanted U.S. forces to block two critical access routes in Panama City and provide air cover to prevent pro-Noriega forces from coming to the general's aid once the coup had been launched. American officers passed the requests to Washington.

The initial contacts had occurred in Panama City on Sunday, October 1. It was just that day that General Colin Powell took over as Chairman of the Joint Chiefs. On the NSC staff, beset once more with differences between its area specialist and the State Department, continuity was interrupted two days before when Everett Briggs, the NSC Latin America man, resigned. Bernard Aronson, State's assistant secretary for the region, had had a tough fight for Senate confirmation and might not have fully established himself.

Perhaps there was confusion about objectives. On the one hand, there were executive orders on the books prohibiting assassinations. The United States had had to be wary of coup plots because of their potential to lead to such assassinations. This, at least, is reportedly the reason the administration desisted in the spring of 1989 when members of the Senate Select Committee on Intelligence raised that doubt, after CIA officials made informal approaches regarding plans for new covert operations in Panama. On the other hand, there was Bush's open invitation to a coup.

Word reached Defense Secretary Richard Cheney at about 2:30 A.M. on October 2 when Colin Powell phoned him. Cheney passed the news to Brent Scowcroft. President Bush called an Oval Office meeting for 9:00 A.M. He approved blocking the requested routes, but only where they passed inside U.S. military reservations, and only in ways consistent with the Panama Canal treaties. He did not permit any air blockade of the jointly operated Howard Air Force Base. Though General Noriega was under indictment in the United States for his alleged drug links, apparently no decision was made about taking forceful action to apprehend him in the context of a coup attempt. Ultimately the United States would be left open to charges of intervention without having made arrangements to really do the job right.

There was certainly confusion about Panamanian intentions and activities. Washington expected the coup that day, and Cheney has claimed the United States was told the coup would not happen if General Noriega was actually present at PDF headquarters. Instead the coup attempt occurred the next day, October 3, at a moment Noriega was in fact present. The plotters were at least half successful—they took over PDF headquarters and held Noriega for four or five hours.

For Washington the question became whether to take custody of Noriega to bring him to the United States. The plotters had not offered to turn over Noriega and in fact argued about it at PDF headquarters. At the White House just before noon the situation was the subject of a meeting among

Bush, Dick Cheney, Colin Powell, Brent Scowcroft, Bob Gates, and White House Chief of Staff John Sununu. President Bush deferred action on any more forceful intervention. In Panama City a key colleague of Major Giroldi switched sides at this crucial moment. Within the next couple of hours loyalist PDF troops crushed the coup. Major Giroldi and other plotters were executed.

Despite the NSC policy papers, what appears to be missing is a sense of strategy. John Sununu ordered postmortems after the Panama affair, but it was too late for the plotters there. It was also too late for the prodemocracy movement in the People's Republic of China where, again, Bush seems to have responded tactically. That student and worker movement flourished, then foundered, in the first half of 1989. In a visit early that year Bush invited a prominent Chinese dissident to dinner at the U.S. embassy, then canceled the invitation to assuage the Chinese hard-liners. Ambassador to China and onetime NSC operator Winston Lord gracefully took responsibility for the gaffe. Prodemocracy demonstrations continued, with statements of encouragement from Washington, until June, when the PRC government sent in troops to clear the streets of Peking. There were untold numbers of casualties, probably thousands, among Chinese citizens and students. International sympathy for the democracy demonstrators was transformed into opprobrium for the Chinese government.

President Bush's reaction was not the decisive break with the Chinese hard-liners that everyone expected, but merely a decision to suspend various categories of relations with the PRC, notably military sales worth about $800 million. In July, Bush sent Brent Scowcroft on his first diplomatic mission, to Peking to talk to the hard-liners, taking Larry Eagleburger with him. Scowcroft and Eagleburger made a second trip in December, just after the Malta summit. That trip was revealed only when Scowcroft appeared in public toasting the Chinese, while the July trip remained secret even longer, until television reporters stumbled on evidence of the visit.

By then American firms had resumed work on their material for the Chinese in the expectation that trade controls would be lifted. A parade of former officials, including Henry Kissinger, Alexander Haig, and Richard Nixon, traveled to China and advocated reconciliation with the Chinese hard-liners. Like Bush they argue the need to maintain relations with this Asian superpower. In contrast Winston Lord, once Henry's man, now believes that "the United States cannot fully restore relations with China until those responsible for the June debacle and its aftermath are no longer at the helm."

This soft spot for the Chinese is even more striking compared with the administration's caution in the face of the most momentous political development of the decade, taking place simultaneously in Eastern Europe and the Soviet Union. There the Warsaw Pact literally unraveled as Communist governments fell in country after country, Communist parties were dissolved, and the Russians, in pursuit of *perestroika,* looked on benignly.

Zbigniew Brzezinski saw this trend relatively early and has begun to argue that communism is dead.

While this upheaval gathered momentum, the Bush administration pushed its cosmetic proposal for a 29,000-man reduction in U.S. forces assigned to NATO in exchange for "asymmetrical" Soviet reductions of 250,000 men. Since some 14,000 American troops in NATO were working with the nuclear weapons eliminated by the INF Treaty of 1988, the real reductions involved in the U.S. proposal can be seen as marginal indeed. It was not the arms treaty but the Iraqi crisis of 1990 that brought about reductions of U.S. forces in Europe.

In the fall of 1989, President Bush announced he would meet Soviet leader Gorbachev aboard ship in the Mediterranean at the beginning of December. Bush then resisted the suggestion that Eastern Europe be made part of the summit agenda. When the meetings actually occurred at Malta, the political tidal wave was in the act of engulfing East Germany, with consequent dismantling of the Berlin Wall and serious talk of German re-unification. The Bush administration initially opposed German reunification. It also made no move, at least with its budget plan for fiscal year 1991, to redistribute money planned for foreign aid to assist the fragile emerging democracies of Eastern Europe. At the level of basic military *glasnost,* though General Colin Powell attended a conference of East-West military leaders in Vienna in January 1990, NSC staffer Robert Blackwill permitted publication without change of a paper he wrote before joining the NSC that concludes controls on military maneuvers would benefit the Soviet Union more than the United States.

When he announced the Malta summit, Bush admitted that the bureaucracy had been excluded from the planning; in particular, Secretary of Defense Cheney had no knowledge of the matter. Apparently no meeting of the NSC was held. Similarly, no NSC meeting occurred during the October 1989 coup attempt in Panama, or the December coup attempt in the Philippines, when Bush authorized U.S. jet aircraft to prevent coup forces using air support against government troops in Manila. So far as is now evident, there was also no NSC meeting in connection with Bush's most ambitious foreign policy move of his first year—the Christmas 1989 invasion of Panama.

If ever there was a contingency in search of a justification, Panama was it. Plenty of recrimination followed the abortive October coup attempt. Then there was talk of further CIA covert operations against Panamanian dictator Manuel Noriega, and of what constraints the agency was or was not under in its activities in Panama. Though nothing happened on the surface, a new U.S. commander took charge of Southern Command in Panama with secret instructions to revise the contingency plans for military action in that country. Meanwhile, Noriega remained defiant, calling himself Panama's maximum leader and declaring a state of war with the United States. This, combined with the killing of one American soldier and roughing up of a naval officer and his wife, became the justification for Operation Just Cause, the U.S. invasion.

President Bush made his decision for the invasion on December 17. Attired in gray slacks and a blue blazer after a Sunday brunch, the President met in his office at the residence with General Powell and Secretary Cheney. These advisers reportedly told Bush that no small secret operation could guarantee toppling Noriega but that an invasion would unseat the dictator whether or not he was captured. Of course the basic problem with an invasion, then and later, was that it would serve to convince Latin countries that "Yankee imperialism" still flourishes. Secretary of State James Baker was not present to make such an argument. Baker only attended the pro forma Oval Office meeting on the afternoon of December 19 where the President confirmed his decision and reviewed final details.

Far from a neat, tidy package, Just Cause may well go down as a poorly planned mess. The juxtaposition of this resort to force with the Soviet complacency over the disintegration of their hegemony over Eastern Europe is especially stark. It will not help George Bush with history that his NSC system seems organized to implement secret decisions secretly arrived at.

Similar things can be said regarding the first big test of the Bush NSC, the operation called Desert Shield. This reaped the seeds sown by Reagan administration policies in the Persian Gulf during the 1980s, which convinced Iraq it could have its way. Misled by inept U.S. diplomacy, compounded by the failure of the American ambassador to caution Baghdad against any use of force, Iraq invaded and occupied Kuwait on August 2, 1990. President Bush sent American forces to Saudi Arabia to deter further Iraqi adventures. This was intervention writ large, the biggest U.S. military deployment since the Vietnam War. George Bush also assembled an international coalition and expeditionary force and secured United Nations and congressional resolutions justifying his actions.

Key decisions occurred within hours of the initial Iraqi invasion, and within the week President Bush had expanded his goal from defending Saudi Arabia to ejecting Iraq from Kuwait. Brent Scowcroft stayed with Bush during all that time. Other NSC principals met with the President at least twice. It is not clear whether these were actual sessions of the National Security Council. In any case the basic decision had already been made before the second of the meetings. Bush used every pulpit he could reach to escalate his rhetoric, in hopes of inducing Iraq to withdraw, while even Scowcroft abandoned customary invisibility to make unusual numbers of appearances on the weekly television news interview programs. At the time of this writing the United States stood at the verge of total war in the Persian Gulf.

Proper conduct of foreign policy, and sound national security policies, will continue to be crucial. This is true for the United States in Latin America, in China, the Middle East, on arms control, everywhere. The NSC and its staff must contribute to sound policy. Already the lines are being drawn.

In a speech at Georgetown University in the fall of 1989, Lawrence Eagleburger *lamented* the end of the cold war. During that era, he argued, it was easy to tell the good guys from the bad guys and make decisions accordingly. If the national security system is not to be conducive to proper solutions, it must be recognized as part of the problem.

PART IX

▲

THE PRESIDENTS' LIEUTENANTS

In the more than four decades that the United States has had a National Security Council, the cold war has waxed and waned, international problems have changed, much is different from what it was. This narrative has shown the rise of the national security adviser to a place of preeminent stature in the American system of government. In addition, the National Security Council staff, partly as the result of advisers as individuals making history, has acquired an institutional existence and importance few observers have yet accorded it.

In the received wisdom it is Dwight D. Eisenhower who is supposed to have created the post of national security adviser. In fact, Ike gave that job a name but Harry Truman created it. It was also Truman who began, with Averell Harriman, the practice of dispatching security advisers on confidential missions. In turn it was Dwight Eisenhower, not John F. Kennedy, who created the modern keeper of the keys, permitting Gordon Gray in the heat of the Berlin crisis to exercise virtually all the functions of successors from Mac Bundy onward.

In a number of ways the NSC and its staff peaked under Eisenhower, indeed specifically under Gray. Andrew Goodpaster might dispute that, for the general believes that the Reagan NSC system with its array of NSDDs maintained an equivalent body of agreed policies. Under Reagan, however, the system was increasingly dominated by the policy entrepreneurs, subordinates in the bureaucracy and even on the NSC staff who used the NSDDs as tools when they agreed with them, but targets when they did not. In Ike's day, a proper sense of decorum (for want of a stronger word) still existed. The NSC was the *President in council* and not to be trifled with. Far from the received wisdom that the Eisenhower NSC was a moribund paper mill, between Gray and Goodpaster the system had flexibility, security, and a formal mechanism to monitor implementation.

John Kennedy's major innovations were the White House Situation Room and the enhanced NSC staff. Both helped diminish the importance of the NSC. With staff commentaries and the daily cable traffic to draw on, Kennedy changed the focus more to current events, and changed the NSC papers from policy reviews to simple directives. The President's creation of an EXCOM during the Cuban missile crisis merely confirmed the earlier trends.

Lyndon Johnson continued the Kennedy NSC system. Both Presidents used the device of Oval Office meetings to replace the formal NSC sessions. That was indeed an important development in the history of the National Security Council, for such private meetings increased in importance steadily. Ike had used these for crises, to keep them outside the NSC structure for planning. Every one of his successors has followed suit, right down to George Bush who had no NSC meeting during Panama. It is a canard to claim that the National Security Council is a crisis mechanism. But Johnson brought long-range issues into the private forum he called his Tuesday Lunch.

Johnson also developed the device of using NSC staff for operational purposes. He started with Bundy but eventually worked down to the staff level with Robert Komer. Again the conventional view —that Henry Kissinger was the first NSC operative—is incorrect. This President did have the finesse, however, by designating Komer as an independent special assistant, to distinguish his operative functions from those of the regular NSC staff. By the end of Johnson's administration the National Security Council in its modern form was essentially in place.

Henry Kissinger, seconded by Zbig Brzezinski, is responsible for the misconception that there is a structural conflict between national security adviser and secretary of state. Observers who argue this ignore the amicable relations that persisted among Dean Rusk, Bundy, and Walt Rostow, as well as the cooperation *five* national security advisers gave George Shultz. There is no inherent conflict, rather there is a potential for tension between men of power that can only be resolved by mutual goodwill. Two examples demonstrate this: The "structural" conflict evaporated when Scowcroft replaced Kissinger; the conflict during Reagan's administration involved the secretaries of state and defense, both NSC principals, rather than the national security adviser. Ultimately it is the President's responsibility to keep his house in order and banish the conflicts among unruly subordinates. Presidents have compiled a rather poor record in this regard.

▲▲▲

▲▲▲

ince the inception of the National Security Council twenty men have held its top job. This includes two—Sidney Souers and James Lay—who served before there was a "national security adviser." It includes two—Souers again and Averell Harriman—who had the job without the title. It also includes three men who held the job on an acting basis—William Jackson, Robert Komer, and Alton Keel, Jr. During the NSC's first four decades two men have held the job more than once: Robert Cutler and Brent Scowcroft.

At forty-two Mac Bundy was and remains the youngest man ever to become national security adviser. Jack Kennedy was but a year older. Some former officials speculate this relative youthfulness was a detriment, that the trait helped account for the hubris, that they lacked the real experience to think through the problems they suddenly faced as they became the leaders of a superpower. That is an interesting thought but it is only speculation. In fact, Kennedy was seconded by plenty of older officials, people like Rusk and Harriman, so it should not have been a problem. On the other hand, it happens that the *second* youngest keeper of the keys was Richard Allen, who turned forty-five in 1981. That tour proved far less successful than Bundy's. If Richard Nixon had given him the job in 1969, Allen would have been thirty-three. Youth was undoubtedly a reason Nixon turned *away* from Allen, to forty-six-year-old Henry Kissinger. Robert McFarlane was also forty-six when he became security adviser.

In terms of occupation, Mac Bundy's appointment was a departure from the practice of choosing men of affairs. Previously there had not been a clear pattern: Bobby Cutler and Sid Souers were businessmen; Dillon Anderson a lawyer; Gordon Gray a journalist. Bundy set a precedent. From Kennedy through Carter every President selected an academic, excepting Brent Scowcroft who had been a general. Scowcroft became the first military man to serve in this post, but during Reagan's years fully half of his several keepers came from the military.

It has been fashionable in the wake of Iran-Contra to mark down the propensity for error to the military, a temptation to which the joint investigating committee succumbed. Blaming the military for weaknesses in the national security system makes little sense. One could, for example, make an equally strong and unjust case against foreign-born, naturalized

Americans. To establish such strictures and call it a reform is rather pathetic.

Another variant of this argument is to blame the problems on the use of detailees from other agencies. Too many of them, the argument goes, make a narrowly focused NSC staff. However, until 1953 the *entire* NSC staff was made up of detailees and it was never accused of being narrow. There has always been a strong component of detailees but, since Eisenhower, never a dominant one. Even under McFarlane and with John Poindexter's "Navy mafia," the rule of thumb for the NSC staff was about one third military, one third detailees from elsewhere in government, and one third from outside. The use of detailees is inescapable precisely because they have expertise of exactly the kinds the National Security Council staff needs.

More serious are the political questions, the questions of loyalty to President or party as they affect service on the National Security Council staff. In one of the Chinese Communist upheavals a couple of decades ago the conundrum was phrased as "Red versus expert." The NSC policy entrepreneurs demonstrated that policy paralysis can flow from forced ideological purity just as surely as from anarchic tendencies within a bureaucracy. Nor can any system be invincible when the President has no strategy, or is asleep at the wheel.

In the course of sworn testimony before the Iran-Contra joint committee, Admiral John Poindexter declared he had taken into his own hands the decision to divert funds from the Iranian arms deals to the *contra* war. Poindexter wanted to "insulate" Ronald Reagan from the decision "to provide him some future deniability." The reactions voiced by Poindexter's peers were uniformly negative. "This goes way beyond the borderline," Brent Scowcroft observed. Zbigniew Brzezinski told reporters he "could not have conceived of the situation in which I would have done that." It was the same with Henry Kissinger. "I was a far much more assertive security adviser than Poindexter," Henry said, "and I would never have dreamed of making a decision like that."

It was, however, precisely the actions of such characters as Kissinger and Brzezinski that made possible the NSC staff excesses of the Reagan years. This is not to say that national security advisers should take blame for the later excesses, or that they did not themselves respond properly to presidential authority.

To be sure, the buck stopped on the President's desk, not John Poindexter's, so Ronald Reagan must bear the major responsibility for what happened. But the system of making decisions and creating policy ought to have worked to restrain Poindexter, preventing precipitate or illegal action. That the national security policy machinery did not operate in this fashion is again partly Reagan's fault, but partly it resides in the accumulation of NSC history recounted here.

A national security adviser today can be more or less conscious of the responsibility he bears, skillful, capable, or expert in the subject. The times no longer allow the adviser to be anonymous, Sidney Souers's preferred mode, because the post has acquired so much prominence. I. M. Destler, a most accomplished private observer of the NSC system, suggested at the outset of the Reagan years that the post be abolished in favor of the executive secretary provided for in the National Security Act of 1947. One has to ask whether such a course is any longer feasible. The idea of national security and the national security state has acquired a concrete character and meaning never anticipated by those unfortunates who coined the phrase. Today a President who wanted to abolish the post of national security adviser would probably have to fight to do it.

The transformation is apparent just from language: For the very phrase "National Security Council" no longer means what it did in Eisenhower's time. Today most people asked about the NSC would think of the national security *adviser* and his small *staff* of aides in the West Wing and Old Executive Office Building. In Ike's day the NSC was the President in council or, at a minimum, a reference to the NSC principals—the Vice President and secretaries of state and defense.

An adviser's writ goes no further than the President's confidence in him, but that can be very far indeed. Iran-Contra shows that writ can press at the boundaries of legality and cross those of established policy. At the same time the national security adviser's grasp of the issues and day-to-day actions of the bureaucracy make the President dependent on him. It is a very symbiotic relationship the keepers have with their chiefs.

A keeper of the keys serves only at the President's pleasure, of course. But another way to put it is that one of the single most important positions in the American government is being left solely to the vagaries of personal choice.

The logical alternative is to put designees for national security adviser up for the advice and consent of the Senate. Zbigniew Brzezinski favors this, but only as part of a larger scheme that would give more formal powers to the keeper of the keys. The most telling argument against confirmation for the national security adviser is that he belongs to the President's *personal* staff, an entity that ought to be answerable only to the President. Most former NSC staff subscribe to this position. Men who work for the President believe in the presidency.

Presidents certainly need personal staffs and should have them. Government is enormously complex, and the Executive Office of the President is one of the fastest-growing entities in federal government. Also there is good reason to have national security experts on such staffs; a case can be made that a President is entitled to a personal foreign policy representative in addition to his official one, the secretary of state.

Unfortunately there is some ambiguity about the status of the National Security Council and the keeper of the keys. Only the national security adviser and such others who hold presidential appointments can be counted among personal staff. The NSC itself was created by an act of Congress, has its own budget line and authority, and is *not* counted as personal staff *by the White House* when it is a matter of mess privileges or parking spaces along West Executive Avenue. The law creates an NSC to be served by a staff under an executive secretary. *The national security adviser has no existence in law whatsoever.*

Not only does the law not provide for the keeper of the keys, it provides next to nothing for the national security staff. There are no statements clarifying what the NSC staff is, whether it is a personal or an institutional staff, who may be on it (beyond an executive secretary), or what it may or may not do. These matters are simply not provided for in Section 402(c) of the National Security Act, which governs the NSC staff.

Defenders of presidential power object that a President should be free to arrange his own advisers, and would do whatever he wants anyway. Thus Jack Kennedy's great wordsmith, Theodore Sorensen, wrote after Iran-Contra that "formal obligatory structures are neither the problem nor the solution." Similarly, Sorensen notes, "any move to mandate how the NSC should function—in effect instructing the president whom he must and must not hear—would be both unwise and unworkable." This is a conventional view and is the basic reason why both the Tower Board and the Iran-Contra joint congressional committee shied away from recommendations about NSC staff or structure.

The same problem exists in the same National Security Act with respect to establishing ground rules for the Central Intelligence Agency. Setting ground rules *is* a legislative function and it is a proper one, not at all the same thing as creating "formal obligatory structures." Appropriate ground rules would have helped *protect* Ronald Reagan from Iran-Contra.

Examination of the history of the National Security Council reveals that activities undertaken during the Reagan years are not aberrations. The kinds of maneuvers attempted by Richard Pipes, Constantine Menges, or Oliver North have antecedents in the activities of previous national security staffs. Current practices have evolved from past ones, and they will recur, *unless* proper ground rules are set. To regard the Reagan excesses as merely a people problem invites repetition.

Such ground rules should be set by law, not by administrative fiat. Regulations created at the stroke of a pen may be done away with just as swiftly. This is the problem with a solution like Carlucci's edict against covert operations by NSC staff, one of the few reforms the national security adviser instituted after Iran-Contra. Keepers of the keys seek to keep Congress out of the NSC business of regulating the NSC by monopolizing action themselves and denying jurisdiction.

Which brings us to oversight. Here we have another instance of the classic question: Who will watch the watchers? In accordance with a system of checks and balances, a President should not be responsible for regulating himself, which he would be as overseer of the NSC staff. Indeed it is naive to suppose the President would have time or inclination for detailed oversight. The same applies to the national security adviser, who was appointed by the President. The usual practice in American government is that the Congress oversees the executive branch.

Should the NSC staff be subject to oversight? This is a huge question with many ramifications. First we must ask how the national security machinery can best serve the United States into the twenty-first century. National security theorists ask citizens to accept unprecedented infringements of basic rights while asserting that a particular institution, which is *known* to have been at or across the borderline of legality in the past, should not be subject to scrutiny.

Amendment of the National Security Act of 1947 should be the focus of the debate. The law is the place to update the government for the future, and to overcome the mistakes of the drafters of the 1947 act, for this opportunity can be used to insert the ground rules for national security staffs that are missing from Section 402(c). At a *minimum* the law should be amended so that the NSC staff authorized by the law corresponds to the White House national security staff that actually exists. This conclusion is made with full understanding of the difficulty of amending laws, especially those as complex as the National Security Act.

One reform of the law should be to provide a legal basis for the position of national security adviser. With proper consultation between the executive branch and Congress there is no reason a President's desire to personally employ a security adviser cannot be built into the law. The relationship between security adviser and Congress can be spelled out in detail.

What has passed for inquiry thus far is a collection of tangential investigations that did not, could not, or were not allowed to penetrate to the heart of the national security policy process. Instead of central questions of policy and process, overseers have largely focused on corruption and controversy. There was little interest in the 1980 bill to make the national security adviser subject to Senate confirmation, or the 1988 one for congressional access to national security decision documents, whatever they may be called by the administration of the moment. On the executive side the Murphy Commission report of 1975 was the last serious survey, but one so broad it devoted little specific attention to the NSC staff.

Whatever else it did or did not do, it is probably safe to say the Iran-Contra affair demonstrated a national consensus against NSC staff involvement in covert operations. That stricture should be made permanent in charter legislation for the NSC staff.

Another fair subject for the charter legislation is NSC staff lobbying and public information activities. From the beginning of the age there has been a temptation here, though in Truman's day the drive was directed at the Soviets. The mechanisms of psychological warfare were created to combat a perceived enemy but have ended up being used against the American people. To a disturbing degree also, national security operators have allowed these efforts to become intertwined with lobbying for the President's program. Moreover, the psychological warfare mechanisms were not isolated cases but rather a repeated refrain in NSC activities: PSB for Harry Truman; OCB for Dwight Eisenhower; the NSAM-308 Committee and VIG of Lyndon Johnson; the OPD of Ronald Reagan. A ban on the public diplomacy activity by the NSC staff is worth considering.

As for NSC staff lobbying, Presidents have had things too much their own way. The national security adviser has become a heavyweight lobbyist, one who speaks with authority and the prestige of the President. At the same time the keeper of the keys is supposed to be *not* subject to the call of those same legislators he is lobbying. Presidents otherwise make extensive and expensive provision for promotion of their legislative programs. If the national security adviser is to be deemed an additional lobbyist, then perhaps it is fair he *should* be confirmed by the Senate. Such a process would provide keepers of the keys with a first opportunity to establish connections on the Hill. It is worth noting that other presidential advisers of equivalent rank, for example the chairman of the Council of Economic Advisers, *do* routinely testify before Congress.

An additional question to ponder has been raised by the fracas over the national security decision documents. These directives constitute information and the question is: To whom does information belong? The ultimate answer is the American taxpayer. Too many games are being played with information generated by the federal government, its use, and its declassification. This is the stuff of bureaucratic politics, too much of which may stifle American dynamism as we move toward the twenty-first century.

Presidential directives are certainly germane to the work of Congress. All branches of federal government require access to the product of other branches. That is the meaning of separated institutions sharing power, at the heart of the American constitutional system. The executive may have to classify sensitive information, but so long as security can be maintained, classification per se should not constitute valid grounds for denial of access. As for *de*classification, the present system is so riddled with problems, the Freedom of Information Act notwithstanding, that a volume could well be written on its defects.

By no means is the information problem only a barrier between the executive branch and Congress. Maneuvers to affect information are the essence of bureaucratic politics. It is not difficult to understand how actors in the national security game get ideas for their maneuvers. Some difficulties will always exist in setting policy, and in running systems to create and implement policy. But this is no excuse to throw up our hands and say nothing can be done about maneuvers to affect information. Something is wrong with a system in which the Joint Chiefs of Staff feel they need a spy on the NSC staff, as happened under Kissinger. Something is wrong with the system when the NSC principals advise against a weapons sale, the Vice President says he opposed it, and the President says he does not remember it, but the sale occurs anyway *and* the proceeds are diverted to another cause altogether, one previously proscribed by a coordinate branch of government. Unfortunately everyone was afraid to say the emperor has no clothes.

That is what occurred in the Reagan administration. Executive officials succumbed to mass amnesia and congressional investigators lacked the political will to carry their inquiry to the basic organizational level. As George Ball would have said, they refused to ask the "giraffe" questions.

Beyond the giraffe questions lie the real philosophical issues. Does the national security mystique serve the national interest? Is the world too complex for "long-range" policies? Can America afford to be without them? What *is* a valid policy and the national consensus on national security? Cold war nostalgia does not work anymore. That is why there must be a Great Debate. But in the meantime the policy system must be made to work, the giraffe questions have to be answered, for otherwise there is no purpose in consensus on national security. America should not cross the threshold of the millennium with a national security system designed for a bygone era.

A NOTE ON SOURCES

▲▲▲

There is a vast primary and secondary literature on American foreign policy in the postwar period, on specific problems of national security, and on particular incidents, wars, alarums, and excursions. A huge bibliography could have been filled with these items. In contrast the literature that focuses right in on the National Security Council is tiny. Though I like to put bibliographies in my books, under the circumstances I felt it preferable to reserve that space for substance. A fair number of published sources are cited in the notes and, anyway, of greater importance for this work have been collections of documents, oral histories, and my own interviews.

Readers should be forewarned that the NSC studies that do exist are overwhelmingly academic in style and content. The one effort that tries to approach the subject from a more popular standpoint is *Our Own Worst Enemy* (New York: Simon and Schuster, 1984) by I. M. Destler, Leslie H. Gelb, and Anthony Lake. Keith C. Clark and Lawrence J. Legere in *The President and the Management of National Security* (New York: Praeger, 1969) present the text of the 1968 NSC study done for the Institute for Defense Analysis. A political scientist whose work has always been highly useful is Alexander L. George, who in this area has written *Presidential Decisionmaking in Foreign Policy: The Effective Use of Information and Advice* (Boulder, Colo.: Westview Press, 1980). A book that collects a number of the opening statements offered at the Jackson Committee hearings is Senator Henry M. Jackson, ed., *The National Security Council.* Historian Stanley Falk wrote two little-known but important works for the Industrial College of the Armed Forces. They were *National Security Management: The National Security Structure* (Washington, D.C.: Industrial College of the Armed Forces, 1972) by Falk and Theodore W. Bauer; and *National Security Management: The Environment of National Security* (Washington, D.C.: Industrial College of the Armed Forces, 1973). Most recent is *The Presidency and the Management of National Security* (New York: Free Press, 1988). In general it is perplexing that an institution of such importance is so rarely featured in books.

As can be seen from a listing of congressional "investigations" into the NSC (there are only four), this institution had also escaped scrutiny from that quarter. The most substantive was the Jackson Committee's, which includes several volumes of hearings, a report, several more staff reports or collections of readings, and a couple of follow-up staff reports in the later 1960s. The basic citation is United States Congress (86/2) Senate Government Operations, Subcommittee on National Policy Machinery. *Hearings* (and *Report*): *Organizing for National Security.* Washington, D.C.: Government Printing Office (hereafter cited as GPO), 1960. A second congressional inquiry is that concerning the Radford affair, in three parts: USC (93/2) Senate Armed Services. *Hearings: Transmittal of Documents from the National Security Council to the Chairman of the Joint Chiefs of Staff.* GPO, 1974. In 1980 there was a hearing regarding a bill Brzezinski did not take too seriously: USC (96/2) Senate Foreign Relations. *Hearing: The National Security Adviser: Role and Accountability.* GPO, 1980. Finally comes the most recent: USC (100/2) House Government Operations. *Hearing: Presidential Directives and Records Accountability Act.* GPO, 1989. For four decades this record is rather paltry.

Former NSC Executive Secretary Bromley K. Smith spent six years as consultant to the NSC writing the monograph *Organizational History of the National Security Council During the Kennedy and Johnson Administrations.* Washington, D.C.: National Security Council, n.d. [1988]. Sadly this paper does not go beyond basic administrative matters, very much in the style of the similar paper he and Robert H. Johnson produced for the Jackson Committee. In fact, the Smith paper utilizes only the most obvious file sources and neglects much of the documentary holdings by and about members of the NSC staff during those administrations.

Documentary sources consulted during the research for this book were numerous. At the National Archives these were Records Groups 218 (Joint Chiefs of Staff) and 273 (National Security Council). At other archives facilities listings follow.

Harry S. Truman Library:
President's Secretary's File: Intelligence File
President's Secretary's File: Subject File
President's Secretary's File: Korean War
President's Secretary's File: NSC Meetings File
White House Central Files: Confidential File
White House Central Files: Official File
Records of the Psychological Strategy Board
Sidney Souers Papers
Clark Clifford Papers
George M. Elsey Papers
Dean Acheson Papers

Dwight D. Eisenhower Library:
White House Office (WHO): Office of the Special Assistant for National Security Affairs (OSANSA): Presidential Subseries

WHO: OSANSA: Policy Papers Series
WHO: OSANSA: Alphabetical Series
WHO: OSANSA: Subject Series
WHO: Office of the Staff Secretary (OSS): International Series
WHO: OSS: Intelligence Series
WHO: OSS: Subject Series
Ann Whitman File (ACWF): DDE Diary Series
ACWF: Legislative Meetings Series
ACWF: Dulles-Herter Series
ACWF: Cabinet Series
ACWF: National Security Council Series
ACWF: Ann Whitman Diary
White House Central File (WHCF): Official File
WHCF: Confidential File
WHCF: Administrative Series

John F. Kennedy Library:
President's Office File (POF): Departments and Agencies
POF: Staff Memoranda
National Security File (NSF): Agency File
NSF: Country File
NSF: Meetings and Memoranda Series (M&M)

Lyndon Baines Johnson Library:
Vice Presidential Security File
Official File: Harry McPherson File
National Security File (NSF): Agency File
NSF: Aides Files: Memos to the President Series
NSF: Country File: Vietnam Series
NSF: Country File: Laos Series
NSF: Files of McGeorge Bundy
NSF: Files of Walt Rostow
NSF: Files of Robert Komer
NSF: Komer-Leonhart File
NSF: Name File
NSF: NSAMs File
NSF: NSC Meetings File
NSF: Subject File
White House Central File (WHCF): General File
WHCF: Confidential File
Declassified and Sanitized Files Unboxed Folders (DSDUF)
Meeting Notes Files
Tom Johnson's Notes of Meetings Series

National Archives, Nixon Library Project:
President's Office File (POF): Annotated News Summaries
POF: Memos to the President Series
POF: President's Handwriting Series
President's Personal File: Foreign Affairs File 1969–1974
White House Central File (WHCF): Subject File
WHCF: FO, Foreign Affairs
WHCF: Staff and Office Files, Haig
WHCF: White House Special Series, Subject Series, Confidential File

The research for this work was further aided immeasurably by access to
a large number of interview transcripts in the Oral History collections of
the Truman, Eisenhower, and Johnson libraries, and by the author's own
interviews. A Truman Oral History consulted was that of Gordon Gray.
Eisenhower Oral Histories included those of: Vernon A. Walters, Dillon
Anderson, Robert R. Bowie, Admiral Arleigh A. Burke, Robert A. Lovett,
Andrew J. Goodpaster, George Kistiakowski, Thomas C. Mann, Dwight D.
Eisenhower (both Columbia and Princeton interviews), John S. D. Eisen-
hower, James C. Hagerty, Karl G. Harr, Neil McElroy, Thomas S. Gates,
Jr., Nathan S. Twining, James R. Shepley, Chalmers R. Roberts, C. Douglas
Dillon. Johnson oral histories consulted included those of: Matthew Nimetz,
Bromley K. Smith, W. Averell Harriman, Phil G. Goulding, William B.
Macomber, Jr., Clark M. Clifford, Stewart Alsop, Michael Forrestal, Wil-
liam H. Sullivan, Chester L. Cooper, Earle Wheeler, John S. Foster, Jr.,
Maxwell D. Taylor, William P. Bundy, William J. Jorden, James C. Thom-
son, Jr., U. Alexis Johnson, Harold Brown, Cyrus R. Vance, Paul C. Warnke,
U. S. Grant Sharp, Zbigniew Brzezinski, Andrew J. Goodpaster, Donald F.
Hornig. The author's own formal interviews included: Gordon Gray, An-
drew J. Goodpaster, McGeorge Bundy, Walt Rostow, Brent Scowcroft,
William G. Hyland, Harold H. Saunders, Spurgeon Keeny, Jr., Brewster
Denny, Richard K. Betts, Chester L. Cooper, Robert N. Ginsburgh, Gary
Sick, Michael V. Forrestal, Howard Wriggins, Morton H. Halperin, Marcus
G. Raskin, and Robert H. Johnson. In addition the author benefited from
approximately three dozen off-the-record interviews, informal conversa-
tions, and other contacts. Henry A. Kissinger and Zbigniew K. Brzezinski
both declined to be interviewed for this project.

NOTES

▲▲▲

PROLOGUE

21 "We will start killing": quoted in *New York Times,* October 9, 1985, p. A9.

22 "The friends have the four": quoted in David Halevy and Neil C. Livingstone, "The Ollie We Knew," *Washingtonian,* Vol. 22, No. 10 (July 1987), p. 145.

23 "a kind of national court": quoted in Donaldson, *Hold On, Mr. President* (New York: Random House, 1987), pp. 99–100.

26 "helpful translation": quoted in Michael Ledeen, *Perilous Statecraft* (New York: Simon & Schuster, 1988), p. 182.

PART I. BROKERS

30 "most important feature": quoted in Arnold A. Rogow, *James Forrestal* (New York: Macmillan, 1963), p. 230.

30 "would undoubtedly try": quoted in Walter Millis, ed. *The Forrestal Diaries* (New York: Viking, 1951), p. 315.

30 "objectives would be advantaged": Memo, Director, Bureau of the Budget-Truman, August 8, 1947, pp. 2–3. John F. Kennedy Library (hereafter JFKL): John F. Kennedy Papers (hereafter JFKP): National Security File (hereafter NSF): Agency File, box 283, folder: "NSC Organization and Administration 1/30/61–6/31/61."

30 "channel for collective advice": quoted in Steven L. Rearden, *History of the Office of the Secretary of Defense: I: The Formative Years 1947–1950* (Washington, D.C.: Historical Office, Office of the Secretary of Defense, 1984; reprint), p. 120.

33 "ready to utilize": NSC-30, "United States Policy on Atomic Weapons," September 10, 1948, reprinted p. 343 in Thomas H. Etzold and John L. Gaddis, eds., *Containment: Documents on American Policy and Strategy 1945–1950* (New York: Columbia University Press, 1978).

33 "defeat of the forces": ibid. p. 167.

34 "a non-political confidant": Memo, Souers-Truman, undated. Harry S. Truman Library (hereafter HSTL): Sidney W. Souers Papers, box 1, folder: "Souers-NSC 1947–1950." Italics in the original.

36 "quite properly": Harry S. Truman, *Memoirs: Years of Trial and Hope* (New York: New American Library, 1965), p. 78.

36 "without an integrated assessment": Memo, Souers-NSC, December 20, 1949 (declassified October 31, 1980). HSTL: President's Secretary's File: NSC Meetings File, box 209, folder "NSC Meeting No. 65."

36 Merged projects: A separate strategic analysis on thermonuclear weapons issues was ordered by NSC Action No. 270. That project was still pending when completion of the policy paper revealed that it covered much of the same ground. NSC Action 270 was therefore canceled.

38 "since he and General Bradley": Memorandum of Conversation, March 22, 1950. *Foreign Relations of the United States 1950 v. I, National Security Policy*, (Washington, D.C.: Government Printing Office [hereafter GPO], 1977), p. 204.

38 "Johnson listened": Dean Acheson, *Present at the Creation* (New York: Signet Books, 1970), p. 487.

38 "State Department would complete the report": ibid.

39 "the action which can be taken" et seq.: NSC-68, "United States Objectives and Programs for National Security," April 14, 1950, in Etzold and Gaddis, op. cit, pp. 440–442.

40 "revised and strengthened staff organization": ibid., p. 442.

40 "senior staff group": Memo, Lay-NSC, April 17, 1950 (declassified December 14, 1982). HSTL: PSF: NSC Meetings File, box 208, folder "NSC Meeting No. 57."

40 "in a position to reflect fully and accurately": ibid.

40–41 JCS views: The Chiefs instead supported an organization similar to their own Operations Deputies, wherein each principal would have an assistant. They also wanted the unit constituted only on an ad hoc basis, and only for NSC-68. Finally, they objected to representatives having to devote their full time to NSC work. Memo, JCS-Johnson, April 20, 1950 (declassified December 14, 1982) HSTL: PSF: NSC Meetings File, box 208, folder: "NSC Meeting No. 57."

41 "discouraged free discussion": ibid.

42 "he was completely trustworthy": quoted in Merle Miller, *Plain Speaking* (New York: Berkley Books, 1974), p. 311.

43–44 "accepted the President's position" et seq.: reprinted in Truman, op. cit., p. 400.

47 "a full time man": Lucius D. Battle, Memorandum of Telephone Conversation, February 5, 1951 (declassified January 4, 1981). HSTL: Acheson Papers, box 66, folder: "Memorandums of Conversation, February 1951."

47 "not sure that enough consideration" et seq.: Memorandum of Discussion at 72nd NSC Meeting, November 24, 1950 (declassified October 27, 1982). HSTL: PSF: NSC Meetings File, box 220, folder: "Memos for the President, 1950."

47–48 "did not advocate that the Joint Chiefs of Staff be excluded" et seq.: Summary of Discussion at 80th NSC, January 18, 1951 (declassified November 3, 1983), HSTL: PSF: NSC Meetings File, box 220, folder: "Memos for the President, 1951."

48 "a most reluctant bride": Acheson, op. cit., p. 655.

50 "BIG . . . MAGNANIMOUS": "Outline of Strategic Plan to Win the Present World Struggle," n.d., p. 2. Capitalization in the original. Attached to letter, Shane McCarthy-Matthew J. Connelly, September 21, 1950. HSTL: PSF: NSC Meetings File, box 210, folder: "NSC Meeting No. 72."

51 "matters relating to coordination": NSC-59, "The Foreign Information Program and Psychological Warfare Planning," December 20, 1949 (declassified January 20, 1984), p. 13-4. HSTL: NSC Records, box 18, folder: "CIA Comments on Gray Report on PSB."

52 "national psychological warfare organization" et seq.: NSC-74, "A Plan for National

Psychological Warfare," July 10, 1950 (declassified May 27, 1977), p. 7. HSTL: PSF: NSC Meetings File, box 210, folder: "NSC Meeting No. 77."

52–53 "assignment to a single official" et seq.: Memo, Lay-NSC, "The National Psychological Effort," December 28, 1950 (declassified September 30, 1980), pp. 1, 3, 4. HSTL: PSF: NSC Meetings Series, box 210, folder "NSC Meeting No. 77."

53 "PSB must be the central place": quoted in Edward P. Lilly, "The Psychological Strategy Board and Its Predecessors: Foreign Policy Coordination 1938–1953," in Gaetano L. Vincitorio, ed., *Studies in Modern History* (New York: St. John's University Press, 1968), p. 365.

54 "you just forget about policy": quoted in John Prados, *Presidents' Secret Wars* (New York: William Morrow, 1986), p. 87. Additional discussion of the PSB may be found therein at pages 83–90.

55 "could not think strategically": Lilly, op. cit., p. 371.

55 "somewhat abortive": Gordon Gray, Eisenhower Oral History (#342), p. 11.

56 "we have not insisted": Raymond B. Allen, "Closing Lecture: The Total Problem," August 15, 1952 (declassified June 18, 1979). HSTL: WHCF: Confidential Files, box 31, folder: "Psychological Strategy Board."

56 "anything the Board approves": ibid.

PART II. IKE'S HIDDEN HAND

57 "look here, Charlie": quoted in Patrick Anderson, *The President's Men* (Garden City, N.Y.: Doubleday, 1968), p. 135.

61 "of which Macmillan published two": quoted in Robert C. Cutler, *No Time for Rest* (Boston: Little, Brown, 1966), p. 67.

61 "the NSC would be converted . . . tantamount to an executive . . . agency": paper, "Organization of the National Security Council: Role of the NSC Staff," n.d., p. 5. Dwight D. Eisenhower Library (hereafter DDEL): Dwight D. Eisenhower Papers (hereafter DDEP): WHCF: Official File, box 318, folder: "72-F: National Security Council (1953)."

62 Cutler recommendations: Memo, Cutler-DDE, March 16, 1953. *Foreign Relations of the United States 1952–1954. v. II: National Security Policy, Pt. 1.* Washington D.C.: GPO, 1984), pp. 245–258.

63 "pyramid": Dillon Anderson, "The President and National Security," *The Atlantic Monthly* (January 1956), p. 44. The term "Policy Hill" was widely used at the time and coined by Bobby Cutler.

63 "Every policy proposal": ibid. Anderson's speech was revised for publication by Cutler and NSC staffer Charles A. Haskins.

64 "a veritable mare's nest": Cutler, op. cit., p. 266.

64 Jackson (PCFIIA) Report: *New York Times,* July 1, 1953.

65 Executive Order 10483, September 3, 1953.

65 "You'd be amazed": Goodpaster interview, "Organizing the White House," in Kenneth W. Thompson, ed., *The Eisenhower Presidency* (Lanham, Md.: University Press of America, 1984), p. 72.

65–66 "my own Sergeant Major" et seq.: Goodpaster interview, in ibid., pp. 65–66.

66 "I would ask nothing more": quoted in Sherman Adams, *First Hand Report* (New York: Popular Library, 1962), p. 60.

67 "that is a policy matter": Goodpaster interview in Thompson, op. cit., p. 81. See also Goodpaster's comment in Samuel Kernell and Samuel L. Popkin, eds., *Chief of Staff* (Berkeley, Calif.: University of California Press), p. 111.

68 "If you give me a week": quoted in Piers Branden, *Ike* (New York: Harper & Row, 1986), p. 397.

69 "organized absenteeism": Richard T. Johnson, *Managing the White House* (New York: Harper & Row, 1974), pp. 74–119.

70 "Bobby Cutler told me" et seq.: Letter, Souers-Raymond P. Brandt, April 12, 1966. HSTL: Sidney Souers Papers, box 1, folder: "Souers Correspondence 1953–1972."

71 "We've got to do something": Walt Rostow interview, September 13, 1988.

73 "operations plan": Lilly, op. cit.

75 "on ice for a while": Cutler, Memorandum for the Record, July 2, 1954. DDEL: DDEP: White House Office (hereafter WHO): Office of the Special Assistant for National Security Affairs (hereafter OSANSA), NSC Series, Administrative Subseries, box 4, folder: "Consultants 1954–1956 (4)."

76 "killing as it may be" et seq.: Cutler, Memorandum for the President, April 7, 1958. DDEL: DDEP: WHO: OSANSA: Special Assistant Series; box 5, folder: "April 1958 (1)."

77 "a respectable point of view": Robert H. Johnson interview, December 8, 1987.

77–78 "expressed little sympathy" et seq.: Gray, Memorandum of Meeting with the President, August 26, 1959 (declassified May 25, 1982). DDEL: DDEP: WHO: OSANSA: Special Assistant Series; Presidential Subseries, box 3, folder: "Meetings with the President 1958 (3)."

78 "exclusions": Gray-Foster Dulles, Memorandum of Conversation, October 10, 1958 (declassified April 3, 1981), DDEL: DDEP: WHO: OSANSA: Special Assistant Series; Chronological Subseries, box 5, folder: "October 1958."

79 "a line against any contacts" et. seq.: Gray, Memorandum of Meeting with the Vice-President, July 28, 1958. DDEL: DDEP: WHO: OSANSA: NSC Series, Administrative Subseries, box 5, folder: "NSC—General."

81 "secure and protect": quoted in Richard J. Barnett, *Intervention and Revolution* (New York: New American Library, 1972), p. 164.

83 "sprawled back in the chair" et seq.: Cutler paper, op. cit., pp. 9, 10.

83 "I assured him": Nathan F. Twining, *Neither Liberty nor Safety* (New York: Holt, Rinehart & Winston, 1964), p. 64.

84 "I am ordering this column" et seq.: quoted in Charles W. Thayer, *Diplomat* (New York: Harper & Brothers, 1959), p. 34.

84 "Since Berlin in 1945": Robert Murphy, *Diplomat Among Warriors* (New York: Pyramid Books, 1965), p. 445.

84 "Well Done!" *The United States Navy: Keeping the Peace* Washington, D.C.: Naval Historical Division, 1968; message reprinted, p. 33.

86 "their next provocative move": Dwight D. Eisenhower, *Waging Peace: The White House Years 1956–1961* (Garden City, N.Y.: Doubleday, 1965), p. 292.

86 "just the statutory NSC members": Goodpaster, Memorandum of Conference with the President, August 11, 1958 (declassified November 17, 1976). DDEL: DDEP: ACWF: DDE Diary Series, box 22, folder: "Staff Notes, August 1958."

87 "I had lived with this problem": Eisenhower, op. cit., p. 334.

88 "our whole stack will be in the pot": quoted in ibid., pp. 338–339.

89 "advanced the ball considerably": Gray, Memorandum of Meeting with the President, March 20, 1959. DDEL: DDEP: WHO: OSANSA: Special Assistant Series, Presidential Subseries, box 4, folder: "Meetings with the President 1959 (4)."

89 "Would it be desirable" et seq.: ibid.

90 "extreme reluctance" et seq.: Gray, Memorandum of Meeting with the President, March 27, 1959 (re March 24). Ibid.

90 "sitting around the periphery": Gray, Memorandum of Meeting with the President, March 27, 1959 (re March 25). Ibid.

92 "capability of individuals effectively to operate": Memo, Cutler-Persons, "Comments on a Speech by Sen. Henry Jackson," June 5, 1959, p. 1. DDEL: DDEP: WHO: OSS: Subject Series, Alphabetical Subseries, box 18, folder: "NSC v. I. (6)."

93 "all reasonable efforts" et seq.: Attachment to Memo, Gray-Persons, June 11, 1959. DDEL: Ibid.

93 "Constitutional privilege": Letter, DDE-Jackson and attached "Proposed Guidelines," July 10, 1959. DDEL: DDEP: WHO: OSANSA: NSC Series, Administrative Subseries, box 5, folder: "NSC—General (6)."

94 "astute and sure-footed": Henry M. Jackson, ed., *The National Security Council* (New York: Praeger, 1965), p. 14.

94 "clear and firm in his response": Gray, Memorandum of Meeting with the President, January 27, 1960 (re January 26). DDEL: DDEP: WHO: OSANSA: Special Assistant Series, Presidential Subseries, box 4, folder: "1960—Meetings with the President v. I (7)."

95 "on numerous occasions" et seq.: Letter, Souers-Lay, July 7, 1960. HSTL: Papers of Sidney Souers, box 1, folder: "Souers: National Policy Machinery." Italics in the original.

PART III. KEEPERS IN CAMELOT

97 "constructive criticisms" et seq.: quoted in Henry M. Jackson, ed., *The National Security Council* (New York: Praeger, 1965) p. xiii.

100 "I've got a lot to do": Walt Rostow interview, September 13, 1988.

101 "open the subject up": Memo, Bundy-JFK, January 24, 1961. John F. Kennedy Library (hereafter JFKL): John F. Kennedy Papers (hereafter JFKP): National Security File (hereafter NSF): Agency File, box 283, folder: "NSC Organization 1.18.61."

102 "tending the door": ibid., p. 2.

103 "held your command": Goodpaster interview, December 15, 1987.

103 "Che learned more than we": Marcus Raskin Interview, April 2, 1987.

107 Kennedy tapes: According to his secretary Evelyn Lincoln, Kennedy had recording equipment installed in the Oval Office and Cabinet Room because he was a history buff. That was in July 1962. Some 248 hours of tape exist that cover 300 meetings, and 12 hours have 280 phone calls. Of the Cuban crisis, tapes of meetings on October 18 and 27 have been transcribed, but classification problems and manpower shortages do not

yet permit additional tapes to be released. The Kennedy Library maintains that 100 to 150 hours of work are required to transcribe each hour of tape (see Fox Butterfield, *New York Times,* October 27, 1983).

107 "take it right out": Transcript, p. 182. Marc Trachtenberg, "The Influence of Nuclear Weapons in the Cuban Missile Crisis," *International Security,* Vol. 10, No. 1 (Summer 1985).

108 "I never heard an expression": Maxwell D. Taylor, "Reflections on a Grim October," *Washington Post,* October 5, 1982.

109 Rostow-Nitze postmortem: Edward Weintal and Charles Bartlett, *Facing the Brink* (New York: Charles Scribner's Sons, 1967), p. 54.

110 "an appalling percentage" et seq.: memo, Bundy-O'Donnell, January 5, 1962, JFKL: JFKP: NSF: Agency File, box 283, folder: "NSC Organization and Administration 12/27/61–11/22/63."

112 GATO: John Kenneth Galbraith, *A Life in Our Times* (Boston: Houghton Mifflin, 1981), p. 441.

112 "cogency as a debater" et seq.: Arthur M. Schlesinger, Jr., *A Thousand Days* (New York: Fawcett Books, 1967), pp. 299, 465.

113 "talk the president's language": Sorensen, Speranza Lecture, May 9, 1963, p. 19. JFKL: JFKP: NSF: Meetings and Memoranda Series (hereafter M&M), box 326, folder: "Theodore Sorensen 1961–1963."

114 "We were few enough": quoted in Herbert S. Parmet, *JFK: The Presidency of John F. Kennedy* (New York: Dial Press, 1983), p. 88.

114 "more than one part of the government": Letter, Bundy-Kissinger, January 28, 1961. JFKL: JFKP: NSF: M&M, box 320, folder: "Staff Memoranda, Henry Kissinger 5/61."

115 "I can think of no way": Note, Ash-Bundy, May 26, 1961. JFKL: JFKP: NSF: M&M, box 320. Ibid. Kissinger's Harvard office did not meet federal standards for facilities to store highly classified materials.

115 "main lines of our policy" et seq.: Kissinger, Memorandum of Conversation with Mr. Conway of Newsweek Magazine, November 17, 1961. Ibid folder: "Staff Memoranda, Kissinger 11/61–12/61."

115 "recent Russian arms deliveries": Memo, Lucius D. Battle-Bundy, January 10, 1962. Ibid., folder: "Staff Memoranda, Kissinger 1/62."

116 "Soviet arms deal had to be stopped": Transcript of Remarks by Henry A. Kissinger Before the Board of the Research Institute of America, p. 2. DDEL: DDEP: WHCF: Subject Series, box 7, folder: "Atomic Energy and Bomb (10)."

117 "Chester Bowles with machine guns": quoted in Schlesinger, op. cit., p. 391.

117 "Marc is going to be our conscience": Raskin interview, April 2, 1987.

118 "If this group": quoted in *Washington Post,* July 30, 1986.

119 "Some people thought": McGeorge Bundy interview, January 28, 1988.

119 "enable me to provide the sort of support you need": Memo, Komer-Bundy, June 21, 1961. JFKL: JFKP: NSF: M&M, box 321A, folder: "Staff Memoranda, Komer 6/15/61–7/23/61."

120 "You're going to the Middle East" et seq.: quoted in Merle Miller, *Lyndon: An Oral Biography* (New York: G. P. Putnam's Sons), pp. 291–292.

120 "My Ankara *faux pas*": quoted in ibid., p. 293.

120 "I'm through being polite": Memo, Komer-Kaysen, June 7, 1962. Capitalization and underlining in the original. JFKL: JFKP: NSF: M&M, box 321A, folder: "Staff Memoranda: Komer 6/62."

121 "To the extent that we are 'NSC' ": Memo, Komer-Bundy, May 6, 1963 (declassified December 1985), JFKL: JFKP: NSF: M&M, box 322, folder: "Staff Memoranda: Komer 3/63–5/63."

123 "nourish a spirit": quoted in William Attwood, *The Twilight Struggle: Tales of the Cold War* (New York: Harper & Row, 1987), p. 255.

123 "How secret can a standing group stay?": Dingeman, Memorandum for the Record, April 23, 1963 (declassified October 24, 1975). JFKL: JFKP: NSF: M&M, box 314, folder: "NSC Standing Group Meetings, General 4/63–5/63."

123 "all necessary means": U.S. Congress (94/1) Senate Select Committee to Study Governmental Operations with Respect to Intelligence Activities. *Interim Report: Alleged Assassination Plots Involving Foreign Leaders* (Washington, D.C.: GPO, 1975), pp. 170–171.

125 "*the* special military representative": David Halberstam, *The Best and the Brightest* (New York: Random House, 1972) p. 163.

126 "like two professors": Walt W. Rostow, *The Diffusion of Power 1957–1972* (New York: Macmillan, 1972), p. 274.

127 "the risks of backing in to a major Asian war" et seq.: Cable, Taylor-JFK, n.d. *The Senator Gravel Edition: The Pentagon Papers: The Defense Department History of United States Decisionmaking* on Vietnam (Boston: Beacon Press, n.d. [1972]); reprinted (hereafter cited as Gravel Pentagon Papers Vol. II), p. 92.

127 "I had no enthusiasm": Maxwell D. Taylor, *Swords into Plowshares* (New York: W. W. Norton, 1972), p. 238.

127 "put on the witness seat": ibid., p. 245.

127 "the Vietnam problem": George W. Ball, *The Past Has Another Pattern* (New York: W. W. Norton, 1982), p. 366.

127 "in general accord": Taylor, op. cit. p. 246.

127 "clear objective" et seq.: McNamara-JFK, November 8, 1961. Gravel Pentagon Papers, Vol. II, pp. 108–109.

128 "hell-bent into a mess": Ball, op. cit., p. 367.

128 "It's just like taking a drink": quoted in Schlesinger, op. cit., p. 505.

128 "a losing horse": quoted in George McTurnan Kahin, *Intervention* (New York: Knopf, 1986), p. 136.

128 "If this doesn't work": quoted in Rostow, op. cit., p. 278. Plans 1 to 5 were SEATO defense plans of which No. 5, which Rostow ardently supported, provided for inserting ground troops into Laos. Plan No. 6 would have been a direct strike upon North Vietnam (ibid.).

129 "an exceedingly good bet": Memo, Schlesinger-Bundy, January 5, 1962. JFKL: JFKP: NSF: M&M, box 320, folder: "Staff Memoranda: Forrestal 1/62–5/62."

129 "I really want you to be my ambassador": David Halberstam, *The Best and the Brightest* (New York: Random House, 1972), quoted p. 190.

PART IV. LYNDON JOHNSON'S VANTAGE POINT

137 "about as peaceful": Lyndon B. Johnson, *The Vantage Point:* (New York: Harper & Row, 1972), p. 22.

137–138 "grab the microphone" et seq.: U.S. Congress (95/2) Senate Select Intelligence. *Hearings: National Intelligence Reorganization and Reform Act of 1978* (Washington, D.C.: GPO, 1978), p. 77.

138 "one page teaser": Memo, Komer-Bundy, November 27, 1963 (declassified October 29, 1986). Lyndon Baines Johnson Library (hereafter LBJL): Lyndon Baines Johnson Papers (hereafter LBJP): NSF: Name File, box 6, folder: "Komer Memos v. I (2)."

138 "reconstruct the type of organization": Letter, Gray-Don Wilson, December 4, 1974. DDEL: Gordon Gray Papers, box 2, folder: "Gordon Gray."

139 "meetings were like sieves": quoted in Doris Kearns, *Lyndon Johnson and the American Dream* (New York: New American Library, 1977), p. 335.

142 "just like the Alamo": quoted in Phillip Geyelin, *Lyndon Johnson and the World* (New York: Praeger, 1966), p. 237.

143 "more than any other organization": Johnson, op. cit., p. 194.

144 "very special" et seq.: Tad Szulc, *Dominican Diary* (New York: Dell Books, 1965), pp. 80–81.

145 "if you gents": quoted in Bradley H. Patterson, Jr., *The Ring of Power* (New York: Basic Books, 1988), p. 119.

145 "I had failed to anticipate": George W. Ball, *The Past Has Another Pattern* (New York: W. W. Norton, 1982), p. 329.

146 Napoleon and Frankenstein: Szulc, op. cit., p. 262.

147 "interrupted civil war": quoted in ibid., p. 278.

150 "Clashing, exploratory": Walt W. Rostow, *The Diffusion of Power 1957–1972* (New York: Macmillan, 1972), p. 360.

152 "knowledgeable, wise": Memo, Rostow-LBJ, July 24, 1968. LBJL: LBJP: NSF: Name File, box 7, folder: "Rostow Memos."

152 "delicate Kennedyites" et. seq.: Richard Goodwin, *Remembering America* (Boston: Little, Brown, 1988), p. 258.

153 "They're already in the air" et seq.: quoted in ibid., p. 406.

153 "I never gave him permission" et seq.: quoted in ibid., pp. 600–601.

154 "general assistant to the President": List, "White House Staff Assignments," August 8, 1966. LBJL: LBJP: WHCF: Confidential File FG 11-5/MC, box 19, folder: "FG 11-8-1 Staff Aides."

154 "pass to him in the international field": Memo, Moyers-Bromley Smith, March 1, 1966, LBJL: LBJP: NSF: Name File, box 7, folder: "Moyers Memos."

155 "I'll bet you five dollars": quoted in Edward Weintal and Charles Bartlett, *Facing the Brink* (New York: Charles Scribner's Sons, 1967), p. 134.

155 "We've had enough of this" et seq.: quoted in ibid., pp. 125–126.

156 "at least knows better" et seq.: Bundy-LBJ, August 4, 1965. LBJL: LBJP: NSF: Memos to the President, box 4, folder: "Bundy, v. 13 (August 1965)."

156 "disturbing sign" et seq.: Memo, Chase-Bundy, June 14, 1965. LBJL: LBJP: NSF: Files of McGeorge Bundy, box 18-9, folder: "Teach-In (May–June 1965)."

157 "a British brigade in Vietnam": Bundy-LBJ, July 28, 1965. LBJL: LBJP: NSF: Memos to the President, box 4, folder: "Bundy, v. 12 (July 1965)."

157 "a tiger for work" et seq.: Bundy-LBJ, September 14, 1965. Ibid., folder: "Bundy, v. 14 (September 1–22, 1965)."

158 "the term 'NSC staff' ": Bundy-LBJ, March 15, 1965. LBJL: LBJP: NSF: Memos to the President, box 3, folder: "Bundy v. 9 (March–April 15, 1965)."

160 "As for the work you fellows have been doing": quoted in Leonard Mosley, *Dulles* (New York: Dell Books, 1979), p. 336.

164 "I don't pose as a philosopher": *Washington Post,* August 7, 1960.

166 "the junior member ends up" et seq.: Memo, Saunders-Rostow, April 8, 1966. LBJL: LBJP: NSF: Name File, box 7, folder: "Saunders Memos."

167 "My first suggestion": Memo, Rostow-LBJ, April 29, 1966. LBJL: LBJP: NSF: Memos to the President, box 7, folder "Rostow v. 1 (April 1966)."

167 "two new ideas by Friday": Rostow interview, September 13, 1988.

167 "would be instructed" et seq.: Memo, Rostow-LBJ, April 19, 1966 (declassified September 13, 1985). LBJL: LBJP: NSF: Memos to the President, box 7, folder: "Rostow, v. 1 (April 1966)."

167 "jawboning session": James Thomson, Johnson Oral History, AC81-98, p. I, 36–37.

168–169 "Mr. Rostow opened" et seq.: Excerpts from unsigned (Thomson) "Minutes of a Meeting of the National Security Council Staff, Spring 1967," LBJL: LBJP: Memos to the President, box 16, folder: "Rostow, v. 27 (May 1–16, 1967)."

169 "nothing really effective": Memo, Rostow-LBJ, May 1, 1967. Ibid.

170 "ablest young Negro" et seq.: Memo, Bundy-Rusk, November 30, 1965. LBJL: LBJP: NSF: Memos to the President, box 5, folder: "Bundy v. 17 (November 20–December 31, 1965)."

170 "I don't always want to be Tonto": Rostow interview, September 13, 1988. The reference is to characters in *The Lone Ranger*, a television program that was popular during the 1950s; even earlier it was a radio dramatization show.

173 "nothing in this incident": Memo, Wriggins-Rostow, January 9, 1967. LBJL: LBJP: NSF: Name File, box 8, folder: "Howard Wriggins, 1967."

173 "You are working against us" et seq.: Memo, Saunders-Rostow, May 16, 1967 (declassified November 5, 1986). LBJL: LBJP: NSF: Name File, box 7, folder: "Saunders Memos."

176 "All our intelligence people" et seq.: quoted in Johnson, op. cit., p. 293.

177 "We cannot imagine": Letter, Johnson-Eshkol, June 3, 1967 (declassified April 5, 1982). LBJL: LBJP: NSF: NSC Histories: Middle East, box 18, folder: "ME, v. 3, Tabs 96–110."

178 "It was his judgment": Saunders, Memorandum for the Record, November 17, 1968 (declassified October 23, 1984). Ibid.

178 "If it wasn't necessary": Harry McPherson, *A Political Education* (Boston: Houghton

Mifflin, 1988), pp. 414–415. McPherson dates this June 6 but the context makes clear the events described occurred on the first day of the war.

179 "the politicians don't try" et seq.: Robert Ginsburgh interview, December 6, 1988.

179 "Johnson . . . never believed": Walt Rostow, Memorandum for the Record, November 17, 1968 (declassified October 23, 1984), p. 3. LBJL: LBJP: NSF: NSC Histories: Middle East Crisis, box 18, folder: "ME Crisis, v. 3, Tabs 96–110."

180 "it would not be useful": George Christian statement and McGeorge Bundy interview, June 7, 1967. LBJL: LBJP: NSF: NSC Meetings File, box 2, folder: "Meetings v. 4, Tab 53, 6/7/67."

181 "Wriggins Doctrine": Howard Wriggins interview, March 10, 1988.

182 "very crucial moment": quoted in Johnson, op. cit., p. 302.

182 "the lowest voices he had ever heard": Saunders, Memorandum for the Record, October 22, 1968 (declassified February 26, 1982) NSC History, op. cit., box 19, folder: "Crisis v. 7, Appendixes G-H."

183 "Same old shit": quoted in Roger Morris, *Uncertain Greatness* (New York: Harper & Row, 1977), p. 12.

185 "I get great support": Memo, Bundy-Rusk, December 1, 1965. Op. cit.

185 "sometimes you need such people": Rostow interview, September 13, 1988.

185 "the level of Presidential appointments": Bundy memo, op. cit.

187 "Humanity cannot tolerate": quoted in Glenn T. Seaborg and Benjamin S. Loeb, *Stemming the Tide* (Lexington, Mass.: Lexington Books, 1987), p. 137.

187 "no special measures": quoted in ibid, p. 147.

187 "tops": ibid., p. 149.

189 "wandered . . . through . . . the woods": Johnson, op. cit., p. 478.

190 McNamara comment at luncheon of the Arms Control Association, November 29, 1988; Rostow, op. cit., pp. 386–387. For McNamara and the charts see B. Bruce-Briggs, *The Shield of Faith* (New York: Simon & Shuster, 1988), p. 282. For a thorough discussion of the Tallinn ABM intelligence dispute see the author's *The Soviet Estimate* (Princeton, N.J.: Princeton University Press, 1986).

192 "in the nearest future": quoted in Johnson, op. cit. p. 485.

193 "not let quibbling": quoted in Seaborg and Loeb, op. cit., p. 435.

195 "give immediate thought to" et seq.: Notes on Emergency Meeting of NSC, August 20, 1968 (declassified May 5, 1987). LBJL: LBJP: Tom Johnson's Notes of Meetings, box 2, folder: "Aug. 20, 1968—NSC."

196 "one last dramatic demonstration" et seq.: Richard Nixon, *RN* (New York: Warner Books, 1979), Vol. 1, p. 428.

196 "It's too bad we waited": quoted in John Newhouse, *Cold Dawn: The Story of SALT* (New York: Holt, Rinehart & Winston, 1973), p. 102.

Part V. VIETNAM

199–200 "I told my advisers" et seq.: Lyndon B. Johnson, *The Vantage Point* (New York: Harper & Row, 1972), p. 414.

200 "Macomberesque" et seq.: Gravel Pentagon Papers, Vol. II, pp. 164–165. Francis Macomber is the foolhardy protagonist in an Ernest Hemingway short story. He dies hunting a tiger.

200 "win their contest": NSAM-273, quoted in Johnson, op. cit., p. 45. See also *The Pentagon Papers as Published by the New York Times* (hereafter cited as Pentagon Papers) (New York: Bantam, 1971), p. 232.

200 "as anxious as Kennedy": George W. Ball, *The Past Has Another Pattern* (New York: W. W. Norton, 1982), p. 374.

201 "*Plans for Covert Action*": Report, McNamara-LBJ, December 21, 1964, paragraph 6. Pentagon Papers, p. 273. Italics in the original.

201 "Let's go to work": Michael Forrestal interview, March 11, 1988.

202 "visions of the Mississippi": Chester L. Cooper, *The Lost Crusade* (New York: Dodd, Mead & Co., 1970), p. 229.

204 "key problems" et seq.: quoted in Robert Johnson, "Escalation Then and Now," *Foreign Policy*, No. 60 (Fall 1985), p. 135.

205 "produced a very large crop" et seq.: quoted in William H. Sullivan, *Obbligato: Notes on a Foreign Service Career* (New York: W. W. Norton, 1984), pp. 181–182.

206 "execute general war plans" et. seq.: Joint War Games Agency (of the JCS), *Final Report: Sigma II-64,* October 1, 1964 (declassification date NA) LBJL: LBJP: NSF: Agency File, box 30, folder: "JCS Wargames v. II (1)."

206 "situation was more serious": Maxwell D. Taylor, *Swords into Plowshares* (New York: W. W. Norton, 1972), p. 310.

207 "We seek an independent": NSAM-288, March 17, 1964. Pentagon Papers, p. 283.

207 "a good letter then": quoted in Cooper, op. cit. pp. 234–235.

209 "wonder and surprise": ibid., p. 239.

209 "beginning to rattle Hanoi": Deptel 336, August 3, 1964. Reprinted in *U.S. News and World Report* (July 23, 1984), p. 60.

209 "I not only want retaliation": quoted in ibid., p. 63.

209 "Johnson was engaged much too early": Haig in Kernell and Popkin, *Chief of Staff,* op. cit. p. 31.

209–210 "North Vietnamese are reacting" et seq.: Summary of Discussion at 538th NSC, August 4, 1964 (declassified December 9, 1980). LBJL: LBJP: NSF: NSAMs and NSC Meetings, box 1–2, folder: "NSF: NSC Meetings."

210 "It became very clear": quoted in *U.S. News and World Report*, op. cit., p. 63.

210 "For all I know": Joseph C. Goulden, quoted in *Truth Is the First Casualty* (Chicago: Rand McNally & Co., 1969), p. 160. LBJ actually told George Ball only a few days after the incidents, "Hell, those dumb, stupid, stupid sailors were just shooting at flying fish!" (quoted in Ball, op. cit., p. 379).

210 "repel any armed attack": P.L. 88–408 (78 Stat. 384), August 10, 1964.

211 "provocation strategy": quoted in Pentagon Papers, p. 312.

212 "faced with the question": Taylor, op. cit., p. 321.

212 "it was now necessary" et seq.: Bundy, Memorandum for the Record, September

14, 1964 (declassified September 14, 1977) LBJL: LBJP: NSF: Memos for the President, box 2, folder: quoted in "Bundy v. 6."

212 "one gloomy opinion followed another": quoted in Johnson, op. cit., p. 120.

212–213 "disheartened him": Bundy Memo for record, op. cit.

213 "American boys to the fighting" et seq.: quoted in Cooper, op. cit., p. 248.

214 "fast full squeeze" et seq.: McNaughton draft paper, "Action for South Vietnam," November 6, 1964. Pentagon Papers, pp. 365–368.

214 "the signal we wish to send": Letter, Rostow-McNamara, November 16, 1964. Pentagon Papers, pp. 418–419.

214 "I was persuaded": Johnson, op. cit., p. 121.

215 "don't you think" et seq.: Michael Forrestal interview, March 11, 1988.

216 "pretty well convinced" et seq.: quoted in George McTurnan Kahin, Intervention, pp. 272–322.

216 "keep plugging" et seq.: McNaughton, "Draft Observations Re South Vietnam After Khanh's Re-Coup," January 27, 1965. Gravel Pentagon Papers, Vol. III, pp. 686–687.

216 "thrashing around": Thomson Oral History (AC81–98), pp. I, 18.

216–217 "the sense in the White House": quoted in Kahin, op. cit., p. 275.

217 "dead center": Cooper, op. cit., p. 256.

217 "reeling": ibid., p. 257.

217 Allen Whiting's warning: Kahin, op. cit., p. 277. Cf. David Halberstam, The Best and the Brightest (New York: Random House, 1972), p. 519.

218 "the attack has opened many eyes": Summary of Discussion at 545th NSC, February 6, 1965 (declassified December 8, 1980). LBJL: LBJP: NSF: Meeting Notes File, box 1, folder: "Feb. 6, 1965, 7:45 P.M." Mike Mansfield spoke of giving the problem to the United Nations or the Geneva powers at a subsequent NSC the next day. The record does not indicate that Mansfield made the objections that David Halberstam (pp. 591–592) attributes to him. Similarly, Max Taylor's reported advocacy of troops in November 1964 (see Taylor, op. cit., pp. 484–487) is not borne out by official records declassified so far.

218 "sustained reprisal" et seq.: Memo, Bundy-LBJ, February 7, 1965. Pentagon Papers, pp. 423–427.

218 "what was the difference between Pleiku": quoted in Halberstam, op. cit., p. 533.

219 "enunciated rather firmly": U.S. Grant Sharpe, Strategy for Defeat (San Rafael, Calif.: Presidio Press, 1978), p. 62.

220 "giraffe" questions: Ball, op. cit., p. 376.

220–221 "exhausting the 1964 target list" et seq.: Paper, Ball-LBJ, October 5, 1964. Reprinted in George Ball, "Top Secret: The Prophecy the President Rejected," The Atlantic Monthly (January 1972), pp. 36–49.

221 "benign tolerance": Ball, The Past Has Another Pattern, p. 384.

221 "further frontal opposition": ibid., p. 389.

221 "follow a particular course": ibid., p. 505, fn. 8.

221 "If we limit ourselves" et seq.: Memo, Bundy-LBJ, February 16, 1965 (declassified

November 14, 1977) LBJL: LBJP: NSF: Memos to the President, box 2, folder: "Bundy, v. 8 (Jan.–Feb. 1965)."

221 "pyrotechnic display of facts": Ball, *The Past Has Another Pattern*, p. 392.

222 "essential elements" et seq.: quoted in Johnson, op. cit., p. 133.

223 Vietnam white paper: "Aggression from the North," Department of State Publication 7839. Reprinted in Marvin E. Gettleman, ed., *Vietnam* (Greenwich, Conn.: Fawcett Books, 1965), pp. 284–316.

223 "ripples of support": Cooper, op. cit., p. 265.

224 "no more a secret": I. F. Stone, "A Reply to the White Paper," *I. F. Stone's Weekly*, March 8, 1965. Reprinted in Gettleman, op. cit., pp. 317–323.

224 "whether massive air strikes would accomplish anything": Editorial, *New York Times*, February 28, 1965.

224 "can't be eight hundred pages long" et seq.: William J. Jorden, LBJ Oral History (AC 79-39), pp. 8–9.

224 "No such publication could have accomplished": Cooper, op. cit., p. 264.

224 "citizen's white paper" et seq.: Reprinted, Marcus G. Raskin and Bernard B. Fall, eds., *The Vietnam Reader* (New York: Vintage Books, 1965), pp. 129–136.

225 "where the appointment was": Letter, Bundy-Raskin, March 26, 1965. LBJL: LBJP: WHCF: General File, box 63, folder: "FG11-5 NSC (11/23/63–12/2/65)."

225 "merely a budgetary device": Robert Komer, Kennedy Oral History; cited in I.M. Destler, Leslie H. Gelb, and Anthony Lake, *Our Own Worst Enemy* (New York: Simon & Schuster, 1984) pp. 190–191.

226 "engine" and "caboose": pp. 56–57. Cf. Henry Graff, "Decision in Vietnam," *New York Times Magazine*, July 4, 1965.

227 "lost or won cleanly": Memo, Rostow-Rusk, May 20, 1965. Pentagon Papers, pp. 447–448.

227 "far from an unmitigated advantage": Cable, Taylor-Rusk (Saigon 3334), April 14, 1965 (declassified August 14, 1979). LBJL: LBJP: NSF, folder: "Open McGeorge Bundy Memos on Vietnam."

227 "Things are in the saddle": quoted in Ball, *The Past Has Another Pattern*, p. 395.

227 "Before we commit": ibid.

228 "willing to go overboard": quoted in ibid., p. 396.

228 "element of stability and strength" et seq.: Memo, Bundy-LBJ, June 30, 1965 (declassified July 17, 1980). LBJL: LBJP: NSF: folder: "Open McGeorge Bundy Memos on Vietnam."

228 "you will want to listen hard": Memo, Bundy-LBJ, July 1, 1965 (declassified October 27, 1982). LBJL: LBJP: NSF: Memos to the President, box 4, folder: "Bundy v. 12 (July 1965)."

231 "You have your two cards to play": Cable, Smith-Bundy, February 12, 1966 (declassified August 30, 1976). LBJL: LBJP: NSF: International Meetings Series, box 1/2, folder: "President's Honolulu Conference."

231 "Mr. Vietnam" et seq.: Memo, Cooper-LBJ, March 3, 1966 (declassified July 25,

1984). LBJL: LBJP: NSF: Memos to the President, box 6, folder: "Komer v. 21 (March 1–31, 1966)."

231 "I'm going to put you in charge": quoted in Bob Brewin and Sydney Shaw, *Vietnam on Trial* (New York: Atheneum, 1986), p. 234.

231 "I enjoy reading history": Marginal note on memo, Komer-Bundy, December 28, 1966. LBJL: LBJP: NSF: Name File, box 6, folder: "Komer Memos v. II (1)."

232 "Blowtorch Bob": Gravel Pentagon Papers, Vol. III, p. 567.

232 "He knew his onions": Memo, Komer-Moyers, September 6, 1966. LBJL: LBJP: NSF: Files of Robert Komer, box 4, folder: "Moyers-Christian."

232 "I read him the riot act": Memo, Komer-Moyers, October 14, 1966. Ibid.

232 "we couldn't help but do better": Memo, Komer-Christian, February 7, 1967. Ibid.

233 "more optimistic than ever": quoted in Gravel Pentagon Papers, Vol. III, p. 575. Italics in the original.

234 "The Lord knows": General William C. Westmoreland, *A Soldier Reports* (New York: Dell Books, 1980), p. 281.

234 "your mind is settling": Memo, Bundy-LBJ, November 27, 1965 (declassified February 12, 1981). LBJL: LBJP: NSF: Memos to the President, box 5, folder: "Bundy v. 17 (11/21–12/31/65)."

234 "Johnson is for peace": Memo, Bundy-LBJ, December 4, 1965 (declassified February 12, 1981). Ibid.

235 "someone moving throughout the world" et seq.: Meeting Notes, December 17, 1965 (declassified April 23, 1982). LBJL: LBJP: Meeting Notes File, box 1, folder: "Dec. 17, 1965, 9:41 AM."

235 "I can understand what McNamara is living with" et seq.: Meeting Notes, December 18, 1965 (declassified March 20, 1986). Ibid., folder: "Dec. 18, 1965."

236 "Jesus, I don't know": Chester Cooper, LBJ Oral History (AC 74–200), Vol. I, p. 20.

236 "They all said very strongly": Memo, Bundy-LBJ, December 27, 1965. LBJL: LBJP: NSF: Memos for the President, box 5, folder: "Bundy, v. 17 (11/21–12/31/65)."

236 "Since we have endured": ibid.

237 "an idea into the town": Memo, Rostow-LBJ, May 6, 1966. LBJL: LBJP: NSF: Memos to the President, box 7, folder: "Rostow v. 2 (May 1–15, 1966)."

237–238 "an experience in 1944": Memo, Rostow-Rusk/McNamara, May 6, 1966 (declassified November 4, 1985). Ibid.

238 "a softening political-diplomatic track": Memo, Rostow-LBJ, May 10, 1966 (declassified November 4, 1985). Ibid.

238–239 "a decision on bombing is not being made" et seq.: Summary of Discussion at 559th NSC, June 17, 1966 (declassified June 16, 1986). LBJL: LBJP: Meeting Notes File, box 1, folder: "June 17, 1966, 6:05 P.M."

239 "your Gettysburg Address": Memo, Rostow-LBJ, June 3, 1966. LBJL: LBJP: NSF: Memos to the President, box 8, folder: "Rostow v. 5 (May 27–June 10, 1966)."

239 "I have perhaps the least claim" et seq.: Memo, Rostow-LBJ, June 15, 1966. Ibid., folder: "Rostow v. 6 (June 11–20, 1966)."

239 "almost had a heart attack": quoted in Merle Miller, *Lyndon,* p. 534.

240 "terrible" influence and "played to Johnson's weaker side": quoted in ibid., p. 413.

240 "need in the next eighteen months": Memo, Henry Owen, "1864–1967," March 14, 1967. LBJL: LBJP: NSF: Memos to the President, box 14, folder: "Rostow v. 24 (Mar. 16–31, 1967)."

240 "the analogy would call for": Memo, Rostow-LBJ, March 17, 1967. Ibid.

240 "accompanied by military and political progress": Unsigned [Owen] Memo, "Decision in Vietnam," March 18, 1968 (declassified July 25, 1979). LBJL: LBJP: NSF: NSC Histories, March 31 Speech, box 48, folder: "v. 4, Tabs N–Z and AA–KK."

241 "a question of fact": Letter, Eugene V. Rostow-Walt W. Rostow, September 13, 1966. LBJL: LBJP: NSF: Memos to the President, box 10, folder: "Rostow v. 13 (Sept. 15–30, 1966)."

242 "before we get into any new target systems": Memo, Rostow-LBJ, January 23, 1967 (declassified March 23, 1981). LBJL: LBJP: NSF: Country File: Vietnam, box 75, folder: "2EE—Primarily McNamara Recommendations."

242 "aerial Dien Bien Phu" et seq.: Memo, Rostow-LBJ, May 19, 1967 (declassified March 23, 1981). LBJL: LBJP: NSF: Country File: Vietnam, box 75, folder: "2EE—Primarily McNamara Recommendations."

243 "felt humiliated": Bui Diem with David Chanoff, *In the Jaws of History* (Boston: Houghton Mifflin, 1987), p. 174.

243 "imbedded in concrete": Cooper, op. cit., p. 311.

244 "direct U.S.-Hanoi gambit" et seq.: Memo, Rostow-LBJ, November 17, 1966. LBJL: LBJP: NSF: Memos to the President, box 11, folder: "Rostow, v. 15 (Nov. 1–30, 1966)."

244 "I still believe": Memo, Rostow-LBJ, January 14, 1967. Ibid., folder: "Rostow v. 18 (Jan. 1–14, 1967)."

245 "incredulous and irate": Cooper, op. cit., p. 362.

245 "pathetic graffiti": ibid., p. 364.

245 "they're having cigars" et seq.: quoted in Cooper Oral History, op. cit., Vol. II, p. 28.

245 "I'm not kidding you!": ibid.

246 "You can't do this": quoted in ibid., p. 29.

247 "lead promptly to productive discussions": quoted in George C. Herring, ed. *The Secret Diplomacy of the Vietnam War: The Negotiating Volumes of the Pentagon Papers* (Austin: University of Texas Press, 1983), p. 75.

249 "detailed briefing of the press" et seq.: Cable, Saigon 7867, October 7, 1967 (declassified November 28, 1983). LBJL: LBJP: NSF: Country File: Vietnam, box 99, folder: "7E(1) b Public Relations Activities 9/67–10/67."

249–250 "best data available": Rostow Memo, November 1967. LBJL: LBJP: WHCF: Confidential File: ND19/CO 312, box NA, folder: "Situation in Vietnam (Oct.–Dec. 1967)."

250 "psychological strategy committee": Don Oberdorfer, *Tet!* (New York: Avon Books, 1972), p. 117.

251 "success offensive": ibid., p. 119.

251 "Don't mourn, Organize!": Memo, Rostow-LBJ, January 16, 1968. LBJL: LBJP: NSF: Name File, box 7, folder: "Rostow Memos."

252 "the field commander is the man at the wheel": Memo, Rostow-Wheeler, January 30, 1968. LBJL: LBJP: NSF: NSC Histories, box 47, folder: "Mar. 31st Speech, v. 2, Tabs A–ZZ."

252 "third phase" et seq.: Cable, Westmoreland-Wheeler (MAC 01464), February 1, 1968 (declassified June 11, 1979). Ibid.

253 "U.S. opinion steady on course": Memo, Rostow-LBJ, February 5, 1968. LBJL: LBJP: NSF: NSC Histories: March 31 Speech, box 47, folder: "v. 2, Tabs A–Z and AA–ZZ."

253 "prove": The theme of journalistic responsibility for defeat at Tet, restated by such participants or observers as General Phillip B. Davidson or Gunther Lewy, was first advanced by Peter Braestrup, in *Big Story* (New Haven: Yale University Press, 1983). Braestrup was right to criticize reporters' frequent "rat pack" mentality and failure to detach themselves more from their stories, but his thesis fails to take into account MACV and Washington's own deliberate efforts, playing to these weaknesses, to slant the news. The Tet battles revealed this slant and led much of the press to automatically discount official pronouncements. It is noteworthy that the U.S. Army's official history of this aspect of the war, recently released, concludes: "In the end, President Johnson and his advisers put too much faith in public relations" (William M. Hammond, *The U.S. Army in Vietnam: Public Affairs: The Military and the Media 1962–1968* [Washington, D.C. Center of Military History, 1988], p. 388).

254 "force Westy to commit to battle" et seq.: Memo, Rostow-LBJ, February 7, 1968 (declassified August 29, 1980). NSC History, op. cit. Rostow's italics. The specific phrase "This is it" Walt used to agree with the basic thrust of analysis of a piece in the British newsmagazine *The Economist*. Elsewhere in the same memo Rostow claimed, "This is a battle which may determine the shape of Asia for a very long time."

254 "how do you explain this": Memo, Rostow-LBJ, February 12, 1968 (declassified August 29, 1980). Ibid.

255 "indirectly let the North Koreans know" et seq.: Memo, Ginsburgh-Rostow, February 26, 1968 (declassified July 8, 1980). Ibid., folder: "v. 3, Tabs A–QQ."

256 "a lot of Harry McPhersons": Memo, McPherson-LBJ, October 27, 1967. LBJL: LBJP: NSF: Country File: Vietnam, box 127, folder: "Vietnam [March 19, 1970 Memo] (1)."

257 "great fall-off in support" et seq.: Meeting Notes, March 20, 1968 (declassified August 16, 1985). Ibid.

257 "has not come up with a plan" et seq.: George Christian Meeting Notes, March 22, 1968 (declassified October 11, 1983. LBJL: LBJP: Meeting Notes File, box 2, folder: "Mar. 22, 1968."

258 "I believe it is the consensus": quoted in Harry C. McPherson, *A Political Education* p. 432.

258 "we can no longer do the job": Meeting Notes, March 26, 1968. LBJL: LBJP: Meeting Notes File, box 2, folder: "Mar. 26, 1968."

260 "You're free of it already": Walt Rostow interview, September 13, 1988.

PART VI. KING RICHARD AND PRINCE HENRY

261 "without the concurrences": Kissinger memo to the President-elect, December 27, 1968. See Henry A. Kissinger, *White House Years* (Boston: Little, Brown, 1979), p. 41–42.

262 "quiet and deliberate" et seq.: Letter, Anderson-Nixon, September 3, 1968. DDEL: Gordon Gray Papers, box 1, folder: "Dillon Anderson (1)."

264 "agnostic": Kissinger, op. cit., p. 42.

265 "rough roads lay ahead": U. Alexis Johnson with Jef O. McAllister, *The Right Hand of Power* (Englewood Cliffs, N.J.: Prentice-Hall, 1984), p. 514.

265–266 "five minutes' conversation": Kissinger, *White House Years*, p. 45.

267 "bureaucratic logjam": I.M. Destler, "Can One Man Do?" *Foreign Policy*, No. 5 (Winter 1971–1972), p. 31.

267 "enough of a shake to the bureaucracy" et seq.: Henry Kissinger and Bernard Brodie, eds. *Bureaucracy, Politics and Strategy* (Los Angeles: University of California Security Studies Project, 1968); reprinted in Morton Halperin and Arnold Kanter, eds. *Readings in American Foreign Policy* (Boston: Little, Brown, 1973), p. 92.

268 "excessive reliance on tactical considerations" et seq.: *Foreign Affairs*, January 1969; reprinted in Henry Kissinger, *American Foreign Policy* (New York: W. W. Norton, 1969), pp. 116, 112, 134. It is instructive that Kissinger dropped *only* this piece when editing later editions of the collection.

270 "how ignorant we were": quoted in *Newsweek* (February 7, 1972), p. 15.

270 "guerrilla wins if he does not lose" et seq.: Kissinger, *American Foreign Policy*, pp 104, 122.

270–271 "in the event of the assassination": NSSM-22, "Contingency Plans for Vietnam," February 13, 1969 (declassified February 27, 1981). NARA: Records Group 273, NSC Records, box 4, folder: "NSSMs."

273 "my only connection with Metternich": Oriana Fallaci, "Henry Kissinger: Women, Power, the War," *New York Post Magazine*, December 23, 1972.

273–274 Kissinger's views on tactical nuclear weapons: Henry Kissinger, *Nuclear Weapons and Foreign Policy* (New York: Harper & Brothers, 1957) pp. 174–233, esp. 190–195 and 199–202. Paul Nitze's scathing review of this study in *The Reporter* led Kissinger to threaten a libel suit. Among Nitze's objections was that Henry had misunderstood the destructive power of tactical nuclear weapons. As Nitze has since recounted: "Henry had no realistic idea how destructive a 500 KT [kiloton] bomb would be" (Paul Nitze, *From Hiroshima to Glasnost* [New York: Grove Weidenfeld, 1989], p. 298). Kissinger expressed later views in his *The Necessity for Choice* (New York: Harper & Brothers, 1960), p. 81; and in *The Troubled Partnership* (New York: Doubleday/Anchor, 1966), p. 181.

275–276 "I *was* naive" et seq.: quoted in Seymour Hersh, *The Price of Power* (New York: Summit Books, 1983), p. 13.

276 "Just the way Mac Bundy handled me": quoted in David Halberstam, *The Best and The Brightest* (New York: Random House, 1972), p. 63.

277 "equivalent of being sent on vacation": John Lehman, *Command of the Seas* (New York: Charles Scribner's Sons, 1988), p. 381.

280 "disciplined my anarchic tendencies": Henry Kissinger, *Years of Upheaval* (Boston: Little, Brown, 1982), p. 107.

282 "I call it the Madman Theory": quoted in H. R. Haldeman with Joseph DiMona, *The Ends of Power* (New York: Dell Books, 1978), p. 122.

283 "I've been in office now for hours": quoted in Hersh, op. cit., p. 98.

285 "inherited procedures their chance to fail": quoted in John Newhouse, *Cold Dawn* (New York: Holt, Rinehart & Winston, 1973), p. 159.

286 "a dawning recognition": Hersh, *The Price of Power*, quoted p. 117.

286 "inordinately proud" et seq.: William G. Hyland, *Mortal Rivals* (New York: Random House, 1987), p. 39.

287 "the main problem": Kissinger, *White House Years*, p. 525.

288 "first-class blunder" et seq.: ibid., pp. 542–543.

290 "avenues other than": Reprinted in Nixon, *RN*, Vol. 1, p. 483.

291 "desultory" and "unattainable": Kissinger, *White House Years*, p. 285.

291–292 Kissinger's preferred version: Kissinger, *White House Years*, pp. 468, 517. Kissinger made this identical claim in an October 10, 1979, television interview with David Frost broadcast on NBC (Program Transcript, pp. 25, 34). In a piece he published in *The Economist* (September 8, 1979), Henry's claim is that North Vietnamese attacks occurred all over Cambodia east of the Mekong within ten days of Sihanouk's ouster. He also used the figure of 100,000 North Vietnamese troops in Cambodia. Contemporary Pentagon official estimates of North Vietnamese strength were 25,000 to 40,000, and high CIA estimates were 63,000. Cf. Jonathan S. Grant et al., eds. *Cambodia: The Widening War in Indochina* (New York: Washington Square Press, 1971), pp. 228–229. In the historiography of the Nixon administration the true revisionists have become the principals themselves, dedicated to creating a version of events that makes their actions seem more plausible.

292 North Vietnamese movements: Truong Nhu Tang with David Chanoff and Doan Van Thai, *A Viet Cong Memoir* (New York: Harcourt, Brace, Jovanovich, 1985), pp. 177–185.

293 "lurching toward a decision": Roger Morris, *Haig: The General's Progress* (N.p.: Playboy Press, 1982), p. 140.

294 Historical dispute: See the very revealing account by Wolfgang Saxon, "Kissinger Revised His Book More Than He Reported," *New York Times*, October 31, 1979. This article shows conclusively that Dr. Kissinger changed the manuscript of his *White House Years* both to suggest that the invasion decision-making began later than it did, and to counter the charges about United States bombing of Cambodia raised by William Shawcross. According to the Saxon piece, Kissinger actually castigates Shawcross for alleged charges the journalist did not make, at least in the places Kissinger refers to in the Shawcross book. The Shawcross account is in *Sideshow: Kissinger, Nixon and the Destruction of Cambodia* (New York: Simon & Schuster, 1979). In a letter to the editor of *The Economist*, excerpted in the *New York Times* (September 29, 1979), Kissinger found the Shawcross account "absurd" and "obscene." Peter Rodman debated the subject with Shawcross in the June 1981 issue of *The American Spectator*. Kissinger resumed the attack in the second volume of his memoirs, reprinting correspondence by American diplomats and Air Force General John Vogt, plus a cable from State to Phnom Penh, intended to show that U.S. air operations in Cambodia remained under close control, thus presumably refuting *Sideshow*'s contentions (*Years of Upheaval*, pp. 1220–1230). In reality all the sound and fury signifies very little, since it pertains to the very narrowest points of the (unknowable) direct destructiveness of American bombing on Cambodian populations. The thesis that U.S. *intervention* led to the destruction of Cambodia, the basic thrust of the Shawcross account and its broadest criticism, is not confronted or refuted by technical objections to Shawcross's documentation, especially in view of repeated official admissions by the Department of Defense that both strategic and tactical bombing raids had been conducted in Cambodia and the records falsified. Columnist

Anthony Lewis sounded the right note in a column on Kissinger's objections he titled "Out, Damned Spot!" (*New York Times,* September 24, 1979).

294 "no consideration" et seq.: Kissinger, *White House Years,* p. 484.

294 "highest level concern" et seq.: quoted Shawcross, *Sideshow,* p. 138.

295 "No Dis Khmer": *New York Times,* May 5, 1970.

296 "Our peerless leader has flipped out": quoted in Morris, *Haig:* op. cit., p. 141.

296 "This is my bleeding hearts club" et seq.: quoted in Hersh, op. cit., p. 188.

297 "it's your ass": quoted in Morris, op. cit., p. 141.

297 "musing": Kissinger, *White House Years,* p. 498.

297 "see that movie one more time": quoted in Marvin Kalb and Bernard Kalb, *Kissinger* (New York: Dell Books, 1975), p. 186.

297 "cowardice of the Eastern Establishment": quoted in Roger Morris, *Uncertain Greatness: Henry Kissinger and American Foreign Policy* (New York: Harper & Row, 1977), p. 174.

298 "What . . . did you say to Henry?": Hersh, op. cit., p. 191.

298 "You've just had an order" et seq.: quoted in Morris, *Haig,* p. 141.

298 "implementing authority": Kissinger, *White House Years,* p. 500.

299 "We know Henry's very upset": quoted in Kalb and Kalb, op. cit., p. 188.

299 "integral" et seq.: William Safire, *Before the Fall: An Inside View of the Pre-Watergate White House* (New York: Belmont Tower Books, 1975); reprint, pp. 185–186.

300 "we are all the president's men": quoted in Morris, *Haig,* p. 142.

301 "Henry came in" et seq.: Transcript, *New York Times,* May 13, 1977.

304 "international credibility": quoted in Kissinger, *White House Years,* p. 597.

306 "Bob, look at this" et seq.: quoted in Haldeman with DiMona, op. cit., pp. 125–126.

306 "what actions we can take": Note, Nixon-Kissinger, quoted in Nixon, *RN,* Vol. 1, p. 602.

307 "time-wasting": Kissinger, *White House Years,* p. 642.

308 flawed base definition: Elmo R. Zumwalt, *On Watch* (New York: Quadrangle Books, 1976), p. 311.

309 Nixon on Kissinger and women: Memo, Nixon-Alexander Butterfield, February 9, 1971. Reprinted in Bruce Oudes, ed., *From: The President: Richard Nixon's Secret Files* (New York: Harper & Row, 1989), p. 215.

310 "Americans admire the cowboy": Kissinger interview with Oriana Fallaci, op. cit. This interview was actually conducted on November 4, 1972.

310 "in the spirit the president intended": Kissinger interview with Gaylord Shaw, quoted in "The Long Journey of Henry Kissinger," *New York Post,* May 6, 1972.

313 "Here we go again": Nixon Marginal Note, White House News Summary (hereafter cited as News Summary), date NA. Nixon Library Project (hereafter NLP): Nixon Papers: President's Office File (hereafter POF), box 30, folder: "September 1969."

313 "Get this to some of the faint hearts" et seq.: Nixon Note, News Summary, n.d.

(March 1969). NLP: Nixon papers: POF, box 30, folder: "January–March 1969." Nixon's emphasis.

314 "Isn't this the time?": Nixon Note, News Summary, n.d. (September 1969). NLP: Nixon Papers: POF, box 30, folder: "September 1969."

314 "Did anyone on your staff talk": Nixon Note, News Summary, n.d. (September 1969), pp. 6–7. NLP: Nixon Papers: POF, box 30, folder: "September 1969."

314 "When Henry gets back tell him": Nixon Note, News Summary, June 20, 1972, p. 6. NLP: Nixon Papers: POF: box 41, folder: "June 7–23, 1972 (2 of 2)."

314 "McClosky is no friend of ours": White House News Summary, February 5, 1970. NLP: Nixon Papers: POF, box 31, folder: "February 1970."

314 "Thieu made good on his promise" et seq.: Nixon Note, News Summary, June 20, 1972, p. 4. Ibid. Author's italics.

315 "in the long run a more productive policy": Memorandum, Nixon-Haldeman, June 2, 1971. Reprinted p. 261 in Oudes, ed., *From: The President.*

315 "very sophisticated" et seq.: H. R. Haldeman, "Fresh Notes, Re: Leaks," February 3, 1970. Reprinted in Oudes, op. cit., p. 93.

317 "Nixon wondered aloud": quoted p. 279 in John Ehrlichman, *Witness to Power* (New York: Pocket Books, 1982).

317 "I was all the way up to speed": Elmo R. Zumwalt, Jr., *On Watch* (New York: Quadrangle Books, 1976), p. 370.

318 "kind of unacceptable risk": Kissinger, *White House Years,* pp. 664–665.

319 "stunned surprise": Kissinger, *White House Years,* p. 670.

319 "If I ever carried": U.S. Congress (94/2) Senate. Select Committee to Study Governmental Operations with Respect to Intelligence Activities. *Interim Report: Alleged Assassination Plots Involving Foreign Leaders* (Washington, D.C.: GPO, 1976), pp. 227–228.

319 "make the economy scream": Richard Helms Notes of Meeting, September 15, 1970. Ibid., p. 227.

320 "felt they were free to continue": Kissinger, *White House Years,* p. 676.

320 "I don't see why we need": quoted in Hersh, op. cit., p. 265. This quotation comes directly from the minutes of the 40 Committee meeting, records never kept before Nixon's administration. It was found by Church Committee investigator Gregory Treverton sitting in a cubicle surrounded by CIA security officers. Previous Special Group records had been limited to sparse notations of projects approved or rejected, etc. According to Treverton, it was Kissinger who had insisted the 40 Committee begin recording actual summaries of discussion.

320 "cool but correct": Edward Korry, "The Sell-Out of Chile and the American Taxpayer," *Penthouse* (March 1978), p. 88.

320 "conception, planning, and execution": Kissinger, *White House Years,* p. 683.

321 "nature of the Chinese Communist threat": NSSM-14, "U.S. China Policy," February 5, 1969 (declassified September 19, 1980). NARA: RG-273, folder: "NSSM-14."

321 "possibly we should move up": Nixon Note, News Summary, April 4, 1970, p. 1. NLP: Nixon Papers: POF, box 31, folder: "April 1970."

321 "without any notice": Memo, Nixon-Kissinger, November 22, 1970. Nixon, *RN,* Vol. 2, p. 10.

322 "Kissinger rolled his eyes": ibid., p. 15.

322 "It was painful enough": Kissinger, *White House Years,* p. 728.

327 "you've had enough exposure": Sonnenfeldt recollections. John W. McDonald, ed., *U.S.-Soviet Summitry: Roosevelt Through Carter* (Washington: Foreign Service Institute: Center for the Study of Foreign Affairs, 1987), p. 82.

327 "There are no secret agreements": quoted in John Prados, *The Soviet Estimate* (Princeton: Princeton University Press, 1986), p. 231.

328 "working on the accuracy" et seq.: U.S. Congress (96/1) Senate. Foreign Relations Committee. *Hearings: The SALT II Treaty, Part I* (Washington, D.C.: GPO, 1979), p. 198.

328 "What in the name of God": *Department of State Bulletin* (July 29, 1974), p. 215.

329 "can you do it without leaking" et seq.: McDonald, ed., *U.S.-Soviet Summitry,* p. 76.

329 "Anatoli, we have been warning": quoted in Kissinger, *White House Years,* p. 1117.

330 "North Vietnamese are taking a very great risk" et seq.: quoted in Tad Szulc, *The Illusion of Peace: Foreign Policy in the Nixon Years* (New York: Viking Press, 1978), p. 548.

330 "a not very subtle hint": Zumwalt, op. cit. p. 384.

330 Told David Frost: David Frost, *I Gave Them a Sword: Behind the Scenes of the Nixon Interviews* (New York: Ballantine Books, 1978), pp. 115–116.

330 "We cannot afford any breast feeding": Transcript, "Briefing by Dr. Henry Kissinger to Members of the White House Staff," April 26, 1972, p. 1. NLP: Nixon Papers: WHCF: Staff and Office Files: Haig, box 44, folder: "General Speech Material (2 of 5)."

331 "all but one of his staff": Nixon, *RN,* Vol. 2, p. 81.

331 "The NSC meeting was obviously a charade": U. Alexis Johnson with Jef Olivarius McAllister, *The Right Hand of Power* (Englewood Cliffs, N.J.: Prentice-Hall, 1984), p. 535.

332 "tough, watershed decision": Memo, Nixon-Kissinger, date NA. Reprinted in Nixon, *RN,* Vol. 2, pp. 85–86.

333 "No one has a right": quoted in Kissinger, *White House Years,* p. 1335.

333 "It appears that this is feasible": Memo, Laird-Kissinger, October 15, 1972 (declassified April 6, 1978).

334 "Operation Big Lie": quoted in Hersh, op. cit., p. 593, fn.

335 "We believe peace is at hand": Text, *New York Times,* October 27, 1972.

335 "dangerous course which your Government": Letter, Nixon-Thieu, October 29, 1972. Reprinted in Nguyen Tien Hung and Jerrold L. Schecter, *The Palace File* (New York: Harper & Row, 1986), pp. 379–380.

335 "It is unrealistic to assume": Letter, Nixon-Thieu, November 14, 1972. Reprinted in ibid., p. 386.

336 "Nixon hardly focused" et seq.: quoted in Allen E. Goodman, *The Lost Peace* (Stanford, Calif.: Hoover Institution Press, 1978), pp. 145, 147.

336 "my absolute assurance": Letter, Nixon-Thieu, November 14, 1972, op. cit.

336 "We will respond with full force": Letter, Nixon-Thieu, January 5, 1973. Reprinted in Hung and Schecter, op. cit., p. 392.

336 "The U.S. will respond vigorously": Letter, Nixon-Thieu, January 17, 1973. Reprinted in ibid., p. 395.

337 "decent interval": Frank Snepp, *Decent Interval* (New York: Random House, 1977).

339 "Victorian middle-class mentality": Kissinger interview with Fallaci, op. cit.

340 "would run counter to all Nixon's ideas" et seq.: Kissinger, *Years of Upheaval,* p. 420. Kissinger is confusing here, claiming on the same page that Nixon planned to appoint Rush and then that "Rush was too little known to be promoted." Kenneth Rush had been Richard Nixon's law professor at Duke University.

342 "speech was more hortatory" et seq.: Wilfrid L. Kohl, "The Nixon-Kissinger Foreign Policy System," *World Politics,* Vol. 28, No. 1 (October 1975), pp. 16, 18–19.

344 "use the war to start a peace process": Kissinger, *Years of Upheaval,* p. 468.

344 "Neither of us fooled the other": ibid., p. 485.

344 "reliable sources": Kalb and Kalb, *Kissinger,* p. 527.

344 "middle levels": Kissinger, *Years of Upheaval,* p. 486.

344 "events had gone beyond": ibid., p. 493.

344 "Israelis must not be allowed to lose": quoted in ibid., p. 495.

345 "Over the next two days": William B. Quandt, *Decade of Decisions* (Berkeley, Calif.: University of California Press, 1977), p. 179.

346 Authoritative account: Matti Golan, *The Secret Conversations of Henry Kissinger* (New York: Bantam Books, 1976), pp. 75–76.

346 "could have delayed my departure": Kissinger, *Years of Upheaval,* p. 544.

346 "History will not record": ibid., p. 548.

347 "smoke issuing from nose": quoted in ibid., p. 557.

347 "I presume she is wild with anger": quoted in Golan, op. cit., p. 82.

347 "Israelis could not help but interpret" et seq.: Golan, op. cit., p. 87, and Kissinger quoted in ibid., p. 86. Kissinger reports he indicated he would understand if there were a few *hours'* slippage while he flew home (*Years of Upheaval,* p. 569). The impression given the Kalb brothers was that (1) the IDF had taken advantage of *Egyptian* violations; (2) Kissinger insisted to Golda upon "scrupulous" observance of the cease-fire; and (3) that Kissinger determined to "stop" the Israelis and "save" the Third Army (*Kissinger,* pp. 549–550).

348 "If you find it impossible": quoted in Kissinger, *Years of Upheaval,* p. 583.

348 "*I* sent a letter": Nixon, *RN,* Vol. 2, p. 498. Italics added.

350 "Kissinger model": cited by reporter Thomas L. Friedman in *New York Times,* March 27, 1989.

351 "I am not conducting my office": quoted in *New York Times,* June 7, 1974.

351 "My judgment is that": *The New Republic,* July 6, 1974; reprinted in John Osborne, *The Last Nixon Watch* (Washington, D.C.: New Republic Books, 1975), p. 156.

351 "churlish": Kissinger, *Years of Upheaval,* p. 1120.

352 "Do you want to start a revolution": quoted in Edward R.F. Sheehan, *The Arabs, The Israelis and Kissinger* (New York: Reader's Digest Press, 1976), p. 167. When an early version of Sheehan's work appeared in the journal *Foreign Policy,* Kissinger disavowed it and denied any connection. In fact, Sheehan recounts, Henry had met with him several times, had allowed him on shuttle flights, and had had him briefed with secret materials by Roy Atherton or Hal Saunders on *at least twenty* occasions. Indeed the transcripts of discussions of which Sheehan uses fragments could have come from no other place. Once the controversy began, the State Department announced its reaction: to reprimand Atherton and Saunders. Atherton was also prevailed upon to inform Sheehan he had been acting only on his own judgment in providing the reporter information based upon secret records. This seems unlikely.

352 Kissinger startled: Kissinger, *Years of Upheaval,* p. 646.

353 "You must stay here": quoted in Nixon, *RN,* Vol. 2, p. 669.

356 NSC meeting, September 13: Ford administration records place this meeting on September 14, while Alex Johnson (*Right Hand of Power,* p. 603) puts it on the thirteenth.

357 "abandoned YMCA camp": Gerald R. Ford, *A Time to Heal: The Autobiography of Gerald R. Ford* (New York: Berkley Books, 1980), p. 209.

359 "certainly favored the Soviet position": Raymond L. Garthoff, *Detente to Confrontation* (Washington, D.C.: Brookings Institution, 1985), pp. 446–447.

359–360 "What I'd like to know" et seq.: quoted in Lehman, op. cit., p. 168.

361 "preliminary": Letter, Nixon-Pham Van Dong, February 1, 1973. Reprinted in *New York Times,* May 20, 1977.

363–364 "Vietnam is falling to pieces" et seq.: quoted in Ford, op. cit., p. 244.

364 "like getting nine women pregnant": quoted in Hung and Schecter, op. cit., p. 296.

364–365 "use of United States military airpower": Memorandum, Weyand-Ford, April 4, 1975 (declassified November 19, 1980). Reprinted p. 468, Hung and Schecter, *The Palace File,* op. cit.

365 Kissinger objects: Ford, op. cit., p. 245. A later study by the House Committee on Foreign Affairs, however, questions whether evacuation constituted a situation of danger of imminent hostilities, and also whether the information Ford finally *did* provide constituted adequate "consultation" under the law (*Special Study: The War Powers Resolution* [Washington, D.C.: GPO, 1982], pp. 183–185).

366 "a very sober interagency meeting" et seq.: Cable, Kissinger-Martin, April 18, 1975. Reprinted in David Butler, *The Fall of Saigon* (New York: Simon & Schuster, 1985), p. 271.

366 "your best efforts": Cable, Kissinger-Martin, April 19, 1975. Reprinted in ibid., p. 276.

366 "I will be hanging": Cable, Kissinger-Martin, April 19, 1975. Reprinted in ibid., p. 283.

366 "trickling Americans out slowly": Cable, Kissinger-Martin, April 20, 1975. Reprinted in ibid., p. 299.

369 "we have a little problem": quoted in Robert T. Hartman, *Palace Politics* (New York: McGraw-Hill, 1980), p. 324.

369 "broad political impact": *Time* (May 26, 1975), p. 12.

370 "Has anyone considered": quoted in Ford, op. cit., p. 271.

371 "attempts to second-guess": quoted in *New York Times,* October 6, 1976.

377 "fulcrums with which to pry" et seq.: Robert H. Johnson, "The National Security Council: The Relevance of Its Past to Its Future," *Orbis,* Vol. 13, No. 3 (Fall 1969), p. 732.

PART VII. BETWEEN POWER AND PRINCIPLE

379 "as far as foreign policy goes": quoted in Jules Witcover, *Marathon* (New York: New American Library, 1977), p. 636.

381 "consciously or unconsciously" and "no role for them": Zbigniew Brzezinski, "Revolution and Counterrevolution," *New Republic* (June 1, 1968), p. 158.

381 "death rattle of historical irrelevants": *Newsweek* (May 12, 1969), p. 72.

381 "dispassionate scholarship": ibid.

381 "historically obsolescent": ibid.

382 "peaceful engagement": Zbigniew Brzezinski, *An Alternative to Partition* (New York: McGraw-Hill, 1965), passim.

383 "overlapping" and "dynamic setting": Zbigniew Brzezinski, "Peace and Power: Looking Toward the Seventies," *Encounter* (November 1968).

383 "victim of the technetronic revolution": Zbigniew Brzezinski, *Between Two Ages* (New York: Viking Press, 1970), p. 35.

383–384 All quotes from *Between Two Ages:* "eschatology" p. 64; "Luddites" p. 108 ff.; "emotion and necessity" p. 109; "Violent Left" p. 249; "organized coercion" p. 250; "human growth and nourishment" p. 272.

385 On jobs: Zbigniew Brzezinski, *Power and Principle* (New York: Farrar, Straus, and Giroux, 1983), pp. 4, 10, 12.

385 "I want you to do me a favor" et seq.: quoted in ibid., p. 4.

385 Brzezinski on Ball and Warnke: ibid., pp. 8, 11–12.

385 "would not be obtaining": ibid., p. 13.

386 "I will try to sensitize": quoted in ibid., p. 13.

387 "floating seminar": Richard Burt, "Zbig Makes It Big," *New York Times Magazine* (July 30, 1978), p. 10.

388 "don't envisage my job": *New York Times,* December 17, 1976.

388 "I have got excellent advisers": Text, *Time* (August 8, 1977), p. 25.

390 "real arms control" et seq.: Strobe Talbott, *Endgame: The Inside Story of SALT II* (New York: Harper & Row, 1979), p. 58.

391 "Good, let's do that": quoted in ibid., p. 59.

393 "unconstructive and one-sided" et seq.: quoted in Cyrus Vance, *Hard Choices: Critical Years in America's Foreign Policy* (New York: Simon & Schuster, 1983), p. 54.

393 "gave the affair a surreal quality": William G. Hyland, *Mortal Rivals: Superpower Relations from Nixon to Reagan* (New York: Random House, 1987), p. 212.

394 "I truly believe": Brzezinski News Conference, April 1, 1977; Text, Roger P. Labrie, ed., *SALT Handbook: Key Documents and Issues 1972–1979* (Washington, D.C.: American Enterprise Institute, 1979), pp. 443–444.

394 "engage here in a critique": ibid., p. 450.

394 "our damnedest effort": ibid., p. 449.

394 "if I wasn't [surprised]": ibid., p. 451.

394 "with the benefit of hindsight": Brzezinski, Power and Principle, p. 162. Italics added.

394 "Looking back on this episode": Hyland, op. cit., p. 215.

395 "there goes Washington" et seq.: quoted in Talbott, op. cit., p. 155.

396 Brzezinski recommends Seignious: Power and Principle, p. 307.

397 "Do you know where you've reached us, Zbig?": quoted in Talbott, op. cit., p. 243.

398 "whenever such denial impedes verification": Text, SALT II Treaty, Article 15, section 3. Vienna, June 18, 1979. Italics added.

399 "Some suggest": Ford speech, undated. Text, Washington Post, September 26, 1979. Ford's italics.

399 "much of the foundation of this agreement": quoted in New York Times, September 29, 1979.

399 "starting in your own end zone": quoted in New York Times, July 6, 1979.

400 "I never felt the Carter White House": Wayne S. Smith, The Closest of Enemies: A Personal and Diplomatic Account of U.S.-Cuban Relations Since 1957 (New York: W. W. Norton, 1987), p. 127.

401 "impose" linkage: Brzezinski News Conference, March 1, 1978. Text; Labrie, op. cit., p. 547.

402 "If State objected": quoted in Smith, op. cit., p. 168.

404 "to my amazement": Brzezinski, Power and Principle, p. 347.

404 "significant": Vance Letter, July 26, 1979. U.S. Congress (96/1) Senate Foreign Relations Committee. Hearings: SALT II Treaty. Washington, D.C.: GPO, 1979), Pt. 1, p. 615.

405 "You may not want to hear this": Brzezinski Weekly Report, September 26, 1979. Reprinted in Power and Principle, p. 565.

405 "The group did meet": Brzezinski, Power and Principle, p. 350.

405–406 "My fellow Americans": Text, New York Times, October 2, 1979.

406 "most disagreeable comments" et seq.: Brzezinski, Power and Principle, p. 351.

407 "more sophisticated appraisal": ibid., p. 177.

408 "my own predisposition": ibid.

408 "Where are the criteria?": quoted in Thomas Powers, "Choosing a Strategy for World War III," Atlantic Monthly (November 1982), pp. 86, 87.

409 "an ominous inclination": Carter Wake Forest Speech, March 17, 1978. Text, New York Times, March 18, 1978.

410 "SALT lies buried in the sands of the Ogaden" et seq.: Brzezinski, Power and Principle, p. 189.

410 "never accepted a defeat": Hodding Carter, "How Jimmy Carter's Foreign Policy Bit the Dust," Washington Post, January 5, 1987.

410 "Brzezinski's Brzezinski": *New York Times,* February 3, 1980.

411 "Brzezinski's poacher" et seq.: Ibid. Cf. *New York Times,* March 2, 1980.

411 "doctrinal innovation": Brzezinski, *Power and Principle,* p. 457.

411 "Harold Brown has now become": Brzezinski Diary, quoted in ibid., p. 458.

412 "anti-American events of 1964": Vance, op. cit., p. 141.

413 "If I could have foreseen": Jimmy Carter, *Keeping Faith: Memoirs of a President* (New York: Bantam Books, 1982), p. 184.

415 "dissociation": Anthony Lake, *Somoza Falling* (Boston: Houghton Mifflin, 1989), p. 70.

415 "feel good" policy: ibid. The following material relies primarily on Robert A. Pastor, *Condemned to Repetition* (Princeton, N.J.: Princeton University Press, 1987).

417 "Put your concerns in a memo": quoted in Pastor, op. cit., p. 67.

419 "the peso stops here": quoted in ibid., p. 135.

419 "decisive": ibid., p. 141.

419 "the first time in a year" et seq.: ibid., p. 157.

419–420 "anxiety had caused him to abandon": ibid., p. 162.

420 "baton being passed" et seq.: quoted in ibid., p. 172.

420 "It's too bad the Shah": Vaky Comments at Panel "U.S. Diplomacy and Political Change," Conference, Society of Historians of American Foreign Relations, June 26, 1986.

421 Kissinger's vague "studies": U.S. Congress (100/2) House. Committee on Veteran's Affairs. *Final Report: Americans Missing in Southeast Asia* (Washington, D.C.: GPO, 1988), pp. 112–118, esp. pp. 113–115. The term "studies" occurs in the Message from Richard Nixon to Pham Van Dong, February 1, 1973. Declassified and Text published in *New York Times,* May 20, 1977.

422 "global or regional hegemony": Memo, Carter-Brzezinski, May 17, 1978; reprinted in Brzezinski, *Power and Principle,* following p. 547.

423 "code of détente": quoted in *New York Times,* May 29, 1978.

423 "not just a professor": quoted in Brzezinski, *Power and Principle,* p. 220.

424 "*not* to convey . . . alarm": ibid., p. 409. Italics in the original.

424 "paper tiger": ibid.

425 "My trip to the Golan": ibid., p. 84.

426 "a shining light burst": Carter, *Keeping Faith,* p. 282.

426 "We have reached such a moment": Letter, Sadat-Carter, October 21, 1977. Reprinted in William B. Quandt, *Camp David: Peacemaking and Politics* (Washington, D.C.: Brookings Institution, 1986), pp. 140–141.

426 Journalists account: Eitan Huber, Zeev Schiff, and Ehud Yaari, *The Year of the Dove* (New York: Bantam Books, 1979).

427 "quite an argument": Carter Diary, February 3, 1978. Quoted in *Keeping Faith,* p. 306.

429 "Sadat is leaving": quoted in Carter, *Keeping Faith,* p. 391.

430 "The Libyan mess": ibid., p. 548.

431 "Brzezinski seemed to seethe" et seq.: quoted in *New York Times,* September 18, 1980.

433 "Carter Doctrine": State of the Union Address. Text, *New York Times,* January 24, 1980. David Newsom has said that the first he ever heard of a Carter "Doctrine" was when he read the text of the speech in the newspaper.

434 "people who are determined" et seq.: quoted in *New York Times,* February 4, 1980.

435 "island of stability": quoted in Jimmy Carter, *Keeping Faith,* p. 437.

436 "not in a revolutionary": U.S. Congress (96/1). House Permanent Select Committee on Intelligence. *Staff Report: Iran: Evaluation of U.S. Intelligence Performance Prior to November 1978* (Washington, D.C.: GPO, 1979), quoted p. 7.

436–437 "strange as it may seem": Gary Sick, *All Fall Down* (New York: Random House, 1985), p. 60.

437 "exactly who is the opposition": quoted in Scott Armstrong, "The Fall of the Shah (series): Vance Deflects a Call for Toughness," *Washington Post,* October 28, 1980.

437 "doctrinal dislike of the Shah": Brzezinski, *Power and Principle,* p. 355.

437 "Thinking the Unthinkable": William H. Sullivan, *Mission to Teheran* (New York: W. W. Norton, 1981), p. 201.

438 "To Cy, Zbig, Stan—": quoted in Stansfield Turner, *Secrecy and Democracy* (Boston: Houghton Mifflin, 1985), p. 113.

438 "a bureaucratic initiative": Brzezinski, *Power and Principle,* p. 368.

439 "one other thing" et seq.: quoted in Sick, *All Fall Down,* pp. 102, 103.

439 "Wisdom may be more than an open mind": ibid., p. 104.

439 "when travel is substituted for thought": George W. Ball, *The Past Has Another Pattern* (New York: W. W. Norton, 1982), p. 457.

439 "worst idea I ever heard": ibid., p. 461.

440 "as an old friend": ibid., p. 462.

440 "an impeccable source" et seq.: Vance, op. cit., p. 328.

441 "while delaying basic choices": Brzezinski, *Power and Principle,* p. 370.

441 "In selecting Ball": ibid., pp. 370–371.

442 "flying Dutchman": quoted in Robert D. McFadden et al., *No Hiding Place* (New York: Times Books, 1981), p. 255.

442 "Kissinger in his subtle fashion": Brzezinski, *Power and Principle,* p. 474.

442 "Zbig bugged me on it": quoted in ibid., p. 474.

443 "first critical phase of the operation": Brzezinski Diary, April 23, 1980; quoted in *Power and Principle,* p. 426.

444 "coordination also means subordination": Brzezinski, *Power and Principle,* p. 534.

PART VIII. THE YEARS THE LOCUSTS ATE

449 "The policy formulation function": quoted in *New York Times,* November 19, 1980.

450 "I'll look to you, Al": quoted in Alexander M. Haig, Jr., *Caveat: Realism, Reagan and Foreign Policy* (New York: Macmillan, 1984), p. 12.

450 "the Secretary of State be your Vicar": Talking Paper for Meeting, 10 A.M., January 6, 1981. Reprinted in "The Document That Sowed the Seeds of Haig's Demise," *Washington Post*, July 11, 1982.

451 "helm is right here": quoted in Laurence I. Barrett, *Gambling with History* (Garden City, N.Y: Doubleday, 1983), p. 117.

451 "We've got to straighten this out": quoted in Larry Speakes with Robert Pack, *Speaking Out: Inside the Reagan White House* (New York: Charles Scribner's Sons, 1988), p. 7.

451 "I was standing right next to him": quoted in Barrett, op. cit., pp. 117–118.

451 "I am in control here": quoted in Haig, op. cit., p. 160.

452 "Haigspeak": Virtually every Haig press conference or impromptu statement brought at least one neologism, not least of them the word "caveat" itself, which Haig used as a verb, as in "let me caveat that comment." As for the term "vicar," Haig claims to have borrowed it from Paul Nitze's testimony before the Jackson Committee in 1960 (Haig, op. cit., p. 53). Nitze in fact had used that term to refer to a person who acted as a sort of chief of staff for foreign and defense policy, a role Nitze thought belonged to the secretary of state (Jackson Committee Hearings, Pt. 1, pp. 857, 867) but which subsequent to 1960 had largely been subsumed into the job of national security adviser.

452 "you are my foreign policy guy": quoted in Haig, op. cit., p. 144. Nancy Reagan, in a 1989 memoir, has stated her belief that the Haig appointment was her husband's worst error during his first term in office.

452 "job was really substituting for the president": Bush News Conference, December 14, 1988. Text, *New York Times*, December 15, 1988.

452 "Allen's Folly": David Aaron, *State Scarlet* (New York: G. P. Putnam's Sons, 1987), p. 278. Cf. *New York Times*, March 16, 1987.

454 "the better evidence indicates": Text, "Conclusions of Probe," *Washington Post*, May 24, 1984.

455 "If you're looking for action" et seq.: quoted in *New York Times*, March 4, 1981.

456 "better use of the president's time": quoted in *Washington Post*, July 12, 1981.

457 "To live on this kind of sufferance": Haig, op. cit., p. 85.

457–458 "In the forty year history": General Robert L. Schweitzer Deposition, March 17, 1987. *Report of the Congressional Committees Investigating the Iran-Contra Affair* (hereafter cited as Iran-Contra Report), Appendix B (hereafter cited as "Depositions" with a volume number) (Washington, D.C.: GPO, 1988), Vol. 24, pp. 349–350.

458 "Who would you get to replace Dick?": quoted in Helene von Damm, *At Reagan's Side* (Garden City, N.Y.: Doubleday, 1989), pp. 201–202.

459 "exactly the wrong thing to say": Schweitzer Deposition, op. cit., p. 330.

460 "the greatest danger that the republic has ever faced": quoted in *Washington Post*, October 21, 1981.

460 "that morning in the White House Mess": Schweitzer Deposition, op. cit., p. 335.

463 "seventy-two hours": quoted in *Washington Post*, January 6, 1982.

463 "become a heavy": quoted in *New York Times*, January 10, 1982.

464 "The NSC's Mid-Life Crisis": *Foreign Policy*, No. 69 (Winter 1987–1988).

464 "Clark, on behalf of the president" et seq.: Walter Raymond Deposition, September 3, 1987. Iran-Contra Report, Depositions, Vol. 22, p. 43.

465 "more effective governmental instrumentalities": quoted p. 10 in Robert R. Parry and Peter Kornbluh, "Iran-Contra's Untold Story," *Foreign Policy,* No. 72, Fall 1988.

467 "major public diplomatic effort": NSDD-102, "U.S. Response to Soviet Destruction of KAL Airliner," September 5, 1983 (declassified April 1, 1986). National Archives: Records Group 273: NSC Records, folder: "NSDD-102."

469 "conducting a second foreign policy": Haig, op. cit., p. 306.

469 "You've won a lot of battles": quoted in ibid., p. 307.

469–470 "For weeks I sat there and listened": Michael K. Deaver with Mickey Herskowitz, *Behind the Scenes* (New York: William Morrow, 1987), p. 165.

470 "Mr. President, I have to leave": quoted in ibid., pp. 165–166.

472 "I shouldn't even have gone": quoted in David C. Martin and John Walcott, *Best Laid Plans: The Inside Story of America's War on Terrorism* (New York: Harper & Row, 1988), p. 113.

472 "On the ground in Beirut": quoted in ibid., pp. 112–113.

473 "sky is falling": ibid., pp. 119–120.

475 "Soviet-Cuban militarization": Reagan Speech, March 23, 1983. Text, *New York Times,* March 24, 1983.

475–476 Grenada Documents; "expect change in criticisms": Paul Seabury and Walter A. McDougall, eds. *The Grenada Papers* (San Francisco: Institute for Contemporary Studies, 1984), pp. 178–180. The Government Printing Office edition of these papers is not widely available and is not cited here. That edition is the one Michael Ledeen and other consultants formally worked on. It is worth noting that, in the moment of United States victory in Grenada, it was said in Washington that at the forty-minute Bishop-Clark meeting, "Clark rejected Bishop's proposal for a joint U.S.-Grenada Commission but held out the possibility of greater American flexibility if the tone of Bishop's rhetoric became friendlier" (*Washington Post,* October 26, 1983).

477 "which could include nuclear weapons": quoted in Constantine Menges, *Inside the National Security Council* (New York: Simon & Schuster, 1988), p. 70.

478 "Constantine, tell the State Department": quoted in ibid., p. 79.

479 "humane deinstitutionalization" of a "communist dictatorship": ibid., p. 81.

479 "seemed not to grasp what I meant" et seq.: ibid.

479 "Preposterous" et seq.: quoted in Larry Speakes, op. cit., p. 152.

479 "Poindexter had hung me out to dry": Speakes, p. 150.

481 "McFarlane's first tasks": *U.S. News and World Report* (October 31, 1983), p. 12.

482 Reagan interview: "What Managers Can Learn from Manager Reagan," *Fortune* (September 15, 1986).

482 "modified limited hangout": McFarlane in fact agreed in an interview that his method could "probably" be characterized by that phrase. See Jane Leavy, "McFarlane and the Haunting Glare of Truth," *Washington Post,* May 7, 1987.

482 "wasn't a member" and "My own credibility": quoted in ibid.

483 "Many people have come to think": Iran-Contra Hearings: McFarlane, p. 1.

483 "fundamentally opposed individuals": quoted in *Washington Post*, April 18, 1986.

484 "What if we begin" et seq.: Martin Anderson, *Revolution* (New York: Harcourt, Brace, Jovanovich, 1988), p. 97.

485 "charged political climate" and "continued paralysis": Robert C. McFarlane, "Effective Strategic Policy," *Foreign Affairs*, Vol. 67, No. 1 (Fall 1988), p. 37.

485 Joint Chiefs meet Reagan: Hedrick Smith, *The Power Game: How Washington Works* (New York: Random House, 1988), pp. 607–609.

485 "We should protect the American people": quoted in ibid., p. 607.

486 "in five minutes": The crack was frequently noted and quoted, as by John B. Oakes, "Mr. Reagan Bombs," *New York Times*, August 18, 1984.

487 "evil empire": Reagan Speech, Mar. 8, 1983; in actuality the President asserted the Soviet Union was "the focus of evil in the modern world" and that it remained an empire. Text, *The New York Times*, Mar. 9, 1983.

487 "international situation is white hot" and "never . . . in the postwar decades": quoted in *Washington Post*, August 8, 1986.

487 "If the Reagan Pattern Continues": *New York Times*, January 1, 1984.

487 "Harsh words have led some": Reagan speech, January 16, 1984. Department of State, "Current Policy," No. 537, 1984.

489 "alternative interpretations" and "no binding commitment": *Washington Post*, October 22, 1985. See also the detailed study by Strobe Talbott in his *The Master of the Game* (New York: Knopf, 1988), pp. 185–373.

489 "almost fell off [his] chair": *Washington Post*, October 22, 1985.

490 "written in 1972" et seq.: *Washington Post*, February 6, 1987.

490 "approved and authorized": quoted in ibid.

491 "Withhold true objectives from staffs": Memo, Poindexter-McFarlane, November 27, 1984. Iran-Contra Hearings: Poindexter, reprinted p. 416. This intention presumably applied only with respect to Central American policy.

491 "Where I went wrong": Iran-Contra Hearings: McFarlane, p. 270.

491 "walk in the woods": See Strobe Talbott, *Deadly Gambits* (New York: Knopf, 1984), pp. 116–151.

495 "I didn't get much sleep": quoted in Regan Deposition, March 3, 1987. Iran-Contra Report, Depositions, Vol. 22, p. 698.

495 "I had words with Mr. McFarlane" et seq.: ibid. Some observers describe this incident as having occurred on the occasion of the Soviet shooting of U.S. Army Major Arthur D. Nicolson. Either version is possible—both times McFarlane woke Reagan.

496 "some kind of a commie": McFarlane Testimony. Iran-Contra Hearings: McFarlane, op. cit., p. 270.

496 "permitting" the NSC to function: Menges, op. cit., p. 20.

497 "how anyone could object" et seq.: Summary of Discussion, NSPG. June 25, 1984. Text released in the course of the Oliver North Trial. Text: "Excerpts from North Trial Documents," *New York Times*, April 14, 1989.

498 "You are causing all this trouble!": quoted in Menges, op. cit., p. 130.

498 "Constantine, your actions": quoted in ibid., p. 165.

499 "monitor Ollie": Abrams Testimony. Iran-Contra Hearings: Abrams, p. 11.

499 "white propaganda": Memo, Miller-Pat Buchanan, March 15, 1985 (declassified October 9, 1987). Iran-Contra Report: Appendix A: Documents, Vol. 1, pp. 587–588. The Guilmartin article itself is reprinted at p. 589. Defenders of Guilmartin, a search-and-rescue pilot with two tours in Vietnam and a colonel in the Air Force Reserves, point to this expertise in helicopter tactics. Neither that affiliation and skill nor his connection with S/LPD is made explicit in the article.

503 "deal" and "judicious": New York Times, March 2, 1986.

503 "we should reiterate": quoted in New York Times, March 7, 1986.

503 "redraw the map of North Africa": Robert Gates memo quoted by Bob Woodward and Don Oberdorfer in Washington Post, February 20, 1987.

504 "Look, Admiral": quoted in ibid.

505 "Proportionality" et seq.: quoted in Seymour Hersh, "Target Qaddafi," New York Times Magazine (February 22, 1987), p. 71.

505 "such unhappiness over here" et seq.: quoted in Bob Woodward, Veil: The Secret Wars of the CIA (New York: Simon & Schuster, 1987), p. 443.

506 "You learn to be cool": quoted in Washington Post, November 30, 1986.

507 "a military man's view of the job": Scowcroft interview, October 4, 1988.

508 "Maybe": quoted in New York Times, March 21, 1987.

509 "Can you imagine": William Safire, "In the Tangled Web," New York Times, February 5, 1987.

509 "three-ring circus" et seq.: quoted in Washington Post, October 2, 1986.

510 "paranoid and ineffective" et seq.: quoted in ibid.

511 "visibly disturbed": Woodward, op. cit., p. 474.

511 "Why not invite" et seq.: quoted in ibid.

511 "collision course": Wall Street Journal, August 25, 1986. John Walcott (coauthor with David Martin of Best Laid Plans), who wrote the original story in the Journal together with Gerald F. Seib, reports that the phrase "collision course" was his own and was based upon a mistaken analysis. Walcott thinks he was not deliberately fed disinformation, although one official he spoke with said something similar. Walcott also confirms that Howard Teicher was not the source of his information (see Martin and Walcott, op. cit., p. 380).

511 "not authorized": New York Times, August 29, 1986.

511 "felt it was a good thing": quoted in ibid.

512 "veracity of that entire story": Reagan interview. Text, Washington Post, October 3, 1986.

512 "did not plan or conspire": Washington Post, October 15, 1986.

512 "I also think": Memo, Teicher-McFarlane, May 28, 1985. Quoted in the Report of the President's Review Board (Tower Board), New York Times edition (New York: Bantam Books, 1987), p. 116.

513 "absurd": quoted in ibid., p. 119.

514 "retrospective" finding: The device of the retrospective finding which Poindexter admits destroying, and associated concepts such as a "mental" finding, were discussed ad nauseam during testimony and depositions to Iran-Contra investigating committees by John Poindexter, Edwin Meese, Stanley Sporkin, other CIA lawyers, and John McMahon.

516 "You are not keeping the agreement": quoted in Tower Board, p. 330.

517 "Don't be too downhearted": quoted in ibid., p. 337.

520 "His body language was more eloquent": Jacqueline Tillman Deposition, April 2, 1987. Iran-Contra Depositions, Vol. 26, p. 1208.

520 "vague recollection": John Poindexter Deposition, June 17, 1987. Iran-Contra Depositions, Vol. 20, pp. 1304–1305.

521 "firecracker costs": Memo, Owen-North, July 2, 1984. Iran-Contra Hearings: McFarlane, reprinted, pp. 776–777.

521 "exercise absolute stealth": North Travel Voucher, August 28, 1984. Text, *New York Times*, April 16, 1989.

525 "people are stealing here" et seq.: quoted in Felix Rodriguez Testimony. Iran-Contra Hearings: Calero et al., pp. 303, 304.

527 "If we agree": quoted in *New York Times*, October 26, 1986. Former ACDA director Kenneth Adelman provides an inside account of Reykjavík in his book *The Great Universal Embrace* (New York: Simon & Schuster, 1989), an account that is sadly flawed owing to its polemical approach. In regard to the question of Reagan agreeing, Adelman is misleading, citing the minutes quoted here, but putting them alongside the comments of several other participants and observers, in effect disguising the authoritative nature of the record released. Adelman's account also raised anew the question of who and what *is* the authority. If Reagan *agreed* to eliminate all nuclear weapons and Shultz went along with him, who were Adelman and the other entrepreneurs to overrule them? The ACDA chief dismisses the United States President's agreement as an inaccurate description of the United States offer (pp. 80–82). In his own memoir (*An American Life*. New York: Simon & Schuster, 1990, pp. 675–679) Ronald Reagan is ambiguous about what exactly happened at Reykjavík. He generally follows claims subsequently made in his name without reconciling these with contrary indications known at the time. For example, the "curveball" that broke up the conference, according to Reagan (p. 677) was Gorbachev's insistence the United States "give up" SDI. He makes no effort to square this with Soviet willingness to settle for a provision of specific duration that the sides continue to observe the ABM Treaty. Reagan also writes that he objected to elimination of battlefield nuclear weapons along with all the others because these were needed by NATO, then relates that Gorbachev promptly countered with an offer to reduce Soviet conventional forces in Eastern Europe, leaving the impression this combination would have been acceptable. In sum the Reagan account suggests that he negotiated for the abolition of *all* nuclear weapons while leaving completely unmentioned the frantic postsummit efforts of the image makers (including seventy-one media events, fifty-three of them featuring Donald Regan, George Shultz, or John Poindexter) to create a different impression.

527 "most sweeping and generous": quoted in Speakes, op. cit., p. 148.

528 "Some of us are like a shovel brigade": quoted in ibid., p. 149.

529 "Well done!": Poindexter PROFS note, August 6, 1986. Quoted in Tower Board, p. 468.

530 "It will blow over": quoted in Donald Regan, *For the Record* (New York: Harcourt, Brace, Jovanovich, 1988), p. 26.

530 "In the presence of the President": Iran-Contra Report, p. 294.

531 "The clear intent": Poindexter Deposition, op. cit., p. 1105.

531 "Ollie's asked to look at some documents": Kenneth de Graffenreid Deposition, June 19, 1987. Iran-Contra Depositions, Vol. 8, pp. 1026–1027.

532 "I would not pull those documents": James R. Radzimski Deposition, August 11, 1987. Iran-Contra Depositions, Vol. 21, p. 866.

532 "I would never ask you": quoted in ibid., p. 867.

532 "All those System-IV documents!": quoted in ibid., p. 906.

534 "It's a terrible mess": quoted in Regan, op. cit., p. 38.

535 "Ollie has given me enough hints": quoted in Jane Mayer and Doyle McManus, *Landslide: The Unmaking of the President 1984–1988* (Boston: Houghton Mifflin, 1988), p. 347.

535 "I'm sorry it's come to this": quoted in Regan, op. cit., p. 42.

536 "What we're trying to find out" et seq.: Text, "Excerpts from Session with President's Panel," *New York Times,* December 2, 1986.

537 "What happened in this case" et seq.: Text, "Excerpts from the Tower Commission's News Conference," *New York Times,* February 27, 1987.

538 "The root cause": Henry Kissinger, "Not Its Power, but Its Weakness," *Washington Post,* December 21, 1986.

538 "honest, convincing" et seq.: Reagan speech, March 4, 1987. Text, *New York Times,* March 5, 1987.

541 "broadest possible range": Letter, Carlucci-Brooks, April 30, 1987. Reprinted in U.S. Congress (100/2) House. Government Operations Committee. *Hearing: Presidential Directives and Records Accountability Act* (H.R. 5092) (Washington: GPO, 1989) p. 11.

541 "a thorough review": Letter, Carlucci-Brooks, May 15, 1987. Reprinted in ibid., pp. 12–13.

541 "not altogether clear": Letter, Carlucci-Wright, August 7, 1987. Reprinted in ibid., pp. 21–22.

542 "doctrines of separation of powers": Letter, Powell-Brooks, August 3, 1988. Reprinted in ibid., p. 25.

543 "Like asking Qaddafi": Memo, Powell-Weinberger, June 18, 1985, marginal note. Iran-Contra Depositions, Vol. 21, pp. 317–318.

543 "The hell we do!": quoted in Lou Cannon, "Antidote to Ollie North," *Washington Post Magazine* (August 7, 1988), p. 38.

543 "a heck of a homework quiz": David Wallechinsky, "It Can Be Done: Have a Vision," *Parade* (August 13, 1989), p. 4.

544 "risks of inaction": Colin Powell, "The NSC System in the Last Two Years of the Reagan Administration," in James P. Pfiffner et al., *The Presidency in Transition* (New York: Center for the Study of the Presidency, 1989), p. 214.

546 "weren't able to do": quoted in *New York Times,* December 25, 1988, quoted p. 17.

546 Powell and Noriega: Cannon, op. cit., p. 41.

547 "moral" operation: quoted in *Washington Post,* October 28, 1988.

548 "We're going to take": Bush News Conference, November 23, 1988. Text, *New York Times*, November 24, 1988.

549 "I realized on day one": quoted in *Washington Post*, April 2, 1989.

552 "I'm very relaxed" and "the President is not trying to make quick headlines": quoted in *New York Times*, February 22, 1989.

552 "The Strategy Morass": editorial, *Aviation Week and Space Technology* (April 24, 1989), p. 9.

552 MILITARY BUDGET TO PRECEDE: *Washington Post*, April 10, 1989.

554 "the United States cannot fully restore relations": Winston Lord, "China and America: Beyond the Deep Chill," *Foreign Affairs*, Vol. 68, No. 4 (Fall 1989), p. 12.

PART IX. THE PRESIDENTS' LIEUTENANTS

564 "insulate" et seq.: quoted in *Washington Post*, July 21, 1987.

565 Destler suggestion: I.M. Destler, "A Job That Doesn't Work," *Foreign Policy*, No. 38 (Spring 1980), pp. 80–88.

566 "formal obligatory structures" et seq.: Theodore C. Sorensen, "The President and the Secretary of State," *Foreign Affairs*, Vol. 66, No. 2 (Winter 1987–1988), p. 243.

INDEX

▲▲▲